# Foreword to the Third Edition

Timesharing schemes now exist in more than 70 separate jurisdictions. The industry is a rapidly growing and now established section of the global leisure market. An analysis of the law, practice and procedure in the major relevant jurisdictions presents any author with a herculean task, which is perhaps why, ten years from the publication of the First Edition, this is still the only work of its nature in the world. The task has only been made possible by the support, encouragement and active participation of friends and colleagues in the industry.

The chapter on UK timesharing has been revised by Howard Lederman of Counsel from whom I have received much valuable advice over the years, and Edward Davies of Interval was particularly helpful in updating the Exchange Organisation material. Eric Tomsett of Messrs Touche Ross, a well-known expert on taxation of timesharing, has revised this section, and David Anderson advised regarding poll tax and rates. I must also thank Robert Kaprow for his assistance and advice. Professor MDA Freeman of University College London prepared the chapter on conflict of laws, Stephanie A Madsen of the American Land Development Association and Craig M Nash updated the chapter on USA timesharing which had been prepared with the assistance of Jeffrey B Stern, a partner in the Washington law firm of Ingersoll & Bloch to whom I am indebted for the specimen American timeshare scheme reproduced as Appendix B. Pedro Planas Lera and Paul Chaloupecky of the London law firm Edmonds Bowen & Company assisted with the preparation of the Spanish and French chapters respectively. Valentini Koussoulas-Gontikas and Anna Maria Fulgoni, acknowledged experts in their field, contributed the Greek and Italian sections respectively, and I shall greatly miss the late David Ferrier, who advised regarding Australian timeshare. On this occasion, the South African section was revised by Johann Havemann. Others who contributed to or influenced the preparation of this work include Colonel Geoffrey Gilhead, Secretary General of the Timeshare Developers Association, Ron Haylock and Colin Collins of RCI, Stefan Voulgaris, President of the Greek Timeshare Association, Wilhelm Froon, Wilfred Meynell, Hermenegildo Altozano, Lupicinio Rodriguez, Catherine Francois, Thanassis Gontikas, Drs Jorges Mota and Cunha Reis, Peter Arthur, Gaby Norton,

Wulstan Berkeley, Paula Woodgate, Sigfrido Espejo, Michel Alexandre, Lee Penrose, Nick Croydon and David Corlett. There were of course many others too numerous to mention who have contributed to the bulging filing cabinets of material and with sound and friendly advice.

I am also grateful to the American Land Development Association and the National Association of Real Estate Licence Law Officials for allowing me to reproduce as Appendix H the NTC/Narello Model Timeshare Act and the ARRDA Model Timeshare Resale Broker Regulation legislation.

I should like to pay a particular tribute to the penetrating insight, vision and humour of Simon Bowen of Edmonds Bowen & Company, Craig Nash, President of Interval, and Tony Sorrentino, President of Worldex, without whom this book would still be gracing my pending tray.

Finally, on this occasion, I must thank my secretaries Vicki Parsons and Jane Hayes who typed the manuscript and my wife Nicole, who has lived through it all for the third time.

**JAMES EDMONDS**
January 1991

# Contents

# Table of Cases

## USA

# Table of Statutes

# Chapter One

# Introduction to timesharing

## Background

It is often claimed that the concept of timeshare was originated by a British developer in Spain but, according to most popular accounts, the first timeshare development in the world was started in 1965 at Superdévoluy, a ski resort in the French Alps. The Société des Grands Travaux de Marseille are said to have launched the concept with the slogan 'Ne louez plus la chambre—achetez l'hotel, c'est moins onereux' which may be loosely translated as 'Don't book a room—buy the hotel, it's cheaper!' The concept of timesharing did not attract much enthusiasm until it was brought to the USA in the early 1970s with three projects in Miami, Florida. The idea was introduced there at an opportune moment, at a time when inflation had virtually destroyed the conventional market for second homes by pricing them out of reach of the average purchaser, as a result of which developers found themselves with a large amount of such property on their hands. Multi-co-ownership, or timesharing as it soon came to be called, while multiplying the sales effort required, brought the property price within the reach of the average purchaser and, in theory, substantially improved the developer's profit margins.

### Factors leading to growth of timeshare industry

What really made the concept a success however was the creation in the USA at this time of the two timeshare exchange networks, Interval International in Miami and Resorts Condominiums International in Indianapolis. The concept of one or two weeks' right of use of an apartment, even on a shared ownership basis, was not really a viable product on its own however attractively furnished and priced. The purchaser would be limited to visiting the same apartment at the same time, year after year. Even with a system of exchanging weeks within a resort, or rental programmes, the concept was too restrictive to catch on. It was the exchange organisation with 'swaps' of time between an ever growing range of different resorts, which proved to be the missing ingredient. The vast majority of resorts are affiliated to either of the two exchange networks, each of which have a range of many hundreds of resorts worldwide. Both networks are so large that no individual timeshare owner could possibly visit every resort in a lifetime. Almost every conceivable variant of the holiday experience is catered for, and for the most part in high quality accommodation. The cost of arranging exchanges is relatively trivial and both networks publish annual audited statistics demonstrating a success rate of well over 95 per cent.

The concept was given even more impetus by the twin phenomena of the late twentieth century—increased leisure time and low cost travel. The exchange networks found that, with the enormous 'buying power' of their rapidly growing membership base, they were able to offer their members preferential travel rates and a range of other benefits.

Indeed, the rapid growth in the services provided by the exchange organisations (see Chapter 4) coupled with the diversification of the exchange organisations into offering travel and insurance arrangements, has moved the timesharing industry significantly closer to the 'package holiday' business whilst for the most part offering a better quality product, for less money and with the consumer retaining far greater control over his holiday arrangements. A share of the ownership of an apartment or villa, fitted out to standards which even the most fastidious second home owner would consider extravagant, has been brought within reach of the majority of the travelling public. They are now offered an extraordinarily wide range of choice as to type of accommodation and location. Even after purchase, through the use of sophisticated computer technology, they are not confined to their eventual choice. They can, for a trivial additional cost, enjoy as an alternative the use of similar accommodation in many different resorts throughout the world, and are presented with a list of alternatives which grows daily.

Not surprisingly perhaps, timesharing has caught on in a big way. The English Tourist Board (ETB) states: 'market research has shown that the trend is towards self-catering holidays—not only for economic reasons but also because of the freedom it offers. In particular there is a growing need for up-market, luxury accommodation and the Board sees timesharing as a way of achieving this high standard to meet the demand'.

Price is of course another important factor. The outright purchase of an apartment or villa is, for most people, a very significant investment, and for something which they are only able to make use of for, on average, two or three weeks a year. The solution of the problem is simple. It is not necessary to pay for the entire cost of the accommodation. Instead the purchase is restricted to the time when the purchaser is able to use it. The buyer does not have to pay for what is not used. This is the key which unlocks the barriers to the new opportunities presented by low cost travel and increased leisure time. As stated in a government report (Ontario Ministry of Industry and Training): 'The practicality of timesharing is obvious and rather stunning in its simplicity'.

The Office of Fair Trading (OFT) indicated in its June 1990 report that the average cost of one week's timeshare in pounds sterling varied between £3,035 for a low season week in a studio sleeping two, and £4,720 for a similar week in high season. Comparable figures for a three bedroom apartment, sleeping eight, were £5,490 and £9,760 respectively. The range of prices varied enormously however—from £250 to £5,500 for the low season studio weeks to between £650 and £6,380 for high season in a studio, with three bedroom apartment prices varying between £2,635 to £11,200 (low season) and £4,250 to £16,250 (high season).

## Statistics

The first UK timeshare project was started in 1976 at Loch Rannoch in Scotland; the first to be set up in England was in 1979 at Torquay. By 1989 there were nearly 200,000 UK owners (about half the European ownership base), 62 per cent of whom owned timeshares in Spain and Portugal. There were some 500 European resorts by then, 270 of them in Spain and Portugal and 77 in the UK. The new concept touched a common chord in countries all over the globe, and timesharing was seen to rank amongst the world's largest industries, and to have a greater growth potential than almost any other industry. More than two million people now own a timeshare and in the last seven years the world industry has grown at an average annual rate of 31 per cent, an impressive rate of growth by any standards. There are approximately 2,500 property timeshare developments in some 70 countries, and international sales for the year 1990 were estimated to be comfortably in excess of £2 billion. Two-thirds of the world's resorts are in the USA but research carried out by investing institutions indicated that in the last decade of this century, Europe has the greatest potential for growth, and the European industry is expected to treble within the next few years, even disregarding the newly emerging East European market. According to research carried out by Richard Ragatz Associates the average age of the typical timeshare purchaser is 50, with more than 70 per cent of purchasers being over 40. The great majority come from the higher socio-economic categories. Typical timeshare owners are a middle-aged married couple with a professional or technical background who have no children living at home. A sizeable proportion are retired.

The industry statistics demonstrate that the overwhelming majority of timeshare owners are happy with their purchase, less than 5 per cent being dissatisfied. In his June 1990 survey the then Director General of Fair Trading reported: 'The majority of timeshare owners who wrote to my office were entirely content with what they had bought and had enjoyed trouble-free holidays for a number of years'.

## Image

However, there is undoubtedly another side to the coin. Just as happened in the early days of the industry in the USA before legislation and a general clean-up of the industry, the industry in Europe suffers from a particularly bad image problem caused by a minority of unscrupulous entrepreneurs. It is the methods used in Europe to sell timeshare, methods which by and large have been eliminated from the American market, which have caused the most controversy. The Director General reported that:

> evidence before me indicates that too often:
> —direct mailshots have been seriously misleading about both their purpose and the 'awards' on offer;
> —companies have engaged in aggressive or deceptive behaviour;
> —people who have not understood the true purpose of the advertising have been enticed into attending a sales presentation;
> —sales staff have been encouraged and trained to engage in high-pressure techniques which seek to control the buyer's behaviour and suppress natural decision making; and
> —incomplete, misleading and untrue information (normally given orally) has been used to induce people to buy and to make unduly hasty buying decisions.

Added to the above, there is no generally accepted formula of law governing how timeshare schemes are created and marketed. It is the purpose of this book to analyse the various laws which do exist and comment on those which are proposed, to guide those whose task it is to set up the legal framework for establishing and marketing timeshare schemes, or those having to advise timeshare purchasers.

It must be said that this simple idea—timesharing—presents those engaged in the business of drafting such schemes with some of the most complicated and wide-ranging difficulties which any legal practitioner is likely to encounter. This book will not provide all the answers but it does describe most existing methods of constructing a timeshare plan, the problems which have been encountered so far and some of the pitfalls which lie in wait. It also describes the problems which are currently becoming evident in the industry and which will eventually have to be faced and surmounted.

Timesharing is a diverse subject which contains a little of everything in an age when most legal practitioners tend to specialise. The author has been quoted as saying: 'timesharing is a new-rooted legal tree springing from a shadowy and still unexplored crevice between the laws of real property and the law of personalty, branching in every direction and reaching up into the airy world of private international law'. There is very little in the way of precedents on timesharing, and hardly any specific timesharing case law in Europe. Such professional publications as have appeared, have almost invariably been too specific as to a particular point or too general to be of much value for the newcomer.

## Aims of this work

The scarcity of legal literature on the subject seems, at first sight, extra-ordinary. Nevertheless it appears that this work is still the foremost, indeed perhaps the only, attempt at a guide to international timesharing for the legal profession. That a work on the subject is necessary is beyond dispute. There are various solutions to the problem of structuring a timesharing plan and often such schemes have been put together in a fragmented way. A review of the various plans will, it is hoped, make it easier to understand the range of possibilities available and the advantages and disadvantages of each solution. There is no universally accepted common form of timesharing plan, although in some countries, notably in the USA, uniform regulation of plans has been made practicable by the ALDA-Narello Model Timesharing Act. The Director of Legal Affairs of the National Timesharing Council of the American Land Development Association is quoted as saying: 'Timesharing is so unique in its legal structure and the peculiarities of title conveyancing that statutes specifically addressing these issues are required'. This proposition applies *a fortiori* in Europe.

The problems of cohesion in Europe are much more difficult due to its different legal systems and languages, but the European leisure industry would benefit considerably if the EEC were to establish a common policy and framework and monitoring systems for such plans. A considerable number of timeshares are sold across national borders and too often the purchaser has no option but to rely on the good faith or financial soundness of the property developer, which has on occasion been lacking. It is still the case that few legal practitioners have experience in advising on such plans, especially those of an international nature. Even developers who make a point of advising prospective customers to take legal advice are fairly safe as regards the probability of their plan being too closely examined on behalf of an individual timeshare purchaser, because of the expense involved. This book is designed to be useful in such circumstances by explaining to the legal practitioner the rationale behind the structuring of timesharing schemes and establishing the criteria for deciding whether the client is likely to be adequately safeguarded. Any reputable developer can provide a satisfactory means of guaranteeing the purchaser's position but as the law now stands in most parts of the world, including the UK, this is not a legal requirement. Not all developers are reputable and not all reputable developers are convinced of the need for such provision, despite the financial collapse of even very substantial developers.

This book is confined to commentary on each area of law as it affects timesharing but without attempting a full and detailed exposition of each subject. This is much better left to the authors of the standard works on each area of law, and those to whom reference has been made are listed in the bibliography.

It is obviously not practicable to attempt to provide any in-depth analysis of foreign legal systems. The purpose has been to explain how overseas timesharing plans are constructed, and in so doing to touch upon the areas of foreign law involved, how they govern the construction of foreign plans and what problems and pitfalls still affect the operation of such plans. No solicitor should attempt to draft a timesharing plan affecting property in a foreign jurisdiction, or which is to be marketed to nationals of a foreign jurisdiction, without the active co-operation of a lawyer familiar with the law of that jurisdiction.

Nor is it practicable to cover separately every country where timesharing plans exist, but it is hoped that the background knowledge of timesharing gleaned from these pages will provide the reader with the necessary foundation from which to approach international timesharing plans based in any country throughout the world. The book is designed to be of assistance to all responsible for advising in this area, whether the client is a developer, a purchaser or a marketing consultant. Finally, it will be of interest to those prospective timeshare purchasers who require something more than the average sales-orientated explanation of timesharing.

## The concept of timesharing

In the early days of timesharing there was considerable discussion as to whether timesharing would be sold as 'ownership in property', as a 'holiday accommodation arrangement' or as 'an investment'. The peculiarities of English law which prevent the transfer of freehold interests to timeshare purchasers have stopped UK timeshares being marketed on a direct freehold ownership basis but this is not always the case in other areas of the world. From the purchaser's point of view the acquisition of a timeshare should never be presented as 'an unbeatable investment proposition'. It is not, and buyers who purchase on the strength of such an assertion are likely in the main to be disappointed. All that may fairly be said is that buying a timeshare will to some extent keep down the cost of future holidays. Nevertheless, timeshares have been sold as investment opportunities accompanied by impressive looking graphs and tables referring to the historical rise in the value of property, but over-strenuous attempts to sell timesharing in this way, at least in the UK, may involve the risk of proceedings being taken against the developer and all others concerned owing to the imposition of sanctions against such activities contained in the Financial Services Act 1986.

It has been suggested that the cost of a typical timeshare can be broken down into 45 per cent marketing and allied costs, 25 per cent developer's profit and a mere 30 per cent for the cost of the land, the property development and the fixtures and fittings. On the basis of those figures, therefore, the timeshare property itself will have to more than treble in value before a situation could be arrived at where the timeshare purchasers would get their 'investment' back if the property were sold and the proceeds divided among the timeshare owners. Most developers offer a chart setting out the weekly price for each unit and if these are aggregated and the total compared with the price of a similar unit in the same area purchased outright, it should be possible to arrive at a conclusion as to the merits of the purchase as an 'investment in property'.

Nevertheless the phrase 'investment in property' still crops up from time to time in the sales brochures but the concept is illusory when so much of the investment is not directly invested in real property. The word 'ownership' loses the significance normally ascribed to it. It would be easy in such circumstances for the buyer to confuse 'ownership' with 'property investment' and 'security' with 'investment potential' but this is not the nature of the beast. Timesharing is something new, with an identity all of its own not to be confused with its parental origins. The timeshare promoter is in the holiday/leisure industry, rather than in the property industry, and the product he sells is holidays. It is true that he needs property to conduct his business, but so do countless other businesses, from cinemas to tobacconists. What really matters is the protection and safeguarding of the timeshare buyer's defined rights. Frequently this can be better achieved through other methods than creating the illusion of theoretical 'ownership of property'. Having said this, there are in existence schemes which should more properly be called 'co-ownership plans' rather than 'timesharing plans'. These involve only a small number of purchasers, perhaps about six, who together acquire a property. Very often there is no great sales effort required; the sales commission and developers' 'mark up' are not too far removed from the commission payable on a normal sale/purchase and there is a closer relationship between the co-owners. In those circumstances it is perhaps more appropriate to link the transaction with 'property ownership' in its traditional sense. However, this guide concentrates on mass timeshare, where up to 51 individual weeks are being sold in each unit.

According to one survey, in response to a questionnaire asking why they had purchased a timeshare, 71.4 per cent of respondents indicated that their motive was 'to save money on future vacation costs'. 50.6 per cent gave as one of their most important reasons the existence of the exchange system, 49.6 per cent felt investment or resale opportunity to be a big advantage, while only 34.5 per cent gave as a reason that they liked the timeshare unit and only 19.8 per cent that they 'liked recreational facilities'. The survey stated: 'Respondents appear primarily concerned with flexible vacation plans, while at the same time being interested in holding down future vacation costs. Holiday timesharing is perhaps the only type of recreational real property which simultaneously offers these advantages'. (Richard L Ragatz Associates Inc, *United Kingdom Timeshare Purchasers: Who They Are, Why They Buy*). The survey further indicated that the percentage of persons buying one week and those buying two weeks were equal (39.2 per cent). A very large proportion (60.8 per cent) stated that they intended to buy two or more additional weeks of timeshare. It may seem surprising that nearly half of the timeshare purchasers interviewed gave investment or resale opportunity as an important reason for purchasing a timeshare. One could no doubt argue that the encouragement of unrealistic expectations is, in the long term, detrimental to the industry.

**Advantages**

The advantages of timesharing to the purchaser are far more practical than theoretical investment opportunities or the idea of 'owning' property. The main advantage is of course that the capital cost of a timeshare is a good deal less than the cost of buying a similar holiday unit on an outright purchase. Since most people can only enjoy a limited period of holiday each year, timesharing is a convenient way of not having to pay for the unused and wasted time when the property would otherwise be vacant. Obviously a premium has to be paid for this benefit which is, as mentioned above, quite substantial, but nevertheless it brings down to an affordable level some of the advantages of actually owning a holiday property.

Another advantage is that the burden of maintaining a holiday property is undertaken initially by the developer and thereafter by the management company. The costs of management are spread out among all the timeshare owners and therefore not only is the capital cost of the holiday period smaller, but also the cost of maintenance is greatly reduced, while the time and effort involved in simply managing a second home are eliminated. Most timeshare units will be fairly lavishly equipped compared to the average second home and this too is because the cost is spread out among so many people.

Also, most developers offer additional facilities (swimming pools, golf courses, skiing, etc) which are either included within the maintenance charge or at special reduced rates. Many developments provide maid service and babysitting etc and other facilities for children which it would be difficult for a second home owner to arrange just for the period of a particular vacation. The replacement costs of furnishings and equipment will also be less burdensome as they are spread out among the various owners.

Another important advantage is that most plans will allow access to the exchange schemes referred to in Chapter 4 which enables the timeshare owner to swap his time period whenever he wishes for a different time in the same resort or in any one of a number of resorts around the world so there is not the commitment to holiday in the same place each year, which is forced on many second home owners by virtue of the size of their investment.

However, the most important advantage is cost, both in acquiring the timeshare right and for future holidays.

Some of the features of conventional second home ownership are also present. The right is usually transmissible and the timeshare owner usually has the right to rent out his time period either to friends or on a commercial basis. A sense of community will be present since the timeshare owner is likely to see many of the same people each year and of course can entertain family and guests at the timeshare villa or apartment.

### Disadvantages

The disadvantages of timesharing from the purchaser's point of view are that the investment is unlikely to show much capital appreciation at least in the short or medium term. Resale, especially in the early years when the timeshare purchaser would be competing with the developer's marketing effort, may not be practicable at or near the acquisition cost.

It should be said, however, that in a new development the early buyers may be offered a preferential price and, although they may have to wait several years thereafter they may be able to sell at a profit. In the UK, since 1979, there is no doubt that some of the earlier purchasers have been able to resell in this way.

In the USA the discount offered to the first purchaser has sometimes been elevated to the status of a rather clever marketing strategy. The developer will offer the timeshare at a certain price (the maximum discounted price) at the outset. Then, every three months or so the developer will increase the price. The effect of this is remarkable. The initial buyers will have made a profit, albeit unrealised or perhaps unrealisable. They will tell their friends and this generates more potential purchasers. A sense of urgency is created—buy now before the price goes up again! In a small number of projects, the technique has worked so effectively that the developer's staff have been able to buy in at the beginning, sell out at the end of the development period and make a profit. The author has not seen such techniques widely applied in Europe, however, and marketing techniques in Europe, so far at all events, are rarely comparable in scale with those employed in the USA. There, as many as 80 highly trained and highly paid sales personnel may concentrate on one development and achieve sell out in 12 months. In Europe, the author's experience is that sell out may take three to four years and the sales team often consists of only a handful of people. It is, however, becoming increasingly common for highly organised offshore marketing organisations and developers to take over existing timeshare plans or commence new timeshare plans in Europe using sophisticated, often 'high pressure' sales tactics. Such tactics have brought the industry into disrepute in many American states and it is rather worrying that these sales techniques, many of them now banned in America, have been imported into Europe.

The furnishings and fixtures and fittings in a timeshare unit are subject to much greater usage than they normally would be and therefore have to be replaced more frequently. This should be reflected in the maintenance charge, and there is of course always a chance that the timeshare buyer's immediate predecessor in time may not be as thoughtful about looking after the property as one would wish and the timeshare buyer will be following his predecessor for a good many years. This gives rise to a problem which often weighs heavily on the mind of a prospective purchaser; control over the maintenance expenditure and indeed over the level of maintenance undertaken may be limited. The budget for the maintenance may have been initially grossly understated so as to provide sales or reduce the developer's contribution in respect of unsold time periods and could rise substantially as soon as the development has been sold. The purchaser will need some assurance that the quality of management will continue once the developer has sold all the units, bearing in mind that, with the heavy usage of the timeshare unit, the condition of the unit and the fixtures and fittings may deteriorate rapidly in the absence of a competent management and replacement policy.

The timeshare unit does not belong to the timeshare owner in that sometimes, for example, there is a prohibition against pets, the unit cannot be refurnished or redecorated to taste and there is often no provision for storage of clothes etc, so that in that sense it is much like hotel accommodation.

There is more risk of something going awry in regard to the purchaser's right of ownership of his timeshare than there would be in the case of a conventional purchase. The scheme documentation in many instances in Europe is hardly comprehensible, sometimes even by the draftsman, and often of uncertain effect. Even if the scheme documentation is effective it is usually impracticable to investigate ownership of property, especially where the purchase is across a national border, simply because the expense and time involved outweigh the cost of the timeshare. The author at one time believed that the American concept of title insurance might be applied, but in practice considers such insurance is of no value in Europe. It is not, as one might have supposed, an insurance that the timeshare buyer's title is secure. It is merely an insured statement of the condition of title at a particular historical point in time.

**The developer**

From the developer's point of view timesharing means that his sales market is vastly expanded since so many more people can afford to buy a timeshare than can afford to buy a conventional second home. He will also be able to sell the project for a considerably greater sum on a timeshare basis than would be achieved if the development were to be sold conventionally. To achieve this happy result, however, a considerably greater proportion of time, effort and money must be spent on marketing the project since each unit will have to be sold to perhaps 30 different purchasers as opposed to just one, and this is why marketing cost is such a large element in the final price of each timeshare. The management problems for the developer are more akin to running a hotel than a conventional development and sales operation and because of the difficulty of arranging finance, the developer may have to provide help of this nature for some timeshare purchasers.

At some point also the developer will have to make a decision as to when to commit a unit for sale on a timeshare basis, since once a timeshare period in a unit has been sold, that unit will effectively be blocked from sale on any other basis.

However, the greater usage of timeshare resorts will mean that restaurant facilities, gift shops, car hire and other facilities which might not normally be very profitable, will be elevated into profitability by the greater volume of occupation of the development.

Finally there is an environmental advantage to timesharing which is often overlooked in that much less space is occupied by a number of people using the same timeshare project than would be occupied if each timeshare purchaser were to acquire a separate unit on a conventional basis.

## Definition

A timeshare is one of a series of similar and exclusive rights to use property in succession granted to a number of persons, all of whom are entitled to a like right for a specified period of time in each year over a period of years or in perpetuity. Usually, but not invariably, this is linked with direct or indirect beneficial ownership of the property by all persons entitled to such right of use, such right being granted in consideration of a premium coupled with an obligation to contribute to the maintenance of the property.

There have been few statutory attempts to define timesharing but a 'timesharing plan' is defined for the purposes of the Real Estate Timesharing Acts CH721 Florida Statutes as:

any arrangement plan or similar device, but not including any exchange programmes, whether by membership, agreement, tenancy in common, sale, lease, deed, rental agreement, licence, right to use agreement, or by any other means whereby a purchaser in exchange for consideration, receives a right to use accommodation or facilities, or both, for a specific period of time less than a full year during any given year, but not necessarily for consecutive years, and which extends for a period of more than three years.

The California 'Subdivision Land Act' defines a timeshare project, a timeshare estate and a timeshare use as follows:

(a) A "Timeshare Project" is one in which a purchaser receives the right in perpetuity, for life, or for a term of years, to the recurrent, exclusive use or occupancy of a lot, parcel, unit or segment of real property, annually or on some other periodic basis, for a period of time that has been or will be allotted from the use or occupancy periods into which the project has been divided.

(b) A "Timeshare Estate" is a right of occupancy in a timeshare project which is coupled with an estate in the real property.

(c) A "Timeshare Use" is a licence or contractual or membership right of occupancy in a timeshare project which is not coupled with an estate in the real property.

An important feature of timesharing is that the interest may either be a personal one or else an interest in immovable property and in many circumstances in various jurisdictions this distinction is critical in order to discover how the creation and sale of the right is to be treated for tax purposes and how far the ownership of the right is protected in the event of the insolvency or bankruptcy of its grantor. A timeshare which is regarded as being an interest in immovable property is almost invariably treated in a different way than if it is understood to be a mere personal right but this is a distinction which may have escaped the notice of the timeshare buyer at the time of purchase, and he may not understand all the implications of the distinction.

**Development of timeshare law**

The original American approach was to recognise this distinction and therefore to divide timesharing schemes into categories, 'time-span ownership' on the one hand and 'right to use' on the other. The former implies some direct or indirect interest in the timeshared property by the timeshare owner and the latter implies that the timeshare owner has a mere personal interest.

The implications of this division and the definitions of a timeshare in the USA are examined in Chapter 8. Whilst this approach recognised the distinction between timeshares which are and are not interest in immovable property, this legal distinction operated to the disadvantage of the consumer. The current thinking is that the consumer wishes to acquire his annual vacation, and should not be prejudiced by the choice of formula by which his object is to be achieved. The American case of *Sombrero Reef Club Inc* v *Allman* (see Chapter 8) resulted in demands for a further reform of the American system, so as to give 'right to use' timeshare owners similar protection to that afforded to those who happen to have purchased a 'timeshare estate'. In the *Sombrero* case, right to use contracts were considered executory, thus allowing the debtor in possession to reject them. The Model Act (see Appendix H) does not make this distinction and regulates 'right of use' and 'time-span ownership' in essentially the same manner. A 'timeshare' is defined in the revised Model Act as 'the right, however evidenced or documented, to use and occupy one or more timeshare units on a periodic basis according to an arrangement allocating such use and occupancy rights between other similar users'.

The Portuguese authorities created a new species of legal right *in rem* by Decree No 355/81 of 31 December 1981 (as amended by Decree Nos 368/83 of 4 October 1983 and 130/89 of 18 April 1989) so as to establish a formula for timesharing schemes that could exist alongside schemes relying on personal or 'obligational' rights. The preamble to the 1981 law states (in translation):

> what is intended ... is to create a new right—the right to periodical habitation—which, in practice, is equivalent to a regime of divided property, no longer divided into horizontal segments, but into time quota shares ... in effect and in synthesis, this right is characterised by being a real right, whose regime does not need to be complemented by conventions or clauses of an obligatory nature, and is evidenced by a property certificate which, by a simple endorsement or registration, is transmissible or chargeable, thus acquiring the negotiable characteristics of a moveable asset.

Unfortunately, as will be seen, the legal infrastructure in Portugal, the lack of ordnance survey type plans and maps and the embryonic land registry facilities prevented the system from working satisfactorily and, even with the amendments contained in Portuguese Decree No 130/89 of 18 April 1989, it is still for all practical purposes extremely inconvenient to create timesharing in Portugal by means of a land registry controlled system.

In Greece, with Timeshare Law 1652/86, the Greek authorities have attempted to set up the timesharer's right as a lease. They have succeeded in creating a system which seems completely unworkable by itself, although with some fairly creative draftsmanship a system has been devised which, although highly unsatisfactory, may enable timesharing plans to be structured in Greece. In the author's opinion the industry in Greece may never develop unless there are radical changes to the law, and it is likely that the major developers will choose Turkey or other mediterranean countries in preference to Greece. Indeed, the state of Greek timesharing law may well have contributed indirectly to the current growth in the Turkish timeshare holiday industry. Certainly, it is one of the reasons why Greece has not benefited to any great extent from the high level of investment and up-market tourism which timesharing brings with it.

In Bermuda the Timesharing (Licensing and Control) Act 1981 (1981: No 60) provides that:

> "Timesharing scheme" means any premises or complex of premises (whether contiguous to each other or not) and the grounds appurtenant thereto operated as a single business venture for the accommodation of purchasers and let for occupancy in exchange for a consideration given in advance by a purchaser who receives in return a right to occupy and use the facilities of the scheme for a specified period of not more than six months during any given year.

The Bermuda Act, while not actually creating a new right, nevertheless contains such stringent and detailed provisions in regard to timesharing schemes, that by their nature they recognise timesharing as a particular type of transaction which requires special protection and control.

In the UK the only statutory definition of timesharing is that contained in the GLC (General Powers) Act 1984, which is discussed in Chapter 2. Recognition of timesharing as a new concept is limited to the context of planning law in the areas of the 32 London Boroughs.

The report from the UK Office of Fair Trading states that: 'Timeshare is the right to use accommodation at a holiday development (usually known as a "resort") for a specified number of weeks each year over a specified period of time (or in perpetuity). For this right "owners" pay a developer an initial lump sum which varies at a particular resort according to the time of the year and the size of accommodation, together with an annual maintenance fee'. The OFT report goes on to make a number of recommendations for legislation, which are examined hereafter.

However, the most remarkable development in Europe has undoubtedly been the issue by the Spanish authorities of a new draft law (reproduced here as Appendix F) the implications of which are explored in Chapter 10. It is to be hoped that this proposed new law will be approved as drafted by the Spanish Parliament and, further, that it will serve as a model for other European jurisdictions. The new draft law will provide comprehensive protection for timeshare purchasers, whether they are acquiring a real or a personal right. At the same time, it incorporates sufficient flexibility to encourage rather than hinder the development of this vital new industry.

## Variation of timesharing plans

Timesharing is mainly concerned with real property but there are in existence timesharing plans relating to boats. Under such plans the boat is held in trust for a period, often of ten years, during which the timeshare owners have a right to use the boat for a specified period. At the end of the ten years the boat is sold and the proceeds distributed among the timeshare owners. Similar plans exist in relation to caravans. Other less common forms of timesharing are those related to golf courses, where the time period is a specified block of minutes on a daily or weekly basis and there have been similar schemes in relation to squash courts.

Property timeshares are more often divided into weekly periods and in order to facilitate use of the exchange opportunities offered by Interval International and Resorts Condominiums International, these weekly periods have been standardised. A copy of the standard chart is reproduced as part of the precedent of the 'Club with Trustee' plan (see page 327). Some plans have been structured to provide fixed weeks in every year, while others involve revolving periods where the rights are for a specified period of two weeks in one year, the following two weeks in the next year and the following two weeks in the next year, and so on. Usually, revolving plans provide for two weeks in the high season and two weeks in the low season and the high season weeks gradually become the low season weeks and *vice versa*. This rather curious arrangement is aimed at evening out the price of each week in a revolving plan. Since low season weeks are usually extremely difficult the sell, more and more developers are offering what at first sight seem extraordinarily low prices for out of season weeks and, in order to recoup their cost, are charging disproportionately large fees for the high season weeks.

Some plans, such as that run by an organisation known as Hapimag, involve points systems whereby the timeshare buyer purchases a certain number of points and then makes an annual booking using those points. High season weeks cost more points than low season weeks, but of course under some systems of this nature, the timeshare buyer loses the security of a specific weekly period and his particular chosen week may not always be available.

Another scheme, known as the Holiday Property Bond, is a single premium whole-life insurance policy. According to the OFT report a proportion of the premium is invested in fixed-interest securities and another proportion in around 400 properties in 17 locations. As at December 1988 there were 9,346 bondholders, 94 per cent of whom were UK residents. The allocation of properties to bondholders uses a points system and bondholders pay a non-profit user charge to cover maintenance of the property for each week of holiday they take. A capital sum is repaid to the bondholder's estate upon death; the amount of the repayment is determined by a fixed scale which reflects the holder's age when the policy was taken out. The bonds unit price is quoted daily in the *Financial Times* and bondholders can encash these units at any time after two years. Again the particular chosen week may not always be available and, according to *The Times* of 20 May 1990 there is a 25 per cent front end charge, after which 60 per cent of the remainder goes to a property fund and the remaining 40 per cent to Euro-bonds to cover the scheme running costs.

Some plans offer the timeshare owner the right to enjoy his timeshare in perpetuity while others provide for the underlying investment to be sold after a defined period and the assets distributed among the timeshare buyers. As will be seen, the type of plan set up will dictate whether the interest can be in perpetuity. In Spain under the *escritura* system of condominium co-ownership, each co-owner will have a statutory right to call for a sale of the property, and the maximum period for which any agreement to postpone sale can endure is ten years, although it is open for the parties to come to another agreement at the end of each ten year period, to postpone the sale for up to a further ten years. The Spanish systems will however be revolutionised if the new draft law comes into effect (see Chapter 10 and Appendix F). In the UK, under a trust plan, the maximum period will be the perpetuity period chosen under the Perpetuities and Accumulations Act 1964 (usually 80 years). In both cases, it is possible to structure plans in a different way, so as to avoid these rules if they are thought to be inconvenient.

In all cases the developer has a choice as to whether he parts with the freehold interest or whether he retains an interest in the plan, eg by merely creating a lease of the project for a defined term of years, which will then form the asset being transferred. In this event the developer must balance the value of his retained interest against any diminution in the value of the individual timeshares. Again, in such instances, the timeshare purchaser may be at risk unless the lease contains sufficiently detailed safeguards against arbitrary forfeiture and in the UK if the lease is non-assignable, it may not be possible to register it under the Land Registration Act 1925. In some instances, the timeshare buyer will be offered his timeshare for a defined period of say 20 years, in return for his premium, with an option to extend for a further period on payment of an additional premium.

In other cases, where the developer may wish to retain ownership and control of the asset being timeshared, the timeshare purchaser may only be issued with a timeshare licence. The difficulties and dangers of this course of action are examined in the next chapter. More usually such bare right to use plans are coupled with a proprietary club, with the membership certificate being in the form of a licence to occupy the timeshare unit subject to the provisions of the rules. As will be seen, there is very little protection in Europe for purchasers of timeshares under such licence schemes, as generally the timeshare owner cannot prevent the developer from mortgaging or alienating the property. In the USA the problems caused by defaulting developers operating such 'right to use' plans has prompted changes in legislation designed to give a measure of protection to buyers in such circumstances.

More usually in the UK the asset to be timeshared is vested in a trustee with the developer, having parted with his interest in the asset, merely having a right to sell club membership certificates representing the total available time to be sold. The club timeshare plan operating with a trustee is currently the most popular in the UK. There are one or two leasehold plans in which the timeshare is represented by a discontinuous lease, (see Chapter 2). Mention must also be made of corporate plans involving the creation of a public limited company, the shares of which carry with them the right of occupation of the timeshared unit. A similar type of corporation, the Société Civil d'Attribution, was the foundation for almost all timesharing in France, but the concept has been found to be seriously flawed (see Chapter 9).

In larger plans the timeshare right may only be to occupy a particular type of apartment or villa, instead of an identified unit, and this of course gives the developer more flexibility, although it poses problems of security for the timeshare buyer.

New variations on the timesharing theme appear almost on a weekly basis, and it is this lack of uniformity which makes it so difficult to give the consumer the protection which, in modern times, he is entitled to expect. There is no uniform system which could be imposed either in the UK or any other country. It is even more impracticable to contemplate the creation of some uniform worldwide plan other than a set of general principles. Nevertheless, all timesharing plans have a number of common features and the eventual goal is that the consumer is protected, and gets some guarantee as to the set of rights which he believes he acquires when he purchases a timeshare. It is easy to identify the areas which operate to his disadvantage.

First, there are a number of legal rules which affect timesharing, but were enacted when the concept was not within the contemplation of the draftsmen of these rules. As a consequence of this, schemes have to be tailored to comply with these rules and often this leads to a lack of simplicity and major areas of uncertainty affecting some schemes currently in operation. Each plan needs to be examined in the light of customary or common law, and statute law. The tax treatment of such plans, especially international plans, offers a particularly good example of an area which often gives rise to difficulty. Securities legislation, planning law, and conflict of laws offer other examples. Legislative intervention such as that proposed by the Spanish authorities could do much to smooth the path of the developer who wishes to set up a properly constituted plan, and to help develop the industry for the benefit of the public.

Secondly, as matters now stand in most of Europe, timesharing plans may be set up by developers who do not have, and do not acquire, the necessary ability to make their plans successful. Such developments are often small, badly constructed and poorly managed, and end in disaster for all concerned. Inadequate financial backing, over-optimistic cash flow forecasts and unfulfilled promises feature largely in amateur operations, even if actual dishonesty is not always present. The control of this minority of timeshare developers must in the end be a matter for legislation. American experience has shown that the difficulty and cost of complying with such legislation is far outweighed by public confidence leading to public acceptance of the concept and vastly increased sales.

It was with consumer protection in mind that the Timeshare Developers Association (TDA) was formed from the merger of the pre-existing trade organisations to be the consumer 'watchdog' and to set and to police standards throughout the timeshare industry. In the end, however, the Director General of Fair Trading concluded in the June 1990 report that he proceeded on the basis that TDA 'could not bring about the remedies which I am convinced are needed for the whole of the timeshare market' and that there was no 'real argument against the need for legislation'. This has led to the demise of TDA and the fact that the UK government is shouldering the burden and assuming the responsibility, at least so far as the purchasers are concerned, will no doubt be greeted with relief by many in the industry. The current view is that legislation is the only answer, although there remains a peripheral role for self-regulation.

# Chapter Two

# Timesharing in the UK

## Co-ownership and timesharing

The structure of timeshare ownership in England and Wales stems from the way in which co-owners of land hold their interests. It is helpful to consider the law relating to co-owners as it might be applied to a timeshare scheme.

In England and Wales interests in land are divided into legal and equitable estates. Since the Law of Property Act 1925 ('the 1925 Act') the only form of co-ownership of a legal estate that can exist according to the law of England and Wales is in the form of a joint tenancy. The object of the 1925 Act and the other associated legislation passed at that time was to enable a purchaser of land to deal with the owner of the legal estate without having to investigate the title of the persons entitled to the equitable estate (such as co-owners of undivided shares in the land) who were hidden behind the 'curtain' of the legal estate. Section 1(6) of the 1925 Act provided that legal tenancies in common could no longer exist: 'a legal estate is not capable of subsisting or of being created in an undivided share in land'. Section 36(4) of the Settled Land Act 1925 provides that an undivided share in land shall not be created except behind a trust for sale. As a consequence of this, the legal estate in an undivided share in land is held by trustees holding as joint tenants upon trust for sale. The beneficial ownership of the subject matter of the tenancy in common is converted from land, into the proceeds of sale.

Section 34(2) of the 1925 Act provides that where land is expressed to be conveyed to any persons in undivided shares after the commencement of that Act and those persons are of full age, the conveyance shall operate as if the land had been expressed to be conveyed to the grantees or, if there are more than four grantees, to the first four named in the conveyance as joint tenants on the statutory trusts. Consequently if an attempt is made to convey freehold land to more than four timeshare owners, the legal estate will vest in the first four named timeshare owners. Those four timeshare owners would hold the legal estate on the statutory trusts in trust to sell the land, with power to postpone the sale, and to hold the net rents and profits until sale and the ultimate proceeds of sale upon trust to give effect to the beneficial and equitable rights of persons for whom the land was held (see s 35 of the 1925 Act).

Nevertheless, the interests of such a co-owner (a timeshare owner whose interest is in the proceeds of sale) may be regarded as an interest in land for the purposes of enforcing a judgment under the Charging Orders Act 1979 (see *National Westminster Bank* v *Stockman* [1981] 1 WLR 67. It seems that the creditor of a co-owner who obtains an order charging the co-owner's interest may apply for an order for the sale of the land under s 30 of the 1925 Act instead of appointing a receiver of the co-owner's interest and waiting for the receiver to apply for such an order (see *Midland Bank plc* v *Pike* [1988] 2 All ER 434 and also *Perry* v *Phoenix Assurance plc* [1988] 3 All ER 60). Clearly such an application by a creditor could place many timeshare schemes based on co-ownership in jeopardy, unless an appropriate mechanism for preventing forfeiture of the interest of the defaulting timeshare owner in such an event were present.

However, in theory any co-owner (such as a timeshare owner) or their creditor or trustee in bankruptcy could apply for an order for sale of the freehold or superior leasehold title under s 30 of the 1925 Act, in the event that they could show that the purpose of the trust had come to an end or that their voice should prevail in equity (see *Re Holiday* [1981] Ch 405 and *Re Evers Trust* [1980] 3 All ER 399). On the other hand, a sale may not be ordered where the co-owners have covenanted for a particular purpose which has not come to an end, or where the exercise of the trustee's power is considered to be *mala fides* (see *Re Buchanon Wollaston's Conveyance* [1936] ChD 211, for example).

In Scotland, it is possible in principle to create common ownership of land amongst many owners each having separate title to a fraction of the undivided whole. The principal drawback is that in the absence of agreement the co-owner of land held in common with others has a right to apply for the division of the land and a sale, if physical division is not possible or equitable.

For these reasons a timesharing system in the UK operating on the basis of the transfer of the freehold direct to the timeshare owners would be impracticable without very sophisticated provisions between them. The solutions which have been found involve the vesting of the legal estate in the developer or a third party (such as a custodian or professional corporate trustee), and the timeshare purchaser's interest is represented by membership of a club or as a beneficiary under a detailed trust (or both of the foregoing), or as a lessee or licensee of the timeshare developer.

There are five main ways in which timeshare schemes are in practice operated in the UK.

## 1 Club plans

These are the most widely used method of timesharing in the UK—usually they take the form of a members' club which must be distinguished from a proprietary club. In the case of the proprietary club the developer retains title in the development and grants membership to timeshare purchasers. Such club members would merely have a contractual right to use club property but normally no direct beneficial or protected interest in the property, which would remain in the ownership of the club's proprietor, the developer. A proprietary club structure would therefore be unsatisfactory for timeshare schemes.

In the case of a member's club, the structure most usually adopted is for the developer to become the founder member and immediately transfer title to the development to a trustee for the benefit of the ordinary club members. The developer will appoint the club members and issue them with membership certificates to evidence their interest. Whilst it is theoretically possible for the developer to incorporate the members' club (as a company limited by guarantee), in which the members' rights are set out in the articles and/or the constitution, the practical problems of this method have generally been found to outweigh any advantage over the conventional club/trustee structure, and could now give rise to difficulty if the OFT proposals are adopted (see Chapter 3).

## 2  Licences

This method may be arranged by the developer simply granting licences to the timeshare purchaser to use the development and issuing the timeshare purchaser with a 'holiday licence agreement' to reflect the rights granted. More usually, the development is vested in a trustee for the benefit of the licensees.

## 3  Leases

This plan is based upon a discontinuous lease and if it succeeds in its intention, provides the timeshare purchaser with a legal estate in land. Such a scheme aims to produce a landlord and tenant relationship between the developer and timeshare purchaser to which many of the normal incidents will be found to apply.

## 4  Company plans

This method is organised on the basis that the development is vested in a public limited company so that the timeshare purchasers become shareholders. Such schemes are provided for in France but are rare in the UK, due to a number of factors: the detailed requirements of the Companies Acts relating to prospectuses and the offering of shares for sale to the public; the taxation implications of such a sale and, more recently, the requirements of the Financial Services Act 1986.

## 5  Property bonds

This method of structuring enjoyment of real property for a large number of different individuals for successive periods during a year is very different from the ordinary kind of timeshare scheme, and it is marketed as an 'investment' and as an alternative to the conventional system. Under the property bond the purchaser pays an annual premium which is invested in funds managed by or on behalf of the developer very much in the manner of a life assurance policy. The principal difference of course is that the bond entitles the purchaser to use of one of a portfolio of properties usually in resort or holiday locations, for a period of time each year. Some of these bonds also provide life assurance cover. The bonds on the market at present provide the opportunity to use properties both within the UK and abroad as part of the portfolio. They also provide for the bond holder to encash and surrender the bond very much in the manner of a conventional life assurance policy or unit trust.

These five methods of timesharing will be examined in detail later in this chapter. Before doing so it is appropriate to consider the subject of planning permission for timeshare developments in the UK.

## Planning permission

The first issue which will face any developer of timeshare accommodation within England and Wales is whether planning permission will be required at all. In most cases establishing such facilities will entail development which requires permission and does not fall within the deemed permission provisions of the General Development Order (1988).

In considering any application for planning permission, the local planning authority will have regard to the local and structure plans in deciding whether to grant permission and if so what conditions to impose. The principles adopted in considering applications for permission for hotels, guest houses, holiday accommodation and other tourist facilities may well be relevant to applications for timeshare developments. As many such developments in the UK are located in or near tourist resorts or areas of outstanding natural beauty, the principles which are applied to residential 'tourist' development in those areas are likely to be of particular relevance.

Certain local authorities, particularly in London, are known to impose conditions upon grants of permission for new residential accommodation seeking to restrict use of the accommodation by occupiers to that of main residence and specifically excluding use of the accommodation for timeshare purposes, or holiday lettings or short-term lets.

### ETB guidance

The ETB publish a development guide (DG24) entitled *Obtaining Planning Permission* and a further guide entitled *Holiday Home Development* which, although published some time ago, are of assistance in outlining the principle issues. In their guide entitled *Developing Timeshare* (DG34), they state:

> Applications for planning permission for a timesharing scheme would be considered as for any other self-catering development for year-round occupation and the decision would probably be based on similar criteria.
> Discussions were held with several local planning authorities around the country

to obtain their views on the general principles of timesharing. Most were favourably inclined to the principle of this type of development.

Although the manner in which an owner disposes of his self-catering accommodation is of no concern to the planning authority (indeed they have no right to enquire), if they are aware that a timesharing scheme is envisaged, it may tip the balance in its favour since such a development might be expected to bring year-round benefits to the local economy.

Some authorities may require a legal agreement with the developer restricting the occupation of any one unit by the same occupier to a certain maximum number of weeks. This would be to avoid any form of permanent use by a single occupier.

Replacing existing static caravans with new large timesharing mobile homes or chalets could be welcomed where it has the effect of up grading the sites. In these circumstances mere replacements may not require planning permission but an application for an extension of permitted occupancy to twelve months a year from a shorter period will be necessary if the existing planning permission and/or site licence currently specify the latter. The planning authorities consulted indicated that they could see no reason why such permission should normally be withheld.

Whilst most local planning authorities consulted were favourably disposed towards timesharing schemes, seeing advantages over the traditional caravan site and "second home" arrangement, it must be stressed that planning applications for such schemes would be subject to all the normal restraints concerning design, location, access, availability of services and so on. Since the accommodation is likely to be occupied all the year round, the authorities may request that the standard should be similar to that required for permanent occupation, for whether the occupants are one family or fifty families the accommodation would be in full-time use.

The ETB also state, under the heading 'Factors that may Appeal to the Planning Authorities', that:

Since most developments are occupied all the year round by those who are likely to take a pride in ownership, developments—both buildings and the surrounding area—should be of superior design and maintained to a high standard. The opportunity of year-round patronage for local tradesmen may be regarded as a welcome feature in addition to the creation of job opportunities within the area.

### Legislative provisions

One issue which is far from clear is whether specific planning permission is required for the conversion of existing premises into a timeshare development. Section 22(1) of the Town and Country Planning Act 1971 ('the 1971 Act') defines the term 'development' to mean, *inter alia*, 'the making of any material change in use of any building or other land'. Section 23 of the 1971 Act provides that, subject to certain exceptions, planning permission will be required for any development.

If hotel accommodation is changed to residential accommodation for example, then this will probably amount to development and a material change of use requiring permission. The change will be to either class C2 'residential institutions' or C3 'Dwelling houses (where people live as a family or not more than six live as a single household)' from class C1, namely 'use as a hotel, boarding house, or guest house or hostel where, in each case, no significant element of care is provided', within the Town and Country Planning (Uses Classes) Order 1987 (see also the guidance on the Uses Order given in the Department of Environment Circular 13/87). The term 'care' is defined in art 2 of the 1987 Order to mean, *inter alia*, personal care for people in need of such care and consequently is unlikely to apply to accommodation used on a timeshare basis. Alternatively, the view may be taken that the timeshare user is *sui generis* (see art 3(6) of the 1987 Order and art 13 of Circular 18/87), so that any material change to that kind of user requires permission. Given the views expressed in the discussions with the ETB it is thought unlikely that such an approach would be adopted. The issue is far from academic, as hotels in England and Wales have been known to change their use to timeshare purposes.

What is not entirely clear is whether a timeshare development with a hotel amounts to material change of use requiring permission. The term 'hotel' is defined for the purposes of the Hotel Proprietors Act 1956 as 'an establishment held out by the proprietor as offering food, drink and, if so required, sleeping accommodation, without special contract, to any traveller presenting himself who appears able and willing to pay a reasonable sum for the services and facilities provided and who is in a fit state to be received'. The Act provides that such an establishment shall be deemed to be an inn for the purposes of the rights and liabilities attaching to inns and innkeepers.

In common parlance the word 'hotel' is often loosely used to refer to establishments which are not inns, such as a residential or private hotel. Furthermore, in the context of grants for the provision and development of new hotels under the Development of Tourism Act 1969, an establishment is not treated as a hotel 'unless its facilities and services are offered to the public generally, that is to say, to any person who wishes to avail himself of, and appears able and willing to pay a reasonable sum for the provision of services and facilities and is in a fit state to be received' (see s 16(2) of that Act).

It is provided by art 3 of the 1987 Order that the use of land or buildings for a purpose within the same class is not to be taken to involve development of the land. It must be at the very least arguable that outside London, such a difference of user with a building would not amount to a material change of user outside the scope of class C1, subject to the extent of the timeshare operation. On the other hand if the timeshare user is considered as *sui generis*, then the use within the building may be argued to have materially changed so as to require permission.

It is instructive to consider the distinction between use as bedsitting rooms and use for hotel purposes which was an issue before the Divisional Court in *Mayflower Cambridge Ltd* v *Secretary of State for the Environment* (1975) 30 P & CR 28, in the context of a purpose built block some of which was used for lettings on a weekly basis. In that case at page 31, Lord Widgery CJ held:

I have no doubt that this is well understood and is acceptable as an ordinary use of English, namely that the real difference between use as bedsitting rooms and use for the purposes of a hotel turns on the stability or instability of the population in the premises and the extent to which they are making the individual flatlets their homes. The essence of a hotel is that it takes transient passengers. Of course there may be an individual here and there who stays for a long time if it suits him, and there are buildings which are wrongly described as hotels or as residential hotels. But the basic feature of a hotel as the word is used in the English language is that it contains a transient population because it is there to serve people travelling who require short stays only.

By contrast the bed-sitting room in the way in which the phrase is used in English is somebody's home. It is where somebody lives, it is where somebody remains for substantial time. Accordingly one has in bed-sitting room use a far more stable population than one has in hotel use.

Although those Acts do not appear in the judgment, it seems quite clear that as the word 'hotel' was construed before the 1987 Uses Order, it is not limited by the definitions in the Hotel Proprietors Act 1956 or in the 1969 Act. Lord Widgery CJ made it clear that the provision of a restaurant, maid service and porterage are not necessary to establish hotel use. Under this definition, timeshare owners would certainly seem to qualify as transients, so that a change of user of part of the accommodation with a hotel to timeshare use might not require permission.

Before the 1987 Uses Order, some planning officers had expressed the view that the question also depended on the degree and nature of the change of occupation and on factors such as whether the timeshare accommodation is self-contained, whether it is self-catering and the extent to which the facilities in the hotel continue to be used by timeshare owners. It would be argued that the timesharing accommodation is not ordinarily available to members of the public so that it is not a hotel. However, it is doubtful whether this is an instrinsic part of the definition of a hotel, given that most timeshare users will wish to use it on a fairly transient basis. In any event unsold timeshare periods may continue to be used as part of the hotel. It is thought, however, that since the 1987 Uses Order the distinction between bed-sitting rooms and hotels has ceased to be of great significance, and that outside London there must be a good case for arguing that permission is not required for such an change of use. The view that permission is not required for the use of part of a hotel for timesharing purposes has been adopted by some local planning officers.

Nevertheless in at least one case a planning authority has decided that turning over part of a hotel to a timesharing scheme constituted a material change of use for which planning permission was required. The factors which the planning authority took into account when considering the application for permission are noteworthy, namely the arrangements for the use of the timeshare apartments in conjunction with other facilities of the hotel, which made it unlikely that they would be used for long-term residential development. This approach may well be followed by other authorities when considering applications for planning permission, especially where the timesharing scheme involves a large number of short-term timeshares rather than the sale of 'property' to a small number of purchasers.

In the event that the use of residential accommodation (see use class C3—dwelling houses) is changed to timeshare accommodation (which may fall within the C1 use class) it may well be that there is a material change of use: compare *Birmingham Corp* v *Habib Ullah* [1964] 1 QB 178 and *Panayi* v *Secretary of State for Environment* [1985] JPL 783. The last case also contains useful statutory and case law references to the meaning of the term 'hostel', which it is submitted will place most timeshare accommodation (which is intended to be more than 'basic and inexpensive') outside the meaning of that term in the C1 use class. It is settled law that the intensification of an existing use may amount to a material change in use if it is sufficiently obvious as to 'affect the definable character of the land and its use': see *Guildford RDC* v *Penny* [1959] 2 All ER 111, *James* v *Secretary of State for Wales* [1966] 3 All ER 964 and *Dyble* v *Minister for Housing and Local Government* [1966] EG 457 concerning change of use of land from part-time to full-time. See also art 9 of Circular 13/87. It is not essential to the classification of premises as a dwelling house that the premises be used as a home. In *Gravesham BC* v *Secretary of State for Environment* [1983] JPL 306, reference was made to a holiday cottage which was visited only at weekends and for a summer holiday but which nevertheless continued to be regarded as a dwelling house. Even so, the transient nature of the occupation may give ground for the argument that the timeshare use is in fact hotel user within class C1.

Within Greater London the position is clearer. Section 25 of the Greater London (General Powers ) Act 1973, as amended, provides that the use as temporary sleeping accommodation of any residential purpose in Greater London for a period of less than 90 days by way of trade, involves a material change of use requiring planning permission. In addition, the creation of a timesharing scheme of residential property within the Greater London area is expressly deemed to be a change of use which requires planning permission by the Greater London Council (General Powers) Act 1984, s 5 which provides as follows:

5—(1) For the purposes of section 22(1) of the act of 1972 there is a material change of use of a dwelling-house in Greater London, if not subject to a timesharing scheme it becomes so subject.

(2) For the purposes of this section a dwelling-house becomes subject to a timesharing scheme when any person is granted a right entitling him to occupy the dwelling-house or any part of it for a specified week or other period in every year during which the right subsists.

(3) In this section 'dwelling-house' includes a flat.

Coupled with the current restrictive policy towards the conversion of owner-occupied residential premises to any other use, such a provision is likely to prevent or severely restrict the conversion of existing residential premises to timesharing within the Greater London area. The district plans of many local authorities contain a policy commitment against allowing residential property to be used for holiday accommodation. For example, s 5.7.2 of the Royal Borough of Kensington & Chelsea's district plan states:

> The Council will not normally grant planning permission for the conversion or change of use of residential properties suitable for permanent residence of the Borough into accommodation used for holiday lets, business flats, or other housing for those whose permanent home is outside the Borough...

As against that or any other local plans, no doubt the applicant for permission will attempt to support his case by citing the relevant parts of the development guides, the fact (if applicable) that the local tourist board has given a grant towards the project, or other support, the contents of the circular on the development of tourism (13/79) and any guidance given on the development of tourism and hotels in the draft strategic planning guidance for areas such as London and Merseyside. In relation to any plan involving timesharing of residential accommodation where planning permission has not been obtained, there may well be uncertainty in the outcome of the application if a determination under the Town and Country Planning Act 1990, s 145 (the 1990 Act) has not been obtained (see below).

In relation to the conversion of only some of a number of apartments in the block to a timesharing use, perhaps the last word might be left with Justice Gardner in the American Case of *Laguna Royale Owners Association* v *Darger* (174 case RPTR 136 4th Dist App Div 2 28 May 1981) who in a dissenting opinion referring to a timesharing scheme of an apartment in a block said:

> The use of a unit [in a condominium] on a timesharing basis is inconsistent with the quiet enjoyment of the premises by the other occupants. Timesharing is a remarkable gimmick. P.T.Barnum would have loved it. It ordinarily brings in enormous profits to the seller and in this case would bring chaos to the other residents ... If as an occupant of a condominium I must anticipate that my neighbours are going to change with clock-work regularity, I might just as well move into a Hotel—and get room service.

This certainly seems to be a comment worthy of consideration. The transient nature of the occupancy would seem to indicate that there would be a change of use from that of the dwelling house to hotel within the C3 class (see the *Mayflower Cambridge Ltd* case above) apart from the question of nuisance and breach of covenant in the leases of the apartments.

Some timeshare schemes in England and Wales are based around buildings of considerable age and history. In such cases, it is also necessary to consider the issue of listed building consent, and enter into consultations with English Heritage. The application for permission might also have to pay special regard to the preservation and enhancement of the character of the building or of the area if the building was located in a conservation area (see s 277 of the 1990 Act and *Steinberg* v *Secretary of State for the Environment* [1989] JPL.

One way around the uncertainties of the planning process is to enter into an agreement with the local planning authority under s 53 of the 1971 Act. In the context of large scale developments this is clearly one option, although obviously the local planning authority will often require a substantial *quid pro quo* as part of such an agreement. At least one major timeshare development in

England has been brought about in association with a local authority where the authority initially took title to the freehold of the development.

The other main alternative available to a developer seeking to crystallise the position so far as planning permission is concerned, is to make an application to the local planning authority under s 145(1) of the 1990 Act, which provides that:

> If any person who proposes ... to make any change in the use of land wishes to have it determined whether ... the making of that change would constitute or involve development of the land and if so, whether an application for planning permission in respect thereof is required. .. he may either as part of an application for planning permission or without such application apply to the local Planning Authority to determine that question.

Appeals for such determinations are decided by the Secretary of State and thence, on points of law only, by the High Court under s 290 of the 1990 Act. The application for a determination under s 145 must be made in writing and the local planning authority must give written notice of the determination, stating the grounds and drawing attention to the right to appeal, within two months of the application (art 25 of the General Development Order 1988).

It is strongly recommended that this statutory procedure is followed in the context of applications for permission for timesharing accommodation. The main drawback may be the delay which any such application to a local authority can entail.

## Timeshare holiday leases

The concept of the timeshare holiday lease or discontinuous lease is one which has been afforded judicial recognition (see *Smallwood* v *Sheppards* [1985] 2 QB 627 (CA) and *Cottage Holiday Associates Ltd* v *CCE* [1983] 2 WLR 861, Woolf J). Precedents for timesharing leasing schemes may be found in the standard conveyancing precedent texts. However, because of the problems and uncertainties which have beset this form of timeshare scheme in practice, it is now hardly ever used by developers of schemes involving large numbers of units of accommodation, although one developer in the UK operated a scheme which purported to grant a lease together with a share in the management company to the timeshare purchaser.

One variation of the leasehold scheme is practice exemplified in the case of *PC & VI Cretney* v *CCE* (1984) VATTR 271, where the developer transferred the freehold to a trustee bank, took a lease back from the trustee and thereafter marketed not only the right to occupy the property for one or more weeks each year by way of an underlease, but also the right to undivided shares (units) in the new proceeds of sale. Both operations were held to be taxable supplies for VAT purposes.

**Lease or licence?**

Clearly this is an area where care must be taken to avoid creating a licence (see *Manchester City Council* v *National Car Parks Ltd* (1982) EG 1297 (CA))where discontinuous business use of a car park for certain hours of each day was held not to grant the appellant the exclusive possession necessary to create a lease.

The law in the area of the distinction between lease and licence is now governed by the decision of the House of Lords in *Street* v *Mountford* [1985] AC 805, which is the starting point for any consideration of this issue, at least in the context of residential accommodation. In essence, an intention to grant exclusive possession for a fixed or periodic term is essential to the grant of a lease. However, there may be an exceptional circumstance which negates the grant of a lease and indicates, for example, that the occupier was a lodger, or that there was no intention to create legal relations. The grant of a right to share residential premises with others, albeit with exclusive possession of one part of the accommodation, may not be sufficient to create a tenancy, joint or otherwise (see *AG Securities* v *Vaughan* [1988] 3 WLR 1205 (HL). It is also clear that the courts will not uphold terms which in form rather than in practice deprive the occupier of exclusive possession and were inserted solely for the purpose of evading the Rent Act 1977, and now presumably the Housing Act 1988 (see [1988] 3 WLR at 1216 (HL).

In the light of these decisions, a cautious timeshare purchaser may well wish the developer to insert a clause into his lease granting exclusive possession for the period of time over which the particular premises are to be used by him. It is doubtful, however, whether even such a declaration would be sufficient to convey exclusive possession, notwithstanding the decision in *Cottage Holiday Associates* (above). The labels that the parties attach to the incidents of their relationship are but one factor which the court takes into account in deciding whether a lease or licence is created.

**Assured tenancies**

Timeshare leases of this kind now granted would not create assured tenancies under the Housing Act 1988 (the 1988 Act) because such a tenancy would almost certainly amount to a holiday let, which is excluded from the category of assured tenancy by Sched 1, para 9 of this Act. Furthermore, an assured tenancy would not be created as the timeshare purchaser would not be occupying the accommodation as his only or principal dwelling. A timeshare lease entered into before the commencement of the 1988 Act will not have created protected tenancy under the Rent Act 1977 because of the holiday let provisions (see s 9). The severe penalties (criminal, and civil liability for damages) imposed by the 1988 Act for unlawful eviction without due process of law do not apply to licences or tenancies for exclusive holiday use (see ss 30 and 31 of the 1988 Act).

Timeshare leases are, almost without exception, expressed to be for the holiday user. In theory, however, the user clause might well be different and the assured tenancy provisions applicable, if there was no such restriction.

### Protection for the timeshare purchaser

Leases of this nature offer some advantages to timeshare purchasers (and to any mortgagees) in that they are afforded a considerable degree of statutory protection against arbitrary re-entry or forfeiture by the landlord, or by any person claiming through, under, or in trust for the landlord—eg a liquidator or trustee in bankruptcy, or a superior landlord (see in particular the Law of Property Act 1925, s 146, the Leasehold Property (Repairs) Act 1938, s 1, the County Court Act 1984, ss 138–140, the Common Law Procedure Act 1952, ss 210–212 and the Supreme Court Act 1981, s 38).

However, the conventional form of protection—by registration as a long lease at the Land Registry—will not be available if the view is taken that the lease is for a term of less than 21 years.

Where the timeshare lease is for a period in excess of 21 years it is necessary to consider whether it is to be construed as one for successive terms or for one continuous term. The Law of Property Act 1925, s 149(3), provides that:

> a term, at a rent or granted in consideration of a fine, limited after the commencement of this Act to take effect more than 21 years from the date of the instrument purporting to create it, shall be void, and any contract made after such commencement to create a term shall likewise be void; . . .

In *Smallwood* v *Shephards* (above), Wright J described a lease granting the right of occupation for three successive bank holidays as 'an agreement for a single letting (although the period of the agreed letting was not continuous) at a single rent'. Section 149(3) does not appear to have been considered. Woolf J in the *Cottage Holiday Associates* case (above), did not find it necessary to consider the application of that section in the context of timeshare leases of holiday cottages. He approved of the view that 'although a lease could be regarded as continuing for more than 21 years, the interest because it was discontinuous did not do so'. For the purposes of the VAT legislation (Finance Act 1972, s 46 and Sched 4, group 8) he distinguished between the lease which created the interest (which did continue for more than 21 years) and the interest (which did not).

This approach to the meaning of the phrase 'term of years' means that the provisions of the Landlord and Tenant Act 1985, s 11 are applicable to timeshare leases of this kind. However, it places such timeshare leases outside the benefit of the provisons of the Leasehold Property (Repairs) Act 1938, s 1, which only applies to leases granted to a lessee for a term certain of not less than seven years.

In theory then, the application of s 149(3) of the 1925 Act remains an issue where the term of the purported grant is in excess of 21 years. For that reason the draftsmen of timeshare leases have in the past sought to provide for the event that the lease is found to be granted for successive terms some of which would take effect over 21 years from the date of the instrument, but introducing a clause declaring that the lease takes effect as a lease for the holiday period in each term of 20 years from the commencement date and thereafter as a licence on the same terms for 60 years commencing on the expiry of the lease. A similar effect might be achieved by the insertion of an option to renew after 20 years: compare *Re Strand and Savoy Properties* [1960] Ch 582 and *Weg Motors* v *Hales* [1960] Ch 582 and *Weg Motors* v *Hales* [1962] Ch 49.

The protection afforded by Part II of the Landlord and Tenant Act 1954 would not appear to apply to timeshare leases so far as they are restricted to holiday use. The position might be different if the user clause were otherwise—compare *Manchester City Council* v *National Car Parks Ltd* above. It is understood that some organisations make use of residential accommodation in large cities such as London on a timeshare basis for the purpose of providing leisure facilities for executives. Such an arrangement would have to be considered separately.

Similarly, the provisions of the Leasehold Reform Act 1967 will not be applicable in the case of holiday accommodation, if only because the condition of the occupation being used as a main or only residence in the ten years before the application for enfranchisement will not be satisfied. Different user clauses and a higher level of occupation throughout the year than might normally be expected in the context of holiday accommodation might make this view worth reconsidering.

Timeshare leases would seem not to be affected by the perpetuities rule: see the Perpetuities and Accumulations Act 1964, s 8(1) which provides that the rule 'shall not operate to invalidate a power conferred on trustees or other persons to ... lease any property for full consideration'.

The Unfair Contract Terms Act 1977, ss 2–4 (relating to the prohibition and regulation of attempts to exclude and restrict liability for death, personal injury and other liability) will not apply to a timeshare lease 'so far as it relates to the creation or transfer of an interest in land'. On the footing that the timeshare lease is construed as a licence, provisions which seek to exclude liability for negligence causing loss or damage will be enforceable only in so far as they satisfy the statutory test of reasonableness (see s 11 and Sched 1 to the 1977 Act). Equally, provisions in a licence construed as a lease which work to exclude or restrict liability for breach of contract or to modify contractual performance may also be enforceable only so far as they satisfy that test. Slightly different provisions of the Unfair Contract Terms Act 1977 apply in Scotland.

In addition, the normal remedies for misrepresentation at common law, in equity, and under the Misrepresentation Act 1967, will apply to the negotiation and entry into a contract for the timeshare lease. It seems that the Unfair Contract Terms Act 1977, s 8 would be applicable to the contract for the timeshare lease, which is sometimes made subject to the standard form national conditions (see *Walker* v *Boyle* [1982] 1 WLR 495, for example). All new contracts for the grant of a timeshare lease will have to comply with the Law of Property (Miscellaneous Provisions) Act 1989 which, amongst other things, repeals s 40 of the Law of Property Act 1925 and requires that all contracts for the sale of land must be in writing and signed by the parties.

In the past, timesharing leases sometimes provided for the freehold in the development to be transferred to the management company, which was effectively owned by all the timeshare lessees. This sometimes created problems with regard to capital gains tax liability on the disposal of the lessee's interest in the timeshare scheme. It is thought that such a provision may have had a negative effect upon a developer's ability to raise finance secured on the freehold. Value added tax is payable on the grant of a timeshare lease (see the *Cottage Holiday Associaties* case above).

So far as the developer is concerned, the value of the development as security for borrowing is materially diminished by the grant of a timeshare lease. A mortgagee will only be able to realise his security on the freehold of the development subject to the leasehold interest of the timeshare purchasers granted with its consent—assuming of course that the timeshare purchaser holds under a lease.

**Maintenance**

In relation to leasehold timeshare schemes, the provisions of the Landlord and Tenant Act 1985, ss 11–16 (as amended by s 116 of the Housing Act 1988) should be considered. Section 11(1) of the 1985 Act implies covenants in the lease which oblige the landlord to keep the structure and exterior of the dwelling house in repair and to maintain in proper working order installations for the supply of water, gas, electricity, for sanitation, space heating and heating water. Woolf J in the *Cottage Holiday Associates* case accepted that the logical consequence of his decision was that the implied repairing obligations imposed by the predecessor to these sections would apply to timeshare leases of the kind under consideration. In theory, these provisions prevent the enforcement of maintenance charge provisions relating to such repairs. In some cases, however, the cumulative total of the timeshare weeks purchased might exceed seven years, whilst some developers might seek to take advantage of the exemption from the benefit of these provisions provided by s 13(2)*(c)* of the 1985 Act where there is an option to renew for a period which, together with the original term, exceeds seven years.

It is submitted that in the context of the Landlord and Tenant Act 1985, the distinction between a lease which may continue for (say) 80 years, and the interest or tenancy which subsists in the land for only the total of the timeshare weeks which are the subject of the lease, is not one which is of assistance. The relevant sections of the 1985 Act apply to 'a lease of a dwelling-house . . . for a term of less than seven years'; and it seems clear, even on the view adopted in the *Cottage Holiday Associates* case, that the term of some timeshare leases would extend to a period in excess of seven years, where more than one weekly period in a year was the subject of the lease.

It has been suggested that the accommodation which is the subject of a timeshare lease is not a dwelling house because it is only used as temporary holiday accommodation. That argument is not supported by the words of McCullough J in *Gravesham BC* v *Secretary of State for the Environment and Michael O'Brien* [1983] JPL 307 at 308, who said the following in the context of the issue whether the General Development Order 1973 had granted deemed permission for a particular building as a dwelling house:

> Consider a building which anyone would acknowledge was a dwelling-house. If it was not being lived in because, for example, the occupants were on holiday or because they had two houses and spent half the year in each, it remained a dwelling-house. Take a common situation where a family had a second house in the country which was only visited at weekends, in the summer months and for a summer holiday. This was clearly a dwelling-house. So the intention to use one's house, or the practice of using it throughout the year was not essential.

He distinguished this from hotels and holiday camps which did not have the facilities required for day-to-day private domestic existence.

Section 11 of the 1985 Act is subject to the proviso that any covenant by the *lessee* for the repair of the premises is of no effect so far as it relates to the obligations imposed on the landlord by s 11(1) of the 1985 Act, or unless and to the extent that it imposes on the lessee a requirement to carry out works or repairs for which the lessee is liable by virtue of his duty to use the premises in a tenant-like manner or to keep in repair and maintain anything which the lessee is entitled to remove from the dwelling house.

The county court may make an order authorising inclusion in a lease or agreement collateral to a lease 'provisions excluding or modifying in relation to the lease, the provisions of s 11 with respect to the repairing obligations of the parties if it appears to the court that it is reasonable to do so, having regard to all the circumstances of the case, including the other terms and conditions of the lease' with the consent of the landlord and the tenant (see s 12 (2) of the 1985 Act). It is thought that the approach taken by the courts to this section might well be similar to that taken to an agreement or lease contracting out of the protection granted by Part II of the Landlord and Tenant Act 1954 when the application is put before the court under s 38 of that Act.

In the event of uncertainty as to whether s 11 of the 1985 Act applies to a particular timeshare lease, it is possible to apply to the county court for a declaration to determine this issue, notwithstanding the fact that no other relief is sought pursuant to the procedure under s 15 of the 1985 Act. In principle, timeshare purchasers holding under the appropriate lease might be able to raise the landlord's failure to comply with the s 11 repairing obligations as a defence to possession and forfeiture proceedings based upon failure to pay maintenance or service charges. In practice, this uncertainty is likely to prove deeply unattractive to developers and, more importantly, to their mortgagees or financiers.

The landlord under the timeshare lease will most probably owe a duty of care to all persons who might reasonably be expected to be affected by defects in the state of the premises or the timeshare development, as he will owe an obligation to the tenant for the maintenance or repair of the premises (see the Defective Premises Act 1972, s 4(1). The nature of the duty is to take such care as is reasonably necessary to keep lessees or their invitees free from personal injury or from damage to their property caused by a relevant defect, although that duty is subject to the landlord being in a position where he knows, or ought to have known, of the relevant defect. Where the landlord is the developer or a trustee holding title to unsold weeks or accommodation in the development or the common parts, or even a maintenance company to whom title to the development has been transferred, any of these bodies may attract a liability under s 4 of the 1972 Act or as occupiers of the premises which are within their control under the Occupiers Liability Acts 1957 and 1984.

In England, Wales and Northern Ireland, such a landlord will not be able to rely upon a notice or other form of disclaimer attempting to exclude or restrict liability for damage to property of a visitor to the development, except in so far as it satisfies the test of reasonableness (see s 2(2) of the Unfair Contract Terms Act 1977). There is no equivalent section in that Act which applies to Scotland (see *Robbie* v *Graham & Sibbald* [1989] 38 EG 124, where this anomaly was highlighted). This might be of significance where sports and other facilities in a timeshare development are (as sometimes happens) open to other members of the public, or simply to guests of the timeshare purchasers.

In any proceedings in which the tenant of a 'dwelling', such as a timeshare apartment, alleges a breach of a repairing covenant on the part of his landlord relating to any part of the premises in which the dwelling is comprised, the court may order specific performance of the covenant, notwithstanding that the breach may relate to a part of the premises not let to the tenant and despite the equitable rule restricting the availability of the remedy, by virtue of s 17 of the 1985 Act. It is thought that in principle, this provision may enable a timeshare lessee to compel his landlord (whether it be the developer, trustee or other body) to carry out repairing obligations. It is noteworthy that it applies to a 'dwelling' and not simply a dwelling house, so that even if timeshare accommodation cannot be categorised as a dwelling house within ss 11–16 of the 1985 Act, the express covenants may be relied upon to found a claim for specific performance. It should be emphasised that where the maintenance or repair obligations are taken on by a maintenance company or trustee which is not the landlord of the timeshare purchaser, the remedy under the 1985 Act is not open to the timeshare purchaser.

The other main method available to a timeshare lessee to compel a landlo'' to carry out repairs, is to apply on an (interlocutory) application for appointment of a receiver to manage the development under Supreme (
Act 1981, s 37(1) as in *Hart* v *Emelkirk Ltd* [1983] 1 WLR 1289 and *D*(
*Bluelake Investments* (1985) EG 275 462. Where the timeshare a''
dation consists of premises forming the whole or part of the buildi''

building or part contains two or more 'flats' the lessee may apply for the appointment of a receiver or manager of the premises pursuant to the Landlord and Tenant Act 1987, s 24 and Part II where there is default by the landlord in his obligations under the lease, and it is appropriate to make such an appointment.

## Service charges

The law concerning service charges in leases relating to residential accommodation has gone through a number of changes in the past few years. The position is now governed by the Landlord and Tenant Act 1985, ss 18–30, as amended by the Landlord and Tenant Act 1987. These provisions now apply to service charges in respect of dwellings, and are no longer restricted to flats. It is thought that the definition of 'service charge' in s 18(1) of the 1985 Act is wide enough to include the maintenance and service charge provisions of most timeshare schemes based on leases. There is detailed provision for the regulation of the calculation of service charges and the provision of information, estimates to tenants or to a recognised tenants' association, and for consultation with tenants in respect of works exceeding a particular value (see s 20 of the 1985 Act, as amended). Proceedings for declarations as to the reasonableness of costs incurred, of the standard of services or works for which costs are incurred and of advance payments of costs may be brought before a county court by virtue of s 19 of the 1985 Act, as amended. Failure to comply with the duties imposed on landlords as to provision of a written summary of costs in s 21, the inspection of accounts and supporting documents and information under s 22, the making of a request for information relating to costs to the superior landlord under s 23 is a summary offence punishable by fine (see s 25). Schedule 3 makes provisions in favour of tenants of dwellings relating to insurance similar to the provision in respect of service charge. Default in respect of some of those provisions is also a criminal offence.

Section 42 of the 1987 Act provides that all sums in respect of service charges and any investments representing the sums are to be held on trust by the payee. This only applies where tenants of two or more dwellings may be required to contribute to the same costs by the payment of service charges. There is provision for what happens to any surplus on dissolution of the fund or termination of the lease.

In principle, these provisions are thought to be applicable to timeshare apartments held on leases. The fact that there is a holiday user does not mean that they do not qualify as dwellings within the amended s 30 of the 1985 Act (see the definition of 'dwelling' given in s 38 of the 1985 Act, and the *Gravesham BC* case above). Needless to say, none of these provisions would apply if the lease were held to be a licence. The provisions of the 1985 and the 1987 Acts do not apply in Scotland or Northern Ireland.

It is also thought that in principle the provisions of Part I of the Landlord and Tenant Act 1987, providing for the right of first refusal in favour of qualifying tenants on disposals by the landlord, would apply to those timeshare schemes which operate by granting leases of flats, as defined in s 60 of the 1987 Act. In theory this could place a developer who subsequently seeks to transfer the freehold of the development to the trustee or to a purchaser at risk. In practice, no doubt, developers take advantage of the exemptions from the relevant disposals subject to rights of first refusal granted by the 1987 Act (such as transfers to associated companies) which developers of ordinary complexes of flats would also seek to rely upon.

If the approach of Woolf J (in the *Cottage Holiday Associates* case) to the timeshare leases is followed, so that the interest or the term extends in most cases for a period of less than seven years, the lessees of the timeshare apartments will be unable, so far as they were otherwise qualifying tenants, to apply for an order compulsorily vesting their landlord's interest in a person nominated by them in accordance with Part III of the Landlord and Tenant Act 1987. Such a right only applies to long leases which are defined to mean a lease for a term certain exceeding 21 years by s 59 of the 1987 Act. The same is true of the right to apply to the court for a variation of terms of a long lease under Part IV of the 1987 Act.

Part VI of the 1987 Act also makes provisions with respect to the information with which landlords are obliged to provide tenants. Of particular relevance to tenants of timeshare accommodation is the requirement that written demands contain an address for the landlord within England and Wales at which notices (including notices in proceedings) may be served on the landlord, by the tenant (see ss 47 and 48 of the 1987 Act). Some timeshare developers operate through companies based in countries with favourable tax regimes or from areas closer to home such as the Channel Isles or the Isle of Man. To some extent such provisions may be self-enforcing. In the period before compliance, rent is not treated as being due. This is of obvious significance to a tenant who is seeking relief in respect of complaints about the management of the accommodation where the landlord (whether he be the developer trustee or maintenance company) is a corporation based outside England and Wales without an address for service within that territory. The tenant is also given the right to search (and take copies from) the Land Register for the name and address of the landlord (s 51 of the 1987 Act, which inserts a new s 112C into the Land Registration Act 1925. This may be of particular assistance to a tenant of timeshare accommodation faced with a landlord who wishes to remain anonymous.

### Shares in the management company

Some developers accompany the grant of a timeshare lease with the transfer of a share in the management company which is contracted to perform the maintenance functions. This scheme is similar to that sometimes used in the sale of apartment leases in blocks of flats in England and Wales. It has yet to be resolved whether this amounts to the carrying on of investment business within the terms of ss 1 and 3 and Sched 1 to the Financial Services Act 1986 ('the 1986 Act'). Such an activity is unlawful unless carried out by a member of, or under the approval of, a self-regulating organisation or other authorised institution. At first sight the sale of the shares in the management company would appear to fall within the term 'investment business', although probably not within 'units in a collective investment scheme' as defined by s 75(6)(g) and Sched 1, para 6 of the 1986 Act. An outline of the consequence of the illegality and other restrictions placed upon the carrying on of investment business by the 1986 Act may be found in Chapter 3.

## Timeshare holiday licences

This category of plan is of central importance to the overwhelming majority of timeshare developments in the UK which operate by way of club membership in favour of the timeshare purchaser, coupled with a trust of the development and the property of the club in favour of the timeshare purchasers. It seems reasonably clear that such an arrangement will be construed as creating a contractual 'holiday' licence of the development (see particularly *American Real Estate (Scotland) Ltd* v *CCE* [1980] VATTR 88, where such a view appears to have been accepted).

Timeshare leases which do not fall to be construed as such will almost certainly be considered as licences. In that event, unless the timeshare accommodation concerned is held by a trustee (so that the licensee becomes a beneficiary under the terms of the trust) there is an obvious danger that the licence will be determined upon the bankruptcy or insolvency of the licensor, thus leaving the timeshare licensee without any effective means of enforcing the right to use the apartment. For this reason, unless the timeshare accommodation is held by a trustee, many 'timeshare holiday licences' should be approached with caution.

A grant of the right to use residential premises in return for consideration which does not confer the right to exclusive possession or enjoyment will create a contractual licence, in the absence of exceptional circumstances. It is also possible for a licensee to be granted exclusive possession. Neverthless, it might be argued that the circumstances surrounding the grant of a right to use an apartment on the timeshare basis indicate that the grant of exclusive possession is referrable to a relationship other than a tenancy. For example, it would be strongly arguable that the provision of services by the developer or a service company such as food and cleaning make the timeshare purchaser the equivalent of the lodger mentioned by Lord Templeman in *Street* v *Mountford*. On the other hand, the argument runs that lettings for the period and purpose of a holiday have not been categorised as licences simply on account of the discontinous and temporary nature of the occupation. It appears to be settled law since *Smallwoods* v *Sheppards* (above) and the

*Cottage Holiday Associates* case, that in principle a timeshare arrangement can constitute a lease.

It is often difficult to determine whether a transaction relating to the occupation of property creates a licence or a lease, but after the decision in *Street* v *Mountford* the onus falls upon those who seek to assert that exclusive possession of residential accommodation is consistent only with a licence to establish that the relationship is not one of landlord and tenant. The criteria which were applied to the finding of a licence in the past, such as whether the grantor has the power to grant a lease, no longer assume the importance which they did before *Street* v *Mountford*. Nevertheless, Lord Templeman did indicate that where the grantor had no power to grant a tenancy this may have been sufficient to negate the intention of the parties to create legal relations necessary to establish a tenancy (see [1985] AC 809 at 821 B). This may be important where a licence to use accommodation on a timeshare basis is granted by a service or maintenance company or the developer company, and the owner of the land was a director of any of those companies in his personal capacity or any other individual. Perhaps it may still be argued that these are the 'exceptional circumstances' which Lord Templeman referred to in his speech in *Street* v *Mountford* which would preclude the existence of a lease where exclusive possession had been granted: *Torbett* v *Faulkner* [1951] 2 TLR 659 and *Finbow* v *Air Ministry* [1963] 1 WLR 697.

It is now clear that whether the intention of the parties was to create a lease or a licence is not the relevant issue. Save in exceptional circumstances, the only relevant intention is that to grant exclusive possession of residential accommodation, together with rent and a term (see *AG Securities* v *Vaughan* above). Even the existence of rent is not a pre-requisite for the grant of a tenancy (see *Ashburn Antstalt* v *Arnold* [1988] 2 All ER 147 (CA)). However, the approach of the House of Lords in *Street* v *Mountford* has not been adopted without qualification in the context of business premises (see *Dresden Estates* v *Collinson* [1971] 1 EGLR 45, (1988) 55 P & CR 47, and compare *Dellneed* v *Chin* (1987) 53 P & CR 172, for example). In such a context the court may well be more willing to find that it was not the intention of the parties to grant exclusive possession. It is thought, however, that most timeshare accommodation will be treated as residential (holiday) accommodation for this purpose and not as business occupation which might qualify for protection under the Landlord and Tenant Act 1954.

The label which the parties put on the relationship is not decisive. Nevertheless, a written agreement conferring exclusive possession or failing so to do, will be good *prima facie* evidence of the parties' intentions so far as that issue was concerned—the onus will lie on the person seeking to disturb a plain statement on the face of the document (see *Buchmann* v *May* [1978] 2 All ER 993 and *Mikeover Ltd* v *Brady* [1989] 39 EGLR 92). The court will aim to detect what Lord Templeman in *Street* v *Mountford* described as a 'sham' or 'artificial device', which he subsequently described as a 'pretence' in the *Antoniades* v *Villers* appeal (see above) designed to avoid the Rent Acts. The

Rent Acts and now the Housing Act 1988 are most unlikely to apply to lettings or licence arrangements for timeshare accommodation for other reasons already stated. It is unclear how the courts will approach clauses in timeshare licences which purport to deny the timeshare purchaser exclusive occupation or contain declarations that services will be provided and that there is no intention to grant exclusive possession or create a relationship of landlord and tenants: compare the terms of the agreement in the *Antoniades* v *Villers* appeal, and the approach of the courts to a declaration in an agreement relating to the shared use of residential accommodation that no landlord and tenant relationship was intended, in *Nicolau* v *Pitt* [1989] 21 EG 71.

It is clear that where a number of documents confer rights on different persons relating to the occupation of the premises these may be construed together (see the *AG Securities* v *Vaughan* appeal and *Stribling* v *Wickham* [1989] 27 EG 81 (CA)). In the context of timeshare purchasers the existence of separate agreements relating to maintenance or other written agreements relating to occupation of the particular apartment for the same time period during a year may need to be construed together.

It is also clear that in considering documents for the purpose of deciding whether a tenancy or a licence has been created and whether or not an agreement genuinely represents the intention of the parties, the surrounding circumstances should be considered including relationships between prospective occupiers, pre-document negotiations, the nature and extent of the accommodation and the actual method of occupation (see *AG Securities* v *Vaughan, Alslan* v *Murphy*, nos 1 & 2, *Duke* v *Wynne* [1989] 38 EG 109 (CA) and *Nunn* v *Dalrymple, The Times*, 3 August 1989).

In other words, whether the timeshare purchaser has exclusive possession as a matter of fact is still an important question. In England and Wales (although apparently not in Scotland), the fact that the right of exclusive possession is discontinuous does not appear to be an objection to the existence of a lease. In the *Cottage Holiday Associates* case, mention was made of the fact that the modern tendency in office lettings was to restrict occupation to normal business hours and to prevent occupation at weekends; no suggestion was made that this prevented a lease from arising. On the other hand the Court of Appeal in *Manchester City Council* v *National Car Parks Ltd* (above) thought that the restriction of use of a car park to the hours of 12.01 am and 2 am and 7 am and 12 pm daily was sufficient to indicate that the parties did not intend to and did not in fact grant exclusive possession of the car park (see also *Taylor* v *Caldwell* (1963) 3 B & S 826 and *Smith* v *Northside Developments* (1987) 283 EG 1211). This must be contrasted with the case of *Westminister Corp* v *Southern Railway* [1936] AC 511, where it was said that the occupier of a station bookstall who was only allowed access when the station was open could nevertheless be regarded as a tenant.

The surrounding circumstances may be relevant in the context of a timeshare licence. Periodic payments, covenants against assigning or underletting albeit qualified, covenants as to quiet enjoyment and a right of re-entry may all be consistent with a lease rather than a licence of a right to use a garage forecourt: see *Shell Mex and BP Ltd* v *Manchester Garages Ltd* [1971] 1 All ER 841 (CA), for example. Lord Templeman in *Street* v *Mountford* considered that the agreement in that case was personal in its nature and created personal privilege if it did not confer a right to exclusive possession of the filling station. It may also be relevant whether the accommodation is self-contained and identifiable. If the timeshare purchaser's agreement only specifies a particular type of accommodation, rather than a defined unit, or if the period of occupation is governed by the acquisition of points or a booking system rather than a specific time period in a particular apartment, which is a feature of some timeshare schemes in the UK, these factors would point to the existence of the licence rather than a lease in a specific property. The failure of an agreement to grant the right to use a specific apartment is thought by the authors of one leading text to indicate that the occupant is a lodger who has no exclusive possession.

It may still be relevant to consider *Marchant* v *Charters* [1977] 1 WLR 1181, where a bed-sitting room was occupied on terms that the landlord cleaned the rooms daily and provided clean linen each week in a 'self-catering residential hotel'. The Court of Appeal held that the occupation of a room on those terms consituted a licence. Lord Denning, MR in that case said that the test of whether a tenancy was created depended upon the nature and quality of the occupancy in the light of all the circumstances and whether it was intended that the occupier should have a stake in the room, or permission personally to occupy. Lord Templeman in *Street* v *Mountford* held that that was the wrong test—the only test was whether on its true construction the agreement confers on the occupier exclusive possession. He held however that the actual decision in *Marchant* v *Charters* was sustainable on the ground that the occupier was a lodger and therefore not a tenant. It might well be said that an agreement granting the right to occupation of a self-catering timesharing apartment with the benefit of services such as cleaning, clean linen, access to a restaurant on site and other services was in a similar position. The nature of the written agreement would have to be considered.

If the document is regarded as having created a licence, then it will be necessary to consider which category of licence has been created. A threefold classification of licences was put forward in *Hounslow LBC* v *Twickenham Garden Development Ltd* [1971] Ch 233, namely licences coupled with an interest, contractual licences and bare licences. The only relevant category in the area of timeshare accommodation is likely to be a contractual licence, as all timeshare contracts will be supported by consideration and are most unlikely to be coupled with the grant of interest in land. Nevertheless, a licensee's interest can be protected as against the licensor by injunction (see *Varrall* v *Great Yarmouth BC* [1980] 3 WLR 258, for example). Whether this relief will be granted depends upon the construction of the terms of the contract. Most purchasers of licences relating to timeshare accommodation will wish to ensure that the licence is only revocable by the licensor prior to determination of the term in exceptional and specified circumstances (perhaps on expiry of a period of time after service of a notice setting out the grounds of alleged breach and giving appropriate opportunity to remedy the breach in similar terms to the notice under the Law of Property Act 1925, s 146. Subject to the exceptions relating to holiday occupation mentioned earlier, such a timeshare licensee is protected by the Protection from Eviction Act 1977 (as amended by the Housing Act 1988) (see *Warder* v *Cooper* [1970] 1 Ch 495). In relation to timeshare agreements concerning occupation of caravans or other mobile homes, the Mobile Homes Act 1983 and the Caravan Sites Act 1968 should also be considered.

There are circumstances in which contractual licences may be enforced against third parties (such as purchasers from or mortgagees of the licensor of the timeshare apartment or a liquidator or trustee in bankruptcy) who take with notice of the licence, but these are restricted to those where the court will impose a constructive trust upon the third party: see *Binion* v *Evans* [1972] Ch 359, and *Ashburn Anstalt* v *Arnold* (above). The suggestion of Denning LJ (as he then was) in *Errington* v *Errington & Woods* [1952] 1 KB 290, that there was a line of authority supporting the proposition that equity would intervene to prevent a third party who was a purchaser for value without notice, was rejected in the *Ashburn Anstalt* case.

However, it is clear from the *Ashburn Anstalt* case that the actual decision in the *Errington* case could be justified on the basis that the third party was bound by an estoppel founded upon a representation made as to the occupation of the licensee, or that the licensee held an interest in the land under the doctrine of constructive trusts. The latter doctrine may only bind a purchaser of the freehold to the timeshare apartments if it is aware of the interest held by the timesharers or of a trust in their favour.

A timeshare licensee is unlikely to be in a position to take advantage of the doctrine of estoppel in the event of a purchaser acquiring an interest in the freehold of the timeshare development, unless circumstances arise whereby a vendor of the timeshare licence (the developer or his agents) makes representations which induce a timeshare licensee or prospective timeshare licensee to act to his detriment or otherwise change his position. The developer and the purchaser of the development may be bound by those representations, despite the absence of consideration or even privity: compare *Brikkom Investments* v *Carr*, and *Midland Bank* v *Farmpride Hatcheries Ltd* (1980) 260 EG 493.

A timeshare licence may be registrable under the Land Charges Act 1972 as a class C(iv) estate contract. However, if the licence is under seal or for less than three years and may be construed as a lease, it is not registrable as an estate contract, as the legal estate if it exists has already been created and the licence will not amount to a 'contract to convey or create a legal estate' within s 2(4) of the 1972 Act. A licence for a period of more than three years, not being under seal will be 'void for the purpose of conveying or creating a legal estate' (see s 52(1) of the Law of Property Act 1925), but may operate as a contract to create such an estate.

The timeshare licence is almost certainly not registrable as a class D (iii) equitable easement, defined as an easement right or privilege over or affecting land, creating or arising on or after 1 January 1926 being merely an equitable interest (see s 2(5) of the Land Charges Act 1972). Such an equitable easement does not embrace a ' . . . right liberty or privilege arising in equity by reason of the doctrine of mutual benefit and burden or arising out of acquiescence or by reason of a contractual licence' (see *ER Ives Investments Ltd* v *High* [1967] 2 QB 379, approved in *Shiloh Spinners* v *Harding* [1973] AC 691). No other registrable classes would appear to have any application to a timeshare licence.

## Land registration

It is also necessary to consider how far timeshare holiday leases and licences are registrable under the Land Registration Acts 1925 and 1986. The three categories of interest under the scheme of the Land Registration Acts are:

1 Registered or registrable interests.
2 Overriding interests, not capable of protection by registration.
3 Minor interests.

### 1 Registered or registrable interests

As we have seen in the *Smallwood* v *Shepards* and the *Cottage Holiday Associates* cases, timeshare holiday leases are capable of existing as legal interests and, subject to argument about the length of the term exceeding 21 years, they are registrable interests being 'estates capable of subsisting as legal estates' within the Land Registration Act 1925, s 2. It is understood that this view has been accepted by one district land registry in relation to a leasehold scheme within their area. On the other hand, in at least one other scheme the timeshare 'leases' have been refused registration as such, and are only protected by a note of the fact in the Charges Register that the land is subject to rights of intermittent occupation.

On the other hand, if the arrangement is not capable of registration as a lease of more than 21 years or as a licence, requiring registration see s 70(1)*(k)* of the 1925 Act, as amended, in relation to 'short' leases, and s 70(1)*(g)* of the 1925 Act in relation to licences. The former section only protects the timeshare purchaser who holds under a lease where a rent or a fine is reserved. The latter section protects 'the rights of every person in actual occupation of the land or in receipt of the rents and profits thereof save where enquiry is made of such person and the rights are not declared'. However, in most cases the timeshare purchaser will not be in actual occupation for most of the year or possibly even for several years if he has taken advantage of one of the timeshare exchange schemes to take the benefit of his weeks at another timeshare apartment in this or another country. It is possible that he may seek to say that he was in receipt of the rent of his apartment if he 'sublets' his right to use the apartment for a particular year, but otherwise his position under s 70(1)*(g)* may well be considered to be tenuous (see *City of London Building Society* v *Flegg* [1987] 1 WLR 1266 (HL), where the rights of the parents of the mortgagors and joint tenants in occupation were held to have been overreached by the execution of legal charges in favour of subsequent mortgagees by two joint tenants). Contrast *Williams & Glyn's Bank* v *Boland* [1981] AC 487, where minor interests of wives in actual occupation were held not to have been overreached by the execution of a legal charge by one trustee, in each case their husbands.

## 2  Overriding interests

Section 48(1) of the 1925 Act provides that 'any lessee or other person entitled to or with an interest in a lease of registered land, where the term granted is not an overriding interest, may apply to the Land Registrar to register notice of such lease in the prescribed manner ...' In this connection a point to be considered in relation to some schemes is whether s 8(2) of the 1925 Act (as amended by the Land Registration Act 1986) applies. That section provides that:

> Leasehold land held under a lease containing a prohibition or restriction on dealings therewith inter vivos shall not be registered under the Act unless and until provision is made in the prescribed matter for preventing any dealing therewith in contravention of the prohibition or restriction by an entry on the register to that effect, or otherwise.

It used to be the case that where a developer granted a headlease of timeshare accommodation to a service company, with the timeshare interests being represented by licences issued by the service company, there would often be a prohibition against assignment in the headlease. Owing to the operation of the predecessor to this section the service company would not in the circumstances have had a registrable interest against which the interests of the licencees could be noted. The position is changed by the amended section which enables an application for registration to be made in respect of leases granted before, as well as after, the commencement of the 1986 Act.

## 3  Minor interests

'Minor interests' are defined by s 2(xv) of the Land Registration Act 1925 as interests 'not capable of being disposed of or created by registered dispositions and capable of being overriden (whether or not a purchaser has notice thereof) by the proprietors unless protected as provided by [the] Act and all rights and interests which are not registered or protected on the register and are not overriding interests ...'. These are no longer capable of entry on the minor interests index which has been abolished.

There are four possible ways in which timeshare interests may bind a purchaser from the grantor of the timeshare interest with notice of the timeshare purchaser's rights—notices, cautions, inhibitions and restrictions.

The grantor of a timeshare licence or lease or even of club membership relating to use of the timeshare development may apply to the registrar to have an entry put on the register to the effect that no disposition of the timeshare development shall be effected except in specified circumstances, such as the consent of the timeshare purchasers or of a committee of those purchasers. This provides a potentially valuable means of protecting the interests of timeshare purchasers, but the consent of the grantor of the timeshare interests will obviously be required to effect such a registration.

## Notices

In the event that the grantor of the timeshare interest has a registered interest in the freehold or superior leasehold title to the timeshare development and his consent cannot be obtained, and the timeshare interest is not capable of registration under s 48 of the 1925 Act, the timeshare purchaser could apply for notice of his interest to be entered on the register. The Land Registration Act 1925, s 49, lists the rights capable of protection by notice as an extension of s 48, and a timeshare purchaser's interest may be registered by notice if either it would have been capable of registration as a land charge under the provisions of the Land Charges Act 1972, or if the registrar can be persuaded that his rights should be protected by notice under the Land Registration Act 1925, s 49*(f)*, as falling within the sweeping up provisions of 'creditors notices and any other right, interest, or claim which it may be deemed expedient to protect by notice instead of by caution inhibition or registration'.

At the time of first registration the registrar has a duty to enter a notice on the register of rights already affecting the land (Land Registration Act 1925, s 70(2) and rule 40 of the Land Registration Rules). However, as time goes on and less and less land in England and Wales is the subject of first registration, the utility of this provision to timeshare purchasers will be diminished. In most cases, the developer will have acquired title to the timeshare development and proceeded to first registration, if appropriate, before the grant of any rights to timeshare purchasers.

## Cautions

The timeshare purchaser may apply for a caution against dealings or against first registration to be entered against the title to the development. The effect of the registration of a caution of the first kind is that no dealing in the registered land can take place until the cautioner has been warned by written notice. Within 14 days (or such other period not less than seven days as the registrar may direct) of the warning by the registrar the cautioner must 'show cause why the caution should continue to have effect'. The same 'warning off' procedure applies in the case of cautions against first registrations and dealings, and is likely to be the more important method of protecting the timeshare purchaser's interest in the long term.

The registrar may remove either type of caution from the register if no cause is shown, or if he arrives at the view that the cause is not sufficient to warrant the caution remaining. In theory the registrar may call a hearing to adjudicate on the matter. The view has been expressed that it might be possible for the registrar to make registration subject to the rights of the cautioner even though those rights would not be capable of being recorded by the more straightforward means of a notice (see Dawson and Pearce, *Licences Relating to the Occupation of Use of Land*, page 198). In practice, what sometimes happens where there is a dispute as to the validity of a claim or right or interest upon which the caution is founded, is that the registrar will refuse to remove the caution and leave it to the party seeking to have the caution vacated to apply to the court to under the Land Registration Act 1925, s 83, or under the inherent jurisdiction of the court. Such an application may be on motion, and will almost inevitably entail a consideration of the merits of the cautioner's claim (see *Alpenstow Ltd* v *Regalian Properties* [1985] 1 WLR 721, for instance).

**Inhibitions**

Inhibitions are temporary notices preventing dealing with land until some specified event and are not appropriate to the particular circumstances of timeshare purchasers.

**Restrictions**

In principle the registered proprietor of the timeshare development or a charge thereon could apply to have restrictions imposed upon the entry prohibiting dealings unless the consent of particular persons is sought, or a particular thing or matter is done or notice has been given. In practice there would appear to be little incentive to the developer to inhibit his freedom to deal with the title to the timeshare development by such an entry, although in theory such a procedure could be used to protect the interest of the timeshare purchaser.

In order to protect the timeshare purchaser's interest in the light of the uncertainties accompanying licences, it may be safer to supplement the licence with an express trust for the benefit of the timeshare purchaser, preferably under the auspices of a custodian trustee holding title to the development, and more usually as part of a 'club' timesharing scheme which is discussed in the following paragraphs.

# Timesharing club plans

These fall into one of the three categories discussed below, namely:

1 Unincorporated members' clubs.
2 Incorporated members' clubs.
3 Proprietary clubs.

**Unincorporated members' clubs**

Unincorporated members' clubs are:

> associations of a peculiar nature. They are societies the members of which are perpetually changing. They are not partnerships; they are not associations for gain; and the feature which distinguished them from other societies is that no member as such becomes liable to pay to the funds of the society or to any one else any money beyond the subscriptions required by the rules of the club to be paid so long as he remains a member. It is upon this fundamental condition, not usually expressed but understood by everyone, that clubs are formed;

per Lord Lindley in *Wise* v *Perpetual Trustee Co Ltd* [1903] AC 139, at page 149.

A members' club does not have a separate legal personality distinct from that of its individual members. For this reason, generally speaking, a members' club cannot sue or be sued, or hold property in its own name. Invariably a members' club will nominate one or more of its members to be a representative party to proceedings by or against the club on terms that the named members are indemnified by the other members of the club, to avoid the necessity of joining each of the members as parties (see Rules of the Supreme Court (RSC), Ord 15, r 12 and Ord 5, r 5 of the County Court Rules). Contrast the position in Scotland where an unincorporated association carrying on business under a descriptive name may sue and be sued in that name (see the Sheriff Courts (Scotland) Act 1913, Sched 2, r 11. In England and Wales the property of a members' club will usually be held by nominated members on trust for the purposes of the club.

In the case of timesharing schemes the custodian trustee holding the property of the club may be appointed at the outset by the developer, usually an independent trust corporation such as those operated by the clearing banks or one of the trust corporations which specialise in providing such a service in the field of timesharing schemes, such as Holiday Property Trustee Ltd or Timeshare Trustees (International) Ltd. The trust deed will often be a relatively sophisticated document providing for detailed rights of indemnity for the trustee, charging provisions, exemption clauses in respect of the trustee's liability and restricting the powers of the trustee to permit mortgaging or pledging of the development.

There are exceptions to the general principle that a members' club is not regarded as a separate legal personality from its members, such as those embodied in the Value Added Tax Act 1983, s 31, and trade unions and employers' associations are regarded as a being in special position (see the Trade Union and Labour Relations Act 1974, ss 2 and 3) although these are unlikely to be relevant to timesharing schemes. Squatters operating in the form of an unincorporated association have been held liable for rateable occupation of premises: see *Westminster City Council* v *Tomlin, The Times*, 25 July 1989, and the cases cited there. The same may be true of a club of timeshare purchasers. Unincorporated associations such as clubs may also be treated as a separate legal personality for a charge to corporation tax (see *Blackpool Marton Rotary Club* v *Martin* [1988] STC 823 and *Conservative Central Office* v *Burrell* [1982] 1 WLR 522, for example).

The members of a club are usually represented by an elected committee under the terms of the constitution of the club. This feature is common in many timeshare schemes operated on the basis of clubs where such a committee may be the only effective way in which the 'members' (the timeshare purchasers) will have some control over the management of the development. Such an elected committee is essential in the case of a licensed club: see the Licensing Act 1964. In theory it is possible for the committee to be the body charged with holding the property of the club, although in practice a trustee will often be used for this purpose to ensure stability, continuity and performance of monitoring and record keeping functions. In addition, a fully independent trustee may be in a position to 'hold the ring' between members of the club and developers who are in dispute, to prevent either taking any precipitate action with the title to the development. Having said that, many timeshare purchase agreements governed by a club membership scheme will incorporate a clause enabling any party to refer any differences or disputes to arbitration before an independent third party such as the President for the time being of the Law Society.

The committee will invariably be the agent of all of the members of the club for the purposes and upon the terms set out in the constitution (see *Fleming* v *Hector* (1836) 2 M & W 172). If the committee act outside the powers and authority given to them in the constitution, they may well find themselves personally liable on any contracts entered into on behalf of the club. However, the constitution will often empower the committee to enter into contracts for the defined purposes of the club. Each member has a contract with all the other club members on the terms set out in the constitution.

The conventional wisdom is that a club member has, in the absence of specific contractual provision, no obligation to contribute to club funds or to any deficiency or liability of the club so far as such funds exceed the subscriptions due from him under the rules of the constitution. However, in practice and in the context of the timeshare scheme members' club, such a rule will probably be mitigated by the right of the trustee to exercise his right of lien or indemnity against the trust property (such as the freehold or superior leasehold title to the development) in respect of any liability incurred by the trustee in the course of the trusteeship or in respect of the trustee's legitimate fees. Where the trustee is a clearing bank or other financial institution, the trust deed will invariably provide for the trustee's fee and charges to receive a priority over other liabilities or a guarantee of payment of its fees by the developer. Such a lien is sometimes expressed to be by way of a first charge on the trust fund.

The founder members—usually the timeshare developer and his representatives—will form the first committee, establish the club and approve the initial constitution. The founder members will represent the developer's interests and will often be exempted by the rules from the ordinary requirements of election. The first committee of the club, formed by the founder members, will, on behalf of the club, enter into the arrangements for the appointment of trustees to hold the club property for the benefit of club members, and also enter into the contract with a management company. The management company will deal with the day-to-day administration of the timeshare development. Unless the rules provide a right of indemnity, or the creditor agrees otherwise, the committee will be personally liable on contracts with third parties (see *De Vries* v *Corner* (1865) 13 TLR 636). The committee members may also be liable to third parties in tort. In *Browne* v *Lewis* (1896) 12 TLR 455, the plaintiff was injured as the result of the collapse of a stand at the club ground. The committee had negligently employed an incompetent contractor to repair the stand and the plaintiff sued the committee as representatives of the whole club. The claim was held to succeed against the committee members and they were found to be personally liable. However, much will depend upon the terms of the rules of the club and in the ordinary course of events a members' club is not liable to its members for injuries suffered on the club's premises in the absence of negligence (see *Robertson* v *Ridley, The Times*, November 1988.

The rules of the members' club are a matter of contract between the members and the courts will not lightly interfere with their operation, except possibly where the rules of discretion apply; compare *Gaiman* v *National Association of Mental Health* [1971] Ch 317 and *Shepperd* v *South Australian Amateur Football League* (1987) 44 SASR 579. Having said that, the assistance of the courts is often invoked on questions of interpretation of the rules of a club, or in circumstances for which no provision is made in the rules. Attempts in rule books to exclude the jurisdiction of the courts have met with little success in the past (see *Lee* v *Showmens Guild of Great Britain* [1952] 2 QB 329, for example). It is thought, however, that provisions for arbitration in the club rules or constitution are likely to be an effective means of avoiding recourse to the courts over matters such as responsibility for damage to individual apartments and complaints about maintenance charges.

It will be important that the rules are comprehensive, and one of the principal tasks of the draftsman or of the adviser representing the timeshare purchaser will be to check that provision is made in the rules for all foreseeable eventualities and for effective, speedy and cheap resolution of any disputes that may arise.

Parliament has intervened to some extent in the nature of rules of clubs within the UK, making it unlawful for a club with 25 or more members to discriminate on the grounds of race (the Race Relations Act 1976, s 24). Non-profit making clubs are exempt from the provisions prohibiting discrimination on the grounds of sex (the Sex Discrimination Act 1975, s 34. Furthermore, the club rules should make it clear that the primary object of the club is the use and enjoyment of the timeshare development by the members and not commercial gain, to avoid falling foul of the Companies Act 1985, s 716(1), which provides that:

No ... association ... consisting of more than twenty persons shall be formed for the purpose of any business ...[which] has for its object the acquisition of gain by the ... association ... or by the individual members thereof, unless it is registered as a company under this Act ...

Precedents for the documents required to establish an unincorporated members' club appear in Appendix A.

### Constitution

The first document is the club constitution or rules. This provides for the club property to be transferred to a trustee and for the club to issue 51 'holiday certificates' for each unit of accommodation. The holiday certificates are then transferred to the developer in consideration for his arranging for the transfer of the property to the trustees. The developer then issues the holiday certificates to the timeshare purchasers as and when each holiday period is sold. The constitution goes on to set out the detailed rules as to rights of occupation by club members, the appointment and powers of the committee, the obligations of the club members, proceedings at meetings and so forth.

### Trust deed

The trust deed is a document which vests the club property in the trustee for the benefit of the members of the club. It should comply with a number of basic principles of trust law to avoid any challenge to its legality or validity. First, the deed must identify the subject matter of the trust, the beneficial interest to be held on trust and the beneficiaries of the trust, all with certainty. The position of unincorporated associations was specifically considered in *Re Recher's Will Trusts* [1972] Ch 526, where four possible methods of a club or unincorporated association holding property were canvassed. In the case of a timesharing scheme the two most likely situations are that the property is held on trust for future and present members or on terms that the property is held for the existing members beneficially on the basis that the property is held as an accretion to the funds of the association to which the members are contractually bound *inter se* by the rules or constitution; see also *Leahy* v *AG for New South Wales* [1959] AC 457.

Secondly, the trust deed must satisfy the rule against remoteness of vesting, ensuring that the interests of the beneficiaries vest within the perpetuity period (usually 80 years). See generally Morris and Leach, *The Rule against Perpetuities*, or Megarry and Wade, *The Law of Real Property*. An unincorporated club scheme must comply with the rule against perpetuities, otherwise the transfer of the club property to the trustees will be void. Accordingly, the trust deed and constitution of most club-based timesharing schemes will restrict the initial operation of the club and of the trust to a perpetuity period not exceeding 80 years (see the Perpetuities and Accumulations Act 1964, s 1. The rule against remoteness of vesting does not occur in Scottish law, although there is a restriction on the accumulation of income. It is possible to provide for an extension of the period either during or at the expiry of the perpetuity period without infringing the rule against perpetuities and where there is restructuring of a scheme based upon a members' club this is sometimes done.

It is clearly important that the trust deed gives timeshare purchasers *locus standi* to apply to the court to enforce the trust, as members of the club or otherwise (see *Re Lipinski's Will Trust* [1976] Ch 235 and *Re Denley's Trust Deed* [1969] 1 Ch 373). In England and Wales, unless the perpetuity period is selected and the trust specifies what is to happen at the expiration of the trust period, the trust will not be valid, and the property may be found to be held on a resulting trust for the benefit of the developer. Most trust deeds and constitutions relating to timeshare schemes will include detailed provisions for termination of the trust and club both before and at the expiry of the perpetuity period, on terms that there is a sale and divisions of net assets in the proportions in which the timeshare periods are held by the timeshare purchasers.

It should be appreciated that transfer of the title to the development to the trustee may not be an absolute protection to the timeshare purchaser against the insolvency of the developer. In England and Wales, where the transfer occurs within two years of the onset of the insolvency the transfer, if it was at an undervalue, may be challenged under the Insolvency Act 1986, s 238, and the court is empowered to make such order as it thinks fit for restoring the position to what it would have been had the developer not made the transfer. In addition, the transfer may be construed as a preference where it was not an undervalue capable of challenge under s 239 of the 1986 Act, if it occurred within six months of the onset of insolvency. In this event, a similar order restoring the position can be made by the court. As is noted elsewhere, these difficulties may be overcome if the developer grants the trustee a lease of the development at the outset.

It is important that the constitution and any other rules of the club are as detailed as possible. It goes without saying that club property cannot be disposed of otherwise than in pursuance of the club rules or with the consent of all of the members, not just a majority (see *Murray* v *Johnstone* 23 R (Court of Sessions) 981). From a practical point of view most constitutions also provide for variation of the club rules, usually by majority vote, which may be the means of achieving a desired objective. On the other hand some constitutions provide that changes to the rules which affect contributions or the trustee directly or indirectly, require the approval of the trustee.

*Management agreement*

The management agreement will be of special importance to the timeshare purchaser, who will want to know the extent of his liability for future maintenance of the development and the restrictions on the potential for abuse by the management company or developer. The parts of the Landlord and Tenant Act 1987 relating to service charges for dwellings provide guidance on what can be achieved in the way of protection for the timeshare purchaser.

*Purchase agreement*
The purchase agreement is the means by which the timeshare purchaser contracts to acquire his interest in the timeshare development, and at the same time agrees to abide by and comply with the membership obligations set out in the constitution. A substantial number of developers who operate within the UK will have had purchase agreements which comply with the Code of Ethics produced by the now defunct TDA which, most notably, provided that the timeshare purchaser had a right to withdraw or cancel within the five day 'cooling-off' period after the agreement is signed. The OFT has suggested that this period be extended to 14 days—see Chapter 3.

*Holiday certificate*
The final document is the holiday certificate which has endorsed on it a form of transfer.

These documents are discussed separately and should be given individual attention by any timeshare purchaser or his adviser. In practice, however, they are often to be found as part of the same booklet or leaflet entitled 'constitution', and undoubtedly will be construed together as part of one overall scheme should there be any conflict or differences between the terms of the individual documents.

The club/trustee form of timeshare scheme is the most popular for timeshare developments in England and Wales. It is also used in a very similar form in Scotland, where the perpetuity rule does not apply, so the duration of the trust, and hence the scheme, can be extended beyond the 80 year period allowed by the Perpetuities and Accumulations Act 1964 in England and Wales. It is interesting to consider the decision in *American Real Estates (Scotland) Ltd* v *CCE* (1980) VATTR 88, where, in the context of a timeshare scheme relating to a development at a castle in Scotland structured on a club membership basis, it was held that the grant of a 'holiday certificate' did not confer upon the holder a 'major interest' or heritable right in land for the purposes of the VAT legislation applicable at that time. It appears to have been accepted that the holiday certificate evidenced licence to occupy the land.

The members' club timeshare scheme is also used in other European jurisdictions, and some of the major developers use this scheme with variations, with Scottish law as the governing law in respect of timeshare developments in territories such as Spain. This practice is permitted by the proposed new Spanish law (see Chapter 10).

*Effects of the Financial Services Act 1986*
There is one unresolved question which may detract from, or add to, the overwhelming advantages of this structure of timesharing scheme, depending upon one's viewpoint. It is arguable that the marketing of club membership in a scheme of this kind amounts to the carrying on of investment business within ss 1 and 3 of the Financial Services Act 1986 ('the 1986 Act'), and this is prohibited unless the persons involved in the transaction and its promotion

are members of the recognised self-regulating organisations or other authorised institutions. Thus, where shares in the developer (a company) or one of its subsidiaries which held title to the timeshare development are subsequently transferred to the custodian trustee, it may well be that membership of the club would in effect carry with it as a beneficiary of the deed of trust, a right over, or interest in, shares in a company which is deemed to constitute an investment, for the purpose of s 1 and Sched 1, paras 1 and 11 to the 1986 Act. In fact, where the developer simply transfers title to the development to the trustee, the provisions of the 1986 Act will probably not apply, and it appears that the problem may in any event be avoided by constituting the title holding company as a company limited by guarantee, not having a share capital.

The trust deed and constitution are almost certainly not a collective investment scheme within the meaning of s 75(6)*(g)* and Sched 1, para 5 of the 1986 Act. The predominant purpose of the arrangements in such a timeshare scheme will be to enable persons participating in them to share in the use or enjoyment of a particular property or properties.

The application of the 1986 Act or other similar regulation to the marketing of interests in timeshare schemes is something which many in the industry have thought to be long overdue. However, it is doubtful whether the existing self-regulatory organisations (SROs) have the experience or specialised expertise in the area of marketing timeshare schemes or the application of the 1986 Act to deal effectively with the regulation of the conduct of business in this area. Were a developer or 'marketeer' selling timeshare schemes to become a member of one of the recognised SROs, the documentation would have to comply with the Conduct of Business Rules produced by the SRO concerned. However, the Financial Services Act 1986, which is concerned with 'investments', is not appropriate to the timesharing industry. This is certainly the conclusion of the OFT, whose suggested special regulations are examined in Chapter 4.

**Incorporated members' clubs**

Incorporation under the Companies Act 1985 may be with liability limited by shares or by guarantee. It has been noted elsewhere that there is a distinct risk that in the incorporation of a members' club, it may assume the form of a proprietary club, with the company being the proprietor. The membership of the club could in theory be different from the shareholders of the company from time to time and the character of the club may be lost (see generally, JF Josling and L Alexander, *The Law of Clubs*, 6th edn (Longman 1986)).

There is also the possibility of a charge to corporation tax on the basis that the company was carrying on a business which should be considered. The mere incorporation of a company for the better carrying on of a members' club does not automatically change the nature of the club so as to transfer any surplus into a profit (see *Jones* v *South West Lancashire Owners Association Ltd* [1927] AC 827).

It is generally thought that non-profit making associations such as professional and trade associations are best suited to the company limited by guarantee, not having a share capital. If it were decided to incorporate a timeshare scheme operating through a members' club, a company limited by guarantee would appear to be the option which would avoid complicated provisions about rights attaching to shares, share transfers, dividends and so on. It may be possible to preserve the essential nature of the members' club on incorporation in this way—compare *Trebano Working Mens Club & Institute Ltd* v *McDonald* [1940] 1 KB 576 at page 579. In practice it should be a requirement that every member of the club also becomes member of the company. Such a company is still subject to the provisions designed to prevent unfairly prejudicial treatment of the members or some of the members in the Companies Act 1985, s 459, so there may be some measure of protection available to timeshare purchasers who find that the founder members or other members are taking steps prejudicial to their interests as members of the company. The existence of this remedy cannot replace the greater protection afforded to members of a club who are granted a holiday certificate where there is a substantial and independent trustee. It goes without saying that where the members' club is incorporated in the form of a company limited by share capital, the remedy may also be available under s 459.

In England and Wales the problems relating to the rule against perpetuities are also sidestepped by incorporation, but there is some cost in complying with the annual return and audited accounts provisions of the Companies Acts.

In the case of a company limited by guarantee, arrangements between the timeshare purchasers should be dealt with in the constitution of the club and not in the articles of association, although this is not always the case. In these circumstances, there would be no actual or deemed share capital so that the provisions regulating advertisements for shares and the contents of a prospectus in Part III of the Companies Act 1985 (replaced by Part V of the 1986 Act, which is only partly in force at the time of writing) would not apply. Similarly, because what would be offered for sale by the developer to the timeshare purchaser would not be 'shares' or 'rights to or interests in' share capital, within the definitions contained in s 1, and Sched 1, paras 1 and 11 to the 1986 Act, there would be no need for the developer to be a member of an SRO or authorised institution.

Failure to adhere to the requirements of the 1986 Act may lead to the contract being declared unenforceable as against the timeshare purchaser, who would be able to recover any monies or property paid or transferred by him under the agreement, together with compensation for any loss sustained by him as a result of having parted with it (see s 5 of the 1986 Act). Non-compliance with the provisions of the 1986 Act is also (subject to the defence that the person took all reasonable precautions and exercised all due diligence to avoid the commission of an offence) a criminal offence punishable by a fine and/or imprisonment by virtue of s 43 of the 1986 Act. In the event that the interest in the timeshare scheme is deemed to be an 'investment', there is also criminal liability for knowingly making misleading, false and deceptive statements or concealing material facts, or recklessly (dishonestly or otherwise) making a statement, promise or forecast which is misleading, false or deceptive where a timeshare 'investment' agreement is in prospect (see s 47 of the 1986 Act). These provisions cannot apply unless the timeshare plan gives the purchaser a right to, or interest in, shares, or is considered to be a 'collective investment scheme'.

It is worth noting that one form of scheme adopted in England and Wales features a members' club in the form of a company limited by guarantee in conjuction with custodian trustees who issue the holiday certificates, and hold a lease of the title to the timeshare development in terms of a trust deed which refers to and incorporates the provisions of the articles of association of the club company. The club company in turn contracts with the maintenance company for the performance of the functions of maintenance of the development. This is clearly a further laudable attempt to provide the timeshare purchaser, who otherwise holds under a contractual licence, with a degree of security. In theory, on liquidation of a developer, the timeshare purchasers would be protected since the liquidator would be subject to the lease in favour of the trustees. As an additional measure of protection, where some of the units may be unfinished at the time of entry into the timeshare purchase agreement, such a scheme may be coupled with a performance bond by which the surety (such as a clearing bank) undertakes to refund monies to timeshare purchasers if there is unacceptable delay or default in the construction of the development or parts thereof by the developer.

### Proprietary clubs

In this scheme a developer is the owner of the club, which is invariably a company, and uses it as the vehicle through which to carry on the business of providing services to the club members. The property in the timeshare development is usually retained by the developer in the name of the club company. The club company will remain in the ownership and control of the developer and the club members will accordingly have little, if any, control over the activities of the developer mortgaging or otherwise disposing of or dealing with the title to the development. There are obvious risks to the timeshare purchaser in this form of structure, not least of which is the lack of priority or security in the event of the liquidation of the developer's club company. The timeshare purchasers would rank as unsecured creditors in such an eventuality despite their 'club membership'. It is possible that they may be in the position of contractual licensees but it is doubtful whether this would provide them with any rights which would bind a liquidator or purchaser of the development—compare *Re Sharpe* [1980] 1 All ER 198. In view of the poor measure of protection for the timeshare purchaser entailed in this scheme, it is hardly ever used in practice in the UK.

## Corporate plans

Another significant variant of the timesharing plan is the corporate plan, which is set up on the basis that a public company is formed and the timeshare purchasers become shareholders in the public company. Each share entitles the shareholder to enjoy the right of use and occupation of a defined part of the company's property for a defined period, as set out in the memorandum and articles of association. This type of plan is less common in the UK owing to the necessity of complying with the prospectus provisions of the Companies Act, but schemes of this nature based on the Société Civile d'Attribution are used in France—although with limited success. Timeshare purchasers and developers should take care to ensure that the companies or individuals involved in any part of the promotion or marketing of such a scheme are members of an SRO or otherwise authorised for the carrying on of investment business under the 1986 Act. A share in a company is specifically defined as an 'investment' by Sched 1, para 1 of the 1986 Act.

Briefly, the statutory requirements of a public limited company are as follows:

1  The memorandum must state that the company shall be a public company.
2  The name of the company must end with the words 'public limited company' (or the Welsh equivalent).
3  The allotted capital must not be less than the authorised minimum (currently £50,000).
4  Each of the allotted shares must be paid up at least as to one quarter of the nominal value and the whole premium.
5  The company must be registered as a public company.

The shares do not of course need to be listed for stock exchange dealings, but if they are, the company will have to enter into a listing agreement. However, the normal way of disposing of the shares will be by way of direct offer to the public by way of prospectus.

The company will not be able to commence business without a trading certificate (see the Companies Act 1985, s 117(1)).

The rules and regulations which govern public limited companies are too numerous in extent and detail to be set out in this general guide but the reader is directed to the standard works on the subject (in particular Palmers' *Company Law*, 24th edn, 1987).

The document of major importance in a corporate timesharing scheme is the prospectus. The Companies Act 1985, s 744, defines this as 'any prospectus, notice, circular, advertisement, or other invitation, offering to the public for subscription or purchase any shares or debentures of a company'. It is unlawful to issue to the public any form of application for shares in or debentures of a company unless it is with a prospectus. The form and contents of the prospectus must comply with the provisions of Sched 3 to the 1985 Act (see s 56 of the 1985 Act generally, and Part V of the 1986 Act when wholly in force. Contravention of the provisions in the 1986 Act is an offence and creates a civil liability. See also Parts IV and V of the 1986 Act.

In relation to overseas timeshare schemes, the requirement in the Companies Act 1985, s 72 relating to subscription shares in or debentures of a company incorporated outside Great Britain applies also to offers for sale (see ss 64, 65 and 79 of the Companies Act 1985. This may trap the sale of foreign company schemes to UK purchasers whilst these sections are in force. They are soon to be replaced by Parts IV and V of the 1986 Act which are not completely in force at the time of writing.

The precise requirements as to the contents and form of a prospectus are set out in the standard texts on the subject. The overall objective is that those purchasing shares in a public limited company operating a timeshare scheme will be in better position than those buying shares in a private company to know the value of the purchase and any difficulties or problems likely to arise. However, possibly because of the complex legislation surrounding the marketing of shares in such a company and the novel taxation implications, such schemes operating through a public limited company in the UK, are rare. For a brief glimpse of such a scheme in operation before the intervention of the Financial Services Act 1986, refer to the decision in *Court Barton plc v CCE* (1985) VATTR 148, where it was held that the sale of shares in a plc timesharing scheme were taxable supplies for the purposes of VAT.

## Property bonds

These are a relatively recent development in the holiday home industry in the UK, although they have been in existence in a smaller form since about 1983. They are marketed on the basis that they are not the equivalent of a timesharing scheme, but nevertheless share the same objectives, namely to enable the purchaser of the bond to enjoy use of holiday or resort accommodation for a period or periods each year, without the need to make an outright purchase of a particular property with the level of expenditure that involves. Whether they succeed in offering the advantages of timesharing will depend on whether there is sufficient accommodation available to satisfy the holiday requirements of bondholders.

The nature of the scheme is that a life assurance company, fund company, the promoters and a trust corporation— often based in the Channel Islands or other territories with low or neutral tax regimes—enter into a deed of trust. The life assurance company issues a policy and the fund company manages the funds and decides what proportion are to be invested in gilts or other securities, and what proportion in properties for the resort or holiday locations. The trust deed may be subject to the law of an offshore territory such as the Channel Islands and may also confine jurisdiction in respect of any disputes arising out of the trust deed or policy to that territory. The trust corporation will hold the assets of the life company (including the deeds of title to the portfolio). There should be express provisions for termination of the appointment of the fund managers or any of the agents or advisers upon default.

There will also be a life policy and rules upon which the bond is operated which will be of contractual effect. The rules will govern matters such as the terms upon which the portfolio properties can be occupied by the bondholder, booking conditions, regulations for the occupation of the portfolio properties, terms of surrender and encashment and the terms on which the rules themselves may be altered. The rules have binding effect upon the bondholder (with or without his consent), and should provide for a dispute resolution procedure. Clearly in those circumstances the identity (and independence) of the trust corporation (which may in practice be responsible for ensuring that the funds are invested in accordance with the fund managers' advice or for resolving disputes) will be critical.

The purchase price of a bond as a payment towards a premium in a life assurance policy which provides cover for the bondholder is in part allocated. The other part of the price goes towards the purchase of a number of units or points which are required to ensure use of the portfolio of properties held by the scheme. The bondholder's right to use a particular property at a particular time of the year will depend not only upon the number of points or units purchased but also, very importantly, upon the number of available properties as compared with the number of bondholders. The more popular resorts and locations in high season require the bondholder to use or purchase more points as a condition of being allowed to apply for an accommodation booking. The allocation of the point or unit values for particular properties within the portfolio is carried out by agents and may vary from year to year. There may be more than one level of bondholder, and a bondholder may be required to pay a user charge on the use of a portfolio property. The provisions for calculating this user charge will need to be considered very carefully by the prospective bondholder. They may turn out to be an unexpected burden. Unlike timeshare club schemes there may not be provision for audit and publication of maintenance charges or the costs that go to make up the user charge on a yearly basis.

It may be important to ensure that the number of portfolio properties is sufficient for the number of bondholders. It is thought that in practice the bond works like some timeshare schemes which do not allocate a right to use a particular property at a particular time of the year, so that booking will operate on a first-come-first-served basis. There may be a cancellation fee for bookings which are not taken up within a specified time.

It should be noted that the bond may not be affiliated to an exchange organisation, so that it is important for the prospective bondholder to be sure that he is satisfied with the range and location of portfolio properties. The right to purchase or lease other portfolio properties or to sell existing portfolio properties will almost certainly be given to the fund managers (or others) in the trust deed so that the choices available to a bondholder may change.

There is a right to encash or surrender the value of the property bond, usually after a fixed period such as two years. This right can be deferred by the life assurance company for a period of time.

It has been suggested that the property bond has some advantages over the conventional timeshare schemes, and that it may legitimately be considered to be more of a medium- to long-term investment upon which a return on capital invested may ultimately be obtained. However, compared with unit trust schemes which invest in property, the charges on the fund may well be considerably higher once fees have been paid to the fund managers, promoters, marketing agents and the trustee(s) and the life assurance company. The level of the fees payable should appear in the trust deed, and it is thought that the administration costs of operating a scheme providing for the successive occupation of large numbers of bondholders throughout the year would be considerably greater than unit trusts or other life policies which invest in property.

The proportion of the assets of the bond which are actually invested in gilts or income-producing investments for the purpose of the return on encashment in the bond should be carefully considered. It may be 40 per cent or lower, and only the remainder of the net assets will be invested in the property portfolio. There may also be an introductory charge for the bondholder. However, like other property based funds, the bond may be listed in the financial media so that the bondholder is able to obtain some idea of the performance of his investment. Unlike other bonds or unit trusts, or for example a pension with associated life assurance cover, the fund managers may not be backed by a well-known insurance company with a track record of investment in property and gilt edged funds, and the value of the bond may well depend upon the number of bondholders wishing to surrender.

In respect of a trust corporation, life assurance company, promoter or agent based abroad, the prospective bondholder should expect to see that they are members of an appropriate SRO (such as FIMBRA) or otherwise authorised under the Financial Services Act 1986 for transacting investment business, if they are marketing investments within the UK. Needless to say, within England and Wales the life assurance company would have to comply with the provisions of the Insurance Companies Act 1982 and, the Financial Services Act 1986, s 130. The alternative route to authorised dealings and advertisements of life policies under the 1986 Act in the event that the life assurance company is based abroad, is where the territory has been designated by the Secretary of State so that the domestic legislation of that territory is deemed to be sufficient to protect the policyholders. The Isle of Man has been made a designated territory for this purpose. There is some measure of protection in authorisation under the Financial Services Act 1986 in that all the SROs have set up a compensation fund for investors (up to a limit of £48,000 per claim) in the event of default of their members.

To comply with most SRO Conduct of Business rules, contracts for bonds entered into within the UK should contain a 'cooling off' period, allowing the prospective bondholder to withdraw without liability within a specific time period (such as a month) after entry into the contract.

## The management contract

The management of a timesharing project presents some unique problems. Each week, generally on the same day, one set of owners will leave to be replaced by a new set who check in. It is important therefore to leave a gap between check-out time and check-in time. If the check-out time is at noon and check-in is at 4 pm, then there will only be four hours for a large number of units to be cleaned and for the linen to be changed, and so forth. The developer should consider this aspect carefully in reviewing the draft scheme documentaion, to ensure that he will be able to cope with the problem.

Every year, most timesharing developments set apart a one or two week period in which to carry out essential maintenance and redecoration. A decision has to be made as to whether to close the whole development or else to stagger the maintenance period between the different blocks of units. A staggered system may lead to problems with adjoining owners and will not deal effectively with repairs to communal facilities such as recreation centres, swimming pools, tennis courts and so on.

Until the development is sold out the developer will be forced to assume liability for payment of the service charge for the unsold units. To do otherwise would either throw an unacceptable burden on the existing timeshare purchasers or lead to a deterioration in standards. This unrecoverable service charge can be a considerable burden on the developer who may prefer to give away unsaleable off-season weeks rather than to continue to accept liability for the service charge relating to them. This is one of the reasons why year round resorts are becoming more popular, and why developers often provide additional facilities so as to make resorts attractive to visit out of season.

The individual apartments and villas will be much more heavily utilised than a unit under single ownership, and perhaps even more than hotel accommodation. The unit will require more frequent redecoration and the furnishings will require replacing more often than is the case in conventional developments. It will be necessary to detail a replacement policy for each item perhaps dividing items into those which are to be replaced daily, weekly, monthly, quarterly, half-yearly, annually and tri-annually. One particularly well-managed scheme has a replacement schedule set out in three-yearly intervals until a 15 year cycle is reached.

Maintenance charges will weigh heavily on the mind of the prospective timeshare purchaser. It is no longer sufficient merely to specify a figure and state that it will only rise with inflation. It will be necessary (even if there is no obligation) to provide a full explanation as to how the service charge is made up, to allay any suspicion that the service charge has been artificially reduced during the period of the sales programme in order to spare the developer's contribution and to assist in the generation of sales.

The management contract or the rules of the timesharing organisation should give the purchaser some degree of control in the management of the development. This may be difficult to achieve in the early years when the developer will need to retain control, but thereafter the continuance of the management company or its replacement should preferably be in the hands of a committee elected by the timeshare purchasers. Such matters should usually be entrusted to a management company; the timeshare purchasers will not be able to deal with the management themselves directly and the developer may have no further interest once the development is sold out. Ideally, the management agreement should define clearly the exact nature of the company's duties, how it is to be remunerated and how it can be replaced.

The management contract should be framed with the terms of the Supply of Goods and Services Act 1982 in mind. The company will usually be a party to the purchase agreement entered into between the timeshare purchaser and the developer, and the management contract between the developer and the company may well be incorporated into that agreement. Attempts to exclude or restrict liability for breaches of the management contract against the timeshare purchaser may well be subject to the provisions of the Unfair Contract Terms Act 1977, to the extent that the management contract does not relate to an interest in land, or to the formation of a company or unincorporated association, or its constitution, or to the rights of its members.

Apart from maintaining the development, the management company can be used to perform a number of other necessary functions. It can assume responsibility for collecting the maintenance charge, apply the penalties imposed in the case of non-payment and act as arbitrator in the case of disputes between members, perhaps with a right to appeal to the committee of members. It should be empowered to deal with the various problems which can arise in the management of a development, such as extracting payment for damage or destruction to a timeshare unit carried out by a timeshare purchaser or his guest. It should also have a contingency plan to cover members against the possibility of another member, for one reason or another, not leaving on time, or of a particular unit becoming uninhabitable. It may also have responsibility for ensuring that the development remains adequately insured at all times. The accounts of the management company or other organisation entrusted with the management functions, should be audited and a copy of the audit report and accounts circulated to all the timeshare purchasers. Finally, the management company should collate all the various guarantees and warranties in regard to the equipment at the development and assume the responsibility of enforcing those when the need arises.

It is often found that the maintenance charge is index-linked. Provided that such index linking is for a defined period and the developer has the resources available to discharge any excess, the practice is difficult to criticise as it does provide the timeshare purchaser with some degree of assurance as to the level of the maintenance charge. However, it seems inherently wrong to link the maintenance charge for any length of time to a standard which may not reflect the actual management costs, since either this will result in an unnecessary surplus, or, perhaps worse, a shortfall leading to a deterioration in the services provided. Both of these points will be of importance to a timeshare purchaser who may be thinking of re-selling his interest at some time in the future. Most management contracts also contain a rather sophisticated mathematical formula for calculation of the management charge, to allow for the addition of units, varying sizes of units and the variation in the number of timeshare purchasers.

Some management contracts provide for the creation of a sinking or reserve fund out of maintenance charges for renewal and replacement of items involving relatively large amounts of (capital) expenditure. In principle, this is a sensible aid to planning for the maintenance of the development and may 'even out' any variations in the maintenance fee that would otherwise be required. However, the creation of such a fund may have adverse taxation consequences for the developer or its assignee or even to the trustee of the fund, unless structured carefully. There may be a measure of protection to the timeshare purchasers in such an arrangement where the monies are held on trust in the event of liquidation or bankruptcy of the management company/ organisation—compare *Re Chelsea Cloisters Ltd (In liquidation)* (1980) 41 P & CR 98 (CA). It is suggested that the example of s 42 of the Landlord and Tenant Act 1987, whereby *all* service charges are held on trust by the management company or organisation, may be an even greater protection for the timeshare purchasers against such an insolvency, a view shared by the OFT.

It is recommended that the problem of maintenance be faced at an early stage; that the system is seen to work fairly, and that the timeshare purchasers be provided with a detailed explanation as to how it works, since experience shows that maintenance arrangements are a major factor in the decisions to purchase. Some schemes have adopted the system now used in many residential blocks of flats or developments, namely that of providing the timeshare purchaser with an estimated figure for management charge and management expenditure in the following year and at the end of the year accounting for actual expenditure.

Even if the timeshare purchaser's title to his timeshare interest may be unaffected by the liquidation or bankruptcy of the developer, if the insolvency occurs in the earlier stages of the sales programme there is an obvious risk that the contributions due in respect of the unsold timeshares will not be made. In view of this risk the developer should consider some form of independent guarantee or bond to timeshare purchasers. In this connection it is interesting to compare the use of a performance bond provided by a developer for the benefit of the timeshare purchasers' club with the aim of guaranteeing construction of the whole of the development. It is thought that such a bond could be adapted or extended to provide a guarantee of the management charge contributions.

# The marketing contract

The form of contract made between a timeshare developer and a marketing company, or 'marketeer', will necessarily vary greatly, depending on the particular circumstances in each case. However, it may be helpful to note some of the considerations which are relevant when negotiating or drafting such a contract.

## The need for a procedures manual

To a large extent the success of the operation depends upon co-operation between the timeshare developer and the marketeer, and disputes are more likely to be avoided if the arrangements between the parties are set out in as much detail and with as much clarity as possible. All kinds of unexpected problems will present themselves during the course of the selling programme, and these will involve some variations of the arrangements. It is important that these are minuted and agreed, so as to avoid communication breakdowns. Once the main provisions of the agreement have been drawn up it is wise for the parties to include a reference to a procedure manual. The procedures can be revised and agreed between the parties from time to time, and an updated and comprehensive manual of procedures should be circulated to all interested parties. In the main agreement the parties should agree not to depart from the procedures laid down in the procedures manual without prior (written) agreement. Care should be taken to avoid drafting such a provisions in a way which could be construed as merely an agreement to agree and hence imply that it was unenforceable on account of uncertainty.

## Parties, governing law and disputes

The identity of the parties at first sight poses no problems. However, the parties who negotiate the contract may not necessarily be those who enter into it. For example, it is often the case that the timeshare developer will be a subsidiary or associated company of the company with whom the contract is negotiated. Consequently, the marketeer may require a guarantee from the parent company. Again, the marketeer may wish to contract in the name of a tax haven corporation, but as the identity of the key personnel may be important to the developer, some provision in this respect may need to be inserted and these provisions may have tax implications. In the case of overseas developments where the marketing is directed to purchasers within the UK, there may be room for choice of a number of different laws and jurisdictions to govern the arrangements. Generally speaking, the locations of the parties' assets will govern the choice of law and jurisdiction, so as to avoid the danger of trying to obtain a judgment in one jurisdiction and then seeking to enforce it in another. With the advent of the Civil Jurisdictions and Judgements Act 1982 this consideration may not have such great significance as between parties whose assets are located in parts of Europe to which the Act applies.

Schemes which entail marketing timeshare interests falling within the provisions of the Financial Services Act 1986 should include provisions binding the marketeer to adhere to the regulations made under that Act or by the relevant SRO, where and to the extent that the Act applies. Similarly, those developers which are members of a trade association may wish to make it a term of the agreement that the marketeer adheres to the Code of Ethics published by that organisation. The contract should also contain some provision for arbitration to allow for a relatively swift and informal dispute resolution.

### Tax and exchange control

These areas are particularly important in relation to overseas schemes. As will be seen from the comments in Chapter 6, the employment of an agent in the UK who has power to bind the seller may mean that the developer will be taxable as if he were trading in the UK. The nature of the services provided in the UK are also material in this connection. If, as is often the case, the agent is carrying out marketing in more than one jurisdiction and the developer is located in a jurisdiction which has exchange control laws, payment to a marketeer in a 'foreign' currency may require central bank permission. In some circumstances, the level of external payments is regulated for example to the level of 10 per cent or 15 per cent of the sales price, so that a way must be found to overcome this problem. The solution often lies in the way in which the scheme is structured and the way in which approach is made to the central bank. However, receipt of funds abroad by the seller or marketeer may in some cases be a criminal offence unless all necessary permissions have been obtained.

### Provision of facilities by the developer

These need to be agreed at the outset. They may include matters such as the construction and availability of show apartments or villas, the erection of signs giving directions to the development (for which planning permission may be required) the provision of site office facilities (the need for a 'closing room' is examined in Chapter 5), accommodation for sales personnel, transport, entertainment for prospective purchasers, access to the developer's own sales records, assistance in obtaining work permits if required, membership of an exchange organisation, access to other parts of the development, the provision of telexes, telephones and other office equipment, and so on. In addition, an advertising budget needs to be drawn up and there must be provisions for the approval of advertisements which may be of particular importance if the advertisements have to comply with s 57 of the Financial Services Act 1986 or for example the existing Portuguese and proposed Spanish legislation.

The form of sales contract will be material to the marketeer, as will the terms upon which finance can be offered, whether or not credit card payments can be accepted, and who is responsible for credit card commissions. General information as to the project, such as proper calculation of the management charge, schedule of furnishing, standard of finishes, plans, other amenities to be offered, and as to the legal structure of the timeshare project, all need to be made clear to the marketeer. He in turn must ensure that his sales personnel are familar with these matters. When and how the inventory is to be made available for sale should be set out clearly in the agreement.

## Accounting and records

It is generally undesirable that the marketeer should have direct access to the timeshare purchasers' funds, but at the same time accounts of all funds received need to be kept. In addition, sales records must be maintained, preferably computerised, and records of all leads and how they have been generated must be kept, together with the performance of each individual sales person. Large numbers of people will have to be told about or shown over the timesharing projects. If the closing ratio is 10 per cent (ie 10 per cent of all leads actually purchased) and there are 30 purchasers in each apartment (some buying one and some three weeks) a hundred unit development will probably involve contacting some 30,000 people (or probably double that number since most purchasers are married couples). The marketeer must also be under an obligation to provide weekly sales reports and returns and, where an expense allowance is granted, budgets and expense returns. Each prospective purchaser involves a good deal of administration time and paperwork, consequently there should be a minimum deposit policy. Needless to say, the point at which the commission is earned and the point at which it is payable must be clearly identified.

## Marketing methods and controls

The timeshare developer must allow purchasers a period within which to cancel, otherwise bad publicity may result. Such a 'cooling-off' period also provides some measure of protection against the side effects of 'hard sell tactics'. The policy in respect of cancellations must be established in the agreement and, where there is a cancellation fee, it should be decided who is to be entitled to it. The agreement should cover the possibility of misrepresentations by sales personnel, perhaps by way of an acknowledgment of representations. The marketeer should also be asked to provide a series of warranties in respect of liabilities that may be incurred on behalf of the principal.

The 'follow up' procedure needs to be agreed. Purchasers should be contacted upon their return home and procedures for completion explained to them. They will need to know whom to contact in the case of complaint. House magazines, news letters and other promotional literature need to be prepared and costed.

The marketeer should also have a Consumer Credit Act licence. All aspects of the marketing plan should be covered in detail in the agreement, including the arrangements for customer inspection visits, provision of accommodation and services to customers, and so forth.

Whilst the marketeers will generally require complete autonomy over the management of the sales personnel, a disputes procedure should be set up and the developer should have a voice in the disciplinary procedures, since bad marketing practices will often adversely affect the reputation of the developer.

## Duration extent and termination

Usually the agreement will be made for a defined period, with provisions for extension or termination dependent upon performance. Performance clauses vary enormously but are usually two-tier geared to monthly and annual returns, the latter usually involving an incentive bonus. Obviously, performance has to be linked with inventory supply. The developer should be careful to provide for phasing of sales, so that a minimum number of sales and a minimum number of weekly periods in each season ('high', 'low' and 'shoulder') are sold before the next phase of the inventory is released to the marketeer. It is a common mistake to allow the marketeer to sell out all the 'cream' weeks such as high season weeks, which are always the easiest to sell, leaving the developer with a large number of unsold low season weeks. Since the developer will be responsible for paying the management charges in relation to unsold timeshare weeks, as few weeks as possible should be left unsold before moving on to the next phase.

It often happens that marketing takes place in respect of units which have not yet been constructed or completed. On the one hand, the developer would obviously like to be in a 'pre-sale situation'; on the other hand the practice is dangerous if practised to too great an extent. This is because, generally speaking, the marketeer cannot afford to wait for commissions until physical completion of the units, and until the units are physically completed, the purchase prices relating to timeshare sales in those units, are, or should be, left in a blocked account, so that the developer will have to fund the commissions either from his own pocket or from sales in completed units. Getting this part of the agreement right will enable the marketeer to decide upon the level of personnel required on the one hand, and avoid overtrading and cash flow problems on the part of the developer on the other.

The agreement should also define the territory within which the marketeer has an exclusive right to sell (if the right is indeed exclusive). The provisions of art 85 of the Treaty of Rome should be borne in mind in case they become relevant in this connection. Lead generation proposals should be carefully examined to ensure that they do not infringe legislation regulating betting, gaming and lotteries within the UK.

The termination provisions should be divided into two categories: those events which will entitle one party to terminate automatically, and those where it is appropriate to allow for a period of notice during which the breach may be remedied.

## Conclusion

The foregoing is merely a summary of the considerations involved in working out the negotiation and preparation of the marketing contract. Experienced advice is always essential, especially where one or other of the parties is new to the field. There are two halves to the equation. One consists of getting the structure of the scheme itself right and the other of arriving at a well thought out marketing plan allied to a comprehensive marketing agreement and experienced marketeers. If too much attention is paid to marketing and not enough to structuring the likely result will be impressive initial sales followed by muddles, legal claims and the ultimately financial collapse. Conversely, if the structuring is good from the legal point of view but the marketing support is inadequate, a good deal of money will have been spent to no purpose.

Finally, new laws governing sales to UK nationals, or made within the UK, are contemplated in the near future (see Chapters 3 and 10). The timeshare scheme and the marketing agreement should be planned with those provisions in mind, otherwise adapting to the new regime may prove to be impracticable, or highly expensive.

# Chapter Three

# Protection of a timeshare purchaser

The cost of acquiring a timeshare unit varies enormously, from as little as a few hundred pounds to many thousands of pounds. Whatever the price, in the majority of cases, the timeshare buyer is asked to assume, very much as an article of faith, that provided he pays the price, he will eventually obtain secure ownership of the unit or units offered by a developer. Timeshare purchasers are naturally concerned as to whether they may safely buy a timeshare unit in, eg, Spain, Portugal, Cyprus, Switzerland or elsewhere. Independent professional advice is often difficult to obtain, especially overseas, and it is often impracticable to make even the simplest enquiries at the local land registry or municipal authority. Apart from language difficulties, the cost of such investigations and particularly a full title search, are not generally warranted by the size of the investment, and in any event are likely to cause purchasers and timeshare developers unacceptable delays. The size or apparent substance of the developer is hardly an adequate guarantee that all will be well. There have already been substantial insolvencies among major timeshare developers in the short history of timesharing and of course some developers may operate schemes through local subsidiaries where, even if the parent company were to accept responsibility, disputes would have to be arbitrated under local foreign law. This raises questions of private international law of potentially fearsome complexity referred to in Chapter 7.

A timeshare buyer will hardly ever have the opportunity to make his own enquiries as to whether such basic services as water, gas, electricity, let alone any luxury amenities such as golf courses and swimming pools, really do belong to and go with the timeshare unit which is being purchased. Even if a developer has been admitted to qualify for the benefits of an exchange organisation, no guarantee is given that the purchaser's rights are protected.

Again, the fact that a developer may be under-capitalised may not always be apparent, especially when there is a strong forward sales programme. It is of course highly unsatisfactory to rely to any great extent on future sales to finance current development, since over optimistic sales forecasts are only too easy to draw up. *A fortiori*, if the developer is able to, he collects and utilises the proceeds of sales of units before they are even constructed or before he has completed the purchase of the development land and obtained all necessary permission for the proposed contribution. Circumstances such as these will continue to arise in the absence of statutory controls.

## Trade protection

The European Holiday Timeshare Association (EHTA) was the first European organisation to be formed with detailed criteria for prospective members and strict rules based upon American legislation, with full-time personnel, a compensation fund and a low cost arbitration scheme similar to that of the Association of British Travel Agents (ABTA). Its members were developers, marketing companies, trust companies and the exchange companies. In November 1987, after lengthy negotiations, it joined forces with a newly formed group of major developers and a small trade association, to become the Timeshare Developers Association (TDA).

The TDA had voting rights weighted in favour of the larger developers, excluded marketing companies and trust companies from membership, but adopted much though not all of the EHTA regulation. Its avowed aim was to become a self-regulatory organisation. The rigours and commercial disadvantages of self-regulation, unsupported by any legislative intervention, made it impossible to achieve the market domination essential to success, a fact recognised by the Director General of Fair Trading who, in a report published in June 1990, advocated a legislative framework for the UK industry. The report prompted a rethink as to how the industry should be represented. At the time of writing this review has not been completed but already, in October 1990, the TDA has resolved to wind itself up. A new association, the Timeshare Council, has been set up by some former TDA members and other parties. It is planned that the new body will have a far wider membership base, which will lend support to an early legislative framework within which some degree of self-regulation would be possible.

Trade associations have also been formed in other jurisdictions:

**Australia:**   National Holiday Ownership Council Ltd
First Floor, 2 Clarke Street
South Melbourne VIC 3205
Australia
Tel: 010 613 693 5433/Fax: 010 613 696 7615

**Bahamas:**   The Bahamas Timesharing and Development Council
(BTDC)
PO Box F2058
Freeport
Grand Bahama Island
Bahamas
Tel: 010 1 809 3528425; and

PO Box N10600,
Nassau
NP Bahamas
Tel: 010 1 809 3262340

**Canada:**      National Timesharing Council of Canada (NTCC)
Suite 1903
PO Box 12
Toronto Dominium Centre
Toronto
Ontario M5K 1AB
Canada

**France:**      Association Realisateures d'Immobiliers En Propriete
Saisonniere (ARIPSA)
97 Avenue Victor Hugo
75016 Paris
France

**Germany:**     Timeshare-Verband
c/- Lawyer Wolfgang Boelke
Widenmayerstr 5
D–8000 Munich 22
Tel: 010 49 8922 85307

Christian Grams
Press Speaker
Timeshare Verband
PO Box 120737
D 4100 Duisburg 12
West Germany
Tel: 010 49 2034 30715

**Greece:**      Greek Timeshare Association
11 Alopekisstr
10675 Athens
Greece
Tel: 010 301 7221558/Fax: 010 301 7220613

**Ireland:**     Irish Property Timeshare Association (IPTA)
Knocktopher Abbey
Co Kilkenny
Ireland
Tel: 056 28618

**Malta:**  Central Mediterranean Timeshare Association (CMTA)
Ramba Bay Hotel
Marfa
Malta
Tel: 010 356 473521/2/3

**Portugal:**  Associacao Nacional dos Industriais De Turismo de
Hapitacao Periodica (ANITHAP)
Portuguese Timeshare Association
Vale Do Lobo
Centro de Servicos Valverde 8100
Almansil
Portugal
Tel: 010 351 89 9484

**South Africa:**  National Timeshare Committee (NTC)
503 Carlton Centre
Johannesburg 2001
South Africa
Tel: 010 27 11 3312637

**Spain:**  Associacion de Promotores de Multipropiedad de
Andalucia
c/o Calypso Decoracion
Urbanizacion Calypso
Centro Commercial Valdepinos
Crta de Cadiz km 197
Mijas Costa, Malaga
Tel: 010 3452 83351/Fax: 010 3452 836077

**USA:**  American Resort and Residential Association
1220 'L' Street NW Fifth Floor
Washington DC 2005
USA
Tel: 010 1 202 371 6700/Fax: 010 1 202 289 8544

## The OFT report

The Office of Fair Trading, in a report published in June 1990, made the following recommendations:

**R1** All timeshare developers, or their agents, should be under a statutory obligation to provide a prospectus with comprehensive and accurate written information, in clear and understandable language, about the resort, its title, facilities, and other matters under the headings specified below. Where no provision is made under any one of these headings this should be stated. Where relevant the prospectus should be an accurate summary of the contract(s). The existence of the prospectus should be clearly referred to in all advertisements for timeshare, including direct mail. It must be posted or handed to the purchaser before he or she signs a timeshare contract. The prospectus should also be available to anyone who asks for a copy. Failure to provide the prospectus before the contract is signed should render the contract voidable. The specified headings are:

(a) *Title*. The nature of the developer's title and details of any mortgages or other encumbrances on the property. Whether planning permission has been granted. Name and address of any solicitor or other authority who has verified this information.

(b) *Purchaser's interest*. The legal structure of the timeshare being sold, the nature and length of the purchaser's interest, what will happen to the resort when the period of the timeshare comes to an end, and the arrangements to be made in the event of the property not being available for occupation at any time.

(c) *Price*. The total cost to the purchaser, listing separately the cost of all the different types of accommodation on offer at different times of the year, together with any discounts available and the conditions under which discounts are given. The cost of renting accommodation and using the communal facilities should also be shown. The date and amount of any planned future price increases should be given together with any mandatory administrative or legal fees. Any other costs not covered elsewhere in the prospectus should be shown.

(d) *Resort Calendar*. for at least the next 50 years, unless the duration of the timeshare is shorter.

(e) *Financial Protection*. Details of the protection offered under R3-R6.

(f) *Owners Association*. Arrangements made for representing interests of owners. Explanation of extent of the developer's interest in the association and how this is to change with time. Whether and at what point owners will eventually have responsibility for running the owners committee. Methods of voting for the owners committee. Arrangements for making management accounts available to owners.

(g) *Description of Resort*. Groundplan of resort, showing how much has been built so far and what further building is planned. Number of units of accommodation to be built, and size, so that prospective purchasers may have some idea of how many other people will be using the resort. A description of all communal facilities which exist or are planned, with expected dates for completion. A clear statement of which facilities belong to owners and which belong to the developer or some other person. If facilities are to be shared with people who are not timeshare owners, or if any are closed at certain times of the year, this should be stated. If owners are allowed to use facilities outside their week(s) of ownership this should be stated. Brief factual description of locality including transport links.

(h) *Maintenance*. The amount currently charged for maintenance, and the basis on which charges are and will be assessed. What services are covered by annual maintenance charge. Any services (such as electricity) not covered by the annual charge. Information about any contribution to be provided by the developer, including the extent of any subsidy of costs, any amount to be put aside for a sinking fund, and owners' rights to see the documents on which the accounts are based. Whether the developer or a third party is to provide the service. The consequence for the owner of failing to keep up payments.

(i) *Exchange*. Factual description of any exchange arrangement (including annual cost), any free membership given by developer, and the exchange fee. Any rejoining charge to be levied after ownership has been allowed to lapse should be stated. If no exchange arrangement exists this should be stated.

(j) *Rental and resale.* Description of any rental and resale programme in operation, including registration fee, if any, and developer's commission. Who runs the programme, if this is not the developer. If a resale programme is in operation, average resale prices over the past 12 months must be shown. If a programme is planned for the future, the date at which it will come into operation and the minimum period it will run for. If no programme is planned this must be stated.

(k) *Withdrawal from contract.* The prospectus should provide details of the cooling-off period (see R2) and explain how purchasers should exercise their legal right to withdraw from the contract during this time. The prospectus should also explain purchasers' rights in the event that the prospectus is not provided, is inaccurate or conflicts with the contract.

The request for a prospectus is, in itself, unobjectionable. Some developers and marketeers will no doubt put in hand the preparation of that document immediately, without waiting for legislation, and a simpler document is required by the proposed new Spanish law (see Chapter 10). The information should be readily available for most resorts.

The OFT report continues:

**R2** All timeshare purchasers should be allowed to withdraw from their contract without penalty within a minimum of 14 calendar days from its date of signing. Developers could offer a longer cooling-off period if they wished.

It is extremely unlikely that the marketeers will accept the administrative delays and complexities involved in a long cooling-off period. The EEC Commission at the time of writing were drafting a proposed directive on unfair contract terms which is to incorporate a seven day cooling-off period for consumers who have agreed to purchase a timeshare interest. One assumes that the industry itself, whilst finding 14 days unacceptable, could accept seven days. After all, the purpose of the cooling-off period is to allow time for reflection, and seven days should be ample for this purpose. It seems hard that the developers are not to be allowed to make some small administration charge to cover the costs of cancellation, and such costs will undoubtedly have to be passed on to those who do purchase, which seems hardly fair.

The report effectively recommends involving an independent stakeholder:

**R3** Legislation should require that payments made to purchase timeshare should be suitably safeguarded. This could take the form, for example, of insurance or bonding to indemnify the purchaser in the event of the contract not being completed, or payments to be paid into an account maintained by an independent stakeholder of suitable standing and repute. This person might be, for example, a trustee, a bank or other appropriate corporate body, a solicitor or professional accountant. The payments should not be passed to the developer until completion of the contract for the timeshare or until the timeshare unit is ready for occupation, whichever is the later. Failure by the developer to comply with these requirements should be a criminal offence.

The involvement of an independent stakeholder is absolutely essential, as otherwise the purchaser will either have to make a value judgment on the worth of the bond or other insurance, or alternatively the statutory regulation will need to be complex and finely drawn to cover all loopholes. The best guarantee that the purchaser can have is the independence and reputation of the stakeholder. The other branch of this recommendation is that purchasers' funds are not to be released until the unit is ready for occupation. It has been common practice for purchasers' funds to be used towards building expenditure and a number of undercapitalised developers are going to be hard pressed to comply with this provision. It could well have the effect of making the completion of some projects impossible, but this is a price which will have to be paid if the industry is to get itself on to a proper footing. The level of the required accounting service, covering inventory data, sales, resales, upgrades, cancellations, financed sales, etc should not be underestimated by those wishing to act as stakeholder. Sophisticated computerisation will be required, with a legal and customer services department to deal with the numerous queries which arise in practice.

The report continues:

**R4**  Where title to timeshare accommodation does not already reside with the owners, that title should be free of all undisclosed or future encumbrances and held by an independent person of suitable standing and repute on behalf of the owners. Failure by the developer to comply should be a criminal offence.

A large number of timeshare schemes in Europe are so structured that the developer retains the right to sell or mortgage the property in such a way as to overreach the rights of the member owners, and usually in such circumstances the property is available to the creditors of the developer. This recommendation effectively makes the involvement of a trustee mandatory.

It has been common practice for many developers to use management charges for their own purposes, as part of their cash flow. The dangers of this are obvious and the OFT report recommends:

**R5**  Until used for the intended purpose, management fees paid by the owners should be declared by statute to be held on trust for the owners and should be held in a client account in the same way as the Estate Agents Act 1979 requires estate agents to hold clients' money. Similar provisions as to keeping of accounts should apply.

The report also makes it clear that monies collected for owners and not from them require to be safeguarded:

**R6**  Monies held on behalf of owners by any person providing a rental or resale service at a resort, including resale brokers or any other agent operating on behalf of the developer or owners association, should be declared by statute to be held on trust for the parties to the transaction and should be held in a client account in the same way as the Estate Agents Act 1979 requires estate agents to hold clients' money. Similar provisions as to keeping of accounts should apply.

The report goes on to outline the current position regarding the Trade Descriptions Act 1968:

**R7** The Trade Descriptions Act 1968 should be amended to apply strict liability for mis-statements about services, accommodation and facilities.

**R8** The Trade Descriptions Act 1968 should be amended so that award schemes are brought within the Act.

**R9** It should continue to be an offence under the Trade Descriptions Act 1968 to make a false statement in respect of the future supply of any services. A false statement shall be deemed to be made when the services are not supplied within the time specified, or when services are supplied which do not correspond to the description. If a trader has supplied services which do not correspond to the description it shall be a defence to show that before supplying the services the recipient of the services was notified of the changes and the recipient's agreement to the changes was obtained.

The Fair Trading Act 1973 is also examined:

**R10** An improved Part III of the Fair Trading Act 1973 (on the lines shortly to be proposed by the Director General) would be the best long stop control to stamp out the worst abuses in the field of timeshare. If such proposals are not implemented, consideration should be given to measures targeted specifically at the sector to prevent unfit traders from marketing timeshare.

It is proposed that Part III of the 1973 Act be amended to enable the Director General of Fair Trading or the local trading standards authorities to take injunctive action when traders break their legal obligations to consumers. The proposals 'will also seek to extend the grounds for such action to include trading practices which are deceptive, misleading or unconscionable. The latter category would include, for example, practices which involve undue pressure to enter a transaction or exploitation of consumers' inability to protect themselves through lack of understanding of the nature of the transactions'. (*OFT Timesharing Report June 1990*, page 107). Failing amendment of the Act, specific further timeshare legislation is proposed to ban unfit traders.

The report continues:

**R11** Consideration should be given to the use of criminal law to deal with those who procure the execution of timeshare contracts in circumstances where there has been failure to comply with the proposed statutory requirements about the provision of a prospectus and a cooling off period.

It remains to be seen whether this proposal will be embodied in legislation. As presently envisaged, it is widely drawn, and could trap lawyers and advisers as well as marketing agents.

The report also recommends further legislation on timeshare:

**R12** Further legislation to regulate aspects of timeshare more closely should be considered if adequate steps to improve standards have not been taken by those directly or indirectly involved.

Presumably the Director General considers that the threat of further legislation will be enough to persuade the industry to make greater self-regulatory efforts. Whether this will in fact occur is doubtful.

## OFT proposals for self-regulation

The Office of Fair Trading put forward a number of suggestions for self-regulation:

S1    Organisations at whom these suggestions are directed should write to this Office within the next six months to outline the steps they are taking to implement them.

S2    Developers, and marketing companies acting as their agent, who promote resorts by direct mail should use only agencies recognised by the Direct Mail Services Standards Board, or members of the British List Brokers Association or the British Direct Marketing Association.

S3    Developers, and marketing companies acting as their agents, should ensure that all their advertisements (including direct mail) comply with the British Code of Advertising Practice, the British Code of Sales Promotion Practice and the DMSSB guidelines on timeshare promotions and any guidelines that may be published by these or similar bodies in the future. In particular:

    (a) advertisements (including direct mail) concerned with promoting the sale of timeshare should say so explicitly;

    (b) timeshare advertisements, including direct mail, which offer incentives to members of the public attending a sales presentation should indicate clearly any expenses or conditions which attach to the incentive;

    (c) timeshare advertisements, including direct mail, should not mislead recipients about their chance of receiving a particular award.

S4    The advertising and direct mail regulatory bodies should undertake a concerted campaign of publicity to make their role in regulation better known to the public and business in general.

S5    To meet increasing demand from the public, perhaps promoted by further publicity, the direct mail industry should consider ways of increasing the funding of the Mailing Preference Service. The Post Office should consider its responsibility as a carrier of advertisements, for example through the imposition of a levy on the direct mail industry, to ensure all who use this medium contribute to funding for the Mailing Preference Service.

S6    The Post Office should consider examining the contents of mailings sent under schemes set up under section 28 of the Post Office Act 1969, including Mailsort, and should refuse to carry them if there are repeated breaches of the British Advertising Code of Practice and/or the British Code of Sales Promotion Practice.

S7    Persons canvassing on behalf of timeshare resorts should be paid sufficient salary to avoid over-dependence on commission. Developers should ensure canvassers are required not to importune or obstruct people.

S8    All timeshare purchasers should be allowed to withdraw from their contract, if signed overseas, without penalty within 14 calendar days of returning to the United Kingdom or 28 days from signing, whichever is the lesser. Developers may offer a longer cooling-off period if they wish.

S9    Vetting procedures should assess resorts from the perspective of the interests of owners, in particular protection of money, title and the rights of owners (and in particular the rules and status of the owners association) as well as the developer's title and financial viability. Such vetting should be carried out by competent independent persons, preferably appointed by an independent organisation such as the appropriate Law Society.

S10 Developers should co-operate fully and freely with the vetting or checking procedures of organisations they are members of or affiliated to.

S11 If the developer or management company retains ownership of part of the resort and fails to carry out its repair obligations owners should have the right to commission an independent expert survey, and undertake any repair works found to be necessary, at their own expense. The costs would be recoverable from the developer or management company, whichever is in default.

S12 Trustees should provide information about resorts for which they act, promptly and fully, to anyone with a legitimate interest in having the information, for example owners and prospective owners at the resorts and their solicitors, exchange companies, owners associations, management companies or resale brokers.

S13 Trustees, finance houses, solicitors, professional accountants and exchange companies should use their power and influence to ensure that developers or marketers provide a prospectus to prospective owners, offer a cooling-off period, have satisfactory arrangements for safeguarding consumers' money or have funds available for the completion of the resort.

S14 Trustees, finance houses, solicitors and exchange companies should require as part of their agreement with a developer, if they do not already do so, that the nature of their involvement with the timeshare developer or resort is not misrepresented. They should actively monitor this requirement. Parent companies, for example banks owning trustee companies, should monitor compliance with this recommendation.

S15 An owners association should be established, and should have elected an owners committee, no later than one year after the first timeshare unit is sold. At the latest the owners should take over the running of the resort from the developer when 50 per cent of the units have been sold.

S16 Developers should only be able to vote for units which are constructed and ready for occupation. They should not be able to exercise, as of right, proxy votes on behalf of owners.

S17 The chairman of an owners committee should be a representative of the owners and not of the developer.

S18 The developer should make available, on request, to the chairman of an owners committee a list of all owners, so that he or she may communicate with them. The developer should also undertake to send any communication to owners on the chairman's behalf.

S19 Elections to the owners committee should take place annually. The original members of an owners committee may be appointed by the developer, but at least one third of the committee members must retire annually by rotation although they should be free to submit themselves for re-election.

S20 Any proposal by developers to institute changes at resorts which are likely to change their atmosphere or the kind of service they provide should first be submitted to the owners committee for approval, and then to the next AGM of the owners association.

S21 The owners committee should assume responsibility for the preparation of annual accounts and budgets which should be sent, together with reports thereon by a qualified auditor, to owners within three months of the end of each financial year. If it is necessary to set an initial management charge before budgets and accounts have been circulated, the auditor should report on whether the initial rate of charge is reasonable in the light of the available information; and when rates of charge are subsequently changed, these changes should be related to the figures in the circulated budget.

**S22**  The management charge should be based on actual costs which have been reasonably incurred with the exception of provision for a sinking fund (see S24). It would be permissible for the charge to be tied to an index of charges produced by a government department or other independent agency for two years out of three, but every third year the charge should be re-assessed against actual costs.

**S23**  The developer should pay the management charge for all unsold weeks. This payment should not be described as a 'subsidy'.

**S24**  Developers should provide that an adequate proportion (generally at least 15 per cent) of all money collected through the management charge should be placed in an interest-bearing sinking fund and retained exclusively for any future structural repairs and refurbishment of the resort.

**S25**  Developers should ensure that from the outset the agreement between the management company and owners association allows either side to withdraw at a maximum of six months' notice.

**S26**  Developers should introduce a rental programme within one year of the first units being sold, and a resale programme within three years.

**S27**  Developers should consider the active promotion of both rental and inspection programmes.

**S28**  No developer or resale broker should require owners wishing to resell or rent their timeshare to enter into an exclusive agreement.

**S29**  Developers should respond promptly to any reasonable request from a resale broker for a copy of the prospectus and any other promotional material about the resort.

**S30**  Developers should consider allowing one or more of the established resale brokers to operate their resale programme.

**S31**  The exchange companies should reconsider the inclusion of exclusivity clauses in their affiliation agreements. Developers and owners should consider affiliating their resorts to both exchange companies, and to any new exchange company which may be formed.

**S32**  The exchange companies should consider providing a grading system for affiliated resorts.

**S33**  The industry should pay greater attention to the need to establish and retain a salesforce well versed in the product and trained to sell without using high-pressure techniques.

*Extracts from this report are reproduced by kind permission of the Office of Fair Trading.*

It is suggested that these recommendations be embodied in a code of practice but there will clearly have to be a good deal more discussion within the industry before such a code could be drawn up. Many of the suggestions appear impracticable, and arguably demonstrate a lack of research or understanding on the part of the OFT, and some would, if adopted, work to the active disadvantage of existing and prospective owners. The view has been expressed that some of the suggestions have been made to provoke discussion rather than acceptance. No doubt the new Timeshare Council will create an industry-wide debate, and formulate an industry approach to these issues, once it is firmly established.

## Relevant legislation

### Unfair Contract Terms Act 1977

This Act provides a remedy against some types of exemption clauses, specifically those which attempt to exclude liability for misrepresentation Section 8 provides:

> 8—(1) In the Misrepresentation Act 1967, the following is substituted for section 3—
>> 3 If a contract contains a term which would exclude or restrict—
>>> (a) any liability to which a party to a contract may be subject by reason of any misrepresentation made by him before the contract was made; or
>>> (b) any remedy available to another party to the contract by reason of such a misrepresentation,
>> that term shall be of no effect except in so far as it satisfies the requirement of reasonableness as stated in section 11(1) of the Unfair Contract Terms Act 1977, and it is for those claiming that the term satisfies that requirement to show that it does.

The Act goes on to provide a test for 'reasonableness'. If the term is found to be unreasonable in accordance with the test the term will be void, and s 11(5) of the Act provides: 'It is for those claiming that a contract term or notice satisfies the requirement of reasonableness to show that it does'. Nevertheless, although the Act has been in force for more than 12 years there is little in the way of precedent as to how it is viewed by the courts. In two cases—*Smith* v *Eric S Bush* and *Harris* v *Wyre Forest District Council* [1989] 2 All ER 514 HL—where clauses in two contracts between lenders and valuers purporting to exclude liability to the borrower for negligence were held to be unreasonable, and the valuers unable to rely on them, the effect of the Act was reviewed.

### Misrepresentation Act 1967

In order to contribute an actionable misrepresentation, the representation must be one of a past and present fact and not a statement as to the future (*Sanders* v *Gall* (1952) CPL 343, *Angus* v *Clifford* (1891) 2 Ch 449 *Beesly* v *Hallwood Estates Ltd* (1960) 1 WLR 549). However, a statement of intention can be regarded as a statement of fact if when made it was not possible to give effect to it (*Edgington* v *Fitzmaurice* (1885) 29 ChD 459). Statements of opinion are not normally actionable, but if it can be shown that a reasonable man in possession of the same facts could not have expressed such an opinion or that the opinion was not honestly held, it may be actionable (*Smith* v *Land and House Property Corp* (1884) 28 ChD 7) and a statement of opinion published as if it were a fact may be actionable (*Reese River Silver Mining Co Ltd* v *Smith* (1869) LR 4 HL 64). Unless the contract is one *uberrimae fidei*, where there is a fiduciary relationship or a duty of utmost good faith, non-disclosure by itself does not constitute misrepresentation (*Percival* v *Wright*

(1902) 2 Ch 421), but failure to inform a representee that a change in circumstances has occurred which has rendered false an originally true representation can be misrepresentation (*With* v *O'Flanagan* (1936) Ch 575 and *Davies* v *London Provincial Marine Insurance Co* (1878) 8 ChD 469). The remedy for material misrepresentation is rescission of the contract although that remedy may not be available if the representee is held to have affirmed the contract in some way, as for example making use of the timeshare. Damages are also recoverable if the representation was fraudulent (*Derry* v *Peek* (1889) 14 App Ch 337 and, since the Misrepresentation Act 1967, for negligent misrepresentation. Section 2 of the Act reads:

2—(1) Where a person has entered into a contract after a misrepresentation has been made to him by another party thereto and as a result thereof he has suffered loss, then, if the person making the representation would be liable to damages in respect thereof had the misrepresentation been made fraudulently, that person shall be so liable notwithstanding that the misrepresentation was not made fraudulently, unless he proves that he had reasonable ground to believe and did believe up to the time the contract was made that the facts represented were true.

(2) Where a person has entered into a contract after a misrepresentation has been made to him otherwise than fraudulently, and he would be entitled, by reason of the misrepresentation, to rescind the contract, then, if it is claimed, in any proceedings arising out of the contract, that the contract ought to be or has been rescinded the court or arbitrator may declare the contract subsisting and award damages in lieu of rescission, if of opinion that it would be equitable to do so, having regard to the nature of the misrepresentation and the loss that would be caused by it if the contract were upheld, as well as to the loss that rescission would cause to the other party.

(3) Damages may be awarded against a person under subsection (2) of this section whether or not he is liable to damages under subsection (1) thereof, but where he is so liable any award under the said subsection (2) shall be taken into account in assessing his liability under the said subsection (1).

As for what constitutes 'reasonable grounds for belief' that the facts represented were true see *Greenwood* v *Leather Shod Wheel Co* (1900) 1 ChD 421, *Brown* v *Raphael* [1958] 2 All ER 79, *Howard Marine and Dredging Co Ltd* v *Ogden & Sons (Excavations) Ltd* [1978] QB 574, but contrast *Wall* v *Silver Wing Surface Arrangements Ltd* (1981) (unreported).

**Trade Descriptions Act 1968**

The Act makes it a criminal offence to make certain false and misleading statements. Prosecutions are normally brought by trading standards officers, but it is open to individuals to bring a private prosecution. Successful prosecutions do not entitle the person to compensation, although the court has power to make compensation orders under the Powers of the Criminal Courts Act 1973 and a conviction can also be used in evidence in a court claim brought by a consumer. Section 14 of the Act reads as follows:

14—(1) It shall be an offence for any person in the course of any trade or business—

    (*a*) to make a statement which he knows to be false; or

    (*b*) recklessly to make a statement which is false; as to any of the following matters, that is to say—

        (i) the provision in the course of any trade or business of any services, accommodation or facilities;

        (ii) the nature of any services, accommodation or facilities provided in the course of any trade or business;

        (iii) the time at which, manner in which or persons by whom any services, accommodation or facilities are so provided;

        (iv) the examination, approval or evaluation by any person of any services, accommodation or facilities so provided; or

        (v) the location or amenities of any accommodation so provided.

  (2) For the purposes of this section—

    (*a*) anything (whether or not a statement as to any of the matters specified in the preceding subsection) likely to be taken for such a statement as to any of those matters as would be false shall be deemed to be a false statement as to that matter; and

    (*b*) a statement made regardless of whether it is true or false shall be deemed to be made recklessly, whether or not the person making it had reasons for believing that it might be false.

  (3) In relation to any services consisting of or including the application of any treatment or process or the carrying out of any repair, the matters specified in subsection (1) of this section shall be taken to include the effect of the treatment, process or repair.

  (4) In this section 'false' means false to a material degree and 'services' does not include anything done under a contract of service.

Actionable statements are not confined to statements inducing the entering into of a contract; they may include statements made after the contract was completed (*Breed* v *Cluett* [1970] 2 All ER 662). Whilst s 14 does not apply outside the UK, for the purposes of the Act a statement is made when it is communicated to someone (*R* v *Thomson Holidays Ltd* [1974] QB 592). Material posted from abroad, for example, may include statements made at the time they are read. Prosecution in such cases could take place if the maker of the statement or someone responsible for circulating it were within the jurisdiction. Inducements to purchase, such as prizes, free gifts and other award schemes are not within the ambit of s 14 because they are not 'services, accommodation or facilities'. (*Westminster City Council* v *Ray Allen (Manshops) Ltd* [1982] 1 WLR 383; *Newill & Another* v *Kicks* (1983) 148 JP 308, and *Kinchin* v *Ashton Park Scooters Ltd* (1984) JP 540. The prosecution must prove that the false and misleading statement was made knowingly or recklessly, so this is not a strict liability offence although the OFT recommends that this be changed (June 1989 Report—*Timesharing*). As to knowledge, see *Wings Ltd* v *Ellis* [1984] 1 All ER 1046. The statement may be made about the provision by third parties of the matters referred to in s 14 (*Bambury* v *Hounslow Borough Council* [1971] RTR 1 (DC)). The statements complained of must be of a serious nature, false to a material degree and not just a breach of peripheral warranties (*R* v *Clarksons Holidays Ltd* (1972) 57 Cr App Rep 38;

*Beckett* v *Cohen* [1973] 1 All ER 120). The impression created in the mind of the representee is important, 'not the meaning which they might, on analysis, bear to a trained legal mind' per Viscount in *British Airways Board* v *Taylor* [1976] 1 All ER 65. It is not necessary for the statement to be made dishonestly to be made 'recklessly' or even that it was made 'careless whether it be true or false' but only that the advertiser did not have regard as to whether the statement was true or false (*MFI Warehouses Ltd* v *Nattrass* [1973] 1 All ER 762). A statement of intention as to the future is not covered by the Act (*R* v *Sunair Holidays Ltd* [1973] 2 All ER 1233).

### Control of Misleading Advertisements Regulations 1988

The regulations provide that the Director General of Fair Trading is required to consider complaints (other than frivolous or vexatious ones) about misleading advertisements. The Director is not required to consider complaints about commercial radio or television advertisements or cable advertisements. Before he considers a complaint the Director may require to be satisfied that appropriate means of dealing with the complaint have been tried and that, despite being given a reasonable opportunity to do so, those means have not dealt with the complaint adequately. (Such means might include complaining to a local authority trading standards department or to a self-regulatory body, such as the Advertising Standards Authority. It is, however, for the Director to determine what means he considers appropriate in any particular case.) In dealing with complaints the Director is required to bear in mind all the interests involved including, in particular, the public interest and the desirability of encouraging the control, by self-regulatory bodies, of advertisements (r 4).

The Director is given power to bring proceedings for an injunction to prevent the publication or continued publication of an advertisement which he considers misleading. He is required to give reasons for his decision to bring or not to bring proceedings for an injunction (r 5).

The advertisement must be published in connection with a trade or business, to promote the transfer or supply of goods or services, immovable property, rights or obligations, and must be likely to affect the economic behaviour of the reader by its deceptive nature.

### Consumer Protection Act 1987

The Act provides for two offences, in s 20(1) and (2) which read:

20—(1) Subject to the following provisions of this Part, a person shall be guilty of an offence if, in the course of any business of his, he gives (by any means whatever) to any consumers an indication which is misleading as to the price at which any goods, services, accommodation or facilities are available (whether generally or from particular persons).
(2) Subject as aforesaid, a person shall be guilty of an offence if—
(*a*) in the course of any business of his, he has given an indication to any

consumers which, after it was given, has become misleading as mentioned in subsection (1) above; and

(*b*) some or all of those consumers might reasonably be expected to rely on the indication at a time after it has become misleading; and

(*c*) he fails to take all such steps as are reasonable to prevent those consumers from relying on the indication.

The Department of Trade has published a code of practice setting out the principles to be observed. Prosecutions are brought by trading standards officers and the courts are empowered to take into account whether the code of practice was observed. The Act may catch those awards or offer schemes which do not indicate the cost involved, eg 'free' car phone or satellite dish without any indication that there is a mandatory installer, instalment and possibly rental charge, or 'free' hotel accommodation without any indication that as a condition of the offer all meals must be paid for at the hotel, whether or not consumed.

## Financial Services Act 1986

Sections 3 and 4 of the Act provides that 'investment' business may only be carried on by 'authorised persons', that is persons licensed by a self-regulatory organisation set up pursuant to the Act or by the Securities and Investment Board itself. The section reads as follows:

**3**     No person shall carry on, or purport to carry on, investment business in the United Kingdom unless he is an authorised person under Chapter III or an exempted person under Chapter IV of this part of this Act.

**4**—(1) Any person who carries on, or purports to carry on investment business in contravention of Section 3 above shall be guilty of an offence and liable—

(*a*) on conviction on indictment, to imprisonment for a term not exceeding two years or to a fine or to both;

(*b*) on summary conviction, to imprisonment for a term not exceeding six months or to a fine not exceeding the statutory maximum or to both.

(2) In proceedings brought against any person for an offence under this section it shall be a defence for him to prove that he took all reasonable precautions and exercised all due diligence to avoid the commission of the offence.

Section 5 goes on to make unenforceable agreements made in contravention of the Act as well as for the recovery of money and property and compensation in such circumstances. What then are 'investments'? The word is defined in Part 1 of Sched 1 of the Act, so far as is relevant to timesharing, as:

## Investments

*Shares etc*
1 Shares and stock in the share capital of a company.
*Note* In this paragraph "company" includes any body corporate and also any unincorporated body constituted under the law of a country or territory outside the

United Kingdom but does not include an open-ended investment company or any body incorporated under the law of, or any part of, the United Kingdom relating to building societies, industrial and provident societies or credit unions.

. . . . .

### Instruments entitling to shares or securities
4 Warrants or other instruments entitling the holder to subscribe for investments falling within paragraph 1, 2 or 3 above.
*Notes*
(1) It is immaterial whether the investments are for the time being in existence or identifiable.
(2) An investment falling within this paragraph shall not be regarded as falling within paragraph 7, 8 or 9 below.

### Certificates representing securities
5 Certificates or other instruments which confer—
  (*a*) property rights in respect of any investment falling within paragraph 1, 2, 3 or 4 above;
  (*b*) any right to acquire, dispose of, underwrite or convert an investment, being a right to which the holder would be entitled if he held any such investment to which the certificate or instrument relates; or
  (*c*) a contractual right (other than an option) to acquire any such investment otherwise than by subscription.
*Note* This paragraph does not apply to any instrument which confers rights in respect of two or more investments issued by different persons or in respect of two or more different investments falling within paragraph 3 above and issued by the same person.

### Units in collective investment scheme
6 Units in a collective investment scheme, including shares in or securities of an open-ended investment company.

### Options
7 Options to acquire or dispose of—
  (*a*) an investment falling within any other paragraph of this Part of this Schedule;
  (*b*) currency of the United Kingdom or of any other country or territory;
  (*c*) gold or silver; or
  (*d*) an option to acquire or dispose of an investment falling within this paragraph by virtue of (*a*), (*b*) or (*c*) above.

. . . . .

### Long term insurance contracts
10 Rights under a contract the effecting and carrying out of which constitutes long term business within the meaning of the Insurance 1982 c. 50 Companies Act 1982.

. . . . .

### Rights and interests in investments
11 Rights to and interests in anything which is an investment falling within any other paragraph of this Part of this Schedule.

*Notes*
(1) This paragraph does not apply to interests under the trusts of an occupational pension scheme.
(2) This paragraph does not apply to rights or interests which are investments by virtue of any other paragraph of this Part of this Schedule.'

Investment business is then defined by Part II of Sched 1 as follows:

**Activities constituting investment business**

*Dealing in investments*
12 Buying, selling, subscribing for or underwriting investments or offering or agreeing to do so, either as principal or as an agent.

*Arranging deals in investments*
13 Making, or offering or agreeing to make—
  (*a*) arrangements with a view to another person buying, selling, subscribing for or underwriting a particular investment; or
  (*b*) arrangements with a view to a person who participates in the arrange-ments buying, selling, subscribing for or underwriting investments.

*Notes*
(1) This paragraph does not apply to a person by reason of his making, or offering or agreeing to make, arrangements with a view to a transaction to which he will himself be a party as principal or which will be entered into by him as agent for one of the parties.
(2) The arrangements in (*a*) above are arrangements which bring about or would bring about the transaction in question.

*Managing investments*
14 Managing, or offering or agreeing to manage, assets belonging to another person if—
  (*a*) those assets consist of or include investments; or
  (*b*) the arrangements for their management are such that those assets may consist of or include investments at the discretion of the person managing or offering or agreeing to manage them and either they have at any time since the date of the coming into force of section 3 of this Act done so or the arrangements have at any time (whether before or after that date) been held out as arrangements under which they would do so.

*Investment advice*
15 Giving, or offering or agreeing to give, to persons in their capacity as investors or potential investors advice on the merits of their purchasing, selling, subscribing for or underwriting an investment, or exercising any right conferred by an investment to acquire, dispose or, underwrite or convert an investment.

*Establishing etc. collective investment schemes*
16 Establishing, operating or winding up a collective investment scheme, including acting as trustee of an authorised unit trust scheme.

Section 75 of the Act defines a 'collective investment scheme' as follows:

**75**—(1) In this Act "a collective investment scheme" means subject to the provisions of this section, any arrangements with respect to property of any description, including money, the purpose or effect of which is to enable persons taking part in the arrangements (whether by becoming owners of the property or any part of it or otherwise) to participate in or receive profits or income arising from the acquisition, holding, management or disposal of the property or sums paid out of such profits or income.

The section then goes on to define in more detail what is and what is not a 'collective investment scheme', specifically providing in s 75 (6)(*g*) that the following are not included:

(*g*) arrangements the predominant purpose of which is to enable persons participating in them to share in the use or enjoyment of a particular property or to make its use or enjoyment available gratuitously to other persons;

Any timeshare scheme set up on the basis that timeshare purchasers acquire shares in a limited company, wherever incorporated, or rights to or interests in shares, is likely to be caught by the Act. Other than schemes involving shares, most schemes are likely to come within the exemption of s 75 (6)(*g*) unless it can be demonstrated that the scheme is sold as a money making investment, or that the predominant purpose of the scheme is the making of profit.

## Data Protection Act 1984

The Act established a Data Protection Register and a Data Protection Tribunal. Anyone holding certain kinds of computerised information must be registered. Entries in the register must state the purpose for which the information is to be used, the sources from which data users will obtain the information, the people to whom they may wish to disclose it and any countries to which they may wish to disclose it. Data users must comply with the following eight principles, Sched 1, Part II:

*The first principle*
1—(1) Subject to sub-paragraph (2) below, in determining whether information was obtained fairly regard shall be had to the method by which it was obtained, including in particular whether any person from whom it was obtained was deceived or misled as to the purpose or purposes for which it is to be held, used or disclosed.
   (2) Information shall in any event be treated as obtained fairly if it is obtained from a person who—
      (*a*) is authorised by or under any enactment to supply it; or
      (*b*) is required to supply it by or under any enactment or by any convention or other instrument imposing an international obligation on the United Kingdom;

and in determining whether information was obtained fairly there shall be disregarded any disclosure of the information which is authorised or required by or under any enactment or required by any such convention or other instrument as aforesaid.

*The second principle*
2 Personal data shall not be treated as held for a specified purpose unless that purpose is described in particulars registered under this Act in relation to the data.

*The third principle*
3 Personal data shall not be treated as used or disclosed in contravention of this principle unless—
    (*a*) used otherwise than for a purpose of a description registered under this Act in relation to the data; or
    (*b*) disclosed otherwise than to a person of a description so registered.

*The fifth principle*
4 Any question whether or not personal data are accurate shall be determined as for the purposes of section 22 of this Act but, in the case of such data as are mentioned in subsection (2) of that section, this principle shall not be regarded as having been contravened by reason of any inaccuracy in the information there mentioned if the requirements specified in that subsection have been complied with.

*The seventh principle*
5—(1) Paragraph (*a*) of this principle shall not be construed as conferring any rights inconsistent with section 21 of this Act.
    (2) In determining whether access to personal data is sought at reasonable intervals regard shall be had to the nature of the data, the purpose for which the data are held and the frequency with which the data are altered.
    (3) The correction or erasure of personal data is appropriate only where necessary for ensuring compliance with the other data protection principles.

*The eighth principle*
6 Regard shall be had—
    (*a*) to the nature of the personal data and the harm that would result from such access, alteration, disclosure, loss or destruction as are mentioned in this principle; and
    (*b*) to the place where the personal data are stored, to security measures programmed into the relevant equipment and to measures taken for ensuring the reliability of staff having access to the data.

*Use for historical, statistical or research purposes*
7 Where personal data are held for historical, statistical or research purposes and not used in such a way that damage or distress is, or is likely to be, caused to any data subject—
    (*a*) the information contained in the data shall not be regarded for the purposes of the first principle as obtained unfairly by reason only that its use for any such purpose was not disclosed when it was obtained; and
    (*b*) the data may, notwithstanding the sixth principle, be kept indefinitely.

The Data Protection Registrar is of the opinion that if members of the public ask a list owner to suppress their personal information and this is not done, the fair processing aspects of the first principle have been breached and the Registrar also considers the requirement in the first principle to obtain information fairly may have been breached if the data user collects information without revealing its purpose, for example, not revealing that the purpose is for direct mail advertising or circulation of prize competitions.

## Fair Trading Act 1973

This Act created the office of the Director General of Fair Trading. Section 34 provides:

*Action by Director with respect to course of conduct detrimental to interests of consumers*

34 —(1)  Where it appears to the Director that the person carrying on a business has in the course of that business persisted in a course of conduct which—

   (a)  is detrimental to the interests of consumers in the United Kingdom, whether those interests are economic interests or interests in respect of health, safety or other matters, and

   (b)  in accordance with the following provisions of this section is to be regarded as unfair to consumers,

the Director shall use his best endeavours, by communication with that person or otherwise, to obtain from him a satisfactory written assurance that he will refrain from continuing that course of conduct and from carrying on any similar course of conduct in the course of that business.

(2)  For the purposes of subsection (1) (b) of this section a course of conduct shall be regarded as unfair to consumers if it consists of contraventions of one or more enactments which impose duties, prohibitions or restrictions enforceable by criminal proceedings, whether any such duty, prohibition or restriction is imposed in relation to consumers as such or not and whether the person carrying on the business has or has not been convicted of any offence in respect of any such contravention.

(3)  A course of conduct on the part of the person carrying on a business shall also be regarded for those purposes as unfair to consumers if it consists of things done, or omitted to be done, in the course of that business in breach of contract or in breach of a duty (other than a contractual duty) owed to any person by virtue of any enactment or rule of law and enforceable by civil proceedings, whether (in any such case) civil proceedings in respect of the breach of contract or breach of duty have been brought or not.

(4)  For the purpose of determining whether it appears to him that a person has persisted in such a course of conduct as is mentioned in subsection (1) of this section, the Director shall have regard to either or both of the following, that is to say—

   (a)  complaints received by him, whether from consumers or from other persons;

   (b)  any other information collected by or furnished to him, whether by virtue of this Act or otherwise.

Section 38 also allows action to be brought against a director, manager, secretary or controller of a company who is an accessory to any offence committed by a company.

The Act is of limited effect, however, because the Director General cannot rely upon the acts of a trader which are lawful but nevertheless unfair.

### Consumer Credit Act 1974

The provisions of this Act are examined in more detail in Chapter 5. Those of greatest relevance to timesharing consumer protection are the possibility of a cooling-off period, the right under s 75 for buyers in certain circumstances to claim against the lending source for damages and compensation for misrepresentation or breach of contract by the seller, a right of rescission of the purchase contract if the credit is refused in a related 'linked agreement', and the powers of the Director General of Fair Trading to refuse or cancel a consumer credit licence to a trader who has a record of criminal offences involving fraud or dishonesty or contravention of consumer legislation or discrimination or engaged in business practices which are 'deceitful or oppressive or otherwise unfair or improper (whether unlawful or not)'.

Any attempt to contract out of the consumer protection measures in the Act is void under s 173 (1) and s 39 (2). It is an offence to carry on, whilst unlicensed, any business for which a Consumer Credit Act licence is required.

### Estate Agents Act 1979

The Act applies to agents (with specified exceptions) involved in the sale of an 'interest in land'. This is restrictively defined by s 2:

2—(1) Subject to subsection (3) below, any reference in this Act to disposing of an interest in land is a reference to—
  (a) transferring a legal estate in fee simple absolute in possession; or
  (b) transferring or creating, elsewhere than in Scotland, a lease which, by reason of the level of the rent the length of the term or both, has a capital value which may be lawfully realised on the open market; or
  (c) transferring or creating in Scotland any estate or interest in land which is capable of being owned or held as a separate interest and to which a title may be recorded in the Register of Sasines;
    and any reference to acquiring an interest in land shall be construed accordingly.
  (2) In subsection (1) (b) above the expression 'lease' includes the rights and obligations arising under an agreement to grant a lease.
  (3) Notwithstanding anything in subsections (1) and (2) above, references in this Act to disposing of an interest in land do not extend to disposing of—
    (a) the interest of a creditor whose debt is secured by way of a mortgage or charge of any kind over land or an agreement for any such mortgage or charge; or
    (b) in Scotland, the interest of a creditor in a heritable security as defined in section 9 (8) of the Conveyancing and Feudal Reform (Scotland) Act 1970.

The Act does not therefore apply in the case of sale of overseas timeshare interests, which will not come within the statutory definition of an interest in land. Most timeshare schemes are so structured that the purchaser does not acquire an interest in land, but where the discontinuous lease structure is used this may well come within the definition.

Where the Act applies, the Director General has power to make a prohibition or warning order against an unfit agent. Section 13 (1) provides that clients' money received by any person in the course of estate agency work is held on statutory trusts and there are regulations as to the keeping of clients accounts, auditing and accounting for deposit interest, and generally as to the conduct of business of estate agents.

### Lotteries and Amusements Act 1976

With certain exceptions, s 1 of the Act makes lotteries illegal. There is no statutory definition of a lottery but the definition generally used is that it is a scheme for distributing prizes by chance where people taking part make a payment or give consideration in return for obtaining their chance of a prize. This could potentially catch people who have to attend a timeshare presentation to collect their prizes, consideration being afforded in travelling expenses and time, but there is no recorded case under English law of a prosecution on this basis. In the USA, where similar legislation exists and similar tests apply, federal law has been interpreted, broadly speaking, to require money to change hands for an offence to be committed (*FCC* v *American Broadcasting Co* (1954) 347 US 284) but various states have held that attendance at a sales presentation provided sufficient consideration. The point remains to be tested in the UK.

## Title insurance

Title insurance is not, as its name might suggest, continuing insurance of good title. It is an insured statement of the condition of title *at a particular (historical) point in time*. It is sometimes used as a marketing aid and may in fact be nothing more than that. If the insured statement is that, as at a certain date 'A' had good title to land, that is of limited value to a purchaser of a right to occupy, if 'A' can subsequently mortgage or sell the land, or if the land is available to the creditors of 'A'. It is also of no value to the purchaser to be supplied with an insurance certificate if, on inspection of the policy, the certificate does not relate to the land to be subjected to the right of occupation. Consequently, if title insurance is offered, it should be treated with considerable caution and does not obviate the need for thorough investigation. It would be of assistance in such cases to ask for copies of the documentation on the basis of which the policy is issued, a copy of the master policy and the last audited accounts of the company actually issuing the policy, whether or not that company is a subsidiary of another company.

# The timeshare trustee and the timeshare owners

### Special duty of care

In most timesharing plans involving a trustee, the trustee will normally be a corporation, either a bank or insurance company or specialist trustee acting as a custodian trustee. A custodian trustee is defined as a corporate trustee under the Trustee Act 1925, ie a custodian trustee pursuant to the Public Trustee Rules 1911. A custodian trustee must have an issued capital of £250,000, of which not less than £100,000 must be paid up in cash. The paid trustee owes a special duty of care to the timeshare owners. As it was said in *Re Waterman's Will Trusts* [1952] 2 All ER 1054 per Harman J 'I do not forget that a paid trustee is expected to exercise a higher standard of diligence and knowledge than an unpaid trustee and that a bank which advertises itself largely in the public press as taking charge of administrations is under a special duty'.

The existence of this special duty of care was reaffirmed by Brightman J in *Bartlett* v *Barclays Bank Trust Co Ltd* [1980] Ch 515:

a higher duty of care is plainly due from someone like a Trust Corporation which carries on a specialist business of trust management. The Trust Corporation holds itself out in its advertising literature as being above ordinary mortals. With a specialist staff of trained trust officers and managers, with ready access to financial information and professional advice, dealing with and solving trust problems day after day, the trust corporation holds itself out, and rightly, as capable of providing an expertise which it would be unrealistic and unjust to demand from the ordinary prudent man or woman who accepts, probably unpaid and sometimes reluctantly from a sense of family duty, the burdens of trusteeship. Just as, under the law of contract, a professional person possessed of a particular skill is liable for breach of contract if he neglects to use the skill and experience which he professes, so I think that a professional corporate trustee is liable for breach of trust if loss is caused to the trust fund because it neglects to exercise the special care and skill which it professes to have.

It is not necessarily a defence that the trustee has obtained legal advice before embarking on a particular course of action. Lawrence L J in *Re Windsor Steam Coal Co (1901) Ltd* [1929] 1 Ch 151 stated: 'even if the appellant had himself taken the best possible advice and had made a payment acting on such advice, I am of the opinion that that would not be sufficient to excuse him having regard to the fact that he was a trustee, paid for his skill and services in performing his duties'.

It is common for the trust deed to contain exclusion clauses designed to protect the trustee from actions at the suit of the club members or third parties. However, the effectiveness of such exclusion clauses has been modified by statute. The trustee may not be able to exclude entirely the common duty of care under the Occupiers' Liability Act 1957. Further, purported exclusions in relation to the validity of the title of the trustee to the trust property (which goes to the essence of the trusteeship), or attempted blanket coverage against liability for anything done in good faith, will be of doubtful value in the light of the provisions of the Unfair Contract Terms Act 1977 and of the special duty of care which exists.

In relation to actions concerning club property the trustees will be the proper plaintiff or defendant and it will not be necessary to join the members (RSC Ord 15, r 14(1)). It will be the duty of the trustees or their counsel to put before the court any considerations which may affect the interest of any of the timeshare owners (*Meller* v *Daintree* (1886) 33 Ch 200). However, although a judgment against trustees is *prima facie* binding on the timeshare owners, the timeshare owners will not be bound in respect of a transaction which they have good ground for impeaching as against the trustees (*Re De Leeuw* [1922] 2 Ch 540) and leave of the court will be required before enforcing the judgment against any person who was not a party to the action (RSC Ord 15, r 12(3)).

Whilst the transfer of property by a developer to trusteees in connection with the establishment of a timeshare scheme will normally protect beneficiaries against claims by creditors of the developer, nevertheless the provisions of the Insolvency Act 1986 need to be considered. Sections 238–241 in the case of companies, and ss 339–342 in the case of individuals allow the courts a discretionary power to set aside transactions at an undervalue or transactions which have been designed to give fraudulent preference. In the case of companies s 238 (5) provides however:

> (5) The Court shall not make an order under this Section in respect of a transaction if it is satisfied—
>    (a) that the company which entered into the transaction did so in good faith and for the purpose of carrying on its business, and
>    (b) that at the time it did so there were reasonable grounds for believing that the transaction would benefit the company.

The Act contains provisions designed to have a similar effect in relation to individuals. The Act provides that no transactions occurring outside five years from the date of the bankruptcy petition (s 341(*a*)) and in the case of a company occurring outside two years from the date of the petition for an administration order or commencement of winding up (s 240(*a*)(i)) may be set aside.

### Trustees' right to indemnity

Trustees of a members' timeshare club are not, unless the rules of the club provide otherwise, entitled to an indemnity from the club members. In the absence of an express provision, an individual member is not under any legal or equitable obligation to indemnify the trustees. Thus, where a trustee pays rent under a lease of club property a trustee cannot look to the club members for reimbursement (see *Wise* v *Perpetual Trustee Co* [1903] AC 139). This is a departure from the normal rule that trustees are entitled to claim an indemnity from their beneficiaries. Timeshare club trustees do however have the normal lien on the club property which they hold in so far as this covers their liability incurred as club trustees.

However, almost invariably the provisions of the trust deed and/or the club constitution contain standard indemnity clauses for the trustee. The trustee is not normally responsible for failure of management and has no obligation to make any disbursements from its own funds, but nevertheless if management is not carried out effectively the trustee is inevitably drawn into the problems which arise. Apart from the administrative burden, there is always the possibility of claims for taxes or services or (in Spain) employment protection compensation being attached to the trust property. In those circumstances the trustee may be inclined to provide temporary *ex gratia* assistance to the timeshare owners. To cover such cases it is obviously extremely important that the indemnity provisions in the trust deed and/or club constitution are widely drawn and moreover, that the trustee has regard, in accepting the trust, to contingency arrangements in the event of management failure.

### Role of trustee or escrow agent

The trustee, escrow agent or stakeholder plays a vital role in any of the following situations which arise in timeshare schemes:

1 Where a contract for the acquisition of the timeshare is conditional upon a minimum number of timeshare units being sold for that particular unit.
2 If the timeshare unit itself is not yet completed or furnished.
3 If certain of the facilities of the development which are advertised to belong to the development have not yet been completed.
4 If legal formalities have to be completed before the title to the timeshare can be effectively vested in the purchaser.

In the case of smaller timeshare schemes the escrow agent can conveniently be the developer's solicitor but in a scheme of any size, the number of transactions involved will necessitate employment of an agent with the necessary accounting facilities. In case of schemes which employ a custodian trustee, the trustee may be prepared to act as escrow agent. The rights and obligations of the escrow agent should be clearly set out so that there is no doubt in the minds of either the purchaser or the developer as to the circumstances in which the monies will be released. In cases of dispute, the escrow agent may be able to be relieved of his responsibility by paying the money into court pursuant to RSC Ord 85 (see The Supreme Court Practice 1991) or alternatively the escrow letter or contract could specify some alternative arbitration procedure.

Another area of concern for the escrow agent will be, in the case of non-UK schemes, the relevant exchange control regulations of the country concerned. The agent should ensure—especially where the agent has assets in the country concerned—that it is acting in accordance with the exchange control regulations of that country. If there is any doubt, then a clearance letter should be obtained from the central bank or other competent authority. The agent should also be aware of any changes in the legislation of the country in which the timeshare development is situated which may affect not only the practical operation of the scheme but also the obligations of the escrow agent himself.

Therefore, the duties and responsibilities of trustees in relation to timesharing schemes are onerous. Splitting the roles of escrow agent and trustee between different parties is undesirable, since it often leads to confusion as to who is, and who is not, a beneficiary of the trust. In order to tackle the job properly, the trustee will need to employ specialist and experienced staff to establish and police correct procedures. Failure to do this, particularly in the case of trusts relating to overseas projects, can lead to the trust assets becoming subject to taxation, to the detriment of existing beneficiaries. In addition to the assets of the trust, the trustees' reputation is bound up with the success of the timesharing project and many major banks are now unwilling to take on the burden of trusteeship of a timesharing project for this reason. The rules relating to the conduct and qualification of trustees vary greatly between one jurisdiction and another and in isolated cases, owing to the failure of a developer to identify a party prepared to take on the trusteeship, it has been possible for the developer himself to form a 'trust' company, usually without any substantial assets other than an impressive-sounding name. It goes without saying that the security afforded to a timeshare purchaser in a trustee scheme rests heavily on the independence, capitalisation and level of expertise of the trustee.

**Independent specialist trustees**

The gap left by the reluctance of some major banks to become involved has led to the formation of specialist trust companies. The largest of these in Europe is:

Timeshare Trustees (International) Ltd
Bourne Concourse,
Peel Street,
Ramsey
Isle of Man
Tel : 0624 814555
Fax : 0624 814823

The development of independent specialist trustees is an important stage in the growth of the timesharing industry. Their expertise in the structuring of a project and their knowledge of the likely pitfalls to be encountered in its administration often mean that procedures and documentation become more standardised and reliable. Increased availability of finance for purchasers and for developers is facilitated by this process.

The independent trustee is likely to be able to provide specialist expertise in various jurisdictions, and a sophisticated 'back office' facility with specially programmed computers, a facility which would take the average developer or marketeer several hundred thousand pounds to develop, and an inordinate expenditure of time not justified on a case-by-case basis.

A specialist trustee should be able to:

1 process sales contracts in different jurisdictions and in different countries and different languages;
2 maintain a current inventory database;
3 deal with cancellations, upgrades, refunds, etc;
4 provide statistical information and compare it with the particular project, eg cancellation rates for individual sales people measured against their peers and industry averages;
5 provide an advance warning to the resort on a weekly basis as to who will be visiting and what property will be vacant;
6 collect management charges;
7 assist developers to find marketeers and *vice versa*;
8 assist owners associations whose resort runs into problems;
9 process consumer finance applications in different currencies in different jurisdictions; and
10 assist developers in arranging project finance.

## Advice for the timeshare purchaser

The ETB publishes a Code of Caution and Guidance in relation to holiday timesharing. A copy may be obtained from them by application to:

Department D
The English Tourist Board
4 Grosvenor Gardens
London SW1W ODU

The Code contains 15 articles, as follows:

1 If gifts are used to promote the project, be cautious.
2 Watch the seller's investment claims.
3 Carefully consider extra costs, sometimes termed closing costs, progress commissions or financing arrangements.
4 Be particularly alert to the fees and arrangements for management and maintenance and how they could increase over the life of the timesharing. In particular, check whether there are funds for major refurbishments and repairs.
5 How frequently will the accommodation be refurbished and how many other weeks will be unlet for annual maintenance?
6 Check that annual maintenance charges include insurance cover for the cost of comparable accommodation if, for whatever reason, the unit is unavailable for your use.

7  Do not surrender to pressure.
8  Remember that the exchange arrangements, with other timesharers in other places, cannot be guaranteed.
9  Enquire into the track record of the seller, the developer and the management company.
10 Be particularly careful if building, equipping, or furnishing of the timeshare properties and 'promised' ancillary facilities are not complete.
11 Be very careful to find out precisely what your rights are if the builder or the management company has money troubles or in some way defaults.
   12  Make sure that you have a written contract signed by all the parties.
13 Make sure that the seller is the owner, and if the seller is not the owner, be absolutely satisfied as to who is the owner of the freehold. Make absolutely certain that there is not a mortgage on the property.
14 Take special care if you are buying from an existing timeshare owner.
15 Have it spelled out, beyond misinterpretation, the actual period during which you, the purchaser, will be entitled to occupy the premises each year.

Each of the articles is followed by explanatory advice in amplification. The legal adviser will be particularly concerned with the areas mentioned in the last five articles. The first step will of course be to obtain and examine all the timeshare documentation and associated sales literature. It is surprising how often the prospective purchaser is not given copies of all the relevant documentation, even upon request The documents and associated literature should then be examined with the following checklist in mind.

*1  Is the developer a member of a trade association?*
If so a copy of the sales rules of the association should be obtained in order to ascertain what protection and assistance is afforded to purchasers from members. It is also wise to check that the developer is a member in good standing.

*2  Is the purchaser legally bound to purchase?*
It will be necessary to examine any contract which has been signed and to check whether a deposit has been paid and if so, to whom. Find out whether there is a rescission option. A number of developers do include an option for the purchaser to withdraw from the transaction. In some countries, notably USA and Bermuda, there may be a legislative right to rescind. In the UK, if the provisions of the Consumer Credit Act 1974 apply, there may be a right to rescind pursuant to ss 57–73 (see Chapter 5). It is also necessary to see if there are any penalties on rescission, and to ascertain how far these may be enforceable. Consideration will have to be given as to what is the proper law of the contract (see Chapter 7).

*3  Is the vendor obliged to sell?*
On occasion the contract will provide that the vendor has an option to rescind if he is unable to find sufficient purchasers. Obviously any financial arrangements for the purchase should be contingent upon the vendor

irrevocably agreeing to complete the sale, and a reasonable time limit imposed on or before which the contract is to be rescinded or to become unconditional.

### 4 Has the timeshare unit been constructed?

In circumstances where the villa or apartment has not been constructed, or furnished, or where agreed facilities such as swimming pools, tennis courts, etc which have been promised are not yet in existence, it should be a term of the contract that the purchase price, or an agreed proportion of the price dependent on the circumstances, should be held safely in escrow. The terms of the escrow and the conditions for the release of the monies should be carefully formulated for the avoidance of doubt. Where the purchase price is expressed otherwise than in sterling, the question as to who is to bear the exchange risk should be settled.

### 5 What is the nature of the timeshare being sold and of the purchase formalities?

The organisation of the timeshare scheme needs investigation to see whether it affords protection to the purchaser. If the right is a personal right, are the timeshare units held in trust and is there any responsible trustee? If not, what is the position if the developer defaults? Will the purchaser's position be prejudiced in such circumstances? Does the developer own the property of which the timeshare unit forms part and has satisfactory evidence of title been produced? Is it practicable to verify title and that planning and byelaw permissions have been obtained? Is the property free from encumbrances and are all main services in existence and connected?

### 6 Is title insurance being offered?

If title insurance is being offered, it is essential to examine the nature of the risks being covered. Title insurance is only an insured statement as to the condition of the title at a particular, historical, point in time. In a 'right to use' scheme, the developer's title may be in order but if the property is nevertheless liable to be seized by the developer's creditors, the title insurance may not be of any practical value whatsoever. Examine the master policy to check that the particular unit is covered, and for copies of the documentation on the basis of which the policy was issued, and obtain a copy of the last accounts of the company actually issuing the policy as opposed to any related company.

### 7 What steps have been taken to vest title to the timeshare in the purchaser?

It is necessary to ascertain whether there is a registration procedure and who is to be responsible for carrying out these procedures so far as they are necessary to vest title effectively in the purchaser. It is also necessary to see whether any special formalities need to be complied with before the purchase can be completed, eg military permission in Spain, etc. The registration procedures need to be examined to see that they provide a sufficient safeguard for the purchaser. It is also necessary to ascertain the fees, costs and taxes associated with the transfer of title to the buyer and the registration of the title into the buyer's name. These should be detailed and the amount and breakdown explained to the purchaser. It should be made quite clear who is to be responsible for payment. In circumstances where this is someone other than the purchaser, the availability of the necessary funds and the assurances that they will be properly directed needs to be examined.

*8  Does the contract provide that no payment is to be released to the vendor*
    *until title has been transferred and registered in the name of the purchaser?*

If not, what assurance is given that title will be achieved by the purchaser and that third parties will not intervene between transfer and registration? In some countries the interval between transfer and registration can be as much as or more than a year. Therefore, unless there is some notice procedure, the execution of which can be verified, there is an obvious danger. To overcome this problem, some form of escrow arrangement may be proposed. If this is so, then the terms of the escrow, and the status of the escrow agent should be examined.

*9  Is there sufficient indemnity against charges which might affect the*
    *property?*

For example, plus valia tax in Spain, road charges, gas, electricity, water charges and sewerage, community charges, service charges, etc. In Spain, even employees' compensation plans may be attached to the property.

*10  What is included in the purchase price?*

The contract should specify as to whether or not the purchase price includes title to the furnishings, fittings and equipment. There should be a schedule of these annexed to the contract and the schedule should be checked to make sure that it is satisfactory and complete.

*11  Planning controls*

It will be necessary to advise the purchaser whether the development and the sales operation fully complies with all local laws.

*12  Exchange control*

Check whether the method of payment complies with local exchange control regulations. In this connection will the purchaser be able to repatriate his funds on sale? Will any evidence be required in such event, eg evidence of prior payment in 'foreign' currency? If so, this evidence should be kept with the documents evidencing title. In particular, an important point to note, is whether the full timeshare price will be disclosed in all the documentation.

*13  Resale service*

Does the developer offer a resale service? How does this operate? What guarantees of resale, if any, are given? Has a resale track record been established and what evidence has been given to the purchaser in this connection?

### 14 Exchange facilities
Is the development affiliated to one or other of the two exchange organisations (Interval International or Resorts Condominiums International)? Who is responsible for payment of the membership fees and annual dues? When will the buyer receive his membership card?

### 15 Management and administration
What is the annual management charge? What has this been historically and what is the current year's estimate? Has a schedule been provided as to how often the fixtures, fittings and furnishings will be replaced? Is there a detailed breakdown of the service charges available and is it satisfactory? How is the proportion attributable to the timeshare calculated? Does the developer have an obligation to pay the service charge on unsold units? How long does this obligation continue? What happens when it stops? Is the developer of sufficient substance to meet this obligation and has a fund been set aside by way of guarantee? Is any independent guarantee as to this obligation being offered? Is there a similar fund to cover replacement of fixtures, fittings and furnishings and for structural repairs etc? Is it adequate? Who holds this sinking fund? Is it held in trust or does the developer have access to it?

Who controls the management? Is there an owners' association? Does it have power to dismiss incompetent managers? Who controls the owners' association—is it the owners or the developer? Are there any 'extras' to pay, eg for use of the facilities forming part of the development? What is the cost of, and is the membership available to, neighbouring facilities, eg golf courses etc?

### 16 Finance
Does the purchaser have sufficient funds to make the purchase? Will he have to arrange finance and if so what are the terms and how certain is the availability of such finance? If finance is offered by the developer, on what terms is such finance offered and are these the best terms available? What rights will exist against the finance company if the developer defaults (see Chapter 5 and the consumer's statutory rights under the Consumer Credit Act 1974)? What is the proper law of the finance contract (see Chapter 7)?

### 17 Insurance
Does the developer offer any insurance, eg against damage or destruction of the unit? How is the purchaser insured against non-availability of use?

### 18 The choice of development
Does the developer have a good track record? Has he constructed other developments? Has the purchaser visited other developments by the same developer and talked to timeshare purchasers there? Are they satisfied with the

way things have gone? If not, what are their major grounds for dissatisfaction and are the same grounds likely to apply to the proposed timeshare purchase? Is the developer financially sound? What did their last accounts look like?

Is the resort itself popular? Are there other timeshare developments nearby? Why is the proposed purchase better than others which may be available? How easy is it to get to the development? Is it served by rail? Is there an airport nearby? Are there charter flights or cheap tickets available for the season in which the timeshare is being purchased? Are there other nearby amenities—shopping, restaurants, etc or will the buyer be forced to rely solely on those provided in the development?

What is the standard of the accommodation offered? Are the furnishings and equipment likely to last? Is the resort strictly seasonal or will it be popular all year round? How does the aggregate purchase price of the timeshare units compare with the purchase price of similar whole ownership units. How does the price compare with the price of other timeshares? Are any existing timeshares which individuals have purchased being resold? If so, at what price and what is the reason for resale?

*19  Change in amenities*
Are the timeshares likely to be affected by development in the area, ie new roads, railways, or, for example, tower blocks between the development and the sea, etc?

*20  Reasons for purchase*
Is the purchaser buying timeshare for the right reasons? Does he really understand the timeshare concept or is he hoping for some 'investment' opportunity or to try and use the timeshare primarily for trading within the exchange system?

*21  Miscellaneous*
Does the buyer need to make a separate will as, for instance, in Spain, to prevent transfer problems on death? Is the time period clearly identified? Is it subject to change and does it fit in with the purchaser's requirements, eg children's school holidays etc?

## Conclusion

No doubt other questions will arise in the mind of a prospective purchaser's legal adviser. In case of doubt or difficulty the developer should be asked to arrange to provide a satisfactory assurance from a responsible person, eg his solicitor.

The advice which it is necessary to give a client must obviously depend upon the circumstances but if it is possible to lay down 'golden rules' these might be as follows:

1 Unless the developer is a member of a trade association which is able to provide the required information, a full evaluation of the timeshare scheme will invariably be necessary. A prospectus, as recommended by the OFT, would be invaluable and should be demanded.
2 The purchaser should be quite clear about the reasons for his purchase of a timeshare and the reasons for the purchase of a particular timeshare in contrast to others on offer.
3 The purchaser should not part with his money until title to a completed timeshare and all ancillary rights is guaranteed. He should be satisfied from his own investigations as to the developer's track record, by talking to other purchasers and so forth, that there is and will continue to be adequate and continuing maintenance of the property.

# Chapter Four

# The holiday exchange service

The success of the resort timesharing industry is due in large part to the existence of holiday exchange companies. The relationship between the holiday timeshare product and the exchange service is one of mutual reliance: one could not exist without the other. Exchange adds an extra dimension to timeshare: it answers the question often posed by potential buyers: 'What if I don't want to come back to the same resort year after year?' Research shows that timeshare is virtually impossible to sell without the exchange facility. Exchange enables timeshare owners to visit different parts of the world, holiday at different times of the year, visit their own resorts at different seasons—and enjoy a range of additional useful services and benefits provided by the exchange companies.

Although timesharing made its debut in the 1960s in Europe, the exchange concept was virtually non-existent until the early 1970s, when timesharing was introduced in the USA. This is where the concept of an independent holiday exchange service was created. Resort timesharing was seen as a solution to the problems of some US condominium developers, who were facing an inventory surplus and an economic crunch that made ownership of a holiday home prohibitive for most consumers. But developers and purchasers were first reluctant to become involved in the new industry because, without an exchange service, it involved having a holiday at the same place and at the same time each year. Exchange proved to be the missing link. The variety and flexibility it offered gave resort timesharing the additional appeal it needed to capture widespread acceptance from both resort developers and the general public. The flexibility afforded by exchange membership grows each year as new resorts are developed and as they become affiliated with the exchange companies. Most developers, large and small, will agree that affiliation with an independent exchange company is essential. From a marketing standpoint, consumer research has consistently revealed that one of the primary motivations for a timeshare purchase is the ability to exchange.

There are two major exchange networks in existence; Interval International (II) and Resort Condominiums International Inc (RCI). Because the two companies operate differently, they will be explained in separate sections of this chapter.

# Interval International (II)

Interval International (II) is a subsidiary of Leaguestar plc, a UK-based company whose business philosophy is to provide a comprehensive range of services to the timeshare industry, without engaging itself directly in the development or marketing of timeshare. Interval International is known as 'the Quality Exchange Network' and relies for product differentiation from its competitors on its demanding quality standards for acceptance of a resort, and in allowing the resort to continue as part of the network. Interval International started operations in the USA in 1976 as part of the Worldex Corporation and commenced operations in Europe in 1978.

Interval International has over 900 member resorts (with more than 250 of these located in Europe) and around 600,000 individual family members worldwide. Operations for the Americas and Pacific are controlled by Interval International Inc in Miami, Florida, whereas European operations are centred on Interval's London headquarters. The group also have offices and representation in California, Colorado, Hawaii, Mexico, Argentina, Brazil, New Zealand, Queensland Australia, Japan, Thailand, Korea and (in Europe) France, Germany, Italy, Spain (mainland and Canaries), Portugal, Greece and Scandinavia.

Interval International offers its members the unique flexibility of two exchange system methodologies, offered under the title of 'Dual Exchange'. The two exchange methods available to users of Dual Exchange are 'Deposit First' and 'Request First'.

## Deposit First

Members are encouraged to use 'Deposit First' if they want 'maximum flexibility' in when to make an exchange request, when to travel on an exchange holiday or if they simply want to deposit the week(s) owned and request later. Members using Deposit First may deposit their holiday period at any time from one year to 60 days (14 days with Late Deposit) before the start of the period. They may enter an exchange request at the time of deposit or subsequently, at their convenience. Depending on when the deposit was made, a request can be entered any time from a year before to a year after the home resort dates. Requested travel dates can also be from a year before to a year after the home resort dates.

Members using Deposit First relinquish their home holiday periods to the Interval system immediately upon deposit. The home period will not be returned, even if a subsequent exchange request cannot be fulfilled. (In those circumstances, a member would be entitled to continue making exchange requests, within the 'window' allowed, until a suitable exchange was obtained.) Members using Deposit First also are required to adhere to Interval's colour codes when making requests, unless requesting on a Flexchange basis (see page 103).

Finally, members who have deposited their home holiday period receive priority over members using the Request First method, if two members giving up otherwise comparable space are competing for the same holiday availability. The exchange application requires members to provide Interval with a selection of at least three different resorts and two different holiday areas. A member may be confirmed automatically into any of the chosen resorts or any resort in the area choices, including the additional choices.

The rules are slightly different for owners at an Interval International Five Star resort. They have to provide only a minimum requirement of three different resorts and one holiday area, but as many additional areas may be given as desired, and these may contain the resort choices. Interval will not confirm a Five Star owning member to a resort from one of his area choice(s) without his prior agreement. Interval still may confirm him automatically to any of his resort choices. The rules governing date choices and colour code compatibility are the same for all members.

### Request First

Members are advised to use 'Request First' if they want a guaranteed holiday at either an exchange resort or at their home resort and if they want to be able to request any resort or date regardless of colour code. Like Deposit First, this method offers certain advantages to the exchanging member, and imposes certain restrictions on him. Members using Request First may enter an exchange request from a year before their home resort dates. They may also request to travel from a year before their home dates, up to the dates themselves. Their home holiday periods are not given up to the exchange system until their chosen exchange has been confirmed. If no suitable exchange can be found, the member will still be able to holiday at his home resort. Use of Interval's colour code is optional to members using Request First. It is recommended that members follow the codes, in order to maximise their chances of successful confirmation. However, this is entirely at the member's discretion. If two members giving up otherwise comparable space are competing for the same holiday availability, priority will be given to a member using the Deposit First method, as a member using Request First will still be able to go to his home resort if disappointed in his exchange request.

As with Deposit First, members must provide a selection of at least three different resorts and two different holiday areas, and the holiday areas must not contain any of the resort choices. They can provide as many more holiday areas as they like, and these may contain the resort choices. They may be confirmed automatically into any of the chosen resorts or any resort in the area choice, including the additional choices. Again, owners at an Interval International Five Star resort have to provide only a minimum requirement of three different resorts and one holiday area. The chosen holiday area must not contain any of the resort choices, but members can give as many additional areas as they wish and these may contain the resort choices. Interval will not confirm a Five Star owning member to a resort from one of his areas without his prior agreement. Interval still may confirm him automatically to any of his resort choices. Date choices may be all the same or may differ, but must all fall before or on the holiday period offered in exchange. This requirement is made so that, in the event of no suitable exchange becoming available, members will still be able to holiday at their own resort.

**Interval's Colour Codes and Sleeping Capacities**

Before entering any resort/area and date combinations, members need to check with Interval's Colour Codes that the areas requested, or the areas in which resort choices are located, are in equal or lesser demand than the holiday period they have deposited, for their selected dates. For each resort the year is divided into peak season, which is colour-coded red; shoulder season, which is colour-coded yellow and off-peak season, which is colour-coded green. Members owning red time can exchange into red, yellow or green time, but those owning yellow time are normally restricted to yellow and green time, unless they use the 'request first' method. Similarly, owners of green time may not normally exchange their time for red or yellow.

The maximum number of people who may travel is determined by the sleeping capacity of the home unit, according to Interval's standard to two people per private sleeping area. The size of the unit received in exchange will be no less than that required to accommodate the actual number of people in the party, following the same standard. Owners at Five Star resorts may indicate that they will not accept a unit of a smaller capacity, according to Interval's standard, than their home unit.

In general, flexibility and accuracy are the keys to exchange success. By being flexible members maximise their exchange options; the greater the choice members give to the exchange department, the better the chance they have of receiving the confirmation they desire.

Those are the *differences* between the Deposit First and Request First methods, within the Dual Exchange system. What both methods have *in common* is access to over 900 quality-tested resorts in more than 45 countries around the world. The system is designed to offer the highest opportunity for exchange success. The quality of the exchange service is the key to member satisfaction and consequently the individual membership renewal and retention rate on which the exchange organisations primarily rely for their income.

**'Flexchange'**

Interval also runs a programme which enables its members to access the exchange system at short notice, for those who are unable to plan too far ahead or simply prefer to make their holiday arrangements at short notice. Flexchange also helps members who were planning to travel to their home resort but find shortly beforehand that they must postpone their travel plans.

Flexchange can be arranged between 59 and seven days before the date on which a member wishes to travel, and can be used whether a member is depositing first or requesting first. When a member has made a deposit between 59 and the minimum permitted 14 days before his home holiday dates, known as a Late Deposit, then he is required to use Flexchange when utilising that deposit. A member wishing to arrange a Flexchange should telephone the Interval International exchange department having first provided himself with his Annual Holiday Planner, his credit, charge or debit card and, if he is an owner at a 'floating time' resort who has not previously deposited his home week, a written reservation from his home resort.

Having ascertained that the member's travel dates fall within the Flexchange 'window', the exchange representative servicing the call will then check, either that the member has already deposited time, or that the home dates the member is offering in exchange fall at least 14 days after the travel dates he is requesting. These conditions fulfilled, the representative will check all availabilities for the areas and dates that interest the member. If an acceptable availability is found an instant confirmation is issued, and the exchange fee debited to whichever card facility the member is offering.

Colour Code restrictions on members using Deposit First do not apply where Flexchange is concerned, whether they have used late or regular deposit. However, it is unlikely that the most highly demanded locations or periods will be available on Flexchange, as they will probably have been previously used by the Interval system.

**Alternate Week Exchange**

There is another special exchange service. This is Alternate Week Exchange. This service is for members wishing to travel only to their home resort, but not in the week that they own. Again the service is available to members whether they are Depositing or Requesting First.

**Exchange communication**

Interval International always acknowledge in writing any communication received from members. If a deposit is received, a deposit number will be issued; if an exchange request, a letter of acknowledgment will be sent, giving all the details of the exchange as they are entered in the system. While an exchange request is being processed, Interval write to the member every 30 days to advise of progress. This continues until they can issue a confirmation and its accompanying Change of Place Kit, full of information about the exchange resort and its surrounding area. Detailed directions and check-in times are included. If Interval are unable to fulfil a request, a denial notice will be issued 45 days before the latest travel date requested.

**Resort affiliation procedures**

In order to become affiliated to Interval so that purchasers can enjoy the benefit of its exchange programme, the developer completes a preliminary application form which includes a fairly detailed description of the development. This is sent to Interval with, in Europe, a deposit on account of the affiliation fee. If the resort appears to meet the minimum standards required by Interval, they will arrange for inspection; otherwise the deposit will be refunded. Upon inspection, Interval state that they use a 'Quality Rating Survey' to evaluate resorts, concentrating on the key factors of location, accessibility, exterior and interior characteristics, marketability, management and exchange desirability. Interval are looking for a high quality of development. The buildings and the furnishings of the development must not be of the lower grade package holiday type. Interval will also want to take a detailed look at the developer's planning of the project and will want to be reasonably satisfied that the targets set by the developer are going to be reached. They will need to ensure that the project has been sufficiently well researched in terms of establishing that there is a market for the product on offer, and that the marketing and sales organisation of the developer are going to be adequate. They will need to know whether the management is going to be competent enough to deal with a timeshare scheme. It will also be necessary to form a view about the location of the development; it is not practicable to sell a development on a timeshare basis if it is isolated from a known tourist area, if there are insufficient local attractions, or if the development does not have amenities within itself, eg golf courses, swimming pools, sauna, tennis courts, etc to compensate for the fact that it is not in a known tourist or recreation area.

As mentioned earlier, Interval has established a 'Quality Rating Survey', originally designed in conjunction with the Cornell University School of Hotel Administration in the USA, which analyses standards of a resort and its location under a series of headings with over 400 considerations taken into account. Some of these factors are discussed in the following paragraphs.

*Resort desirability*
Interval assess the attractiveness of the greater resort area, (usually the area of approximately 50 miles radius of the actual timeshare location). This includes the ease of access, main attractions, sightseeing opportunities, restaurants, shopping and nightlife. A key factor considered is the overall reputation of the area and its attractiveness to holidaymakers as a destination.

*Site desirability*
There is an in-depth review of the advantages and disadvantages of the timeshare development's precise location, and the impact they may have on the consumer's holiday is fully considered. The proximity of the site to main attractions is assessed, as well as convenience, quality of surroundings,

safety and security. The resort setting and views which are afforded are also examined.

### Factors desirability
The quality and attractiveness of the timeshare resort are evaluated. There is a review of the building, the grounds and public space. The extent of indoor and outdoor amenities and facilities weigh heavily in the criteria.

### Unit desirability
The overall quality of the timeshare accommodation, including layout, design and interior furnishings, are assessed; size, cleanliness and privacy are important factors. Interval also looks at the planning and the durability of the decor and furnishings and their ability to maintain their appeal. This element of the evaluation accounts for in excess of 30 per cent of the overall scoring.

### Guest services
The amount and quality of what in the hospitality business are called 'soft amenities' are taken into account. Sports and social activities and housekeeping arrangements are evaluated. Other services, such as travel information, rental cars and babysitting are scored in assessing the level of sophistication of the resort.

### Final rating
In order for the resort to be recommended as a potential member of Interval 500, it must score around 80 per cent or above. The results of the survey are run on a computer programme and the scores achieved for the various factors are weighted to take into account the varying holiday requirements of the type of timeshare holiday resort involved, ie lakes and mountains, ski, sun and beach, rural or urban. Following the evaluation, an Interval 500 membership committee comprising Interval's senior officers must give final approval of a resort with a majority vote for acceptance into Interval 500. Approximately the top 20 per cent of Interval affiliated resorts are awarded a five star quality status. These are resorts which have demonstrated an exceptionally high standard of accommodation, on-site facilities and management standards.

The advice which Interval, with their worldwide experience, can give is of the utmost value to the developer. If the scheme is unlikely to prove successful, then it will cause problems for Interval, who depend for their income on membership satisfaction. Consequently Interval will give the developer an informed and detached view about his chances of success, frequently having to advise a developer that his scheme, at least as originally envisaged, will not be successful in their view. On occasion they have advised sale on a whole-ownership basis, thus turning an unworkable timeshare development into a viable whole-ownership sales operation. If the resort passes muster, the developer is presented with the affiliation contract for completion and signature. The contract is set out in clear and unambiguous language and will be the basis of a long-term relationship between the developer and Interval.

**Interval contract**

The salient points of the Interval contract are:

1 That all purchasers at the affiliated resort are automatically enroled for membership of the exchange company for an agreed period, usually ranging from one to three years. The promoter also pays a one-off affiliation fee.
2 The promoter usually has to provide a certain amount of space at the development without charge, which provides a working reserve within the exchange system, thus making exchanges easier and confirmation rates high.
3 The provision by the promoter of a minimum level of new member enrolments per annum (normally in the region of 200 enrolments after two years).
4 Adherence to standards of service, appearance, cleanliness and management of timeshare units and associated amenities.
5 That the timeshare resort will attain at least a minimum number of timeshare units, to be able to provide an overall quality of holiday experience to fulfil the required quality standards.
6 Affiliates must honour all confirmed exchangees into their resorts. If a confirmed exchange cannot be honoured by a resort the affected member must be given alternative accommodation of a similar size and quality for the same time period—at the expense of the affiliate.
7 Affiliates must provide all exchange members and their guests with the same rights and privileges and at the same rates as are afforded to their resort owners.

The exchange companies are also likely to make enquiries as to:

1 How title to the property which is the subject of the resort affiliation agreement is held and the nature of the occupancy rights to be granted to purchasers at the project.
2 Whether the legal structure and marketing of the project is in compliance with all local laws both where the property is located and where the property will be marketed.
3 Whether the purchase price will be held or guaranteed by an independent third party of standing until the purchaser's rights are fully constituted and vested in the purchaser. These are often referred to as escrow arrangements.
4 Whether the legal structure protects purchasers' interests in the project for the duration of the timeshare programme, and a statement that such purchasers shall be entitled to the undisturbed use of the units, amenities and facilities in the event that the affiliate fails to perform, becomes

bankrupt or sells the property, or if mortgages or liens are recorded on the property.

5 Whether the person executing the resort affiliation agreement has the authority to bind the affiliate.

However, purchasers cannot rely upon these enquiries, which are merely designed for 'corporate comfort' and as part of the information required by the exchange organisation when making a commercial judgment as to whether or not to accept or continue with affiliation. The exchange companies are not responsible if the timeshare scheme collapses or if satisfactory standards of service are not provided at the resort.

Once the resort has become affiliated, so long as the developer complies with the affiliation agreement, the member timeshare purchaser has access to all the benefits of the Interval exchange programme. Membership involves an annual or multi-year membership fee—three or five years (averaging £30 per annum)—and if the exchange service is used an exchange fee for each confirmed week exchanged.

Interval publishes a quarterly magazine *European Traveller* (*Traveller Magazine* in the USA) as well as an annual directory of resorts. Through another Leaguestar plc subsidiary, Worldex Travel Centres, Interval operates the Interval Travel Club which enables member families to access low cost air fares, discounts on car hire, cruises etc.

The developer is also given sales presentation support in the form of an extensive programme of on-going assistance. The comprehensive annual directory of resorts is available in ten languages and used at point-of-sale as a demonstration of the range of resorts accessible. A top quality video is also used at point-of-sale to demonstrate how the exchange system works. Interval also tours its resorts regularly to give sales updates, and organises regional seminar-style presentations.

Enquiries in Europe should be addressed to:

*Until 30 August 1991:*
Interval International Ltd
25/31 Knightsbridge
London
W1X 7LY
Tel: 071–235 5567
Fax: 071–823 1501
Telex: 297984 EXCHANG

*From 31 August 1991:*
The Leaguestar Building
4 Citadel Place
Tinworth Street
London
SE11 5EG

## Resort Condominiums International Inc (RCI)

RCI is a privately owned company based in Indianapolis, USA which services more than 1,500 affiliated resorts, representing over 750,000 individual members. As with Interval, RCI maintains a global presence.

**Standard of affiliation**

Affiliation is open to resorts offering whole ownership, fractional ownership and/or timeshare ownership programmes. Prospective affiliates must prove that their developments conform to RCI's requirements from the physical, financial, consumer protection and managerial standpoints before they are accepted into the exchange programme. An RCI affiliation fee is remitted by the resort. The initial affiliation agreement is in effect for a period of five years. The agreement is automatically renewed until termination is requested either by the affiliate or by RCI. Either party must be given a minimum of 12 months' notice of termination of contract.

**Developer obligations**

To remain in the RCI exchange programme, affiliates must fulfil specific obligations. Failure to comply with the RCI requirements could lead to an indefinite suspension of exchange programme privileges for affiliates and their owners. Continued compliance problems will generally lead to disaffiliation.

1 Dual affiliation is discouraged. RCI maintains that affiliation with more than one exchange service causes operational problems and difficulties for resorts and confusion for holiday owners.
2 A minimum of 100 RCI members must be enrolled (and their enrolment fees remitted to RCI) by the affiliate on or before the first anniversary date of affiliation. Resorts that fail to meet this requirement are charged a month service fee until the minimum number of enrolments has been achieved.
3 Affiliates must provide a specific number of holiday units (free accommodations) to RCI as working resource for the exchange programme. Resorts are required to supply such reserve space until they are 90 per cent sold.
4 Resorts must be able to prove at any time that they have been and are being truthful in their product descriptions. This includes an accurate representation of the RCI exchange programme to owners and prospective purchasers.
5 RCI affiliation developments must consist of at least ten units. This requirement is waived for resorts that are of exceptional quality and that are located in destinations which are in high demand.
6 Affiliates must honour all confirmed exchanges into their resorts. If a confirmed exchange cannot be honoured by a resort the affected RCI member must be given alternative accommodation of similar size and quality—and for the same time period—at the expense of the affiliate. Affiliates must provide all RCI members and their guests with the same rights and privileges and at the same rates afforded to their resort owners.
7 All requests for exchanges at the affiliated resort—both internal exchanges and external exchanges—must be processed through RCI.
8 All disputes are subject to arbitration.

**Marketing and sales support**

In addition to the exchange programme, RCI affiliates can take advantage of a variety of marketing support tools designed to assist them in their sales efforts. These include a video production explaining resort timesharing and exchange services; a full travel agency service offering low cost fares and insurance; a variety of publications including a members' magazine published quarterly, and the *Annual Directory of Resorts* giving information on exchange opportunities. RCI also organises conferences and seminars.

**Enrolment of members**

Affiliated resorts are required to enrol their owners in the RCI exchange programme at the time of sale. This adds immediate value to the timeshare purchase and ensures that new purchasers will receive materials about RCI exchange opportunities in a timely fashion. The initial period of enrolment is for the year of purchase, plus from one to four years, depending on the terms of the resort's affiliation agreement. All memberships operate on a calendar year basis. Following the initial enrolment period, RCI members must renew their membership annually to continue participating in the exchange programme. Renewal rates are available for one, three or five years.

**The mechanics of the RCI exchange system**

RCI have only one exchange system which works very much like the Interval 'Deposit First' system, but without the 'Request First' system. As with the Interval Deposit First system, the year is divided for each resort into colour-coded time divisions. RCI use red colour coding for peak season, white for shoulder season and blue for off-peak season. Subject to the 'late exchange' provisions mentioned hereafter, owners of red time can exchange into red, white and blue time, owners of white time into white and blue time, and owners of blue time only into blue time.

Each week is also assigned a value, which RCI calls its 'trading power'. This value is based on five factors: season, size, holiday experience profile, demand and deposit time. The seasonal division is as explained above. The size factor has two elements: firstly the maximum number of people a unit can accommodate and secondly the number of people who have direct access to a bathroom without passing through another sleeping area, such as a sitting room with a convertible sofa bed. In the RCI Directory, for example, the accommodation capacity may be described as '6/4'. This means that the unit could sleep six as maximum, but only four would have direct access to a bathroom. The 'holiday experience factor' is assessed using replies to cards circulated to members. Demand is assessed by comparing the week with other weeks in the system. In the RCI system, deposit time is a very important factor. RCI believe that the earlier the member deposits his week, the greater the 'trading power'. A week deposited two years in advance will have a higher trading power, and thus a greater likelihood of certain requested exchanges than, for example, one made nearer the holiday date.

Weeks which have not been allocated 45 days prior to their start date fall into the 'late exchange' category. This means that their 'trading power' has reached a level which can be accessed by all members, who can then have access to resorts and dates with higher values. However, if a member is confirmed into a larger apartment he can only travel with the same size group as could occupy his home unit. RCI exchange confirmations are personal to the member. If the member wishes to allow another person or persons to use the exchange, a guest certificate must be obtained from the RCI. Guest certificates are not transferable, and will not be issued to anyone who owns time at a resort affiliated to RCI but who is not an RCI member. Two other restrictions imposed by RCI are noteworthy. RCI members may not normally exchange into the same resort more than once every four years, and certain resorts do not allow exchanges from other resorts located in the same geographical area.

### Exchange cancellations

The 1991 RCI terms of membership provide that once a member deposits his timeshare 'he relinquishes all rights to use the timeshare holiday deposited with RCI and RCI shall be entitled in its absolute discretion to use the relevant premises for inspection visits or other corporate purposes, or for the purpose of renting out the accommodation to third parties and all income received by RCI for renting out the accommodation shall be the property of RCI'. However, if given written notice, and if the holiday period has not been confirmed to another member or used by RCI in accordance with the above mentioned conditions, and if the member has not received a confirmed exchange, then RCI would allow the withdrawal of the deposit, but no exchange fee would be refunded. A confirmed exchange may be cancelled on not less than two days prior written notice, and then the member can request an alternative exchange, but would have to pay an additional exchange fee in those circumstances.

Enquiries in Europe may be addressed to RCI at:

RCI (Europe) Ltd
Clarendon House
8–12 Station Road
Kettering
Northamptonshire
NN15 7HA
Tel: 0536 310101

## How successful are the exchange systems?

Success rates for exchanges under the II and RCI schemes are said to be comparable; both systems claim high percentages of successful exchanges (around 98 per cent). There is no doubt that the exchange systems do work. Both organisations depend on consumer satisfaction for their income and increase in membership and have a vested interest in continually improving the services which they offer.

It is important to appreciate the fact that a 98 per cent success rate does not mean that the member has a 98 per cent chance of getting the week he wants at the particular resort of his choice. His chances in this respect will depend on the desirability of his own unit and the competition for the unit of his choice.

## Does exchange network size matter?

It is often said that, even if a timeshare owner used his exchange network every year, he would have to live to the ripe old age of 1,500 plus to visit every RCI resort, or else to 900 plus to visit every Interval resort! Clearly, adequate choice is presented with the first few hundred affiliations, and thereafter the most important consideration is quality. With either RCI or Interval there is an extremely wide choice. In summary, the exchange system works successfully and supplies an added attractive dimension to timesharing which a developer must provide to ensure a successful scheme.

The terms on which the two major exchange organisations operate are obviously subject to change and some of the detail in this chapter may well be out-of-date at the time of going to press. The reader is therefore advised to contact the two organisations direct for updated information and for advice on their current full range of services.

## Other exchange possibilities

The larger timeshare developers will often offer an in-house exchange programme. Club Hotel, one of the major French timeshare developers, offers an in-house exchange facility involving over 20 different locations. They offer 'La clef de l'échange'—'The exchange key'. Each year the owner of the timeshare in one of the Club Hotel units is sent a circular. This allows him to surrender his next following time period to the management of the timesharing company of which he is a member, in exchange either for a fee or for an order to take advantage of the exchange facility. With the circular is sent a list of developments, each of which is linked to an annual chart divided into colour-coded weeks. Those weeks not coloured are not within the exchange system. The very high season is coded red, high season is coded yellow, middle season is blue and low season is green. Exchange is possible between timeshares colour-coded with the same colour. 'Red' season can also exchange with any other season, whatever its colour code. 'Yellow' season can exchange with any season except 'Red'. 'Blue' may exchange with any colour except red or yellow and 'Green' is restricted to exchange with any other green colour-coded unit.

Exchanges are further restricted to those with similar types of accommodation, depending upon the number of persons each unit can accommodate. The type of accommodation is sub-divided into two-person, four-person and six-person units. In order to make the system workable it will be apparent that the restriction of the exchange system in respect of time zones and size of accommodation prevents owners of off-season timeshares in smaller accommodation from trading up, whilst still retaining a general freedom of the owners of timeshares in the high season (who will of course have paid more for their timeshares).

Under the Club Hotel system the timeshare owner remains responsible for the maintenance charges attributable to the timeshare which he owns but must conform to the regulations affecting the timeshare to which he is making an exchange visit. He also pays a modest arrangement fee to Club Hotel. When requesting an exchange, the timeshare owner lists the first three desired exchanges in descending order of preference, on the understanding that Club Hotel will come back to him with alternative suggestions should none of the three choices be available.

## Consumer liability in England

At the time of writing, there is no reported case in England arising out of claims by exchange organisation members who find that, for one reason or another, their exchange visit results in a spoilt holiday, or arising out of the failure of a resort to meet expectations. It might be helpful, therefore, to consider the position of the exchange organisation in such an eventuality and to explore the extent of the liability of the exchange organisation.

### Tour operators and travel agents

Most cases arising out of unsuccessful holidays have involved either tour operators or travel agents and before attempting to examine the possible extent of liability of the exchange organisations, it may be helpful to review the current position of both of these. A tour operator is normally in the business of selling 'package holidays'. It is the tour operator who makes arrangements for accommodation, transport, meals and other elements in a holiday. These are packaged together and sold to the public. Usually the ingredients of the package are set out in a colourful brochure prepared by the tour operator and sold to the public either direct or via a travel agent. The tour operator generally maintains an on-site representative and supervises all aspects of the holiday including transport to and from the airport and often, in addition, provides local entertainment. The on-site representative has the job of ensuring that the customers' needs are properly met, that the customer has a trouble-free holiday and that any local difficulties are sorted out to his satisfaction. The representative will usually accompany customers from the destination airport to the destination hotel.

Some of the largest tour operators are members of an organisation known as the Tour Operators Study Group (TOSG), all of whom are members of the Association of British Travel Agents (ABTA). Customers of ABTA have recourse to the ABTA Travel Agents Fund, which protects their customers against the insolvency of other ABTA members. Additionally, if the tour operator makes available 'as a principal or an agent, accommodation for the carriage of persons or cargo on flights in any part of the world' (Civil Aviation Authority Act 1982, s 71(1)), he is also required to obtain an air travel organisers' licence (ATOL) and again will have to provide a bond to protect customers against the consequences of default.

*Statutory obligations*
The liability of tour operators is governed by a number of statutory obligations. Section 14 of the Sale of Goods Act 1979 provides that where goods are sold in the course of business, they should be reasonably fit for the purpose for which they are supplied. Since a tour operator normally provides meals as part of the 'package', the contract is, *inter alia*, one for the sale of goods.

Section 13 of the Supply of Goods and Services Act 1977 provides that 'In a contract for the supply of a service where the supplier is acting in the course of business, there is an implied term that the supplier will carry out the services with reasonable care and skill'.

Additionally, the Trade Descriptions Act 1968, s 14(1) provides statutory obligations which have been examined in Chapter 3. Section 24(1) of the Act, however, provides that:

> In any proceedings for an offence under this Act it shall, subject to sub-section 2 of this Section [giving notice to the Prosecution that the Defence will be relied upon], be a Defence for the person charged to prove:
> (a) that the commission of the offence was due to a mistake or to reliance on some information supplied to him or to the act or default of another person, an accident or some other cause beyond his control; and
> (b) that he took all reasonable precautions and exercised all diligence to avoid the commission of such an offence by himself or any person under his control.

Apart from the civil claim to which any misrepresentation may give rise, s 2(2) of the Misrepresentation Act 1967 allows a person to whom an innocent misrepresentation has been made to recover damages. This liability cannot be excluded except in so far as the exclusion clause 'satisfies the requirements or reasonableness as stated in s 11(2) of the Unfair Contract Terms Act 1977' (Misrepresentation Act 1967, s 3, as amended by the Unfair Contract Terms Act 1977, s 8).

Section 11(2) of the Unfair Contract Terms Act 1977 provides that in determining whether a contract term satisfies the requirement of reasonableness, regard shall be had to various matters specified in Sched 2 of the Act. In relation to services, they are listed as follows in that Schedule:

*(a)* the strength of the bargaining position of the parties relative to each other, taking into account (among other things) alternative means by which the customer's requirements could have been met.

*(b)* whether the customer received an inducement to agree to the term, or in accepting it had an opportunity of entering into a similar contract with other persons, but without having to accept a similar term;

*(c)* whether the customer knew or ought reasonably to have known of the existence and extent of the term (having regard, among other things to any custom of the trade and any previous course of dealing between the parties);

*(d)* where the term excludes or restricts any relevant liability, if some condition is not complied with, whether it was reasonable at the time of contract to expect that compliance with that condition would be practicable.

*Case law*

The leading cases on tour operator liability are *Jarvis* v *Swan Tours Ltd* [1973] 1 All ER 71); *Jackson* v *Horizon Holidays* [1975] 3 All ER 92; *Adcock* v *Blue Sky Holidays* (unreported, 13 May 1980); *Chesneau* v *Inter-home Ltd* (unreported, June 1983); *Askew* v *Intasun North* (unreported, Ashby-De-La-Zouche County Court, November 1979); *Levine* v *Metropolitan Travel* (unreported, Westminster County Court, November 1980); *Bragg* v *Yugotours* (1982) CLY 777); *Harvey* v *Tracks Travel* [2 CL 84] and finally *Wings Ltd* v *Ellis* [1984] 3 WLR 965. They seem to establish the principle that a customer can sue a tour operator not only in respect of his own loss, but also in respect of the loss suffered by people who accompanied him on holiday, and that he will be able to recover general damages for loss of enjoyment. Where the tour operator is selling the customer not a mere package of assorted services, but the expectation that the customer is likely to have a good time, the tour operator will be liable if that reasonable expectation of having a good time is defeated. As was said in *Jarvis* v *Swan Tours Ltd*: 'To quote the assurance which they gave regarding the Morlialp House-Party Centre "no doubt you will be in for a great time when you book this houseparty holiday". The result was that they did not limit themselves to the obligations to ensure that an air passage was booked, that hotel accommodation was reserved, that food was provided and those items would measure up to the standards they themselves set up. They went further than that. They assured and undertook to provide a holiday of a certain quality for "gemutlickeit" (that is to say, geniality comfort and cosiness) as its overall characteristic and a "great time", the enjoyable outcome which would surely result to all but the most determined misanthrope' (per Edmund Davies LJ).

Tour operating is a highly competitive business but the liability of tour operators to their customers for representations about the quality of the 'package' on offer is certainly much higher than liability for implied promises made in other transactions. One can readily think of inferences which are not actionable, for example, that a packet of monosodium glutamate and other assorted chemicals can turn a neglected housewife into a loved cordon bleu cook. The tour operator is selling a comparable fantasy to some degree, but the courts have held that in their particular business, the reality must at least approximate to the fantasy on offer. Apart from the obligation not to make claims about the quality of the holiday which turn out not to be true, there is also very strict liability, under s 14(1) of the Trade Descriptions Act 1968, to ensure that every single statement of fact is absolutely accurate. This stringent interpretation of the Act is a matter of policy. As was said in *Wings* v *Ellis* (per Lord Scarman):

> It is no exaggeration to say that the social impact of the class of business which I have described and in which the respondent company is engaged has been immense. It has brought about a dramatic change in the life-style of millions. People rely on the brochures issued by the companies engaged in this highly competitive business when choosing their annual holidays abroad, some choose to travel great distances to far-away places very different from anything which they have experienced at home upon their faith in a description which they have read in a brochure but which they cannot check.

The defence of innocence, or lack of knowledge, is unlikely to succeed if raised by a tour operator, since the tour operating company is deemed to have the knowledge of all of its employees, whether or not they communicate that knowledge to the 'directing mind' of the company. As Lord Scarman said in *Wings* v *Ellis* (at page 979/980) '... knowledge of the "directing mind" of the business is not a necessary ingredient of an act prohibited by the Statute ...' and he went on to quote Viscount Reading CJ in *Mousell Brothers Ltd* v *London & North Western Railway Co* [1917] 2 KB 836, 844 that it may well have been the intention of the legislature 'in order to guard against the happening of a forbidden thing, to impose a liability upon a principal even though he does not know of, and is not a party to the forbidden act done by his servant ...' The tour operator will usually have staff on-site and will arrange many visits to the resort featured in the brochures. Consequently, the degree of imputed knowledge is far greater than that which would be imputed to a travel agent, who is not involved in arranging holidays, but merely sells the holiday arrangements already arranged by the tour operator.

The services offered by a tour operator are substantially different, both in nature and in the degree of responsibility accepted, from those offered by the travel agent. The tour operator is not acting as an agent. There is certainly no contract of agency between the tour operator and the customer, nor is the tour operator an agent of the hotelier who provides the accommodation. It may be said that the travel agent is, by definition, an agent, though the question of who is the travel agent's principal (that is, is it the customer or the tour operator) is one which is not free from doubt. Certainly members of the public do regard the travel agent as their agent and consider that the travel agent is there to arrange a contract between themselves and the tour operator. It can be argued that the public view is correct by analogy with the case of *Anglo-African*

*Merchants Ltd* v *Bayley* [1970] 1 QB 311, where it was held that insurance brokers selling to customers policies offered by different insurance companies were agents of the insured not of the insurer, even where payment to the agent was in the form of commission from the insurer. The position remains questionable, however.

The agent will also have a liability similar to that of the tour operator under s 14 of the Trade Descriptions Act 1968. That is, he must ensure that statements made to customers are accurate, though in the case of the travel agent those statements are derived from information given to the travel agent by the tour operator. The tour operator will consequently be liable to indemnify the travel agent in respect of liability arising out of inaccurate statements. Moreover the travel agent will normally have available the defence afforded by s 24(1) of the Act. The travel agent, because he purports to act as an expert in arranging travel contracts, has a duty of care to the customer: 'it should now be regarded as settled that if someone possessed of a special skill, undertakes, quite irrespective of contract, to supply that skill for the assistance of another person who relies upon such a skill, a duty of care would arise' (per Lord Morris of Borthy Gest, *Hedley Byrne Co Ltd* v *Heller & Partners Ltd* [1964 AC 465]. In effect, this is the principle codified as s 13 of the Supply of Goods and Services Act 1977.

The position of the exchange organisation is clearly analagous to that of the travel agent. The exchange organisation does not package up a holiday or sell a holiday dream and is plainly an agent of the exchange member, by whom he is paid. It seems, then, that the obligations of the exchange organisation depend upon the extent to which the organisation owes a duty of care, and the extent to which such duty as does exist has been modified by agreement.

In the first instance, the governing law between an exchange network and its members may not be the law of England and Wales, if there is an express choice of some other system of laws in the membership agreement. Such a choice is likely to be binding on the member (see Dicey and Morris Rule 180(1)). The Unfair Contract Terms Act 1977 does not alter what would otherwise be the proper law of the contract, as may be seen from its terms, particularly when comparison is made between sub-ss 27(1) and (2) and in the context of international exchange networks carrying on transnational business. The question as to whether any contractual liability has been excluded by the terms of the contract will therefore be determined by the proper law. If this is English law, the question as to how far exemption and exclusion clauses will protect the exchange network have been dealt with in Chapter 3. There must be considerable doubt as to whether the exchange networks have a duty of care to their members or to third parties. The starting point for consideration of this issue is that a claim in tort on behalf of a timeshare owner would detail a claim to damages for pure economic loss. Such a claim will not be entertained by the courts unless it falls within the category of cases arising from negligent mis-statement as in *Hedley Byrne & Co Ltd* v *Heller* (above) (see also *D & F Estates* v *Church Commissioners* [1988] 2

All ER 992 (HL) and *Murphy* v *Brentwood District Council, The Times*, 27 July 1990).

It is most unlikely that an exchange network will be held to owe a duty of care in respect of any promotional literature issued by it or a developer of the resort in so far as statements in such material might indicate that the network had endorsed or approved or otherwise satisfied itself as to the resort.

The approach to this issue has recently been considered by the House of Lords in *Caparo plc* v *Dickman* [1990] 2 WLR 358 and in *Smith* v *Bush* [1989] 2 WLR 790. Traditionally, the first component of such a duty of care traditionally has been foreseeability of loss. The second requirement necessary to establish a duty of care in such a case is proximity. This has been taken to mean not physical proximity, but 'such close and direct relations that the act complained of directly affects a person whom the person alleged to be bound to take care would know would be directly affected by his careless act' (see *Donoghue* v *Stevenson* [1932] AC 562, at 561).

It would probably be a central ingredient to establishing a sufficient degree of proximity where the loss is economic that there was reliance on the part of the timeshare owners upon the statements of the exchange network (see *Hedley Byrne* v *Heller* and *D & F Estates Ltd* v *Church Commissioners* above).

There are a number of significant differences from the factual matrix in *Smith* v *Bush* and the exchange network's relationship to timeshare owners at the resort. There is usually no payment by the timeshare owners at the resort to the exchange network for the timeshare. Many of them will (one hopes) have consulted qualified advisers before purchase, and those who did not, will not have been canvassed by agents by or on behalf of the exchange network. Even if it was forseeable that timeshare owners would rely upon statements made by the exchange network or the fact of the exchange networks' association with the resort, as manifested in use of its logo and publications in the sales literature and material, this of itself is not conclusive as far as the issue of whether a duty of care is owed is concerned: compare *Morgan Crucible* v *Hill Samuel Bank Ltd, Financial Times*, 27 July 1990 (Hoffman J).

There is considerable doubt as to whether a duty of care could be imposed on an exchange network. There must be a world of difference between a valuer of residential property who prepares a report upon which he knows the prospective purchaser will rely and has paid for, and the exchange network's process of vetting resorts applying for affiliation or membership, which process is to ensure the efficient working of the exchange system and the reputation of the exchange organisation rather than as an additional report on title for individual interval members or prospective members who purchase timeshare interests at any particular resort. The case of *Mariola Marine Corp* v *Lloyd's Register of Shipping, The Times*, 21 February 1990, Phillips J, should also be considered. Here, no duty of care was found to be owed to the prospective purchasers by the Lloyd's Register in respect of the accuracy of the value of a ship on the register as there was not held to be insufficient proximity. However, it is not possible to give a definitive view without considering the nature of the statements which may be complained of, and the circumstances of their publication. Silence as to the inadequacies of the resort is unlikely of itself to ground liability in tort: compare *Banquet Caesar Ullman SA* v *Skandia (UK) Insurance Co, The Times*, 26 July 1990.

There may be an issue as to whether English law applies and this will depend on exactly where the allegedly negligent statements were published. Accordingly to English law, the generally accepted rule is that acts and statements are actionable in England first if, had the act been done in England, it would have been actionable as a tort, and secondly, that it is actionable according to the law of the country where it was done (see Dicey and Morris Rule 205, *Boys* v *Chaplin* [1969] 3 WLR 322 and compare *Minister Investments* v *Hyundai Precision & Industry Co* [1988] 2 Ll R621 concerning negligent statements made abroad but relied upon within the UK), but see Chapter 7 where these issues are further explored.

## Conclusion

It would seem, therefore, that the nature of the functions and responsibilities of an exchange network are such that its liability to members and third parties is limited in the extreme, and fraught with conflict of laws problems. Perhaps for this reason there is no recorded instance of a successful claim, by a member against an exchange network, being adjudicated.

# Chapter Five

# Financing and a timeshare development

According to one survey approximately 68 per cent of US purchasers obtained financing for their timeshare purchases, whereas in the UK, in the early years of timesharing, the comparative figure was only around 7 per cent (Richard I Ragatz Associates Inc. *United Kingdom Timeshare Purchasers: Who They Are, Why They Buy* (1981)). Increasingly, however, purchasers are being offered finance and the current percentage of sales so financed is now estimated to be greater than 50 per cent for UK purchasers. In addition, there are now many larger timeshare developments comprising between 100 and 1,000 units and in order for these to operate successfully, finance must be offered to purchasers.

The timeshare interest has not generally been regarded as 'good security' for a loan in the UK because only about one-third of the cost of a timeshare is represented by the underlying value of the timeshare property. About one-third of the balance is represented by the developer's sales costs and the remaining third comprises the developer's overheads and profit. In many respects this is rather a blinkered way of looking at a transaction of this kind, in that it is based on the notion that timeshare developers are selling 'property' rather than a new holiday concept. There is a section of the timeshare market which is involved in the selling of property, in the sense that it is putting together a small number of purchasers, perhaps up to six in number, with the intention of purchasing a property between them. This, however, is not mass-market timesharing in the true sense. The value of the timeshare is not directly related to the underlying property valuation. It depends upon how easily the investment can be realised by sale. This in turn depends upon the success of the development and on whether the seller has to compete with the developer's own marketing of unsold timeshares.

There are two ways in which the developer can make the timeshare more attractive as security. Firstly, he can arrange to provide a resale service through the management company. In the early stages of development this may operate in competition with the developer but if a track record of successful resales is established, this in itself will be a valuable added advantage for the prospective purchaser of a new timeshare and will also demonstrate to prospective lending sources that a viable resale market exists. Secondly, the developer may offer the lending source a right of 'recourse'.

Under a recourse arrangement the developer agrees with the finance company to take back finance agreements which go sour and the developer's recourse is an important factor in arranging low cost financing. The experience seems to be that rather less than 1 per cent of timeshare purchasers fail to honour their obligations, so that the finance company's right of recourse to the developer is not an onerous obligation. Initially the finance company may keep a retention from the finance paid to the developer, or may accept fresh sales in lieu of requiring a cash refund on recourse. The arrangement also speeds the process of financing which, in the UK, can take six weeks or more if a second mortgage is involved.

Under the US system of financing the developer, rather than the finance company, deals with the credit check on the prospective purchaser. Often the developer will have obtained information regarding the purchaser's financial circumstances from the sales interview. Frequently the deposit on the purchase is paid by use of the purchaser's credit card, which some developers regard as a sufficient means when coupled with the information obtained at the interview, of establishing the credit-worthiness of the prospective purchaser.

Timesharing systems usually operate so that it is not possible to dispose of the timeshare except with the consent and knowledge of the developer. A timeshare is not a portable asset, like a car or a boat. The developer obtains the purchaser's signature to the finance agreement and transfers the timeshare to the purchaser. So far as the latter is concerned, the transaction is completed. American experience shows that it is far easier to make a financed sale in this way, as the purchaser is less likely to change his mind once away from the sales site. In the USA, however, the purchaser generally has a right to rescind the arrangements within a specified period. A similar provision operates in the UK if the agreement is a 'cancellable agreement', ie one to which Consumer Credit Act 1974, s 67 applies. The developer sends the agreement to the finance company which then, within an agreed period, pays the developer that part of the purchase price which has been financed.

Sometimes, the developer will collect the finance payments on behalf of the finance company at the same time as collecting the service charge or maintenance payments, and often other charges (for instance in respect of holiday insurance and the like) are included in the total amount charged to the purchaser. Sometimes the finance company performs this service for the developer. In the USA, a third party may take over this administrative burden and provide a similar service to a number of developers and finance corporations.

The finance company may require, as part of the recourse agreement, a percentage of the finance to be withheld from the developer so as to establish a recourse fund. Experience however shows that the number of financed agreements on which the purchaser defaults is of the order of only 1 per cent, so that the percentage of the retention is generally very small. The developer may be offered the option of credit insurance but will often prefer to assume the risk himself. If there is default, the developer is usually afforded the option of replacing the defaulting agreement with a fresh agreement to a new purchaser, rather than having to refund the finance directly to the finance company. In respect of the small number of purchasers who do default, the finance company often sends out a first reminder letter to the defaulter. If the defaulter fails to respond, a second letter will be sent and the developer will be informed. At this stage the developer will contact his customer and find out what has gone wrong. He will have the sales file before him so he will know something of the background of his customer. If the purchaser is unable or unwilling to pay the balance owed, the developer will offer to take back the timeshare and settle the finance agreement so as to avoid the purchaser being pursued by the finance company. If the purchaser defaults fairly soon after the agreement is entered into, the developer retains the deposit and any payments already made, but he may still incur a small loss because of the expense of resale. He may try to avoid this, assuming he operates a resale programme, by persuading the purchaser to bring his payments up-to-date and to continue them whilst placing the timeshare in the resale programme. In that way the purchaser may not lose to the same extent. If the default takes place when a substantial amount of the finance has been paid off, the developer may take back the timeshare and offer a percentage of the resale price to the purchaser when the resale is made.

If the purchaser proves completely intractable, the finance company will pursue him in the usual way and the developer will have to meet the costs involved to the extent that they are not eventually recovered from the purchaser. Such cases comprise only a tiny minority of the 1 per cent of the purchasers who do default: most appear to be amenable to reason. The Ragatz survey has shown that the overwhelming majority of timeshare purchasers are home-owners in well paid employment and not likely to default on their obligations. This system works very well in the USA and in the jargon of the trade, American Finance Corporations say that : 'Timeshare paper is the best paper we have'. As a result, they are keen to lend, and a glance through, for example, the American magazines *Resort Timesharing Today* and *ALDA*, which contain numerous advertisements from finance companies offering timeshare finance, makes this readily apparent. The more sophisticated financing schemes available in the USA may go some way towards explaining the rapid expansion in the industry there, although it must also be said that American tax law, which affords the buyer tax relief on the loan interest and on the element of tax in the maintenance charge, and has no equivalent of VAT, must also be a contributory factor.

The UK and elsewhere in Europe have still not achieved this level of sophistication. The signs are though that some overseas finance companies wish to expand their operations into Europe, so it may be that circumstances will change.

The English Tourist Board publishes various useful guides to assist developers in arranging finance, one of which—Guide No DG32 *Services of the Clearing Banks for Developers in Tourism*—they intend to update on a six-monthly basis. There is also *Financing Tourist Projects* available from Department D and booklet DG18 *How to Approach a Bank for Finance.* Applications for these should be addressed to:

English Tourist Board
4 Grosvenor Gardens
London SW1W 0DU

In the UK, a number of companies run schemes in conjunction with an endowment assurance policy. Borrowing is usually arranged for up to 90 per cent of the purchase price for the timeshare, with the repayments spread over perhaps ten years. This arrangement has the advantage that the timeshare purchaser may obtain tax relief on the endowment loan assurance policy premiums and of course in the event of his or her death during the repayment period, the loan would automatically be paid off. The endowment policy provides additional security to the lending source but the cost is prohibitive. The developer is in the business of selling insurance and not timeshares. Furthermore, such loans were often restricted to more than £5,000 to avoid the provisions of the Consumer Credit Act 1974, and since 19 May 1985, when the limit was increased to £15,000, this restriction can in practice no longer be applied.

It is always possible for home owners in the UK to apply to their building societies or banks for a loan or an increased loan on the security of their property. This is usually the cheapest way of raising money for a timeshare purchase, but the homeowner should remember that loans used otherwise than for the purchase of a principal private residence do not qualify for the tax relief. Moreover, the procedure is frequently cumbersome and time-consuming. The timeshare industry requires more convenient and readily available financing facilities for purchasers.

Difficulties arise where a timeshare developer wishes to arrange finance because, if the lending source is a UK bank or finance company, or if the borrower is resident in the UK, the provisions of the Consumer Credit Act 1974, s 75, may apply. The implications of the Act are examined later in this chapter, but briefly, this section provides that if the finance is provided pursuant to arrangements made between the developer and the finance company, a timeshare buyer will have the same claim against the finance company as he has against the timeshare developer in the event of the latter's default. In other words, if the title to the timeshare proves not to be secure, or if the development is not completed, or if all the representations made by the timeshare developer are not made good, the buyer may be able to write off the loan and sue the finance company for damages.

It is therefore extremely important for the finance company to ensure that the development is soundly structured, that the whole timeshare project is properly evaluated, and that the timeshare purchasers are provided with some independent assurance as to the rights acquired in the purchase of a timeshare.

In view of these difficulties, some developers 'write their own paper'—that is, enter into loan agreements direct with the purchaser. Such agreements, if subject to UK law, will also be subject to the Consumer Credit Act 1974. Timeshare developers in such circumstances will no doubt hope to assign the loan agreements—the 'receivables'—to a bank or finance company and thus obtain the capital represented by timeshare sales. But here again the finance company assumes the obligations of the developer, as the assignee will be a 'creditor' pursuant to s 189(1) of the Act.

## Effects of the Consumer Credit Act 1974

The availability of finance for timeshare purchasers is obviously an important factor in any timeshare development marketing plan. The effects of the Consumer Credit Act 1974 always require careful consideration at the outset. The Act and the regulations made thereunder are of considerable complexity. All that can be provided here is some examination of the relevant provisions of the Act in so far as they relate to timesharing.

Subject to certain exceptions, the Act covers all consumer credit agreements, and provides for a system of licensing in respect of persons or corporations granting or arranging credit, a series of statutory protections for the consumer and a requirement, set out in detailed regulations, governing the form of consumer credit agreements, the information which they must contain and the way in which credit business is sought. The Act contains a number of important definitions.

### Debtor-creditor-supplier ('DCS') agreement (s 12)

A DCS agreement is any credit agreement where the supplier of the goods or services is connected with a lender who finances those goods and services. It may be a two-party DCS agreement, where the creditor and supplier are one and the same (eg where the timeshare developer gives credit to the timeshare purchaser direct) or a three-party DCS agreement, where the timeshare developer (the supplier) has made arrangements with a finance company for finance to be provided to his timeshare purchasers.

### Debtor-creditor ('DC') agreement (s 13)

A DC agreement is one where there is no connection between the supplier of the services and the provider of the loan.

### Restricted and unrestricted use credit (s 11)

A restricted use credit is one where the credit may only be used for a certain purpose. Credit card purchases and transactions in which the loan is paid directly to the timeshare developer or to his order are restricted use credits. Any other agreements will constitute unrestricted use credits.

**Credit broker (s 145)**

Anyone who introduces a prospective debtor to a person who carries on a consumer credit business is a credit broker. This definition covers introductions to a credit broker, so that anyone introducing the purchasers to a credit broker, as opposed to introducing them to a finance company direct, is himself a credit broker and is subject to the provisions of the Act.

**Linked transaction (s 19)**

All transactions financed by a DCS agreement or entered into in compliance with the term of the consumer credit agreement constitute linked transactions.

**Multiple agreement (s 18)**

A multiple agreement is one containing provisions placing part of the agreement within one area of the Act and other parts in other areas of the Act. If, for example, credit protection insurance is offered as part of the arrangement and the premium is covered by the finance agreement, the whole agreement will be a multiple agreement.

**Negotiator (s 56)**

A credit broker or supplier in a DCS transaction is deemed to be the agent of the creditor, not of the consumer.

**Cancellable agreement (s 67)**

A debtor may cancel a credit agreement and a linked transaction within five days of completing it (or within five days of receiving a copy thereof pursuant to s 63(2)) unless:

1 It is secured on land or;
2 It is signed on the trade premises of either the creditor, the negotiator or the supplier.

In relation to timesharing, the Act does not apply to the transactions involving:

1 A loan exceeding £15,000 (s 8(2)) as amended by Consumer Credit (Increase of Monetary Limits) Order 1983)).
2 Loans to corporate bodies (s 8(1). See the definitions in s 189(1)).
3 Where the lender is one of the class specified in s 16(1) (notably building societies and insurance companies) and:
   (a) the loan is for the purpose of the purchase of land or the provision of dwellings on land; and
   (b) the loan is secured by a land mortgage on the land.

For the purpose of 3 above, the only form of timeshare which may qualify as 'land' is a leasehold timesharing scheme. A share in a corporation is obviously not an interest in land, nor is a club membership certificate, even where the timeshare property is held by a trustee (see *American Real Estate (Scotland) Ltd* v *The Commissioners* (1980) VATTR 88, at page 91)).

## The need for a Consumer Credit Act licence

The provision of credit by the timeshare developer to the timeshare buyer will mean that the developer requires a licence under category 'A'—consumer credit business. If a timeshare developer, or his marketing agent, arranges credit for the timeshare buyer, each will require a licence under Category 'C'—credit brokerage.

If either the timeshare developer or the marketing agent wishes to canvass for purchasers off the trade premises (eg off-site personnel contract 'OPC' selling), the licence will need to be endorsed with permission accordingly. The forms of application may be obtained from:

The Office of Fair Trading,
Consumer Credit Licensing Branch
Government Buildings
Bromyard Avenue
Acton
London
W3 7BB
Tel: (071) 242 2858

The Office of Fair Trading also publishes a number of explanatory booklets. The fee for a licence for a corporation is currently £150 for the first category of business applied for, plus £10 for each additional category and for the endorsement referred to above. The other categories of business are 'B'—consumer hire business, 'D'—debt adjusting and debt counselling, 'E'—debt collecting and 'F'—credit reference agency. It will obviously be necessary to consider whether to obtain a licence for these additional categories of business.

The licence covers all lawful activities carried out in the course of the business, whether directly by the licensee or by his employees. Where agents are employed, as a general rule, because a licence is required to 'carry on a business', each agent who runs a business on his own account needs a licence, unless the agent's activities are merely an extension of his principal's business. The question is one of fact to be determined in each case but almost invariably an agent who represents more than one principal requires a licence. In view of the penalties imposed for carrying out licensable activities without a licence, a timeshare developer should employ only marketing agents who are properly licensed.

Trading without a consumer credit licence in circumstances where such a licence is required is an offence punishable on indictment by imprisonment for a term not exceeding two years, or a fine or both (ss 39 and 167). Any offence by a body corporate is also an offence by any actual or deemed officer of that corporation if it is committed with his consent or connivance or because of his neglect.

In such circumstances, the credit agreement will not be enforceable without an order from the Director General of Fair Trading permitting the agreement to be treated as if the creditor had been licensed. The Director has a discretion as to whether he grants such an order and in exercising his discretion must take into account various factors set out in the Act, including the degree of culpability of the trader in not obtaining a licence.

Currently, Consumer Credit Act applications seem to take in excess of six weeks to process. Since it amounts to credit brokerage if one introduces people to other credit brokers, there is no easy way around the problem if a licence is needed, so that long delays may occur before selling activities can start, unless a licence has been obtained in advance. The need for a licence should therefore be considered at the early stages of planning a timeshare project.

## Formalities relating to a Consumer Credit Act agreement

Part V of the Act and numerous Statutory Instruments made thereunder, lay down various rules which have to be complied with on the making of a consumer credit or consumer hire agreement and specify that the agreement itself must be in a certain form and executed in a special way. The debtor must be given a copy of the agreement when he signs it. If the creditor has not signed the agreement when it is signed by the debtor, then within seven days of the agreement being executed by the creditor, the debtor must be sent a further copy of the agreement. Failure to comply with these formalities means that the agreement is improperly executed and is not enforceable without a court order.

## Timeshare purchaser's right of cancellation

The timeshare purchaser will have a right to cancel the agreement unless either:

1 it is secured on land or is a restricted use agreement financing the purchase of land, or is a bridging loan in connection with a purchase of land; or
2 it is signed at the business premises of either the creditor or owner or negotiator or party to a linked transaction other than the debtor or a person associated with the debtor.

If the timeshare purchase agreement itself contains a contractual right of cancellation, the consumer credit agreement associated with it will also be cancellable and all the formalities relating to cancellable agreements will apply. Cancellable agreements should be avoided wherever possible. One way of achieving this is to have a 'closing room' or office at the timeshare development and to make sure that the credit agreements are signed in that office and nowhere else.

If the agreement is cancellable it must contain a statutory notice reminding the debtor of his rights to cancel the agreement (s 64 (1)(a)). The debtor must be given a copy of the agreement when he signs it. If the agreement is thereupon completed because the creditor has signed it at the same time, the creditor must send by post to the debtor within seven days a separate notice of cancellation rights. If the agreement is not concluded, because it has not been signed by the creditor, the creditor must send a further copy of the agreement to the debtor within seven days. In short, the timeshare purchaser must be provided either with a copy of the executed agreement when it is signed by himself and the creditor, followed by a notice of cancellation rights by post, or alternatively, a copy of the executed agreement by post incorporating a notice of cancellation rights. Failure to comply with these provisions may mean that the agreement will be unenforceable. If the copies have been provided but do not contain the notice of cancellation rights or if the separate notice of cancellation rights is not served, the agreement will clearly not be enforceable (s 127 (4)(b)). If the notice of cancellation was given but the relevant copies were not provided, it is possible for the creditor to make an application to the court under s 127 (4)(a). There does appear however to be a conflict between the provisions of s 127 (4)(a) and s 127 (4)(b) of the Act and if there are to be cancellable agreements, it will be essential to have a tight method of policing the procedures and seeing that they are properly observed.

If a cancellable agreement is entered into by mistake (for example, if the purchase contract does not contain a right of cancellation, but the credit agreement was signed off the trade premises) it seems clear that the agreement will be unenforceable by virtue of s 127 (4)(b).

The timeshare purchaser may cancel the credit agreement (and the timeshare purchase agreement, which will be a linked transaction) within five days of receiving the second copy of the agreement or the separate notice of cancellation rights. The right of cancellation is exercised by the timeshare purchaser posting a notice to the creditor or owner, or to the negotiator, or any person who in the course of his business acted for the timeshare purchaser in negotiating the agreement

## Finance company liability

Section 75 of the Act provides, *inter alia*, as follows:

(i) If the debtor, under a debtor-creditor-supplier agreement falling within Section 12 *(b)* or *(c)* has, in relation to a transaction financed by the agreement, any claim against the supplier in respect of a misrepresentation or breach of contract, he shall have a like claim against the creditor who, with the supplier, shall accordingly be jointly and severally liable to the debtor.

(ii) Subject to any agreement between them, a creditor shall be entitled to be indemnified by the supplier for loss suffered by the creditor in satisfying his liability under Sub-Section (i), including costs reasonably incurred by him in defending proceedings instituted by the debtor...

The section does not apply if the cash price of the timeshare exceeds £30,000—most timeshare sales will therefore come within the limit.

Section 75 applies to the situation where the timeshare developer has made an arrangement with the finance company for his timeshare sales to be financed by the finance company. In other words it applies to three-party DCS agreements.

If the timeshare developer is able to limit his liability with appropriate exclusion clauses, the liability of the finance company will similarly be diminished. It is important to note that only claims in respect of misrepresentation or breach of contract are covered by the section so that no claim arises in respect of breach of statutory duty, negligence or fraud other than in respect of misrepresentation.

The liability of the creditor is confined to the transaction financed by the DCS agreement. A timeshare plan will usually contain provisions for ongoing management services to be provided under a separate management agreement, and as these services will not normally be financed by the Consumer Credit Act agreement, breaches by the management company or failure by the management company to provide the services in line with its obligations will not normally entitle the timeshare purchaser to make a claim against the finance company. In order to assess its liability the finance company will therefore have to consider exactly what is being sold by the timeshare developer to the purchaser and what representations are made at time of sale. So far very few claims have been made under s 75 and provided that the timeshare plan documentation makes it quite clear what is being provided and it can be clearly established that no misrepresentations were made, liability may not be quite as fearsome as might be supposed.

In the case of overseas timesharing schemes where the timesharing rights are governed by foreign law, s 75 of the Act may still apply if the finance source is a UK-based bank or finance company or if the timeshare purchaser is resident in the UK. In such circumstances any liability of the timeshare developer to the timeshare purchaser is established under the rules of the law governing the purchase agreement, which may be less onerous than English law so far as the timeshare developer is concerned. These issues need to be examined in the context of the conflict of laws (see Chapter 7).

## Charge cards and credit cards

A distinction needs to be drawn between charge cards (eg American Express or Diners Club) where payment is due from the customer upon delivery of the bill, and credit cards (eg Access and Visa) where the customer has an opportunity of repaying the debt over a period of time (four or more instalments). The provisions of credit by credit card companies comes within the Act and accordingly s 75 applies. For this reason, credit card companies are generally unwilling to allow their cards to be used for the purchase of timeshares or for the payment of deposits. However, it may be worthwhile approaching such companies, who will no doubt consider each case on its own merits.

## Recovery of possession of the timeshare

The timeshare buyer must be supplied with a default or termination notice (ss 76 and 87–89 of the Act) before any action is taken to terminate the agreement or enforce any security. Recovery of possession of 'goods' or 'land' will require a court order.

'Land' is defined as including 'an interest in land and in relation to Scotland includes heritable subjects of whatever description' and, apart from the leasehold schemes, the timeshare interest is unlikely to be regarded as land in this context (see *American Real Estate (Scotland) Ltd* v *The Commissioners* above).

'Goods' are defined as in the Sale of Goods Act 1893, s 62(1) which provides that 'goods include all chattels personal other than things in action and money, and in Scotland all corporeal movables except money . . . .' In England and Wales the timeshare is likely to be regarded as a 'thing' or 'chose' in action. The restrictions on the recovery of goods or land without a court order referred to in ss 90 and 92 of the Consumer Credit Act 1974 are not therefore thought to apply.

Section 16(5)(c) of the 1974 Act provides that orders may be made to exempt transactions where 'an agreement has a connection with a country outside the UK'. No order has yet been made specifically relating to timeshare schemes.

Paragraph 5 of the Consumer Credit (Exempt Agreements) Order 1980 provides that:

> The Act shall not regulate an agreement made in connection with a trade in goods or services between the United Kingdom and a country outside the United Kingdom,

or within a country or between countries outside the United Kingdom, being an agreement under which credit is provided to the debtor in the course of a business carried on by him.

Apart from the timeshare not coming within 'a trade in goods or services', the average timeshare buyer will not be obtaining credit in the course of a business carried on by him. Consequently, finance agreements with a UK purchaser, or with a UK developer or involving a UK finance company will either be debtor/creditor agreements or else debtor/creditor/supplier agreements, where the proper law is English law or otherwise where the *lex fori* is England, to the extent that the provisions of the Act are regarded as procedural rather than substantive.

Where the proper law of the transaction is English law, eg where a club system is operated under UK law even where the trustee is non-resident, the finance company will have to ensure compliance with the Act. This means that in these circumstances even overseas developers will require a licence. Again, the proper law of the finance agreement may be English law, whereas the agreement between the developer and the timeshare purchaser may be regulated by a foreign law. Conversely, a foreign buyer may be purchasing a timeshare in a UK development and financing the purchase with a bank or finance company in his home country where the bank or finance company has an understanding with the developer (a debtor-creditor-supplier agreement). Questions arising in these circumstances will need to be resolved in accordance with the rules governing conflict of laws (see Chapter 7).

# Chapter Six

# Taxation

In this chapter we shall look at some of the salient features of UK tax law in so far as they apply to timesharing. We shall examine the different types of taxation and their separate effect on both the developer and the timeshare purchaser. The tax position of both parties will depend largely not only on how the scheme itself is constructed but also on the identity, residence and other circumstances of the developer and the timeshare buyer. The following must in no sense be regarded as a substitute for proper taxation advice, which should always be obtained at the outset both by the developer and by the timeshare purchaser.

Taxation considerations need to be discussed and evaluated at the formative or planning stages of any development, as they are likely to dictate the structure to be adopted. The developer should give some thought to the purchaser's taxation position—by reducing such problems the developer will maximise the marketability of his project. Once the structure is in being, it may be impossible or impracticable to change it if a tax problem arises or if some aspect has not previously been considered, and this could obviously be disastrous to the profitability or even the viability of the whole scheme.

The timeshare purchaser should also be aware of the tax implications of 'holiday investment'. Timeshare is a relatively new and growing industry in the UK and hence the tax treatment has not yet been properly defined either by statute or by case law or by Inland Revenue practice. Professional advisers therefore need to examine the various existing Taxes Acts and related case law and interpret their likely effects on the timeshare industry.

It is a very difficult area and in many instances the tax authorities themselves have not yet decided how they will interpret the law. As any tax adviser will confirm it is often crucial not only to know the relevant law, but also to know how this law is to be applied in practice. The reader will appreciate that the phraseology used in the timeshare development business is not always precise and the law will follow the text of the documents as a whole. The title by which they are described will not always be accurate and can be disregarded. With these caveats in mind and subject to the need to obtain specialist advice in each case, it may be helpful to review the main areas of taxation and how they are likely to affect the timeshare project.

# Value added tax

Value added tax (VAT) was introduced in the UK on 1 April 1973 by means of the Finance Act 1972. Subsequent Finance Acts have amended VAT legislation and the Value Added Tax Act 1983 (VATA 1983) consolidated all previous legislation with effect from 26 July 1983. Value added tax is not a sales tax, nor even a tax on value added (ie profit or gain) but a tax on certain classified transactions. It is charged on any supply of goods or services made in the UK and on the importation of goods into the UK (VATA 1983, s 1). For any particular transactions to fall within the scope of VAT and thus become chargeable, several conditions need all to be satisfied.

## 1 Supply of goods or services

There must be a 'supply of either goods or services'. There is no definition of the word 'supply' in the VAT legislation, although the word is considered to include all forms of supply, but not anything done otherwise than for a consideration. Where consideration passes but there is not a supply of goods, the supply is one of services (which includes the granting, assignment or surrender of any rights) (VATA 1983, s 3(2)). However, the grant, assignment or surrender of a major interest in land is treated as a supply of goods (VATA 1983, Sched 2, para 4).

## 2 Taxable supply

The supply must be a 'taxable supply', which means any supply of goods or services other than an exempt supply (VATA 1983, s 2 (2)). Taxable supplies include those liable to VAT at the standard rate, currently (1991) 15 per cent and the zero rate—0 per cent. An 'exempt' supply is a supply of goods or services which specifically falls under one of the Group headings contained in Sched 6 of the VATA 1983 (this Schedule lists the various groups of exemptions). A person who makes exempt supplies only is therefore not a taxable person, cannot be registered for VAT (VATA 1983, s 2 (2)) and therefore must not charge VAT to customers and cannot recover VAT incurred on expenditure. In cases where a trade makes both exempt and taxable supplies, the special rules of 'partial exemption' apply and normally only a proportion of VAT suffered is reclaimable. These special rules on partial exemption are beyond the scope of this book and specialist advice should be obtained if it appears that partial exemption is likely to be relevant.

There is a major distinction to be drawn between exempt supplies and those eligible for zero-rating. A person who only makes zero-rated supplies may be liable (or eligible) to register for VAT and recover in full VAT incurred on expenditure, subject to specifically blocked items, eg the purchase of a motor car.

## 3 Tax must be chargeable on the taxable supply

To be within the charge to VAT, a supply of goods or services must be made within the UK. The place of supply of goods depends on where the goods are when the vendor contracts to supply them (VATA 1983, s 6). A supply of services is treated as made in the UK if the supplier of the service 'belongs in' the UK. Consequently, a supply of services is treated as made outside the UK if the supplier 'belongs in' a country other than the UK (VATA 1983, s 6 (5)).

A supplier of services is treated as 'belonging in' the UK if he has a UK business establishment (including a branch or agency or some other fixed establishment) and no such establishment elsewhere. He is also deemed to belong in the UK if he has such establishments in more than one country, but the establishment which is most directly concerned with the particular supply in question is in the UK. When the supplier has no business establishment in any country, he belongs where his usual place of residence is located (s 8 (2)). The term 'usual place of residence' in relation to a corporate body is the country in which it was legally constituted (s 8 (5)(*b*)).

Where a supplier owns the freehold or leasehold interest in a house, flat, chalet or other building used to provide timeshare accommodation, Customs & Excise consider that the property constitutes a business or other fixed establishment for VAT purposes. Consequently the place of supply for these transactions is determined by the location of the accommodation provided. This has the effect that timeshare businesses who are otherwise located overseas may have a liability to register for VAT in the UK if they supply timeshare accommodation in buildings located there. In the same way, timeshare operators located in the UK with properties overseas may find that local VAT or other taxes apply.

The usual place of supply rules outlined above were modified with effect from 1 April 1988 in respect of 'designated travel services' provided by 'tour operators' (the VAT (Tour Operators) Order 1987 SI 1987 No 1806). The term 'tour operators' is not defined in law. However, Customs & Excise interpret these provisions to apply, *inter alia*, to persons who buy in timeshare accommodation from a third party and resell the services either singly or as a package in the role of principal. Supplies falling under the tour operator's scheme are treated as supplied in the member state of the European Community in which the tour operator has established his business (VAT (Tour Operators) Order 1987 SI 1987 No 1806, art 5 (2)).

Persons who are treated as making these supplies in the UK are required to account for output tax on the margin of their standard rated supplies. However, no VAT is due in respect of zero-rated transport facilities provided within a package or relating to timeshare accommodation located outside the European Community. The recovery of input tax incurred by tour operators on the purchase of margin scheme supplies is restricted in full. Furthermore, the calculation of output tax due by such persons is most complex. Specific advice should be taken by tour operators.

## 4 Supply must be by a taxable person

It must also be noted that before VAT is chargeable on a taxable supply of goods or services, the supply itself must be made by 'a taxable person'. A 'taxable person' is 'a person who makes or intends to make taxable supplies for which he is, or is required to be, registered (VATA 1983, s 2). A 'person' (this includes a sole proprietor, partnership, limited company, club, association or charity) making or intending to make a taxable supply of goods or services in the course or furtherance of a business is required to be registered for VAT if his taxable turnover, or prospective turnover, exceeds, or is expected to exceed, certain prescribed limits (referred to later in this chapter). A timeshare developer therefore will normally fall within the scope of VAT whereas an individual reselling a timeshare unit will not as a rule come within its scope, as the resale is unlikely to have taken place 'in the course or furtherance of a business'.

The VATA 1983, s 47 provides that the term 'business' includes any trade, profession or vocation. In determining whether a business exists for VAT purposes the existence of an intention to make a profit is irrelevant (*Commissioners* v *Morrison's Academy Boarding Houses Association* [1977] SLT 197). In this case a company's affairs were so managed that neither a profit nor a loss would accrue, but it was held that the company was liable to account for VAT on the value of its supplies. The activities which the company carried on concerned the making of taxable supplies to consumers for a consideration and thus the company was carrying on a 'business'. The fact that the company did not intend to make a profit did not alter the fact that taxable supplies were being made. It must also be noted that it is the person (as already defined) who is required to register for VAT purposes, not the business which is being carried on. Where a person operates several dissimilar businesses all of the business activities must therefore be covered by one registration (*Commissioners* v *Glassborow* [1975] QB 465).

The position may be summarised, in simple terms, by saying that value added tax is chargeable on any supply of goods or services made in the UK where it is a taxable supply made by a taxable person in the course or furtherance of any business carried on by him (VATA 1983, s 2 (1)).

## Further provisions of VATA 1983

Section 47 of VATA 1983 provides that (subject to certain exceptions relating to political, philanthropic and related activities, not pertinent to the scope of this book) the following are deemed to be the carrying on of a 'business':

1 The provision by a club, association or organisation (for subscription or other consideration) of the facilities or advantages available to its members; and
2 The admission, for a consideration, of persons to any premises. (See the *Eric Taylor Testimonial Match Committee* v *The Commissioners* [1975] VATTR 8 VAT Tribunal).

The duty to furnish returns and to do anything which is required to be done by a club, association or organisation managed by its members or a committee of its members is the joint and several liability of:

1 every member holding office as President, Chairman, Treasurer, Secretary or any similar office; or in default of any thereof;
2 every member holding office as a member of a committee; or in default thereof;
3 every member.

These provisions should be noted and borne in mind by any timeshare owner who accepts an office and the necessity of requiring a tax indemnity should be considered.

It will be seen therefore that, *prima facie*, the trustee, club and leasehold arrangements all fall within the VAT net. The arguments in practice have turned on whether instead of being treated as standard rated supplies, the sales of timeshares are exempted from VAT or whether such sales could be zero-rated. VATA 1983, Sched 6, Group 1 provides that there shall be exempted from value added tax: 'The grant of any interest in or right over land or of any licence to occupy land, other than:' There then follows a number of exceptions, most of which relate to non-residential buildings, but two of the exceptions are as follows:

(c)   the provision in an hotel, inn, boarding house or similar establishment of sleeping accommodation or of accommodation in rooms which are provided in conjunction with sleeping accommodation or for the purpose of a supply of catering;
(d)   the provision of holiday accommodation in a house, flat, caravan, houseboat or tent;

Most timesharing schemes involve the provision of holiday accommodation. Attempts to argue that the section refers to the transient supply of accommodation and not the sale of timeshare interests has not met with any success (*American Real Estate (Scotland) Limited* v *The Commissioners of Customs & Excise* [1980] VATTR 88).

## Zero-rating

Item 1 of Group 8 of Sched 5 of the VATA 1983, however, provides that there shall be zero-rating in respect of:

the grant by a person constructing a building—
(a)   designed as a dwelling or a number of dwellings; or
(b)   intended for use solely for a relevant residential purpose or a relevant charitable purpose;
of a major interest in, or in any part of, the building or its site.

VATA 1983, s 48 (1) defines 'major interest' as including the fee simple or a tenancy for a term certain exceeding 21 years (in Scotland, the estate or interest of the proprietor of the dominium utile or, in the case of land not held on feudal tenure, the estate or interest of the owner, or the lessee's interest under a lease for a period exceeding 21 years).

Note 7 to this group, effective from 1 April 1989, excludes from zero-rating the supply of a qualifying major interest granted under terms by which the grantee is not entitled to reside in the building, or part thereof, throughout the year. This removes any possibility that supplies of timeshare accommodation may qualify for zero-rating. Prior to this date, a timesharing lease for one week per year for a period of 80 years was held not to be the grant of a major interest in land (*Cottage Holiday Associates Limited* v *Customs & Excise Commissioners* [1983] 2 WLR 86). The fact that the total period of occupation envisaged under the lease was 80 weeks, and therefore below the 21 year threshold, was decisive. It would have been interesting to see the tribunal's reaction to a claim that a purchaser of a timeshare on a lease of 999 years, which entitled him to a two week period of occupation each year, was being granted a zero-rated major interest in land under Sched 5, Group 8, Item 1 of the VATA 1983. It appears that such an argument had a good chance of prevailing up to the legislative change effective from 1 April 1989.

Consequently, club membership timeshare schemes involving the grant of a licence even where the property is held by a trustee for the benefit of the timeshare holders, amount to the standard rated provision of holiday accommodation and not to a zero-rated supply as the grant of a major interest in land (*American Real Estate (Scotland) Limited* v *The Commissioners*, above). However, the provisions of VATA 1983, Sched 4, para 9 should be borne in mind. Para 9 reads as follows:

9 (1) This paragraph applies where a supply of services consists in the provision of accommodation falling within paragraph (c) of item 1 of Group 1 in Schedule 6 to this Act and:

   that provision is made to an individual for a period exceeding four weeks; and
   (a) throughout that period the accommodation is provided for the use of the individual either alone or together with one or more other persons who occupy the accommodation with him otherwise than at their own expense
   (b) (whether incurred directly or indirectly).

(2) Where this paragraph applies:—
   (a) the value of so much of the supply as is in excess of four weeks shall be taken to be reduced to such part thereof as is attributable to facilities other than the right to occupy the accommodation; and
   (b) that part shall be taken to be not less than 20%.

The object of the provision was to ensure that hoteliers with long-term residents were put in a similar position to landlords providing rented accommodation; the draftsmen had clearly not contemplated timesharing at the time the section was drafted. In practice, in the case of long-term occupancy, the Commissioners seem to require the standard rate of 15 per cent to be charged in the first four weeks, and thereafter will in most cases accept that 80 per cent of the charge for the next ensuing weeks is in respect of the right to occupy the accommodation—and that therefore VAT at the standard rate would only apply to the remaining 20 per cent value of the supply for those ensuing weeks.

So far, at least, no developer has yet had the courage to test this theory. The section refers only to 'accommodation in a hotel, inn, boarding house or similar establishment'. Customs appear to hold the view that timeshare transactions fall outside this category. It could be argued that the term hotel should be given a quite wide definition (see Chapter 2 and *Mayflower Cambridge Limited* v *Secretary of State for the Environment*, above). Although the point was not argued in *American Real Estate (Scotland) Ltd* v *The Commissioners* [1980 VATTR 88] there would appear to be a case for suggesting that the section applies to most timesharing developments.

### VAT and plc timesharing plans

The final type of arrangement to be considered in relation to VAT is the plc timesharing plan, that is where the timeshares are represented by shares in a public company. At first sight these supplies would appear to fall within VATA 1983, Sched 6, Group 5, Item 6 which exempts 'the issue, transfer or receipt of, or any dealing with any security or secondary security being: (a) shares, stock, bonds, notes (other than promissory notes), debentures, debenture stock or shares in an oil royalty; or ...).'

Consequently, supplies of shares in a plc timesharing arrangement are *prima facie* exempt from VAT. In informal discussions, however, Customs & Excise have indicated that they would seek to draw a distinction between the price paid for the underlying value of the shares and the value of the services provided by the corporation to the shareholders, ie for the use of the corporate property. Their argument appears to be that one must look at what, as a matter of 'substance and reality', was the true nature of the goods or services provided in return for the payment received (see *Customs & Excise Commissioners* v *Automobile Association* [1974] 1 All ER 1257; *Barton* v *Customs & Excise Commissioners* [1974] 1 WLR 1447; [1974] 1 All ER 1257; [1974] 3 All ER 337, DC). In *British Railways Board* v *Customs & Excise Commissioners* [1977] WLR 588 a student paid £1.50 plus 15p VAT for a card which entitled her to a right to travel half-fare for the next six months. The supply of transport by BR is zero-rated (VATA 1983, Sched 5, Group 10, Item 4). It was held that the £1.50 paid for the card was to be regarded as part payment in advance for the supply of transport and hence was zero-rated. The question as to what in substance and as a matter of fact a payment is made for depends 'upon the legal effect of the transaction considered in relation to the words of the statute: and that is a question of law' (per Lord Denning MR at page 591). Consequently, the state of mind of the parties is irrelevant. Lord

Denning commented on the *Automobile Association Case* (above) and *Barton v Customs & Excise Commissioners* (above) where the club members' subscription entitled them to several publications (zero-rated) as well as services, and went on to say (at page 592):

> The proper question is: "What is the consideration for the payment of the subscription?" The answer in the case of these associations is: It is the supply of the literature and other benefits. Insofar as literature is supplied, it is zero-rated. Insofar as other benefits are supplied, they are liable to pay Value Added Tax. Apportionment is necessary to decide how much to each.

In the case of a plc timesharing arrangement Customs & Excise are likely to argue that in reality what is being supplied is (at least in part) holiday accommodation, and to that extent the transaction is chargeable as falling within VATA 1983, Sched 6, Group 1, Item 1(d). It might be possible to counter-argue that the security, ie the share in the plc, has a substantial separate value as a security and to the extent of that value would be exempt. It would appear that the exercise of valuing each share without the appurtenant right to occupation of the holiday accommodation would have to be gone through, and this is likely to require some negotiation with the Commissioners. As predicted in an earlier edition of this book, Customs & Excise has now succeeded in establishing that the sale of shares in a plc timesharing plan is a taxable supply (see *Court Barton plc* v *Customs & Excise Commissioners* VATTR 1985 Lon/83/243).

## VAT registration

VATA 1983, Sched 1, para 1, as amended by subsequent Finance Acts, exempts from the requirement to register, and hence to charge, for VAT, a person who makes taxable supplies in the course of business (whether zero-rated or not) which fall below a certain threshold. The Finance Act 1990 increased the thresholds for registration to £25,400 per annum with effect from 20 March 1990. The figure is inclusive of the VAT which should be applicable. As a rule, the developer will therefore fall within the VAT net but the individual reselling a timeshare will usually come within the exemption limit (even in the most unlikely event that he is found to be making a supply in the course of business).

The maintenance or service charge levied by a timeshare organisation in the UK constitutes consideration for a taxable supply in the ordinary way, being a supply of services. The charge is regarded as part of the consideration for the right to occupy the accommodation.

It must be noted that the Isle of Man has adopted a VAT system and UK legislation applying to VAT similarly applies to the Isle of Man under a corresponding Act of Tynwald. The Isle of Man in effect must be regarded as part of the UK for the purposes of VAT.

## Corporation tax

The normal rules of corporation tax will apply to a 'corporation' (as defined) carrying on a timesharing development. Detailed comment as to how the system operates is not within the scope of this book, but it may be helpful to make some comments of special reference to timesharing. The corporate timesharing developer is regarded as obtaining an income from carrying on a trade under the standard provisions of the Income and Corporation Taxes Act 1988 (ICTA 1988). All normal deductions against such income may be claimed (ICTA 1988, s 74). The developer will be able to deduct payroll, consultancy, advertising and financing costs as well as the cost of the development and contributions in respect of unsold units from his receipts from timeshare sales and any other income chargeable to corporation tax.

Corporation tax for the financial year ending 31 March 1991 is charged at the rate of 35 per cent. The rate for small companies' profits is 25 per cent on profits up to £200,000. The corporation tax rate of 35 per cent applies to profits over £1,000,000. Where a company's annual profits are between £200,000 and £1,000,000, the effective tax rate on the total profits is between 25 per cent and 35 per cent as calculated in accordance with a formula set out ICTA 1988, s 13.

### Calculation of profit

The profits of a UK company are calculated by reference to an 'accounting period'. This is normally the period covered by a company's annual accounts apportioned, if necessary, on a time basis between the financial years ending 31 March in which the accounting period falls (ICTA 1988, s 8 (3)). For corporation tax purposes a 'company' is defined as any corporate body or unincorporated association. It should be noted that where an accounting period is less than 12 months, the figures previously mentioned of £1,000,000 and £200,000 are reduced proportionately (ICTA 1988, s 13 (6)). Furthermore these profit thresholds are divisible by one plus the number of 'associated companies' which the company has in an accounting period. A company is an 'associated company' of another if both are under common control or if one of them has control of the other (ICTA 1988, s 416). Dormant companies are excluded but a company may be associated with another even if the association existed for one day only of a mutual accounting period. These provisions must not be overlooked. If a UK timeshare development group consists of several companies (some of which may not even be trading in the timeshare industry) the number of associated companies may considerably reduce the level of profits on which the lowest rate of corporation tax (ie 25 per cent) is payable. Serious consideration should therefore be given by a UK corporate timeshare developer to operating the timeshare development through a separate company which is not associated with other companies within the statutory definition. In this way, the timeshare developer company may make profits of up to £1,000,000 per annum without having to pay the highest rate of corporation tax on all its profits.

A UK corporate timeshare developer, rather than deciding to break away from other companies, may in turn decide to form a 'group'. Companies are 'members of a group of companies' if one is the 75 per cent subsidiary of the other or both are 75 per cent subsidiaries of a third company (ICTA 1988, s 413 (5)). A '75 per cent subsidiary' means a corporate body of which not less than 75 per cent of the ordinary share capital is owned directly or indirectly by another body corporate (ICTA 1988, s 838). The advantages of a group of companies arise from the provisions allowing the timeshare developer to offset trading losses made by one member of the group against profits made by another member of the group. Special rules apply to the apportionment of profits and losses when companies join or leave a group. The rules are technical, and professional taxation advice should always be obtained if such a move is envisaged. The structuring of the ownership of a UK corporate body intending to become involved in the timeshare industry is of major importance. It can also have serious effects on any other companies controlled by the promoters. Good tax planning is advised whenever new companies are set up. Thought should also be given to changing the ownership of existing timeshare development companies.

*Advance corporation tax*
One point to be borne in mind in relation to public company timesharing schemes is the possibility of the public timesharing company being liable to a charge to advance corporation tax. Where a company in the UK makes a 'qualifying distribution' it is liable to pay advance corporation tax to the Collector of Taxes (ICTA 1988, s 14). The rate is currently one third of the distribution. There is the possibility of the Revenue saying there is a charge to tax based on the notional rental income of the timeshare property and it is wise to clear this point with the Revenue at an early stage where it is likely to arise.

*Close companies*
Where close companies are concerned the current legislation will normally be of little effect. It is unlikely that timesharing companies will be 'close investment holding companies', which are denied the benefit of the 'small companies' corporation tax relief and are subject to restrictions in respect of the tax credits on their dividends.

In the case of an incorporated members' club (as opposed to a proprietary club), the maintenance charge itself should not be subject to tax, as has already been noted. If, however, these funds are left on deposit any interest arising therefrom will be liable to corporation tax in the normal way.

**Companies incorporated abroad**

In the context of corporation tax, we have so far dealt only with the taxation of UK resident companies, though the timeshare development itself may be undertaken in the UK or overseas. Consideration should, however, be given to various other overseas matters. The mere fact that a company is incorporated abroad does not necessarily mean that it is not a UK resident company. Further, if an overseas trader has an agent in the UK, this can be relevant in determining the tax situation of that overseas trader. There are three main sets of possibilities. One must determine whether:

1 the non-resident is trading in the UK or with the UK;
2 the non-resident, if trading in the UK, is liable to income tax or corporation tax on its profits. It is frequently overlooked that a non-resident company can be liable to income tax on its UK profits;
3 the taxable profits are assessable on the non-resident direct or in the name of the agent.

Deciding whether a non-resident is trading with the UK or in the UK is a difficult question in a complicated area. Ultimately it is a question of fact to be determined by the Commissioners of the Inland Revenue in respect of each particular case. There is no statutory definition. A company resident outside the UK is not liable to UK corporation tax except on profits arising from a trade carried on in the UK through a branch or agency, or on gains arising from a disposal of assets situated in the UK which relate to that trade (ICTA 1988, ss 6 and 11). A non-resident company may be liable to income tax in respect of income arising from a source in the UK. A company resident in the UK is chargeable to corporation tax on both its UK and overseas profits, whether or not remitted to the UK (ICTA 1988, s 70(1)). It can be seen that it is a matter of importance whether a company is resident in the UK or whether it is non-UK resident.

From 15 March 1988 all UK incorporated companies are automatically UK resident, except that certain UK incorporated companies which were carrying on business before that date and were non-resident until 15 March 1993, or in some cases indefinitely if they became non-resident in accordance with a treasury consent. Prior to 15 March 1988 the sole test of corporate residence was whether or not the central management and control of the company's business was located in the UK. From that date, this test continues alongside the new test relating to UK incorporation such that there is a dual test of corporate residence.

*De Beers Consolidated Mines* v *Howe*
The Inland Revenue's views on this matter are set out in a Statement of Practice SP1/90, dated 9 January 1990 and entitled *Company Residence*, which describes the case law test used by the Inland Revenue as follows:

> The test of company residence is that enunciated by Lord Loreburn in *De Beers Consolidated Mines* v *Howe* [1906] 5 TC 198 at the beginning of this century:
> "A company resides, for the purposes of Income Tax, where its real business is carried on . . . I regard that as the true rule; and the real business is carried on where the central management and control actually abides."

The 'central management and control' test, as set out in *De Beers* has been endorsed by a series of subsequent decisions. In particular, it was described by Lord Radcliffe in the case of *Bullock* v *Unit Construction Company* [1959] 38 TC 712, at page 738:

> as precise and unequivocal as a positive statutory injunction ... I do not know of any other test which has either been substituted for that of central management and control, or has been defined with sufficient precision to be regarded as an acceptable alternative to it. To me ... it seems impossible to read Lord Loreburn's words without seeing that he regarded the formula he was propounding as constituting the test of residence.

Nothing which has happened since has in any way altered this basic principle: under current UK case law a company is regarded as resident for tax purposes where central management and control is to be found.

It will be noted that the *De Beers* tax case, which is now over 80 years old, has established the important principle that the residence of a company may be determined by the place 'where the central management and control actually abides'. The Inland Revenue's comments in their Statement of Practice under the heading 'place of central management and control' are therefore all-important, and they are quoted in full:

> In determining whether or not an individual company is resident in the UK it thus becomes necessary to locate its place of "central management and control". The case law concept of central management and control is, in broad terms, directed at the highest level of control of the business of a company. It is to be distinguished from the place where the main operations of a business are to be found, though those two places may often coincide. Moreover the exercise of control does not necessarily demand any minimum standard of active involvement: it may, in appropriate circumstances, be exercised tacitly through passive oversight.

*Other case law*

Successive decided cases have emphasised that the place of central management and control is wholly a question of fact. For example, Lord Radcliffe in *Bullock* v *Unit Construction Company* (above) said that 'the question where control and management abide must be treated as one of fact or "actuality" (page 741)'. It follows that factors which together are decisive in one instance may individually carry little weight in another. Nevertheless the decided cases do give some pointers. In particular a series of decisions has attached importance to the place where the company's board of directors meet. There are very many cases in which the board meets in the same country as that in which the business operations take place and central management and control is clearly located in that one place. In other cases central management and control may be exercised by directors in one country though the actual business operations may, perhaps under the immediate management of local directors, take place elsewhere.

The location of board meetings, although important, is not necessarily conclusive. Lord Radcliffe in *Bullock* v *Unit Construction Company* (above) pointed out (page 738) that the site of the meetings of the directors' board had not been chosen as 'the test' of company residence. In some cases, for example, central management and control is exercised by a single individual, for example when a chairman or managing director exercises power formally conferred by the company's articles so that the other board members are little more than cyphers; or by reason of a dominant shareholder. In those cases the residence of the company is where the controlling individual exercises his powers.

In general the place of directors' meetings is significant only in so far as those meetings constitute the medium through which central management and control is exercised. If, for example, the directors of a company were engaged together actively in the UK in the complete running of a business which was wholly in the UK merely because the directors held formal board meetings outside the UK, the company would not thereby be deemed to be resident outside the UK. While it is possible to identify extreme situations in which central management and control plainly is, or is not, exercised by directors in formal meetings, the conclusion in any case is wholly one of fact depending on the relative weight to be given to various factors. Any attempt to lay down rigid guidelines would only be misleading.

### Inland Revenue approach

Generally, where doubts arise about a particular company's residence status the Inland Revenue adopt the following approach:

1 They first try to ascertain whether the directors of the company in fact exercise central management and control.
2 If so, they seek to determine where the directors exercise the central management and control (which is not necessarily where they meet).
3 In cases where the directors do not exercise central management and control of the company, they then look to establish where and by whom it is exercised.

SP1/90 concludes:

In outlining factors relevant to the application of the case law test, this statement assumes that they exist for genuine commercial reasons. Where, however, as may happen, it appears that a major objective underlying the existence of certain factors is the obtaining of tax benefits from residence or non-residence, the Revenue examines the facts particularly closely in order to see whether there has been an attempt to create the appearance of central management and control in a particular place without the reality.

The test examined in this statement is not always easy to apply in present day circumstances. The last relevant case was decided over 20 years ago, and there have been many developments in communications since then which in particular may enable a company to be controlled from a place far distant from where the day-to-day management is carried on. As the statement makes clear, while the general principle has been laid down by the Courts, its application must depend on the precise facts.

The foregoing quotations from the Inland Revenue's Statement of Practice should be examined seriously by any timeshare developer who believes that merely because his company was incorporated outside the UK, the company is not resident for UK tax purposes.

*Where do trading operations take place?*
One must also consider whether in substance the trading operations giving rise to profits take place in the UK or abroad. If those operations take place in the UK then the company is trading in the UK and if they take place abroad then the company is trading with the UK. Two main situations can be distinguished:

1 If the contracts for the goods or services are made in the UK, then invariably, even if all the services are performed abroad, the non-resident is trading in the UK;
2 Where the contract is made abroad one has to look at what is actually done in the UK. If what is done in the UK in substance produced the profit or part of the profit, a non-resident is still regarded as trading in the UK even where the contract was made abroad.

When dealing with the timeshares in an overseas property, it is considered that provided the contracts relating to the sales of timeshares are all concluded abroad, an overseas company would find it easier to establish that it was not trading in the UK.

Quite clearly, the less that is done in the UK the better, if non-resident status is to be achieved. If a central administrative office is needed in the UK, it is essential to make sure that the office does not have authority to conclude contracts and does not in fact conclude contracts in the UK. When contracts are concluded abroad, it is preferable to ensure that the contracts go direct from the non-resident to the UK purchaser, rather than via the administrative office. A copy of the correspondence can be sent to the UK office for information only. There is no reason however, why advertising cannot be carried on in the UK. In this connection the words of Lord Herschell in the case of *Grainger and Son* v *Gough* [1896] 3 TC 311, 462 (HL)) are relevant:

I do not think ... that the solicitation of custom in this country by a foreign merchant would in all cases amount to an exercise by him of his trade "within" this country. The learned Counsel shrank from maintaining that if, for example, he sought custom only by sending circulars to persons residing here or advertising in a British newspaper, he could on that account be said, within the meaning of the statute, to be exercising his trade in this country. They would argue circumstances that he had appointed agents in this country who regularly solicited and received orders and transmitted them to (the principal). If in each case the other circumstances are the same, the contract of sale being made abroad and the delivery taking place there, I find myself quite unable to see how the mode in which orders are solicited and obtained, whether by an agent or by circulars or by advertisements, can make the difference and cause the trade in the one case to be exercised, and in the other case not to be exercised, within this country.

Finally, it should be noted that a company which is not resident in the UK but which trades in the UK through a branch or agency is liable to corporation tax on chargeable profits from the branch or agency. Where a timeshare project includes any overseas implications it must, in conclusion, be stressed that serious consideration needs to be given to the question of its resident or non-resident status.

## Capital gains tax, income tax and inheritance tax

These taxes are more likely to affect the purchaser than the developer, as the developer may well be a corporation and therefore liable to corporation tax rather than income tax. Further, as we have seen, the developer will be treated as carrying on a trade in land and his profits will therefore be taxed as trading profits under Schedule D, Case 1.

## Capital gains tax

Where the purchaser is concerned, the sale of his timeshare constitutes a disposal of a chargeable assets and he is therefore liable to capital gains tax on the consequent 'gain'. For individuals, capital gains tax is charged as if the gain were the highest part of their income. A company which acquires the timeshare for its own purposes (as opposed to a company trading in the timeshare industry) is liable to corporation tax on any capital gains at the same rate as applies to income. Individuals are exempt from capital gains tax on the first £5,000 of their annual gains (for 1990/91—see Finance Act 1990, s 64). The gains taxable in any year are the total amount of chargeable gains arising in the tax year of assessment, after deducting capital losses for the year and any unrelieved capital losses brought forward from earlier years. Therefore a timeshare purchaser considering disposing of his timeshare may offset against any gain arising on the disposal, a capital loss incurred in the same tax year or any earlier year insofar as it has not already been relieved.

### Other considerations

In calculating the capital gain on the sale of a timeshare three further considerations need to be examined

### 1 Bentley v Pike

Following the decision in *Bentley* v *Pike* [1981] STC 360, it is clear that where an overseas timeshare has been sold, the original cost and the proceeds realised (if the transaction was not in sterling) must be converted at the exchange rate prevailing at the date of acquisition and disposal. If a disposal takes place overseas and the proceeds are left overseas and not brought back to the UK until some months later, the actual amount eventually remitted to the UK in sterling, is irrelevant. The capital gain will be based on the exchange rate applicable on the actual date of disposal and must be calculated in sterling.

*2 Indexation provisions*

The indexation provisions introduced by the Finance Act 1982 and extended by the provisions of the Finance Act 1985 allow for the cost of a timeshare to be notionally increased in line with the Retail Price Index over the period of ownership (or since March 1982 if the timeshare was purchased prior to then). The taxpayer may claim to calculate the indexation allowance due by reference to the market value of the timeshare as at 31 March 1982, rather than by its cost. Such a claim must be made within two years of the end of the year of assessment in which the disposal took place. It appears that, once made, such an election is irrevocable. Put simply, if a timeshare purchase was made prior to March 1982 and its value as at that date was greater than its cost price, an election should be made to have the indexation allowance calculated by reference to its March 1982 value.

*3 The 50 years rule*

The capital gains tax treatment on a disposal of a timeshare will depend on whether there is less than 50 years left unexpired when the disposal takes place. If there is less than 50 years, the timeshare is treated as a wasting asset for capital gains tax purposes and the total cost of the timeshare is not allowable as a deduction. Instead the original cost is to be amortised, using the special leasehold depreciation table provided in the Capital Gains Tax Act 1979, Sched 3. The subsequent amortised cost will then be an allowable deduction. If the timeshare has more than 50 years unexpired on the date of disposal there is no need to apply the depreciation tables and the original cost will be deductible.

## Inheritance tax

A resale of the purchaser's timeshare on an arm's length basis and for market value should not give rise to a charge to inheritance tax. Inheritance tax (formerly capital transfer tax) was introduced by the Finance Act 1975 and is charged on gifts made after 26 March 1974 and on transfers on death occurring on or after 13 March 1975 (when it replaced estate duty). The tax is chargeable on transfers made by individuals domiciled in the UK irrespective of where the assets themselves are situated. Thus a UK-domiciled individual should be aware that his timeshare asset will form part of his estate on death for inheritance tax purposes even though the timeshare may relate to overseas property.

From 18 March 1986 the scope of inheritance tax on lifetime transfers has been very substantially reduced. For lifetime transfers occurring on or after that date, inheritance tax will only apply if:

1 the transferor does not survive for at least seven years after the transfer;
2 the transferor reserves an interest in the property; or
3 with respect to certain transfers into trust.

There is a nil rate tax band which is applicable both to transfers on death and cumulative lifetime gifts. Currently this nil rate tax band covers the first £128,000 of chargeable transfers in any ten-year period. Chargeable transfers are accumulated over a ten-year period. Once ten years have passed since the making of a gift, the value of that gift is eliminated from the cumulative total carried forward for inheritance tax purposes.

## Income tax

Apart from a possible income tax charge on benefits-in-kind, examined below, the only income tax considerations likely to arise in connection with purchasing a timeshare will be where income is derived from the sub-letting of the timeshare itself. Income received by a UK resident in respect of sub-letting is normally chargeable to income tax whether or not the asset is situated in the UK. If the asset is situated overseas it is immaterial whether or not the income is remitted to the UK, unless the recipient of the income is domiciled outside the UK or, being a Commonwealth citizen or a citizen of the Republic of Ireland, is not ordinarily resident in the UK (ICTA 1988, s 65 (4)).

Assuming the income from sub-letting a timeshare is taxable, presumably under Schedule D, Case VI, various expenses are allowable against such income. Unless there is in fact income from letting, no interest relief will be available in respect of a loan used to acquire the timeshare in the first place. ICTA 1988, s 354 grants interest relief on a loan used to acquire property, provided the property concerned is let at a commercial rent for more than 26 weeks in any period of 52 weeks comprising the time at which the interest is payable and falling wholly or partly within the year of assessment.

Furthermore, when the property is not so let it must either be available for letting, under repair, or being used as a main residence of the borrower. It is therefore virtually impossible for a timeshare purchaser to satisfy these requirements, bearing in mind that he may only have a right to occupy the relevant property for a few weeks in each year. Even where a timeshare purchaser has acquired the right to occupy a property for, say 30 weeks a year, he would not only have to let his timeshare for more than 26 weeks but would also have to prove that during the remaining weeks' occupation the timeshare constituted his main residence. Therefore, it can be seen that if no sub-letting takes place no interest relief will be granted on a loan used to acquire the timeshare. An argument by a taxpayer that the timeshare was his private residence should not even be contemplated. It is possible that some concessionary relief in practice be given by the Inland Revenue in respect of that part of the interest paid that an be shown to be attributable to the period of letting. Other expenses wholly relating to the period of letting rank as deductible expenses so that, for instance, a management charge paid for a period during which a timeshare is let is allowable against letting income.

## Corporate Purchasers

There is a growing tendency in the UK for companies to purchase timeshare for the use of directors and employees. The purchase price of the timeshare itself is not considered deductible in computing the trading profits of the purchasing company, because the purchase price is a capital, rather than a revenue, payment. Invariably, single lump sums are paid to acquire an identifiable asset, comparable to a lease acquired on a payment of a premium. However, management charges are considered to be a deductible expense from trading profits as they are incurred in maintaining an asset belonging to the company. Interest paid by a company on a loan used to acquire a timeshare would also appear to be an allowable deduction provided that the interest is paid to a UK bank or other qualifying lender as the interest constitutes a charge on profits under (ICTA 1988, s 338).

Resale of a timeshare acquired by a company may give rise to a capital gain chargeable to corporation tax (see above under the heading capital gains tax). The same capital gains tax rules apply to companies and individuals in respect of gains arising from a sale of timeshare rights, except that companies are not entitled to the annual gains exemption of £5,000. A company can offset a trading loss incurred in an accounting period against a chargeable gain arising during the same accounting period (ICTA 1988, s 393 (2)). A trading loss incurred in an accounting period may be carried back and offset against unrelieved chargeable gains arising in the previous accounting period (ICTA 1988, s 393 (2) and (3)). There is therefore some measure of relief available against any gains arising from the resale of a timeshare by a corporate purchaser. It must be remembered that if a corporate purchaser were to sell timeshare rights regularly, the Inland Revenue might consider the company to be trading, ie in the buying and selling of timeshares, so that any profits would be chargeable to corporation tax (under Schedule D, Case 1, rather than as chargeable gains).

Once the corporate purchaser has acquired the timeshare its actual use will determine the tax consequences. If the corporate purchaser makes the timeshare available for use by a director or an employee, a charge to tax on the director or employee will arise under Schedule E under the provisions charging benefits in kind. Tax will be charged under ICTA 1988, s 145 and the charge will be based on the gross rateable value of the property. Section 145 (2) states that the assessable benefit is: 'The rent which would have been payable for the period if the premises had been let to him at an annual rate equal to the annual value as ascertained under Section 837 of the Taxes Act.'

For UK timeshares it would therefore appear that the charge for one week is

1/52 of the gross rateable value, although a deduction can be made in respect of any rent paid by the director or employee to the company. Directors and higher-paid employees using the timeshares would be liable to a further charge under ICTA 1988, s 154 in respect of their use of furniture, utensils, etc and of the consumption of electricity, heating or gas and of the provision for them of cleaning and other services. The amount of the charge in respect of the use of furniture and utensils, is calculated by reference to the 'annual value of the use of' those assets under ICTA 1988, s 156 (5) (b). That part of the management charge which is attributable to those assets will not, it is thought, be taken into account again under sub-s (5) (b). It is considered that notwithstanding the definition of 'annual value' in s 156 (5) (b) no addition should be made by reference to 20 per cent of the market values of those assets, otherwise an element of double taxation will arise. It is considered that s 156 (5) and (6) should be read subject to sub-s (2), so that, while the cost of the benefit 'in any year' is calculated by reference to annual value, only so much of that annual value as corresponds to the fraction of the year during which the accommodation is available for use by the employee will be brought into account when taxing that employee.

The position will however be different in the case of foreign timeshares. Although ICTA 1988, s 145 still determines the position, the annual rent cannot be treated as the gross rateable value, as rateable value figures will not usually be available for overseas property. In such circumstances it is considered that the director or employee will be treated as being in receipt of emoluments equal in amount to the rent which would have been payable in the period of the director's or employee's use if the property had been let at an annual rental under a lease at arm's length.

It must also be mentioned that if a director or employee has the use of a timeshare period the cost of which exceeds £75,000 then it is considered that, in addition to the director or employee being chargeable to income tax under s 145 (as mentioned above), there may also be an additional Schedule E charge under s 146. This additional charge is based on the excess of the cost of the timeshare period, used by the director or employee, over £75,000. The excess over £75,000 is multiplied by the 'official rate' of interest in force at the beginning of the tax year (which at the time of writing is 16.5 per cent). The resultant figure is then treated as an additional charge under Schedule E. The additional charge under s 146 may well prove to be a very penal one and should be avoided, simply by ensuring that no director or employee is provided with the use of timeshare periods costing more than £75,000.

It must be remembered that it seems to make no difference in the context of the benefit-in-kind taxing provisions whether the director or employee did or did not actually use the timeshare periods available. The fact that the periods were available for use is enough for them to be caught by these taxing provisions.

However, the reader must not forget that the tax charge on the director or employee in respect of a benefit-in-kind will generally be less than the value of the benefit itself. Also, if the recipient of the benefit had bought the timeshare period himself, the cost price would have to be found from his net income after tax and it is clear that any tax payable on the benefit will be cheaper than the cost of the timeshare periods themselves.

The possible taxation implications are far reaching. Although this chapter highlights the many areas which need to be examined, the reader, whether he be a developer or a purchaser, is advised to seek individual professional taxation advice.

## Rates and community charge ('poll tax')

The earliest timeshare properties both in Scotland and in England and Wales were valued as dwelling houses for rating purposes. This came as no surprise to anyone; the properties were regarded by developers and purchasers alike as multi-ownership holiday homes (the term 'timeshare' did not arrive in the UK until much later) so it was logical that they should be rated in the same way as holiday homes in single ownership. This method of valuation continued in England and Wales until 1 April 1990 when Community Charge (or poll tax) was introduced for domestic properties, and at the same time there was a general revaluation of all non-domestic properties.

In the terms of the Local Government Finance Act 1988, which introduced the Community Charge in England and Wales, it is provided that second homes are to be subject to what is known as the Standard Community Charge, which is between one and two times the ordinary Personal Community Charge, depending upon the discretion of the charging authority. Most charging authorities in practice have fixed their Standard Community Charge at twice the ordinary Personal Community Charge. However the Department of the Environment, which has been responsible for overseeing the introduction of the Community Charge in England and Wales, has taken the view that timeshare properties in England and Wales should instead be subject to commercial rates, and in the revaluation which has taken place at 1 April 1990, all timeshare properties have been valued as commercial properties with resultant high increases in their rateable values.

The TDA had made representations to the Department of the Environment against the decision to treat timeshare properties as being subject to commercial rates rather than the Standard Community Charge, and there were indications from that correspondence to date that the Department may have made the mistake of treating timeshare properties as being owned and occupied by the developer rather than by the timeshare owners. At the time of writing, the primary objective is seen as ensuring that the Department is fully aware of the true legal identity of the owners and occupiers of the properties.

Events have taken a similar course in Scotland, which has separate legislation on Rates and Community Charge, but there the timing has been slightly different. In the early 1980s at least one regional assessor in Scotland sought to value timeshare properties as commercial for rating purposes. This was resisted and a compromise was reached whereby neither side made any admissions in regard to the arguments of the other. However in Scotland there was a general revaluation of all properties, both domestic and commercial, at 1 April 1985, and in that revaluation all timeshare properties were valued as commercial with resulting high increases in rateable values. All these revaluations were appealed against but because of the enormous number of appeals in relation to all types of property the first hearing on a timeshare property did not take place until November 1989. This related to the Forest Hills Trossachs Club and came before the Lands Tribunal for Scotland which decided in favour of the assessor. The decision has been appealed to the Lands Valuation Appeal Court for Scotland from which there can be no further appeal but at the time of writing a date has not been fixed for the appeal hearing.

In between times the Community Charge was introduced into Scotland. It commenced on 1 April 1989, a year earlier than in England and Wales. The view taken by the Scottish Office at the time was that timeshare properties should be subject to commercial rates rather than Standard Community Charge. From telephone conversations with officials in the Scottish Office it appears that this view was to a large extent based on advice from the Scottish assessors to the effect that timeshare properties were valued for rating purposes as commercial rather than domestic properties. This decision cannot be analysed properly until the result of the Forest Hills appeal to the Lands Valuation Appeal Court is known, but even if that appeal were to decide that the properties in question should be treated as commercial for the purposes of the 1985 revaluation in Scotland, it is still possible that they should be treated as 'domestic subjects' for the purposes of the Abolition of Domestic Rates etc (Scotland) Act 1987 and thus as subject to the Standard Community Charge.

Both in Scotland and in England and Wales it may be that for timeshare properties to be treated as subject to Community Charge some alterations would be required to the Statutory Regulations and Orders made under the Acts which introduced the Community Charge in each jurisdiction, but if the existing Regulations and Orders or the Government's interpretation of them proceeded upon a fundamental misunderstanding of the true legal nature of timesharing in the UK, then there is no reason why such changes should not be made.

# Chapter Seven

# Overseas timesharing and conflict of laws

Overseas timesharing may well give rise to problems which involve the application of a body of law known as private international law or conflict of laws. These problems will have to be solved by applying principles governing conflict of law issues, which have of course been developed to take account of problems considerably wider in scope and depth than those of international timesharing. The rules of conflict of laws which have grown up over more than a century, have not been codified to any great extent, nor reduced to statutory form. They are thus found in the common law and, on the whole, present a complex and sometimes confused picture. Nevertheless, certain general rules have been established, rules which should prevent conflict reaching the point of litigation.

## The proper law of the contract

Most substantive matters of international timesharing will be matters of contract law. In English conflict of laws, most matters relating to contract are governed by a flexible rule known as the 'proper law of the contract'. In the leading case of *Mount Albert Borough Council* v *Australasian Temperance and General Mutual Life Assurance* [1938] AC 224, Lord Wright said that this was 'that law which the English or other court is to apply in determining the obligation under a contract'. Indeed, it is possible for the parties to agree that different contractual issues should be governed by different laws, and the circumstances may require different questions to be submitted to different laws. But in any complicated international timesharing problem there will be a primary system of law and this is designated 'the proper law of the contract'.

English law, like most European systems, emphasises that the autonomy of the parties is the most important issue. Accordingly, within limits, the parties are free to choose their own governing law. In English law it has been recognised since at least 1796 that parties may expressly select the law by which their contract is to be governed. In the modern leading case of *Whitworth Street Estates* v *James Miller & Partners* [1970] AC 583, Lord Reid said at page 683:

parties are entitled to agree what is to be the proper law of their contract. There have been from time to time suggestions the parties ought not to be so entitled, but in my view there is no doubt they are entitled to make such an agreement and I see no good reason why, subject though it may be to some limitations, they should not be so entitled.

There are, however, some limitations to this freedom of the parties. In the leading case of *Vita Food Products* v *Unus Shipping Co* [1939] AC 277, Lord Wright said: 'It is difficult to see what qualifications are possible, provided that there is no reason for avoiding the choice on the ground of public policy'. It has been accepted since this case that autonomy is accordingly qualified by:

1  *bona fides*,
2  legality, and
3  public policy.

All of these matters are, however, uncertain; it is not clear what any of them means and certainly no English court has refused to accept an express choice of English law for the proper law of the contract in any reported case to date. It should be added that as yet the *Vita Food* provision has not been applied directly to an express choice of a foreign law but there is clear consensus amongst the writers that the principle which applies to the express choice of English law should also apply to the express choice of some other system of law.

In addition to expressly choosing a proper law of the contract it is also possible for parties to incorporate into their contract foreign law. This is a different technique from the express choice of foreign law and has significantly different effects. Parties may, having already created a contract which is valid, incorporate within it the provisions of a foreign law other than the proper law as a term or terms of the contract. The incorporation may be effected in a number of ways; by the verbatim transcription of the relevant provisions, or by a general statement that the rights and liabilities of the parties shall in certain respects be subject to the chosen law. For example, parties to a contract may expressly provide that their duties as to performance should be governed by, for example, French or Swiss law. Whether a particular term incorporated in this way is valid and effective is a matter for the proper law to determine. It has long been established that this right of incorporation may be freely exercised (*Dobell* v *SS Rossmore* [1895] 2 QB 408). Once incorporated, the foreign statute becomes a set of contractual terms and has to be construed as such.

They remain constant and so are unaffected by any change in the relevant foreign law incorporated. This contrasts with the express choice of foreign law. It is well established that the proper law must be a living law and must be applied as it exists when the contract is to be performed and not as it was when the contract was made.

If the parties do not expressly choose a proper law, one may be implied.

Dicey and Morris, in the leading English text on private international law, state as follows:

When the intention of the parties to a contract with regard to the law governing the contract is not expressed in words then their intention is to be inferred from the terms and nature of the contract and from the general circumstances of the case and such inferred intention determines the proper law of the contract.

In *Jacobs* v *Credit Lyonnais* [1884] 12 QBD 589, Bowen L J put it thus: 'the only certain guide is to be found in applying sound ideas of business, convenience and sense to the language of the contract itself, with a view to discovering from it the true intention of the parties'. In some cases an implied common intention can be found and in others it is impossible to find one. Judges may even disagree in the same case as to whether an implied common intention can be found. Thus, for example in *Amin Rasheed Shipping Corp* v *Kuwait Insurance* [1983] 2 All ER 884 the judges differed as to whether it was possible to imply a common intention. What factors fall to be considered to elicit a common intention? One common factor relied on is that the parties have agreed that any disputes will be submitted to the courts of, or arbitration in, a particular country. Such a choice of jurisdiction clause is a powerful implication that the law of that country should be applied on the principle *qui elegit judicem elegit ius*, but 'strong as the implication may be it can be rebutted as other implications of intention can be rebutted. It is not a positive rule of law which is independent of the intentions of the parties' (per Lord Diplock in *Compagnie Tunisienne De Navigation* v *Compagnie Armement Maritime* [1971] AC 573). Apart from the choice of jurisdiction or arbitration clauses there are other factors that the courts may consider; eg the form of a contract, its language and its style. Even so, because a form of contract has to be interpreted in accordance with English rules, this does not mean that the proper law must now necessarily be English. The residence, the nationality of the parties, the nature, location and the subject matter of the contract, a connection with a preceding transaction—all these are matters which have been relied upon in decided cases to lead the court to the conclusion that the parties do have an intention, although they have not expressed it. There is also a general maxim: *ut res magis valeat quam pereat*. This means that there is a general presumption in favour of that law which is most effective. So the fact that a contract or term of the contract is valid under one possible law and void under another possible law is evidence, though it is not conclusive evidence, that the parties intended their contract or that term of their contract to be governed by the law by which the contract or term was valid (*Coast Lines* v *Hudig & Veder* [1972] 2 QB 34, 50–51).

Where there is no choice of proper law the position is as stated by Dicey and Morris: 'Although the intention of the parties to a contract with regard to the law governing it is not expressed and cannot be inferred from the circumstances, the contract is governed by the system of law with which the transaction has its closest and most real connection'. In *Mount Albert Borough*

*Council* v *Australasian Assurance Society* (*above*) Lord Wright said: 'the court has to impute an intention in order to determine for the parties what is the proper law which as just and reasonable persons they ought or would have intended if they had thought about the question when they made the contract'. In *The Assunzione* [1954] P 150 at 176 Singleton LJ said:

> one must look at all the circumstances and seek to find what just and reasonable persons ought to have intended if they had thought about the matter at the time when they made the contract. If they thought that they were likely to have a dispute, I hope it may be said that just and reasonable persons would like the dispute determined in the most convenient way and in accordance with business efficacy.

The court will take into account many factors, including the place of contracting, the place of performance, the places of residence or business of the parties, the nature and the subject matter of the contract, and any other matter which is relevant to the particular circumstances of the case. There are no firm rules. One difficult matter, which has only arisen in litigation in the last few years, concerns the question as to what is the time for determining the proper law for contract where there is no express choice and none can be implied. This question arose in *Armar Shipping* v *Caisse Algerienne* [1981] 1 All ER 498. The Court of Appeal held that there must be a proper law of the contract, a governing law, at the time of making that contract. If, says Lord Justice Megaw:

> ... at the time when the contract was made, the question remained undecided whether the general adjustment was to be made in England or the United States or in Germany or somewhere else, then the fact that it was subsequently decided by one of the parties that the venue should be England cannot be a relevant factor in the ascertainment of the proper law at an earlier date. As a matter of legal logic, I find insuperable difficulty in seeing by what system of law you are to decide what, if any, is the legal effect for an event which occurs when the contract is already in existence with no proper law, but instead with a floating non-law.

Although there are no decided cases expressly on the point, it is likely that one of the facts which would weigh heavily with the court forced to impute a proper law in the case of international timesharing would be the place where the property was located. It would be wrong, however, to say that there was a presumption in favour of *lex situs* in contracts of this nature even though they clearly relate to immovable property. Indeed it would be fair to say that presumptions, though once fashionable, are now out of fashion and largely rejected.

## Interests in land

A dispute involving a contract relating to land needs to be distinguished from one involving the question of title to the land. In the case of a dispute relating to title to land, a court will always apply the *lex situs*. In countries other than those in which the English system of land law has been applied, an English settlement of land therein will be ignored in so far as it exceeds the limitations locally sanctioned (*Earl Nelson* v *Lord Bridport* (1843) 49 ER 1039; *Re Miller* [1940] 1 Ch 511).

As a general rule, English courts have no jurisdiction to entertain an action for the determination of the title to, or rights to possession of, any immovable property situated outside England. There are, however, two exceptions to the exclusion of such jurisdiction. If a court has jurisdiction *in personam* over a defendant, the court has jurisdiction to entertain an action against him in respect of a contract or an equity affecting foreign land. The jurisdiction is substantially confined to cases in which there is either a contract or an equity between the parties. For example, an action by a lessor to recover rent due under a lease of foreign land, or an action by a vendor or purchaser of foreign land for specific performance of a contract of sale, or by a vendor or purchaser of equities for a declaration that the defendant holds foreign land as a trustee, or an action to redeem or foreclose a foreign mortgage, are all cases which an English court would consider itself to have jurisdiction and competence to hear. Whether a personal obligation is such as to affect the defendant's conscience is a matter to be determined solely by English law.

An English court will not refuse to exercise its equitable jurisdiction merely because the right is not recognised by the *lex situs*. However, performance of the English decree must be possible in the country where the property is situated. The futility of ordering a defendant to perform some act which would be forbidden by the *lex situs* is obvious. Furthermore, there must be privity of obligation between the parties. The personal obligation which is the basis of the English court's jurisdiction must have run from the defendant to the plaintiff. For example, if A agrees to sell foreign land to B, there is no doubt that A incurs personal liability that is justiciable in England but if A sells the foreign land to X there is no personal equity which B can enforce against X. A good example of this is the leading case of *Deschamps* v *Miller* [1908] 1 Ch 856. In addition, the jurisdiction cannot be exercised if the court cannot effectively supervise the execution of its decree, so that it will not order the sale of foreign land at the instance of a mortgagee. On the other hand, it will order the foreclosure of a mortgage, decree specific performance of a contract to sell foreign land and make an order for the inspection of foreign land. There are decided cases which hold that each of these actions is permissible. It should be added that there is no English authority on the converse question, namely whether the decree of a foreign court purporting to operate *in personam* on the parties to some contract or equity affecting English land can be enforced in England.

Reference has been made to movables and immovables. It should be pointed out that these are the concepts that are used within the international framework of the conflict of laws. The distinction is close to, but differs from, that between realty and personalty. For example, a leaseholder's estate is an immovable for the purposes of conflict of laws despite the fact that we would regard it under English domestic law as personalty. Timesharing schemes can be construed either as interests in immovables, for example under the condominium scheme in Spain, or as interests in movables, for example shares in a corporation owning property in Spain. We cannot state for certain in what way an English court would regard them.

## Mandatory clauses

At this point we must return once again to the question of the proper law. As was indicated earlier, the amount of statutory intervention in the area of contract law in relation to international matters is very limited. However, in 1977 the United Kingdom Parliament passed the Unfair Contract Terms Act and this may have some considerable importance in the area of timesharing.

The Act imposes severe restrictions on the validity of exemption clauses in many kinds of contract, and restates the control of exemption clauses earlier found in the Supply of Goods (Implied Terms) Act 1973 in contracts for the supply or sale of goods that were originally imposed by the 1973 Act. The Act provides in s 27(2) that the Act has effect notwithstanding any contractual term purporting to apply the law of some country outside the United Kingdom if:

1 the term appears to be imported wholly or mainly for the purpose of enabling the party imposing it to evade the application of the Act, or
2 in the making of the contract one of the parties 'dealt as consumer' and was habitually resident in the United Kingdom, and the essential steps necessary for the making of the contract were taken there.

It should, however, be noted that the Act does not as such strike down the choice of a foreign law; it leaves it to take effect, subject to the controls of the Act. However, the criterion in s 27(2)(a) may well lead an English court to strike down the foreign choice of law clause in its entirety. The question as to what happens then is the subject of some considerable and continuing academic controversy. The controls of the English Act must be applied, but it does not necessarily follow that English law is now the proper law of the contract. For example, parties choose French law because they think that the English law is undesirable as a result of the controls contained in the 1977 Act. The question that then arises is: what if the chosen foreign law has tighter controls on exemption clauses than the 1977 Act? For example, the foreign law declares them void in circumstances where they clearly satisfy the test of reasonableness contained in the 1977 Act. It is argued in the leading text on this subject (Cheshire and North, *Private International Law*, page 470) that the exemption clause can be relied on because s 27(2) states: 'this Act has effect notwithstanding the choice of foreign law' and the Act in effect says that a clause which is reasonable can be relied on.

## Procedure and substance

A further distinction to which attention must be given is that between procedural and substantive law. Where English law is the *lex fori* (law of the place where the action is tried), procedural law of the proper law will be ignored and the procedural laws of England will be applied instead. This is not as straightforward as it seems, because English law will sometimes classify as a procedural rule what a foreign system of law regards as a substantive rule, and as a result ignore it. This frequently happened in the past when English courts were somewhat insular in their approach to foreign rules of law. It is to be hoped that such an approach would no longer be taken today and indeed from recent case law there is evidence that a new international approach is taking root.

Section 2 of the Law of Property (Miscellaneous Provisions) Act 1989 has repealed s 40 of the Law of Property Act 1925. The latter provided that a contract for the sale or disposition of an interest in land was unenforceable by action unless evidenced by a memorandum in writing which contained certain specified information. Section 2 of the 1989 Act provides that a sale or other disposition of an interest in land can only be made in writing and only by incorporating the terms which the parties have expressly agreed in one document or, when contracts are exchanged, in each of them. Thus, it will no longer be possible to have an oral contract evidenced in writing. Note the use of the word 'expressly' indicates that implied terms (eg a term for vacant possession) need not be included. A major difference between s 40 and the new s 2 is that s 40 was a rule of evidence: non-compliance meant that the contract was unenforceable by action. Non-compliance with the new provision will mean that the contract will be invalid; in effect there will be no contract.

The new English rule is thus one of substance, whereas it was possible to interpret the previous English rule as one of procedure. This should mean that we will only apply the rule in s 2 to timeshare contracts the proper law of which is English law. Accordingly, any rule of a foreign system of law providing for the contract to be in writing or for registration or the like is likely to be interpreted by an English court as a rule of substance. It will therefore be upheld by an English court in any situation where the foreign legal system is the proper law of that timeshare contract. There is little danger that we will in the future interpret such provisions as rules of procedure and thus ignore them in English courts.

## Foreign law as fact

It must be appreciated that where the *lex fori* is English and the *lex causae*, that is the law which governs the question, is that of another country, the law of that other country must be established as a matter of fact. As far as English courts are concerned, foreign law is a matter of fact so that it has to be pleaded and proved to the satisfaction of the judge.

If a party wishes to rely on a foreign law, he must plead it as he would any other fact on which he relies. If he does not do so, a court will decide a case containing a foreign element as though it were a purely English domestic case. It will ignore the foreign law totally. English courts, of course, take judicial notice of the law of England but they do not take judicial notice of any foreign law. Thus, foreign law must be proved in each case unless it is admitted, even if there is a previous English decision in which the same rule of foreign law has been before the court and satisfactorily proved. Indeed, it has happened that different decisions have been reached in different cases on different evidence of the same rule of foreign law. If there is already a decision of foreign courts on that matter of foreign law, weight will obviously be given to it, but in a case of conflict the English courts will decide the issue even where it remains unresolved in the country concerned. For example, in the case *Re Duke of Wellington* [1947] Ch 506, an English Chancery judge found himself faced with deciding a difficult matter of Spanish law that had never been decided in a Spanish court.

Who can prove foreign law? The question as to who is a sufficient expert has not been satisfactorily resolved by English courts. Although, no doubt, the court has a discretion, the general principle has been that no person is a competent witness unless he is a practising lawyer in the particular legal system in question, or unless he occupies a position or follows a calling in which he must necessarily acquire a practical working knowledge of the foreign system of law. In other words, practical experience has been held to be sufficient qualification (the *Sussex peerage Case* (1844) 11 C 1 & Fin 85).

A view has been taken by the courts that academic knowledge of foreign law does not qualify a person to be an expert witness. However, it has now been made clear (see the Civil Evidence Act 1972, s 4(1)) that evidence as to foreign law may be given by a person who is qualified to do so on account of his knowledge and experience 'irrespective of whether he has acted or is entitled to act as a legal practitioner there (see also Practice Direction Foreign Law (affidavit) [1972] 1 WLR 1433)

The evidence of the expert may exceptionally be given by affidavit but it is usually given orally and he is accordingly open to cross-examination. Although he must state his opinion as being based on his knowledge or practical experience of the foreign law, he is allowed to refer to foreign codes, decisions or treatises for the purpose of refreshing his memory, but in such an event the court is free to examine the law or the passage in the book in question to arrive at its own view as to its correct meaning. Even if the expert evidence is not contradicted by other expert testimony, the court may examine the text to reach its own conclusions on the foreign law, although generally there will be a reluctance to reject such testimony, unless the court takes the view that the evidence as to the foreign law is absurd. If there is a conflict of testimony between the expert witnesses on either side, the court must place its own interpretation on the foreign law in the light of all the evidence given. In all cases the court has both the duty and the right to examine and criticise the evidence.

Only recently, has the question of proof of foreign law in an appellate court been examined. This was done by Simon P who said:

> foreign law is, it is true, regarded in English Courts as a question of fact; and appellate courts are slow to interfere with trial courts on questions of fact; but that only applies with particular force as regards the assessment of relative veracity and the judgment of matters of degree. Where the inference of fact depends on the consideration of written material, an appellate court is at no particular disadvantage compared to a trial court and would regard itself as freer to review the decision of the trial court [Parkasho v *Singh [1968] P 233 at 254*].

### Renvoi

If an English court decides that the *lex causae* is a foreign system of law, another question may arise, that is, what is meant by that system of law. If an English court should decide in a timesharing case that the Spanish law applies, does this mean Spanish internal law (the law that would be applied by a Spanish court to a purely domestic case) or is this reference to be taken to include also the Spanish rules of private international law?

This raises the rather academic problem of *renvoi*. There are a number of views as to what an English judge should do. It is probably the English law (but it is by no means certain) that an English judge should take the law of Spain to mean the law which a Spanish judge would administer if he were seised of the matter. This is sometimes known as 'the foreign court theory of *renvoi*' or the English doctrine of *renvoi*. It is extremely unlikely that such a problem will arise in practice but those concerned with international timesharing should be aware of the possibility. The English *renvoi* doctrine has been applied mainly in the area of wills and intestate succession, and although it has been applied in one or two other areas as well it does seem unlikely that it will intrude into this area. Certainly, it has been held that the principal of *renvoi* has no place at all in the field of contract (*Re United Railways of Havana and Regla Warehouses Ltd* [1960] Ch 52, 96–97).

## Jurisdiction

The law on jurisdiction varies from country to country. It would be impossible in a book of this nature to state what the jurisdiction rules of the courts of other countries are. Needless to say, should it be thought necessary to pursue an action in a foreign country, it would be advisable to seek legal advice from a person in that country familiar with those rules.

As far as the law relating to jurisdiction of the English court is concerned, this has been complicated by the Civil Jurisdiction and Judgments Act 1982. This came into operation in England at the beginning of 1987 and affects questions of jurisdiction where they are concerned with 'contracting states' of the EEC which have ratified and put into operation the Brussels Convention of 1968. Our rules of jurisdiction therefore differ in accordance with whether the defendant is 'domiciled' in a contracting state or not. If he is not domiciled in a contracting state the rules of jurisdiction which apply are those of the old common law. It is therefore necessary to describe both the EEC rules of jurisdiction and the common law rules of jurisdiction. It should be added that the description of the EEC rules of jurisdiction applies to other EEC countries as well. So where a timesharing agreement concerns property in any EEC country the jurisdiction rules of the Brussels Convention apply equally in that country as they do in England. The Brussels Convention applies 'in civil and commercial matters whatever the nature of the court or tribunal'. There is no definition in the Convention of 'civil and commercial matters'. There can, however, be no doubt that matters relating to timeshare agreements will come within the scope of the Convention.

Where the defendant is domiciled in a contracting state the bases of jurisdiction under the Convention will apply and not the traditional rules of jurisdiction of the forum. Where the defendant is not domiciled in a contracting state, in general the traditional rules of jurisdiction of the forum will apply (in our case the rules of the common law).

Where the defendant is domiciled in a contracting state, art 2 in s 1 contains the most important basis of jurisdiction under the Convention, namely that a defendant domiciled in a contracting state is subject to the jurisdiction of the courts of that state. If the defendant is to be sued in the courts of a contracting state other than that of his domicile, art 3 provides this can only be done by virtue of the bases of jurisdiction set out in ss 2 to 6. In the case of the United Kingdom it is specifically provided in art 3 that, against such a defendant, jurisdiction can no longer be founded on the presence of the defendant in the forum. It is also implicit from that article that service out of the jurisdiction under RSC Ord 11 cannot be used. Article 3 does not refer to the domicile of the plaintiff. It accordingly follows that, for example, someone who is domiciled in one of the states of the USA, although not domiciled in a contracting state, would have to use the bases of jurisdiction under the Convention if he wished to sue in a contracting state a defendant who was so domiciled.

Articles 2 and 3 require courts to decide whether a defendant is domiciled in a contracting state. Section 41 of the 1982 Act contains a provision for determining when an individual is domiciled in one of the countries of the United Kingdom. It provides that he is so domiciled, if and only if:

1 he is resident in the United Kingdom; and
2 the nature and circumstances of his residence indicate that he has a substantial connection with the United Kingdom.

The latter requirement is presumed to be fulfilled if the individual has been resident in the United Kingdom or in a part of it for the last three months or more, unless the contrary is proved (see s 41 (6)). If the individual is not domiciled in the United Kingdom it then has to be seen whether he is domiciled in another contracting state. There are no provisions for determining this in the 1982 Act because art 52 of the Brussels Convention provides that, in order to determine whether a party is domiciled in another contracting state, the courts are to apply the law of that state.

As regards companies, s 42 (3) determines when a corporation has a seat in the United Kingdom. It states that it has a seat, if and only if:

1 it was incorporated in the United Kingdom and has its registered office, or some other official address there; or
2 its central management and control is exercised in the United Kingdom.

Section 42 (6) determines whether a corporation has its seat in a state other than the United Kingdom; this could be in a contracting or in a non-contracting state. It uses the same criteria as those in s 42 (3). The fact that s 42 (6) applies to determine whether a corporation has its seat in a contracting state follows from art 53 of the Brussels Convention, which requires contracting states to apply their own concept of a seat even to the question of whether a company has its seat in another contracting state. There is a problem with this: eg England may regard the company as having its seat in France, whereas France, which may have different concepts of a seat, may regard the company as having its seat in England. To solve this problem s 42(7) provides that a corporation has a seat in a state other than the United Kingdom if it is shown that the courts of that state would not regard it as having its seat there.

Where the defendant is not domiciled in a contracting state, art 4 states that the jurisdiction of courts of each contracting state shall, subject to the provisions of art 16, be determined by the law of that state. So, if an Englishman wishes to sue a New York domicilliary in England, he will have to do so under the traditional common law rules of jurisdiction and not under the rules provided by the Brussels Convention. It should be added that the Brussels Convention rules are more generous to the plaintiff, so that it may be easier to sue in this country an individual or a corporation which has entered into a timeshare agreement with an English person than to sue an equivalent person or corporation from a contracting state.

Article 4 requires the courts of contracting states to ascertain when a defendant is not domiciled in a contracting state. Once it has been decided that an individual defendant is not domiciled in the United Kingdom (that is under our definition), and is not domiciled in another contracting state (under the definition of domicile applied in that state), it follows that the defendant must be domiciled in a non-contracting state.

There is one exception to the rule that national bases of jurisdiction apply where the defendant is not domiciled in the contracting state. This is contained in art 16 of the Brussels Convention which gives exclusive jurisdiction in certain circumstances regardless of the defendant's domicile. As one of the grounds of exclusive jurisdiction relates to immovables this has an important impact upon the area with which we are concerned. Discussions of exclusive jurisdiction must however be postponed until the primary basis of jurisdiction is considered. It is to this that we will now turn.

Article 2 provides that 'a person domiciled in a contracting state shall, whatever their nationality, be sued in the courts of that state'. The Convention thus adopts the principle that, in general, persons should be sued in the courts of the contracting state where they are domiciled. Their physical presence in a contracting state is not sufficient to ground jurisdiction: the defendant must be domiciled there. This is in striking contrast to the traditional rules of the common law, under which physical presence in England even for a short period of time is enough to ground jurisdiction.

Although art 2 uses the words 'shall ... be sued', these words should not be taken too literally, for there are other bases of jurisdiction and these show that the defendant may, indeed in some circumstances must, be sued in the courts of a contracting state other than that of his domicile. Indeed, where *Lis pendens* applies, a court of a contracting state is required to decline jurisdiction, even where that court is the court of the contracting state in which the defendant is domiciled. To ascertain whether the defendant is domiciled in the contracting state under art 2, reference must be made to ss 41 and 42 of the Civil Jurisdiction and Judgments Act 1982 and art 52 of the Brussels Convention. These have been discussed in some detail already. Where the contracting state in which the defendant is domiciled is the United Kingdom, the modified convention will apply to allocate jurisdiction between the courts of England, Scotland and Northern Ireland. This allocation of jurisdiction will be considered further later in this chapter.

**Special jurisdiction**

In addition to the basic ground of jurisdiction based on domicile, the Brussels Convention provides for special jurisdiction. Trial is permitted in the courts of a contracting state other than the one in which the defendant is domiciled when the grounds for special jurisdiction are satisfied. Article 5 provides that a person domiciled in the contracting state may be sued in another contracting state in seven specified situations. The ones which are of relevance to a time share agreement are:

1 Article 5(1) in matters relating to contract, in the courts for the place of performance of the obligation in question.
2 Article 5(3) in matters relating to tort, delict or quasi-delict in the courts of the place where the harmful event occurred.
3 Article 5(5) as regards a dispute arising out of the operations of a branch,

agency or other establishment, in the courts for the place in which the branch, agency or other establishment is situated.

As far as art 5(1) is concerned 'the obligation in question', whose place of performance is in question, is the obligation which is the basis of the action. Jurisdiction is conferred on the place of the performance of the obligation in question and not on the place of the breach. If there is a breach in England of contractual obligations to be performed elsewhere, eg by express or implied repudiation, then, under the Convention, jurisdiction will be conferred on the place of performance and not, by this reason alone, on England as the place of the breach. This jurisdiction may be invoked even if the existence of a contract is denied by the defendant. In *Effer spA* v *Kantner* [1982] ECR 8025 the dispositive holding was that the plaintiff may invoke this jurisdiction 'even when the existence of a contract on which the claim is based is in dispute between the parties'.

Article 5(3) states that the court has jurisdiction, in matters relating to tort etc, where the damage occurred or where the event which gave rise to the damage occurred. The provision is unlikely to be invoked within the context of overseas timesharing unless as an incident of that timesharing a tort such as negligence or nuisance is committed. Should that occur the place of damage connotes the place where the physical damage is done or the recoverable economic loss is actually suffered. It is pointed out by Dicey and Morris that even though in a sense a plaintiff may suffer economic loss at the place of his business, that is not of itself sufficient to confer jurisdiction on that place, the reason being that otherwise the place of business of the plaintiff would become another basis of jurisdiction almost automatically.

### Branches, agencies and other establishments

Further, the court has jurisdiction to determine a dispute arising out of the operations of a branch, agency or other establishment, if the branch, agency or other establishment is situated in that contracting state. Two important questions arise here. First, what is a 'branch, agency or other establishment'? Secondly, what disputes arise out of its operations? As to the first question it is clear that the concept must be interpreted by Convention standards and not by purely national concepts (see *Somafer SA* v *Saar-Ferngas SG* [1978] ECR 2183, 2190). The obvious case of a branch bearing the same business name and staffed by employees of the main undertaking requires no further comment, but more difficult cases arise. The European Court has declined to extend the concept of a branch to distributors or sales agents for goods of foreign companies. In *De Bloos Sprl* v *Bouyer SA* [1976] ECT 1497 the court held that one of the essential characteristics of a branch or agency was the fact of being subject to the direction and control of the parent body, that the concept of establishment 'should be interpreted in a similar way', and that an exclusive distributor was therefore not a branch of the manufacturer. In *Clanckaert*

*Willems PVA Trost* [1981] ECT 819, the same court held that an independent commercial agent who merely negotiated business was free to arrange his own work and decide what proportion of his time to devote to the interest of the undertaking which he had agreed to represent, and was representing at the same time several firms competing in the same manufacturing marketing sector, and who merely transmitted orders to the parent undertaking without being involved in the terms of their execution, did not have the character of a branch, agency or other establishment within the meaning of art 5(5). In addition to the element of direction and control, the European Court has required the element of the 'appearance of permanency'. In the *Somafer* case, the court held that the concept of branch, agency or other establishment implies a place of business which has the appearance of permanency, such as the extension of a parent body, so that third parties do not have to deal directly with such parent body but may transact business at the place of business constituting the extension.

To deal with the second question, ie whether the claim arises out of the operations of a branch, agency or other establishment, in the *Somafer* case the European Court explained that the concept of operation included matters relating to rights and contractual or non-contractual obligations concerning the actual management of the agency, branch or other establishment itself, such as those relating to the situation of its building or the local engagement of staff to work there. It also included those relating to undertakings which had been entered into at the place of business in the name of the parent body and which had to be performed and the contracting state where the place of business was established and also actions concerning torts arising from the activities in which it was engaged. The wording of art 5(5) suggests that jurisdiction is granted to the courts of the place of the branch in relation to any contract entered into by it. However, the European Court seems to have limited the jurisdiction to cases where performance is to take place in the same state as the branch. It will be seen that as a result of this interpretation, in matters of contract, art 5(5) adds little to art 5(1) (the provisions of contract). It is also thought to be the case that an essential element of the agency, branch or other establishment's jurisdiction is that it is designed for the benefit of third parties, and not for intra-company or intra-firm disputes. All this of course means that where the timeshare agreement has been entered into by a branch, agency or other establishment in a country outside England, the courts of that country will have jurisidiction in addition to the jurisdiction conferred by other provisions.

Thus we have seen that the primary ground of jurisdiction is domicile and there are other grounds for jurisdiction under art 5. However, in relation to timeshare agreements, the most important basis of jurisdiction to note may well be that in art 16(1) of the 1968 Convention, which provides that in proceedings which have as their object rights *in rem* in, or tenancies of, immovable property the courts of the contracting state in which the property is situated have exclusive jurisdiction. But what are immovables, or what actions have as their object rights *in rem* in, or tenancies of, immovable property will not be a matter for national law, but must be determined by interpretation of a uniform convention concept. This is at the very least implicit in two important decisions of the European Court namely those in *Sanders* v *Van Der Putte* where it was held that a dispute over the lease of a florist business in a shop did not come within art 16(10), because the principal aim of the lease was the operation of a business and secondly in *Rösler* v *Rottwinkel*, where it was held that short term holiday lettings were tenancies for the purposes of art 16(1). The latter decision is of great importance to the timeshare agreement.

On one level, it is obvious what comes within the scope of art 16(1). Actions involving title or possession clearly do so. On the other hand, it is equally clear that an action for damage caused to an immovable piece of property does not. Similarly, art 16(1) is not, it is thought, concerned with an action relating to the purely contractual aspects of a property transaction, eg an action for the payment of damages for failure to complete a purchase or even an action for specific perfomance of a contract relating to an immovable. Thus, if two Englishmen agree on the sale of a house in Italy from one to the other, one could sue the other in England for failure to complete or for an order requiring completion. However, if an order for possession were required it seems that they would have to go to the Italian courts. Article 16(1) was developed by Continental lawyers with civilian concepts in mind and the question of equitable rights does not easily fit into the scheme developed by those who framed the Brussels Convention. But in all probability equitable interests which are equivalent to property rights in immovables will fall within art 16(1) if the action which is being brought is designed to ensure that they are upheld as against the whole world.

### *Rösler* v *Rottwinkel*

As far as timeshare agreements are concerned, it is the case of *Rösler* v *Rottwinkel* [1986] QB 33 that must particularly concern us. In that case, it was held that art 16(1) applied to all disputes concerning the respective obligations of lessor and tenant under the lease, and in particular those which related to the existence and interpretation of leases, their duration, return of possession of the property to the lessor, the repair of damage caused by the tenant, the recovery of rent and other charges such as charges for water, gas and electricity. However, art 16(1) does not apply to disputes which are only indirectly connected with those of the property, such as claims for damages for loss of the enjoyment of a holiday and travel costs (matters which were in dispute in *Rösler* v *Rottwinkel*).

In *Rösler* v *Rottwinkel* it was also held that art 16(1) applies to short-term holiday lettings. This might lead to the conclusion the the the article will also apply to disputes which relate to timeshare agreements relating to immovable property. However, whether it does or not must depend on the nature of the arrangements. For example, if the arrangement can be conceptualised as amounting to co-ownership it will certainly fall within art 16(1): if on the other hand the arrangement amounts to no more than a company share scheme then it will probably not come within art 16(1). Support for this view is to be found in the standard text by Dicey and Morris (page 921).

### States outside the Brussels Convention

The dicussion of jurisdiction has thus far confined itself to cases where the parties involved are domiciled in one of the contracting states of the Brussels Convention. Most timeshare agreements, at least those within Europe, will now come under the umbrella of the Brussels Convention. But a timeshare agreement relating to a country outside the contracting states, eg relating to a property in Malta, Yugoslavia or Florida, will still fall under the traditional common law rules of jurisdiction. It is to these that we must now turn.

At common law, English courts are competent to try an action in three situations:

1  where there has been service of a writ upon a defendant present within the jurisdiction;
2  where the defendant has submitted to the English court's jurisdiction;
3  where there has been service of a writ out of the jurisdiction under RSC Ord 11.

Each of these will be looked at in turn.

As far as individuals are concerned, a writ may be served upon a defendant who is present within the jurisdiction. Even the transient presence of a person in England is sufficient to render him amenable to the jurisdiction of the English courts. If a writ is served, for example, on an American during a visit of a few hours to London, an action may then be brought against him in his absence, notwithstanding that the matter is totally unrelated to anything that has occurred in England. This has to be read subject to the now developed doctrine of *forum non conveniens.*

In the case of a partnership, the plaintiff may serve the writ on an individual partner who is present in England, or on the partnership firm under RSC Ord 81. This permits the writ to be served upon one or more of the partners, or upon the person having control of the business at the principal place of business in England, or by posting to the firm at the principal place of business within the jurisdiction, whether or not any member of the firm is out of the jurdisdiction. Therefore, service which is effected upon the person in control of the English business operates as a valid service upon all the partners, even in the case of a foreign firm all the members of which are resident abroad. Further, service upon upon one partner present in England is effective against the co-partners out of the jurisdiction. As far as companies are concerned, a company registered in England under the Companies Act 1985 (CA 1985), is regarded as present in England and service of a writ can be effected by sending it to the registered office of a company (CA 1985, s 725(1)). The position of a foreign company or corporation is less simple. To facilitate the service of a writ upon an 'oversea company', CA 1985, s 691 obliges it to file with the Registrar of Companies the names and addresses of some one or more persons authorised to accept service of process on its behalf. So long as the name of such person remains on the file, service of a writ upon him renders the company subject to the jurisdiction of a court, even though the company no longer carries on business in England.

If, however, a company fails to register with the obligations laid down by CA 1985, or if the persons on the register cease to be resident here or die, or they refuse to accept service, the writ may be served on the company by leaving it at or posting it to 'any place or business established by the company in Great Britain' (CA 1985, s 695). In *The Theodohos* [1977] 2 Lloyd's Rep 428, it was held that the procedure for service laid down in what is now the CA 1985 was the only procedure available here in the case of an oversea company with a place of business here. The CA 1985 procedure can only be used when the foreign company is 'an oversea company'. According to CA 1985, s 744 an 'oversea company' means:

1 a company incorporated elsewhere than in Great Britain which, after the commencement of this Act established a place of business in Great Britain, and
2 a company so incorporated which has before that commencement, established a place of business and continues to have an established place of business in Great Britain at that commencement.

It may therefore become important to decide whether a foreign company has established a place of business in Great Britain. What this means has become clearer from some recent decisions. In *South India Shipping Corp Ltd* v *Export-Import Bank of Korea* [1985] 1 WLR 585, the defendant bank was incorporated in Korea and conducted its main business in that country. It rented an office in London for the purpose of gathering and providing information as well as liaising with other banks. The plaintiff company, which was incorporated in India, sent a writ by post to the defendant bank's office in London. It was held by the Court of Appeal that the writ had been duly served upon the defendant, since the defendant had established a place of business here under the Companies Act 1985. The question of when a foreign company established a place of business in Great Britain was treated by the Court of Appeal as being simply one of fact. It refused to establish any rigid list of requirements which would have to be satisfied in the individual case. In the *South India* case the defendant had both premises and staff in Great Britain and carried on activities here. The fact that these activities did not consitute a substantial part of the foreign company's business and were merely incidental to the defendant's main objects was not considered an objection to their satisfying the test. Ackner LJ said that: 'Parliament has placed no express qualification or limitation on the words "a place of business" and there seems no good reason why we should employ one' ([1985] 1 WLR 585 at 591]). More recently the question arose in the case of (*Re Oriel Ltd* [1986] 1 WLR 180). In this case the Court of Appeal held that a specific location for the business is necessary in order to come within the terms of CA 1985. The establishment of a place of business is said to imply some degree of continuity and a location recognisable to outsiders. It is said that the owning of the land in England was not enough and that it had to be shown that the business of the foreign company was habitually carried on from that land. It was also held that the private residence of one of the directors of the company can consitute a place of business if the company transacts business from it.

In addition to jurisdiction based upon presence, English courts have jurisdiction where the defendant submits to the jurisdiction. This can be done in a number of ways. For example, by entry of unconditional appearance or instruction of a solicitor to accept service on one's behalf or commencement of an action as plaintiff, giving the court jurisdiction over a counter-claim. The person who appears merely to contest the jurisdiction of the court does not submit to it (see *Re Dulles' Settlement* [1951] Ch 842). Submission may also be inferred from the terms of the contract. This is, of course, common with international contracts, including overseas timesharing contracts. Parties cannot, by submission, confer jurisdiction on the court to entertain proceedings beyond its authority. For example, the defendant cannot submit to jurisdiction when what is at issue is title to foreign land (see Civil Jurisdiction and Judgments Act 1982, s 30).

### RSC Order 11

The English court will also have jurisdiction where leave to serve the defendant out of the jurisdiction has been obtained under Order 11 of the Rules of the Supreme Court (RSC). This specifies a number of grounds upon which service out of the jurisdiction may be allowed in the discretion of the court. Comment here will focus upon the main grounds which permit service of a writ upon the defendant who is abroad, the emphasis being on those cases which are most likely to affect someone concerned with a timeshare agreement.

There are a number of grounds under Ord 11 which deal with contract. They are:

1  Where 'the claim is brought to enforce, rescind, dissolve, annul or otherwise affect a contract, or to recover damages or to obtain other relief in respect of the breach of a contract in the following cases:
    (a)  where the contract 'was made within the jurisdiction';
    (b)  where the contract 'was made by or through an agent trading or residing within the jurisdiction on behalf of the principal trading or residing out of the jurisdiction',

(c) where the contract 'is by its terms, or by implication, governed by English law'. This means that the proper law of the contract is English law. It should be stressed that the courts have shown considerable reluctance to exercise their discretion under this head, to the extent that it has been held that the plaintiff has a particularly heavy burden to discharge when showing good reasons justifying service out of the jurisdiction; and

(d) where the contract 'contains a term to the effect that the High Court shall have jurisdiction to hear and determine any action in respect of the contract'.

2 Where 'claim is brought in respect of a breach committed within the jurisdiction of a contract made within or out of the jurisdiction, and irrespective of the fact, if such be the case, that the breach was preceded or accompanied by the breach committed out of the jurisdiction that rendered impossible the performance of so much of the contract as ought to have been performed within the jursidiction.'

There is also a clause of RSC Ord 11 dealing with tort. This allows for service out of the jurisdiction when 'the claim is founded on a tort and the damage was sustained or resulted from an act committed within the jurisdiction'.

There are also grounds of RSC Ord 11 dealing with property. These are:

1 Where 'the whole subject matter of the transaction is land situate within the jurisdiction (with or without rents or profits) or the perpetuation of testimony relating to land so situate'. The most obvious example of this would be an action to recover land (see *Agnew* v *Usher* (1884) 14 QBD 78).

2 When 'the claim is brought to construe, rectify, set aside or enforce an act, deed, will, contract, obligation or liability affecting land situate within the jurisdiction'. It has been held that the rule includes an action against an assignee of a lease for breach of covenant to repair (*Tassell* v *Hallen* [1892] 1 QB 321), to a claim by a tenant of a farm to recover compensation for improvements (*Kaye* v *Sutherland* (1887) 20 QBD 147), and to an action to enforce obligations under a declaration of trust in respect of land which has been sold at the time of the action (*Official Solicitor* v *Stype Investments (Jersey) Ltd* [1983] 1 All ER 629). However, an action for the recovery of rent and an action concerning royalties in respect of the production of oil have both been said to fall outside this particular group (see *Agnew* v *Usher*, as above, and *BHP Petroleum Ltd* v *Oil Basins Ltd* [1985] VR 725).

There is also jurisdiction under Ord 11 where 'the claim is made for a debt secured on immovable property or is made to assert, declare or determine proprietary or possessory rights, or rights of security, in or over movable property, or to obtain authority to dispose of movable property situate within the jurisdiction'. This would cover, for example, a claim for a debt secured on immovable property, an example might be an action for non-payment of a bank loan secured by the mortgage of a house.

It is also possible for the property heading of Ord 11 to be used where 'the claim is bought to execute the trusts of a written instrument, being trusts that ought to be executed according to English law and of which the person to be served with a writ is a trustee, or for any relief or remedy which might be obtained in such action'. It will be noted that there is no need for the property subject to the trust to be situated in England.

## Conclusion

Even if the plaintiff can establish that the defendant comes within one of the grounds under Ord 11, the court will still have to be pursuaded to exercise its jurisdiction. It is now clear that service out of the jurisdiction will only be allowed when England is the most appropriate forum (see *Spiliada Maritime Corp* v *Cansulex Ltd* [1986] 3 WLR 972, 985). In (*Amin Rasheed Corp* v *Kuwait Insurance Co* [1984] AC 50 at p72) Lord Wilberforce said: 'the court must take into account the nature of the dispute, the legal and practical issues involved, such questions as local knowledge, availability of witnesses and their evidence and expense'. It is also necessary to look at the expense and inconvenience to a foreign litigant of attending a trial in England. In addition, the courts have considered the connection that the parties in the cause of action have with this country and with any alternative fora. If English law is the applicable law to the dispute this may of course point to England as being the appropriate forum for the trial. If, on the other hand, trial in England would lead to a multiplicity of proceedings, with concurrent actions, involving the same parties and the same issues, taking place both in England and abroad, this would be a ground for exercising the jurisdiction against allowing service out of the jurisdiction (see *The Abidin Daver* [1984] 1 AC 398).

Where parties have agreed to submit their disputes under a contract to the jurisdiction of a foreign court, an English Court will need very strong reasons to allow one of them to go back on his word and attempt to sue in England.

The courts are not supposed 'to embark upon a comparison of the procedures or methods, or reputation or standing of the courts of one country as compared with those of another' (see the *Amin Rasheed* case per Lord Wilberforce at page 72); however, two considerations will be looked at by the courts. First, there is the question of whether justice will be obtained in a foreign court. If it seems likely that the plaintiff will not receive a fair trial abroad, for political or other reasons, the court may well exercise its discretion in favour of the application for service out of the jurisdiction, even though both parties to the suit are foreigners and even though their rights fall to be determined by foreign law. Second, there is the question of whether the plaintiff will obtain a legitimate personal or juridicial advantage from trial in

England. In the *Spiliada* case Lord Goff said: 'the Court should not be deterred from refusing leave in Order 11 cases simply because the Plaintiff will be deprived of an advantage, such as high damages or a more generous limitation period, provided that the Court is satisfied that substantial justice will be done in the available and appropriate forum abroad'.

# Chapter Eight

# Timesharing in the USA

The legal structure of timeshare offerings in the USA divides into two basic forms, one which conveys a fee interest in real estate to the buyer and the other which conveys a 'right-to-use' the property. This distinction between the two basic forms of timesharing interest was incorporated into the 1979 version of the ALDA-Narello Model Act. That Model Act labelled the two systems of timesharing 'timeshare estates' and 'timeshare licences' and defined them as follows:

1 A timeshare estate means a right to occupy a unit or any of several units during five or more separated time periods over a period of at least five years, including renewal options, coupled with a freehold estate or an estate for years in a timeshare property or a specified portion thereof.
2 A timeshare licence means a right to occupy a unit or any of several units during five or more separated time periods over a period of at least five years, including renewal options, not coupled with a freehold estate or an estate for years.

Each category of timeshare interest has several sub-forms which have been developed or adapted to suit the demands of the marketplace, the requirements of lending institutions, and the rapid emergence of state timeshare laws. The fee or ownership interests obviously call for more complex documentation, bringing with them all the appurtenances of real estate ownership. The right-to-use forms have simpler documents, but have been perceived as providing less protection to purchasers and less security to lenders. Notwithstanding the differing legal structures however, consumer legislation now generally regulates all systems in a similar manner.

## Fee interests

Fee interests have generally three sub-forms: a traditional tenancy-in-common interest, sometimes referred to as time span ownership; interval ownership; and the concept of the estate for years.

### Tenancy-in-common

The tenancy-in-common or time span ownership approach to creating a timesharing structure is the one most commonly employed. Each timeshare purchaser receives an undivided ownership interest in the real property and, by separate documents, the co-owners regulate their mutually exclusive rights to use the property for the time period specified by the timeshare plan.

There are two difficulties associated with this type of timeshare project. As in Europe, a tenancy-in-common is viewed as a temporary state and tenants-in-common have a right to partition—to require that the timeshare property will either be physically divided or, if this is impracticable, that the property be sold and the proceeds divided. In considering this a right of partition, US lawyers have to consider pre-1925 English legislation—An Act for Joint Tenants and Tenants In Common 1539.31 Henry 8 CI and English Common Law (eg *Turner* v *Morgan* [1803] 8 VES 143).

In the early years of US timesharing, this right to partition was considered a nuisance. Occasions on which it may be exercised are not immediately obvious, but nonetheless real. Since 'low-season' weeks are less expensive than 'high-season' weeks, the owner of a low-season week might wish to exercise his right so as to achieve the same share in the proceeds of sale of the timeshare apartment as the owner of a high-season week. If he was not minded to do this, then his creditors might take a different view. Some states find that there is an implied agreement not to partition in a timesharing plan and most plans incorporate an express agreement not to partition, but the enforceability of such implied or express agreements is not entirely clear and the only safe answer is legislative intervention. Such provision is contained in the ALDA/Narello Model Act, art 2–104 which provides: 'No action for partition of a timeshare may be maintained except as permitted by the timeshare instrument or by art 2–105(d)' Article 2–105(d) provides that, *inter alia*, subject to the provisions of the timeshare instrument, the partition will be on the basis of the proportion of market value of each timeshare. The Florida Real Estate Time Sharing Act, s 721.22 provides that no action for partition of any timeshare unit will lie unless otherwise provided in the contract between the seller and the purchaser. Similar legislation exists in most other states.

### Interval ownership

Interval ownership involves the concept that any estate in property is also divisible in time as well and in length, width and height. This concept is analagous to early English concepts of 'springing' and 'shifting' uses relates back to and the Statute of Uses of 1536. Interval ownership, unlike tenancy-in-common, creates in the same deed a legal estate in the land, coupled with a future tenancy-in-common. At the end of the period of the timeshare plan, the owners become tenants-in-common and can either elect to continue as tenants-in-common or renew the timeshare plan or cause the property to be sold and the proceeds distributed. This concept of interval ownership has not received unanimous judicial approval. In a decision of the Barnstaple County Superior Court, Massachusetts, it was held that: 'The inclusion of time as a limiting factor upon the rights ... has no support in the common law or any analogy derived therefrom' and accordingly it was ruled that interval ownership was not a real interest in land under the Massachusetts Condominiums Law (*Joseph B McCabe and Anor* v *Board of Assessors of the town of Provincetown*, Mass SUP CT No 417999 5 August 1983) This decision was upheld by the Massachusetts Appellate Tax Board in an opinion rendered on 4 November 1986. In 1987, a timesharing statute was enacted in the state which specifically enabled timesharing interests. Interestingly, the case resulted in more favourable property tax treatment as the condominiums were eventually assessed as whole units, rather than individual timeshare interests.

### Estate for years

Under the concept of the estate for years, the timeshare buyer receives a lease for a specified period, with a tenancy-in-common interest in remainder. In many ways, therefore, the same effect is achieved as in the interval ownership plan, without the necessity to incorporate the concept of springing and shifting uses.

An anotated precedent for a fee or ownership timesharing plan is incorporated as Appendix B. This timeshare plan represents the 'state of the art' in relation to ownership timeshare plans, and it complies with a definition of a timeshare estate contained in the Florida Real Estate Time Share Act as 'a right to occupy a timeshare unit, coupled with a freehold estate or an estate for years with future interest in a timeshare property or a specified portion thereof'.

# Right-to-use

Right-to-use plans also divide into three main sub forms namely 'vacation lease', 'vacation licence' and 'club membership', the latter dividing further into proprietary and non-profit organisations.

### Vacation leases

In this type of timeshare plan the buyer is granted a discontinuous lease over a specified number of years, usually between 10 and 40 years, after which title reverts to the developer. Such leases constitute a legal interest in land, which is capable of being recorded in the Title Registry. If recorded, the lessee will be given priority in respect of charges or encumbrances registered against the land subsequent to the date of the recording of the vacation lease, but in many timeshare plans the vacation lease will contain a specific prohibition against recording, thus enabling the promoter to use the timeshare property as security for financing the project.

**Vacation licences**

Vacation licences are in many respects similar to non-recordable (ie non-registrable in a land registry) vacation leases. The distinction between vacation licences and vacation leases is much the same as the distinction between licences and leases examined in the context of English law in Chapter 2. Licences are a personal interest and not generally assignable. As was stated in one case: 'A licence is, however, merely a personal privilege to do some particular act or series of acts on land without possessing any estate or interest therein. ... Also, a licence is, ordinarily, revocable at the will of the licensor and is not "assignable" (*Lehman* v *Williamson*, COLO, APP–533 P 2 D 63 (1975). It will be seen at once that vacation licences give very little protection to the licensee in the event of the failure of the licensor.

**Club membership**

Club membership, sometimes known as vacation plan timesharing, may either be similar to the UK proprietary club or alternatively may be organised on a quasi ownership basis, as in the case of a co-operative, which in many ways is similar to an incorporated members' club plan. In the former case, the timeshare buyers are issued with a licence to use the club's facilities for a defined time at the end of which the developer may either renew the membership certificate or sell the membership to another buyer. The co-operative or incorporated members' club type plan, on the other hand, affords its members rather more protection. Usually, the club/co-operative is perpetual and organised on a non-profit making basis. The purchasers will have a right of direction and control of the organisation, and transfer of their rights will, by virtue of the type of system employed, generally be uncomplicated and inexpensive, unlike the position of a purchaser in an ownership plan who will have to comply with conveyancing formalities and registration procedures.

It is also appropriate to mention at this stage the limited partnership timesharing concept. A limited partnership is a novel idea when applied to timesharing. The general partner is the developer, who has a fiduciary relationship with all the timeshare purchasers, who become the limited partners. This system is not without its disadvantages, however. In particular, the limited partners may have no say in the management operation of the timeshare development without running the risk of losing their limited liability status. It is difficult to build adequate consumer safeguards into such a system. It appears to be a widely held view that such limited partnership plans do present too many problems to form a viable basis on which to construct a timesharing plan and during the 1980s this concept has fallen into disuse.

Right-to-use plans came under review by the courts in the Florida case of *Sombrero Reef Club* v *Allman* 18 BR 612–1982. Approximately 200 buyers had acquired right-to-use licences entitling them to the use of club facilities for a period of 30 years on payment of an initial premium and an obligation to pay a maintenance charge during the residue of the 30 year period. Allocation of the timeshare units to members was arranged on a booking system instead of on the basis of a defined specific unit allotted at the outset. The Federal Bankruptcy Law (Chapter 11 USC s 365) permits the rejection of an executory contract by a trustee or debtor in possession and (despite much argument as to the precise nature of the timeshare club members' interest) they were held (because of their continuing obligation to pay maintenance charges) merely to have had an executory contract and accordingly their interest became forfeited without compensation. The case was cited in similar proceedings in other states and has caused grave concern not only to buyers but also to developers, since lenders, in view of the case, were reluctant to grant finance to buyers for such right to use interests and the consequent drop in sales had in turn a 'knock-on' effect in pushing some developers closer to financial difficulties. The case prompted the change in federal bankruptcy law referred to later in this chapter (see page 189).

In the 1970s, right-to-use forms of timesharing plan were perhaps more common because of their relative simplicity, flexibility and (then) lack of exposure to regulation. The development of more sophisticated documentation for fee interests, allowing for greater flexibility of use on the part of the timeshare owner, such as floating time, one day use periods etc, has contributed to the growth of fee projects rather than right-to-use schemes. Today, more than 80 per cent of US timeshare resorts convey a fee interest. The right-to-use forms are still found in hotel projects where conversion to fee interest is difficult or unsuitable.

## State activity

The majority of American states have enacted legislation to protect timeshare purchasers. Such legislation is under continuous review. Although no state has adopted any Model Act in its entirety, many parts of existing and proposed legislation have included concepts extracted from provisions contained in the existing state laws and the Uniform Law Commissioners Model Real Estate Time Sharing Act (URETSA). In addition, a Model Act co-sponsored by the National Time Sharing Council of the American Resort and Residential Development Association (ARRDA) and the National Association of Real Estate Licence Law Officials (Narello) (known as the Alda/Narello Model Act) first appeared in 1977 and was approved as a Uniform Act in 1979. A revised version was published in February 1983 and is much more comprehensive and consumer orientated. Both have been used as resource material for many state laws and regulations.

**The Alda/Narello Model Act 1979**

Since the 1979 version of the Alda/Narello Model Act has been given so much weight by various state legislatures and may serve as a model for legislation in Europe, it is helpful to comment upon its major provisions.

The definitions relating to timeshares contained in the Act have been mentioned previously and it has been noted that the 1979 Act divided all American timeshare plans into one of two categories: ownership plans on the one hand and right-to-use plans on the other.

The Act provided a considerable measure of protection for the timeshare buyers. However, the principle on which it had been drafted was that the buyer had to be given all necessary information to make an informed decision about the purchase, whilst leaving the developer free to limit his liability provided that any such limitations were clearly set out. The developer had to issue an 'offering document' (which is roughly equivalent in its aims to a UK company prospectus) to the buyer at the outset. There was a cooling-off period during which the buyer had the option of rescinding the contract. The Act also covered the assessment and auditing of the maintenance charge payable by each timeshare buyer provided for the monitoring of timeshare project advertising and established the machinery for a state licensing and control system for all timeshare projects.

The 1979 Act established the machinery for a state administration agency and for all timeshare developments to be registered with that agency. It set out the powers and duties of the regulatory authority, covering not only developers within the state, but also sales made or selling operations conducted within the state.

The Act suggested solutions to problems parallel to those encountered by the timesharing industry in Europe.

**The Alda/Narello Model Act 1983**

As mentioned above, the 1979 Model Act, which has been the basis for so much state legislation, was superseded in 1983 by a revised Model Act which contains a number of stricter provisions. The new Act is divided into eleven articles. The revised version appears as Appendix G, so that it is unnecessary to detail the provisions here, but in summary the articles provide as follows:

1   Definitions. It should be noted that the former distinction between 'right-to-use' and 'ownership' plans is absent, and essentially all plans are regulated in the same manner.
2   Sales of timeshares only by licensed real estate brokers. A licence is also required to market a timeshare development, and a copy of this licence must be supplied to each purchaser. In order to obtain the licence the developer must submit to the regulatory authority the plan documentation, a title report, project budget and reports concerning zoning legislation compliance etc.

3   Regulation of the sales documentation, prevention of blanket incumbrances affecting timeshare purchasers, a five day mandatory rescission period and detailed trust and escrow provisions preventing the release of funds until the purchaser's title is protected.

4   Regulation of advertising practices.

5   Warranties to be given by the developer as to the promises made in the sales documentation, and in regard to the standard of building construction etc.

6   An obligation of good faith on the developer and sanctions against any breach of this obligation.

7   Detailed powers for the regulatory authority to intervene and to investigate developers and developments, including a power to ban further operations and suspend real estate brokers from operating.

8/9   Information on exchange schemes.

10   Detailed requirements as to the content of the timeshare documentation and provisions to overcome technical difficulties, eg the right of partition referred to earlier, and to termination of a timeshare plan.

11   Amendment of the operation and management provisions in the earlier Act and certified accounts and budgets to be supplied to all purchasers.

The revised Model Act has been reviewed by a majority of the state legislatures with some of its provisions being adopted in whole or in part. It goes beyond the principle established by the first Model Act that the first thing to do is to have full disclosure, and thereafter the maxim *caveat emptor* applies, since it provides for a number of mandatory procedures and warranties and safeguards which require detailed examination, investigation and supervision by the regulatory authority.

Because of local concerns and political realities, many states have opted not to include provisions from these Model Acts, but have merely drawn from the concepts espoused in the model legislation and rely just as much on the particular state's condominium and land sales acts. The 1980s have provided the timesharing industry with more legislative and regulatory activity than most industries experience over several decades. Almost all legislative and regulatory initiatives have been and should continue to be on a statewide basis for the foreseeable future, although a bill designed to regulate timesharing federally was introduced in Congress during 1982, it was never pursued in subsequent years. However, certain federal laws affect timeshare development and sales, which will be discussed later in this chapter.

Prior to 1983, 10 states had adopted timeshare laws. In 1982, Arizona, Connecticut, and Hawaii enacted substantive laws or amendments addressing timeshare rules. Oregon also tackled the industry by adopting comprehensive administrative rules. By the end of 1990, fully 37 states had enacted specific laws, amendments, or rules to regulate timesharing. Eleven other states continued to regulate timesharing through condominium, securities or land sales statutes. Only Alaska, which regulates timeshares on a case by case basis, and Wyoming, which only applies its real estate licensing requirements, remain out of the mainstream of regulatory activity.

During the 1983 legislative sessions, timeshare legislation was introduced in 24 states. It should be noted that many of these states introduced several proposals. Of these bills legislation was enacted in the following states: Alabama, Arkansas, Colorado, Georgia, Louisiana, Maryland, Misissippi, Nevada, North Carolina, Oregon, South Dakota, Utah, Washington and Wyoming. In addition, Virginia, Tennessee and Florida amended their existing timeshare laws with Florida enacting by far the greatest changes. Other states saw their bills defeated for various reasons and many re-introduced legislation during the next legislative sessions. State legislative activity continued at a slower pace throughout the remaining years of the decade. By 1990, nearly every state with a significant level of timeshare development or marketing activity had enacted laws and rules to regulate the industry.

In 1984 there was a heightened interest on the part of the local governmental authorities in the field of timesharing. The stance of California's cities that timeshare owners and their guests should be subject to both *ad valorem* real property taxes and transient occupancy taxes is an example. This trend has continued to some extent—although not to the extent the industry feared—through local communities attempting to ban timesharing, attempts to enact excessive occupancy taxes, and increased *ad valorem* property taxes.

Timeshares in Florida were often valued on the basis of adding together their full sales prices, without a suitable deduction for sales and marketing costs and unusual financing costs, as allowed under Florida tax law. Further, the methods of assessing timeshares for *ad valorem* tax purposes varied greatly from county to county. Not only timeshare developers, but also timeshare owners, complained loudly of their high taxes. After several years of effort, the industry finally saw passage of some relief in 1988.

While timeshare weeks are still assessed individually, assessors are required to look first to the resale market to determine value and, if no suitable resale market exists, the assessor must use a deduction of 50 per cent from the purchase price for sales and marketing costs. It should be noted that this presumption of 50 per cent is rebuttable, and may be challenged by either the assessor, developer or timeshare owner.

Some states are also looking to apply various forms of sales taxes to timesharing. Right-to-use forms are often a target, whereas fee interests may be exempt under state law. In an unprecedented action, Wisconsin enacted legislation in 1989 which applied a sales tax to fee timeshare interests which offer a floating use, as well as taxing the maintenance fees for all types of properties. The state's timeshare industry is expected to challenge the amendment in the 1990 legislative session, particularly since charging a sales tax on maintenance fees can result in taxing an owner's real estate taxes which are often billed with the maintenance. This and any similar initiatives generally

result from state governments looking to timesharing for increased government revenues.

**Timeshare abuses**

The state governmental authorities lobby vigorously for provisions allowing
for rule-making authority since they do not want to be required to pursue a
legislative remedy which would seriously inhibit a desire to act quickly in order
to mitigate serious abuses and harm to the public. There has been, and will
continue to be, debate over agency rule-making authority. Even though each
state has its own set of politics and particular concerns, there are several areas
particular to the industry which practically all state governmental bodies and
elected officials attempt to address through some sort of governmental control
in some cases to the point of 'overkill', a term used by US participants which
describes laws designed to remedy the abuses of a few unscrupulous operators
to the detriment of the truly legitimate businesses.

*High pressure selling*
Firstly, laws or rules target the hard-sell, high pressure sales techniques which
are, unfortunately, used too frequently in sales operations. Most states
address this issue by a non-waivable purchaser rescission right. This 'cooling-
off' period ranges from three days in California and Nebraska, to 15 in
Connecticut, Tennessee and Maine, with the most common being five days.
The states base the length of the rescission period on such factors as the level of
complaints, political pressures, whether the purchasers live in or outside the
state and, in some instances, industry studies and testimony. Such industry
testimony indicates that approximately 90 per cent of the rescissions occur
within 72 hours of sale. The rescission period has definitely reduced the volume
of complaints in those jurisdictions where it has been imposed and properly
enforced.

*Misrepresentation*
The second area of state concentration is the problem associated with
misrepresentations regarding investment potential, ease of resale and
exchange, as well as the total cost of the timesharing plan. Virtually all states
have utilised the disclosure-orientated approach in the form of a public
offering statement to inform the consumer. It is felt that such detailed
disclosure, coupled with the use of a non-waivable rescission period, should be
sufficient to protect the consumer. The trend by states with a history of
substantive regulation such as Florida, California, Hawaii, Oregon and New
York, as well as several others, is the requirement that the public offering
statement be filed and approved by the administering agency before a
developer may be permitted to commence sales. This trend has increased and
has been followed by all but a few states.

*Advertising ethics*

The third area of uniform concern and increased regulation is advertising. This includes general advertising as well as those promotions which include the elements of chance, consideration and prize. In fact Florida banned the issue of such devices in timeshare promotions as of 1 January 1985. Curiously, by 1989, the industry in Florida had so matured that state regulatory officials appeared willing to allow the use of sweepstakes again, provided proper controls were in place. The industry, however, showed some reluctance to reintroduce sweepstakes, given the serious abuses of the past. Chance, consideration and prize are the three elements which make up an illegal commercial lottery under federal (10 USC, s̃1301)—and most state—laws. The key element of the three is 'consideration'. Federal law—governing 'sweepstakes' and other gift and prize promotions—has been interpreted to mean that where a participant is not required to make a payment, purchase an item, or exert substantial performance, the element of consideration is not present (*FCC* v *American Broadcasting Co* (1954), 347 US 284): therefore no lottery exists. Simply speaking, federal law has looked primarily to money changing hands to find 'consideration' where the states have tended to look to 'performance' by the participant as well. This broader view has directly affected timeshare promotions since a prospective buyer is often required to drive to a resort location (which could be two or three hours away) to obtain his prize or gift. Since prize and chance are usually clearly present on the face of the promotion, finding the required drive to the resort is 'consideration' makes the plan an illegal lottery—a criminal violation. This gives the states considerable power over the promoter, particularly when a government agency must respond to consumer complaints that they 'travelled all that distance' for a gift or prize which was either misrepresented or was not available as promised.

Florida's approach is the strictest taken by the states, one which has singled out timeshare sales as opposed to other sales of property. Their law is included as Appendix G. Prior to the effective date of the ban, Florida had required 'sweepstakes' programmes to be pre-filed and approved by the Division of Florida Land Sales and Condominiums before use. In addition, 'sweepstakes' carried a hefty filing fee. Most other states require prior approval before use or simultaneous filing with use and mandate the use of specific disclosures to purchasers regarding the purpose and conditions of the offer. A number of states prohibit the use of 'sweepstakes' or any other 'free' gifts when a licensed real estate broker/salesperson is involved in the sale. This prohibition applies to the sale of all forms of real property thus avoiding potential constitutional issues which attorneys have raised in Florida. However, an Illinois case involving Coldwell Banker, a major real estate brokerage firm, held that the state's prohibition against brokers offering free gifts to potential clients was unconstitutional.

Interestingly, Louisiana's law, enacted in 1983, did not require sales of timeshares to be conducted through licensed broker/salespeople, but created a special registration procedure administered by the Real Estate Commission establishing a new class of timeshare salespeople.

### Product delivery

The fourth area of state concern is product delivery. Escrow and bonding requirements are the primary means of accomplishing this goal, with Florida, California, Hawaii and New York leading the states with comprehensive requirements. In addition, Florida now substantially prohibits the use of monies received from the consumer for construction purposes. An alternative assurances provision is provided for under the statute, but if the industry's experience in Florida is any indication of the Division's flexibility, there will be a very limited number of developers eligible to receive such alternative assurances. These escrow and bonding requirements are extraordinarily important if the project is being marketed in several states where all could arguably assert jurisdiction over the sale of the timeshares. Since the overwhelming trend is for more off-site marketing because of local market saturation, there will be a greater need for multi-state registrations. The practical problems of simply keeping up with the ever-changing state requirements are obvious, but problems of conflicting state laws are more complicated than can be indicated here.

### Sales licensing

The fifth area which is covered uniformly by states is sales licensing. The trend is clearly to require licensed real estate broker/salespeople to sell all forms of timesharing. Most states do, however, provide for the owner/developer exemption for salaried employees. A few states, such as Alabama, Louisiana, Nevada and South Carolina and Tennessee have created special timeshare sales registration and/or examination requirements as an alternative to real estate brokers' licensing. Many industry professionals prefer a special limited share sales licence since most real estate brokers are not interested enough or, in the absence of specific courses, sufficiently educated in the concept. The licensing issue has been a major stumbling block politically when such timeshare legislation is considered. In addition, there is continued controversy over whether or not individuals merely setting up appointments over the telephone or handing out leaflets encouraging a sales prospect to attend a timeshare sales presentation should be fully-fledged real estate brokers/salespeople. Logic would imply that they should not, and the Florida legislature agreed by enacting an amendment setting up a special licence for individuals engaged only in this function. The issue still continues in other states however.

### Administration

Another important area which has received much attention recently is concern over the administration of timeshares. Although no state law has adequately addressed management thus far, for the regulatory agencies it is the single most talked about issue. California, however, has addressed management and budgets in great detail by way of regulation. There is little doubt that the states will be enacting detailed, comprehensive management and budgetary provisions in proposed legislation, as well as in amendments to existing laws. The greatest concern is, however, whether too much damage will be sustained before meaningful regulatory controls find their way into the marketplace.

As may be apparent, several states have enacted laws which single out and treat timesharing development and sales in a different manner to other forms of real estate, for instance the 'sweepstakes' prohibition, removal of the owner/developer exemption under the real estate licensing laws (which was ultimately held to be unenforceable), as well as the prohibition of the developer from utilising in excess of 10 per cent of the deposit for construction purposes in the state of Florida. In addition, some states, including Maryland and Louisiana, have excluded timesharing claims made with the state's Real Estate Guarantee Fund. Such funds are maintained by many states to provide relief to consumers in their claims against real estate licensees. Maryland's action was prompted by the so-called 'Seatime fraud', which resulted in millions of dollars being claimed under their fund. The New York Attorney General's bill, introduced during the 1983 session, banned the sale of the no fee (right-to-use) form of timesharing. As mentioned this was in response to *Sombrero Reef Club, Inc* v *Allman* (18 Bankruptcy 612), which case held that the trustee, under Chapter 11 bankruptcy proceedings could reject the right-to-use 'vacation licences' since the court deemed them executory in nature. The result of this case cast the purchasers as no more than unsecured creditors. This proposal was not well received by the industry since an outright ban seemed too severe at a time when no viable structuring alternatives existed and when progress was being made to amend the Bankruptcy Code discussed later in this chapter. Although most timeshare marketeers agree that fee ownership is the more marketable form of timesharing in the USA at this time, the existing hotel market may provide the industry with tremendous growth potential. Holiday Inn, Marriott and Princess hotels have already entered the timesharing market and other major chains are seriously considering timesharing. It is of course difficult to adapt fee interest type plans to hotel timesharing projects.

## Property taxes

Last, but certainly not least, is the most important issue facing the industry and consumers alike—property taxes. Tax notices in connection with timeshare interests in Florida reflected increases of up to 600 per cent from 1982 and 1983. The problem continued until passage of the 1988 legislation. Tax reform legislation is ultimately the only way to address this dilemma which, if not corrected, will affect the viability of the timeshare concept. The problem is not unique to Florida but has become one of the greatest legal issues nationwide.

California industry participants attempted to pass legislation amending their revenue and taxation code related to property taxation during the 1983 legislative session. The California legislature found that the purchase price of a timeshare included features and services that are not real property in addition to the ownership of realty. As is the case in other states, there was a lack of uniformity among county assessors in the method by which these non-real property items were to be excluded from the purchase price of the timeshare in valuing the real property portion of the interest. After an intensive owner consumer letter writing and lobbying effort the California legislature enacted legislation which states:

> ... the full value of a timeshare estate of timeshare use may be determined by reference to condominiums, cooperatives, or other properties which are similar in size, type and location to the property subject to timeshare ownership and are not owned on a timeshare basis. The aggregate assessed value of all the timeshare estates or uses relating to a single lot, parcel, unit or other segment of real property shall be determined by adding (1) the fair market value of the similar lot, parcel or unit, or other segment not owned on a timeshare basis, and (2) an amount necessary to reflect any increase or decrease to the market value attributable to the fact that the property is marketed in increments of time, or by any alternative method which will determine the real property value without regard to any non-real property items which may be included.

It was hoped that the tax assessors would appraise timeshare property fairly, but the results thus far have not been encouraging for the industry. Various last minute amendments by the tax assessors lobby virtually eliminated any relief to timeshare owners and developers alike.

**Resale of timeshares**

By the end of the 1980s another issue had come to the fore, which was only vaguely contemplated in the early days of the industry. That issue is the development of a viable secondary—or resale—market for timesharing. By 1989, more that 1.3 million people in the US owned timeshares. A survey completed in November 1989 by Ragatz Associates for the American Resort & Residential Development Association (ARRDA) showed that 13 per cent of timeshare owners had their properties actively for sale, with another 17 per cent 'considering' selling. Previous surveys by other groups showed a higher number of 'for sale' timeshares. Further, there was disappointingly little evidence of an active resale market. And timeshares which were sold were often sold at less than their original price with a few exceptions in high demand, low supply areas.

The problem was exacerbated by the growth of unscrupulous listing companies—companies which for a fee of from $200–$400 in advance promised to resell consumer's timeshares readily and at a profit. Unfortunately, many of those promises were not being fulfilled. On the other hand, developers began to face the fact that timesharing could simply not be sold with a resale angle or investment pitch. As a result, ARRDA developed both a model resale act (see Appendix H) and initiated an educational programme for both developers and consumers on the fact that timesharing was not intended to be a real estate investment, but a vacation product whose value was in its use through the years. Florida was the first to pass the model resale legislation in 1989, and the Act was circulated to state attorneys general and real estate regulators, with additional actions expected in the 1990s. Further, federal authorities took steps against several resale companies in late 1989, with three companies being sued by the Federal Trade Commission for unfair and deceptive acts and practices, and another company being indicted on 18 counts of mail fraud, wire fraud, conspiracy and bank fraud.

## Federal activity

### Internal Revenue Service

In addition to the highly volatile state regulatory arena some important issues related to timesharing were recently addressed at federal level. These issues include Internal Revenue Service ('IRS') rulings regarding the Rule of 78s and their impact on some newer tax shelter plans. IRS positions have been set out as regards the taxation of right-to-use club memberships, federal regulations authorising increased Savings and Loan (S & L) participation in timesharing, amendments to the federal bankruptcy law in order to protect right-to-use consumers, as well as increased activity on the part of the Federal Trade Commission.

The Rule of 78s is a method of allocating loan interest to different time periods of a loan. Using this method, interest for a given period is calculated by multiplying total interest for the entire term of the debt (T) by the following fraction: the numerator representing the remaining periods of debt (RP) and the denominator of which is the sum of the periods' digits over the life of the loan. Thus, T x RP/SD (sum-of-the-digits) = I (interest for the period). The Rule derives this name, from the fact that the digits from 1 to 12 (on a one year loan) total 78. The use of the Rule has a front-end loading effect as the following example illustrates. Assume a 30 year loan for $100,000 at 12 per cent interest, with equal payments of $12,414 to amortise it fully. With an economic accrual of interest, the first year's interest is $12,000 (12 per cent of $100,000). Using the Rule of 78s, however, results in interest of $17,575. This comes from multiplying total interest of $272,420 by the following fraction: 30 (30 years remaining) over 465 (sums of digits from number of years from 1 to 30).

With regard to the Rule of 78s, the IRS has now generally disallowed this method of interest allocation and does not allow interest deductions for any year in excess of the amount represented by the economic accrual of interest. The one exception where the Rule of 78s will still be permitted is for certain short-term loans as set forth in Revenue Proc 83–40. These loans must be for a term not to exceed five years, have no balloon at the end, be self-amortising with level payments made at least annually, and treat interest as earned, upon pre-payment or otherwise, under the Rule of 78s. The position taken in this revenue ruling could well be challenged. As it stands, however, it undermines the use of the Rule of 78s in certain tax shelter offerings, including some involving timeshare properties which have been used in recent years. In fact, the US Department of Justice has brought suits against at least two timeshare tax shelter promoters on this very issue.

Another area affecting timesharing development and the subject of recent IRS positions is the deduction of marketing costs in connection with right-to-use timeshare programmes, as well as the developer's inclusion as income of promissory notes in the year delivered. The IRS issued an internal memorandum with respect to the Paradise Palms Vacation Club. The IRS ruled that the seller had to deduct its marketing costs over years on a *pro rata* basis (ie, not at once in the year when incurred, but fractionally over the life of the timeshare scheme) and could not immediately recover such marketing costs. This is particularly onerous to timesharing development due to the extraordinarily high marketing costs. The service's position regarding *Paradise Palms* is consistent with its previous position set forth in the *Windrifter* case which was formally released as Private Letter Ruling 7803005. In both cases, the government refused to acknowledge that there had been a sale of timeshare ownership and viewed the transfer as being more of a prepaid rental or lease transaction.

In addition, the *Paradise Palms* ruling held that the seller, irrespective of his method of accounting, would be required to recognise as income all cash received as well as the fair market value of the promissory notes delivered as payments. Thus, the face value of the notes must be included in the developer's income in the year of delivery even though the notes may not be cash equivalents (ie discounted by sale or hypothecation) or even collected. And, further, the expense of the sale must be spread over the life of the timeshare. This means the maximum income is taxed during the year with only a small portion of the expenses available to offset the income.

*Savings and loan activities*
On the brighter side, however, the Garn-St Germain Depository Institutions Act, signed into law in October 1982, provides the legal foundation for the potential growth in Savings and Loan (S & L) activities involving timesharing. Thereafter, the Federal Home Loan Bank Board adopted regulations which provide the operative framework that implements the new S & L powers. This new regulation can be found at 48 Fed Reg 23032 (1983). However, the deregulation of S & Ls ultimately resulted in massive insolvency for many institutions, thus an S & L 'bailout' law was enacted in 1989. Under the provisions of that law, S & Ls must keep at least 70 per cent of their assets in residential property. At the time of writing, it is unclear whether timesharing could be included in the 70 per cent although ARRDA was lobbying actively for such inclusion.

*The Bankruptcy Code*

When the outcome of the *Sombrero Reef* bankruptcy case was known, industry professionals were justifiably concerned. As previously mentioned, the court's opinion reduced all of the right-to-use timeshare purchasers to the status of unsecured general creditors with virtually no hope of any recovery from the bankrupt developer. In addition to finding that right-to-use timeshare contracts were executory, pursuant to s 365(a) of the Bankruptcy Code, and could be rejected by the debtor, the court also found that the Florida law designed to protect the consumer (through non-disturbance provisions) was pre-empted by federal law and thus invalid. Therefore, the only solution was to push for an amendment to the federal bankruptcy law.

During the latter half of 1982, the timeshare industry's legislative advocate in Washington DC, ARRDA, was successful in securing the introduction of federal legislation to ensure the necesary protections for the consumer in the event of developer default. Through the industry's efforts in 1983, bills were introduced in the Senate by Senator Orrin Hatch and in the house by Representative Bill McCollum. In addition, a modified version was included in Senator Robert Dole's Omnibus Bankruptcy Improvement Act of 1983.

Although there were some variations among these pieces of remedial legislation, the primary objective of all these bills was to ensure that in the event of developer bankruptcy, the timeshare consumer had the right to continue the use and enjoyment of the timeshare project. This was accomplished by language which treated timeshare agreements in the same manner as leases and sales of real property under the Bankruptcy Code. The timeshare bankruptcy legislation was finally signed into law by President Reagan on 10 July 1984.

## Federal Trade Commission

Last but not least, the Federal Trade Commission (FTC) under the FTC Act, s 5 is granted broad powers to regulate persons, entities and industries which are engaging 'in unfair or deceptive acts or practices in or affecting commerce'. The FTC has been quite active in the timesharing industry in recent years and it is quite possible that federal scrutiny of timesharing may increase even further.

The FTC's interest in timesharing dates back to late 1975 when the agency announced it was investigating 'promoters and sellers' of various types of timeshare plans. No real action was taken until September 1981 when the FTC filed a civil complaint against the Paradise Palms Vacation Club and 12 individual and corporate defendants. Among the charges made by the FTC were that the defendants had misrepresented escrow arrangements; the location, value, and ownership of the timeshare units; and the operation and availability of an independent exchange network. When the case finally came to trial, one of the key defendants was literally 'banned' from participating in the timeshare industry by the court. In short, the FTC has, and has exercised, broad enforcement and remedial powers to protect consumers against what it regards as 'unfair and deceptive practices'. While the FTC Act does not define these types of practices, considerable guidance is available from case laws and a number of trade regulation rules and guidelines. A timeshare practitioner concerned with timeshare marketing practices might review the following:

1 Synopsis of FTC Decisions relevant to Vacation Promotion (approved 16 December 1980 in file 812 3042).
2 Cooling-Off Period for Door-to-Door Sales, 16 CFR S429 (applicable only to right-to-use forms of timesharing).
3 Preservation of consumer Claims and Defenses, 16 CFR S433 (applicable only to right-to-use forms of timesharing).
4 FTC Advertising Guidelines:
    (a) use of the word 'free' and similar representations,
    (b) guides against deceptive pricing,
    (c) guides against bait advertising,
    (d) endorsements and testimonials in advertising.

The FTC also administers two other laws which apply to timesharing transactions. The FTC's responsibilities under these laws are limited to enforcement of non-bank, non-financial institution creditors, ie timeshare companies which offer credit to their buyers. The Equal Credit Opportunities Act (15 USC, s1691) basically prohibits discrimination in the extension of credit on the basis of race, colour, religion, national origin, sex, marital status, age or source of income. The Act also prohibits discouraging credit applicants on any of the prohibited bases. Since many timeshare marketing programmes try to 'pre-qualify' recipients of their mailings, advertising has contained conditions which transgress the ECOA. For example, an advertisement which says: 'To participate in this programme, you must be between the ages of 25 and 65, gainfully employed, and married,' would exclude single, young or retired persons. While there has been no major litigation in this area, both the FTC and the US Department of Justice view these kinds of conditions as potential or actual ECOA violations, thus necessitating careful drafting of conditions. The ECOA's thrust is to make creditors focus primarily on an applicant's 'creditworthiness'.

Nearly every timeshare offering is also subject to the Truth-in-Lending Act (15 USC, s1601). The goal of the Act is simple: to provide consumers with standardised information about the cost of credit. The Act itself, its implementing Regulation Z, and 'official staff commentary' is highly detailed, complex and arcane. The disclosure forms consumers see are indeed simple to read, but their preparation is not and competent advice is invaluable. There are serious penalties for failure to disclose information and for failure to disclose it properly. The Act also mandates very particular disclosures when credit is publicly advertised. Fortunately, these procedures are fairly straightforward. The FTC has, however, been quite active in reviewing advertisements for compliance and issuing warnings of more serious enforcement action if violations are not corrected.

## Department of Housing and Urban Development

Any timeshare programme should also be reviewed in the light of two US civil rights Acts—the Fair Housing law (Title VIII of the 1968 Act) and the Equal Accommodations law (Title II of the 1964 Act). Both prohibit discrimination in housing or accommodation on the basis of race, colour, religion, sex or national origin. In 1984, two cases against timeshare marketeers and developers were brought by the US Department of Justice charging, primarily, race discrimination. In 1988, the Fair Housing Act was amended to include 'handicap' and 'familial status' as categories which may not be discriminated against. Familial status generally refers to the presence of children under 18 years of age. Further, the amendments expanded the definition of a dwelling unit to cover condominiums, co-operatives, and mobile homes specifically and the Department of Housing and Urban Development (HUD) had stated that timesharing was included in the definition. The amendments also increased HUD's enforcement authority and established monetary penalties of up to $50,000 for violations.

Whilst one other law should be considered, most timeshare projects, if properly structured, would be exempt. This is the Interstate Land Sales Full Disclosure Act (15 USC, s1701) which has been applied to condominiums which are being sold prior to actual completion of the units. The Act can apply where the timeshare plan involves the sale of vacant land or the sale of unbuilt units, unless the sales contract provides for them to be constructed within two years, with the purchaser having a right to rescission if the construction is not completed within that time. The Department of Housing and Urban Development (HUD) do issue 'no action letters' in appropriate circumstances. In fact, there has been considerable litigation on the jurisdiction issue, particularly in the state of Florida, with no absolute conclusions reached. While timeshared condominiums have not become embroiled in the litigation, they need not be exposed to the problem at all with proper planning and documentation.

## Classification of timeshares as securities

In the early days of US timesharing, there was grave concern over whether timeshares might be classified as securities under federal (and state) law. Section 5(a) of the Securities Act 1933 provides:

> (a) unless a registration statement is in effect as to a security, it shall be unlawful for any person, directly or indirectly—
> (1) To make use of any means or instruments of transportation of communication in inter state commerce or of the mails to sell such security through the use or medium of any prospectus or otherwise; or

(2) to carry or cause to be carried through the mails or in inter state commerce, by any means or instruments of transportation, any such security for the purpose of sale or for delivery after sale.

The Act defines the term 'security' as:

any ... bond, debenture, evidence of indebtedness, certificate of interest or participation in any profit sharing agreement, collateral trust certificate ... investment contract ... certificate or deposit for a security ... or any certificate or interest or participation in, temporary or interim certificate for, receipt for, guarantee of, or warrant or right to subscribe to or purchase any of the foregoing.

The Securities Acts of 1933 and 1934 govern 'investment contracts' and the sale of any interest or investment 'commonly known as a security'. There were two tests, known as the 'Howey test' and the 'Hawaii Market Center Test', which were to be applied in order to ascertain whether the transaction is affected by the securities legislation. In *SEC* v *Howey Co* 328 US 293 (1946) it was stated that:

An investment contract for the purposes of the Securities Acts means a contract, transaction or plan where a person invests his money in a common enterprise and is led to expect profits solely from the efforts of the promoter or a third party, it being immaterial whether the shares in the enterprise are evidenced by formal certificates or by nominal interests in the physical assets employed in the enterprise.

In a typical timeshare plan, the investment by the purchaser will be present but the expectation of profit may depend to a large extent on the promotional material. This is the reason why developers will avoid alluding to the possibility of profit or even demanding that the purchaser provide a written acknowledgment that he was not motivated by the expectation of profit in making his purchase. The third branch of the test, that profits are to be produced by the promoter or a third party, will make it important to distinguish between management of the enterprise by the promoter, eg in right-to-use plans, and management by the purchasers, eg in fee ownership plans.

Following the California case of *Silver Hills Country Club* v *Sobieski* (55 CAL 2d 811 1961), in *State* v *Hawaii Market Center Inc* (485 P 2d 105 1971), it was stated that:

... an investment contract is created whenever:-
(1) an offeree furnishes initial value to an offeror and
(2) a portion of this initial value is subject to the risks of the enterprise, and
(3) the furnishings of the initial value is induced by the offeror's promises or representations which give rise to a reasonable understanding that a valuable benefit of some kind, over and above the initial value, will accrue to the offeree as a result of the operation of the enterprise, and
(4) the offeree does not receive the right to exercise practical and actual control over the managerial decisions of the enterprise.

It will be seen that this definition casts a wider net. It has been argued that even the expectation that there would be savings as a result of not having to take into account inflation on the cost of equivalent hotel rooms, was a 'valuable benefit' under the *Hawaii Market Center* definition.

It was at one time possible to obtain an opinion from the US Securities and Exchange Commission (SEC)—a 'no action letter'—provided one was able to persuade them that the securities acts did not apply, but it is understood that this procedure is no longer available.

Compliance with the securities legislation, as with the prospectus provisions of the UK Companies Acts, would be a time-consuming and expensive operation. The cost of complying with the federal security laws alone would have stifled the burgeoning industry. Those early fears (unlike the situation in Australia) were never realised. The SEC has in fact never become seriously involved with the timeshare industry. While the agency gives no comfort to developers, attorneys and lenders, neither has it taken any enforcement action against any timeshare properties. The key to this posture at the SEC may be found in a release on condominium securities (Release No 5347, 38 FR 1935, January 1973) which stated as follows:

In summary, the offering of condominium units in conjunction with any of the following will cause the offering to be viewed as an offering of securities in the form of investment contracts:
1 The condominiums, with any rental arrangement or other similar service, are offered and sold with emphasis on the economic benefits to the purchaser to be derived from the managerial efforts of the promoter, or a third party designated or arranged for by the promoter, from rental of the units.
2 The offering or participation in a rental pool arrangement; and
3 The offering of a rental or similar arrangement whereby the purchaser must hold his unit available for rental for any part of the year, must use an exclusive rental agent or is otherwise materially restricted in his occupancy or rental of his unit.

In all the above situations, investor protection required the application of the federal securities laws.

A later US Supreme Court decision states it more succinctly:

The touch-stone [of the existence of a security] is the presence of an investment in a common venture premised on a reasonable expectation of profits to be derived from entrepreneurial or managerial efforts of others. By profits, the Court has meant either capital appreciation resulting from the development of the initial investment or a participation in earnings resulting from the use of investors' funds ... [*UHF* v *Foreman* 421 US 837 (1975)].

In 1989, a Ninth Circuit Court of Appeals opinion somewhat obscured the issue. In *Hocking* v *Dubois* (21 September 1989, US App LEXIS 14159; Fed Sec L Rep (CCH) P94, 710), Hocking purchased a Hawaii condominium on the secondary market from Dubois, a local real estate broker. After purchasing the condominium, Hocking entered into a completely separate rental pool arrangement which Dubois recommended, but to which the real estate broker had no business relationship. When Hocking's investment failed to perform as expected, he sued Dubois alleging securities fraud.

In an *en banc* rehearing before 11 circuit judges, six of the judges concluded Dubois may have offered an investment contract security because the rental pool arrangement was offered 'as part of the same transaction.' The decision has raised concerns that, if broadly applied, it could severely inhibit secondary market transactions for resort condominiums.

This is not to say, however, that no timeshare programme will ever be held to be a security at federal level. (A few timeshare programmes have attempted to be securities in order to make investment and 'profitability' representations.) At least one state, Oklahoma, believes timeshares are securities. A timeshare developer who sells his product promising appreciation profits upon resale, rental potential, and so forth, may find the Enforcement Division of the SEC tapping him on the shoulder. By its very lack of official pronouncements in the timeshare area, the SEC has left the door open for future interpretations responsive to the creativity of the marketplace. Additionally, each timeshare plan must be examined in the light of state securities laws (the so-called 'blue sky' laws).

## Conclusion

In summary, while there is no 'federal law of timesharing' in the US, quite an arsenal of statutes exists which are being applied, or which can be applied to those who go astray. These overlay the specific state timesharing laws and provide additional requirements and remedies. It is by no means a simple regulatory plan, particularly for projects which will be sold in several states. An early review of relevant statutes will have a strong influence on all aspects of the timesharing offering.

There is an increasing tendency to market UK and European timeshare plans in the USA. Of course, if the project is marketed on site, albeit to American nationals, there is no necessity to comply with US law. If, however, the marketing activity takes place in the USA, then there will be a necessity to comply with US Law. Often there will be a requirement to register the project with the state supervisory authority and to provide that authority with an independent appraisal by a qualified expert, including a satisfactory title report, and an assurance as to the protection of the timeshare buyer's interest. Discussions with the regulatory authority will be needed at an early stage and there may even be a requirement that there be on-site inspection by an official of the regulatory authority to be carried out at the expense of the developer.

A developer who intends to market his development in North America will be well advised to appoint an established and recognised attorney and marketing organisation in the USA to advise on the requirements and to ensure compliance with the federal and state legislation. While requirements are similar in each US state, all are technically different demanding considerable expertise and planning, particularly when a multi-state marketing effort is contemplated.

If the developer carries on the business of marketing overseas timeshare plans in the USA, there will be exposure to the risk of US taxation. However, if the arrangement is properly structured, the risk can be minimised if not avoided altogether. Again, the local marketing organisation is likely to be able to provide helpful advice.

Finally, there are two features of American timesharing which demand consideration, if not emulation, in Europe. The first is the much greater availability of timesharing finance. The Richard L Ragatz Association Inc Survey *United Kingdom Timeshare Purchasers; Who They Are, Why They Buy*, showed that 67.6 per cent of US purchasers pay via a loan, the percentage being only 7.2 per cent in the United Kingdom. The second feature is the awareness of the trade associations as to the need for consumer protection legislation, and the way in which such legislation is promoted by the trade associations.

The US market should not be ignored by developers. It is by far the largest timesharing market in the world, with sales of $2 billion for 1989. One study has shown that approximately 25 per cent of American purchasers live more than 1,000 miles from their timeshare development, and that there is a substantial demand in the USA for European timesharing developments.

# Chapter Nine

# Timesharing in France

As we have seen, according to most popular accounts, it was in France that timesharing first came into being, in 1965 at the alpine sports resort of Superdévoluy. In the first few years, the timesharing system in France remained confined to the winter sports region. However, it soon came to be adopted in other tourist areas, in particular the Côte d'Azur. More recently, timesharing in France has gone beyond the bounds of real estate property as such and has been applied to boats, tennis courts, buildings used for commercial purposes or exhibitions, and even to paintings. There are now said to be more than 10,000 timeshare owners in France.

Until recently, French timesharing schemes have been operated, in most cases, under a corporate system in which the timeshare purchasers are the shareholders and exercise their rights pursuant to the company's constitution, which assigns separate rights to each share. This form of company is known as the *Société Civile d'Attribution*.

As might be expected from the country which claims to have invented the idea of timesharing, the French system is well developed and affords a certain amount of statutory protection to the timeshare purchaser expressed mainly in specific legislation on timesharing corporations.

## Ownership and timesharing under French law

The French solution to the timesharing conundrum is based on a corporate structure, owing to the unsuitability of existing property sections of the Code Napoleon. In fact, within the range of the concepts of interests in property under the French Civil Code, neither the original right of ownership in itself, nor, indeed, ownership in undivided shares, co-ownership or the real right of use and occupancy appear to be capable of adapting to the new *de facto* situation created by the advent of timesharing. The last three forms of interest in property were adapted from the right of ownership as set forth in the Civil Code of 1804.

## Concept of time

None of the forms of ownership mentioned above are appropriate because French law does not allow time to be defined as something to which a real right of ownership, as specified in the Civil Code of 1804, can apply. This position derives from the effect of arts 552 *ff* of the Civil Code which define real estate ownership. Under French law, therefore, it is not possible to have a right of ownership over one week which would be regarded as a right of ownership in real property, ie, a real right as opposed to a mere personal right.

While there cannot be a real right of ownership divided in time, it might have been conceivable, but for the difficulties detailed hereafter, to place timesharing either within the framework of ownership in undivided shares, or co-ownership, or alternatively within the real right of use and occupancy. All three of these are adaptations of the right of ownership as defined by the Civil Code, and they have made it possible to keep pace with other developments in real estate practices up to the present day.

If an attempt was made to vest an apartment in the timeshare owners as owners in undivided shares, an immediate problem would arise. In such a case, the timeshare proprietors would be co-owners of undivided shares, wanting to retain ownership in undivided shares as regards ownership of the dwelling, while dividing occupancy thereof into periods. This form of ownership would be governed by art 815 of the Civil Code, as amended by Law No 76–1286 of 31 December 1976, which provides:

> Nul ne peut être contraint à demeurer dans l'indivision et le partage peut être toujours provoqué à moins qu'il n'y ait été sursis par jugement ou convention.

> No party may be compelled to remain in ownership in undivided shares and partition can always be brought about unless it has been postponed by a ruling or agreement.

It would also be regulated by arts 1873 *ff*, which define the conditions under which owners of a property in undivided shares can enter into an agreement concerning their property. Article 1873(3) provides that such an agreement may be concluded for a definite period not exceeding five years. If the agreement is concluded for an indefinite term the property can be severed at any time.

It is therefore clear that a structure of this kind is not stable enough to serve as a basis for a timesharing operation.

## Co-ownership

The next possibility which requires consideration is co-ownership. This is an organised general form of ownership in undivided shares governed by Law No 65–557 of 10 July 1965. The provisions of this Law apply to any building of which the ownership is divided between several individuals. Each owner in condominium holds a right in undivided shares over all of the common parts of the building but is the outright owner of his apartment. Ownership of each apartment would, in a timesharing scheme, have to be attributed to several persons who would share in its possession. The regulations governing ownership in condominium would have to define the period of possession for each person. This would, in practice, be tantamount to creating ownership in undivided shares of each apartment, giving rise to the problem described above with regard to ownership in undivided shares, ie it is a structure that is far too unstable to serve as a basis for timesharing.

### Real right of use

The third possibility is the granting of a real right of use and occupancy. The company owning the estate would assign to its members the right of real possession through an agreement granting alternating occupancy. In this way, the assignees would be placed within a real, as opposed to a personal, property framework. However, these real rights of use and occupancy are governed by arts 625 *ff* of the Civil Code, which impose considerable restrictions on their use. In particular, both transfer and letting are prohibited (arts 631 and 634). Moreover, these rights lapse upon the decease of their holder. It is therefore impracticable to apply this third form of real right to timesharing.

It will be clear from the above that the rights acquired by timeshare owners can exist only as personal rights in French law.

## Timesharing based on a corporate structure

After some 20 years of timesharing in France, the French Parliament decided to pass a specific law governing this matter: Law No 86–18 of 6 January 1986 relates to companies whose purpose it is to allocate to their shareholders the use of buildings to be enjoyed on a timeshare basis.

The aim of this law is to complement existing legislation (ie namely Law No 71–519 of 16 July 1971), without repealing it and other subsequent legislation, most of which is set out in *Code de la Construction et de l'Habitation* (CCH).

The general purpose of the 1971 Law, which is very broad in scope, is to provide for the regulation of various aspects of real estate activities. In particular, it governs the form of any company which can be used as a basis for the conduct of such activities as well as regulating real estate development contracts and the sales of blocks of flats or individual houses. Article 5 of this law (now art L 212–1 of the CCH) provides the legal foundation for a timesharing corporation:

> Les sociétés ayant pour objet la construction ou l'acquisition d'immeubles en vue de leur division par fractions destinée à être attribuées aux associés en propriété ou en jouissance peuvent être valablement constituées sous les différentes formes prévues par la loi, même si elles n'ont pas pour but de partager un bénéfice …

Companies whose purpose is to construct or purchase buildings with a view to dividing them into fractions to be allocated to the members for ownership or possession can be validly constituted in the different forms provided for by the law, even if their purpose is not to share out a profit.

Hence, it has been possible under art 5 to form a company whose constitution provides for the allocation of possession without the allocation of ownership. This interpretation of art 5 is supported by art 11, s 9 of the Law of 16 July 1971 which provides:

Sauf si les statuts ne prévoient que des attributions de jouissance ...

Unless the company's constitution provides only for the allocation of possession ...

By making use, therefore, of art 5, French lawyers have been able to adopt a corporate structure appropriate to timesharing schemes.

Timeshare corporations may be distinguished from other types of corporation by two main features:

1  they are non-profit making, non-trading companies and,
2  the right of possession of one and the same portion of property is divided up over the year between a number of members who use the portion of property in turn at corresponding periods determined by the constitution of the company and by the contract of purchase so that the period of possession is annual.

The Law authorises the choice of any form of company provided for by law. It thus includes both commercial and 'civil' companies.

The 'civil' form is the one most often selected, owing to its greater operational flexibility. The timesharing company is known as a *Société Civile d'Attribution*—literally a 'civil company of allocation'—so called because it is a corporation formed for the purpose of allocating the right of possession and use of its property amongst its members. The 1986 law defines the new rules governing *Sociétés Civile d'Attribution* only to the extent that the rules derogate from the pre-existing legislation for timesharing purposes.

## Scope of the 1986 Law

Pursuant to art 1, the law applies only to:

les sociétés constituées en vue de l'attribution ... d'immeubles à usage principal d'habitation.

companies constituted for the purpose of allocating to their shareholders the buildings to be used mainly for dwelling.

The law would clearly not apply to timesharing set up on a basis other than a corporate one (eg periodic renting) and where the company's objects are other than the timesharing of dwellings (eg tennis courts, golf, yachts). According to art 1 of the 1986 Law, this statute applies mandatorily. Moreover, timesharing companies set up before the 1986 Law came into effect were obliged to modify their constitutions within two years so as to comply with the provisions of this Law (art 34 of the 1986 Law).

The aims of the 1986 legislation are:

1  to strengthen private purchasers' rights of use of the property, and
2  to adapt French company law for timesharing purposes.

First, we will look at the rules relating to the constitution of companies and then secondly, the rules regulating the functioning of companies governed by the 1986 Law.

## Constitution of the company

### Founder members
As a rule, any person legally capable of entering into a contract may set up a company governed by the 1986 Law. However, such a company is very likely to be formed by a professional developer in the course of his normal business.

### Advertising
The founder members of a timeshare company must not describe the shareholders as 'owners' of the site in any document, literature or advertisement intended to inform the general public. They must not use any terms which might confuse or mislead the purchaser as to exactly what his rights are, since the purchase of shares does not give the purchaser any rights over the land and buildings, which are still owned by the company (art 33, para 2).

Breach of the above rule is construed as misleading advertising (*délit de publicité mensongère*) which is a criminal offence under art 44 of Law No 73–1193 of 27 December 1973.

## Structure of the company

The 1986 Law has not created a new type of company. Most companies will be *sociétés civiles* governed by arts 1845 *ff* of the Civil Code, as they are easy to set up and administer. However, there is one important qualification. Article 1857 of the Civil Code sets out a general rule whereby, the civil company's members are wholly liable for the debts of the company.

Article 4 of the 1986 Law derogates from this rule providing that the liability of shareholders for the debts of a company, governed by the 1986 Law, is limited to the amount of capital invested by each of them.

This new statutory provision is an obvious expression of the legislator's concern for consumer protection.

**Objects of the company**

For a company to be governed by the 1986 Law, its objects should fall within the definition set out in art 1 of the Law.

Such a company must be:

> ... constituée en vue de l'attribution, en totalité ou par fraction, d'immeubles à usage principal d'habitation en jouissance par période aux associés auxquels n'est accordé aucun droit de propriéte ou autre droit réel en contrepartie de leurs apports ...

> ... constituted *in order to attribute* wholly or partly buildings to be used principally for periodic occupation by the shareholders although the shareholders would be entitled neither to ownership of the building nor to any real rights in consideration of their contribution to the company's capital ...

The law envisages that a company may acquire a whole building as well as only a part of it on a co-ownership (*co-propriété*) basis. In the latter case the remaining part of the building would belong to a third party and the building as a whole would be governed by a condominium status (Law of 10 July 1965).

Pursuant to art 1, para 2, the main objects of a timesharing company are:

> ... la construction d'immeuble, l'acquisition d'immeuble ou des droits réels immobilier, l'aménagement ou la restauration des immeubles acquis ...

> ... constructing (the company's) buildings, acquiring buildings or real property rights, converting and upgrading acquired buildings ...

The company has three means to implement its purpose (ie to attribute to its shareholders the use of the property on a timeshare basis):

1 to acquire the land and contract with a third party for the erection of the building;
2 to purchase a building to be erected or a building in the course of its completion; or
3 to purchase a building which has already been completed.

In accordance with art 1, para 3, the objects of the company must also include the administration of the property and acquisition of the furniture and other equipment consistent with the purpose of the property. Where a company has been set up for the purposes defined above, the company is mandatorily subject to the 1986 Law.

It should be mentioned that by exception to the general rules as set out in art L 212–7 of Code de la Construction et de l'Habitation, whereby a *Société Civile d'Attribution* is allowed to grant a charge over its property in order to guarantee loans taken out by the shareholders, a company subjected to the 1986 Law cannot undertake to guarantee obligations of any third party (art 2 of the 1986 Law). This provision has been enacted to prevent the developer from allowing the company to guarantee the developer's personal liabilities and thus putting the other shareholders' rights at risk.

## Company capital

There are no specific requirements regarding the company's minimum capital as the 1986 Law (art 1) refers to the general rules of company law. Initially, the answer will depend on the form of company which its founder members have chosen. There is such a requirement for a *Société Commerciale*: the minimum capital for a *Société à Résponsabilitié Limitée* (SARL) is 50,000 French francs and for a *Société Anonyme* (SA) 250,000 French francs. There is no such requirement for a *Société Civile*.

The capital is to be divided into shares of a nominal value, usually in the case of a *Société Civile* fixed at 10 francs each. Specific rules govern the distribution of the company's shares among the shareholders since the shares entitle the shareholders to the use and occupation of the building owned by the company.

Pursuant to art 8 of the 1986 Law:

Les parts ou actions sont reparties entre les associés en fonction des characteristiques du lot attribué à chacun d'eux, de la durée et de l'époque d'utilisation du local correspondant.

The shares are allocated to the shareholders according to the specification of the premises the shareholder is entitled to occupy, the duration of occupation and the time of year the premises are used.

The shares are divided into several groups set out in a *tableau d'affectation des parts sociales* (table of allocation of shares) according to the above criteria.

In accordance with art 8, para 3, the value of shares will be assessed at the date of their allocation to the relevant group.

## Required legal documents

A number of legal documents are required in order for a timesharing company to be established. These are as follows:

1 Articles of association: the articles of association must comply with both provisions of the 1986 Law and the rules governing the type of company which has been chosen. The exact requirements of the articles of association will be specifically dealt with below.
2 *Etat descriptif de la division et tableau d'affectation des parts sociales* (description of the division of the property and table of allocation of shares): the *état descriptif* sets out the geographical division of the property. According to art 8 this document:

Délimite les divers parties de l'immeuble social en distinguant celles qui sont communes de celles qui sont à usage privative.

Defines different parts of the property and distinguishes between the parts for private use and common use.

The *tableau d'affectation* allocates a definite number of shares to each part of the property for private use (ie apartments) having regard to the duration and the period of occupation of the property by each shareholder.

3 Regulations: this document mainly:

... précise la destination de l'immeuble et ses divers parties et organise les modalités de l'utilisation des équipments collectifs [art 8, para 5].

... defines both the purpose of the property as a whole and the purpose of its different parts and sets out the means of use of the collective equipment ...

Finally, the regulations include the rules dividing the maintenance costs amongst the shareholders.

The timesharing company must adopt all the above documents prior to the commencement of building works or prior to the acquisition of an already completed building by the company (art 11 of the 1986 Law).

## Functioning of a company governed by the 1986 Law

This matter will be dealt with under three headings. We shall examine:

1 how to carry out the company's objects (ie legal means for the property to be allocated on a timeshare basis);
2 the legal rules governing the administration of the company;
3 the rights and obligations of shareholders.

### Implementation of the company's objects

Whether it be commercial or non-commercial, a company constituted with a view to conferring allocation based on the rights of occupation of its members may include either the construction of the building or its purchase in its corporate objects.

*Sociétés de Construction*
Article 12 of 1986 Law provides that a company which includes in its corporate purpose the construction of a building, must comply with the requirements of art L 212–10 of the CCH. This means that the company is bound under art L 222–1 of the CCH to conclude a development contract (*contrat de promotion immobilière*) in conformity with the provisions of arts 1831–1 and 1831–5 of the Civil Code and arts L 222–1 to L 222–7 of the CCH.

According to these articles the development contract concluded between the *Société de Construction* and a professional, real estate developer (*promoteur immobilier*), obliges the real estate developer, in consideration of the agreed remuneration, to develop the building for a stipulated price.

Under such a contract, the real estate developer is liable for all charges in excess of the agreed price, for the completion of the building, in accordance with the terms and conditions set out in the contract. This liability is in turn guaranteed by a financial institution.

Where a company acquires an already completed building with the intention of converting it and the value of planned works exceeds 50 per cent of the purchase price of the building, art 12, para 2 of the 1986 Law, also subjects such a company to the above conditions.

*Sociétés d'Acquisition*

In order to avoid the complicated legal and financial structures involved in a real estate development contract, the 1986 Law has authorised a pre-existing method for the constitution of timeshare companies based on purchasing buildings to be completed at a future date rather than on purchasing only the land and providing for the erection of the building.

Article 12, para 3 of the 1986 Law provides that:

> Les sociétés prévues à l'Article 1 qui ont pour objet l'acquisition des immeubles à construire doivent conclure un contrat ou bénéficier d'une cession de contrat conforme aux dispositions des Articles L 261–10 et suivant du CCH. Si la vente a lieu sous la forme de vente d'un immeuble en état futur d'achèvement, le contrat comporte la garantie d'achèvement prevue par l'Article L 261–11 du même code.

> A company defined under Article 1 and whose objects are to purchase buildings to be erected must enter into or be assigned a contract drafted in accordance with Articles L 261–10 and following of the CCH. In the case of the purchase of a building in a future state of completion the contract must include the guarantee of completion provided for by Article L 261–11 of the same code.

In other words a timesharing company can and usually does acquire its assets by way of purchase of a building yet to be erected.

Such a purchase is usually made in the form of a 'sale of a building in a future state of completion' as set out by the Law of 3 January 1967, codified by arts L 261–1 *ff* of the CCH and must provide for a completion guarantee for the benefit of any purchaser.

The completion guarantee is defined in art R 261–17 of the CCH.

> La garantie de l'achèvement de l'immeuble résulte soit de l'existence de conditions propres à l'opération, soit de l'intervention, dans les conditions prévues ci-après, d'une banque, d'un établissement financier habilité à faire des opérations de crédit immobilier, d'une entreprise d'assurance agrée à cet effet ou d'une société de caution mutuelle constituée conformément aux dispositions de la loi modifiée du 13 mars 1917, ayant pour objet l'organisation du crédit au petit et moyen commerce, à la petite et moyenne industrie.
> La garantie de remboursement est donnée par l'un des organismes indiqués à l'alinéa ci-dessus ...

The guarantee of completion of the building derives either from the existence of conditions peculiar to the operation, or from the intervention, under the conditions provided for hereinafter, of a bank, a financing institution empowered to carry out real property credit operations, an insurance company approved for this purpose or a mutual guarantee company set up in accordance with the provisions of the amended Law of 13 March 1917 having as its purpose arrangement of credit for small and medium-sized businesses and small and medium-sized industries.

The guarantee of reimbursement is provided by one of the entities indicated in the above paragraph ...

It can thus be seen from this provision that the guarantee of completion must be provided by one of the entities specified, hence by an entity outside the constructing company. However, according to art R261–18 of the CCH, there is an exception from the requirement to provide an independent guarantee where the following conditions are fulfilled.

a. L'immeuble est mis hors d'eau et n'est grevé d'aucun privilège ou hypothèque, ou
b. Les fondations sont achevées et si le financement de l'immeuble ou des immeubles compris dans un même programme est assuré à concurrence de 75% du prix de vente prévu
   —par les fonds propres du vendeur;
   —par le montant du prix des ventes déjà conclues;
   —par les crédits confirmés des banques ou établissements financiers habilités à faire des opérations de crédit immobilier, déduction faite des prêts transférables aux acquéreurs des logements déjà vendus ...

The guarantee of completion derives from the existence of conditions peculiar to the operation when the latter fulfils one or the other of the following conditions:
a. The building is made watertight and is not encumbered by any preferential claim or mortgage, or
b. The foundations are completed and the financing of the building or buildings included under one and the same programme is insured up to the amount of 75% of the selling price provided for:
   —by the funds of the vendor himself;
   —by the amount of the prices for sales already concluded;
   —by the confirmed loans of banks or financial institutions empowered to carry out real property credit operations, after deduction of the loans transferable to the purchasers of the accommodation already sold ...

Furthermore, in the case of a sale of a building in a future state of completion, the buyer pays the purchase price of the building in stages as the work is carried out. Article R261–14 of the CCH provides in this respect:

Les paiements ou dépôts ne peuvent excéder au total:
   35% du prix à l'achèvement des fondations;
   70% à la mise hors d'eau;
   95% à l'achèvement de l'immeuble.
Le solde est payable lors de la mise du local à la disposition de l'acquéreur; toutefois, il peut être consigné en cas de contestation sur la conformité avec les prévisions du contrat.

Payments or deposits cannot exceed in total:
35% of the contract price when the foundation is completed;
70% when the building is watertight;
95% when the building is totally completed.
The balance is payable when the purchaser enters into actual possession of the building; however, the balance can be placed in escrow in case a dispute should arise as to whether the building was constructed in accordance with contractual provisions.

In practice the developer would form two companies: the first one, a *Société de Construction*, would acquire the land and erect the building on it and the second one, a *Société d'Acquisition*, would purchase the land and building in future state of completion from the first company. Thus, the developer has avoided the requirements of entering into a real estate development contract with a third party, which he would otherwise be obliged to do.

## Administration of a timesharing company governed by the 1986 Law

The administration of a timesharing company will generally depend on the form of the company its founder members have chosen subject to the following exceptions:

### Management

Article 7 of the 1986 Law makes null and void:

> ... toutes clauses de statuts prévoyant la désignation d'une personne physique ou morale autre que le réprésentant de la société pour assumer la mission prévue à l'Article 1er de la presente loi.

> ... any clause of the articles of association providing for the appointment of a natural person or corporate body other than the representative of the company to carry out the duties as set out in Article 1 of this law.

This provision has been enacted to prevent a timesharing company from entrusting a third party with carrying out the company's objects. Therefore, such duties can be carried out only under the responsibility of the company's managers or directors.

Article 5 of the 1986 Law mandatorily provides that the company's manager can only be appointed or dismissed by a majority not less than 50 per cent of the shares.

### Shareholders' meetings

Pursuant to art 13, para 4, the shareholders may always attend the annual general meeting and vote personally or appoint a proxy or vote by correspondence. A manager of the company may not be appointed as a shareholder's proxy.

As the timesharers (shareholders) are generally spread throughout the whole country and live a great distance from each other, it is usually difficult for them to attend general meetings. The 1986 Law attempted to lessen such an inconvenience by providing for an original institution: the appointment of a representative of a period. Given that certain shareholders occupy the property within the same time of the year and they, therefore, have certain common interests, the legislator made a provision for the shareholders to be represented by either one or several of their fellow shareholders at general meetings.

Article 14 of the 1986 Law set out that:

les statuts prévoient que chaque ensemble d'associés ayant un droit de jouissance pendant la même période, peuvent, à la majorité, désigner un ou plusieurs de cet ensemble pour les répresenter à l'assemblée générale.

The articles of association shall provide that each group (class) of shareholders exercising their rights of occupation within the same period, may appoint one or several shareholders chosen among the members of such a group in order to represent that group at general meetings, such representatives being appointed by a simple majority.

The representative of the group of shareholders may be appointed for not more than three years but such an appointment may be renewed.

Notwithstanding the appointment of the representative of the group of shareholders, each shareholder may always attend at and vote at general meetings personally or by a proxy specifically appointed by him for this purpose (art 13, para 4).

By the above provision, the legislator obviously intended to protect the rights of shareholders who have not voted in favour of a representative of their group.

The representative of the group may vote for any resolution at the general meetings except resolutions relating to amendments of articles of association, regulations, disposal of company's assets, winding up the company and alteration of allocation of the shareholders' rights (art 14, para 3 and art 16, paras 2, 4 and 5).

*General meetings and documents to be notified to shareholders*

The general meeting must be held at least once a year. It can only consider resolutions put on the agenda within a reasonable time beforehand and documents duly notified to the shareholders. It should be also noted that the number of votes of each shareholder must always be proportionate to the number of his shares in the capital.

*Majority rules*

As a general rule, all decisions taken at general meetings are taken by a simple majority of the votes of shareholders in attendance, either personally or through their representatives (art 16, para 1).

However, decisions on certain matters require a greater majority. A majority of two-thirds of the votes of shareholders, either voting in person or by proxy, is required for decisions relating to alteration of equipment or altering the common parts of the building (art 16, para 3).

A majority of two-thirds of the share capital (shareholders' votes) is required for any resolution relating to the amendment of articles of association, amendment of the plan which sets out the extent and distribution of the units in which the property is constituted, provisions affecting the rights of occupation of shareholders, extension of the life or winding-up of the company, or changes in the proportion of share capital allocated to shareholders.

In respect of the above decisions, the shareholders who are not founder members of the company shall exercise at least 40 per cent of voting rights (art 16, paras 2, 3 and 4).

### Control organs of the company

Article 18, para 1, provides for constitution of a supervisory board to be appointed from the shareholders other than the managers. Article 18, para 4, provides that an external auditor of the company is to be mandatorily appointed.

### Legal status of shareholders and the transfer of shares

The founder members acquire the shares by subscription to the share capital when the company is incorporated. Normally the founder members are developers who subscribe to the shares for the purpose of selling them to the public. Therefore, there is no need for statutory protection of the founder members.

However, the legislator did intend to protect shareholders who would be acquiring shares in the company at a future date, with the purpose of using their rights to occupy the premises. Thus, art 20 sets out the rather cumbersome requirements, with respect to the selling of shares to the public, to be complied with.

Documents affecting the transfer of shares in the company must contain the following information:

1 the nature of the rights transferred. The address of the property, the residential premises corresponding to the unit, the length and period of its occupation attributable to the transferor, the sale price to be paid to the transferor or creditor as the case may be (unless the transfer takes place as a gift), should all be clearly identified;

2 the state of the transferor's account with the company as certified by the company;

3 The reference numbers allocated to the notary's records of the contract of sale of the property at the time of its acquisition by the company and the documents establishing ownership of the rights of occupation;

4 the memorandum and articles of association and regulations containing an inventory of equipment, fixtures and fittings, and the distribution and extent of the private and common parts of the property, and the schedule of the groups of shares and their allotment as between shareholders;
5 the note describing the characteristics of the property and the residential premises.

The transferor shall deliver to the transferee a copy of all of the above documents and obtain written evidence of their delivery. Alternatively, these documents may be annexed to the contract of sale or to the particulars of sale in the case of a compulsory sale.

The following additional documents must also be delivered to the transferee: the company balance sheet for the preceding financial year, the amount of the charges paid in connection with the unit forming the subject of the sale (or, if these are not available, an estimate thereof) and the inventory of the equipment, fixtures and fittings appurtenant to the unit.

The transferor shall deliver to the transferee a copy of these documents and obtain written evidence of their delivery. Alternatively, the transferor may inform the transferee in writing that these documents are in the hands of the notary, stating the relevant reference in the records of the notary.

If private services aimed at organising the exchange of the period of occupation are advertised by the company, the transferor must specify this in the contract of sale.

The provisions of art 20 are binding on shareholders only in the event of an increase in the share capital of the company. They do not apply to the initial shareholders at the time of the constitution of the company.

*Transfer of shares prior to completion of the property*
The transfer of shares prior to completion of the property and the installation of all the equipment necessary for the normal use of the same, is permitted only between the founder members. Notwithstanding the foregoing, the transfer of shares to third parties may be allowed where the transferor can guarantee, in the event of the failure of one or more founder members to meet calls upon capital, to meet calls for funds made upon him sufficient to carry out the object of the company.

Such a guarantee must be provided by the *bona fide* guarantee of a property finance company, or mutual guarantee company as defined by the Law of 13 March 1917, whose object is to provide credit for small and medium-sized commercial or industrial companies. The requirement of a guarantee is waived in the case where the transferor is itself one of the legal entities cited above.

*Shareholders' rights and obligations*
A shareholder has the unfettered right to occupy or lend or rent the premises during the period allocated to him. Any clause in the articles of association or regulations stipulating otherwise is null and void (art 23).

In consideration of the above rights the shareholder has the following obligations:

1 To contribute in proportion to his rights when calls are made for funds necessary for the acquisition of land for construction or conversion or overhauling of the building (art 3);
2 To contribute towards maintenance and management costs (art 9).

The law divides the costs into two classes: *charges communes* (running or general maintenance costs) and *charges liées à l'occupation* (costs related to occupation). The 1986 Law has not defined any precise legal criteria to distinguish between different classes of costs. In this respect art 9 refers to a governmental decree to be issued at some later stage. Unfortunately, this has not yet happened.

It is submitted that in practice the costs should be divided into:

1 The general running costs of the company and the upkeep and maintenance of the common parts together with related services including management costs, taxes, insurance, repayable on the common areas and the salary of the caretaker, the costs of services, materials and equipment common to the whole property together with the general upkeep of the property, the water rates, the cost of electricity in the common areas including that supplied to the caretaker's flat, and the whole charges of the utility companies' apparatus and the costs of maintenance of the equipment required for the administration of timeshare property.
2 The costs relative to the occupation of individual residential premises such as the cleaning, etc.

*Apportionment of contribution to maintenance costs among shareholders*
A shareholder contributes towards the general maintenance costs according to his share in the company's capital. As has been seen already, such a share would depend not only on the type of private premises (apartment) the shareholder is to use, but also on the duration and the time of year of his occupation.

However, the shareholder is not to contribute towards the costs relating to occupation if he does not actually occupy the premises.

*Default of a shareholder*
Pursuant to art 3, if a shareholder does not contribute in proportion to his rights in the capital when calls are made for funds required, in order to realise the objects of the company or to pay the outgoings set out in art 9, the provisions of art L 212–4 of CCH apply: in such a case a shareholder cannot claim to enter into possession of the portion of the building to which he is entitled nor may he remain in possession of the shares; the debtor's shares can be put up for public sale, subject to the authorisation of the general meeting

(which must vote by a majority representing two-thirds of the company capital on being convened a first time and by two-thirds of members in attendance or voting by proxy, on being convened a second time).

The proceeds from the auction of the shares sold are apportioned, in the first place, to payment of the sums that are due to the company from the defaulting shareholder at the date of the sale. The rights of the company to the sums recovered take priority over all others including, in particular, the rights of any creditor who has granted to the defaulting shareholder a loan secured on his shares.

Notwithstanding the above specific provisions, the company is always entitled to sue the defaulting shareholder for payment under the general provisions of French law governing debt collection.

## Tax regime of companies under the 1986 Law

One has to make a distinction between the tax regime of a timeshare company and that governing the transfer of company shares of such a company.

According to art 35 of the Law of 6 January 1986, unlike other types of property companies, timeshare companies cannot benefit from the tax transparency system contained in art 1655 of the Code Générale des Impôts (CGI). As a result, these companies are theoretically liable to pay corporation tax. In order to establish the practical effects of this rule, one must first ascertain the nature of taxable profit.

Article 239 *Octiès* of the General Income Tax Code (CGI) as amended by art 6–1 of the amending law on finance of 27 December 1975 provides that, when the purpose of a legal entity liable to pay company tax is to transfer to its members free of charge the possession of an item of movable or real property, the net value of the privilege thus conferred is not to be taken into account in order to determine the taxable profit.

Thus, as long as a timeshare company does not receive funds other than those corresponding to the reimbursement by the shareholders of the management and maintenance expenses incurred on their behalf or for the conservation of the company assets, it does not produce any taxable profit and therefore escapes liability to company income tax. It is not required, because of an explicit provision of art 239 *Octiès*, referred to above, to pay the forfeitary minimum annual tax of 3,000 francs. If, however, the company made any profits it would become subject to the company tax and to the forfeitary minimum tax.

The timeshare company is normally exempt from VAT on its expenditure on the management, upkeep and conservation of the property, ie in practice, the monies paid to the company by way of reimbursement of these costs. The exemption from VAT applies only to the services furnished by the company itself; it is therefore not applicable if the services are rendered by a management company separate from the timeshare company.

These exemptions from company tax and VAT apply only on condition that the company does not carry out any income producing operation with third parties, unless these are incidental operations not amounting in value to more than 10 per cent of its total receipts.

### Taxation of the shareholders

In the case of a member using his timesharing personally, he is exempt from income tax as to the net value of the privilege transferred to him by virtue of the Law of 27 December 1975. If, however, a member is a legal entity liable for company tax or tax on industrial and commercial profits, it cannot benefit from this exemption, which applies only to natural persons and the value will therefore have to be added to its taxable profit, according to the value of the benefit in kind granted (unless these properties are shown among its assets and used for the purposes of its activity). Each member is, in addition, liable to pay the 'tax on occupancy'.

A member who rents out his timeshare is treated as a lessor of furnished apartments. The profits realised are deemed to constitute industrial and commercial profits and are taxed as such.

### The tax regime applicable to the transfer of shares

According to art 257–7 of the CGI any transfer of shares carried out during the construction of the development and within five years from the date of its completion is subject to TVA at the rate of 18.6 per cent. The second transfer and subsequent transfers after the completion, as well as any transfer occurring more than five years after the date of completion, are subject to registration dues at the rate of 5.40 per cent to which must be added the regional tax.

Profits realised upon selling company shares acquired by the original members are also subject to income tax or company tax according to the normal tax rules (art 35–1 of the CGI).

In all of these cases, the provisions of the applicable tax laws must also be taken into account if the member is not a French resident, in order to establish, in particular, whether or not a withholding tax is required and, if such a tax is applicable, to determine its amount.

## The 'club trustee' system, adapted for French conditions

In order to be able to offer to the consumer (occupier) long-term guarantees of his initial investment and to ensure proper long-term management of the buildings in which he exercises his right, it is desirable that he is given more security than the mere contractual guarantees which he would be given, for example, in the case of a long-term or renewable rental contract, but whose price is paid in full on signature of the contract.

### Limiting the consumer's risk

In fact, there are no legal means to protect the occupier against the financial collapse of the entity which grants him such periodic lease, and to ensure the management of the building. However, one could limit the risk by giving to the occupier of the apartment an effective means of controlling the management of the building in which his apartment is situated. As has already been said, taking into account existing French legislation, the only structure which can limit such risks is that of the company in which the occupier would be a shareholder.

This is why the concept of investment in holiday property, based on the acquisition of shares of a real property company giving the shareholder rights of occupation in a given apartment for a particular period and at the same time some control over the management of the building, is an idea which at first seems very attractive. However, the legal structure of a *Société Immobiliaire* (real property company) is considered far too rigid to deal with the risks involved in a major development on an international scale.

### The function of the trustee

In order to facilitate investing in holiday property which will be marketed outside France, it is possible to integrate a concept based on French company law within a larger scheme based on trustee law (club trustee scheme) as used in Britain. The latter scheme has already been explained in Chapter 2 but, in short, a trustee holds the building on behalf of an unincorporated and non-profit making body (club) whose sole object is to ensure for its members the exclusive rights of occupation of the building held on trust by the trustee.

The rules governing the constituting and management of a club, and the rules governing the legal relationship between the club and the trustee, are very flexible. They allow, in particular, the acquisition of new properties or the controlled disposition of a property by the club without any substantial formality.

It is also submitted that club members have the same amount of control or influence over the management of a club as do the shareholders of a French company governed by the Law of 6 January 1986.

### Legal problems

As the concept of the trustee does not yet exist under French law, all legal setting up based on this concept has to be governed by English law. However, a new trust law is proposed for France, and a draft of the proposed law is included as Appendix C. The law is expected to be enacted in the near future and, clearly, this draft may be subject to modification. Once enacted, the new law will simplify matters dramatically, but it is as well to examine the current situation.

Currently, the direct use of the trustee system in France would carry a risk of running into major legal obstacles: with regard to the subject matter of the membership contract to the club and the exercise of a member's rights in relation to the timesharing of a building in France.

Pursuant to arts 14 and 15 of the Civil Code, French courts have jurisdiction over matters brought before them by French nationals. Thus, a French timesharer may bring before a French judge a case involving, for instance, a sales contract for club membership or the club constitution.

Given that these contracts are governed by English law, the French judge, in such a case, would have to reach his decision mainly by following the rules of a legal system with which he is not familiar. Such a situation would involve a risk for the parties involved arising from the legal uncertainty as to the outcome of such litigation.

One way of overcoming this problem would be to insert a clause into the contract waiving the French party's rights, under arts 14 and 15. Such a clause inserted into a contract would be deemed to be perfectly valid.

However, the French judge might declare such a clause void if he thought that the subject matter of the litigation put into question the rules relating to the protection of French consumers. It follows therefore, that as long as a timesharing scheme is sold in France and to the French, it must conform to French consumer protection legislation.

Since the purpose of an international timesharing scheme is that it should be marketed in other countries, eg England, it must also conform to the rules of protection for English consumers. It is extremely difficult and risky to try to draw up one contract conforming to the consumer protection legislation of several countries at the same time. Finally, it is likely that the French consumer will be reluctant to invest in a timesharing scheme governed by legal rules that he cannot understand.

## A possible solution

However, it is possible to offset to a large extent the problems described above by combining, in some way, the concept of a French timesharing company with that of the 'club trustee system'. The part of the concept governed under English law is similar to that used in Spain. The main points can be summarised as follows: the developer, referred to as 'sales company', transfers the property to a company specially set up for this purpose called 'owning company', which is 100 per cent owned by the trustee.

At the same time, he will have formed a club whose sole object is to ensure for its members the exclusive rights of occupation of the building held on trust by the trustee. The club is formed by two founder members: a developer and a management company in charge of the administration of the club's business and property.

In consideration for the transfer of the building to the owning company, the trustee will hold the property on trust for the developer who is initially entitled to all the membership rights of the club represented by membership certificates. Each certificate entitles the holder to the right of occupation of a particular apartment in the building for a fixed week in the year.

The club member acquires not only the benefit of the contractual rights as set out in the membership application agreement and in the rules of the club constitution itself, but also acquires a beneficial interest under the deed of trust entered into, on the one hand, by the founder members of the club on behalf of the club and all its members at the time and, on the other hand, by the trustee.

The developer will sell membership rights to the public, charging a membership admission fee, of which he is free to fix the price. The developer is free to increase the size of the initial project as he completes new buildings, by transferring these into a trust in which he will initially receive all the club membership rights. If the promoter finds that he is not successfully marketing the building under the system, he has two solutions:

1  He may always demand that the trustee sells that part of the building in which no sales have yet been made.
2  The developer, as a member of the club, may always rent out the unsold weeks of occupation to which he is entitled, provided that he does not change the function and purpose of the building.

**Guarantees to the purchaser**

If we envisage the marketing of a building in the course of its completion the purchaser should receive the benefit of two alternate guarantees. The purchaser must be protected by a guarantee either that he will be able to occupy the premises on the agreed day or that his entire investment will be reimbursed if the building is not completed within a stated period of time.

To achieve this, proceeds from the sale of membership rights are not received directly by the promoter. The sums paid by the public are placed in an escrow account opened for this purpose by the trustee.

The trustee under the escrow conditions will only release the funds to the promoter upon completion of the building. If completion does not occur within the agreed time period, the trustee as stakeholder will reimburse purchasers all monies paid with interest.

The trustee can, however, partially release funds as the building works advance. To facilitate early release of funds a bank completion guarantee can also be arranged. In this way the guarantees given to the purchaser are identical to the guarantees for completion of the building required by French law. Nevertheless, as the concept is based on the existence of a trust, all the above operations must be submitted to English law, and, for the above stated reasons, it is not recommended that it be sold in France until the new trust law comes into force.

### Creation of a *Société Civile* for French members

With regard to that part of the programme which is to be marketed in France, as opposed to that part which will be marketed outside France, it would be advisable, as the law now stands, to set up a scheme so that club memberships could be individually sold to the French public under French law, thereby preventing any member of the French public bringing before the French courts that part of the structure governed by English law. This may be achieved by incorporating all French members of the timesharing scheme into a *Société Civile* which the developer would set up for this purpose in France.

The *Société Civile* would be incorporated under French law and would comply in particular with the consumer protection rules as set out in the 1986 Law. It would apply as such for the membership in the English timesharing club, since a member may be any legal person whether an individual or a corporate body. The *Société Civile* would purchase from the 'sales company' (the developer) the membership rights related to a specific apartment for the whole calendar year (ie 52 membership certificates for one week each) so as to have absolute beneficial entitlement as against the trustee.

Whereas, the articles of association of the French company and contracts for sale of its shares would be governed by French law, the company's relationship with to the trustee and the English club would be governed by English law. In this way the purchase of occupation rights by a French timesharer would be subject to French law.

The *Société Civile* would enjoy the rights of an ordinary member of the English club. The number of votes in the club's general meetings that the French company would have would correspond to the number of 'purchased' apartments multiplied by 52 (since there are 52 weeks in a year).

We should mention the general principles of French private international law with respect to the relationship between the *Société Civile* on one hand and the sales company, trustee and club on the other.

The choice of English law by the parties should certainly be upheld, since it is consistent with the actual relationship between them. It is unlikely that a French court, which could only be seised by the *Société Civile*, would decide that the choice of jurisdiction clause is null and void as French consumer protection legislation should not be involved and a *Société Civile* does not call for any particular protection.

As regards French consumers, their interests are well protected since the proposed legal framework is subject to French law and the memorandum and articles of association may be drafted so as to take account of all relevant provisions of the Law of 6 January 1986.

However, one source of difficulty may exist concerning the nature of the rights conferring entitlement to the occupation of the property (*l'immeuble 'social'*).

The 1986 Law (art 1, para 2) reads that it only applies to companies whose objects include: '... acquisition of buildings or real property rights over buildings ...'. The French civil company does not appear to own a property right in the property, only a chose in action against the club whose membership certificate the company possesses. Nonetheless, it appears that under the English law of trusts, the company is entitled to require delivery up by the trustee of the part of the property to which its exclusive rights correspond (absolute beneficial entitlement). In any event, it is possible for a French national to own real estate through the intermediary of an English trust in circumstances where the legal relations between the French national and the trustee are governed by English law (cf Paris, 10 January 1970, D1972.122).

A French judge before whom the question might be brought would have little choice but to conclude that the French *Société Civile* complies with the provisions of the Law of 6 January 1986 relating to the definition of its object provided that the rules of the club, or other obligations incumbent on the club, permit the company at its sole discretion to exercise its rights over the apartments as it sees fit and, if appropriate, to sever and dispose of its estate in the property.

Once again, it is worth envisaging other circumstances in which a French court could be seised. Proceedings could be brought by the *Société Civile* in relation to its legal relations with the club or by a member in relation to his legal relations with the *Société Civile*.

There is obviously no difficulty in applying French law to the relationship between the *Société Civile* and its shareholders and to submit this relationship to the French jurisdiction.

The acquisition of the right of use of the property by the *Société Civile* takes place pursuant to a contract for sale of such rights (expressed in membership certificates) governed by English law and incorporating an English jurisdiction clause.

According to the case law now well established by the *Cour de Cassation* the French judge should declare the jurisdiction clause valid and therefore also declare himself as not having jurisdiction over the case (Civ 4 July 1972; Clunet 1972, 843; Civ 7 December 1985, IR 265; Cassation Req du 22 mai 1983; GP 1983, 2, 38).

In conclusion, it is submitted that the international club trustee timeshare scheme incorporating the *Société Civile* has the merit of placing the French consumer in the same position as he would be if he subscribed to shares in a *Société Civile Immobiliaire d'Attribution*.

It ensures compliance with the very demanding requirements of French consumer protection legislation and preserves to a very large extent the flexibility provided for by the English law of trusts. The new law, when enacted, will enable a club trustee system to be established, very much on Anglo-Saxon lines but governed by French law, and will consequently remove the drafting difficulties and complexities referred to above.

## Tax regulations and the club trustee system in France

From the tax point of view the legal structure described above is fairly complicated and may involve the tax regulations of several countries, depending where the different companies which the scheme involves are situated.

For tax purposes the economic relations between different elements of the scheme may be summarised as follows:

1 *The sales company* ('Sales'):
   (a) acquires from a third party a newly completed building;
   (b) transfers this building to the owning company at its acquisition value and, in consideration of this transfer to the owning company (wholly owned by the trustee), Sales receives from the trustee all the membership certificates in the club (representing the occupation rights);
   (c) sells the certificates to the public, making a substantial profit.
   (d) Its profit is the difference between the sale price of all the certificates and the acquisition price of the building.
   (NB: Sales is a founder member of the club with as many votes as it holds membership certificates.)
2 *The owning company*: as a wholly owned subsidiary of the trustee, receives from Sales the property.
3 *The trustee*:
   (a) as parent of the owning company, delivers to Sales the membership certificates of the club, corresponding to the acquisition value of the building;
   (b) holds the shares of the owning company on trust for the club (ie, collectively for the members of the club);
   (c) receives remuneration for its services (the administration of the assets in trust) in the form of 'fees' paid by the club by virtue of a separate contract.
4 *The management company*:
   (a) is a founder member of the club but only holds one membership certificate;
   (b) administers the building according to instructions received from the club to which it must account;
   (c) receives remuneration for this service by virtue of a service contract entered into with the club.
5 *The club*:
   (a) gives instructions to the trustee relating to the administration or disposal of the shares of the owning company (eg the sale of the asset, ie the building of the owning company, or the acquisiton of a new asset);
   (b) gives instructions concerning the actual management of the building to the management company and controls the carrying out of such instructions;

(c) pays all costs relating to the management of the building;

(d) collects from its members the necessary funds to pay the charges mentioned in the previous paragraph; and

(e) in the name of and on behalf of all the beneficiaries of the trust (members of the club), as defined in the deed of trust, gives instructions to the trustee to the effect that the trustee will permit members of the club to occupy the building as stipulated by the membership certificates.

(f) The decisions of the club are taken collectively by its members in accordance with similar rules to those which normally govern a company.

6 *The ordinary members of the club*:

(a) can be domiciled anywhere in the world;

(b) acquire for valuable consideration, the rights of occupation (by reference to weekly periods) relating to given apartments.

(c) The rights of occupation (evidenced by the club membership certificates) are granted to them by the sales company for a price greatly exceeding the corresponding part of the value of the building.

(d) The ordinary members enjoy their rights in kind (ie, they occupy the club's building), but they can also rent the premises to third parties.

How will the above operations be taxed by the French tax authorities with regard to:

1 company tax,
2 VAT,
3 tax under art 990.D of the CGI (3 per cent tax).

## Company tax

*Owning company*

For the sake of administrative convenience, in a typical timeshare scheme, the owning company should be set up in the country where the trustee is incorporated or domiciled.

Since the owning company is the 100 per cent owned subsidiary of the trustee and it makes no profit on the property of the building wherever the owning company is incorporated, it is not subject to any tax by way of company tax.

*Trustee*

The trustee should be incorporated in a country whose legal system includes the concept of trust law, eg England and Wales, Channel Islands, Isle of Man.

The trustee grants to the sales company, membership certificates as consideration for the transfer of the building to the owning company which, as stated above, is the 100 per cent owned subsidiary of the trustee. The trustee makes no direct profit from the operation.

The French tax authorities are not concerned with the trustee's remuneration for services provided (the administration of the assets of the club held on trust) since these services are provided abroad.

## Management company

The management company is subject to the principle of territoriality of tax (art 209–1 of the CGI). Under this principle, the French tax authorities apply two criteria to determine whether the activities of the management company are subject to French company tax:

1 the notion of the established place of business (which could be the case if there was a subsidiary in France etc);
2 the carrying out of a series of related commercial transactions completing a cycle.

Taking into account the location of the building, the management company, whose registered office is situated offshore (eg on the Isle of Man), would risk its activities being taxed on one or other of the criteria. On the other hand, if the management company is situated in England, the tax regime and the place of payment of taxes will be defined by the Anglo-French double taxation treaty.

## Sales company

The sales company will receive from the trustee, as consideration for the transfer of the building to the owning company, the membership certificates of the club of which it is a member. It will sell these certificates to the public and will earn substantial profits from such sales.

The type of tax applicable to these profits and the place where it is charged will be determined by the interpretation given to the sale of the said certificates by the French tax administration.

Pursuant to art 35.1 of the CGI, the French tax authorities are likely to regard the sale of membership certificates as the sale of shares in a *Société Civile immobilier*, since a membership certificate entitles its holder to the use of a building, and a company involved in such a sale is subject to corporate tax on its profits. Moreover, under art 164B of the CGI, revenues from buildings situated in France or revenues from rights relating to these buildings are always considered as revenues arising in France.

Three situations may arise:

1 If the sales company is situated in France it would be subject to the French company tax.
2 If the sales company has its permanent establishment in another country, such as Great Britain, which has passed a reciprocal treaty with France to assist in collection of tax, it would still be subject to normal company tax in France.

3 If the sales company is situated offshore (eg on the Isle of Man) it would be subject to the withholding tax of 50 per cent, as provided by art 244 bis of the CGI.

## VAT on the sale of membership certificates or shares

Article 258–2 of the CGI charges to French property VAT any property transaction or sale of shares described in arts 257–6 and 257–7 of the same Code, regardless of the country in which these transactions have taken place and the nationality of the parties. Therefore, the transfer of the building from sales to the owning company will be subject to French rules governing VAT.

Where these operations are carried out at their nominal value the tax effect will be neutral. The difficulty arises with the transfer of the membership certificates by the trustee to the sales company and their sale by the latter to the public.

Once the tax authorities decide that the club members (including the sales company) are as a matter of fact the holders of the shares or have an interest in an SCI (in these circumstances the owning company), whose allocation ensures the occupation of a building in France, VAT on property will be payable on all transfers of membership certificates wherever they take place.

However, according to certain French tax specialists (*Memento Immobilier Lefebvre Edition* 1989 No 4257): 'with regard to the share capital the location of the building will be deemed to be that of the company's registered office'. If this opinion proves correct, which remains to be seen, the sale of membership certificates by a company not registered in France will not be subject to French VAT on property.

## VAT on other services

*Management company*
The management company's principal activity is the management of the building in France. It is thus entitled to collect the contributions (corresponding to the maintenance charges of the building) from members wherever they are situated.

VAT in France will therefore normally be chargeable on its activities in accordance with the provisions of art 259.A—2 of the CGI.

*Trustee*
The trustee is charged with the management of the shares of a foreign company. Therefore the French administration will not be concerned with these services.

## CGI, art 990D 3 per cent tax

Under art 990D of the CGI, companies whose registered office is situated ouside France and which, whether directly or through intermediaries, possess a building situated in France, or are owners of real rights over such a building, are chargeable to an annual tax of 3 per cent of the market value of the building or the rights.

Companies with a registered office in a country which has entered into a double taxation treaty with France are not liable for this tax.

Under art 990G, the 3 per cent tax is not deductible from company tax. Therefore, it would seem that it is to be additional to the witholding tax of 50 per cent outlined in art 244 bis of the CGI and, of course, with VAT on property if applicable. If one follows the doctrine of the tax authorities relating to transparent companies (see *Memento Fiscal Francis Lefebvre* 1990 Edition No 3450), the tax is not payable by a foreign company situated in a tax haven if its members are situated in a country which has passed a double taxation treaty with France. Therefore, if Sales is situated in Great Britain, the 3 per cent tax will not be payable.

One should, however, add that it stems from the text of art 990D itself, that the amount of tax payable should diminish as membership certificates are sold to people domiciled in countries which have passed such a double taxation treaty. Therefore, in practice, if the sales company is registered in a tax haven, this tax will only be payable during the first years of the life of the club, ie during the sales period.

### Fiscal control

The above observations do not take into account the possibility of the French tax administration scrutinising the practical effect of these operations and the value of the different transactions comprised therein.

Nevertheless, in practice, it must be borne in mind that the building is located in France and the tax authorities can proceed on the basis of a deemed taxation more easily, since they are familiar with corporate timeshare operations.

Further, a deemed imposition will be easier to establish since a portion of the rights of occupation are to be sold in France, and the price of their sale to the public will therefore be known.

## Club trustee system incorporating a *Société Civile* in France

We assume that a *Société Civile* will be established in France having as its assets all 52 certificates relating to a given apartment, by which the *Société Civile* acquires the continuous rights of enjoyment in a fraction of the building.

The sales company (whether English or French) will be the initial shareholder of the *Société Civile* with the total share capital concentrated in its possession. The *Société Civile* will be set up according to the legislation on *multipropriété* companies of 1986. The sales company as initial shareholder will sell the shares of the *Société Civile* to the French public.

With regard to taxation, this operation would be entirely subject to French legislation. The sales company will pay company tax and VAT calculated on capital gains arising from the sale of shares in France.

## Timesharing concepts linked with property purchase on a co-ownership basis

This type of investment is based on the purchase of an apartment in a tourist complex on a freehold basis. The relationship between the owners of different apartments is governed by the co-ownership legislation (Law No 65–557 of 10 July 1965, as amended by Law No 85–1470 of 31 December 1985).

The purchase is coupled with either a lease back agreement (*propriété nouvelle*) or the assignment of the use of the property granted by the purchaser to the management company of the resort (in fact the developer) for a certain number of years (*prépropriété*), whereby the purchaser reserves for himself the use of the property during certain weeks every year.

In order to obtain maximum tax and financial efficiency for the purchaser the apartment should normally be situated in a tourist resort (*résidence du tourisme*) of a certain standard of comfort following the norms established by the Minister of Tourism. The legal definition of such a 'tourist resort' is currently provided by *Arrêté* of 14 February 1986:

(La résidence de tourisme) est un établissement commercial d'hébergement classé faisant l'objet d'une exploitation permanente ou saisonnière. Elle est constituée d'un ensemble homogène de chambres ou appartements meuvlés (collectif ou pavillonnaire), mis à la disposition d'une clientèle touristique qui n'y élit pas domicile.

(A tourist resort) is a commercial establishment of classified residential units used either permanently or by season. It consists of a homogeneous group of furnished rooms or apartments (collective or separate), available to tourists who do not elect to make it their home.

Furthermore, the tourist resort must satisfy the following requirements:

1 It must have a capacity of at least 100 beds.
2 The property is normally held on a co-ownership basis.
3 The co-ownership system must include a long-term commitment to rent furnished premises for a period of not less than nine years.
4 The tourist resort must be used for the purposes of holiday letting and must be managed by a single person, whether an individual or a company.

Based on their amenities and services, the resorts are classified in one of four categories set fourth in the *Arrêté* of 14 February 1986. The classification is made by decision of the Commissioner of the Republic upon notice of the Departmental Commission of Tourism.

## Taxation of tourist resorts

Without going into details of the tax regime governing tourist resorts, such schemes (including, *inter alia*, '*propriété nouvelle*' and '*prépropriété*') have been conceived to provide large tax incentives benefiting both corporate and private investors.

The income from letting the apartments in a resort is considered as industrial and commercial income, (*benefice industriel et commercial*) (arts 151 septiès and 156–1–4 of the CGI).

However, the investor (owner of the apartment) is actually allowed to set off, under certain conditions, the cost of the initial investment against the income generated from renting the premises (art 156–1–4 of the CGI) and VAT paid on the purchase price against VAT charges from the rent (art 273 bis II of the CGI).

## Propriété nouvelle and prepropriété

*Propriété nouvelle* and *prepropriété* are both forms of co-ownership.

### Propriété nouvelle

A typical resort usually consists of one or several plots of land on which are built apartment buildings or bungalows and premises for occupiers' common use and other facilities. The resort is governed by the Law of 10 July 1965 relating to the co-ownership of immmovable property. Finally, the resort would belong to the category of 'tourist resorts' within the scope of the *Arrêté* of 14 February 1986 and would be managed by a professional management company.

The legal structure of the scheme consists of two operations:

1 a contract for the sale of an apartment to be completed in the future, and
2 a lease contract between the purchaser and the management company of the resort.

The term *propriété nouvelle* expresses the indivisibility of these two operations compared to a mere freehold property transfer.

The purchase contract for an apartment in a state of future completion within the resort is entered into by the developer as vendor and, in most cases, a private purchaser. The purchase price is reduced by 20 per cent—30 per cent compared to the standard market value of the apartment. The reduction of the price is granted in consideration of the purchaser granting a lease to the management company for nine to 11 years, the apartment to be subsequently sublet by the management company to ordinary tourists on a weekly basis.

The income resulting from the lease is paid in two ways:

1 In kind: in a typical scheme the purchaser is entitled to occupy the apartment for six to seven weeks per year during the whole term of the lease;
2 In money or money's worth: advance payment of the rent under the lease and reimbursement of the VAT allowed by art 273 bis II of the CGI the amount of which corresponds to the reduction of the price of the apartment.

If the purchaser finances the acquisition by a private loan, he is allowed to deduct the interest of such a loan, up to a certain amount, from his yearly income to be declared to the tax authorities. The purchaser pays no contribution towards the maintenance costs of the resort since this is financed from the income the management company generates from the subletting of the remaining available weeks.

When the lease expires, the owner of the apartment recovers the whole interest in the property and is free either to renew the lease or to sell the property free of any contractual encumbrances.

## Prepropriété

The purchaser acquires an apartment in a tourist resort on a freehold basis and irrevocably assigns the use of the apartment (*cession de l'usufruit*) to the management company of the resort, usually for 12 years. In consideration of the assignment of the use of the property, the purchaser obtains a reduction in the price corresponding to the rental value of the property for 12 years (approximately 50 per cent of its full market value). A part of this reduction is, however, granted in kind. The purchaser opens what is, effectively, an account with the management company from which he is entitled each year to a credit (a voucher) corresponding to the rental value of his apartment for two weeks during the high season. The purchaser is entitled to use the 'credit' in the account to rent an apartment or otherwise use the facilities within the particular resort.

The assignment of the use of the apartment cannot be cancelled before its time. Therefore, the apartment can only be sold within the first 12 years subject to the management company's rights over the use of the property.

Arguably, the *propriété nouvelle* or *prepropriété* should not be classified as a genuine timeshare scheme since the specific feature is to share the occupation rights only among two 'timesharers': the freehold owner and the management company of the resort. Therefore, such schemes can clearly only work if the management company is able to rent out the particular apartment on a traditional tourist resort basis during a significant part of the year.

It is also arguable that whilst a purchaser perceives the purchase of timeshare rights (either in the form of shares in a timeshare company or in the form of a membership certificate or a club trustee scheme) as a holiday investment, the purchaser of an apartment within the scheme of *propriété nouvelle* or *prepropriété* would perceive it as an investment in 'bricks and mortar' and therefore would be greatly influenced by the financial return of the investment.

Finally, the price of a typical apartment purchased in the form of *propriété nouvelle* or *prepropriété* seems to be far higher than the purchase of occupation rights relating to a similar apartment within a timeshare scheme.

## Nota

The French Government has recently decided to introduce trust law into the French legal system. The preliminary draft of the Bill, presented by the Ministry of Justice, suggests the introduction of a new chapter into the French Civil Code (Appendix C). No date, however, has been fixed yet, but the Government is planning to introduce the Bill as soon as possible.

To a large extent, the Bill is inspired by English Common Law. However, as opposed to the latter, the French trust (*la Fiducie*) is not a form of ownership but a mere contract.

Subject to substantial alterations of the initial project, it is believed that the new French trust law may facilitate the introduction of the Club trustee timesharing scheme, which is similar to the scheme used in the UK, in France.

It is also believed that such a scheme, based on the new French trust law, is likely to supersede most of the existing timesharing schemes which are described above since it is (a) relatively simple to set up, (b) flexible and, moreover, (c) having regard to the specific functions of the trustee, it may offer better protection to timeshare users.

# Chapter Ten

# Timesharing in Spain

There are now more timesharing projects in Spain and the Spanish islands than in any other European country and at the same time the largest market for timesharing in Spain is the United Kingdom, although other markets, such as the German one, are increasing their share. It is therefore important to provide some analysis of Spanish law in relation to timesharing.

## Spanish law and timesharing

The first point to make is that there is no specific timesharing law in Spain. The Spanish authorities (in consideration of the increasing importance of timesharing within the tourism industry, which is the most important industry in Spain) are now preparing draft legislation to regulate timeshare activities. The preparation of this legislation so far has been carried out in co-operation with representatives of the industry, as it is the declared intention of the Spanish authorities not to restrict the growth of timesharing. A draft of the proposed new law can be found at Appendix F and will be commented on hereafter. We commence however with an examination of the current law.

### Real rights

If timesharing were to be regarded as one of the types of rights existing in Spanish law, it would have to be included among the real rights as granting to its holders an immediate and direct power over the object of the right and also imposing upon everybody (*erga omnes*) an obligation of respect and abstention, thus distinguishing it from a personal or contractual right. Another characteristic of a real right under Spanish law is the possibility of its registration in the Land Registry which entails a privileged protection of the right.

If a timesharing scheme had to be governed by Spanish law (as opposed to applying a different system of laws, although relating to rights of occupation of property in Spain) it would necessarily be required to have the characteristics of a real right under the Spanish law, since the Anglo-Saxon trust concept is not part of the *lex loci*. Accordingly, it is necessary to address the question of whether it is possible to create new types of real rights under Spanish law.

In principle, Spanish law seems to leave freedom for the constitution of real rights and the modification of those already existing. This view is based on art 2.23 of the *Ley Hipotecaria* (Registration Law) which refers to every existing real right and then adds '*otros cualesquiera derechos reales*' (any other real right), and more clearly on art 7 of the regulations under this law which provides as follows:

> Conforme a lo dipuesto en el artículo 2 de la Ley, no sólo deberán inscribirse los títulos en que se declare, constituya, reconozca, transmita, modifique o extinga el dominio o los derechos reales que en dichos párrafos se mencionan, sino cualesquiera otros relativos a derechos de la misma naturaleza, así como cualquier acto o contrato de trascendencia real que, sin tener nombre propio en derecho, modifique, desde luego, o en lo futuro, algunas de las facultades del dominio sobre bienes inmuebles o inherentes a derechos reales.

> According to the provisions of art 2 of the law, not only will the titles whereby ownership or real rights are declared, constituted, recognised, transferred, altered or extinguished, have to be registered, but any other title relating to rights of the same nature, and also any other action or contract of a real nature which, without having a proper name in law, modifies or may modify in the future some of the rights of ownership over immovable property or rights inherent to real rights.

In practice it is necessary to devise a framework for timesharing by adapting or modifying existing real rights because the tendency of Spanish doctrine and the jurisprudence issued by the Directorate of Registries is to maintain the principle of *numerus clausus* in relation to real property rights; that is to say, not to allow the free creation of such real property rights.

By virtue of the principle of autonomy of will, which governs contracts under Spanish law set out in art 1255 of the Civil Code, there is freedom to create new types of rights, but their recognition as real rights can only be granted by the Directorate of Registries or a law governing their existence. Consequently, timesharing can be created as a contractual right and agreements entered into by the parties will be binding, but the right will not have the nature of an independent real right, in other words as a right *in rem*, in the absence of legislative recognition, unless it can be considered as a variation of an existing real right.

Although timesharing as a special intermittent right applicable to immovable property is still a novel concept, intermittent real rights are known to Spanish law, eg in relation to abstraction of water or use of a well, and in relation to rights of way.

## Ownership

It is necessary at the outset to examine the right of ownership in Spain since timesharing belongs to this class of right. The Spanish Civil Code is based on the Code Napoleon which in turn is based on Roman law. Following the continental legal system, art 348 defines ownership as follows:

La propiedad es el derecho de gozar y disponer de una cosa, sin más limitaciones que las establecidas en las leyes. El propietario tiene acción contra el tenedor y el poseedor de la cosa para reivindicarla.

Ownership is the right to enjoy and dispose of a thing, with no limitations other than those established by law. The owner has a right of action for recovery against the holder and the possessor of the thing.

This definition is not entirely satisfactory since it does not differentiate ownership from other rights which also involve an enjoyment and disposal of a thing.

Ownership is defined as an absolute and exclusive right of enjoyment. The right may be further subdivided into the following:

1 Power of free disposal. It is not only the right to transfer or give the property to other persons, that is to say, to alienate, but the right to limit or encumber the property and the right to alter and destroy it. This must be understood in relation to the limitations of art 7.2 of the Civil Code concerning the abuse of rights or the anti-social use of the same, and also with regard to art 33 of the Constitution which in its second paragraph, having recognised the right of ownership, insists on the social function of the property.
2 Powers of free use. These include the right of use and enjoyment of the property, whether or not this adversely affects the value of this property, eg by extracting minerals.
3 Powers of exclusion. Evidently, the right of ownership implies the power to monopolise the enjoyment of the property and therefore the power to exclude others from this enjoyment. The power of exclusion is channelled through actions of protection of ownership whose object is to prevent interference or distrubance in the enjoyment or use of the property by strangers.

According to the object of the ownership, it is necessary to distinguish between movable and immovable property, since each is subject to different regulation. Immovable property requires special regulations aimed at recording and protecting its disposal. The Land Registry was established, therefore, to publicise transactions of immovable property and also the real rights which affect it. Article 1 of the Registration Law (*Ley Hipotecaria*) provides:

El Registro de la Propiedad tiene por objeto la inscripción o anotación de los actos y contratos relativos al dominio y demás derechos reales sobre bienes inmuebles ...
  Los asientos del Registro ... están bajo la salvaguardia de los Tribunales y producen todos sus efectos mientras no se declare su inexactitud en los términos establecidos en esta Ley.

The Land Registry has as its object the registration or entry of the acts and contracts relating to the ownership and other real rights affecting immovable property . . .

The entries in the Registry . . . are under the safeguard of the courts and they are fully effective unless their inaccuracy is declared in the terms established by this law.

### Transfer of immovable property

Following the Roman system, the transmission of ownership in Spain requires two elements. First, a legal basis or cause, called *título* (title), and secondly the transmission of the possession of the property, called *traditio*. The Civil Code provides in art 609 as follows:

La Propiedad y los demás derechos sobre los bienes se adquiren y transmiten por la ley, por donación, por sucesión testada e intestada, y por consuencia de ciertos contratos mediante la tradición.

Ownership and the other rights affecting the goods are acquired and transmitted by law, by donation, by inheritance—whether testate or intestate—and as a consequence of certain contracts by means of transfer.

As far as the validity or existence of the contract is concerned, the requirements are consent of the parties, ascertained objectives and cause of the obligation established, as expressed by art 1261 of the Civil Code.

As regards the form of the contracts the principle is flexibility as stated in art 1278 which reads:

Los contratos serán obligatorios cualesquiera que sea la forma en que se hayan celebrado siempre que en ellos concurran las condiciones esenciales para su validez.

Contracts will be binding in whatever form they were executed provided that they comply with the conditions essential to their validity.

However, art 1280 of the Civil Code provides:

Deberán constar en documento publico: 1 Los actos o contratos que tengan por objeto la creación, transmisión, modificación o exención de derechos reales sobre inmuebles . . .

A public document will be necessary to give evidence of the following: 1 The acts or contracts whose object is the creation, transmission, modification or exemption of real rights over immovable property . . .

This begs the question as to whether the execution of a public title deed (*escritura publica*) is necessary for the transmission of ownership over immovable property according to art 1280, or whether signature of a simple private contract by the parties is sufficient, pursuant to art 1278. The Supreme Court has repeatedly stated its jurisprudence that the *escritura publica* is not a *sine qua non* for the validity of the contract and that compliance with the terms entered into can be demanded even if there is no *escritura*. Furthermore, art 1279 of the Civil Code provides that parties who have entered into a private contract can in any event compel each other to execute an *escritura publica*.

Although the lack of a public document does not affect the obligations of the parties, as we have seen art 1261 of the Civil Code does not include any kind of requirement in respect of form for the validity or existence of the contract, it has important consequences since in its absence it will not be possible to register the title in the Land Registry and consequently it will not have the registral protection established in art 1 of the Registration Law, (*Ley Hipotecaria*) as seen before. Article 3 of the Registration Law (*Ley Hipotecaria*) reads as follows:

> Para que puedan ser inscritos los títulos ... deberán estar consignados en escritura publica ...

> In order that the titles may be registered ... they should be reflected in a public deed ...

That is to say, the titles which are not duly registered cannot impair the rights of third parties and a title which is duly registered cannot be opposed by another title which is not registered or by claims for an incompatible registration.

It used to be common practice to transfer property by means of a private contract without the purchaser demanding the execution of an *escritura*. The object of this practice was to avoid transfer taxes. Frequently, property changed hands several times without any *escritura* having been prepared. In a small village or town, where all the participants were known to each other, the risks of so doing might have been acceptable in view of the very considerable savings in transfer taxes. Nowadays, however, the practice is uncommon. Two instances of the risks associated with this practice will suffice. First, let us suppose that the first vendor goes bankrupt and the creditors seize the property, still registered in the name of the vendor, in satisfaction of his indebtedness. The purchaser who has acquired that property by means of a private contract and does not have further evidence of the transaction, will have to resort to the courts presenting a third party claim to ownership (*terceria de dominio*) and also a claim for the nullity of the registration as the only means of proving that the property belongs to him. If the creditor's claims have been secured by prior registration of a charge this will be difficult if not impossible. Secondly, a purchaser who has bought a property by means of a private contract only, is not protected if a fraudulent vendor transfers the same property to a second purchaser, registering the second transfer at the Land Registry. In this situation, the law protects the second purchaser whose title is duly registered, provided he has acted in good faith. Therefore, the first purchaser will run the risk of losing the property. This is set out in the second paragraph of art 1473 of the Civil Code.

Consequently, the execution of the *escritura de compraventa* and its subsequent registration at the Land Registry is the only safe guarantee of title to the claims of third parties.

The procedure for the transfer of immovable property in Spain is not particularly complicated. The deed or *escritura* referred to above should be executed and signed before a notary public (*notario publico*). Once signed, it remains at the notary's office and a copy (*copia simple*) is issued at the time of signature, and this is followed a few days later by delivery of an authorised copy ('*primera copia*'—'first copy') which is effective for all purposes. Thereafter notaries can issue, at the request of the parties, authorised copies of deeds which have the same value as the first copy and which are called after their respective ordinal number ('*segunda copia*'—'second copy' and so on). This system protects the parties against the loss of the document. The *escritura* (usually the '*primera copia*') is then submitted to the tax office (*oficina de liquidación de impuestos*) for payment of the corresponding taxes. The document must be submitted for assessment of tax within 30 days of execution, otherwise there will be a penalty (*multa*).

In many cases the Land Registry exercises the function of a tax office with regard to transfers of immovable property. Where this is not the case it should be taken into account that the process of assessment and payment of the taxes on the public deed may often take a year or more and consequently it is not safe to wait until this process is completed before the document is delivered to the Land Registry for registration.

In order to preserve priority, it is wise to have the public deed delivered to the Land Registry immediately after execution for *asiento de presentación* (presentation entry) in the diary book ('*diario*'). Registral protection starts at the moment when the presentation entry is made at the Land Registry in the diary book. Article 254 of the Registration Law (*Ley Hipotecaria*), set out below, must be read in conjunction with art 255:

[Article 254:] Ninguna inscripción se hará en el Registro de la Propiedad sin que se acredite previamente el pago de los impuestos establecidos o que se establecieren por las leyes, . . .

[Article 255:] No obstante lo previsto en el artículo anterior, podrá extenderse el asiento de presentación antes de que se verifique el pago del impuesto; mas, en tal caso, se suspenderá la calificación y la inscripción u operación solicitada y se devolverá el título al que lo haya presentado, a fin de que se satisfaga dicho impuesto.

Pagado éste se extenderá la inscripción o asiento de que se trate y sus efectos se retrotraerán a la fecha del asiento de presentación, si se hubiese devuelto el título dentro del plazo de vigencia del mismo.

Si se devolviese el título después de los sesenta días, deberá extenderse nuevo asiento de presentación, y los efectos de la inscripción u operación que se verifique se retrotraerán solamente a la fecha del nuevo asiento.

En el caso de que por causa legítima debidamente justificada no se hubiese pagado el impuesto dentro de los sesenta días, se suspenderá dicho término hasta que se realice el pago . . .

En estos casos, el asiento de presentación caducará a los ciento ochenta días de su fecha.

[Article 254:] No registration will be made in the Land Registry without the payment of the established taxes or such payment, according to the law, being verified . . .

[Article 255:] In spite of what is contained in the previous article, the presentation entry may be made before the payment of the tax is verified; but in this case, the registration requested will be suspended and the title will be returned to the person who presented it, in order that the said tax be paid.

Once this has been paid, the registration or entry concerned will be made and its effects will be backdated to the date of the presentation entry, if the title has been returned within the period of effectiveness of the same.

If the title is returned after the sixty days, a new presentation entry should be made, and the effects of the registration being checked will be backdated only to the date of the new entry.

If, due to a legitimate reason duly justified, the tax has not been paid within the sixty days, the said term will be suspended until the payment is made ...

In these cases, the presentation entry will expire one hundred and eighty days from its date of registration.

Before entering into the *escritura* and parting with the purchase price, the first step to be taken when acquiring property is to check if the property is actually registered in the name of the vendor and whether it is encumbered in any way. It will be necessary to go to the Land Registry to investigate this, and on payment of a small fee the Registry can provide a *certificado de libertad de cargas*—a certificate showing whether the property is affected by charges and encumbrances and, if so, providing a list and description of them. The Registration Law (*Ley Hipotecaria*) declares the principle of the Land Registry being a public service, and anybody with a legitimate interest can obtain information from the Registry, art 221 states:

Los Registros serán publicos para quienes tengan interés conocido en averiguar el estado de los bienes inmuebles o derechos reales inscritos.

Registries will be of public use for those persons who are interested in checking the situation regarding immovable properties or real registered rights.

It will also be necessary to check on such matters as the identity of the property, planning permission, building licences, availability of water, electricity, telephone and other services. It is also advisable to check on outstanding charges for public works, ie roads, sewers, storm drainage, etc.

The town hall (*ayuntamiento*) maintains an index of local property with an official valuation for each property or catastral value. For reasons explained later, it will be vital to check on the official registered value of the property.

**Appointment of an *abogado***

The prudent purchaser will employ his own lawyer (*abogado*) to check on all these matters. There is no effective practical system for enforcement of undertakings given by an *abogado*, apart from the supervisory and rather nominal role played by the Spanish Advocacy Council (*Consejo General de la Abogacia Española*). This Council in turn supervises the various Bar Associations (*Colegios de Abogados*), who in turn supervise lawyers in their area. No *abogado* can practice in any area for which he is not registered. At present there is no effective system for the control of *abogados*. In some cases *abogados* act for both parties to a transaction, and so the choice of one's legal representative or agent requires a considerable degree of care. There are no requirements for a compensation fund, or for compulsory negligence insurance, or for a separate clients account or annual accountants compliance certificates, such as are required for English solicitors.

## Joint ownership and timesharing

It is evident that a property can belong to a sole individual or to several individuals in condominium (*régimen de copropiedad*). Spanish law does not treat co-ownership as a separate real right, but as a form of ownership.

The system of condomninum regulated by arts 392 to 406 of the Civil Code is supplementary and this means that its provisions will be applicable only in the event of lack of a specific contract or special provisions pursuant to the second paragraph of art 392.

Although a timesharing scheme is a form of condominium, it is not regulated in the terms in which condominum is regulated in the Civil Code, although condominium could be taken as a model. Article 392 of the Civil Code defines the condominium as follows:

> Hay comunidad cuando la propiedad de una cosa o de un derecho pertenence pro indiviso a varias personas ...

> There is condominium where the ownership of a thing or right belongs to several persons in common ...

And it also regulates the legal relationships between the co-owners as regards the rights and obligations of use of the property, its maintenance, administration, etc. The rights of the co-owners are reflected in quotas which represent the ratio in which they can enjoy the property, contribute to the charges and obtain a part of the same should it be divided (or a part of its value if it is indivisible). Article 394 of the Civil Code states as follows:

> Cada participe podrá servirse de las cosas comunes siempre que disponga de ellas conforme a su destino y de manera que no perjudique el interés de la comunidad ni impida a los coparticipes utilizarlas segun su derecho.

> Each co-owner can can use the communal property provided that he disposes of it in accordance with its purpose and in such a way that the interest of the community is not impaired and the other co-owners are not prevented from using it in accordance with their rights.

According to art 397 of the Civil Code:

> Ninguno de los codueños podrá sin consentimiento de los demás hacer alteraciones en la cosa comun aunque de ellas pudieran resultar ventajas para todos.

No co-owner can make alterations to the communal property without the consent of the other co-owners even in the case of such alterations being advantageous for everyone.

The Supreme Court has repeatedly made rulings granting to any co-owner the power to appear in court and exercise or defend the rights which affect the community.

As regards the administration of the common property, the Civil Code establishes as a general rule the principle of majority in art 398:

Para la administración y mejor disfrute de la cosa comun serán obligatorios los acuerdos de la mayoría de los participes.

For the administration and best enjoyment of the communal property, resolutions taken by the majority of co-owners will be binding.

This majority is not the personal majority of the co-owners, but the majority of quotas.

Generally, in a timeshare scheme, the majority system will be substituted by the appointment of an administrator or manager, since the majority system would not be practical in most cases.

The rights to which each co-owner is entitled with respect to his quota are referred to in art 399 of the Civil Code which provides as follows:

Todo condueño tendrá la plena propiedad de su parte y la de los frutos y utilidades que le correspondan, pudiendo en su consecuencia enajenarla, cederla o hipotecarla y aun sustituir a otro en su aprovechamiento . . .

Every co-owner shall have full ownership rights to his or her part, as well as to its rent and profits, including the right to sell, transfer or mortgage it, and also the right to assign its use and enjoyment to a third party . . .

In the event that a co-owner decides to transfer his or her share to a third party, the other quota owners will have a pre-emptive right *derecho de retracto* recognised in art 1522 of the Civil Code:

el copropietario de una cosa comun podrá usar del retracto en el caso de enajenarse a un extraño la parte de todos los demás condueños o de alguno de ellos.

in the event that the portions or parts belonging to the other co-owners or a portion or part belonging to any one of them is sold to a third party, any co-owner of the thing owned in common will have the right of pre-emption as regards the part or parts being sold.

Certainly the condominium regulated by the Civil Code is considered as a transitory state, and therefore the measures whose object is to make the indivision cease and to extinguish the community are favoured by granting to the co-owners the *actio communi dividundo* and the right of pre-emption.

The right of pre-emption in favour of the co-owners would have to be excluded from the legal framework of timesharing, since its exercise would impair the object for which this special community is established. Every co-owner would have to waive this right. Until specific rules are produced in Spain, the provisions of art 6.2 of the'Civil Code are taken to be the legal basis for this waiver.

La renuncia de los derechos establecidos en la ley será válida cuando no se contrarie el interés o el orden publico ni se perjudique a terceros.

The waiver of the rights established by law will be valid provided that it does not go against the public interest or order and it does not impair the rights of third parties.

The provisions of art 6.2 must, however, be read in conjunction with art 400 of the Civil Code as follows:

Ningun copropietario estará obligado a permanecer en la comunidad. Cada uno de ellos podrá pedir en cualquier tiempo que se divida la cosa comun. Esto no obstante será válido el pacto de conservar la cosa indivisa por tiempo determinado que no exceda de diez años. Este plazo podrá prorrogarse por nueva convención.

The co-owners will not be bound to remain in the community. At any time, any co-owner will have the right to ask for partition. In spite of this, any agreement will be valid which stipulates that the thing be kept undivided for a term not exceeding ten years. This term will be renewable by agreement.

Notwithstanding that condominium is regulated by permissive laws and allows flexibility, the transcribed art 400 is considered by jurisprudence and doctrine as a rule of public order and therefore imperative and in no event renounceable by the parties' will. Consequently, the waiver can be established over a period of ten years, which can be extended for a further ten according to the most usual interpretation of this precept, but once this period of twenty years has elapsed, there does not seem to be a way to prevent any co-owner exercising the action of partition of the common property.

A timeshare scheme cannot be dependent on a co-owner's free will to exercise the said action in order to sell the property and divide the proceeds among the other co-owners, and therefore a formula must be found to exclude this possibility. In practice under the Spanish system this is done by obtaining a permanent waiver from the co-owners, but there are doubts about the legality of this as examined above, and about its admission for registration. In respect of this problem the *Dirección General de Registros y Notariado* (General Directorate of Registries and Notaries) in its resolution of 18th May 1983 distinguished between accidental communities, those of an involuntary origin, and voluntary ones, those which have their origin in agreement between parties and that pursue a common objective. The doctrine is not shared by the Supreme Court of Spain (*Tribunal Supremo*). This question is examined later in this chapter in the explanation of the *escritura system* of timesharing.

# Horizontal property and timesharing

Among the various forms of immovable property in Spain there is ownership divided into flats or apartments regulated by the Law of Horizontal Property (*Ley de Propiedad Horizontal*) of 21 July 1960.

This system assigns the ownership of a building to several individuals or companies with a mutual delimitation as regards the enjoyment of the flats or units, but without the usual characteristics of condominium. Each owner will have the exclusive right of ownership over his or her respective house or apartment and will share with the other co-owners the possession of the common elements, ie access ways, swimming pools, tennis courts, etc. In a horizontal property system where exclusive and communal property are combined, the exclusive property is greater, which is not so in the case of a condominium.

### Quotas of participation

A flat or apartment subject to a timeshare scheme will usually form part of a horizontal property community combined with the rest of the development. Consequently, the powers and duties of each co-owner in a horizontal property are comparable to those of each co-owner of a timeshare during the period in which he is occupying the unit. Also, the timeshare owners, according to the provisions of their own community, will have to meet the corresponding cost pursuant to art 9.5, first section, of the Law of Horizontal Property, which provides:

> Serán obligaciones de cada propietario:
> . . .
> Contribuir, con arreglo a la cuota de participación fijada en el título o a lo especialmente establecido, a los gastos generales para el adecuado sostenimiento del inmueble, sus servicios, tributos, cargas y responsabilidades que no sean susceptibles de individualización . . .

> It will be the obligation of each owner to:
> . . .
> Contribute, according to his quota of participation set up in the title or to special provisions, to the general expenses for the adequate maintenance of the block, and the services, taxes, charges and responsibilities which cannot be directly assigned to individuals.

The quota is that referred in art 3, para 4 of the same law when it establishes that:

> . . . A cada piso o local se le atribuirá una cuota de participación con relación al total del valor del inmueble y referida a centésimas del mismo. Dicha cuota servirá de módulo para determinar la participación en las cargas y beneficios por razón de la comunidad . . .

... Each flat or premises will be assigned a quota of participation in relation to the total value of the block and will be expressed in hundredths of the same. This quota will serve as a basis to determine the division in the charges and benefits in respect of the community ...

## Ownership rights

In a horizontal property, the right of every co-owner over his flat or premises is considered as an individual and exclusive right pursuant to art 3 of the law and therefore it could be compared to ordinary ownership. This right, however, is subject to limitations: first, in general terms each owner must (art 96 of the Law of Horizontal Property):

... observar la diligencia debida en el uso del inmueble y en sus relaciones con los demás titulares y responderá ante éstos de las infracciones cometidas por el que ocupe su piso ...

... exercise due care in his use of the block and in his dealings with the other owners; he will be responsible to them for infringements committed by any person occupying his flat ...

Also, art 7 of the Law of Horizontal Property authorises every owner of a flat or premises to carry out works in it provided they do not alter or diminish the security of the building, its general structure, its configuration or external condition, or impair the rights of any other co-owner; and in any event, such owner must notify the representative of the community of owners (who is usually the president) of any works he proposes to carry out. The second paragraph of the same article provides:

... en el resto del inmueble no podrá realizar alteración alguna y si advirtiese la necesidad de reparaciones urgentes, deberá comunicarlo sin dilación al administrador.

... in the rest of the building he will not be allowed to carry out any alteration whatsoever, and whenever he realises that urgent repairs need to be done, he must notify the administrator immediately.

If the works affect communal elements, they will have to be approved by the co-owners in a general meeting.

The last paragraph of art 7 of this law establishes a further limitation as regards the use of the flats:

... al propietario y al ocupante del piso les está prohibido desarollar en él y en el resto del imueble actividades no permitidas en los estatutos, deñosas para la finca, inmorales, peligrosas, incómodas o insalubres.

... the owners or occupiers of the flats will not be allowed to use the rest of the building for activities which are prohibited by the internal regulations of the communal property, and also for activities which are dangerous, immoral, inconvenient, unsanitary or could damage the building.

Jurisprudence has maintained that unless such activities are specifically prohibited in the internal regulations of the community of owners, the co-owner who wishes to stop them will need to prove the inconvenience, the damage, etc of the same (Ruling of the Supreme Court of 10 October 1981). These provisions are of some concern where only some, as opposed to all, apartments in a block are turned over to timeshare. The owners of the remaining apartments could well claim that the increased level of occupancy involved in timesharing creates a nuisance or inconvenience.

Lastly, the owners of flats or premises in a horizontal property can divide these physically in order to make up more reduced and independent units, or they can extend them by amalgamating adjacent units, according to art 8.1 of the Law of Horizontal Property, but for this power to be exercised not only is the consent of the owners concerned required but also the approval of the community of owners, which will also have to set up the new quotas of participation. (Ruling of the Territorial Court of Madrid of 18 February 1974.)

Consequently, all the foregoing demonstrates that the right of ownership of a member of a horizontal property community is limited by the rights of the other co-owners and by the co-ownership of the communal elements.

## Constitution of the system of horizontal property

### Title deed

In order to constitute a horizontal property scheme a public deed (*escritura publica*) will have to be executed before a notary and registered at the Land Registry. A deed of horizontal property can be executed by the builder or developer of the building which is to be sold as flats, as a unilateral act, or alternatively by the various owners of the flats, as a collective act. In either case, the deed can be executed before the building has been completed, provided that the circumstances set out in art 5 of the Law of Horizontal Property exist. Article 5 is set out below:

El título constitutivo de la propiedad por pisos o locales describirá además del inmueble en su conjunto, cada uno de aquellos al que se asignará numero correlativo. La descripción del inmueble habrá de expresar las circunstancias exigidas en la legislación hiptecaria y los servicios e instalaciones con que cuente el mismo. La de cada piso o local expresará su extensión, linderos, planta en la que se hallare y los anejos, tales como garaje, buhardilla o sótano.

En el mismo título se fijará la cuota de participación que corresponde a cada piso o local, determinada por el propietario unico del edificio al iniciar su venta por pisos, por acuerdo de todos los propietarios existentes, por laudo util de cada piso o local en relación con el total del inmueble, su emplazamiento interior o exterior, su situación y el uso que se presuma racionalmente que va a efectuarse de los servicios o elementos comunes.

El título podrá contener, además, reglas de constitución y ejercicio del derecho y disposiciones no prohibidas por la Ley en orden al uso o destino del edificio, sus diferentes pisos o locales, instalaciones y servicios, gastos, administración y gobierno, seguros, conservación y reparaciones, formando un estatuto privativo que no perjudicará a terceros si no ha sido inscrito en el Registro de la Propiedad.

En cualquier modificación del título, y a salvo lo que se dispone sobre validez de acuerdos, se observarán los mismos requisitos que para la constitución.

The constitutive title deed of any property divided into flats or premises shall describe not only the building as a whole, but also each of its units, to which a correlative number shall be assigned. The description of the buildings shall express all the details set up by the property laws, and include all of its installations. The description of each flat or premises shall describe in detail its extent, boundaries, the floor in which it is situated, and its annexes, such as its garage, attic or basement.

The title deed shall also express the quota or share in the communal property allocated to each flat or premises, as set up by the sole owner of the building at the time when the sale of the flats started, or by agreement between all the existing owners, or by award or court decision. The setting up of such quotas shall be made on the basis of the developed and usable area of each flat or premises and its internal or external location, the floor on which it is situated, and the use to which it could reasonably be assumed that its installations or communal elements would be put.

The title deed may also contain rules for the establishment and exercise of, and rules not forbidden by law in relation to, the use of the building, its flats or premises, installations, expenses, management, insurance, conservation and repair. The title deed may thus become a private statute which shall not impair the rights of third parties unless it is registered at the Land Registry.

In case of any alterations to the title deed, and apart from what is hereby ruled as to the validity of the communal decisions, regard shall be had to the same requirements as those necessary for its constitution.

## Administration

Articles 12 to 19 of the Law of Horizontal Property establish the governing system for the community of owners. The law provides for the community of owners to have a chairman, appointed by the co-owners, an administrator or secretary-administrator and the assembly of owners (*junta de propietarios*). The assembly of owners makes the principal decisions affecting the life of the community as provided by art 13 of the law we are examining. They need, at least annually, to discuss the accounts and the budget, and further meetings will be called whenever the chairman or 25 per cent of the owners or a number of owners representing 25 per cent of the quotas may consider it convenient, as specified in art 15. The owners may send a representative to the meetings, authorising such representation in writing as provided by art 14.

The requirements for the adoption of decisions by the assembly of owners are provided by arts 16, 1 and 2 of the Law:

Los acuerdos de la junta de propietarios se sujetarán a las siguientes normas:
1 La unanimidad para la validez de los que impliquen aprobación o modificación de reglas contenidas en el título constitutivo de la propiedad o en los estatutos . . .
2 Para la validez de los demás acuerdos bastará el voto de la mayoría del total de los propietarios que a su vez representan la mayoría de las cuotas de participación . . .

The decisions adopted by the owners' assembly shall be subject to the following rules:

1 All decisions which mean the approval or amendment of the rules contained in the constitutive title deed, or of the statutes of the horizontally divided property, shall be adopted unanimously.
2 The vote of the majority of owners, which in turn represents the majority of quotas, will be sufficient to ensure the validity of the rest of the decisions.

This article is usually construed to mean that unanimity is required only to alter the horizontal property system, that is to say, the regulations regarding communal elements, quotas of participation, etc.

The constitution of a timesharing scheme in one of the flats does not necessarily modify the title constituting the horizontal property, if new quotas are not introduced and only affect the temporal possession of that one flat. Furthermore, as often established by the courts, property is presumed free of charges and those wanting to impose limitations to it will have to prove their claim. Outside the law and the statutes of the community, no restrictions can be imposed on the co-owners (Rulings of the Territorial Courts of Oviedo on 15 October 1971, Madrid on 14 April 1969, Granada on 7 February 1976, and others).

Subject to the foregoing comments, and in the absence of claims by other owners, a timeshare scheme will therefore be generally accepted for a unit included in a horizontal property community.

Lastly, it is important to note that art 396 of the Civil Code and art 4 of the Law of Horizontal Property exclude the right of pre-emption and the action of division from a system of horizontal property. The purpose of these two articles is obvious: this form of property is created for its distribution among the members of the community and cannot be dependent on the free will of an owner to exercise the action of division.

Given the lack of special timesharing regulations, the two articles referred to above could be applied to timesharing by analogy, on the basis that both timesharing and horizontal property respond to the same criteria of diffusion and duration.

# Taxation

There are several taxes levied on the enjoyment of immovable property and the income obtained from the same and on its transmission *inter vivos* or *mortis causa*. Those people (including non-Spanish citizens) owning property situated on Spanish territory will be liable to these taxes.

## Taxes on immovable property

*Wealth tax (impuesto extraordinario sobre el patrimonio de las personas físicas)*
This tax is levied upon the net assets of individuals and is payable annually to the central administration. Its rate is assessed according to an aggregrate scale

starting at 0.20 per cent assessed between 0 and 25 million pesetas and ending at 2 per cent for assets of more than 2,500 million pesetas.

*Income tax (impuesto sobre la renta de las personas físicas)*
This tax is levied on the whole income and gains earned in Spain in the fiscal year, according to the amount of income and to the personal and family circumstances of the individual. It is payable annually to the central administration. The assessment of its rate is made according to an aggregate scale starting at 8 per cent for any income between 0 and 500,000 pesetas and ending at 66 per cent for the portion of income exceeding 12,200,000 pesetas.

The combined total of income tax and wealth tax in the case of individuals subject to personal tax liability must not exceed a certain percentage of taxable income.

*Corporation tax (impuesto sobre sociedades)*
This tax is levied on the property and capital gains of companies. The normal rate payable is 35 per cent. There are however detailed provisions regarding the taxation of non-resident companies.

*Urban tax (contribución territorial urbana)*
This tax affects the ownership of rights over properties of an urban nature (which includes land and buildings) which imply a deemed income. The said income is estimated according to three factors:

1 catastral value, which is the average value of the land and buildings in accordance with indexes given by the town hall;
2 catastral rent, which is 4 per cent of the given catastral value;
3 net return which is obtained by deducting 30 per cent from the catastral rent.

The resulting figure is taxed at a rate of 20 per cent. Again, fines have to be considered if the tax is not paid on time.

*Luxury tax (impuesto municipal sobre gastos suntuarios)*
This tax, when applied to immovable property, is levied on the enjoyment of all types of dwellings exceeding 10 million pesetas in catastral value. It is paid annually to the municipal authorities at the rate of 0.6 per cent of the excess over ten million pesetas of the catastral value.

**Taxes on the transmission of immovable property**

*Transfer tax (Impuesto general sobre las transmisiones patrimoniales y actos jurídicos documentados)*
This tax is commonly known as *derechos reales*. It is levied on transmissions *inter vivos* of all kinds of property and rights. Its current rate is 6 per cent. This tax is of limited importance in practical terms since in the majority of

transactions the vendor acts in a commercial capacity and as such is subject to the payment of VAT (IVA).

*Local capital gains tax (Impuesto sobre el incremento del valor se los terrenos)*
This tax is usually referred to as the *plus valia* and is payable to the local council independently of income tax. The *plus valia* tax amounts to up to 40 per cent of the difference between the catastral value at the date of the last transfer and the recorded price of the current transfer.

The rate is arrived at by dividing the percentage increase in the official value of the land since the previous sale by the number of years between the sales. The local authorities will send in the assessment anything up to eighteen months after the transfer and will look to the recorded owner (ie the purchaser) for payment. The purchaser will have a right of indemnity from the vendor unless, as is very often the case, the sales contract provides for the purchaser to be responsible for this tax. The tax is structured in two ways. First taxing the increase of the value of the land the ownership of which is transferred by any means. Secondly taxing the increase of the value of the land which has been in the hands of a legal person for more than ten years.

*Inheritance tax (Impuesto sobre sucesiones y donaciones)*
This tax is levied both on transmissions *mortis causa* and lifetime gifts and is assessed according to the value of the property transferred and to the relationship between the deceased or donor and the beneficiary. Spanish inheritance taxes are extremely high when a beneficiary is not a member of the deceased's family. The determination of the taxes payable is calculated according to a progressive scale in relation to the value of the property, the degree of the relationship between the beneficiary and the deceased and the value of the current estate of the beneficiary.

*Value Added Tax (Impuesto sobre el valor anadido)*
Value added tax (*impuesto sobre el valor añadido*, in short IVA) is regulated by Law 30/1985 of 2 August, and came into force on 1 January 1986, when Spain joined the European Community.

In brief, it taxes any delivery of goods or services provided by companies or professionals on a chargeable basis in the development of their commercial or professional activity within the mainland territory and the Balearic Islands, and also the importation of goods into the said territories. It does not apply in the Canary Islands or in the Spanish African territories of Ceuta and Melilla. There are basically three applicable rates: the ordinary one being 12 per cent, a reduced rate of 6 per cent, and the increased rate of 33 per cent. The rate applicable to the transfer of immovable property is the reduced type of 6 per cent. This tax will be the most commonly applicable form of transfer tax since in most property transactions the vendor is a professional promotor, developer or builder.

Where VAT is applicable, *impuesto de actos jurídicos documentados* (stamp duty) will be imposed separately. Reference must be made to Law 26/1984 of 19 July, entitled General Law for the Protection of Consumers and Users (*Ley General para la Defensa de los Consumidores y Usarios*), a law which has particularly affected the transmission of immovable property. Article 2, of this law sets out the fundamental rights of every consumer and user and then provides in para 2:

> La renuncia previa de los derechos que esta Ley renonce a los cosumidores y usuarios en la adquisición o utilización de bienes o servicios es *nula*.
> Asimismo son nulos los actos realizados en fraude de esta ley, de conformidad con el artículo 6 del Codigo Civil.

> The prior waiver to the rights, which this law recognises, of consumers and users in regard to the acquisition and utilisation of goods or services is null.
> The actions carried out contrary to this law are also null, pursuant to article 6 of the Civil Code.

In the same Law, art 10 provides that in all contracts there should be good faith and a fair balance in the items exchanged, which *inter alia* rules out:

> En la primera venta de viviendas, la estipulación de que el comprador ha de cargar con los gastos derivados de la preparación de la titulación, que por su naturaleza correspondan al vendedor (Obra Nueva, Propiedad Horizontal, hipotecas para financiar su construcción o su división y cancelación).

> In the first sale of dwellings, the provision that the expenses arising from the preparation of the title documentation, which by their nature are payable by the seller (new building, horizontal property, mortgages to finance their construction or their division and the cancellation of the same), are to be satisfied by the purchaser.

Although in the initial interpretation of this article there was a series of discrepancies with regard to the term *vivienda* (dwelling), it is now accepted that it refers to all transfers of immovable property and consequently it bans the hitherto common practice of dividing the said expenses among the purchasers. It is apparent from the foregoing that this practice would now be illegal and consequently purchasers should refuse to make such payments.

Article 10.4 of the same law provides as follows:

> Serán nulas de pleno derecho y se tendrán por no puestas las cláusulas, condiciones o estipulaciones que incumplan los anteriores requisitos.

> The clauses, conditions or provisions which are not in compliance with the above requirememts, will be null and will be disregarded.

Finally, reference should be made to the recently published Royal Decree No 515 of 21 April 1989 in connection with the aforementioned General Law for the Protection of Consumers and Users. The Royal Decree regulates the information which has to be supplied to customers buying or renting a dwelling. In accordance with the provisions of art 1, the Royal Decree is to be applied for the offer, promotion and advertising carried out for the sale or lease of dwellings in the event that they are made under a business or commercial activity directed at customers. The main purpose of this Royal Decree is to ensure that the offer, promotion and advertising reflect the true nature, conditions and use of the dwelling, including the information concerning its characteristics, and equipment.

Law 39/1988 of 28 December *Reguladora de las Haciendas Locales* (governing local municipal budgets and taxes) has been introduced to modify the existing structure of local taxes. This law creates a financial system directed at the effective fulfilment of the principles of autonomy and financial sufficiency of the local municipal budgets, as is declared in the reasoning (*Exposición de Motivos*) at the start of the text of the law.

The new law creates three taxes:

1 *impuesto sobre bienes inmuebles*, hereafter referred to as IBI (tax on immovable properties);
2 *impuesto sobre actividades económicas* (tax on economic activities); and
3 *impuesto sobre vehículos de tracción mecánica* (tax on motor vehicles).

The IBI involves the elimination of the following existing taxes:

1 *Contribución territorial rustica y pecuaria* (rural contribution);
2 *Contribución territorial urbana* (urban contribution); and
3 *Impuesto municipal sobre solares* (municipal tax on urban land).

The existing *impuesto municipal sobre el incremento del valor de los terrenos* (*plus valía tax*) is being re-structured, substituted by the *impuesto sobre incremento del valor de los terrenos de naturaleza urbana*.

Article 61 describes the IBI:

El Impuesto sobre Bienes Inmuebles es un tributo directo de carácter real, cuyo hecho imponible está constituido por la propiedad de los bienes inmuebles de naturaleza rustica y urbana sitos en el respectivo término municipal, o por la titularidad de un derecho real de usufructo o de superficie, o de la de una concesión administrativa sobre dichos bienes o sobre los serivicios publicos a los que estén afectados, y grava el valor de los referidos inmuebles.

The tax on immovable properties is a direct tax of a real nature, whose taxable value is constituted by the ownership of the immovable properties of a rural or urban nature, situated in the respective municipal boundary, or by the ownership of a real right of use or right over the ground, or by that of an administrative concession over the said properties or over the public services which affect them, and it taxes the value of the aforementioned immovable properties.

The value of the immovable property is determined in accordance with the catastral value as seen above and the general rate applicable is 0.4 per cent for urban property and 0.3 per cent for rural property. These rates can be modified within certain limits by the town hall, depending on the population and services provided by the town hall.

The *impuesto sobre el incremento del valor de los terrenos de naturaleza urbana* taxes the increase in value of urban land shown at the time of transfer of the ownership of the same or at the time of constitution or transmission of any real right affecting the right of ownership over the said land, as indicated in art 105. The rate applicable is determined according to population and the length of time passed since the last transfer, which can be up to 20 years maximum.

Another tax newly created by the same law is the *impuesto sobre construcciones, instalaciones y obras* (tax on construction, installation and building works) which taxes any kind of construction, installation or building work for which a building licence is required, whether the said licence has been obtained or not, and only when it falls to the town hall to issue the said licence. This tax is payable by the owner of the property where the said activities are carried out, or by the applicant for the licence if the latter does not coincide with the former. The rate payable is 2 per cent of the real cost of the works, although this rate could be increased up to 4 per cent in the case of town halls with populations of more than 100,000 people.

The town halls are obliged by this law to make the necessary adaptations before 1 January 1990, which is the date when most of the taxes described will come into force.

## Foreign investment and exchange control regulations

On this matter there is constant up-dating and important changes are likely to occur in view of the full integration of Spain into the EEC. The current regulations are compiled in the Royal Decree of 27 June 1986, No 1265/86 which pursues the mandate established by Law 47/1985 of 27 December which gives the basis for the adaptation of the exchange control regulations to those of the EEC.

The text of this Royal Decree reads as follows:

La Ley 47/1985, de 27 de Septiembre, de Bases de Delegación al Gobierno para la aplicación del Derecho de las Comunidades Europeas, delega en el Gobierno la facultad de dictar normas con rango de Ley sobre las materias reguladas por las leyes . . ., a fin de adecuarlas al ordenamiento jurídico comunitario y en la medida en que tales materias resulten afectadas por el mismo . . . El Presente Real Decreto legislativo pretende, pues, cumplir ese mandato adecuando la normativa española sobre inversiones extranjeras a los principios y criterios contenidos en las normas comunitarias reguladoras de los movimientos de capital.

The Law 47/198, of 27 September, concerning bases of delegation to the government for the application of the law of the European Communities, delegates to the government the power of dictating rules with the category of law with regard to matters regulated by the laws, . . ., in order to adjust them to the juridical order of the EEC and in the way which such matters are affected by the same . . . The present Royal Legislative Decree proposes to fulfil that mandate, adjusting the Spanish law relating to foreign investments to the principles and criteria contained in the European Community Regulations governing the movements of capital.

The Royal Decree establishes a new definition of forms of investment in its art 3: direct investment, portfolio investment, investments in immovable property and other investments. It establishes a regime of freedom subject to an administratative verification procedure for the checking of the true nature of the foreign investment.

As a general rule and for all types of foreign investment, art 4 of the Royal Decree establishes a general principle:

Los titulares de inversiones extranjeras en cualquiera de las formas señaladas ... gozarán del derecho de transferir al exterior, sin limitación alguna:

a)  Los capitales invertidos y las plusvalías obtenidas de las enajenaciones que se realicen.
    ... El derecho de transferencia se podrá ejercer desde el momento en que la inversión haya sido declarada en debida forma para su inscripción en el Registro de Inversiones.
    La Administración sólo podrá denegar el derecho de transferencia cuando, previa comprobación administrativa, resulte que los beneficios y plusvalías se hayan obtenido infringiendo las normas legales del ordenamiento jurídico español.

The foreign investors in any of the indicated forms ... will enjoy the right of transferring abroad, without any limitation:

a)  The capital invested and the surplus obtained from the transfers carried out.
    ... The right of transfer may be carried out from the moment in which the investment has been declared in due form for registration at the Registry of Investments.
    The Administration will only deny the right of transfer when, following administrative verification, it transpires that the profits and surplus have been obtained in such a way as to infringe the legal rules and juridical Spanish order.

The foreign investments will be established in a public document executed before a notary public or authority with notarial functions as declared in art 16, which also determines the persons or entities which have the obligation to declare the foreign investment.

The *dirección general de transacciones exteriores* (general body controlling foreign investment) through the *Registro de Inversiones del Ministerio de Economía y Hacienda* (Investments Registry of the Ministry of Economy and Inland Revenue) is the body concerned with surveying the fulfilment of this law.

All the payments and collections originating from foreign investment will have to be carried out through or by banks, which for this particular purpose will be acting as delegates of the foreign investment authorities.

Chapter 4 regulates investment in immovable property. Article 13 reads as follows:

1. Son libres, sin sujeción a ningun tramite administrativo previo, las inversiones extranjeras que pretendan realizarse mediante la adquisición de bienes inmuebles, salvo lo establecido en el numero siguiente.
2. Son igualmente libres, pero sujetas al tramite de verificación administrativa, las inversiones que tengan por objeto la adquisición de bienes inmuebles por personas jurídicas extranjeras, asi como las inversiones en bienes inmuebles que pretendan realizar las personas fisicas extranjeras, no residentes en España, mediante:
   a) La adquisición de bienes inmuebles de naturaleza rustica
   b) La adquisición de solares, considerados como inmuebles urbanos conforme a la legislación del suelo y ordenación urbana
   c) La adquisición de locales comerciales
   d) La adquisición de más de tres viviendas en un mismo inmueble, o, en general, de más de tres unidades de una misma división horizontal...

1. The foreign investments to be carried out by means of the acquisition of immovable property, may be carried out freely except in respect of that which is established in the following section.
2. Investments which have as their object the purchase of immovable property by legal foreign persons who are not resident in Spain are equally free, but subject to the process of administrative verification, as are investments in immovable properties carried out by foreign individuals, not resident in Spain, in respect of the following:
   a) The acquisition of immovable property of a non-urban nature
   b) The acquisition of plots, considered as urban properties according to planning legislation
   c) The acquisition of commercial premises
   d) The acquisition of more than three dwellings in the same building, or, in general, of more than three units in the same horizontal division ...

The previous Royal Decree has been developed by regulation (*reglamento*) No 2077 of 25 September 1986. In art 12.2.2 the authority of the *Dirección General de Transacciones Exteriores* (general body governing foreign transactions) is established. As regards the proceedings, art 25 is applicable.

It is important to point out art 25 that:

... Presentada la solicitud en forma, la Dirección General de Transacciones Exteriores verificará el proyecto de inversión notificando al interesado su conformidad o disconformidad al mismo, en el plazo de treinta días hábiles a contar de aquélla. Transcurrido este plazo sin que el interesado haya recibido notificación de la resolución, el proyecto se tendrá por verificado y confome.

... Once the application has been presented, the general body governing foreign transactions will verify the investment plan notifying the interested party of its approval or disapproval with regard to the same, within a period of thirty working days from the application date. If this period passes without the interested party having received notification of the resolution, the plan will be considered verified and approved.

Once the foreign investment has been verified, the investment itself has to be carried out within six months from the date of verification and approval unless a different period is specified. After the said period, the verification or approval is considered as expired.

Summarising the regulations of the exercise of the right of transferability abroad, examined above, it should be borne in mind that this right is subject to certain requirements and formalities of which one must take the following into account:

1 The transfer must be made through a delegated banking entity. It is prohibited to carry it out directly.
2 The appropriate administrative authorisation or verification must be obtained.
3 Justification of the foreign money contribution used for the investment must be made. A certificate of the import of the currency (*certificado de divisas*) must be obtained from one of the authorised Spanish banks at the time of the investment. It must be noted that a foreign corporation is not permitted to acquire real property in Spain without first producing this certificate to the notary.
4 A declaration to the Investment Registry of the investment and, where applicable, of the liquidation of it is required.
5 Fulfilment of all fiscal obligations must be shown.

## Condominium system

This is the background to the construction of timesharing schemes in Spain. There are two main ways in which Spanish timesharing schemes have been constructed. First, there is the direct ownership system known as the condominium system, which is based on a set of *escrituras*. Secondly, there is the club system which depends for its effectiveness on a trust set up outside Spain. A timesharing scheme set up according to the *escritura* system establishes the direct ownership of the timeshares by the co-owners and is treated as if it were a condominium as governed by arts 392 to 406 of the Civil Code. It should be borne in mind that in some cases the timeshare scheme is not based on the ownership right, but on other real rights such as the right of use (*usufructo*) or lease rights (*arrendamiento*).

In order to set up this type of system, and taking the right of ownership as the basis of the timeshare scheme, the first step is the execution of a deed of co-ownership which will start off by establishing the identity of the developer or vendor, will then describe the building and will go on to divide the ownership into proportional shares known as *cuotas*, each one giving the owner the right to occupy the dwelling for a defined period of time. This deed will also establish the rules which will govern the community. The following are the most important items in the *escritura*:

### Ownership quotas

Timesharing will be based on the existence of ownership quotas corresponding to time periods, especially weekly periods.

These quotas can be equal in principle, but experience has proved the different economic attraction of the seasons. The existence of high seasons and low seasons will produce a different coefficient or percentage for each of the months of the year, therefore the quotas will be established according to the value which the parties give to each period.

Each quota will have to appear individually, and this could be done, as suggested by the Land Registrars Pedro Sanchez Marin and Pedro Martinez Castro, by accompanying each of the quotas with a notation which identifies it clearly, for instance:

18 per cent, August (18% August)
5 per cent, February (5% February)

The *escritura* could commence as follows:

...................... is the owner of 18% August of the following property.

As regards the occupation of the apartment, if this is to be divided into 52 weekly time units, then period number 1 will be, for example, 12 noon on the first Saturday in the year until 12 noon of the following Saturday, period two from then until 12 noon of the following Saturday and so on.

The shares will, of course, correspond to a minimum period of time and will be indivisible, not only as an institutional requirement, but also in defence of the purchaser. In this respect the criteria of registrars can have a relevant influence in the establishment of the minimum and indivisible shares. The indivisibility of the shares should also be taken into account in transmissions *mortis causa*, assigning the share to a sole inheritor subject to compensating the other beneficiaries. Not all land registrars are prepared to allow registration of this kind of deed.

The following may be noted as an example of a system based on the right of use. The constitution deed would establish the units in the timeshare scheme as affected by a temporary right of use. The right of use would be divided into 51 weeks per year during the period of validity of the right of use. Its *cuota* or share would then represent an undivided portion in respect of a specific unit for a specific time. The general regulations governing the right of use are arts 467 to 522 of the Civil Code, but it must be noted that there are a number of special regulations which apply to the different regions as part of a historical inheritance. One of the main problems in organising a timeshare scheme based on the right of use is that the length of that right is determined by the life of the beneficiary and, in the case of legal persons, for a maximum period of thirty years.

## Administration

The system established by the Civil Code for a condominium does not seem applicable for the administration of this form of ownership. Article 398 provides that 'for the administration and a better enjoyment of the common property, the decision taken by the majority of co-owners will be binding' (*para la administracion y mejor disfrute de la comun serán obligatorios los acuerdos de la mayoria de los partícipes*), and it would be impracticable to call a meeting of all the timeshare owners whenever an administrative decision had to be taken. For the same reason, the administration system established by the Law of Horizontal Property with regard to the meetings of co-owners would be inadequate.

In the deed of co-ownership, therefore, an administrator would be appointed in the section where the rules of the community are established. This deed often also contains the system for the appointment and dismissal of administrators and for the control of the accounts. The owners will decide on the duties and remuneration of the administrators, eg the power to evict an owner who is still occupying the unit when his timeshare period has expired.

In short, it is necessary to create an independent management body in order to obtain greater efficiency and protection of the individual timeshare owners.

The deed of co-ownership will also contain provisions in connection with the participation of the co-owners in the maintenance expenses, replacement of furnishings and fixtures and in general all the community costs. This participation will in any event be proportional to the ownership quotas. The deed can also establish liability for damages to the unit or furniture, and penalties for non-payment or delay in the payment of the maintenance charges.

### Renunciation of the right of pre-emption

As already mentioned, the exercise of the right of pre-emption, which the Civil Code grants to the co-owners in a condominium, is impracticable in a timesharing scheme. This problem is solved in practice by obtaining a renunciation from each timeshare owner, but this system is not free from difficulties. A specific separate renunciation can be obtained from each timeshare owner before transferring his interest and this could be dealt with by appointing an attorney to deal with the necessary consents. However, the more modern method is simply to recite a waiver of pre-emption rights in the *escritura* of co-ownership. There is no case law confirming this practice but, as indicated, it could be based on art 6.2 of the Civil Code.

As the right of pre-emption has been excluded from special communities, as in horizontal property, and in relation to water rights etc, it can be argued that its exclusion from timesharing schemes should equally, by analogy, be admitted since there is a corresponding objective. However, since timesharing involves the sharing of living accommodation, there is also an argument for existing timeshare owners having some control over who is allowed to share their accommodation.

### Impracticability of the action of division

As mentioned above, once the twenty years allowed by the Civil Code for the waiver of the action of division have elapsed, there seems to be no means of preventing a co-owner from exercising this action over the common property. The right to exercise this action is considered non-renounceable and imprescriptible, as maintained by rulings of the Supreme Court of 5 November 1924, 7 October 1927, 15 June 1929, 17 May 1958, etc.

This is a serious drawback to the efficacy of timesharing. To overcome this by analogy one school of thought introduces the application of art 4 of the Law of Horizontal Property. Article 4 only refers to horizontal property, but, so it is said, could be applied to timesharing on the basis of art 4.1 of the Civil Code which provides:

Procederá la aplicación analógica de las normas cuando éstas no contemplen un supuesto específico, pero regulen otro semejante entre las que se aprecie identidad de razón.

The analogous application of the laws will be possible when these do not envisage a specific case but regulate a similar one which may be considered to have the same purpose.

Article 4 of the Law of Horizontal Property is set out below:

La acción de división no procederá para hacer cesar la situación que regula esta Ley. Sólo podrá ejercitarse por cada propietario proindiviso sobre un piso o local determinado, circunscrita al mismo, y siempre que la proindivisión no haya sido establecida de intento para el servicio o utilidad comun de todos los propietarios.

This action of division will not be applicable if it is contrary to the situation regulated by this Law. This power can only be exercised by each co-owner *proindiviso* of a specific flat or premises, limited to the same, and provided that the *proindivision* had not been intentionally established for the service or common use of all owners.

On the basis of the last part of the above article it is argued that in a timesharing scheme the 'indivision' of the property is established precisely with the intention of protecting the common interest of the co-owners. On the other hand, a timeshare is notoriously difficult to re-sell, and carries with it an onerous burden to contribute in perpetuity to the upkeep and maintenance of the property. Further, over a period of time, the property may be effectively unusable without substantial capital expenditure. Failure to allow a compul-sory sale of the property may deprive some owners of the ability to extricate themselves from this liability.

In short, and until specific regulations can resolve this problem, an attempt can be made to ensure the indivisibility of the common property by the inclusion of appropriate items in the co-ownership deed among the rules governing it, on the basis of analogous application of the article mentioned above, although this is only an interpretation and there could be objections to it. While the essence of art 400 of the Civil Code is connected with a vision of the community as a transitory and undesirable situation, on the other hand, the provisions of the Law of Horizontal Property are designed with a view to establishing a permanent and desirable situation as regards the community. The concept of timeshare reflects the second situation rather than the first. Much will depend on the criteria of the relevant land registrars, amongst whom there are differing views as to the validity of such provisions.

**Inclusion of furniture**

It is clear that timesharing involves not only the building but also adequate furniture and fixtures, both constituting in an indissoluble way the object of the ownership, that is to say, we will always be dealing with a furnished unit. This will mean that in a timesharing scheme we will be dealing with both movable and immovable property. Consequently, the concept of a furnished unit implies the existence of furniture adequate to the object of the apartment, the elements of which are usually described in the deed of co-ownership.

The second document in a timeshare scheme of this nature, after the deed of co-ownership itself, will be the private contract for purchase between the developer and the individual purchaser, which should have annexed to it the inventory of fixtures, fittings and furnishings belonging to the property.

In practice, the contract usually provides for a deposit of, say, 10 per cent to be paid to the developer and the balance to be paid on completion of the formalities. The contract will specify the price of the timeshare and, because of Spanish Exchange Control, if the purchaser is a non-resident the price will have to be paid in Spain.

In some cases it has been the practice to base the price on the catastral or artificially low value attributed to the property, this part of the price being paid in Spain and the price for the share of the inventory of fixtures and fittings being paid outside Spain. This arrangement appears to be contrary to Spanish law. The contract will almost inevitably be construed according to Spanish law since it concerns immovable property in Spain.

The third document which is required is the deed of transfer (*escritura de compraventa*) between the developer and the purchaser, whereby a share in the communal property and a timeshare period is conveyed by the original owner to the new purchaser.

The fourth document will be the maintenance contract, which will be entered into by the administrator and a local management company and which will deal with the maintenance and the repairs necessary to keep the unit in good condition. The timeshare purchaser will be concerned to see that this document establishes exactly what work the local administration agent is to perform and how he is to be paid for his services.

The advantages and disadvantages of the condominium timesharing system can be summarised as follows. The main advantage is that, subject to the decision of the local registrar, a timeshare owner can become registered as proprietor in a Spanish Land Registry and to that extent he will obtain the protection under Spanish law afforded to a registered property owner. However, we have already seen some of the difficulties which can be encountered in respect of the registration of the waiver of the right of pre-emption and the division of communal property.

Although the *escritura* system may have the merit of being governed by Spanish law, problems may arise in practice with regard to the administration and control of the community and with regard to the transmission of timeshares.

As regards the administration of the property, except in large developments, the timeshare purchaser is likely to be fairly remote from control of the continuing management of the apartment or villa. He may not have the means of contacting all the other timeshare owners and orchestrating them into some concerted effort to replace bad administrators or managers. This problem is aggravated when the co-owners are nationals of different countries. Whereas in the larger schemes an owners' representative committee or club arrangement will provide the timeshare proprietor with a body concerned to protect his interests, in a smaller development this is usually impracticable. Actions for non-payment of management charges will inevitably have to be conducted in the Spanish courts and any judgment will then have to be enforced abroad. The cost, length and complexity of this process means that if some owners (or the timeshare developer in the case of unsold quotas) do not pay the management charge there is no effective and practicable means of recovering the shortfall. Existing owners will either have to make up the deficiency or accept that the management will not be carried out.

When he purchases his timeshare from the developer, it is up to the purchaser to check the title to the development and all the facilities of the development, such as golf courses, swimming pools, etc. This is usually so time consuming and expensive that the cost is disproportionate to the acquisition cost of the timeshare.

Another disadvantage is the disproportionate expense involved in the transmission of a timeshare. The transfer of a timeshare under the condominium system is a transfer in property and this involves the expense of the preparation of the transfer deed, its registration with the Land Registry, the payment of the transfer taxes and fees and the payment of the notarial fees and the fees of the *abogado* employed. The fees and expenses vary, but are often quite high in relation to the acquisition price for the timeshare. For example, typically, where a new scheme had been set up in the south of Spain, the total of the fees, expenses, tax, etc, amounted to nearly £800 per timeshare. In the timeshare scheme under the condominium system these costs multiply rapidly. Even disregarding *plus valia* tax, assuming a 100 unit development with average sales of 31 or 32 weekly periods for each unit, each involving costs of £500, the total bill will amount to £1.5 million!

Transmission *mortis causa* also involves payment of inheritance tax, which could be a considerable sum, and, if a Spanish will has not been made, probate will have to be proved in Spain before any transfer can take place, involving additional legal costs and fairly lengthy delays.

### Accessibility of the Land Registry

The access of the condominium system of timesharing to the Land Registry involves two main problems, according to the Registrars Messrs Sanchez Marín and Martinez Castro. One concerns its legal nature, and the other problem is one of registral evidence.

*Legal nature*
As we have seen, although timesharing is a form of community, it does not fit into the terms on which this is regulated in the Civil Code, and for this reason the Registries must decide on the registral evidence of those agreements which alter it. It is open to the Registrars to apply art 7 of the byelaws of the Registration Law (*Reglamento de la Ley Hipotecaria*), which provides that 'the acts which modify some of the rights of ownership will also be registrable' (*se inscribirán también los actos que modifiquen alguna de las facultades del dominio*).

*Registral evidence*
The Land Registries must provide adequate publicity for the true legal nature of this form of ownership.

The two Registrars mentioned above understand that there should be a main entry in favour of the developer in respect of the apartment or villa, stating the number of timeshares and the basic rules of organisation of the community. A special folio would be dedicated to entries for the transfer of the individual timeshares.

## Club system

The alternative to the condominium system of timesharing in Spain is the club system. Under this system each apartment or villa is owned by a company limited by guarantee. Membership is vested in trust for the benefit of the club members. The intervention of a trustee, usually a bank or other substantial organisation, will provide some assurance to the timeshare purchaser that his interests are properly protected. The advantage of the club system is that it is considerably less expensive and complicated to set up and provides a much simpler and more flexible framework for the timeshare purchasers to regulate their affairs for the future.

Membership in the club is easily transferable. The right transferred is thought to be no longer an interest in immovable property and can be transferred with the minimum of formality.

As a club member, the timeshare buyer can expect to have some rights under the rules of the club as to the way in which the club is run and he will certainly be part of a larger pressure group than the single co-owner of one apartment. The timeshare buyer will not have to pay the legal costs and taxes otherwise associated with the acquisition of his interest, because these kinds of expenses do not arise under the club system. Usually, club schemes provide for expenditure to be audited and for proper financial controls to be implemented, with a regular system of reporting to club members.

The concept of ownership of property need not necessarily be forgotten in a club scheme, because it can be provided that after a period of years, the apartment or villa may be sold and the proceeds distributed among the timeshare buyers entitled to rights of use in respect of it.

The club system in Spain operates as follows:

1  A management company is formed which will have the obligation to carry out the management of the timesharing apartments for all the timeshare buyers. The management agreement with this company will contain far more detailed and adequate provisions in regard to the activities of the management company and the control of the management company by the club members than is usually found in an *escritura* system.

2  The developing company (together with the management company) becomes founder member of an unincorporated club, the rules of which are set out in a club constitution. The rules of the club contain much more detailed provisions regarding the assets of the club and the rights of the club members than would be found in a condominium type scheme. The constitution also has an appendix which lists the apartments belonging to the timesharing scheme, and has annexed to it the time period chart in which the year is divided into weekly periods, each of which is numbered, and each member must have at least one numbered weekly right of use.

The constitution also provides that the founder member has to form separate offshore companies limited by guarantee (to avoid securities legislation problems associated with the sale of shares) called 'owning companies' and transfer one or more apartments to each owning company. The founder member also has to transfer membership and control of each owning company to an independent trustee.

3  A deed of trust is executed and this document recites the vesting of the properties into the various companies, and the vesting of the companies in the trustee. It will also set out the rights and duties of the trustees vis-à-vis the developer and the timeshare owners.

The trustee executes the declaration of trust, in which the trustee agrees to control the owning companies on behalf of all the timeshare club members and agrees not to allow the properties owned by the owning companies to be sold, mortgaged or otherwise disposed of.

4  The last stage of this scheme is the application for membership under which the prospective member applies to acquire membership of the club from the developer; each member signs an undertaking agreeing, *inter alia*, to comply with the statutes and rules of the club.

If the developer is an offshore entity, it must be careful not to trade in Spain or to have a 'permanent establishment' in Spain, otherwise the developer will be taxable in Spain on all profits made, even if those profits arise from sales activities in other countries, and in such cases, not all the expenses incurred to make the sales will necessarily be deductible from 'profits'. Usually the developer incorporates a Spanish corporation to act as promotional services agent in Spain, and enters into an arm's length promotional services contract under which the Spanish entity is properly rewarded for all activities carried out in Spain itself. The importance of good tax advice cannot be over emphasised.

## Legislation affecting foreign operators

The *Ley General Tributaria* (general tax law), modified on numerous occasions, establishes that tax infringements may be punished even when they occur as a result of negligence. The punishments range from fines to the temporary suspension of professional status or prevention of access to official credit. However, the most severe punishment is described in the Criminal Code *Codigo Penal* in arts 349, 350 and 350 bis. Without going into an extensive analysis of *Delito Fiscal* (tax crime), it should be noted that the most serious cases, such as a fraud against the Inland Revenue, (*Hacienda Publica*), valued at more than 5,000,000 pesetas of undue fiscal benefits, may result in imprisonment.

Finally, the attention of timeshare developers and marketing agents is drawn to the *Ley de derechos y libertades de los extranjeros en España*, or foreigners' law, which came into force on 1 July 1985. This new law codifies the rights of foreigners in Spain, and in particular the hitherto rather easygoing system in effect allowing foreigners and marketing agents to work in Spain without a work permit has been tightened up. Foreigners who work without a work permit are liable to fines, imprisonment and expulsion orders and the employers themselves are also liable to fines and imprisonment. The authority to deal with these matters has been transferred in most provinces to the *Gobernador Civil* (the representative of the *Ministerio Interior*, equivalent to the Home Office). Now that Spain has become a member of the EEC, some of these provisions will no doubt have to be amended in so far as they now apply to EEC nationals and in this respect the applicable regulation is the treaty between the member states of the European Communities and the Kingdom of Spain and the Portuguese Republic concerning the accession of Spain and Portugal to the EEC, signed on 12 June 1985. Articles 55 to 60 of the treaty reflect the transitional provisions regarding the free movement of workers within the community declaring that:

> The Kingdom of Spain and the other Member States may maintain in force until 31 December 1992, with regard to nationals of the other Member States and to Spanish

nationals respectively, national provisions, or those resulting from bilateral arrangements, making prior authorisation a requirement for immigration with a view to pursuing an activity as an employed person and/or taking up paid employment.

The Royal Decree 1099/86 of 26 May 1986 contains specific regulations for entry, residence and work in Spain on the part of citizens of the member states of the EEC. The Decree goes into some detail about the administrative proceedings applicable for obtaining the appropriate permits. It is important to note that, according to this regulation, the sanctions applicable to any infringement of these matters can only be of a monetary nature, ie a fine. Other measures, such as imprisonment or explusion, can only be adopted for reasons of public order, public security, or public health and being based on the regulations covering those areas, and fundamental only in the personal behaviour of the individual concerned and never in financial or economical considerations.

The Treaty of Accession also regulates the transitional provisions regarding the free movement of capital which will eventually end exchange control regulations in Spain. The relevant arts are 61–66 and for this purpose the provisions of the Single European Act are also relevant. It should be borne in mind that despite the liberalisation in the movement of capital, certain administrative requirements such as verification, rather than authorisation, of investments may survive.

## The draft timeshare law

It must be emphasised at the outset that the draft law which will be found at Appendix F is very much a recent draft and is subject to amendment. It is however the first draft of any European law which deals adequately with the concept of timesharing and has detailed consumer protection regulation. It is to be hoped that the Spanish Parliament will enact the draft legislation broadly as it stands. and that the new law will become a model for other European jurisdictions.

### The principle of the law

On of the greatest merits of the new law is that instead of confining the industry to a specific and narrow formula, such as the Greek leasehold right, the French corporate right, or the Portuguese real right, all of which have created major difficulty for the industry in an international context, the new Spanish law instead defines common ingredients for every timeshare scheme and yet at the same time retains essential flexibility. Using the provisions of the new law the timeshare developer can structure a scheme which can be sold in any country. The draftsmen of the new law have recognised the international dimension of the timeshare business, and are the first to do so in a cohesive way.

## The prospectus

A fundamental principle of the new law is that every new timeshare scheme, and after an interim period, every existing timeshare scheme, must have a prospectus which is to be set out in the form of a notarial deed. Article 5 sets out the contents of the 'Prospectus'. The contents of this document will give timeshare purchasers and their advisers for the first time all the basic information required to know exactly what is being purchased. A copy of this Prospectus must be made available to purchasers in a language which they can understand (art 18.1).

## The contract

Article 10 sets out the minimum contents of the contract. Of particular note is that the contract must now contain a mandatory seven day 'cooling off' period which must be notified to purchasers in bold type in the contract.

## The management company

Every timeshare company must now have an authorised management company (Article 36) formed as a Spanish company with a paid up capital of not less than 50 million pesetas. This provision addresses one of the major problems of the timeshare industry, lack of proper management. Those problems are more likely to be found in smaller schemes than in larger schemes, and since the smaller schemes will not generally wish to capitalise a management company to the required extent, this will encourage the smaller schemes to appoint independent management companies. There are provisions in the new law for an annual budget, accounts and audit.

## The legal structure

As has been said earlier in this book, what really matters to timeshare purchasers is not whether the right to be granted is a 'real' or 'personal' right, but that whatever formula is chosen the rights which are to be acquired are properly protected. Very sensibly, the law does not require any specific form of legal structure, only by Article 20, that timeshare purchasers' rights are protected in one of five specific ways which are designed to cover almost every eventuality. The specified methods are:

(a) by, as part of the arrangements, transferring to each purchaser the right of ownership by periods or the usufruct by periods over the unit which is the object of the timeshare contract pursuant to Chapter I;

(b) by, as part of the arrangements, transferring to each purchaser of a timeshare period one share of the company owning the resort pursuant to Chapter II;

(c) by, as part of the arrangements, pledging all the shares of the said owning company in favour of the association of timeshare owners in accordance with Chapter III;

(d) by, as part of the arrangements; granting a mortgage over the property in accordance with Chapter IV in favour of the association of timeshare owners;

(e) by, as part of the arrangements, providing a bank guarantee or insurance policy insuring the full repayment of the full price plus interest at the legal rate in the event of the default by the developer pursuant to Chapter V.

As will be seen from Appendix F, a separate chapter of the new law is provided to regulate each of the five methods.

Method (a) will be utilised when a 'real' right is to be granted. The grant of a 'real' right necessarily involves the purchaser in having to register his right in the Land Registry in order to gain full protection. Consequently this method is unlikely to be used where sales are to be made internationally although having said that some developers will no doubt wish to experiment with ways of overcoming the logistical problem involved in the multiplicity of international registrations. The usufruct in particular is fraught with problems, not least of which is that the Civil Code provides that the right automatically terminates on the death of the owner.

Methods (b) and (c) vary only in detail, but will be used if the right to be granted is to be a corporate right being a share in the company which owns the resort, either directly (method (b)) or indirectly (method (c)). In both cases the developer will have to comply with securities legislation which will be deeply unattractive to many promoters but may be appropriate for some specific larger schemes which are linked with a financial instrument.

Method (d) is the method which preserves the club/trustee system, the system used by almost all timeshare promoters in Spain today. To adapt the conventional club/trustee system will only require that the owning companies create a mortgage in favour of the Owners Association although the detailed wording of the documentation, especially the sales contract, will need to be reviewed, a notarial 'prospectus' drawn up and an authorised management company appointed. One imagines that existing trustees will establish an authorised management company subsidiary and offer both trustee and management services since, to some extent, both overlap.

Method (e) which is the provision of a financial guarantee is only likely to be used as an interim method, pending the establishment of one or other of the foregoing four systems.

Since the provisions of the law are as yet in draft form and the requirements are clearly set out in Appendix F, it is unnecessary for the provisions to be rehearsed in detail in this chapter. The authors of the draft law are to be congratulated in having drafted a convenient and flexible law which will encourage the orderly development of the timeshare industry and which emulates a degree of consumer protection which currently does not exist outside the USA. Clearly an immense amount of time and thought has gone into the drafting, which demonstrates a complete understanding of both the theoretical and practical basis of the timeshare industry.

# Chapter Eleven

# Timesharing in Portugal

## Real rights in Portuguese law

From its inception in Portugal, the Portuguese authorities welcomed timesharing. They recognise that timesharing brings to the Portuguese economy investment of foreign capital, increased tourism revenue and local employment opportunities. The Portuguese National Tourist Office published literature designed to promote the Portuguese timesharing industry in which they say: 'Timesharing reduces the investment in your holiday property. It makes family holidays cheaper. It avoids expense and the deterioration of houses which are used for only one or two months without any income throughout the rest of the year'.

### Legislation

Portugal was the first European country to have created a new form of legal right of timesharing. The preamble to Decree No 355/81 states (in translation) 'This new concept is interesting for several reasons; it will mobilise savings; it will stimulate domestic tourism by offering guaranteed accommodation at accessible cost; and it will encourage Portuguese emigrants and foreign tourists, whose accommodation requirements are of a seasonal nature, to invest foreign currency in Portugal'.

Timesharing is known in Portugal as *direito de habitaçao periodica* (right of temporary habitation or timeshare right). The early laws, Nos 355/81 of 31 December and 368/83 of 4 October, envisioned the timeshare right purely as a right in real property, a right *in rem*. Contractual rights were allowed to exist but were essentially unregulated. With Decree No 130/89 of 18 April, which came into force in May 1989, the law in relation to real rights of timesharing was radically overhauled and also, for the first time, so-called obligational rights, or personal contractual rights, were regulated. The Portuguese law makers still conceive such rights as giving greater protection to timeshare purchasers although on a practical level this is usually not the case. With this in mind it is appropriate to examine the true meaning of the legal expression 'real rights' under Portuguese law.

The terms *direitos reais* (real rights) and *direito das coisas* (law of things) are used in the Portuguese doctrine without differentiation and refer to a kind of legal relation which can be identified by means of its structure and object. The terminology is therefore somewhat inaccurate and there are authors who prefer one or the other. The better view is that the term *direito das coisas* must be used when referring to a group of rules concerning the legal status of things, which are rights of the nature described in arts 202 *et seq* of the Civil Code; it is preferable to use the term 'real rights' when we are referring to a type of rights to be distinguished from other types of rights of a different structure, eg obligational or contractual rights or rights arising from a different source, eg rights in the field of family law or succession law.

The Portuguese Legislature adopted in the Portuguese Civil Code of 1966, the law which governs private legal relationships in Portugal, the term *direito das coisas*, like the German law (in Germany the term used is *sachenrecht*, which literally means law of things) which has exercised a strong influence on the Portuguese Civil Code. The Portuguese Civil Code of 1966 adopts the Germanic classification and divides the Code into five books:

Book I      General part
Book II     Obligation law
Book III    Law of things
Book IV     Family law
Book V      Succession law

It is only necessary to deal with Book III—Law of things—since this contains the rules which are employed to define the boundaries of real rights, and, consequently, the right of temporary habitation (timesharing) and with the provisions of Decree Nos 355/81 and 368/83 and 130/89, which created and adapted this new real property right in Portugal.

Book III of the Portuguese Civil Code consists of six chapters, namely:

I      Possession
II     The right of ownership
III    Usufruct, use and habitation
IV     Emphyteusis
V      Surface right
VI     Predial liens

A detailed explanation of the various rights referred to above is unnecessary, the essential thing being to determine the nature of these rights and how they come to be classified as real rights. A very brief historical explanation will help to explain the nature of the concept.

Roman law used to view all personal juridical situations through the perspective of the action in court. Consequently Roman authors contrasted the action *in rem* with the action *in personam*, ie the 'action against a thing' and the 'action against a person'.

Medieval authors, in turn, reasoning that every action in court should be supported by some sort of right, started to talk of *jus in rem* and *jus in personam*, ie the right which directly falls upon a certain thing and the right of demanding from a person a certain performance or duty. This opposition is enhanced with the so-called Germanic classification of the legal relationship and the contrast between the law of things and the law of obligations becomes perfectly evident. It is therefore appropriate to explain the nature of real rights by contrasting them with the nature of obligational rights.

'Real' rights have the characteristic of conferring on their holders absolute rights, that is to say, rights which must be respected by everyone, by means of the passive universal obligation not to deprive the holder of a real right of the useful enjoyment of it. Therefore, those bound by a 'real' legal relationship are not a pre-determined category, since they are all those who will from time to time deal with the holder of the right and will be obliged to respect the content of those rights. In the case of an obligational right, a separate legal relationship establishes (between two or more defined parties) a complex of rights and obligations, the effect of such relationship being restricted to the relevant parties. Thus it is said that obligational rights are not absolute rights, but relative rights, since they are not *erga omnes*.

Another important characteristic of real rights is the fact that they exist directly over things enabling their holders to take advantage of their characteristics. On the other hand, obligational rights and the power arising from these rights affect directly, positively, or negatively, the conduct of those who have agreed to be bound by them, affecting *things* only indirectly.

Once the general lines for the definition of real rights have been drawn, it is important to say that the ownership right or right of property is the fundamental real right and it is in the rules governing it where the general principles ruling all the real rights, such as typicality and the sequel right (*sequela*), are established. Under Portuguese legislation all other rights are only elements of the various powers contained in the legal definition of the right of ownership.

Article 1205 of the Civil Code provides:

> o proprietário goza de modo pleno e exclusivo dos direitos de use, fruiçao e disposiçao das coisas que ihe pertencem, dentro dos limites da lei a com observancia das restriçoes por ela immpostas.

> The owner enjoys in a full and exclusive way the rights of use, enjoyment and disposal of the things which belong to him, within the limitations of the law and with observance of the restrictions imposed by it.

Consequently, the owner has exclusive enjoyment of all the rights appurtenant to the thing owned. The existence of minor real rights is seen, in the Portuguese doctrine, as what might be described as a compression of the fundamental real right of ownership, which nevertheless maintains the characteristic of expanding again as soon as the minor real right terminates.

Doctrine calls it the 'elasticity factor' and we shall revert to it later on in this chapter. As will be seen, it is such a 'reaction' which is considered to occur between the right of ownership and the timeshare right.

Article 1306, 1, of the Civil Code, deals with the so-called principle of typicality in the following terms:

1. Nao é permitida a constituiçao, com carácter real, de restriçoes ao direito de propriedade ou de figuras parcelares deste direito senao nos casos previstos na lei; toda a restriçao resultante do negócio juridico, que nao esteja nestas condiçoes, tem natureza obrigacional.

This article means that under Portuguese law new real rights cannot be created except by statute. Obligational rights, on the other hand, are governed by art 405, which established the principle of contractual freedom. Consequently, in order to confer upon a right of temporary habitation a 'real' nature, that is to say, in order that it be considered an absolute right, it was necessary to establish it by legislation.

But for the decree laws, the right of temporary habitation could exist only as a contractual right having the characteristics of an obligational right and binding only the parties which created it: it would never have had the characteristics of an absolute right.

It is precisely this characteristic, of real rights, ie that the holder can enforce them unaffected by a right, temporary in nature, that is technically called *sequela* (sequel right). More plainly, it can be said that a real right follows the thing in question throughout and the holder can only lose his right by transfer (*inter vivos* or *mortis causa*) to a third party, the right itself disappearing only with the destruction of the thing itself.

Thus, on an infringement of a right of ownership or any other real right, the owner's consequent claim will always be recognised.

Article 1311 reads:

1. O Proprietário pode exigir judicialmente de qualquer possuidor ou detentor da coisa o reconhecimento do seu direito de propriedade e a consequente restituiçao do que ihe pertence.
2. Havendo reconhecimento de direito de propriedade, a restituiçao só pose ser recusada nos casis previstos na lei.

1. The owner can demand through the courts the recognition of his right of ownership by any possessor or holder of the thing, and the subsequent restitution of what belongs to him.
2. When there is recognition of the right of ownership, a restitution can only be denied in the cases provided by law.

This remedy, which has been designed for the right of ownership, is applied to the rest of the real rights by virtue of art 1315.

In accordance with these principles and with Decree No 355/81 of 31 December, Decree No 368/83 and Decree No 130/89, the holder of a real right, be it the right of ownership or the timeshare right, who is prevented from exercising that right will be able to start legal proceedings to recover whatever has been taken from him (and will also have rights of indemnity). Even whilst an action is pending, or before proceedings are commenced, the holder of a real right also has the right to take other direct steps in order to protect and secure his interest.

The fundamental mistake of the Portuguese law was to insist that only a right *in rem* could adequately protect consumers. This is clearly shown by the preamble of the original Decree No 355/81 of 31 December 1981 which stated (in translation):

> The purpose of this new law is therefore to create a new real estate right—the right to periodic use of property—which in practice is similar to the condominium concept but the division is by timeshares and not by horizontal segments. This law will also provide better legal protection for holders of holiday shares since up to now they have had recourse only to precarious protection of a contractual nature.

As we shall see, a number of important consequences result from this initial error. Timesharing in Portugal as constituted by the decree laws is a real right, not only because the law describes it as such, but also because it has all the required characteristics. It exists directly over a thing; it was created by means of a decree, in this way complying with art 1306 of the Civil Code which enshrines the principle of typicality and finally, as will be seen, it is a right endowed with sequel since the holder of this right can enforce it through a claim action.

## Function of the Land Registry

The existence and transfer of real rights is recorded in the Land Registry. The aim of the Land Registry system is to make public the rights over immovable property in accordance with art 1 of the Code of the Land Registry. This article provides that all real rights which revert over real estates must be publicised, and art 2 of the same Code sets out the matters which must be registered. *Inter alia*, acquisitions and divisions of the right of ownership have to be registered, as must the constitution, acquisition or modification of the rights of usufruct, use and habitation and servitude, the constitution of the horizontal property, etc. It is important to remember that the Land Registry acts as guarantor as to the security and validity of the rights which revert over real estate.

Although art 2 of the Code of the Land Registry did not of course envisage the problem of the registration of timesharing rights in the Land Registry, (at the date of the Code's publication timeshare had not yet been created) art 5,1 of Decree No 355/81 of 31 December 1981 provided, and art 8 of Decree No 130/89 of 18 April now provides, that in relation to each right of temporal habitation the relevant Land Registry office must issue a land certificate which registers the existence of that right and records its encumbrance or alienation. This land certificate will contain the essential elements of the right it refers to.

That is to say, the object and duration, and the main rights and obligations, both of the holder of the right and of the owner of the block of real estate, ie the holder of the right of property.

As in other cases, the Land Registry has the function in relation to this new real right of giving it publicity before third parties and of securing its existence. Registration of the right at the Land Registry is of great importance, since without registration the right is not opposable *erga omnes*.

## Comparison between timesharing and other similar real rights

### Right of ownership and timesharing

The legal definition of the Right of Ownership or right of property has already been given and appears under art 1305 of the Civil Code. As was noted, the 'real' right which involves the greatest range of powers, and provides the owner with an almost unlimited enjoyment of the use of things, is the theoretical right, of ownership.

According to Portuguese theory, the right of ownership compresses itself in order to co-exist with a minor real right and when the minor right is extinguished, the right of ownership automatically extends to its former state. It is precisely this quality of elasticity that is inherent in the creation of a timesharing right, since this right co-exists with the right of the owner of the block of real estate.

The timeshare right gives to its holder the right to occupy a specific property for a specific period of time, and this right will, as soon as it begins to exist, limit the right of ownership, timesharing itself being a real right opposable *erga omnes*.

The main difference between these two real rights is that the right of ownership gives to its holder the full and exclusive rights of use, enjoyment and disposal of the property, whereas the timeshare right gives to its holder the right to use and enjoy the thing for a specific period of time, without the power to dispose of the thing itself. Only the rights of use can be transferred, either for value or gratuitously, *inter vivos* or *mortis causa*. Besides this essential difference, the holder of the timeshare right is not entitled to use the property in whatever way he wishes; he cannot give it a different use from that which the property was designed for nor can he do anything prohibited in the notarial deed, which creates the timeshare right.

One of the reasons for examining the theoretical basis of this new right, is that when the right of ownership co-exists with the timeshare right, either of these rights can be transferred to third parties without involving disturbance of the other right. It follows, therefore, that besides the ability to transfer the right of ownership without affecting the timeshare right, title to ownership of the properties can be mortgaged without the timeshare rights themselves being affected, although the converse is also true.

Development and construction companies often create mortgages over the land where the construction is going to take place, since they need to provide security to creditors when borrowing to finance their business. In the event of bankruptcy of the owner, the mortgage creditor may exercise his rights and so will become the owner of the property. As we have seen, this will not necessarily affect the holder of the timeshare right. Nevertheless, in the event that the mortgage creditor is a bank or any other entity without special experience of this kind of enterprise, endless practical difficulties could in fact arise.

Under Portuguese law it is the person or entity entitled to the right of ownership who is bound to provide the services and rights of occupation to which timeshare owners are entitled by virtue of the ownership of their rights. A foreclosing mortgagee steps into the shoes of the proprietor of the right of ownership of the property and becomes personally liable to undertake the onerous burden of granting the timeshare owners their rights. The mortgagee will have to provide management and funds to carry out the administration and will be liable to be sued by the timeshare owners for any failure to provide such services.

Originally the timeshare owners did not have the right to appoint a manager to administrate. Decree No 130/89 provides that the manager can now be appointed by the majority of timeshare owners (art 26) and under art 29 any timeshare owner can apply for the appointment of a judicial manager if necessary.

**Right of usufruct and timesharing**

According to art 1439 of the Portuguese Civil Code, usufruct is:

o direito de gozar temporária e plenamente uma coisa ou direito alheio, sem altrar a sua forma ou substancia

the right to enjoy temporarily and fully someone else's property without altering its form or substance.

Thus, whereas the owner has three fundamental powers over his property, namely *jus utendi* (use), *jus fruendi* (enjoyment) and *just abutendi* (destruction or disposal), the usufructuary has the first two powers only, and therefore he cannot dispose of the thing. Every usufruct implies a co-existence of real rights and where there is a usufruct it co-exists with a right of ownership deprived of *usus* and of *fructus*.

This is reflected in art 144g of the Portuguese Civil Code, which provides in a quaint and appealing way

O usufrutuário pode usar, fruir e administrar a coisa ou o direito como faria um bom pai de familia, respeitando o seu destino económico.

The usufructuary can sue, enjoy and administer the thing to right as a good father of a family would do, respecting its economic destiny.

There can, therefore, exist over a building or development a right of ownership, a right of usufruct and a timeshare right, and in such a case the last right will limit the usufruct since the timeshare owner will be entitled to use and enjoy the property for a certain period of time.

From the foregoing it will be realised that the timeshare right is more restricted than the right of usufruct, since the latter includes powers to administer the property and is not discontinuous. Usufruct is a continuous right even if terminable (eg on the death of its holder or the expiry of a pre-established period of time).

### Horizontal property and timesharing

In creating the new timeshare right *in rem*, the timeshare laws establish a parallel between this new right and the horizontal property, and also between the social roles which these two rights play. Both rights correspond to a division of ownership and property being a division of space in the case of the horizontal property, and a division of time quotas in the case of timesharing. The emergence and institutionalisation of the concept of 'horizontal property' arises from the construction of blocks of flats, a solution to the housing problems caused by shortage of land.

Article 1414 of the Portuguese Civil Code provides:

> As várias fraçcoes de que um edificio se compoe, em condiçoes de constituirem uniade independentes, podem pertencer a proprietários diverso em regime de propriedade horizontal.

> The various sections into which a building is divided, making up independent units, can belong to different owners in a system of horizontal property.

It is clear from this article and subsequent provisions of the Civil Code that several rights of ownership, which are totally autonomous, can be constituted in a single building over independent sections of it, and a co-ownership is constituted over the communal elements of the building. Thus, the system of horizontal property provides for two circumstances, exclusive ownership of the apartments and co-ownership of the common parts. This is not the case with timesharing, which is a minor real right or a limited real right, and in turn corresponds to a limitation of the ownership right. Consequently, the timeshare laws refer to the owner of the building on one hand and the holder of the timeshare right on the other hand, distinguishing between them and delimiting the rights powers and duties of each *vis-à-vis* the other.

## Portuguese timeshare law

A translation of Decree No 130/89 will be found at Appendix E. The law supersedes and codifies the previous timeshare law relating to timesharing as a real right, and at the same time addresses some of the problems with the earlier law, detailed in the last edition of this work. For the first time the new law contains controls to protect the intending purchaser of a real right, and also for the first time attempts to regulate contractual or obligational rights of timesharing. Whichever route is followed, whether creating the scheme by way of a real or by way of a personal right, the approval of the Directorate General of Tourism has to be obtained. This is a lengthy process and few if any schemes have yet been approved at the time of writing, notwithstanding that new schemes have required approval since May 1989 and existing schemes were required to obtain approval by May 1990. At present, the authorities seem to be taking a relaxed view and have not so far taken any enforcement action. It would seem, however, that purchasers who have not made use of their timeshare may be entitled to avoid their contracts for non-compliance with the law, if they were to acquire a real right which would necessarily be governed by Portuguese law. Other arrangements are not necessarily governed by Portuguese law and will have to be considered in the light of conflicts of laws. On general principles (see Chapter 7) there seems to be no reason to suggest that arrangements between members of an overseas (non-Portuguese) club, with a foreign (non-Portuguese) trustee would be governed by Portuguese law, unless this system of laws was expressly chosen by the governing documentation, which would be very unlikely. The situation is extremely unsatisfactory, but what seems clear is that the Portuguese authorities have made a requirement for approval, without at the same time creating the necessary infrastructure for the processing of applications for approval. A similar problem has existed under previous decree laws, and will no doubt continue to exist under the new law. Whenever an attempt is made to create the timeshare right as a real right, the Land Registries are just not equipped or staffed to handle the volume of work. It may take years to get the title certificates issued, even with the help of *ad hoc* arrangements (which are not unknown in Portugal) whereunder the developer seconds staff to the Registry to help with the work. With this in mind we analyse the provisions of the new law as it is to operate in theory, bearing in mind that practice may vary and, as always, good local advice is essential.

## Real rights under Decree No 130/89

The sales contract must contain information pursuant to art 30 which may be summarised as follows:

1  The identity of the owner of the project, the purchaser, the sales agent (if any) and the manager (if any).
2  The identity of the development and the reference number of the application for classification of the development as a tourist enterprise. Real rights of timeshare are not allowed in any projects, only those qualified under Decree No 328/86 of 30 September (art 2).

3 Extract from the Land Registry description of the development and buildings to be timeshared.

4 The date of opening of the development or, if under construction, the date of the building project approval and the date when the project, or its relevant phase, is to be completed.

5 Description of the unit and an itemised furnishing inventory together with details of amenities to be provided and a summary of the rights and obligations of timeshare owners and the developer, taken from the notarial deed creating the right, or a draft of that deed.

6 Details of the timeshare period contracted to be sold.

7 Details of any mortgages affecting the property.

8 If the property is not completed, whether the purchasers' funds are guaranteed and if so how.

The purchase price is not required to be mentioned, although one imagines that it will be. There is no requirement for a completion guarantee, so purchasers paying developers prior to completion are clearly at risk. Moreover, if the property is mortgaged, the lenders' rights may override the contract, so once again purchasers may be at risk. The new law therefore legitimises a highly unsatisfactory situation, allowing the developer to take purchasers' funds with no completion guarantee, and before title is conveyed.

There is a requirement for a seven day cooling-off period (for proposed sale of real rights only) under art 30.4, but curiously the required information in the contract does not include a mandatory statement advising the purchaser of this cooling-off right, and the revocation must be in writing with recorded delivery within seven days of signing the contract. Most purchasers will be likely to lose their rights simply because they will be unaware of them until after the seven day period has expired.

There is a requirement that the buyers are not told in the documentation that they will become owners of the development. It is not clear precisely what this provision is intended to achieve, although in practice it is likely to cause confusion and translation difficulties.

There is an additional right of rescission at any time between the signing of the contract and delivery of the title certificate or date of notarial declaration of sale, if either the building project approval has not been granted at the date of the contract, or the contract does not contain the required information, or if the contract refers to an 'ownership interest' being sold, notwithstanding that a real right, registrable in the Land Registry, is in fact being sold. In this event the purchaser is entitled to receive double what he has paid, plus interest (at a rate not specified by the law) from the date of payment of the contractual payments until repayment of all monies due under this article (art 32). Why the purchaser is to obtain a windfall profit in these circumstances is not explained and, whilst the position is not free from doubt, it appears that even if the claim for annulment is delivered, at any time before making payment, the developer can block the claim by issuing the title transfer even if the contract did not contain the required information and even if the purchaser was misled as to the nature of the interest to be acquired and conceivably even if the property is mortgaged. It also seems that any monies paid pursuant to the contract which do not relate to the purchase price, for example (as is often the case) if the contract covers temporary alternative accommodation pending construction, can also be recovered twice over if art 32 applies. The article does not make it clear who is liable to make the repayment of the contractual payments and penalty. It is conceivable that the developer may be liable, and the agent (if any) could escape liability, even though the agent may not have accounted to the developer for the funds. The contract between the developer and the marketing agent will need to cover this point. The position in regard to sales made outside Portugal is far from clear. The intending purchaser may have a claim in Portugal against the developer under Portuguese law, but not necessarily a claim against the agent, if the agent is not resident in Portugal. Escrow arrangements, under which money is blocked pending the project licence, are clearly affected, since even if the purchaser is by this means guaranteed a full refund, he nevertheless may have a claim to be paid twice.

Clearly, contractual purchasers of real rights of timesharing are in a highly unsatisfactory position, and their rights, if generous in some respects, are by no means guaranteed. The state itself may impose a fine for breach of art 30, but of a relatively small amount, (100,000 Esc to 200,000 Esc) (art 39). There is also power to ban the development entity concerned from carrying on business for up to two years (art 41) although clearly such action could prejudice existing purchasers.

Article 33 provides that all promotional material, including advertising, must contain most of the information required to be part of the contract including, for example, the itemised list of furnishings. Why the draftsmen of the Act considered this to be necessary is something of a mystery and the provision would, if observed, lead to some large and unwieldy advertising. The author has not seen any advertising which complies with the law, but none is allowed until the directorate of tourism approves a project, and meantime the authorities appear to be turning a blind eye. The penalty for breach is a relatively modest fine of between 50,000 Esc to 150,000 Esc (art 39) and the offending material may be confiscated (art 41).

In order to establish the real right, each separate scheme must have one owner of the land and buildings involved (art 3.1) which must be classified as an aparthotel, tourist village, tourist apartment or tourist complex pursuant to Decree No 328/86. Each timeshare right must not be for a period of less than seven or more than 30 days per annum, but there seems nothing to stop a purchaser acquiring several rights, for example five rights of seven days each. The scheme is to last in perpetuity unless a shorter period is specified, not being less than 20 years. By implication (since each right has to be registered at the Land Registry against each dwelling unit with a named owner) floating time schemes where particular time periods are allocated on a booking system, are not possible to create as real rights. The timeshare rights when created may be issued by the developer to himself or to a third party. Subject to what is said regarding contractual rights hereafter, the *use* of the timeshare period itself may be granted (art 12) as opposed to outright assignment of the timeshare interest. This opens the way to a number of devices designed to avoid the main restrictions and penalties of the law, since the user of a timeshare right would not have the rights of the proprietor of the real right.

The documentation for the real rights scheme must be approved by the Director General of Tourism, a lengthy and difficult process which has already been commented upon. Essentially, the right itself is created by means of a notarial deed containing certain mandatory information (arts 4 and 5). This deed is then to be registered at the Land Registry, who then, in time, are to issue property right certificates, one for each right so created. For example, if the scheme involves 100 apartments, then 5,200 certificates must be issued, and each one entered into the records of the Land Registry. Frequently this work is still done manually. Existing schemes already set up on a similar basis under the previous law must be altered to comply with the new law, but may only be altered so as to comply with the new law with the consent of all the existing registered owners. What is to happen if that consent is not forthcoming is not specified.

Transfers of the right are carried out by a transfer declaration executed before a notary, but only the transferor need execute the declaration. This removes one obstacle under the previous law, which formerly required both parties, one of whom was likely to be a holidaymaker not resident in Portugal, to execute the transfer.

The transferee will still need a lawyer or agent to effect the registration of the transfer without which the right is not valid *erga omnes*. Many thousands of purchasers have left this task to the developer, and when on occasion the developer has failed to register, and has in the meantime created mortgages or sold the property, substantial difficulty has arisen. The registration of the transfer is likely to involve the purchaser in some expense, correspondence and language problems, although some developers have set up special arrangements with local lawyers for the benefit of customers.

## Taxation and real rights

There are in Portugal several taxes levied on income from immovable property. The tax which is relevant here is land tax. In art 1 of the Code of Land Tax (*Código da Contribucao Predial*) it is provided that this tax is levied on:

> Os rendimentos dos prédios situados no contiente ou ilhas adjacentes, divindo-se, de harmonia com a classificaçao destes, em rústicos e urbanos.

> The income from the land situated on the continent or adjacent islands, being divided, according to their classification, into rural land and urban land.

A timesharing development will of course be established on urban land.

According to art 3 of the Code of Land Tax, the income from urban land when leased out is the value of the rent expressed in the usual currency, and when not leased, the equivalent use which the person who can use or enjoy the land obtains from it or has the possibility of deriving from it. Consequently, the timeshare owner will be subject to payment of that part of *predial* tax corresponding to the period during which he has the use and enjoyment of the property or an autonomous section of it. However, according to art 21 of Decree No 130/89, all the taxes or other annual duties levied on the building or development which has been timeshared, although assessed according to the respective income therefrom, are payable by the owner of the property and not by the individual timeshare owner. So the *predial* tax will be payable by the owner and not by the holder of the timeshare right, and the same will apply with regard to the fire tax (*imposto de incendio*) and the municipal taxes (*taxas camarárias*), if any. It is even arguable that as there is no exemption for the income obtained by the timeshare owner by way of rental, that tax on this is payable by the unfortunate owner of the whole building, It seems odd to require the developer to pay tax on rental income realised by the timeshare owners.

With regard to transfers of immovable property, there is in Portugal a conveyance tax and a tax on succession and donations. The conveyance tax (currently 10 per cent) is levied on transfers for value of the right of ownership or parcels of this right on immovable property, according to art 2 of the Code of Conveyance Tax and Succession and Donations Tax (*Código da Sisa e do Imposto sobre Sucessoes e Doaçoes*). The succession and donation tax is levied on gratuitous transfers of movable and immovable property.

According to art 15 of Decree No 355/81, which remains in force pursuant to art 47 of Decree No 130/89, the transfer of a timeshare right is exempted from conveyance tax; gifts and successions *mortis causa* of such a right are not, however, exempted.

## Management and real rights

The new law contains detailed provisions regarding the management of the timeshare resort. Primarily the registered owner of the land and buildings, normally the developer, is made liable and always will be liable so long as he owns the interest from which the timeshare interests are derived. He may appoint a manager, but if he fails to carry out his duties, the timeshare owners may themselves appoint a manager (art 25) and any timeshare owner may apply for the appointment of a traditional manager (art 29). The management charge must include a sinking fund of not less than 2.5 per cent of the amount collected (art 20) against repairs and replacements, and management fees must not exceed 20 per cent of the total management charge (art 18). The management accounts must be audited and copies of the audited accounts distributed to all owners within three months of the year end (art 23), failing which a fine may be imposed (art.39) and the developer or manager banned from carrying on business for up to two years (art 41). A three month rule is likely to be more honoured in the breach than in the observance.

There is also mandatory provision for a guarantee of half the aggregate annual management charge which must be lodged by the developer or the manager with the Directorate General of Tourism. This must be in the form of an insurance bond or a bank guarantee or deposit of funds. The manager or judicial manager may enforce the guarantee in case of need. The guarantee must be updated annually. Curiously, failure to provide the guarantee initially is punishable by a small fine (art 39). The failure to update it if there is an increase in charges is punishable by up to two years suspension from business (art 41).

In the event that the proprietor of the timeshare rights (who in many cases may be owned by the developer) fails to pay, the manager may deny access to the unit until payment is made, if and only if the notarial deed constituting the right contains this power. If the timeshare owner uses the timeshare, or cannot be prevented from using the timeshare, the outstanding charge is a preferred debt, after certain other debts such as legal costs, government charges relating to taxes and certain fiscal charges related to councils (art 19). The law does not provide for a remedy if the timeshare owner does not use the timeshare and does not pay the management charge. This is a fatal flaw. Action against foreign owners in Portugal is likely to be a long drawn out expensive process, and a surprisingly large number of owners simply do not visit their timeshare or pay their charges, especially where the purchase price was small and the management charge substantial. It is puzzling that the draftsmen of the law did not include a right of forfeiture for non-payment. Even more alarming, if the developer fails to pay in respect of the timeshare rights which he owns, there may be a lengthy *inter regnum* before management can be re-established by the owners, and a sufficient number of timeshares may not have been sold so as to make management viable without contributions in respect of the unsold weeks. As we have seen, failure to provide the guarantee deposit is not punished severely. Clearly, therefore, the new law may have protected timeshare owners against overcharging, but the more serious problems which can arise have not been addressed. Finally, in the event of the death of the timeshare owner, his administrators or executors will have a Portuguese estate to administer, with all that this entails.

## Contractual timeshare schemes

There must be considerable doubt as to whether contracts not governed by Portuguese law and entered into between non-Portuguese contracting persons are governed by Decree No 130/89 but the Directorate General of Tourism has expressed the view that they are. On the assumption that this view is correct, the provisions of the law may be analysed, but the view remains to be tested.

If the law applies, contractual timeshare schemes can only be created in relation to that property which could be subjected to the real right system of timesharing. Documentation must be submitted to the Directorate General of Tourism for approval and the selling entity must provide an insurance bond or bank guarantee in the amount of one third of the value of the timeshare rights being sold or 10 million Esc (about £50,000 at the time of writing) whichever is the greater. As a matter of practice, the Directorate General of Tourism usually requires that all the documentation is translated into Portuguese. It should be emphasised that the guarantee relates to the seller's obligations and not the obligations of any third party, such as a trustee or agent. The value in relation to which the guarantee level is to be set is not specified in detail. If the rights are to be sold wholesale to foreign entities for resale to foreign consumers, it seems that in practice the authorities accept the wholesale price if this is thought to be fair on an arm's length basis, instead of insisting upon the valuation being based on the resale price for the purpose of establishing the level of the required guarantee. There are more limited requirements as to what information the contractual documentation must contain, broadly what is required to be set out in the notarial deed creating a 'real right' timeshare scheme. Any contractual owner may apply for the appointment of a judicial manager, who may enforce the guarantee mentioned above, if it exists and has not lapsed. Any purchasers who have not exercised their right of occupation and in respect of which the right has not been legalised (presumably by cure of the breach) can void the contract and claim a double refund with interest if the contractual documentation does not contain the required information or if the requisite approval from the Directorate General of Tourism has not been obtained. There is a fine of between 100,000 and 200,000 Esc for the sale of contractual rights which do not comply with the provisions of the law, and under art 41 the authorities have power to seize the offending documentation. There is no right to ban developers for two years in relation to real rights, and the management provisions and guarantee deposit for management charges are not required in the case of the sale of contractual rights. Also, there is no seven day cooling-off period for contractual rights.

Accordingly, developers wishing to continue with the club/trustee or other contractual schemes should not find it overly difficult to comply with the law, but the major problem, as with the law relating to real rights, is the difficulty in persuading the authorities to process applications in a reasonably diligent manner. The authorities must be aware of the problem, because, so far as the author is aware, no enforcement action has yet been taken, at least at the time of writing.

## Conclusion

If the provisions of Decree No 130/89 were to be strictly enforced it would throw the Portuguese timeshare industry into chaos to the detriment of consumers and promoters alike. At the time of writing it is clearly difficult to advise promoters or consumers as to how they should proceed. What is needed is a rational review of the law, perhaps along the lines of the new draft Spanish law.

# Chapter Twelve

# Timesharing in Australasia, Bermuda, Greece, Italy, Malta and South Africa

## Australasia

Despite the speed and ease of modern travel, the fact that Australia and New Zealand are further away from the rest of the developed world than almost anywhere else has affected their timesharing activities. Thus, while the industry has flourished in this region, a part of the common law world where English is the universal language, American and European business has to date not sought timeshare development opportunities in Australasia to any great extent preoccupied as it must be with its own great mass markets for consumer leisure and lifestyle products.

Nevertheless, Australia, New Zealand and the Pacific Islands present some outstanding opportunities for various forms of shared ownership. Substantial overseas interest in timeshare development, purchase and exchange has begun to appear and American timeshare marketeers, consultants and local entrepreneurs have been active for many years.

The physical and social geography of the area set some important guidelines for timeshare in the region. Thinly populated, the whole Southwestern Pacific hardly comprises more than 20 million people with an American or European cultural orientation. Principal centres of population such as Sydney, Melbourne and Brisbane (all on Australia's Pacific Coast, though at intervals of more than five hundred miles distance by road) are highly urbanised and account for as many as half the people of the region.

These factors, added to the distance of prime resort areas such as Surfers Paradise, Queensland, from the larger cities and the relatively high cost of travel to and within the area, have meant that marketing, in many ways the key to timeshare development success, is relatively expensive and has had to go off-site. This in its turn has attracted significant marketing and sales practice regulatory activity, which may well intensify.

Shared ownership of resort property is not new in the region, having been known on the Australian snowfields as much as 100 years ago. Timesharing as such, however, dates from pioneer country and ranch projects of the late 1960s in New South Wales and has now achieved a measure of product recognition with the public at large, though the detail of its development and legal and financial structuring peculiarities remain surprisingly little known. It is the task of this short account to sketch principal features of the legal landscape and invite the drawing of relevant inferences for developers and consumers and their advisers.

**Legal context**

Australia is a federation of seven states each with its own legislature and judicature in addition to those superimposed nationally by the Common-wealth. For brevity and unless otherwise mentioned, all will be treated as parallel and New South Wales alone cited in state matters, federal law being cited as such. New Zealand is a separate sovereign country whose law is likewise sufficiently parallel in all material matters not to need separate citation here. The Pacific islands, where for instance the claims of traditional owners and restrictions on foreign ownership of real estate are the rule, are a separate matter beyond our present scope.

All Australasian jurisdictions have inherited the common law and have progressively modified it through the classic process of precedent decided cases. All legislatures have been active in making statute law but in the law of real estate, the environment, corporations, trusts, trade practices and the public offering of securities, they are all strikingly similar in their thrust and often their detail. British and American attorneys and financial advisers with land development and business law experience are quickly at home and welcome in the Australasian professions.

**Law of timeshare development**

Timesharing is a flexible concept, fitting a wide variety of developer and end buyer requirements. A freehold owner/developer thus has various options, first as to whether to sell or retain his fee simple interest. If he has a lesser estate in the land and improvements, he may wish to sell that or retain it. The following principles of law will define his options further:

*Title to land*

1  Freehold, leasehold, subleasehold titles in land and licence to occupy land (which is regularly defined to include fixed improvements) are all possible, and strata, cluster and community titles (ie separate title within horizontal and/or communal property regimes) are available for freehold and leasehold property, though the latter is rare.
2  Apart from negligible pockets of common law title which remain proved and passed by deed and conveyance, all title is registered and underwritten by appropriate government agencies. Title registration on the Torrens system, now widely imitated around the world, was first used in Australia. Title insurance on the American model is unknown.
3  Co-tenancy (as joint or in common) is possible without limit as to the

number of persons beneficially interested. Though the point is not entirely free from doubt, the commonly accepted view is that it is possible to contract out of the right of covenants to partition or seek a trustee for sales (eg Conveyancing Act (NSW) 1919–1969, s 66G); and a tenant in common typically has the right to call upon the title registrar to call for issue to him of a separate certificate of his title (Real Property Act (NSW) 1900, s 100).

*Taxation*
Australian and New Zealand tax legislation distinguishes between capital and income and now taxes net gains of both. As part of the development strategy, developers must consider whether they need to set the cost of acquisition of land assets against the proceeds of sale. If so, they must sell a timeshare structured to include a real estate component; and this has been the common case in Australia. Current foreign investment review policy may have relevance: though all foreign ownership proposals at the date of writing require approval regardless of type and size, the Australian federal authorities have a stated policy favouring foreign entrepreneurial joint ventures with Australian residents. Withholding taxes apply to dividend and interest remittances abroad and double taxation arrangements are operative between Australia and most countries likely to be relevant overseas developers investing in Australia.

*Corporations, trusts and business entities*
An owner association, through the constitution and rules of which timeshare rights are appointed among owners and their affairs mutually regulated, can take virtually any corporate form. For reasons to do with the regulation of public offerings detailed below, the public unit trust has been preferred; but public companies limited by shares and/or guarantee, co-operative societies and other entities are possible and right-to-use programmes have been successfully established through differential share classes (prior to the introduction of the most recent forms of capital gains taxation in Australia), redeemable shares being sold at a premium by the developer as timeshares.

There are important matters of detail here which though space does not permit a fuller analysis, should not be glossed over. As a useful generalisation, it can be said that an American or British lawyer practised in his home corporate and condominium documentation would be quickly at home in Australia with the timeshare-relevant substance of any of these entities, as they are defined and regulated by (for instance) the National Companies Codes of Australia.

Many timeshare developers start from situation which is less than ideal and must balance what can be done against what they assess to be an ideally saleable end product. However, marketability is the key to timeshare success and the consensus to date among Australasian developers has been that most buyers want a real estate interest which in practice means a tenancy in common in the fee simple, linked with timeshare rights in the resort property. Right-to-use programmes are in the minority.

In summary and at its simplest in Australian timesharing, the real estate interest to be committed to a timeshare project is normally leased by the developer in virtual perpetuity (or for as long as the timeshare is to last) to the owner's entity, whatever form it takes; the underlying real estate is committed to multiple tenancy in common in a number equivalent to the timeshare to be created, and through the owners' entity, in which they hold shares or units matching their tenancies in common, the owners exercise their timeshare rights.

### Development approval

State and local government have very wide permissive and coercive powers in all matters to do with land development. As in most jurisdictions, application must be made in the approved form with a wealth of supporting documentation to satisfy regulators ever more sensitive to environmental impact. Timesharing is, however, regulated on the same basis as general development and has not achieved any special categoristaion for these purposes, though it tends to generate relatively intensive land use and is controlled accordingly by governments with an increasing awareness of what timesharing is.

### Land sales

Though most state jurisdictions within the region have well developed systems of control of the sale of land and interests in it, the trend has been to leave the regulation of selling land in timeshared form to corporate and securities regulators.

Australia has no equivalent of the US Office of Interstate Land Sales Regulation or any of its European analogues and it has been one of the more fortunate results of timeshare becoming a security that land sales regulators as such have not sought to police it.

It is worth mentioning that state duties are usually payable by purchasers of real estate interests or negotiable securities on a sliding scale up to substantial sums (as much as 5 per cent *ad valorem*). There are no wealth or capital transfer taxes at the time of writing, and none are mooted.

### Law of timeshare selling

### Registered public offering

In practical terms, under Australasian corporate and securities law, all timeshares are treated as marketable securities and, if offered for sale to the public, must only be so offered on the basis of documentation registered with the National Companies and Securities Commission or its equivalent. The reasons briefly are as follows.

Section 5 of the Companies Codes defines a 'timesharing scheme' as: 'a scheme . . .(a) participants in which are or may become entitled to use, occupy or possess, for 2 or more periods during the period for which the scheme . . . is to operate, property to which the scheme. . . relates; and (b) that is to operate for a period of not less than 3 years'; and by the same legislation, a timesharing scheme is to be regarded as a 'prescribed interest'.

The Codes use the concept of 'prescribed interest' to cover on the broadest definitions any kind of participation in a common enterprise or investment scheme: unit trusts, mutual funds, realty and personalty investment syndications. Prescribed interests may not be offered to the public except on the basis of documentation approved by the corporate and securities regulatory authorities.

The principal documents for approval and registration (as stipulated by Divs 1 and 6 of Pt IV of the Australian Codes, New Zealand having separate similar legislation in this behalf) are:

1 *The constituent documents of the timeshare scheme*: To date this has usually been a bulky unit trust deed linking multiple freehold owners in the resort land with units in the trust and incorporating a number of compulsory statutory covenants binding the 'watchdog' custodian trustee and the manager of the scheme (ie the developer), providing for deposit escrows, rescissions, owner democracy, audit and like matters commonly found in trust documentation for more orthodox forms of investment security. The trustee must be a trustee approved under the Code (in practice one of the major public trust corporations) and the manager a not insubstantial public company. The most notable manager covenant *prima facie* required of managers of prescribed interest trusts is that required by s 16891 (b)(iii) of the Code, to the effect that the manager/developer will repurchase the interest in question or cause it to be repurchased within a stipulated time and at a predetermined price, this provision being designed to guarantee buyers a secondary market; but timesharing enjoys special privileges in this, as noted below.

2 *The offer document* (the 'prospectus'): This document, by the Code and its concomitant regulations, is required to contain a wealth of disclosures about the timeshare scheme, title, the resort, the developer and its affiliates and officers, downstream contractual obligations, brokerage paid, maintenance fees, investigating accountant reports and so on. In addition, promoters are required to produce to the regulators unpublished information of all kinds in substantiation of claims made in the published documents.

*Licencing of offerors*

The Securities Industry Codes of Australia regulate dealing in securities and offerors of timeshare and their representatives (their sales and marketing employees) are required to be licenced for the product or products they sell. Apart from showing good character, honesty and due diligence in discharge of licensed functions, this involves various not specially onerous formal compliances, proof of modest net tangible assets and the posting of relatively modest security. A federal government green paper has recommended substantial simplification and deregulation of the licensing regime, but this has lain dormant since 1986 and change does not seem imminent.

### Regulatory exemption

To treat timeshares as fully fledged securities on a par with investment products properly so called may seem draconian, but approval and registration of timeshare documents is not nearly so fearsome an affair as it is for instance in many parts of the USA. In practice, 'regulators' have used their discretions to allow exemption from the strict letter of the Australian Codes (ss 168(2), 170(5) and 215C) with a generous pragmatism. A set of guidelines for the exercise of these discretions has been issued by the National Commission. These guidelines (National Companies and Securities Commission Policy Statements, Release No 117) allow wide exemptions from the full rigour of the Codes if adequate safeguards are provided.

The principal concerns are to ensure:

1 an informed buyer decision; proper handling of purchaser funds pending completion of construction, if applicable;
2 provision for buyer rescission within seven days of purchase;
3 developer responsibility for maintenance levy attributable to unsold inventory on an equal footing with purchasers;
4 disclosure or exemption from buyback obligation; and
5 lesser matters including a requirement for information to be provided on offer of timeshares for resale in the secondary market.

If these are properly provided for and the matter frankly negotiated with the Commissions on a case-by-case basis, exemption is usually available from most of the compliances developers find irksome, among them the buyback guarantee, direct or indirect profit revelations, and lengthy boilerplate disclosure of scheme formalities. Timeshare prospectuses are also permitted to remain current for 18 months, three times the normal statutory limit, with periodic price increases and statutory information updates being simply notified to the Commission. Restrictions of advertising applicable to securities are relaxed.

### Control of selling practices

Australasia is not alone in having experienced a small percentage of forced or misleading sales practices. Throughout the region consumer advocates, together with various departments of state responsible for consumer affairs, have been quick to use the ample legislative weapons at their disposal to regulate the marketing of timeshare by street solicitation, telephone canvassing and other means familiar in other places. Federal trade practices legislation in a dragnet phrase forbids 'misleading and deceptive conduct', and also a wide variety of pressure techniques such as referred selling and certain kinds of gift and prize programmes, and it regulates door-to-door and residential selling. State laws give consumers a wide range of rights and summary remedies that have effectively weeded out the unscrupulous and have kept reputable developers on their mettle.

*Industry self-regulation*
The Australasian Resort Timesharing Council is an industry body formed some ten years ago for the purpose of self-regulation and promotion of industry interests. It maintains a full-time permanent secretariat funded by developers and has made significant progress in recent years in the shaping of government policy, setting of standards and practice in development, marketing and sales and in handling media and consumer relations.

**Conclusion**

Though it has not fulfilled the grandiose predictions made for it in the early 1970s, timesharing has grown steadily and soundly over the last 15 years and established itself throughout Australasia as a viable means of real estate development. Its legal and financial structures have now been clarified and a workable framework for its regulations is in place. The 'chronometric' dimension of real estate has been born and the most innovative development in Australasian land law since the introduction of strata title in 1961 is here to stay. It remains to be seen what further refinements the exigencies of the marketplace and the ingenuity of developers will produce.

# Bermuda

Perhaps the most stringent legislation regulating timeshare anywhere in the world is that in Bermuda. Their Timesharing (Licensing & Control) Act 1981 was enacted on 1 August 1981 and under the enabling provisions contained therein the Timesharing (Licensing & Control) Regulations 1982 have been passed.

The Bermudan authorities have taken a very cautious approach to timesharing and as at July 1982 enforced a moratorium on future timesharing developments other than the three which were then in existence. The Bermuda Department of Tourism announced in July 1982 that the moratorium would remain in effect until such time as assessment could be made of the success or otherwise of the existing operations and until such time as the effectiveness of the Timesharing Act could be determined. Some of the major features of Bermuda's Timesharing Act are as follows:

1   To make provision for the licensing of all timesharing developer/owners, managing agents and marketing agents.

2   To prohibit all forms of timesharing other than the right-to-use or club membership type.
3   To limit the duration of any timesharing operation to 25 years or less.
4   To give the Minister of Tourism the authority to approve or disapprove applications for new timesharing developments and to regulate the amount of inventory coming on to the market at any one time.
5   To provide for compulsory registration of all timesharing sales for which the managing agent is responsible.
6   To provide for a 15 day recission period and a compulsory escrow account in a Bermuda financial institution into which all sales proceeds must be paid during the recission period; after which 35 per cent may be dispersed for marketing; 5 per cent into a post-completion sinking fund (to remain intact for five years after the development is totally completed) and the balance into a trust fund to remain until such time as an occupancy permit is issued in respect of each unit.
7   To provide an annual audit of the monies accrued from maintenance fees and to provide for a percentage of such fees (between 5 per cent and 25 per cent at the discretion of the Minister) to be placed in a trust fund annually for replacement purposes.
8   To provide for the annual inspection of timesharing premises by government tourism officials and to give the Minister of Tourism authority to vary, suspend or revoke a licence.
9   To require that each timesharing property shall be adequately insured to the satisfaction of the Minister of Tourism.
10  To provide for the drafting of regulations to set standards for development, administration, marketing, sales procedures, licensing procedures, management, maintenance, and legal proceedings.

The Miscellaneous Taxes Amendment (Number 2) Act 1981 makes provision for the payment by each timesharing purchaser of a timesharing occupancy tax which amounts to 10 per cent of the sales price. This is a one-off tax payable in advance. The same Act also makes provisions for a timesharing services tax payable annually, in the amount of 5 per cent of the annual maintenance fees. The Government Fees Amendment (Number 2) Regulations 1982 make provision for two fees; one to be paid upon the registration of each timesharing sale ($25) and the other to be paid by anyone wishing to inspect the Timesharing Sales Register ($5). These Regulations also make provision for the payment of licensing fees by the developing owner, the managing agent and the marketing agent. Copies of the Act and Regulations can be obtained on application to:

The Manager
Information Services
Bermuda Department of Tourism
P O Box 465
Hamilton 5
Bermuda

The 1982 Regulations contain extremely detailed provisions covering every aspect of any timesharing scheme, including provisions in regard to the preparation of food, and a prohibition against cracked or chipped dishes (reg 28(3)), equipment which must be provided, down to the number of toilet rolls (reg 42(10)(J), the interior standard of the timesharing unit and the cleaning and maintenance of it. The Regulations are incredibly detailed down to the mandatory provision of a corkscrew and as many coasters as there are glasses (reg 43, Sched (0)).

Nothing like this legislation exists anywhere else in the world and it is difficult to imagine more stringent controls or regulatory provisions. The penalties for infringement range from substantial fines (up to $500 for each day) and imprisonment (up to six months).

# Greece

### Timeshare legal title

The timesharing concept has only recently been exported to Greece and it has been accepted with growing interest. The salient point which is raised in Greek jurisdiction is what kind of legal title may and does a timeshare owner acquire. In principle only two legal titles can secure timeshare ownership: the first is of a contractual character, including leasing rights, and the second is of a real character, ie direct ownership in property. The legal nature of any timeshare title is especially important because many tourist areas of Greece are classified as 'frontier areas' within which foreign nationals cannot acquire direct ownership in property. As of 1986 a specific timeshare law has been introduced (Law 1652/86) followed by administrative regulations that cover such diverse areas as taxation and procedures for state approval of a timeshare scheme.

It will be helpful, therefore, when constructing a timesharing scheme in Greece, to consider certain aspects of Greek law related to acquisition of real rights as well as to foreign ownership of property and to compare them with the rights recognised and regulated by the Timeshare Law 1652/82.

### Real rights in Greek law

Real rights, defined as those which confer an immediate and absolute authority over a thing, are limited in number under Greek law (Civil Code Book 111, Law of Things, arts 947—1345). Real rights, other than those enumerated, cannot be created by private agreement, nor can the content of these rights be altered. In respect of immovables, real rights are:

1 ownership (*kyriotis*),
2 servitudes (*douliae*), and
3 mortgage (*hypotheque*)

Possession, detention and quasi-possession are *sui generis* rights, neither real nor personal. When the power over a thing exhausts all its utility, the right is ownership. When this power exhausts only some part of the thing's utility, the right is a *jus in re aliena*, ie servitude or mortgage. The creation of *jura in re aliena*, even in the performance of an obligation, is a real transaction, and as such subject to the rule of temporal priority (*prior tempora potior jure*).

Real rights, as in other civil law jurisdictions, include two important attributes, the right to follow and the right of preference. The first right, with regard to immovables, enables the owner of a real right to reclaim the thing in the hands of any possessor.

With regard to real security, the right to follow acquires full practical significance, resulting in a tangible difference between hypothecary and ordinary creditors; the rights of a mortgagee continue in respect of the immovable even when that immovable is transferred to a third party.

The right of preference is the prerogative, which the owner of a real right has, to exclude from the enjoyment of property such persons as may have only a personal right or a real right of an inferior rank. Again, in respect of real security, the mortgagees will be paid before other creditors having only personal rights and, amongst several mortgagees, the earlier in time will be preferred.

A particular procedure for registering a mortgage is recognised by law in the event that a creditor is not legally authorised to register a mortgage and the debtor is not willing to enter a mortgage contract. This procedure for pre-registration of a mortgage, known as prenotation of mortgage (*Prosimiosis*), is authorised by a court and is dependent on the condition that the claim of the creditor will have been definitively judged before enforcement of the mortgage.

In everyday practice a prenotation of mortgage is widely used instead of an ordinary mortgage as it offers two main advantages:

1 It is a summary court procedure that saves time for the creditor.
2 It has considerable financial advantages, the cost involved for securing a pecuniary claim amounting to about 7 per cent for registration of a mortgage compared to about 0.6 per cent for registration of prenotation of mortgage.

## Frontier areas' restrictions on real rights

For reasons of overriding national security and the integrity of national territory, a complex set of laws (Presidential Decree 22/24 June 1927, Parliamentary Act 18 February 1927, Legislative Decree 5 May 1926, Law 3250/1924, Legislative Decrees 3/4 September 1924 and Law 1366/1938) prohibits foreigners from acquiring real rights in immovables situated in frontier areas of the Greek state under penalty of absolute invalidity of the transaction. Violation of the prohibition also constitutes a criminal and disciplinary offence by the contracting parties and notaries public involved.

Any district of the Greek state may be classified as a 'frontier area' following a decree upon resolution of the Council of Ministers and until very recently almost 55 per cent of Greek territory qualifies as such. For example, the islands of Corfu (*Kerkyra*) Rhodes and Crete, leading summer resorts, were designated as frontier areas in which foreigners were not allowed to own or acquire any real right, except mortgages. These restrictions have been partially relaxed by Law 1892 of 31 July 1990 which excluded Corfu and a considerable part of the Island of Crete from the effect of the restrictions and also provided that Greeks and EEC Nationals are to be treated identically with regard to ownership, long leases and real charges on immovables situated in frontier areas. Both Greeks and EEC Nationals can acquire and transfer real rights subject only to prior permission of the 'NOMARCH' (local authority). Non-EEC Nationals are still subject to the same restrictions as previously applied to EEC Nationals.

In Greek law, although a lease is a contract and leasing rights are of contractual and not of real character, for the same reasons applicable to ownership rights, non-EEC Nationals are not allowed to own or acquire leases for a period in excess of three years.

Already, a judgment of the Athens High Court (*Areios Pagos* No 524/1983) has extended the applicability of frontier area legislation to include companies registered and domiciled in Greece but controlled or managed by foreigners. To discourage abuse of rights by former owners of land in frontier areas sold to foreigners, a fresh law has been enacted (Law 1540/1985) to the effect that only the Greek state can bring action against purchasers or their successors for invalidity of purchase of land and only for sales effected prior to the publication of Law 1540/1985—ie before 10 April 1985, all sales of property to foreigners and now non-EEC Nationals henceforth being null and void, as explained above.

Greece is a member of the Common Market and consequently these restrictions have been changed, so far as EEC residents are concerned. The Court of Justice of the European Communities had already dealt with this issue by way of its recent decision of 30 May 1989 in Case 305/87 brought by the European Commission against Greece. The Court had ruled that by maintaining in force the laws relating to frontier areas, Greece had violated its obligations under arts 48, 52 and 59 of the EEC Treaty providing for free circulation of services. However, at present, the laws do exist in relation to non-EEC Nationals and it is necessary that they be borne in mind when establishing the legal title held by timesharers.

Of the real rights recognised by Greek law and detailed in the previous paragraph, only a mortgage (including a prenotation of mortgage) is specifically excluded from the prohibition of 'frontier area' laws, foreigners therefore being allowed to acquire and hold such real rights as a mortgage and a prenotation of mortgage on property situated in frontier areas.

Contractual rights and commercial agreements whereby an agreement or a contract is made between a property owner and a client to provide, for example, hotel accommodation and related services fall outside the scope of 'frontier area' laws and can be negotiated and concluded with no restrictions as long as they do not serve the purpose of indirectly violating the said laws.

Such commercial agreements, well known in international hotel transactions under the form of either an *allotment* granted by a hotel to a tour operator or a *management* agreement to run a hotel securing occupancy for the benefit of the owner, are included in the options that will be reviewed in the paragraph dealing with structuring a timeshare scheme in frontier areas.

### Timeshare legislation

The legal title recognised and regulated by Greek law with regard to timesharing is a contract of lease. Any timesharer will acquire a leasing right which—irrespective of its contractual, non-real character—requires registration in the books of property registries securing, in a way, the timeshare's interests. Registration of a long-term lease, ie exceeding nine years, was already included in the Civil Code chapter dealing with a civil law lease which is classified as a specific contract (Civil Code, art 618). At present there are three sets of rules (the timeshare legislation) dealing with timeshare leases:

1  Law 1652/86 on timeshare leases; (the timeshare law) arts 1–7 of this law define and regulate timeshare leases while art 8 ratifies the twelve-year old and 27-article Regulation of Hotelier–Clients Relationship of the Hellenic Tourism Organisation (EOT). Article 9 deals with publication formalities.
2  A Ministerial Decision of the Deputy Minister for National Economy No A9953/DIONOSE/1789 (The Ministerial Decision) issued on the basis of art 4, para 2 of the timeshare law and delegating to the Ministry of National Economy the authority to set out the procedures and minute details of the law's implementation. The 10-article Ministerial Decision provides an all-inclusive guideline system applicable to any timesharing project falling within the scope of the timeshare law.
3  A circular of the Finance Ministry No E10976/5/88 (the Tax Circular) deals with income tax issues and VAT applicability and regulates supporting documentation which must be kept by timeshare resorts.

Applicability of the timeshare legislation is limited to tourist developments licensed to be built and operated by the Hellenic Tourism Organisation (EOT).

The Greek national economy is heavily dependent on tourism generated foreign exchange and, consequently, the tourist industry is heavily regulated by the state. Complex sets of rules providing for site and planning approvals combined with operational controls and mandatory minimum pricing of hotels and other tourist resorts set the trend: within such a framework the timeshare law introduces additional regulations and procedures requiring prior state approvals, combined with costly and lengthy registration formalities before a timeshare product will be introduced in the tourist market.

Obviously, considerable protection is offered to the consumer by way of state controls although both time and cost factors have been criticised as deterring potential private investment in the timeshare industry.

Notwithstanding the short life of the timeshare legislation it is reasonable to say that the market has reacted rather hesitantly to date. Until 1986 five developments were offered to the public on timeshare schemes with a legal structure based on general civil law principles. Under the new law only five more have been added while several applications to timeshare are pending lengthy approvals and authorisations by the EOT at the time of going to press.

Three main factors contributed to the rather slow development of the timeshare industry in Greece, considering that this country is a prime sunbelt location. These are:

1 restrictive legislation, including the timeshare legislation combined with applicability of the frontier area law;
2 inadequate information on timesharing combined with some adverse publicity on certain selling techniques and unsafe structures, although mainly in countries other than Greece; and
3 complicated and expensive procedures required before sales to the public are possible.

However, efforts are made which, based on the experience acquired in the short life of the timeshare legislation, may lead towards liberalisation of the timeshare market and towards faster development of the timeshare industry in Greece.

A few important principles set out by the timeshare law as well as by the Ministerial Decision and the Tax Circular currently regulate the timeshare industry:

Article 1, para 1 of the timeshare law provides that by way of a timeshare leasing contract a lessor undertakes the obligation to provide to a lessee, during the term of the contract, the use of tourist accommodation and to provide to the same lessee related services for a period specified in the contract and a lessee undertakes the obligation to pay the agreed upon lease premium.

Such definition of a lease creates a new, specific kind of lease, ie a timeshare lease. A timeshare lease is a contract which includes elements of a classic civil law lease of the Greek Civil Code (arts 574–618) combined with elements from a contract for hotel services. The latter form of contract, although not specifically defined by Greek civil law, is generally accepted by doctrine and precedent to include a well-defined object, ie to provide appropriate accommodation and personnel in order to service clients either permanently or for a limited period. The definition of a 'client' is not in any way affected by the amount of time such client spends in the hotel accommodation.

As is the case with any other civil law contract, the essential elements of a timeshare lease contract will be defined to include:

1 the parties to the contract,
2 the object of the contract,
3 consideration of the contract,
4 the form of the contract etc.

The parties to a timeshare lease are the lessor/owner of the development of the first part and the lessee of the second part. Both lessor and lessee may be either natural persons or legal entities. This is especially important in the case of the lessee: international experience has shown that it is impractical for each individual timesharer to hold a separate title and what happens in practice is that a legal entity holds the leasing title on behalf of all the timesharers of a development. As previously stated, the legal title acquired by a lessee is not a real right but a contractual leasing right the ownership of which is the object of the contract.

The object of the lease constitutes the foremost obligation of the lessor and is defined as the lessor's obligation to provide use of an immovable thing, such thing being specified as 'tourist accommodation'. The combined provisions of the timeshare law (art 1, cl b) and of the Ministerial Decision (art 1) set out in detail what developments may be classified as tourist accommodation, citing hotels operating in the traditional form, hotels operating in the form of furnished apartments, tourist villages, tourist villas and tourist furnished houses. All such accommodation must have been built and licensed to operate by the EOT and classified at least in the second 'B' category of operation. Greek hotels and other tourist developments are classified on an A, B, C, D, E scale with A being the highest category except for a 'de luxe' category which is outside the scale. The timeshare legislation allows only for a certain percentage of a development to be timeshared with a view that this may lead to a satisfactory level of maintenance and services. For developments built before the timeshare law was introduced, ie before 1986, the percentage allowed to be timeshared is up to 49 per cent of any development's capacity in beds while for newly built developments the maximum percentage is increased to 70 per cent.

The validity of the reasoning behind this restriction may be questionable because there is no reason why state controls of maintenance and service level cannot be carried out irrespective of timesharing and—more importantly—because consumer mentality does not easily accept mixed use of a development by mass tourism and private timesharers, especially with regard to smaller developments.

Further, the Ministerial Decision (art 1, para 3) provides that amenities areas and communal facilities such as reception, lobbies, in-house shops, restaurants, gardens, sports areas, etc cannot be the object and are excluded from a timeshare contract; in the eyes of the authorities this is reasonable and well accepted in international practice. The use of those areas and facilities by a lessee may be allowed under no less favourable terms than those offered to other clients in general.

In order for a tourist development, as previously defined, to become the object of a timeshare lease, a prior permission by the Secretary General of the EOT must be granted to the developer/lessor following an application to that effect. It is important that an application to timeshare a development must include—among other information—draft regulations which will govern the relationship between lessor and lessee for the term of the timeshare scheme (art 2, pt 1 of the Ministerial Decision).

Such regulations must define the services which the lessor is obliged to provide, especially with regard to maintenance and repair of the timeshared accommodation as well as of the communal and recreational areas, notwithstanding the fact that such areas are excluded from the timeshare lease, as previously explained. Refurbishment and renewal of fittings and fixtures must also be provided for in the regulations. Last but not least, arrangements for the employment of adequate personnel and the meeting of regular social security payments, state-run electricity bills, telephone bills and water supply bills as well as of any other expenses that may be incurred, must also be provided for in the regulations. The services to be provided by lessor to lessee are not specified by the timeshare legislation; it is to be assumed, however, that such services cannot be less favourable than the ones usually offered to regular clients of the development and as set out in the EOT regulations for each particular category of tourist development, and in any event such services cannot be less than those required to be provided by a B class development.

Consideration of the contract for the use of the timeshare-leased premises is the lease premium payable by a lessee. This, indeed, is an essential obligation of a lessee as set out in the timeshare legislation. The lease premium must be agreed and paid either in drachmae, the local currency (in the case of a Greek lessee) or in foreign currency in the case of a lessee domiciled or registered (if lessee is a company or other entity) outside Greece.

A lessor is obliged to surrender such foreign currency to be bought by the Bank of Greece against Greek drachmae within one month following payment and the same obligation is imposed on a lessee who, in turn, will sublet the timeshare lease premises to a non-Greek sublessee (art 1, para 3 of the timeshare law and art 6, para 2 of the Ministerial Decision).

The obligation to surrender foreign currency is imposed with regard to the total premium payable to a lessor; however, such premium must not be less than a minimum fixed by the same Ministerial Decision. A rather complicated formula is used in order to define the minimum lease premium payable in foreign currency related to the formal construction cost per bed as set out by the EOT from time to time. Thus the minimum lease premium is defined as: 'the formal construction cost as defined by law 1262/82 per bed multiplied by a coefficient of 2 and further multiplied by a coefficient of 1.5 for the first 15 years of the timeshare lease contract, or by a coefficient of 2 for the period exceeding 15 years'.

The said formal cost will be decreased by 2 per cent per annum for each year following construction and up to a maximum of 20 per cent. This formula is applicable when the term of the lease is for 50 weeks each year while, in contrast, to define a weekly lease premium, the same decision introduces the criterion of 'demand' dividing weeks in each year into three categories:

1 weeks in a low demand season are included in the period between 1 November to 31 March of each year and the corresponding weekly lease premium will be 22 per cent of the previous formula divided by 21, ie the median number of weeks included in that period;
2 weeks in a middle demand season are included in April and October of each year and the corresponding weekly lease premium will be 16 per cent of the said formula divided by 8;
3 weeks in a high season are included in the period from 1 May to 30 September in each year and a corresponding weekly lease premium will be 62 per cent of the said formula divided by 21.

Such weekly lease premium is charged for a studio while the weekly lease premium thus defined will be increased by 50 per cent in the case of one bedroom furnished flats and suites.

As long as foreign currency restrictions are applicable in Greece and until such time as EEC regulations cause some of these restrictions to ease, any violation will be treated as a criminal offence. It is important to have such restrictions in mind when structuring a timeshare scheme in general as well as when defining lease premiums in particular. Lease premiums may be paid in advance at the time of executing the lease contract or may be credited for a maximum period of 18 months.

With regard to the form of the contract, the timeshare law provides that the form of the timeshare lease contract is a notarised deed which is registered in the local property registry, in much the same way as a civil code long-term lease (art 1, para 1 of the timeshare law, cf art 618 of the Civil Code).

Should any other form be executed, eg a non-notarised private document, then the lease will be null and void. This is important, especially with regard to a lessee's protection against either the lessor or any other party who may have a prior real right of a higher rank or a lien on the property. In all those instances a timeshare lease will secure adequate protection if the lease contract is executed before a notary public and is subsequently registered in the appropriate Property Registry. The cost for executing and registering a timeshare lease will be half the normal charge for a civil code lease and will amount to approximately 3.5 to 4 per cent of the lease premium.

As far as the contents of the timeshare lease are concerned, the following requirements must be met, as set out in art 3 of the Ministerial Decision: 'The names, addresses and nationality of the parties must be set out and the leased premises must be identified and described in full together with their equipment and other fixtures'. The term of the contract must be determined in years, and occupation within any one year must also be determined. The amount of the lease premium, the currency in which it will be paid and the terms of payment together with the term of payment of maintenance fees must be included in the timeshare lease contract. Any terms and conditions with regard to assignment of a lessee's rights under the lease contract and with regard to any terms and conditions related to the user of other amenities and communal facilities at the timeshare resort must also be included in the contract. Greek law applicability combined with jurisdiction of the Greek courts are mandatory elements of a timeshare lease contract.

As previously explained, a set of rules regulating the relationship between lessor and lessee must have been previously approved by the Secretary General of the EOT and the regulations document must be annexed to the timeshare lease contract. It has already been mentioned that leasing contracts in excess of three years fall within the restrictions of frontier are a law and as a result no foreigner can acquire leasing rights for a longer period, in such areas.

The timeshare legislation, and in particular art 10 of the Ministerial Decision, specifies that timeshare leases are deemed to be long-term leases with regard to which no foreigner can acquire leasing rights in relation to immovable property situate in frontier areas.

At first sight those provisions may be construed as altogether prohibiting timesharing in frontier areas. However, a more careful research into what kinds of rights are allowed by Greek law to be acquired by a foreigner combining allowed real rights with contractual rights, will determine several options that may be relevant to any timeshare scheme. One such option is by way of setting up a Greek company which is owned by a Greek majority and managed by Greek nationals while minority interest is held by a foreign company acting for and on behalf of timesharers. Obviously there is no reason why such a company may not be entitled to acquire and own leasing rights in frontier timeshare developments, as has been the case in similar precedents with regard to property ownership rights. Of course, there must be additional guarantees and securities introduced in such a scheme in order that satisfactory protection is offered to the individual purchaser while some flexibility is allowed for resort owners and investors. Similar schemes have already been approved by the EOT on the basis of a sound legal structure combining leasing rights with contractual rights secured by mortgages on the development in favour of the timeshare purchasers. Such an example is given in the following paragraphs.

It has been accepted that a Greek company under Greek control with a foreign minority managed by Greeks may lease, for the benefit of its clientele, such number of apartments in a frontier resort as may be allowed to be timeshare leased. There is no legal impediment to such lessee to further allocate the use of the apartments, inclusive of the right to overnights and inclusive of the right to related services to its own clientele. The concept of 'clientele', being not legal but factual may be defined as business usages dictate. In this instance a clientele will be defined as the total number of the timeshare owners of the development and it may include Greeks and foreigners. It may also vary, since clients will come and go, exchanging, transferring or otherwise disposing of their units.

Thus, two independent contracts are entered into: the first contract is a timeshare lease contract whereby the lessee acquires all the leasing rights for the benefit of its clientele. The second contract is a typical hotel agreement whereby the lessee provides occupancy and services to its clientele. The reason for separating the timeshare rights into two independent contracts is the following. Pursuant to art 10, pt 1 of the Ministerial Decision, the provisions relating to foreign ownership rights in frontier areas are applicable with regard to timeshare leases. However, the obvious meaning of that clause is that in order for such provisions to be applicable the commutative conditions laid down by the said legislation must occur, ie there must be:

1  an immovable property, in the sense defined by civil legislation, ie a complex of land and buildings having legal and economic autonomy;
2  either a contract of lease in the sense defined by civil law, such contract excluding the owner or third parties from the use of the immovable property; alternatively there may be a 'cession' of use, which being a factual, non-legal term cannot be treated more strictly than a contract of lease;
3  a foreign lessee acquiring direct rights, as defined, on an immovable, property;
4  a term of the contract exceeding three years on the basis of a 355-day year this being the only 'year' recognised by Greek law.

Under such conditions the scheme already described is obviously exempted from the frontier area restrictions because the terms and conditions previously cited are not accumulated, ie:

1  A foreign client does not acquire direct ownership of an 'immovable' property. In fact, any foreign client enjoys an exclusive right to hotel overnights in a bed within the immovable property, identical to that of any other foreign client of any other frontier area hotel, together with a non-exclusive right to use the amenities and common areas of the hotel, also identical to that of any other client; no rights are acquired on an immovable having legal and economic autonomy.
2  There is no 'lease contract': or 'sublease' or 'cession' of use because any foreign client does not directly contract as a lessee, sublessee or user with the owner of the immovable. The relationship between the Greek company, which acts as a timeshare lessee, and a foreign client is the non-prohibited contract for hotel accommodation and services for a long term.
3  'Clientele' is not a physical person or a legal entity so its nationality cannot be established: neither is the identity of clients known at the time such timeshare lease is entered into. Non-prohibited arrangements of a contractual nature, such as to subsequently secure overnights and related services as well as to secure use of communal areas and facilities to clients, are not relevant to frontier area restrictions. The fact that, according to market usages, such clientele of the lessee is organised as a non-profit

holiday club, (ie an association of persons without legal personality), has no bearing on this issue.

4 There is no term of the contract in excess of three years, because a foreign client—even in the event that same might be construed to acquire directly or indirectly a prohibited right, which is not the case—acquires a right divided in time and limited in time. For example, a week per year and for 30 years obviously equals a term of such right for 210 days and does not exceed the term of 1095 days included in the legal term of 'three years'.

The nature of the contract between the timeshare lessee Greek company and its clientele (even if foreign) is the usual contract for hotel services which, although not defined by civil law, has a generally accepted object: ie to provide appropriate lodgings and personnel to service clients either permanently or for a limited time each. The definition of a person as 'client' is not affected by the amount of time he spends in a hotel. Hotel regulations applicable today do not include any provisions to the effect that a stay in a hotel, including frontier area hotels, by a client, including foreign clients, must be limited in time. Consequently, any client may stay as long as he wishes.

Any views to the contrary might lead to excluding foreign clients from staying in the same frontier area hotels for a number of years—regardless of whether they may be regular clients of hotel owners or clients of a timeshare lessee Greek company, based on the same legal reasoning and for reasons of non-discretionary treatment. Such views, if any, might have extremely adverse financial effects on the private and national tourist economy of Greece as well.

Occupancy by individual timesharers is usually secured by registering substantial real rights on the development, either in the form of a notarised and registered mortgage, by a court ruling allowing registration of a prenotation of mortgage or by a combination of both.

In the following paragraph, an example of structuring a timeshare scheme in a frontier area resort will demonstrate how a club scheme with trustee offers full protection acceptable under both Greek and UK jurisdictions to the satisfaction of the authorities and stakeholders involved.

Upon registration of a timeshare lease, a lessee has the right to enjoy undisturbed use of the timeshare leased premises, subject to payment of the agreed lease premium and the related annual management expenses, while several secondary effects are manifest as well.

One such effect is that heirs and successors of the lessee are allowed to terminate the lease but without recourse to the lease premiums already paid to the lessor (art 2, pt 1 of the timeshare law). Obviously in such cases, heirs and successors of the lessee will not have a further obligation to pay the annual management fees.

Another secondary effect is that in the event of sale of the timeshare lease property and irrespective of the legal title of the new owner, ie by way of a voluntary sale or through a forced sale, a lessee's rights will not be affected and the new owner will be bound to respect the obligations of the initial owner/

lessor (Civil Code, art 618; Code of Civil Procedure, art 1009, pt 1).

With regard to other liens or mortgages on a timeshare property, the law provides that a lessor is entitled to request his creditor, whose claim is secured by the liens, that such liens may be cancelled provided that either a bank letter of guarantee for the total indebtedness or an assignment of the lease premium is offered to the creditor's satisfaction. This facility is offered only when the owner of the mortgage or of any other lien is the Greek state, or a public agency or a bank. Any differences between the parties with regard to mortgage cancellation will be referred to a summary procedure of the tribunal (Law 1652/86, art 3). The EOT currently holds the view that existing liens on developments offered on a timeshare lease basis must be deleted and cancelled within a reasonable time following EOT approval to timeshare the development. Local banks who have a vested interest in the hotel industry holding substantial mortgages on most, if not all, existing developments have not reacted as yet to such procedures.

In order to encourage lessees' control in the administration of the timeshare leased property, the law recognises that lessees, as co-owners of identical rights, will be organised in a general meeting, the rules and regulations of which must be set out in the document of regulations of lessor/lessee relations which must be approved by the EOT and annexed to the timeshare lease contract.

With regard to taxation issues, the Tax Circular gives instructions on income tax to be paid on lease premiums, with VAT applicability and with the supporting documentation to be kept by a developer when he timeshare leases his resort.

As a matter of principle, the Tax Circular establishes that on the strength of a timeshare lease a hotelier is obliged to provide hotel services to lessees on the same basis as to regular clients. Pursuant to this assumption a hotelier will not be construed as being excluded from the economic use of his development. For this reason any income acquired from a timeshare lease will be treated as income generated from commercial activities and income tax will be paid with regard to each fiscal year included in the timeshare lease. In other words, although the lease premium must be paid within eighteen months following execution of the lease contract, for tax purposes it will be spread in as many years as are included in the term of the lease and each year's income will be taxable together with any other income earned during that year (para A, cl 7 of the Tax Circular). The same principle will be applicable with regard to VAT on lease premiums which must be paid at the end of each fiscal year or at the end of the period within which hotel services are rendered to lessees by the owner of the development (para C of the Tax Circular).

The so called 'door book', registering arrival and departure of each individual client, irrespective of nationality, must be kept with regard to timeshare lessees as well as by any timeshare lessor (para B, cl 7 of the Tax Circular). Legal and tax considerations are obviously of importance to any developer and expert advice must be sought at the time of structuring a timeshare scheme, especially with regard to timeshare price and its apportionment between developer and marketeer. Before granting approval to timeshare, the EOT examines the financial aspects of a project and in some instances requires the lease premium to be disclosed prior to approval.

**Greek law and the club trustee system**

Greece is a signatory country of the Convention On The Law Applicable To Trusts And On Their Recognition which was adopted in draft by the Hague conference on Private International Law in October 1984. However, as that Convention has still to be ratified by the Greek Parliament at the date of going to press, the question of whether the club trustee system is compatible with Greek law is relevant.

Organising timesharers in the form of a club with a trustee is indeed compatible with Greek law in general and with the timeshare law in particular. As has been argued in the previous paragraphs, while the lessor under the timeshare law may be an individual and is usually the developer, lessees may be as many as there are weeks in the year. Even when only one composite lease is signed, the use of any apartment is allocated to several persons. The total number of timeshare owners can be construed as a civil society of persons (Civil Code, arts 785—805) which is created under the rules of the timeshare law and upon the terms and conditions set out in the document of the lessor/ lessee regulations annexed to any timeshare lease contract.

There is no legal impediment to the members of such a timeshare civil society selecting a system regulating the relationship between themselves and third parties. On the contrary, a direct argument in favour of such regulation is that the Ministerial Decision (art 2, para 2 and art 3, paras 2 and 7) requires two basic conditions to be satisfied with regard to many joint lessees of the timeshare leased premises: first, that a set of rules governing the lessor/lessee relationship must be annexed to any timeshare lease contract and, secondly, that such rules must set out how lessees' annual meetings will be called as well as with what quorum and what majority their decisions will be taken.

In fact a non-profit holiday club's constitution may set out the rights and obligations of club members and may detail the club's powers, the club's committees, regulate the club members' annual and other meetings etc. An agreement may be added to the effect that the club's affairs will be managed by a management company which will collect the members' annual fees and will be held responsible for supervising the maintenance and operation of the club's holiday premises.

Pursuant to the civil law rules regulating mandate and proxies (Civil Code arts 211 *ff* 713 *ff*), the club's constitution may include an agreement that club members may delegate the power to enter a timeshare lease to one entity, such as a title company, which will hold the timeshare rights for the benefit of the club and for the benefit of the club members. The advantages of executing and registering one composite timeshare lease compare favourably with the system of the registration of separate leases for each individual timesharer and are supported not only by law but by common sense as well.

It is important that a title company's shares and assets are held in trust in order to satisfy the need for protecting each individual timeshare right in such a way that no conflict is allowed to be created between each right and that all identical timeshare rights are collectively protected against third parties, including the lessor of the timeshared apartments.

Obviously the trustee's appointment and the trust deed must be governed by a jurisdiction recognising the concept of trust, eg UK jurisdiction. However, it is useful to remember that a timeshare lease contract must include a clause to the effect that Greek law is applicable with regard to both the lease contract and to the attached lessor/lessee regulations. Apart from that requirement, the timeshare legislation (Ministerial Decision, art 7, para 3) provides that the contracting parties, ie lessor and lessee, may agree on additional protection with regard to a lessee's rights. Such additional protection may be granted by registering real security and encumbrances on the property securing the lease premium; real charges may also secure a lessee's damages in the event of the lessor's default. Additional protection may also be granted by a bank letter of guarantee, or insurance etc. All agreements aimed at giving a lessee additional protection, pursuant to the said clause of the Ministerial Decision, are based on and supported by the doctrine of 'freedom of contract'.

### Structuring a timeshare scheme in a frontier area resort

Structuring a timeshare scheme in a frontier area resort under the timeshare legislation relating to the club trustee system is not simple: nor is it inexpensive or fast to set up.

First of all, the developer must obtain EOT authorisation to timeshare his tourist resort. An application to that effect must be filed with the EOT detailing the apartments which will be entered into the timeshare scheme. The scheme's legal structure must be explained and supporting legal documentation as described above must be filed as well. A period of time varying between two and six months, must be allowed for EOT inspections of planning and building licences and the actual site of the resort before an EOT permit to timeshare is granted.

Secondly, based on the well-known fact that a considerable portion of the timeshare market is British, a structure acceptable to UK jurisdiction must be set up. This is especially important in order to secure the services of a trustee, who will accept the obligation to protect and guard the timesharers' rights and to secure affiliation of the development with an exchange organisation, which is an important feature of the timeshare industry. Both Greek and international markets can then be successfully approached with a legal scheme that satisfies more than one jurisdiction. The system selected in this instance is the club with trustee system, which is widely recognised in Europe.

For reasons of convenience in setting out the rules of the timeshare plan, an unincorporated foreign club is formed, the constitution of which sets out the rights and obligations of the timesharers. Some of the rules relating to timesharers' annual meetings are also included in the document of lessor/ lessee regulations, which after prior approval by the EOT will be annexed to the timeshare lease contract.

Next, a foreign title company is set up, the shares of which are held in trust by an independent trustee for the benefit of timeshare owners. A Greek title company is then set up with a minority holding of up to 49 per cent controlled by foreign title while the majority remains in the control of the developer. Greek title must be managed by Greek directors.

In order to ensure that Greek title and foreign title companies will not become separated, it is provided in the constitution of Greek title that it may not carry out any important acts without the consent of 75 per cent of its owners. Particular care is taken to comply with foreign currency restrictions when determining the lease premium payable by Greek title to the developer.

The question of funding the Greek title company in order to pay the lease premium is resolved by way of a foreign marketing and sales company and arrangements are made to satisfy the financial requirements of both the developer and the marketeer. It is the latter who makes funds available for the Greek title company from the proceeds of timeshare sales. The right to sell the timeshared apartments is part of the sales and marketing agreement between the resort owner and the sales and marketing company. For reasons of convenience, the overall timeshare structure is included in a master agreement detailing the parties to the timeshare scheme and allocating their respective rights and duties.

Greek title enters a timeshare lease contract acquiring rights for the benefit of timeshare owners or—in other words—for its prospective Greek and foreign clients, including exchange clients. The leasing rights acquired are not contained in a collection of many leases for separate timeshare rights, but in a single composite lease encompassing all the timeshare rights in the apartments in the resort. Alternatively, a series of composite leases adjusted to sales progress may substitute for one lease, but essentially in the same spirit.

An important feature of the timeshare lease contract is that it includes substantial penalty clauses entitling the lessee, ie the Greek company, to pecuniary compensation in the event of the lessor's default. Such compensation is then assigned to the foreign title company held in trust by the trustee; in turn, the foreign title obtains a prenotation of mortgage combined with a mortgage on the land and buildings of the resort in security of the assigned potential money compensation. In this way the foreign title company has come to embody the security of all timeshare purchasers, irrespective of nationality.

Any timeshare purchaser buys and acquires membership of a foreign club agreeing to be bound by the club's constitution. By way of a deed of trust, arrangements are made with an independent trustee to hold the foreign title upon trust and, therefore, all the rights and controls upon the timeshared apartments, securing the rights of timeshare purchasers within the rules and the structure of the timeshare scheme, are held in trust for them.

The timeshare lease contract is then registered in the local property registry followed by registration of the prenotation and mortgage in the same registry. Upon completion of those formalities any club membership purchaser, irrespective of his nationality, is protected by three complementary interests on the timeshared apartments: the first is the registered timeshare lease contract; the second is the assignment of penalty clauses under that lease to the foreign title company held by the trustee; the third is the mortgage and prenotation of mortgage securing the money element of that assignment.

Despite its apparent complexity, the timeshare structure described in this paragraph offers significant advantages of consumer protection and investment flexibility. The system allows sales to different nationalities as the demands of the marketplace dictate, while development controls by the EOT combined with registered rights satisfy the need for a long-term, inviolate agreement. On the other hand, the resort owner may place into that structure additional inventory within the resort or even at other resorts as the sales proceed and according to demand.

From the end-user's viewpoint the club trustee system saves individual registration of hundreds of leases. The advantage of combining registered leasing rights allowed to Greek nationals only with contractual rights secured by way of real rights allowed to all nationals is obvious: security, practicability and flexibility are manifest once the structure is in place and it is offered to potential purchasers.

## Alternative timesharing methods

Because the timeshare legislation's applicability is limited to tourist developments licensed by the EOT to operate as class A or B and de luxe categories, some schemes may have to be structured with a view to allowing the timesharing of attractive properties licensed to operate under a less expensive classification altogether outside the scope of EOT licensing.

Structuring such a timeshare scheme is based on the Civil Code doctrine of 'freedom of contract'. As long as a timeshare scheme does not in any way infringe restrictive legislation, it can present several advantages to everybody concerned. There are two such major methods which have already been put to use.

### Allotment method

The first is based on the well-known hotel agreement 'allotment'. An allotment is an agreement between a hotel owner of the first part and a tour operator or any other professional agent or even a group of persons of the second part. The object of the contract is to reserve a number of beds for a determined period of time for continuous occupation by unidentified, various clients at agreed prices. A hotel allotment agreement is regulated by sub-arts 11, 12 and 13 of art 8 of the Timeshare Law 1652/86, which governs relations between hotel owners and hotel clients. Pursuant to the said provisions:

An agreement or a contract between a Hotelier and a Tourist Office or a Travel Agency or a group of clients to reserve a number of beds for a specific period for continuous occupancy by alternate clients (allotment) must include, among other elements:

a) the agreed overnight price, or including breakfast, or including half board or including full board.
b) the type of accommodation (ie single rooms, double rooms, with or without bathroom facilities).
c) the exact length of the occupancy period.
d) the agreed maximum and minimum overnights in each month' [sub-art 11, art 8, Law 1952/86].

A hotelier is entitled to request a deposit of up to 25 per cent of the aggregate amount of the agreement but will be held liable to indemnify the beneficiary in full with interest plus damages, if any, in the event of his failure to provide occupancy of the agreed rooms. In addition, any default will entail severe EOT licensing penalties. In the event, however, of the travel agent's or tourist office's etc default, a hotelier is entitled to money compensation of 50 per cent of the agreed overnight price which can be set off against any deposits received (sub-art 12 of art 8, Law 1652/86).

A travel agent or a tourist office may cancel the allotment in part or in full within a release period of 21 days, provided that notice to that effect is given 21 days prior to the client's arrival date. The same release period is granted in favour of the hotelier if a reservation will not be confirmed by way of a voucher or a rooming list.

Should a travel agent cancel an allotment during low season, a hotelier is entitled to reduce *pro rata* the high season allotment subject to the minimum number of allotted rooms in each month in the high season (sub-art 12 of art 8, Law 1952/86).

*Joint ownership method*
The alternative timesharing method is based on a real right of joint ownership and may be applicable with regard to private properties built outside EOT licensing for building and operation. The system, however, is not applicable in frontier areas because it involves direct ownership rights which cannot as yet be legally acquired and held by foreigners. Under the joint ownership method each of the joint owners will have the right to use the jointly owned property for a predetermined period of time to be agreed between themselves.

Although timesharing between joint owners is a new concept, it can be structured on the basis of the Civil Code provisions relating to joint ownership and the law relating to horizontal property (Civil Code, arts 1002 and 1113 *ff*, Law 3741/29, Legislative Decree 1024/71) in a manner similar to co-ownership of an apartment in a block of flats, where co-owners would agree to be bound by an agreement between themselves as to the exact time and length of each one's occupancy rights.

*Comparison of the two methods*

Under the allotment method the legal title, which will be held by timesharers, is a contract of 'hotel allotment' secured by a mortgage or combined with a prenotation of mortgage. In this method as well, the system of a club with trustee is essential.

Just as in the case of a timeshare lease system (Law 1652/86), under the allotment method the rights of occupation of the timeshared apartments are alloted or granted to a foreign title company by way of a normal unregistered commercial agreement whereby the owner of the apartments agrees to allot or to reserve occupation for the benefit of club members. The shares of the foreign title company are held in trust for the timeshare owners. The timeshare price paid by timesharers in consideration for occupancy rights is secured by a prenotation of mortgage in favour of that company. The value of the mortgage needs to be sufficiently substantial so that during the term of the timeshare scheme, the property is rendered valueless from the point of view of transfer or remortgage. In theory, if the mortgage were to be enforced, the timeshare owners would become entitled to the drachmae proceeds of the property's forced sale.

This necessarily involves a currency risk but this is also true with regard to any other foreign currency transaction; since Greece is a member of the EEC it is possible to link the value of the mortgage to the European Currency Unit (ECU).

The allotment method of structuring a timeshare scheme is not directly excluded from applicability with regard to tourist developments falling within the timeshare lease system (arts 1–7 of Law 1952/86).

However, besides the difference in the legal title held by timesharers under the two systems there is one other important difference: the pricing systems are different as far as price controls and foreign currency controls are concerned and the EOT has not as yet expressed any views on whether timesharing by way of an allotment agreement will be allowed for the de luxe and A and B category developments.

Structuring a timeshare scheme under a joint ownership direct system is much simpler and does not involve the club trustee system: however, it does involve the continuous exercise of legal and managerial skills by the timesharers and imposes on them the task of taking care of their timeshare property. This system may be useful with regard to small, private developments and works in the following way. Each apartment is made the subject of 52 rights of joint ownership, ie as many as the weeks in a year, and each joint owner buys an undivided real right equal to 1/52 of the apartment with the unsold weeks remaining with the developer. In the purchase contract each joint owner agrees to use or occupy the commonly owned apartment for one week only and to respect similar use by the other joint owners. The transfer of the property is effected by a notarised deed which is registered at the local property registry.

When structuring a timeshare scheme, it is essential to consider and evaluate the size, the location and the seasons of a resort before selecting the appropriate timeshare method. In this respect the legal costs and expenses are relevant and it must be mentioned that property transfer tax and expenses exceed 13 per cent on the value of the property as determined by the tax office. That percentage together with public notaries' fees, legal fees, registration and stamp duties is payable upon execution of the property transfer deed. Timeshare lease registration fees and expenses amount to approximately 3.75 per cent on the total lease premiums but registration of a prenotation of mortgage will not exceed 0.6 per cent on the total value of the transaction.

Selecting the proper structure for a timeshare project and carefully balancing the mutual rights and obligations while securing the necessary controls will satisfy the interests of all the parties. On the one hand, the timeshare buyers' rights are protected, whilst on the other hand, the Greek tourist industry and economy benefit from a secure and growing customer base of persons who will be visiting their timeshare resort over a period of years. They will be contributing to the Greek economy not only by payment of their timeshare fees, but also by paying annual management charges and spending foreign currency in the same way as any other high income tourist.

At the same time, in frontier areas, it is usually the case that timeshare owners are not directly acquiring real property in Greece so that the fear from the Greek authorities, that tracts of Greek land in sensitive areas would fall into the hands of foreigners, does not apply, especially with a growing EEC trend towards investment in real property.

## Italy

Timesharing (*multiproprieta*) in Italy is a fairly new concept and only in the last three or four years has it really started to develop. Initially, development was in the hotel timesharing sector although there are now many developments which are specifically for timesharing use.

It is difficult to place timesharing within the context of the Italian legal system. In fact problems have arisen in relation to timesharing because of the difficulty of categorising it in legal terms in the absence of specific timesharing legislation. A definition for it must therefore be sought in fairly old legal provisions which did not, at the time they were enacted, contemplate such an institution. There have been attempts at resolving the juridicial problems relating to timesharing and two main types of timesharing have developed in Italy.

The first type, which is defined as property timesharing (*multiproprieta immobiliare*), reflects many of the institutions of common ownership (*comunione*). Thus the timesharing owner acquires a right of common ownership which is duly recorded in the public property registers and the owner is able to enjoy that property for a predetermined period during the year, every year.

The second type, which is defined as timesharing by shares (*multiproprieta azionaria*), arises from the provisions which apply to companies limited by shares. The property is owned by a company limited by shares (*societa per azioni*) the capital of which is divided into ordinary and preference shares. The owners of the preference shares are entitled to use the property free of charge for a limited period during the year, every year.

Two other types of timesharing may be found in Italy, but their use is decreasing as they have not proved suitable for the purposes of timesharing. They are hotel timesharing (*multiproprieta alberghiera*), under which a quota of the hotel is purchased, but it continues to be run as a hotel; and the other is similar to timesharing (*multiproprieta cooperativa*), which is similar to timesharing by shares, save that the company which owns the property is a co-operative company.

The type of timesharing which is most common at the moment is that of *multiproprieta immobiliare* because of the many problems which have arisen in relation to timesharing by shares as a result of the inflexibility of company law in Italy.

The elements which make up the common ownership (*comunione*) are the joint ownership by several persons of one and the same property, the division of the use of the property into quotas, the respecting of the agreed use of the property, the possibility of delegating the administration of the property to a suitable person and the fact that the property owned cannot be further divided up.

However, problems have arisen in relation to this type of timesharing mainly as a result of art 1111 of the Italian Civil Code of 1942 which provides:

*Scioglimento della comunione*
   Ciascuno dei partecipanti puo sempre domandare lo scioglimento della comunione; l'autorita guidiziaria puo stabilire una congrua dilazione, in ogni caso non superiore ai cinque anni se l'immediato scioglimento puo preguidicare di interessi degli altri.
   Il fatto di rimanere i comunione per un temp non maggiore di dieci anni e valido ed ha effetto per gli eventi causa dai partecipanti. Se e stato stipulato per un termine maggiore a questo si riduce a dieci anni.
   Se gravi circostanze lo richiedono l'autorita giudiziaria puo ordinare lo scioglimento della comunione prima del tempo convenuto.

*Dissolution of common ownership*
   Each participant can always demand dissolution of the common ownership; the court can establish an appropriate period of delay, in no case greater than five years, if immediate dissolution could prejudice the interests of the others.
   An agreement to remain in common ownership for a period of no more than ten years is valid and is also effective against the successors of the participants. If it was stipulated for a greater period this is reduced to ten years.
   If serious circumstances require it, the court can order dissolution of the common ownership before the agreed time.

It is obvious that such a time limit would render this timesharing method impossible. There is, however, a solution and it lies in art 1112 of the Italian Civil Code which provides:

Lo scioglimento della comunione non puo essere chiesto quando si tratta di cose che, se divise, casserebbero di servire all'uso a cui sono destinate.

Things not subject to partition. Dissolution of the common ownership cannot be demanded when things are involved which, if divided, would cease to serve the use for which they are destined.

As a result of this provision, common ownership timesharing contracts usually include an article which provides that if the units are divided up they cannot serve the use and purpose for which they are destined. However, the interpretation of the way arts 1111 and 1112 interrelate is still open and court decisions and legal doctrine do not yet agree on this point.

A bill has recently been lodged before Parliament providing for a law to regulate timesharing in Italy. However, given the long process of approval before it becomes law, if indeed it ever does, it will be some years before we can expect to have specific legislation governing the matter in Italy, and of course in the meantime the above provisions will apply.

When the right to a quota of the property is purchased, the purchaser must accept the timesharing regulations, which contain a series of articles which set out obligations to ensure that dealings between the individual co-owners and between them and the managers of the timesharing property are satisfactory. There are obligations to keep the unit purchased in good order and to deliver it up in such condition to the subsequent timesharing co-owner and should this not be done the costs for putting it in such order can be charged to the person who has not fulfilled this obligation.

The unit cannot be changed in any way and must be kept in a condition suitable for the agreed use. The vendor/owner of the timesharing units can, however, change the unit but cannot do so in such a way as to diminish the enjoyment of the property by the timesharers. The timesharer must furthermore pay the costs of ordinary and extraordinary maintenance according to his quota.

Other common clauses in the regulations relate to the contribution which must be made for expenses by each timesharer and to the appointment of a manager and the granting of powers to him. Furthermore, it may be provided that should expenses not be paid within 20 days of the approval of the expenses budget and should they not be paid within a month thereafter, the manager of the complex can ask for such payment by way of registered letter. Fifteen days after this letter has been sent, if no payment has been made, the manager is entitled under the agreed regulations and the stipulation of the purchased deed to let the unit for the period of time to which the owner is entitled and to use the rent received to pay the said expenses and interest. This power is similar to that granted to the manager of a condominium and in fact, as stated above, this type of timesharing closely resembles that institution.

With all the above types of timesharing but particularly with reference to *multiproprieta azionaria* the problem of what happens upon dissolution of the company or the *comunione* is difficult to resolve. Precedents have held that in the case of a *multiproprieta azionaria* the right to use the property for a fixed period every year is not a real property right but a right connected directly to the ownership of shares. These precedents did not in fact deal with the question of liquidation but with the applicability of VAT on the sale of a timeshare unit. However, by analogy they could be extended to the liquidation, in which case presumably the company would call in all its assets, pay off all creditors and distribute any surplus. Once again this proves the need for specific law on timesharing in Italy.

### Formalities for the purchase of a timesharing unit

A preliminary contract (*compromesso*) is executed between the parties setting out their rights, obligations and duties, establishing the purchase price for the timesharing unit and providing for a deposit to be paid to the vendor. A final contract before a notary (*rogito*) is executed when the purchase monies have been paid in full and this is then registered at the local land registry.

A registration tax (*imposta di registro*) is charged at the rate of 3 per cent on the price of the transfer. The tax is usually borne half by the vendor and half by the purchaser but in some timesharing schemes it is borne entirely by the purchaser. The notary's charges will also depend upon the price and are calculated according to the notarial scale of fees.

Should the property be sold, a capital gains tax known as the *imposta comunale sugli incrementi del valore degli immobili* is payable upon the appreciation of the property from the time it was purchased. It is levied at progressive rates which depend upon the taxable gain, the initial value and the number of years of ownership. Rates vary from 3 to 30 per cent.

### Exchange control regulations

Ministerial Decree No 148 of 10 March 1988 liberalised Italian exchange control regulations to a great extent in line with the setting up of the 1992 Single Market. Communication with the exchange control authorities is no longer necessary, now only a simple declaration needs to be signed, under personal responsibility, declaring the provenance of the funds invested in Italy and their purpose. This has considerably simplified banking procedures and speeded up investments of all types in Italy which formerly required communication and specific approval. Upon the sale of a timeshare unit the initial investment and any increase in value thereof may be transferred freely out of Italy.

## Malta

The tourist industry is of great importance to the Maltese economy and every year the number of tourists visiting the island greatly exceeds the local population. However, for recent historical reasons, over the past few years there has been something of a slump in the industry which has caused problems for many hoteliers. The island is once more becoming popular and the advent of timesharing has accelerated growth in the tourist industry. At the time of writing there are eleven timeshare projects operating or in course of development on the island.

In Malta a timeshare plan must be drafted in compliance with the Maltese Civil Code and various statutory provisions which apply to such plans, notwithstanding that those provisions were enacted without timesharing in mind. The first and most important of these is the Immovable Property (Acquisition by Non-Residents) Act 1974. Section 2 of this Act provides that for the purposes of the Act a 'non-resident person' means and includes:

1  any individual who is not a resident of Malta; and
2  any body or other association of persons, and any authority, institution, organisation, fund, trust, firm and any other entity whatsoever, whether corporate or not, if:
   (a)  it is constituted, formed, established, incorporated or registered in, or under the law of, any country outside Malta, or
   (b)  it has its principal place of residence or business outside Malta, or
   (c)  20 per cent or more of its share or other capital is owned by a non-resident person, or
   (d)  It is in any manner and whether directly or indirectly controlled by one or more non-resident persons.

'Resident of Malta' means an individual who is a citizen of Malta and who is ordinarily resident in Malta.

Section 3 of the Act goes on to provide as follows:

Save as hereinafter provided, with effect from 30 May 1974 a non-resident person may not acquire immovable property by or under any Title, and in any manner whatsoever, whether by Act inter-vivos or Causa Mortis, and including prescription, occupancy or accession; and any Deed, Will or other Act purporting to transfer or transmit any immovable property to a non-resident person, and any devolution or other event having the effect of transmitting immovable property and which but for the provisions of this Act would have transmitted such property in favour of a non-resident person, shall be null and void and be without effects for all purposes of Law and in regard to all persons; and any transfer, payment or other thing made or done or given as part or in consequence of, or as ancillary to, anything which is prohibited as aforesaid shall likewise be null and without effect and, as and where appropriate, the subject matter thereof shall be returned, restored, refunded, cancelled or otherwise dealt with accordingly.

Although later provisions of the Act allow acquisition by non-residents with prior consent of the Ministry of Finance, it is thought that such consent will be difficult if not impossible to obtain. Consequently, it is not practicable to base a plan on a transfer of immovable property to the timeshare owner either directly or indirectly.

The next question to consider is whether some form of leasehold interest might be granted. Here again, difficulties are encountered. Section 1615 (1) of the Maltese Civil Code defines a lease as follows: '. . . (1) The letting of things is a contract whereby one of the contracting parties binds himself to grant to the other the enjoyment of a thing for a specified time and for a specified rent which the latter binds himself to pay to the former . . .' At first sight, therefore, a grant by title of letting can be made in favour of a non-resident, without such letting amounting to an acquisition of immovable property for the purpose of the Immovable Property (Acquisition by Non-Residents) Act 1974. In relation to contracts of leases or letting however, it is important to note at this stage that contracts of subletting are dealt with rather differently under Maltese law, than is the case in some jurisdictions. Professor Caruana Galizia in his commentary on the Maltese Civil Code distinguishes between subletting and assignment as follows:

> Sub-letting is very similar to granting on Lease: Indeed it is a true lease, but subordinate to another, ie the sub-Lessee binds himself to pay the rent which is paid periodically like the rent in the principal Lease, whilst in the case of assignment, any consideration agreed upon is to be paid only once, unless it is divided into instalments, and if the assignment is made gratuitously, the assignee pays nothing saving the assumption on his part of the obligations of the Lessee unless such burden is retained by the Assignor.

Although Section 1702 of the Civil Code provides that 'In the absence of special provisions, the contract of subletting is regulated by the same provisions which regulate the contract of letting and hiring', s 1709 provides that a 'Sub-lessee may not claim against the lessor any of the rights competent to the lessee'. In order that sublessees acquire similar rights to those of the lessor, the rights must be specifically acknowledged by the head lessor.

The essence of the timesharing arrangement is that the timeshare buyer pays a premium rather than an annual rental when he acquires a timeshare and if those rights derive from someone who is himself a lessee, if a substantial rent passes, and the lessee fails to pay it, the purchasers of the timeshares will obviously be prejudiced. At first sight it might be thought possible for a lease to be granted at a premium, ie an advance payment of the rack rent passing, but here one encounters the problem of s 1624 of the Civil Code which provides:

(i) Every payment in advance in respect of rent of rural tenements is null, if any prejudice is caused thereby to the hypothecary creditors of the Lessor or to the person succeeding to the property under an entail, or to whom, in consequence of any dissolution of his right, the property passes.

(ii) Every payment in advance in respect of rent of an urban tenement for more than six months is also null, if any prejudice as aforesaid is caused hereby.

The lessee and *a fortiori* any sublessee cannot prevent the lessor from mortgaging or encumbering the property, and if a mortgagee or, as they are effectively termed in Malta, a 'hypothecary creditor' forecloses, any lessee not paying a market rent is likely to have his interest terminated, and if he has paid a market rent in advance, will have to pay it over again after the first six months.

But for further provisions of the Civil Code mentioned hereafter, it might be possible to contemplate the creation of a timesharing plan based on a lease with the timeshare purchasers being protected by an independent third party bank guarantee in respect of the payment of the rent, or the deposit of the rent in trust over the period of the lease.

However, the danger in leasehold schemes is that the lease may be regarded, under Maltese law, as a contract for emphyteusis. Emphyteusis is defined by s 1576 (1) of the Civil Code: 'Emphyteusis is a contract whereby one of the contracting parties grants to the other, in perpetuity or for a time, a tenement for a stated yearly rent or ground rent which the latter binds himself to pay to the former, either in money or in kind, as an acknowledgement of the tenure ...' This section must be read in conjunction with s 1580 which provides:

(1) Where a tenement is granted for a time exceeding 16 years, or in such manner that the grant may be made to last for more than 16 years, and, in either case, under the conditions which are in accordance with the Provisions of the following Sections of this Title rather than with those relating to contracts of letting and hiring, the grant shall be deemed to be an emphyteutical grant, although the parties shall be termed it a contract of letting and hiring, and any such grant is null if made otherwise than by a public deed.
(2) On the contrary, where a tenement is granted under a title of emphyteusis, the grant shall be deemed to be an emphyteutical grant, notwithstanding the shortness of the period for which it is made and the nature of the stipulations attaching thereto ...

Section 347 of the Civil Code provides: 'The following are immovables by reason of the object to which they refer: (a) The dominion directum or the right of the dominus on the tenement let out on emphyteusis, and the dominium utile or the right of the emphytueta on such tenement ...'.

As we have seen, the Immovable Property (Acquisition by Non-Residents) Act 1974 provides that a non-resident person may not acquire immovable property without the consent of the Ministry of Finance.

Section 1576 (1) of the Civil Code (Emphyteusis) should be contrasted with s 1615 (1) (Leasehold). The distinction between emphyteusis and leasing is that emphyteusis is the grant of property, and leasing is the grant of the enjoyment of property. Emphyteusis is a right *in rem* and leasing is a right *in personam*. Although subject to the obligation to pay a ground rent, the emphyteuta is in the same position as the owner of a property, with all the rights and obligations of an owner. A lessee is merely considered a transient user of the property, with far more limited rights and obligations.

Subject to the conditions of the emphyteusis, the emphyteuta may alter the property (s 1587) make any profit out of it, benefit from any treasure trove (s 1585) and dispose of the property (s 1589). The emphyteuta is bound to 'keep and in due time resort the property in a good state' (s 1586) and 'to carry

out any obligation imposed by law, on the owners of buildings and lands'
(s 1588).

In a tenancy or lease, subject to the conditions of the lease, the tenant's
obligations are less onerous and the lessor is liable for maintenance and
restoration (ss 1628 and 1629). The rights of the tenant are also more
restricted, and improvements cannot be made without the consent of the lessor
(s 1653 (1)). The distinction between emphyteusis and contract of letting often
turns on who is responsible for the carrying out of and the payment of
ordinary and extraordinary expenditure and who has the right to decide and
pay for re-construction and improvements.

The obligations of a lessor and lessee under a contract of letting are set out in
ss 1628 and 1629 of the Civil Code:

> 1628.   The Lessor is bound, by the nature of the contract, and without the necessity
> of any special agreement—
> (a)   To deliver to the Lessee the thing let;
> (b)   To maintain the thing in a fit condition for the use for which it has been let;
> (c)   To secure the Lessee and the quiet enjoyment of the thing during the
> continuance of the Lease.

and

> 1629.   (1) The Lessor is bound to deliver the thing in a good state of repair in every
> respect.
> (2)   During the continuance of the lease, the Lessor is bound to make all repairs
> which may become necessary, except, with regard to urban tenements, the
> repairs mentioned in s 1645, and Lessee shall have expressly bound himself
> to carry out even such repairs.

The rights and obligations of the lessee are further dealt with in ss 1643–1654
of the Civil Code.

Section 1663 of the Civil Code provides: 'If the Lessor sells the thing let, or
alienates it in any other manner, the alienee cannot dissolve the lease, unless
the Lessor has reserved to himself such power in the contract of Lease.'

It follows from the foregoing that it is difficult to base a Maltese timesharing
scheme upon the institution of the lease or letting contract because, on the one
hand, if the term of the timesharing arrangement exceeds 16 years there is a
danger that the contract may be considered to be a grant of emphyteusis and
null and void if not made by public deed and with the consent of the Ministry
of Finance and, on the other hand, the contract would have to be one at a full
market rent which could not be paid as a premium or in advance if the
timeshare owners were to be protected against the claims of hypothecary
creditors.

A mortgage or 'hypothec' is defined by s 2115 (a):

> (a)   A Hypothec is general or special: it is general when it affects all the property
> present and future of the debtor; it is special when it affects only one or more
> particular immovables of the following kind:

(a) Things which are immovable by their nature, and products of such immovables so long as they are not separated therefrom;
(b) The right of usufruct over the said immovables, during the continuance of such right;
(c) The dominium directum over the said immovables given on emphyteuses, and the dominium utile over such immovables.

The distinction between general and special hypothecs is of great importance. Section 2117 of the Civil Code provides:

1 A special hypothec continues to attach to any immovable charge therewith into whosoever's possession such immovable may pass.
2 A general hypothec attaches to the property affected thereby only so long as such property does not pass into the hands of a third party.

The mortgage, as it is understood in Anglo-Saxon terms, is analogous to a special hypothec. It can be created either by contract or as a result of the registration of a judgment in the Public Registry (s 2128) and a general hypothec gives the hypothecary creditor the right to register a special hypothec over particular property of the debtor through his unilateral act (s 2120).

Hypothecs rank according to the date of registration (s 2197(10)). The hypothecary creditor cannot take possession of the property. The hypothecary right is exercised by enforcing the public auction of the property under the authority of the court and obtaining payment from the proceeds of sale.

In the event of a hypothecary creditor enforcing his rights, the tenant would retain his rights under the contract of letting or lease (s 1663) but subject to the provisions of s 1624 of the Civil Code, mentioned earlier, in relation to payment in advance for in excess of six months. Whilst it would be possible for a hypothecary creditor to consent to payment of rent in advance for more than six months, in such an eventuality there would be nothing to stop the creation of a further hypothec during the course of the lease.

In addition to hypothecs, other charges, known as privileged debts, can also be charged against the property. These are dealt with in s 2114; which provides that privileges arise over specific immovables in the following case:

(A) The dominus over the dominium utile of the emphyteutical tenement for the debt due to him by the emphyteuta in respect of ground rent and for the performance of the other obligations arising from the emphyteutical contract;
(B) Architects, contractors, masons and other workmen, over the immovable constructed or repaired, for the debts due to them in respect of the expenses and the price of their work.
The same privilege is competent to the person who has, by means of a public deed, supplied money or materials for the construction, re-construction or repair of the immovable, or for the payment of the workmen employed on such work, provided it is shown by the said deed that the supply was made for that purpose, and it is proved that the work was carried out, or the payments to the workmen made, with the materials or out of the money supplied.
The same privilege is also competent to a third party in possession over the

immovable of which he has been dispossessed, for the repairs and improvements made in or on such immovable. The said privilege, in the case of repairs necessary for the preservation of the immovable extends to the whole amount of the debt; in any case it is limited to the sum corresponding to the increase in the value of the immovable resulting from the works or expenses.

(C) The Vendor or any other alienor, whether under an onerous or a gratuitous title, over the immovables sold, or alienated by means of a public deed, for the whole or the residue of the price, or for the performance of the covenants stipulated in the deed of sale or alienation. The same privilege is competent to the person who has, by means of a public deed, supplied in whole or in part the money for the payment of the price agreed upon, provided it is shown and it is proved that the money taken on loan has been paid to the alienations, the first alienor is preferred to the second, the second to the third and so on;

(D) Co-heirs and other co-partitioners, over the immovables which were the subject of the partition, in case of eviction of the immovables divided between them, and for any compensation or owelty of partition;

(E) The Advocate and the Legal Procurator, for the fees due to them for their services in the action for the recovery of the immovable, and the person disbursing the expenses of the said action, over the immovable, if recovered.

The Ministry of Finance has confirmed that the grant of a hypothec in favour of a non-resident does not require permission, although if the right was enforced, and reduced to money, exchange control permission would be required for the conversion of the currency out of Maltese pounds.

It will be seen from the foregoing that conventional methods of devising a timesharing plan are fraught with difficulty in Malta. The solution to the problem has been found by analogy with tour operating contracts. In a tour operating contract, the hotelier binds himself to allow customers of the tour operator to have occupation of the hotel or other property. There is not usually a direct contractual relationship between the customer and the hotelier. The customer has a contract with the tour operator and the tour operator in turn has a contract with the hotelier. Frequently such contracts can cover a period of several years, but by itself the tour operating contract does not give sufficient protection to the timeshare purchasers in a timesharing scheme, since the timesharing contract may exist for upwards of 30 years. A way has to be found therefore of giving the timeshare buyer the degree of security required. What happens in practice is that the owner of the property contracts with an offshore company to provide accommodation and services to the timeshare buyers. At the same time, in order to secure those rights, the owner grants a special hypothec to the offshore company, which will necessarily be for a value greatly in excess of the whole ownership value of the apartment which is to be the subject of timeshare rights, and will equate to the aggregate of the timeshare prices.

If the shares in the company were owned by the timeshare developer, the future of the company would be bound up with the solvency of the timeshare developer so that as part of the arrangement, the shares in the offshore company are transferred into trust, with the trustees holding the shares on behalf of the timeshare owners. The concept of trust is not known to Maltese law, but as we have seen in relation to the rules regarding conflict of laws, if the company which owns the rights is incorporated in a jurisdiction which recognises trusts, existence of the trust can be recognised in that jurisdiction. The rights and obligations of the timeshare buyer must be set out in detail, and generally this is done as in other jurisdictions by establishing a club and providing that the timeshare buyers become members of the club, and that the trustee holds the shares in the company which has the special hypothec on trust for the members of the club.

It is of the essence of the timeshare concept that the timeshare buyers pay a capital sum for the acquisition of their right, but if this sum were paid over to the owner of the hotel or other accommodation, it would be likely to be taxed at a punitive rate in the year in which it was received, notwithstanding that the obligations of the owner extended over a period of years. Consequently, the sum involved is treated as a deposit against the future obligations of the owner, who may draw against that deposit each year *pro rata* over the period of the timeshare contract. The owner of the property therefore becomes entitled to an annual payment from the deposit, together with an annual maintenance charge paid by each timeshare owner, and usually collected by the promoters of the timesharing scheme and paid over to the owner on an annual basis. This solution provides at one and the same time for the protection of the timeshare owner (since the existence of the special hypothec for a value in excess of that of the property will prevent the property being sold, mortgaged or otherwise disposed of contrary to the interest of the timeshare owners) whilst at the same time proceeds of sales for the timeshares, after payment to the offshore promoters of the scheme, arrive in Malta. The Maltese economy therefore benefits from the inward investment of foreign currency, not only in regard to the 'deposits' but also in regard to the annual maintenance payments. The Maltese tourist industry also benefits since a 'customer base' is created. The timeshare purchasers are people who, over a long period of years, will be coming to Malta to occupy their timeshared accommodation and will also be spending foreign currency in Malta in the same way as any other tourist. The concept has been welcomed in Malta for these reasons. In addition, the concept provides not only a steady and growing group of holidaymakers but also extends the season over which they will visit. At the same time the fears of some sections of the Maltese community, that land and property will be taken over by non-residents, are not justified in the case of the timesharing concept, because the timesharers do not themselves actually own the land or property but merely have their rights to visit it secured.

## South Africa

The timesharing industry in South Africa has grown substantially since first introduced not long before issue of the second edition of this book (1986).

Compared with sales of 46,607 weeks sold out of 67,851 available as at January 1985, the industry has since developed as shown in the table below:

| Year | Supply | | Sold | | % Sold |
|------|--------|------|------|------|--------|
| 1986 **Total** | 88 400 | | 60 000 | | 67 |
| 1987 | + 64 699 | (+73%) | 20 000 | (+34%) | 31 |
| Total | 153 000 | | 80 500 | | 52 |
| 1988 | + 42 000 | (+27%) | + 40 000 | (+50%) | 95 |
| Total | 195 000 | | 120 500 | | 61 |
| 1989 | + 36 350 | (+18,6%) | + 36 000 | (+30%) | 99 |
| Total | 231 250 | | 156 500 | | 68 |

Increasing product differentiation providing more specialised vacation ownership opportunities to specific market segments, with resorts focusing on particular sporting, health and leisure facilities, continues.

Vacation ownership adds most of the new accommodation to the country's tourist infrastructure which places the timeshare sector of the market in the best position to take advantage of rising tourist demand both domestic and international, with exchanges in the latter category being projected to grow rapidly from 1,800 weeks in 1989 to some 4,000 in 1990.

Demographic surveys on reasons for purchasing timesharing in the local market show the following findings indicating a sophisticated purchaser market.

Reasons for purchase (importance rating):

1 saving of future holiday costs: 64%
2 ensure future holidays: 54%
3 local and foreign exchangeability: 51%
4 financial investment: 48%

The most popular way of establishing timeshare schemes is still by means of the share block method; although the club membership method has been used, it is not as popular as is the case in the UK.

The legislature, in enacting timeshare legislation in South Africa, has ensured that the prospective buyer of a timeshare obtains full and accurate disclosure of all relevant information, whatever the method used to effect the scheme may be. A considerable amount of legislation applies to the development of any immovable property. In the field of timesharing the most important statutes are the Share Blocks Control Act No 59 of 1980, the Sectional Titles Act No 95 of 1986 (previously Act No 66 of 1971) and the Property Time Sharing Control Act No 75 of 1983.

Since timesharing schemes are mainly effected by share block and sectional title, these schemes will be discussed in detail; the remaining types of schemes will not be examined.

**Share block schemes and the Share Blocks Control Act**

Most timesharing schemes in the Republic are constructed on a share block basis. One of the reasons for this is that, unlike a sectional title development, a share block development can be effected on both leasehold and freehold property and on property falling either in or outside the area of jurisdiction of a local authority.

The registration requirements are simple and the costs to the timeshare purchaser of becoming a shareholder in a share block company are substantially less than those payable by a purchaser of a sectional title unit. It should be noted that a share block scheme may not be operated in respect of agricultural land without prior consent of the Minister of Agriculture.

At the time of offering shares for sale, a developer is required to state in writing whether or not the share block company intends to effect the opening of a sectional title register and, if so, to secure the costs of opening the sectional title register by the provision of guarantees.

The Share Blocks Control Act was first promulgated when timesharing schemes were not predominant and is therefore more appropriate to schemes where the share block owner occupies a unit on a permanent basis.

The fundamental features of a share block scheme are that the shares in a company which owns or leases land are sold to a purchaser. The purchaser enters into an agreement (known as a use agreement) with the share block company in terms of which the purchaser will be entitled, free of rent and in perpetuity or, where the property is leased by the share block company, for the duration of the lease, to occupy the particular unit to which the share block relates. Timesharing in a share block scheme is a simple variation of this: instead of the purchaser being entitled to occupy the unit, for instance, in perpetuity, the purchaser's occupation is limited to say one, two or three weeks' occupation in a calendar year.

The Share Blocks Control Act applies to every 'share block company', which is defined as a company whose activities comprise or include the operation of a share block scheme which existed on or was commenced after 1 January 1981; ie any scheme in terms of which a share (which means a share in the share capital of the company and includes a debenture) confers a right to use of, or interest in the use of, immovable property.

As with any other company incorporated under the Companies Act No 61 of 1973, a share block company is obliged to have a memorandum and articles of association. In terms of s 7 (1) the main object and main business of a share block company must be to operate a share block scheme in respect of the immovable property owned or leased by it. Section 7 (2) provides that the articles must stipulate that each member is entitled to the use of a defined part of the company's immovable property on which the share block scheme is operated, and on terms and conditions which are contained in a use agreement between the company and that member. Every share in a share block company is required to confer a right to, or an interest in, the use of the company's immovable property and must confer a right to vote at any meeting of the company. In addition, every share in a company in respect of which a share block scheme is brought into operation after the commencement of the Act must confer the same vote as every other share in the company.

Ordinarily, an offer of shares by a company to the public must be accompanied by a prospectus; any person offering shares for sale to the public in a share block company need not publish a prospectus, but is required to make a large number of disclosures to the purchaser. The object of these disclosures is to provide the purchaser with all the relevant information, particularly with regard to the rights and obligations of the purchaser and those of the share block company. Furthermore, the share sale agreement must be accompanied by certain documents such as the use agreement, the latest audited annual financial statements of the share block company and a statement of the amount which each share block purchaser is obliged to lend to the company to enable the company to discharge its obligations.

Section 12 entrenches the right of the shareholders to appoint one director to the board of the share block company if there are fewer than ten members and to appoint two directors where there are more than ten members. The Act recognises that the developer of the share block scheme may be a majority shareholder; accordingly the minority shareholders are given certain rights so that, for example, the wishes of the minority can be made known at all times.

As is to be expected, every share block company is obliged to establish a levy fund which is intended to provide finance for the day-to-day expenses of the company as well as the maintenance and administration of the company and its property. It is common in share block schemes for a share block purchaser to be obliged to lend to the share block company in order to enable the company to discharge its obligations. In order to protect share block holders against unscrupulous conduct on the part of the developer, s 14 (1) provides that a share block company may not increase its loan obligations or encumber any of its assets except with the approval of a resolution passed by at least 75 per cent in number and votes of the members of the company, excluding the share block developer.

In terms of s 8 (1), a share block company has only such powers as may be necessary to enable it to realise its main object and ancillary objects and does not have the power, save with the approval by special resolution of a general meeting of the share block company, to alienate any immovable property of which it is the owner or any of its rights to immovable property of which it is not the owner and in respect of which it operates a share block scheme. Any act of a share block company in excess of its capacity or powers is void.

All monies paid by the share block holder in reduction of the holder's obligations to lend money to the company must be deposited in a separate trust account. This requirement is intended to ensure that the monies so paid are actually used by the share block developer to discharge its obligations and are not used by the developer for other purposes. The directors of a share block company are obliged to ensure that the property of the company is adequately insured against damages. The share block developer, directors and officers of the company are jointly and severally liable for any damages suffered as a result of failure to make such provision. Share block holders will be obliged to contribute a levy to a fund out of which maintenance and day-to-day expenditure is to be met. The amount of the current levy must be disclosed to the purchaser at the time of signing the sale documents.

Similar provisions to those contained in the Sectional Title Act, dealt with below, to protect the interests of tenants are also contained in the Share Blocks Control Act. Provision is made in Sched 1 to the Act for a share block scheme to be converted into a sectional title development where not less than 30 per cent of the members of the share block company so resolve.

There are two fundamental disadvantages to a share block scheme. The first is that, in terms of s 38 of the Companies Act, no company is permitted to give financial assistance in connection with the purchase or subscription for any shares in itself. Accordingly, if a share block holder wishes to sell shares and the purchaser does not have sufficient funds to pay the purchase price immediately, the seller will be forced to grant the purchaser credit; the company cannot in any way give any financial assistance in connection with that sale of shares. As a general rule, the financial institutions have been reluctant to lend money on the security of a pledge of shares in a share block company. Fortunately, this appears to be changing and instances of financial institutions financing purchasers of this nature appear to be becoming more common. In a sectional title scheme the purchaser of a sectional title unit can borrow money on the security of a mortgage bond over the unit and can use the monies so borrowed to pay the purchase price.

A further problem is that the share block holder's right of occupation is based on an agreement between the share block holder and the company. If the company is put into liquidation, any purchaser of the property is not obliged to honour the occupation agreement between the company and the share block holder. The purchase of a share block in a share block company does not vest the purchaser thereof with any real right in respect of the land. As a result the share block holder's rights may be destroyed and he will be left with a claim for damages against the share block company which may prove to be worthless. This problem cannot arise in a sectional title scheme.

Notwithstanding these disadvantages, share block schemes provide an extremely convenient and flexible means for operating a timesharing scheme. Prior to the enactment of the Share Blocks Control Act, share block schemes were justifiably regarded with a certain amount of circumspection. However, the protections afforded to members of a share block company by the Share Blocks Control Act are most welcome and have assisted in establishing the respectability of share block schemes as a useful alternative to sectional title developments, especially in the field of timesharing.

## Sectional title schemes and the Sectional Titles Act

Most modern condominium legislation may be classified as being either dualistic or unitary. In contrast to the unitary system, which involves only one form of ownership, namely co-ownership by all participants in the scheme of both the land and buildings erected on it, the Sectional Titles Act is based on the dualistic system of ownership. The principal feature of the dualistic system is the linking together of two different forms of ownership, namely, separate ownership of a 'section' (the timeshare unit) coupled with the co-ownership of 'the common property' (the land on which the development is situated). Despite the fact that the dualistic system has two different forms of ownership, the two forms are, in law, combined and are regarded as comprising a single entity; the Act prohibits the disposition of the one without the other.

The biggest stumbling block to the introduction of the Sectional Titles Act in South Africa was the fact that the concept of sectional title was contrary to Roman-Dutch common law and the principles of land ownership on which the South African common law of property is based. In the first place it was contrary to the principle *omnia quod inaedificatur solo cedit*, ie whatever is built on the soil accedes to and forms part of the soil. It was also contrary to the principle of ownership being *plena in re potestas* in terms of which the owner is entitled to do as he pleases with the object of his ownership including having the power to destroy. Finally, it conflicted with the principle *cuius est solum eius est e coelo et ad inferos*, pursuant to which the owner of land owns everything above it to the sky and everything below it down to the centre of the earth. All of these problems have, however, been overcome in the Sectional Titles Act.

In terms of the Act, the 'developer' means a person who is the registered owner of land within the area of jurisdiction of a local authority on which is situated or to be erected a building or buildings which he has divided or he proposes to divide into two or more sections in terms of a scheme and includes his successors in title as developer. A 'development scheme' in terms of which a building or buildings situated or to be erected on the land are divided into two or more sections and common property is prepared by a land surveyor or architect. The developer then makes application to the appropriate local authority for approval of the scheme and plan. The function of the local authority is to ensure that the proposed scheme is not in conflict with any other proposed or approved time planning scheme and that an existing building or one proposed to be built is suitable for sectional title development. Although the erection of the building itself is not a prerequisite for approval of the sectional title plan by the local authority, The Registrar of Deeds will not register the opening of the sectional title register unless furnished with a certificate by an architect or surveyor confirming that the building is sufficiently complete for occupation.

In order to protect a purchaser, the Act provides that the developer may not receive any portion of the purchase price prior to not only the approval of the sectional title plan by the local authority, but also the opening of the sectional title register in the deeds registry concerned, unless the developer provides the purchaser with a back-to-back bank or building society guarantee. The effect of this is that if the plan is not approved or the register not opened, the prospective purchaser is assured that his money will be returned. If the developer does not have sufficient financial resources to provide a guarantee, then any portion of the purchase price must be held in trust by the developer's attorney or an estate agent until the plan is approved and the register opened.

Although this legislative innovation prevents self-financing sectional title developments, it was necessary in view of certain schemes which failed as a result of unscrupulous conduct by developers. In order to counteract the stringency of this provision, the Act allows for a scheme to be developed in successive stages so that the transfer of ownership may be registered as each phase is completed; this enables the developer to utilise the profits from the first phase to develop the second and subsequent phases.

With regard to buildings erected or in the course of erection prior to 1981, the developer is prohibited from selling or offering for sale any unit or an undivided share in any unit prior to the opening of the sectional title register. If the developer contravenes the Act in this respect, the sale is void and the purchaser is entitled to reclaim the purchase price. However, the developer is entitled to reasonable compensation for the use the purchaser has had of the unit and for any damage caused to the unit.

In order to protect tenants of units which are to be converted into sectional title units, the Act provides that every tenant is to be notified in writing that the building is to be converted to sectional title, and is to be invited to attend a meeting at which the developer or his agent will be present and available to provide the tenant with information regarding the particulars of the scheme and the condition of the building.

Any unit occupied by a tenant must be offered to that tenant, who has 90 days to accept or refuse the offer to purchase. A protected tenant has 365 days to accept or refuse the offer. If the tenant either refuses or fails to accept the offer, for 180 days the developers may not offer for sale or sell the unit at a price lower than that offered to the tenant unless the developer has first offered the unit at the lower price to the tenant who then has a further period of 60 days to accept or refuse. In addition, the tenant is not required to vacate the premises until the expiry of the 180 or the further 60 day period unless such tenant is in breach of the lease; the developer may not demand a higher rental during that period.

Once the sectional title register has been opened, certificates of registered sectional title are issued to the developer for each unit; any further transfers of units are effected by endorsement of the certificates. The endorsement is effected on the basis of a conveyancer's certificate setting out all relevant details of the transaction.

With effect from the date on which any person, other than the developer, becomes an owner of a unit, a body corporate—the controlling body of the scheme—automatically comes into existence. Every owner of a unit automatically becomes a member of the body corporate. The body corporate is a juristic person whose function is to control, administer and manage the building and to see to the enforcement of the rules governing the use and enjoyment of the sections and common property for the benefit of all owners. Initially, the developer is obliged to register the Sched I and II rules as laid down in the Act, but is entitled to adopt other rules if unit holders agree. Section 48 of the Act provides for termination of a sectional title scheme where, for example, the building or buildings are physically destroyed. In this event, the owners cease to be separate owners of sections but remain co-owners of the land and anything remaining on the land.

If a judgment is granted against a body corporate and the judgment debt is not satisfied, s 47 allows the judgment creditor to apply to join the members of the body corporate in their personal capacities. If so joined, the individual members become liable for the debt in proportion to their respective quotas in their sections.

Sectional title schemes, like share block schemes, can be used to convey occupation of a unit in perpetuity or, in a timesharing scheme, for short periods of say, one, two or three weeks.

However, there is one essential difference between the two types of schemes. In a sectional title scheme the timesharers become co-owners of an undivided share in a particular section comprising the accommodation and an undivided share of the common property. Co-ownership of the asset does not arise in a share block scheme because there is no asset which is owned in common with any person.

The common law of South Africa permits a co-owner of property (the owners of sectional title units in a timesharing scheme are co-owners) to appropriate the whole or any part of the property to his exclusive use without the consent of the remaining co-owners. Furthermore, a co-owner may demand that the relationship between all the co-owners be dissolved so that the property is sold. It is essential in a sectional title timesharing scheme that these two incidents of the common law relating to co-ownership be eliminated from the scheme. This can be achieved with careful drafting, which can also ensure that the rights of subsequent co-owners are eliminated.

Whilst there is no doubt that sectional title schemes are, from the point of view of the purchaser, far more attractive and secure than a share block scheme, the latter is far more flexible and less confined by strict legislative provisions.

## Property Timesharing Control Act

The Property Timesharing Control Act came into operation on 1 March 1984 and applies to the alienation of any timesharing interest on or after that date.

(It is important to note that the word 'alienation' in relation to a timesharing interest means the sale of that interest or the letting of the interest for a period of at least three years.) A timesharing interest in relation to a timesharing scheme, means a right to, or interest in, the exclusive use or occupation of accommodation for determinable periods during any year.

The Act defines a timesharing scheme to mean any scheme, arrangement or undertaking in terms of which timesharing interests are offered for alienation or are alienated and the utilisation of such interests is regulated and controlled under a share block scheme, a sectional title scheme, a scheme involving club membership or any scheme which is declared to be a property timesharing scheme by the Minister of Industries, Commerce and Tourism by notice in the *Government Gazette.*

The two principal features of the Act are that it compels the disclosure of certain information and prohibits self-financing timeshare schemes. With regard to the first feature, the Act provides that an alienation of a timesharing interest must be incorporated in a written contract which contract must contain certain information. For example, the contract must contain a description of the legal basis and duration of the property timesharing scheme and of the timesharing interest which is the subject of the contract, including the period during which and the conditions on which the purchaser is entitled to the timesharing interest.

The seller is also obliged to disclose further information in the contract such as whether the immovable property is owned by the seller or occupied by the seller in terms of a lease; details as to the nature of any encumbrances which the property may be subject to, etc. Finally, the seller is obliged to disclose the place at which, and the hours during which, written details of the scheme and of any rules in relation to the scheme may be inspected, as well as an inventory of any movables which will be available for use by the purchaser in conjunction with the timesharing interest.

Certain provisions in a contract for the alienation of a timesharing interest are void. For example, a provision exempting the seller from liability for any act, omission or representation by any person acting on behalf of the seller, or a provision that any person who acted on behalf of the seller in connection with the sale is deemed to be the agent of the purchaser for any subsequent sale of that timesharing interest.

The prohibition against a self-financing scheme is contained in s 7 of the Act. This section provides that no person is permitted to receive any consideration in respect of the alienation of a timesharing interest unless an architect has issued a certificate that the accommodation to which the timesharing interest relates is substantially in accordance with any applicable and relevant officially approved building plans, town planning scheme and local authority byelaws and is sufficiently complete for the purposes of utilisation of the timesharing interest. A copy of the architect's certificate must also be delivered to the purchaser. If the certificate has not been issued at the time of signing the contract for the alienation of a timesharing interest, the seller is obliged to disclose the latest date by which the certificate will be issued and delivered to the purchaser This date must not be more than three years after the date of entering into the contract. If the seller is unable to deliver the certificate within the promised period, the purchaser is entitled to cancel the contract.

As with sectional title schemes, the stringency of s 7 is mitigated by the fact that the seller will be entitled to receive consideration under the contract if that consideration is deposited in trust with an attorney or an estate agent until issue of the architect's certificate or if the purchaser is simultaneously furnished with an irrevocable and unconditional guarantee by a bank, building society or insurance company.

In terms of s 12 of the Act, the Minister of Industries, Commerce and Tourism is empowered to make regulations regarding various matters. The appropriate regulations came into force on 1 March 1984 and elaborate on certain features of the Act. For example, any advertisement with regard to the alienation of a timesharing interest, must contain certain details of a nature similar to those which must be disclosed in any contract for the alienation of a timesharing interest. Similarly, a developer is obliged, at the time of entering into a sale of a timesharing interest, to make certain information available to the purchaser. This information includes, for example, the site development plan or layout or, where the building has not been completed, a copy of the approved building plans. The developer is also obliged to provide the purchaser with a detailed projection of the estimated income and expenditure in respect of the operation and maintenance of the property timesharing scheme for one year in advance. The projection must be certified as adequate by both the developer and the person who manages the scheme.

Regulation 5 (a) prohibits the sale of timesharing interests in a particular property timesharing scheme unless all available residential accommodation in the immovable property relating to such property timesharing scheme is being utilised for purposes of that scheme. Regulation 5 (b), however, provides that no building or part thereof may be used for the purposes of a property timesharing scheme unless 75 per cent of the owners in a sectional title scheme or shareholders in a share block scheme relating to such building have consented thereto in writing.

These two regulations give rise to some anomalies in interpretation. Regulation 5 (a) ostensibly prohibits 'hybrid schemes', in terms of reg 5 (b), on the other hand, it is apparently permissible for part of a building to be used for the purposes of a property timesharing scheme provided that the requisite 75 per cent of owners in a sectional title scheme or shareholders in a share block scheme have consented thereto in writing.

The remaining regulations do not apply to timesharing schemes which operate on a share block or sectional title basis but will apply to other types of timesharing schemes such as those based on leases or club membership. These regulations oblige the developer to appoint a managing agent. They also provide for the establishment of a management association with effect from the date on which any person, other than the developer, acquires a timesharing interest. The management association is charged with certain duties such as the insurance of the property. It is also vested with the power to establish a levy fund for the operation of the timesharing scheme. Finally, the management association is obliged to prepare or cause to be prepared a detailed budget of the expected income and expenditure of the management association. The budget must be approved at the annual general meeting of the management association.

In terms of reg 10, the developer directs the managing agent until the creation of the management association whereafter the managing agent becomes responsible to the management association.

**Miscellaneous legislation**

There are a number of Acts which apply to every timesharing scheme. For example, the Group Areas Act, No 36 of 1966, strictly controls the areas in which the members of the various race groups in South Africa may own or occupy immovable property. Most, if not all, timesharing schemes have been developed in 'white group areas' and are therefore not available to members of the other race groups unless a special exemption has been obtained from the Minister of Community Development.

In terms of the Subdivision of Agricultural Land Act, No 70 of 1970 no farm property can be subdivided nor can any right to any portion of farm property be granted to any person. The effect of this is to preclude any timesharing scheme being operated on farm property.

The Usuary Act, No 73 of 1968 (previously the Limitation and Disclosure of Finance Charges Act) applies to the sale on credit of a sectional title unit or a share in a share block scheme. Briefly, this Act obliges the grantor of the credit to disclose certain information of a financial nature relating to the rate of interest being charged by the seller as well as any additional finance charges which the seller proposes to levy. The Act also limits the amount of the finance charges which are recoverable from the purchaser to rates which are regarded as not being usurious.

Whilst a purchaser of a timesharing interest who is not resident in the Republic of South Africa will not be obliged to obtain the approval of the exchange control authorities to purchase a timesharing interest, the seller, if resident in the Republic, will be obliged to obtain authority to sell to a non-resident; the authority is normally granted as a matter of course by a commercial banker.

**Fiscal implications**

In terms of the Income Tax Act, No 58 of 1962, income tax is levied in South Africa on all receipts or accruals (other than those of a capital nature) derived from a source within or deemed to be within the Republic of South Africa. The fine distinction between capital and revenue profits which has troubled judges in the English courts for so many years has been equally troublesome in South Africa. Nevertheless it is always important for the developer of a timesharing scheme to keep a close watch on the possibility of the profits arising from the development being subject to income tax.

Broadly speaking, a developer will almost always be subject to income tax on the development profits unless the developer (who will bear the onus of proof) can show that he was realising a capital asset to the best advantage. If the development profits are to be subjected to tax, the developer must be extremely careful to ensure that he obtains a deduction for as many of the costs involved in the development as possible. There are many pitfalls for the unwary developer in this area.

If a close corporation or a person other than a company receives a dividend from a share block company, that dividend will be taxable. Whilst it is most unlikely that a share block company will be distributing a dividend of a conventional nature, it has been argued that the definition of 'dividend' in the Income Tax Act is wide enough to apply to a share block company's granting a shareholder a right of occupation of the company's property. The better view is that this does not constitute a dividend. It is not the current practice of the Revenue to treat this as a dividend.

Where a share block scheme is converted to a sectional title scheme, it has also been argued that the conferral by the company of a right of ownership constitutes a dividend. Again, the better view appears to be that this is not correct and, fortunately, the Revenue shares this view. A further pitfall with regard to conversion arises where the share block company grants credit to the share block holder for any debt which may be due by a share block holder to the company arising out of the conversion. The granting of credit will, in appropriate circumstances, constitute a dividend which is taxable in terms of s 8B of the Income Tax Act.

If a sectional title unit in a sectional title timesharing scheme is sold by a developer (who is taxable on the profit from the sale) in instalments and ownership is reserved to the developer until the last instalment of the purchase price is paid, the developer will be subject to tax in the year in which the sale takes place on all of the profit arising from the sale even though he will not have received the full proceeds. In order to mitigate the severity of this, the developer can apply for an allowance in terms of s 24 of the Income Tax Act, under which the developer may be allowed to deduct from the total profit made on the sale an amount equal to the unpaid balance of the purchase price. The effect of this is to spread the income tax liability of the developer over the cash flow period of the development.

In a share block timesharing scheme, it is customary for the developer to pass ownership in the shares immediately to the purchaser and, as security for the unpaid balance of the purchase price, to oblige the purchaser to pledge back the shares to the developer. In such circumstances the developer will not be entitled to claim the benefit of s 24 allowance because ownership in the shares will have passed immediately to the purchaser. Since the developer gains a significant advantage from the s 24 allowance, the developer must provide that, where shares are sold on instalments, the ownership in the shares will not pass to the purchaser until the last instalment of the purchase price is paid; in such circumstances the developer will be entitled to claim the allowance.

Income tax is levied at a flat rate of 50 per cent on companies and close corporations. The tax is levied on a sliding scale on the income of persons other than companies at a maximum marginal rate of 45 per cent on a married person whose income exceeds R80,000.00 and 45 per cent on an unmarried person whose income exceeds R54,000.00.

The purchaser of a sectional title unit is obliged to pay transfer duty on the sales value of the unit although the Revenue has the right to levy transfer duty at market value should that be higher than the sales price. Where the purchaser is a person other than a company, transfer duty is levied at the rate of 1 per cent on the first R30,000.00 and 3 per cent on the balance in excess of R30,000.00; where the purchaser is a company or close corporation, the transfer duty is 5 per cent. In respect of properties acquired after 1 April 1980, improved properties are exempted from transfer duty where the value is less than R30,000.00 and in the case of unimproved land where the land value is less than R12,000.00.

Stamp duty is payable on the registration of transfer of shares in a share block scheme. The duty is based on the consideration payable for the shares, or the market value of the shares if there is no consideration or if the consideration is less than the market value. The average rate of duty is 1.5 per cent where the duty is paid within 6 months of the date on which the share transfer form is executed and three times that if paid after the expiry of the 6 month period.

In the Republic of South Africa, general sales tax is levied on the sale of all corporeal movable assets. Neither a sectional title unit nor shares in a share block scheme are corporeal movable assets and, accordingly, no general sales tax is payable.

## Conclusion

A sophisticated body of legislation already exists to deal with some of the problems which have been experienced in other jurisdictions. No developer can undertake a timesharing development without expert advice on a large number of statutes. A developer will, in particular, need to be advised on all relevant property and taxation laws.

# Appendix A

# Club scheme documentation

# Appendix A

## XYZ CLUB

## CONSTITUTION

## 1 Definitions

In this Constitution the following expressions shall have the following meanings:

'the Advance Management Charge' means the estimated advance payment under the Second Option in Clause 7 of the Management Agreement annexed hereto.

'the Club' means the XYZ Club.

'the Committee' means the body of persons appointed under Clause 11 hereof.

'the Company' is XYZ Club Sales Limited a company incorporated in [                    ] whose registered office is at [ADDRESS].

'the Constitution' shall mean this Constitution and any amendments hereto made in accordance with the provisions hereof.

'the Deed of Trust' means the Deed in the form annexed hereto or any similar document for the time being in operation and 'Trust Deed' shall be construed accordingly.

'the form of Surrender and Request' means the form as annexed to the form of Membership Certificate annexed hereto as referred to in Clause 15 hereof.

'the Founder Members' are the Company and the Management Company (as hereinafter defined).

'a Membership Certificate' means the certificate in the form annexed hereto more particularly referred to in Clause 8 hereof and 'Certificate' shall be construed accordingly.

'the Management Agreement' means the contract for management services more particularly referred to in Clause 11.4 hereof and any similar document for the time being in operation.

'the Management Charge' means the charge provided for under the Management Agreement.

'the Management Company' is XYZ Club Management Limited a company incorporated in [                    ] whose registered office is at [ADDRESS].

'Members' means the Members from time to time of the Club including the Founder Members unless the context otherwise requires.

'the ordinary Members' means all Members of the Club other than the Founder Members.

'the Owning Companies' means the company or companies the names of which are set out in the Appendix and constituted to hold title to the Apartments and owned or controlled by the Trustee upon trust for the Members in accordance with the Deed of Trust and 'Owning Company' shall be construed accordingly.

'Apartments' means the Studio, one bedroomed, two bedroomed and Duplex Apartments at [ADDRESS], [                    ] referred to in Clause 7 hereof and any other Apartments or residential property in [                    ] from time to time vested in an Owning Company and 'Apartment' shall be construed accordingly.

'the Appendix' A list of Owning Companies and Apartments as provided for in Clause 7.3 hereof, in the form set out in Schedule 1 hereto, revised from time to time in accordance with the provisions of Clause 7.3 hereof.

Except where the context otherwise requires, the words and phrases in this Constitution shall be construed in accordance with the Interpretation Act 1978 (UK) and the headings in this Constitution shall be ignored.

## 2 Name

The Club shall be called 'XYZ Club'.

## 3 Location of the club

The main office of the Club shall be at [ADDRESS], or at such other place as shall from time to time be determined by the Committee of the Club.

## 4 Objects

The Club shall be a non-profit making Club whose object is to secure for its Members the ownership of exclusive rights of occupation of the Apartments for such specific periods in each year as shall be allocated to Members until the dissolution of the Club.

## 5 Membership

The Club shall consist of not more than two Founder Members and of such number of ordinary Members as shall be admitted to membership as hereinafter provided.

## 6 Founder members

The Founder Members of the Club shall be the Company and the Management Company.

## 7 Duties of founder members and appointment of trustee

7.1 The Founder Members shall cause to be conveyed or otherwise transferred to the Owning Companies the Apartments set out against their respective names in the Appendix, complete with such amenities, services, fixtures, fittings, equipment, furnishings, provisions and utensils as they shall reasonably consider appropriate.

7.2 The Founder Members shall arrange for the ownership and control of the Owning Companies to be transferred to or vested in an independent trustee (hereinafter called 'the Trustee') or as the Trustee may direct who will hold the same upon trust for the benefit of the Members of the Club from time to time upon the terms of the Deed of Trust in the form annexed hereto.

7.3 (a) The Founder Members and the Trustee shall maintain an Appendix to the Constitution setting out the names of the Owning Companies, and set against the respective names of the Owning Companies, the address of the Apartment transferred to that Owning Company and the weekly commencement and termination day (as provided in the next following sub-clause) relating to that Apartment. Such Appendix shall be in the form set out in Schedule 1 (or as near thereto as circumstances permit) and shall be revised upon each occasion that further Owning Companies are constituted or further Apartments transferred to Owning Companies and each Appendix or, as the case may be, revised Appendix shall be executed by the Trustee.

(b) The Company shall specify the weekly commencement and termination day in respect of each Apartment upon procuring the transfer of the same to an Owning Company.

7.4 The initial Trustee shall be [NAME AND ADDRESS].

## 8 Rights of occupation

The Company shall procure that the Owning Companies engage in no trading activity whatsoever but shall keep their respective Apartment or Apartments free from any mortgage lien or encumbrance (nor do, suffer or permit to be done anything which might prejudice their ownership of the respective Apartments) and shall permit occupation thereof in accordance with the terms of this Clause as follows:

8.1 Not more than 51 Membership Certificates will be issued for each Apartment designated from '1 to 51' inclusive and each Membership Certificate will entitle the registered holder thereof to occupy the Apartment to which it relates for the weekly period or periods referred to therein in accordance with the provisions of this Constitution for the duration of the Club.

8.2 Such weekly periods will be numbered from 1 to 52 with the weekly period numbered '2' beginning on the second weekly commencement and termination day (determined in accordance with Clause 7.3(b) of this Constitution) in each calendar year. Such periods shall each commence on the weekly commencement and termination day (determined as aforesaid) specified in respect of that Apartment at 16.00 hours and shall end at 10.00 hours on the following weekly commencement and termination day.

8.3 A Certificate covering more than one weekly period shall be deemed to be a series of separate Certificates, one for each weekly period it covers, for all the purposes of this Constitution including ascertainment of voting rights and entitlement upon termination.

8.4 The dates of the said Weekly Periods for the duration of the Club are as set out in the Table of Weekly Periods annexed hereto and any days unallocated to Members for Weekly Periods shall belong to the Company, provided that the Founder Members shall ensure that not less that seven days per annum are available for works of routine maintenance, cleaning and repair for each Apartment.

## 9 First issue of membership certificates to the company

In consideration of the Company causing the ownership and control of the Owning Companies to be transferred to or vested in the Trustee or as the Trustee may direct the Company will initially be entitled to (and shall be liable in respect of) all the Membership Certificates in respect of each Apartment so vested in accordance with the provisions of this Constitution.

## 10 Membership

10.1 Any person (not being a minor) may apply for and be admitted to membership of the Club. A person shall include an incorporated company or body and persons may purchase in joint names in which case they shall both apply for membership.

10.2 No person or persons shall be registered as a holder or holders of a Membership Certificate or be entitled to the benefit thereof unless he or they shall be a Member or Members of the Club.

10.3 Both the Founder Members and the Committee shall have power to admit applicants to membership which each may exercise without reference to the other provided always that such power shall not be exercised so as to result in two Membership Certificates being granted in respect of the same Apartment and the same weekly period.

10.4 In the first instance the Company as initial holder of all Membership Certificates (as provided in Clause 9 hereof) shall issue to Members Membership Certificates and such other evidence of membership as shall from time to time be determined by the Committee. Thereafter Membership Certificates may be transferred from current Members or the representatives of deceased Members in accordance with the relevant provisions of the Constitution, PROVIDED always that a Membership Certificate on issue or transfer must be sealed by the Trustee to be validly issued or transferred.

10.5 Membership of the ordinary Members of the Club shall cease on the occurrence of any of the following events:

(a) the transfer of a Member's Membership Certificate subject to the transferee becoming a Member of the Club; or

(b) the cancellation of a Member's Membership in accordance with the subsequent provisions of the Constitution; or

(c) termination of the Club in accordance with the provisions of Clause 18 of this Constitution provided always that termination as aforesaid shall be without prejudice to any person's rights in respect of a Member's liabilities arising prior to the said determination.

10.6 Any Membership Certificates not issued by the Company to ordinary Members will belong to the Company as an ordinary Member and it will be entitled to all the rights and privileges and subject to all the liabilities of being an ordinary Member and Membership Certificate Holder provided that the Company will not be subject to the obligations attached to any Membership Certificate retained by it in respect of Apartments (unless otherwise provided under the provisions of Clause 18) used for the purpose of maintenance and repair in any year provided that no more than six Membership Certificates in respect of each Apartment may be retained for such purpose. Without prejudice to the foregoing, the Company will be entitled to let out the Apartments to which such unissued Membership Certificates relate or otherwise grant rights of occupation to third parties for the duration of the period of such unissued Membership Certificates.

## 11 Appointment of committee and powers

11.1 The business and affairs of the Club shall (save in so far as the same may have been delegated to a management company as hereinafter provided) be managed by a Committee of not more than five persons, three of whom shall be ordinary Members of the Club and two of whom shall be nominated by the Company and may be ordinary Members of the Club. The Committee shall meet as often as necessary and at least once every 12 months. Any two members of the Committee may call a Committee meeting by notice in writing to all members at least 14 days prior to the date of such Committee meeting and one of the Committee members shall be appointed to act as Chairman of the Committee at the first meeting of the members of the Committee, failing which the Chairman of any meeting of the Committee will be elected by a majority of those members of the Committee present at the meeting in question. Decisions of the Committee shall be on the basis of a majority of those present and, in the event of an equality of votes, the Chairman shall have the casting vote. Three members of the Committee shall form a quorum. Proper minutes of the proceedings at Committee meetings shall be taken.

11.2  The first members of the Committee will be elected at the first general meeting of the Members of the Club which will take place on or before [DATE]. The first annual general meeting of the Members of the Club will be convened by the Founder Members by notice in writing sent to every Member not less than 28 days before the date of such meeting. At that first general meeting the Company's nominee shall preside as Chairman. At the second annual general meeting of the Club and at each subsequent annual general meeting one member of the Committee shall retire and a new member thereof shall be elected. Retiring members may offer themselves for re-election. The order in which the first three members of the Committee retire shall be decided by drawing lots. Thereafter retirement of elected Committee members shall be by rotation, each member retiring at the third annual general meeting to be held after their respective elections. The Committee members nominated by the Company shall cease to be such on written notice being given to them by the Company and the Company shall then nominate a successor or successors to fill any vacancy or vacancies thereby created.

11.3  Save as herein provided, election or removal of members to and from the Committee shall be dealt with only at annual general meetings or special general meetings of the Club and nominations shall be made by any Member of the Club in person at such meeting and shall be similarly seconded.

11.4  The Committee shall have power to do all things that may be necessary for the carrying out of the objects of the Club for its general management and shall be entitled to delegate to the Management Company hereinafter referred to such of its powers as may be appropriate to enable the Management Company to perform its functions. Until such time as the Committee shall have been constituted, the management of the Club and all the powers of the Committee shall be vested in the Founder Members who will on behalf of the Club enter into an agreement with XYZ Club Management Limited in the form annexed hereto or as close thereto as circumstances shall permit for the management of the Apartments and the proper provision of the various amenities and facilities to be enjoyed by the Members and any other property of the Club. The Founder Members on behalf of the Club and on behalf of the Members thereof shall have power to enter into the Deed of Trust referred to in Clause 7 hereof.

11.5  Without prejudice to the generality of the foregoing the Committee shall have the following specific powers:

(a)  At any time to appoint a Member of the Club to fill any casual vacancy amongst the elected members of the Committee occurring through any death, illness, resignation or otherwise. All such persons so appointed shall hold office only until the next following annual general meeting but shall be eligible for re-election for the unexpired portion of the period for which the Committee member whom he was so co-opted to replace would otherwise have been due to serve.

(b)  To make Byelaws at any time for the proper regulation of the Club and such Byelaws shall be binding on all Members of the Club. Such Byelaws shall not conflict with this Constitution and in the event of any apparent conflict the terms of this Constitution shall prevail.

(c)  To appoint such sub-committees as shall be necessary for the carrying on of the management of the Club.

(d)  At any time to suspend for a reasonable period of time or cancel the membership of any Member who in the reasonable opinion of the Committee shall have committed a substantial breach of the provisions of this Constitution or any Byelaws or Regulations hereunder or whose conduct in the opinion of the Committee shall be wholly unbecoming a Member of the Club and who has not remedied the breach of conduct complained of within a reasonable time following a

# THE XYZ CLUB WEEKLY PERIOD CHART

### WEEK NUMBERS

| YEAR | 2 | 3 | 4 | 5 | 6 | 7 | 8 | 9 | 10 | 11 | 12 | 13 | 14 | 15 | 16 | 17 | 18 | 19 | 20 | 21 | 22 | 23 |
|---|---|---|---|---|---|---|---|---|---|---|---|---|---|---|---|---|---|---|---|---|---|---|
| 1981 2009 2037 | 10/1 | 17/1 | 24/1 | 31/1 | 7/2 | 14/2 | 21/2 | 28/2 | 7/3 | 14/3 | 21/3 | 28/3 | 4/4 | 11/4 | 18/4 | 25/4 | 2/5 | 9/5 | 16/5 | 23/5 | 30/5 | 6/6 |
| 1982 2010 2038 | 9/1 | 16/1 | 23/1 | 30/1 | 6/2 | 13/2 | 20/2 | 27/2 | 6/3 | 13/3 | 20/3 | 27/3 | 3/4 | 10/4 | 17/4 | 24/4 | 1/5 | 8/5 | 15/5 | 22/5 | 29/5 | 5/6 |
| 1983 2011 2039 | 8/1 | 15/1 | 22/1 | 29/1 | 5/2 | 12/2 | 19/2 | 26/2 | 5/3 | 12/3 | 19/3 | 26/3 | 2/4 | 9/4 | 16/4 | 23/4 | 30/4 | 7/5 | 14/5 | 21/5 | 28/5 | 4/6 |
| 1984 2012 2040 | 14/1 | 21/1 | 28/1 | 4/2 | 11/2 | 18/2 | 25/2 | 3/3 | 10/3 | 17/3 | 24/3 | 31/3 | 7/4 | 14/4 | 21/4 | 28/4 | 5/5 | 12/5 | 19/5 | 26/5 | 2/6 | 9/6 |
| 1985 2013 2041 | 12/1 | 19/1 | 26/1 | 2/2 | 9/2 | 16/2 | 23/2 | 2/3 | 9/3 | 16/3 | 23/3 | 30/3 | 6/4 | 13/4 | 20/4 | 27/4 | 4/5 | 11/5 | 18/5 | 25/5 | 1/6 | 8/6 |
| 1986 2014 2042 | 11/1 | 18/1 | 25/1 | 1/2 | 8/2 | 15/2 | 22/2 | 1/3 | 8/3 | 15/3 | 22/3 | 29/3 | 5/4 | 12/4 | 19/4 | 26/4 | 3/5 | 10/5 | 17/5 | 24/5 | 31/5 | 7/6 |
| 1987 2015 2043 | 10/1 | 17/1 | 24/1 | 31/1 | 7/2 | 14/2 | 21/2 | 28/2 | 7/3 | 14/3 | 21/3 | 28/3 | 4/4 | 11/4 | 18/4 | 25/4 | 2/5 | 9/5 | 16/5 | 23/5 | 30/5 | 6/6 |
| 1988 2016 2044 | 9/1 | 16/1 | 23/1 | 30/1 | 6/2 | 13/2 | 20/2 | 27/2 | 5/3 | 12/3 | 19/3 | 26/3 | 2/4 | 9/4 | 16/4 | 23/4 | 30/4 | 7/5 | 14/5 | 21/5 | 28/5 | 4/6 |
| 1989 2017 2045 | 14/1 | 21/1 | 28/1 | 4/2 | 11/2 | 18/2 | 25/2 | 4/3 | 11/3 | 18/3 | 25/3 | 1/4 | 8/4 | 15/4 | 22/4 | 29/4 | 6/5 | 13/5 | 20/5 | 27/5 | 3/6 | 10/6 |
| 1990 2018 2046 | 13/1 | 20/1 | 27/1 | 3/2 | 10/2 | 17/2 | 24/2 | 3/3 | 10/3 | 17/3 | 24/3 | 31/3 | 7/4 | 14/4 | 21/4 | 28/4 | 5/5 | 12/5 | 19/5 | 26/5 | 2/6 | 9/6 |
| 1991 2019 2047 | 12/1 | 19/1 | 26/1 | 2/2 | 9/2 | 16/2 | 23/2 | 2/3 | 9/3 | 16/3 | 23/3 | 30/3 | 6/4 | 13/4 | 20/4 | 27/4 | 4/5 | 11/5 | 18/5 | 25/5 | 1/6 | 8/6 |
| 1992 2020 2048 | 11/1 | 18/1 | 25/1 | 1/2 | 8/2 | 15/2 | 22/2 | 29/2 | 7/3 | 14/3 | 21/3 | 28/3 | 4/4 | 11/4 | 18/4 | 25/4 | 2/5 | 9/5 | 16/5 | 23/5 | 30/5 | 6/6 |
| 1993 2021 2049 | 9/1 | 16/1 | 23/1 | 30/1 | 6/2 | 13/2 | 20/2 | 27/2 | 6/3 | 13/3 | 20/3 | 27/3 | 3/4 | 10/4 | 17/4 | 24/4 | 1/5 | 8/5 | 15/5 | 22/5 | 29/5 | 5/6 |
| 1994 2022 2050 | 8/1 | 15/1 | 22/1 | 29/1 | 5/2 | 12/2 | 19/2 | 26/2 | 5/3 | 12/3 | 19/3 | 26/3 | 2/4 | 9/4 | 16/4 | 23/4 | 30/4 | 7/5 | 14/5 | 21/5 | 28/5 | 4/6 |
| 1995 2023 2051 | 14/1 | 21/1 | 28/1 | 4/2 | 11/2 | 18/2 | 25/2 | 4/3 | 11/3 | 18/3 | 25/3 | 1/4 | 8/4 | 15/4 | 22/4 | 29/4 | 6/5 | 13/5 | 20/5 | 27/5 | 3/6 | 10/6 |
| 1996 2024 2052 | 13/1 | 20/1 | 27/1 | 3/2 | 10/2 | 17/2 | 24/2 | 2/3 | 9/3 | 16/3 | 23/3 | 30/3 | 6/4 | 13/4 | 20/4 | 27/4 | 4/5 | 11/5 | 18/5 | 25/5 | 1/6 | 8/6 |
| 1997 2025 2053 | 11/1 | 18/1 | 25/1 | 1/2 | 8/2 | 15/2 | 22/2 | 1/3 | 8/3 | 15/3 | 22/3 | 29/3 | 5/4 | 12/4 | 19/4 | 26/4 | 3/5 | 10/5 | 17/5 | 24/5 | 31/5 | 7/6 |
| 1998 2026 2054 | 10/1 | 17/1 | 24/1 | 31/1 | 7/2 | 14/2 | 21/2 | 28/2 | 7/3 | 14/3 | 21/3 | 28/3 | 4/4 | 11/4 | 18/4 | 25/4 | 2/5 | 9/5 | 16/5 | 23/5 | 30/5 | 6/6 |
| 1999 2027 2055 | 9/1 | 16/1 | 23/1 | 30/1 | 6/2 | 13/2 | 20/2 | 27/2 | 6/3 | 13/3 | 20/3 | 27/3 | 3/4 | 10/4 | 17/4 | 24/4 | 1/5 | 8/5 | 15/5 | 22/5 | 29/5 | 5/6 |
| 2000 2028 2056 | 8/1 | 15/1 | 22/1 | 29/1 | 5/2 | 12/2 | 19/2 | 26/2 | 4/3 | 11/3 | 18/3 | 25/3 | 1/4 | 8/4 | 15/4 | 22/4 | 29/4 | 6/5 | 13/5 | 20/5 | 27/5 | 3/6 |
| 2001 2029 2057 | 13/1 | 20/1 | 27/1 | 3/2 | 10/2 | 17/2 | 24/2 | 3/3 | 10/3 | 17/3 | 24/3 | 31/3 | 7/4 | 14/4 | 21/4 | 28/4 | 5/5 | 12/5 | 19/5 | 26/5 | 2/6 | 9/6 |
| 2002 2030 2058 | 12/1 | 19/1 | 26/1 | 2/2 | 9/2 | 16/2 | 23/2 | 2/3 | 9/3 | 16/3 | 23/3 | 30/3 | 6/4 | 13/4 | 20/4 | 27/4 | 4/5 | 11/5 | 18/5 | 25/5 | 1/6 | 8/6 |
| 2003 2031 2059 | 11/1 | 18/1 | 25/1 | 1/2 | 8/2 | 15/2 | 22/2 | 1/3 | 8/3 | 15/3 | 22/3 | 29/3 | 5/4 | 12/4 | 19/4 | 26/4 | 3/5 | 10/5 | 17/5 | 24/5 | 31/5 | 7/6 |
| 2004 2032 2060 | 10/1 | 17/1 | 24/1 | 31/1 | 7/2 | 14/2 | 21/2 | 28/2 | 6/3 | 13/3 | 20/3 | 27/3 | 3/4 | 10/4 | 17/4 | 24/4 | 1/5 | 8/5 | 15/5 | 22/5 | 29/5 | 5/6 |
| 2005 2033 2061 | 8/1 | 15/1 | 22/1 | 29/1 | 5/2 | 12/2 | 19/2 | 26/2 | 5/3 | 12/3 | 19/3 | 26/3 | 2/4 | 9/4 | 16/4 | 23/4 | 30/4 | 7/5 | 14/5 | 21/5 | 28/5 | 4/6 |
| 2006 2034 | 14/1 | 21/1 | 28/1 | 4/2 | 11/2 | 18/2 | 25/2 | 4/3 | 11/3 | 18/3 | 25/3 | 1/4 | 8/4 | 15/4 | 22/4 | 29/4 | 6/5 | 13/5 | 20/5 | 27/5 | 3/6 | 10/6 |
| 2007 2035 | 13/1 | 20/1 | 27/1 | 3/2 | 10/2 | 17/2 | 24/2 | 3/3 | 10/3 | 17/3 | 24/3 | 31/3 | 7/4 | 14/4 | 21/4 | 28/4 | 5/5 | 12/5 | 19/5 | 26/5 | 2/6 | 9/6 |
| 2008 2036 | 12/1 | 19/1 | 26/1 | 2/2 | 9/2 | 16/2 | 23/2 | 1/3 | 8/3 | 15/3 | 22/3 | 29/3 | 5/4 | 12/4 | 19/4 | 26/4 | 3/5 | 10/5 | 17/5 | 24/5 | 31/5 | 7/6 |

| 24 | 25 | 26 | 27 | 28 | 29 | 30 | 31 | 32 | 33 | 34 | 35 | 36 | 37 | 38 | 39 | 40 | 41 | 42 | 43 | 44 | 45 | 46 | 47 | 48 | 49 | 51 | 52 |
|---|---|---|---|---|---|---|---|---|---|---|---|---|---|---|---|---|---|---|---|---|---|---|---|---|---|---|---|
| 13/6 | 20/6 | 27/6 | 4/7 | 11/7 | 18/7 | 25/7 | 1/8 | 8/8 | 15/8 | 22/8 | 29/8 | 5/9 | 12/9 | 19/9 | 26/9 | 3/10 | 10/10 | 17/10 | 24/10 | 31/10 | 7/11 | 14/11 | 21/11 | 28/11 | 5/12 | 22/12 | 29/12 |
| 12/6 | 19/6 | 26/6 | 3/7 | 10/7 | 17/7 | 24/7 | 31/7 | 7/8 | 14/8 | 21/8 | 28/8 | 4/9 | 11/9 | 18/9 | 25/9 | 2/10 | 9/10 | 16/10 | 23/10 | 30/10 | 6/11 | 13/11 | 20/11 | 27/11 | 4/12 | 22/12 | 29/12 |
| 11/6 | 18/6 | 25/6 | 2/7 | 9/7 | 16/7 | 23/7 | 30/7 | 6/8 | 13/8 | 20/8 | 27/8 | 3/9 | 10/9 | 17/9 | 24/9 | 1/10 | 8/10 | 15/10 | 22/10 | 29/10 | 5/11 | 12/11 | 19/11 | 26/11 | 3/12 | 22/12 | 29/12 |
| 16/6 | 23/6 | 30/6 | 7/7 | 14/7 | 21/7 | 28/7 | 4/8 | 11/8 | 18/8 | 25/8 | 1/9 | 8/9 | 15/9 | 22/9 | 29/9 | 6/10 | 13/10 | 20/10 | 27/10 | 3/11 | 10/11 | 17/11 | 24/11 | 1/12 | 8/12 | 22/12 | 29/12 |
| 15/6 | 22/6 | 29/6 | 6/7 | 13/7 | 20/7 | 27/7 | 3/8 | 10/8 | 17/8 | 24/8 | 31/8 | 7/9 | 14/9 | 21/9 | 28/9 | 5/10 | 12/10 | 19/10 | 26/10 | 2/11 | 9/11 | 16/11 | 23/11 | 30/11 | 7/12 | 22/12 | 29/12 |
| 14/6 | 21/6 | 28/6 | 5/7 | 12/7 | 19/7 | 26/7 | 2/8 | 9/8 | 16/8 | 23/8 | 30/8 | 6/9 | 13/9 | 20/9 | 27/9 | 4/10 | 11/10 | 18/10 | 25/10 | 1/11 | 8/11 | 15/11 | 22/11 | 29/11 | 6/12 | 22/12 | 29/12 |
| 13/6 | 20/6 | 27/6 | 4/7 | 11/7 | 18/7 | 25/7 | 1/8 | 8/8 | 15/8 | 22/8 | 29/8 | 5/9 | 12/9 | 19/9 | 26/9 | 3/10 | 10/10 | 17/10 | 24/10 | 31/10 | 7/11 | 14/11 | 21/11 | 28/11 | 5/12 | 22/12 | 29/12 |
| 11/6 | 18/6 | 25/6 | 2/7 | 9/7 | 16/7 | 23/7 | 30/7 | 6/8 | 13/8 | 20/8 | 27/8 | 3/9 | 10/9 | 17/9 | 24/9 | 1/10 | 8/10 | 15/10 | 22/10 | 29/10 | 5/11 | 12/11 | 19/11 | 26/11 | 3/12 | 22/12 | 29/12 |
| 17/6 | 24/6 | 1/7 | 8/7 | 15/7 | 22/7 | 29/7 | 5/8 | 12/8 | 19/8 | 26/8 | 2/9 | 9/9 | 16/9 | 23/9 | 30/9 | 7/10 | 14/10 | 21/10 | 28/10 | 4/11 | 11/11 | 18/11 | 25/11 | 2/12 | 9/12 | 22/12 | 29/12 |
| 16/6 | 23/6 | 30/6 | 7/7 | 14/7 | 21/7 | 28/7 | 4/8 | 11/8 | 18/8 | 25/8 | 1/9 | 8/9 | 15/9 | 22/9 | 29/9 | 6/10 | 13/10 | 20/10 | 27/10 | 3/11 | 10/11 | 17/11 | 24/11 | 1/12 | 8/12 | 22/12 | 29/12 |
| 15/6 | 22/6 | 29/6 | 6/7 | 13/7 | 20/7 | 27/7 | 3/8 | 10/8 | 17/8 | 24/8 | 31/8 | 7/9 | 14/9 | 21/9 | 28/9 | 5/10 | 12/10 | 19/10 | 26/10 | 2/11 | 9/11 | 16/11 | 23/11 | 30/11 | 7/12 | 22/12 | 29/12 |
| 13/6 | 20/6 | 27/6 | 4/7 | 11/7 | 18/7 | 25/7 | 1/8 | 8/8 | 15/8 | 22/8 | 29/8 | 5/9 | 12/9 | 19/9 | 26/9 | 3/10 | 10/10 | 17/10 | 24/10 | 31/10 | 7/11 | 14/11 | 21/11 | 28/11 | 5/12 | 22/12 | 29/12 |
| 12/6 | 19/6 | 26/6 | 3/7 | 10/7 | 17/7 | 24/7 | 31/7 | 7/8 | 14/8 | 21/8 | 28/8 | 4/9 | 11/9 | 18/9 | 25/9 | 2/10 | 9/10 | 16/10 | 23/10 | 30/10 | 6/11 | 13/11 | 20/11 | 27/11 | 4/12 | 22/12 | 29/12 |
| 11/6 | 18/6 | 25/6 | 2/7 | 9/7 | 16/7 | 23/7 | 30/7 | 6/8 | 13/8 | 20/8 | 27/8 | 3/9 | 10/9 | 17/9 | 24/9 | 1/10 | 8/10 | 15/10 | 22/10 | 29/10 | 5/11 | 12/11 | 19/11 | 26/11 | 3/12 | 22/12 | 29/12 |
| 17/6 | 24/6 | 1/7 | 8/7 | 15/7 | 22/7 | 29/7 | 5/8 | 12/8 | 19/8 | 26/8 | 2/9 | 9/9 | 16/9 | 23/9 | 30/9 | 7/10 | 14/10 | 21/10 | 28/10 | 4/11 | 11/11 | 18/11 | 25/11 | 2/12 | 9/12 | 22/12 | 29/12 |
| 15/6 | 22/6 | 29/6 | 6/7 | 13/7 | 20/7 | 27/7 | 3/8 | 10/8 | 17/8 | 24/8 | 31/8 | 7/9 | 14/9 | 21/9 | 28/9 | 5/10 | 12/10 | 19/10 | 26/10 | 2/11 | 9/11 | 16/11 | 23/11 | 30/11 | 7/12 | 22/12 | 29/12 |
| 14/6 | 21/6 | 28/6 | 5/7 | 12/7 | 19/7 | 26/7 | 2/8 | 9/8 | 16/8 | 23/8 | 30/8 | 6/9 | 13/9 | 20/9 | 27/9 | 4/10 | 11/10 | 18/10 | 25/10 | 1/11 | 8/11 | 15/11 | 22/11 | 29/11 | 6/12 | 22/12 | 29/12 |
| 13/6 | 20/6 | 27/6 | 4/7 | 11/7 | 18/7 | 25/7 | 1/8 | 8/8 | 15/8 | 22/8 | 29/8 | 5/9 | 12/9 | 19/9 | 26/9 | 3/10 | 10/10 | 17/10 | 24/10 | 31/10 | 7/11 | 14/11 | 21/11 | 28/11 | 5/12 | 22/12 | 29/12 |
| 12/6 | 19/6 | 26/6 | 3/7 | 10/7 | 17/7 | 24/7 | 31/7 | 7/8 | 14/8 | 21/8 | 28/8 | 4/9 | 11/9 | 18/9 | 25/9 | 2/10 | 9/10 | 16/10 | 23/10 | 30/10 | 6/11 | 13/11 | 20/11 | 27/11 | 4/12 | 22/12 | 29/12 |
| 10/6 | 17/6 | 24/6 | 1/7 | 8/7 | 15/7 | 22/7 | 29/7 | 5/8 | 12/8 | 19/8 | 26/8 | 2/9 | 9/9 | 16/9 | 23/9 | 30/9 | 7/10 | 14/10 | 21/10 | 28/10 | 4/11 | 11/11 | 18/11 | 25/11 | 2/12 | 22/12 | 29/12 |
| 16/6 | 23/6 | 30/6 | 7/7 | 14/7 | 21/7 | 28/7 | 4/8 | 11/8 | 18/8 | 25/8 | 1/9 | 8/9 | 15/9 | 22/9 | 29/9 | 6/10 | 13/10 | 20/10 | 27/10 | 3/11 | 10/11 | 17/11 | 24/11 | 1/12 | 8/12 | 22/12 | 29/12 |
| 15/6 | 22/6 | 29/6 | 6/7 | 13/7 | 20/7 | 27/7 | 3/8 | 10/8 | 17/8 | 24/8 | 31/8 | 7/9 | 14/9 | 21/9 | 28/9 | 5/10 | 12/10 | 19/10 | 26/10 | 2/11 | 9/11 | 16/11 | 23/11 | 30/11 | 7/12 | 22/12 | 29/12 |
| 14/6 | 21/6 | 28/6 | 5/7 | 12/7 | 19/7 | 26/7 | 2/8 | 9/8 | 16/8 | 23/8 | 30/8 | 6/9 | 13/9 | 20/9 | 27/9 | 4/10 | 11/10 | 18/10 | 25/10 | 1/11 | 8/11 | 15/11 | 22/11 | 29/11 | 6/12 | 22/12 | 29/12 |
| 12/6 | 19/6 | 26/6 | 3/7 | 10/7 | 17/7 | 24/7 | 31/7 | 7/8 | 14/8 | 21/8 | 28/8 | 4/9 | 11/9 | 18/9 | 25/9 | 2/10 | 9/10 | 16/10 | 23/10 | 30/10 | 6/11 | 13/11 | 20/11 | 27/11 | 4/12 | 22/12 | 29/12 |
| 11/6 | 18/6 | 25/6 | 2/7 | 9/7 | 16/7 | 23/7 | 30/7 | 6/8 | 13/8 | 20/8 | 27/8 | 3/9 | 10/9 | 17/9 | 24/9 | 1/10 | 8/10 | 15/10 | 22/10 | 29/10 | 5/11 | 12/11 | 19/11 | 26/11 | 3/12 | 22/12 | 29/12 |
| 17/6 | 24/6 | 1/7 | 8/7 | 15/7 | 22/7 | 29/7 | 5/8 | 12/8 | 19/8 | 26/8 | 2/9 | 9/9 | 16/9 | 23/9 | 30/9 | 7/10 | 14/10 | 21/10 | 28/10 | 4/11 | 11/11 | 18/11 | 25/11 | 2/12 | 9/12 | 22/12 | 29/12 |
| 16/6 | 23/6 | 30/6 | 7/7 | 14/7 | 21/7 | 28/7 | 4/8 | 11/8 | 18/8 | 25/8 | 1/9 | 8/9 | 15/9 | 22/9 | 29/9 | 6/10 | 13/10 | 20/10 | 27/10 | 3/11 | 10/11 | 17/11 | 24/11 | 1/12 | 8/12 | 22/12 | 29/12 |
| 14/6 | 21/6 | 28/6 | 5/7 | 12/7 | 19/7 | 26/7 | 2/8 | 9/8 | 16/8 | 23/8 | 30/8 | 6/9 | 13/9 | 20/9 | 27/9 | 4/10 | 11/10 | 18/10 | 25/10 | 1/11 | 8/11 | 15/11 | 22/11 | 29/11 | 6/12 | 22/12 | 29/12 |

written request by the Committee for him to do so. Any such cancellation or suspension shall be ratified by the Members of the Club at the general meeting next following. For the avoidance of doubt any dispute or difference howsoever arising out of this sub-clause may be the subject of a reference to arbitration in accordance with Clause 21 below but cancellation or suspension may come into immediate effect notwithstanding that such a reference has been made.

(e) To enter into all contracts and agreements which the Committee may deem necessary or desirable in connection with the management of the Club and to apply the funds of the Club in payment of the expenses of management, administration and running of the Club as detailed in Clause 12 except in so far as these powers may have been delegated to the Management Company under the Management Agreement.

(f) To appoint a chartered accountant being a member of the Institute of Chartered Accountants in England and Wales or other appropriate person as auditor to audit the accounts of the Club annually and to appoint lawyers and other professional advisers.

(g) To agree the remuneration of the auditors, lawyers and any other professional advisers from time to time appointed or instructed by or on behalf of the Club and (in the event of failure to agree the remuneration of the Trustee between the Founder Members and the Trustee) to agree the annual remuneration of the Trustee.

(h) To bring, defend, agree to be joined, settle or compromise any proceedings or claims of any kind in relation to the affairs of the Club or the obligations of the Members hereunder or under the Deed of Trust referred to in Clause 7 and in the event of any such proceedings or claims relating to some only of the Members to bring, defend, agree to be joined, settle or compromise the same on behalf of such Members at their respective costs.

(i) In the event of the determination of the appointment of the initial Trustee or of any Trustee subsequently appointed by or on behalf of the Club in accordance with this sub-clause to appoint another body or person as Trustee of the property of the Club.

11.6 The Committee shall maintain or cause to be maintained a register of names and current addresses of Members of the Club indicating when they became Members and when, if appropriate, they ceased to be Members.

11.7 Without prejudice to the generality of the provisions of Clause 11.5(d) hereof in the event of the cancellation of any person's Membership thereunder, the Committee shall use its best endeavours to cause to be transferred that person's Membership Certificate(s) and each Member hereby irrevocably agrees to appoint the Committee as attorney for that purpose and the Committee shall immediately thereafter account for the proceeds thereof to the former member after deduction of reasonable commissions, fees or any other expenses reasonably incurred in connection with the said transfer and all arrears of contributions or other payments or amounts due under the terms of this Constitution owing up to and including the date of transfer.

## 12 Member's liability for payment of management expenses etc

12.1 The Members of the Club shall contribute in accordance with the terms of the Management Agreement to all reasonable costs incurred by the Club including and without prejudice to the generality of the foregoing the reasonable cost of the following:

(a) Maintenance, decoration, cleansing, and (where necessary) repair of the Apartments, services and facilities provided by the Club for the benefit of the Members whether exclusive or in common with others entitled thereto.

(b) Maintenance, repair and (when necessary) replacement of furniture, equipment, utensils, provisions, furnishings, fittings and fixtures in or about or pertaining to the Apartments.

(c) Insurance of the Apartments and the contents thereof for the full reinstatement cost and any other insurance whether or not relating to the Apartments which the Committee or the Company shall consider necessary or appropriate, or for the benefit of the Members including, at the discretion of the Company and/or the Committee and without prejudice to the generality of the foregoing any insurances recommended by the Trustee.

(d) The full amount of the rent payable by the Company or the Management Company (as the case may be) to the Member or Members of the Club in the event of the Company or the Management Company renting weekly periods from an Owner or Owners in order to facilitate maintenance, repair or reconstruction works, such rent to be calculated at the full market rate for the time being in force.

(e) All outgoings incurred in respect of the Apartments including rates, contributions to the community of property owners to which the Apartments belong and any income or other taxes or other charges or impositions whether of an annual or recurring nature or otherwise.

(f) All work and acts which are required to be done to comply with any statutory provisions or the directions or notices of any governmental, local or public authority.

(g) Any reasonable management charges or any other charges whatsoever which may be incurred in the management and preservation of the value of the Club's property and the running of the Club's affairs and any value added tax or like tax or imposition payable in respect of the same (whether under the laws of [                    ] or otherwise).

(h) The establishment and maintenance of a sinking fund for the replacement of capital items of the Club's property.

(i) The establishment and maintenance of any reserve fund requested by the Trustee in accordance with Clause 13 of the Deed of Trust.

(j) The fees and expenses of the Trustee and all other costs, expenses or payments to the Trustee under the Deed of Trust and the fees and expenses of the auditor, lawyers and other professional advisers hereinbefore referred to.

(k) Membership fees of any golf, tennis or other club and/or any trade or professional association pursuant to any arrangements made by the Founder Members or the Committee.

12.2 Each Member shall, if so required by the Management Company, permit the Management Company or, if so required, the Trustee on behalf of the Management Company to collect the Management Charge by means of a direct debit from the Member's bank to the Management Company's bank or as the case may be to the Trustee's bank and for that purpose on demand from the Management Company or the Trustee to supply full details of the Member's bank account and sign and deliver to the Management Company or as the case may be Trustee any necessary authorisation or mandates to the Member's bank.

12.3 Save in so far as the same may have been delegated by the Management Agreement hereinbefore referred to, the Committee shall have sole discretion in deciding what monies should be spent for any of the foregoing purposes and when the same shall be expended.


## 13 Club's powers

The Club shall have the power:
(a) to borrow money,

(b) to grant securities and mortgages over its property,

(c) to purchase, lease or otherwise acquire additional property, and

(d) to sell, lease, grant easements over or otherwise dispose of or deal with its property or any rights over its property.

PROVIDED THAT all the foregoing powers shall be exercisable only upon a decision by not less than a two-thirds majority of votes cast at a general meeting and (within the period of five years from the date of this Constitution) shall not in any event be exercisable without the prior written consent of the Company and the Management Company in each and every case.

## 14 Further obligations of members

The Members of the Club shall automatically be bound by the terms and provisions of the Deed of Trust upon election to membership and such Members shall by the acceptance of this Constitution also be deemed to have accepted the obligations imposed on the Club and the Members by the provisions of the Deed of Trust. Each Member of the Club shall also be subject to the following obligations (and to the intent that such obligations shall continue to bind his estate after his death and until such time as his Membership Certificate shall be transferred to a new or other Member of the Club and notwithstanding that his personal representatives may not themselves be Members):

14.1 To vacate the Apartment to which his Membership Certificate relates at the expiration of the appropriate period of time in each year.

14.2 At all times to observe the regulations relating to the occupation of the Apartments a copy whereof is annexed to this Constitution and all variations, additions and amendments thereto made by the Committee.

14.3 To keep and maintain the interior of the Apartment and all of its contents to which his Membership Certificate relates in a good and tenantable state and condition during the period of his occupancy and to pay or indemnify the Club against any damage, deterioration or dilapidation (over and above fair wear and tear and damage or destruction by fire or any other risk insured against which may have taken place during the period of his occupancy) as to which the Committee or (during such time as the administration of the Club affairs may be delegated to it) the Management Company shall be the sole judge.

14.4 In the event of any repair or maintenance work to be carried out to the Apartment or its contents during the period of a Member's occupancy of the Apartment to allow access on reasonable notice (except in the case of emergency) to necessary workmen and others to enable such work to be carried out provided that any such work will be carried out with all due diligence and speed and will not, save in so far as is reasonable, interfere with Members' enjoyment of their occupation of the Apartments.

14.5 Not in any way to make alterations to the Apartments to which his Certificate relates or the contents thereof.

14.6 To pay for all telephone calls made and for electricity consumed during his occupation of the Apartment. The Management Company may demand a reasonable deposit against such charges and where an Apartment is not metered for electricity may charge on the basis of estimated consumption or may aggregate the same in the management charge.

14.7 To notify the Committee and the Management Company forthwith of any change in his permanent address.

14.8 To pay within one month of the same being demanded the appropriate portion of the cost referred to in Clause 12 hereof incurred by the Club in any year.

14.9 Not to do anything which would make void or voidable the insurance of the Apartment and its contents or any other insurance for the time being in force and relating to the Apartments or which may operate to increase the premium payable in respect of any such insurance and to indemnify the Club and the Trustee against any increased or additional premium which by reason of any such act or default may be required for effecting or keeping up any such insurance and in the event of the Apartment or any other property as aforesaid or any part thereof being damaged or destroyed by any insured risks and the insurance money being wholly or partially irrecoverable by reason solely or in part of any act or default of such Member then and in every such case to pay forthwith to the Club or the Trustee or as directed by either of them (or in the case of a conflict in directions, by the Trustee) the whole or as the case may require a fair proportion to be conclusively determined by a surveyor to be appointed by the Club of the cost of rebuilding and reinstatement of the same as the case may be together with the whole or such portion as aforesaid of the fees of such surveyor.

14.10 During such times as the administration of the affairs of the Club shall be delegated to the said Management Company to pay the Management Company at the times provided by the Management Agreement his due proportion of the Management Charge (including where appropriate the Advance Management Charge) provided for by the Management Agreement and further to pay upon demand any charge falling due under sub-paragraphs 3,6,8 and/or 9 of this Clause. In the event of any of the said sums not being paid by the due date the Committee or the Management Company as the case may be shall be entitled to refuse the Member in question or any other person in his place, occupation of the Apartment to which his Membership Certificate relates until all arrears have been discharged.

14.11 If any Member shall wish to sublet or grant rights of occupation of the Apartment to which his Membership Certificate relates for money or money's worth he shall give prior notice to the Management Company or to such other person as the Owning Company may from time to time direct and any such subletting shall thereafter be undertaken in the name of the relevant Owning Company and the income derived from any such subletting or grant of rights of occupation shall be paid direct to the Management Company or any such other person as aforesaid. The Management Company (or such other person as aforesaid) shall thereafter account to the Member for the income after deduction of any tax which may be levied by the appropriate authorities as a result thereof.

14.12 No Member shall make use of the register of the Members of the Club for any purpose other than Club purposes and for the distribution to fellow Members of the Club of any communication pertaining exclusively to the Club and its administration and in particular no Member shall distribute upon the basis of the register any advertising or promotional material unrelated to Club purposes or make the register available to any third party intending to so distribute.

## 15 Transfer of Membership Certificates

15.1 Any Member may subject to the provisions hereof bequeath or agree to sell or otherwise transfer the rights to which he is entitled pursuant to a Membership Certificate in favour of a third party subject to such third party becoming a Member of the Club and subject to the discharge of the Member's liabilities hereunder up to the date of transfer. In the event of the death or bankruptcy of any Member (or the winding up of a Member being a corporation) his personal representatives, trustee in bankruptcy or liquidator as the case may be may agree to sell such rights to a third party or to vest the same in a beneficiary subject to the third party or beneficiary becoming a Member of the Club.

15.2 In the event of a Member agreeing to sell or otherwise dispose of the rights vested in him pursuant to his Membership Certificate he or his personal representatives, trustee in bankruptcy or liquidator as the case may be shall deliver the relevant Membership Certificate to the Committee or the Management Company or their lawyers with the Form of Surrender and Request endorsed thereon duly executed by such Member, personal representatives, trustee in bankruptcy or liquidator (and stamped if necessary) and by the person to whom such rights are to be transferred or vested in and, upon production of satisfactory evidence of the transfer vesting or other devolution of such membership rights, and upon payment of the fee hereinafter mentioned, the Committee or the Management Company shall within 28 days of such evidence being produced issue a new Membership Certificate in the name of the new Member whose admission shall be ratified at the next following general meeting of the Club. The register of Members of the Club shall be duly completed to register such transfer.

15.3  A reasonable fee may be charged for the registration of the transfer which fee may be revised by the Committee or the Management Company from time to time. A Member may also let the rights of occupation of the Apartment to which his Certificate relates for the whole or a part of the period to which his Certificate relates subject to:

(a) the provisions of Clause 14.11 hereof and

(b) any requisite consent from the appropriate authorities being previously obtained (and the Trustee in no way warrants that any such consent will be forthcoming) but provided that the Member will in any event during the period of such let remain the holder of the Certificate and be primarily responsible for all the obligations incumbent on the holder of the Certificate.

## 16  General meetings of the Club

16.1  The annual general meeting of the Club shall be held at such place in [                    ] or elsewhere as the Committee shall decide on such a date in each year as shall be determined but not so as to cause a period of fifteen months to elapse between each annual general meeting by the Committee (subject in the case of the first such meeting to Clause 11 hereof) and shall be convened by notice sent to all Members not less than 28 days before the date of the meeting together with the Agenda of the business to be conducted at such meeting.

16.2  The Committee may and shall upon a request in writing from the holders of not less than ten per cent in number of the Membership Certificates call a special general meeting of the Club to be convened and held in the manner prescribed for annual general meetings save that 14 days' notice only shall be necessary.

16.3  Notices of special and annual general meetings shall contain copies of the agenda for such meetings and the exact wording of any resolution to be voted upon at the meeting and shall include a form of voting proxy for Members unable to attend. No business other than that specified in the notices of meeting and documents therewith shall be considered at the meeting.

16.4  At every general meeting the Chairman of the Committee (and in his absence a Chairman appointed by a majority of those present at the meeting) shall preside. Each Member shall be entitled to one vote for each Membership Certificate held and voting rights shall be exercised by way of a poll and not by a show of hands. Members will be entitled to appoint a proxy to vote in their stead. A proxy need not be a Member of the Club. At all meetings in the case of an equality of votes the Chairman shall have the casting vote. Any resolution to be proposed otherwise than by the Committee at any annual or special general meetings of the Club shall be submitted in writing to the Committee not less than 21 days before the date of the meeting if it is an annual general meeting or 14 days if it is a special general meeting and shall be signed by the proposer and the seconder. Any resolution involving a change in the Constitution shall require not less than a three-quarters majority of all votes cast. At all general meetings of the

Club the quorum shall be ten Members present in person or by proxy. Minutes of all general meetings will be prepared by the Committee and circulated to all Members of the Club within six weeks of the general meeting.

16.5 The instruments appointing a proxy shall be in writing under the hand of the appointor or his attorney duly authorised in writing or if such appointor is a corporation under its common seal, if any, and if none, then under the hand of some officer duly authorised in that behalf. The instrument appointing a proxy and power of attorney or other authority, if any, under which it is signed or a certified or office copy thereof shall be deposited at the offices of the Club not less than 48 hours before the time appointed for holding the meeting or adjourned meeting at which the person named in the instrument proposes to vote and in default the instrument of proxy shall not be treated as valid. No instrument appointing a proxy shall be valid after the expiry of 12 months from its date.

16.6 Voting at all meetings of the Members including annual general meetings and special general meetings shall be on the basis of the number of Membership Certificates held whether by Founder Members or otherwise, subject to Clause 8.3 hereof. Where a Membership Certificate is owned jointly the vote of the first named joint owner on the Membership Certificate only shall be counted.

16.7 A resolution in writing signed by all the Members of the Club who would be entitled to receive notice of and attend and vote at a general meeting of the Club at which such resolution was to be proposed or by their duly appointed attorney, shall be valid and effectual as if it had been passed at a general meeting of the Club duly convened and held. Any such resolution may consist of several documents in the like form each signed by one or more of the Members or their attorneys and signature in the case of a body corporate which is a Member shall be sufficient if made by a director thereof or its duly appointed representative.

## 17  Audit

17.1 The financial year of the Club shall end on 31 December in each year or on such other date as the Committee may decide. The Committee or the Management Company as the case may be shall cause proper books of account to be kept with regard to:

(a) all sums of money received and expended by the Club and the matter in respect of which such receipts and expenditure take place;

(b) the assets and liabilities of the Club provided that while the First Option under the Management Agreement is in operation accounts need not be kept in respect of matters pertaining exclusively to the First Option.

17.2 Unless all the income and expenditure of the Club in the preceding year (or since the inception of the Club) falls to be dealt with under the First Option referred to in the Management Agreement the Committee shall at the annual general meeting in every year lay before the Club an audited income and expenditure account for the period since the last preceding account (or in the case of the first account since the inception of the Club) together with an audited balance sheet made up as at the same date unless all income and expenditure of the Club falls to be dealt with under the First Option. Every such balance sheet shall be accompanied by proper reports of the Committee and the auditor and copies of such account balance sheets and reports shall not less than 21 clear days before the meeting be sent to all Members at their respective addresses.

## 18  Termination provisions

18.1 The Club shall continue in existence until (a) the [DATE] or (b) a resolution to determine the Club is passed at a general meeting of the Club by not less than a three-quarters majority of all votes cast by or on behalf of ordinary Membership Certificate holders in accordance with the provisions of Clause 16 of the Constitution (whichever is the sooner). Upon termination the Club shall then be wound up and its assets dealt with in accordance with the provisions of this Clause.

18.2 The Trustee shall as soon as practicable cause the sale of the relevant Apartments by the Owning Companies, or, at its sole discretion, cause the sale of the Owning Companies to which the relevant Apartments relate, on the open market.

18.3 The sums realised pursuant to Clause 18.2 (after deduction of all costs and expenses incurred by the Trustee) together with any other funds and unexpended Management Charge apportioned at the sole discretion of the Management Company as relating to the Apartments shall be distributed first in discharge of all liabilities in accordance with the provisions of any Trust Deed for the time being in force and secondly in discharge of all other debts and liabilities of the Club, apportioned at the sole discretion of the Trustee to the respective Apartments.

18.4 The net assets available for distribution after the foregoing provisions of this clause have been complied with (hereinafter called 'the net assets') shall be notionally apportioned to each of the Apartments comprising the property of the Club at the termination of the Club in proportion to the open market value of each Apartment at the termination of the Club.

18.5 The amount of the net assets apportioned to each Apartment aforesaid shall, for the purpose of ascertaining the amount thereof to be distributed to each member, be divided into 51 units of value (each such unit being hereafter referred to as a 'unit of value') and there shall be distributed (subject to the provisions of sub-clause 15.3 of the Deed of Trust) to each Membership Certificate holder one unit of value in respect of each of the said weekly periods to which such Member (or as the case may be Founder Member) is entitled.

## 19 Use of Membership Certificates as security

19.1 Any Member may mortgage, pledge or assign his Membership Certificate as security for any loan or advance (but neither the Founder Members nor the Trustee warrants that such loans are or shall be available) and in such event shall:
(a) notify the Management Company with the name and address of the lender ('the lender') in the form from time to time required by the Management Company and
(b) deposit with the Trustee his Membership Certificate together with a true copy of the mortgage pledge or loan agreement together with an acknowledgment by the Management Company of the notice referred to in (a) above, together with an authority from the Member in the form from time to time prescribed by the Trustee and
(c) pay to the Trustee the fee from time to time prescribed by the Trustee.

19.2 In the event of the Trustee subsequently receiving a request in writing (a 'transfer request') from the lender to that effect, the Trustee shall thereupon transfer the Membership Certificate as directed by the lender.

19.3 Until receipt by the Trustee of a transfer request, the Member shall be entitled to and shall be subject to all the rights and obligations appurtenant to the Membership Certificate save that the Member shall not be entitled to assign or transfer the Membership Certificate without first providing to the Trustee the consent in writing of the lender in the form from time to time prescribed by the Trustee.

19.4 The Trustee, the Founder Members, the Management Company and the Club are hereby jointly and severally conclusively indemnified by the Member and as a separate indemnity by the lender from and against any costs claims and demands whatsoever arising out of compliance with a transfer request and without prejudice to the generality of the foregoing shall not in any way be concerned with any claims which the

Member may have against the lender or which the lender may have against the Member.

19.5 The Trustee may require as a condition of effecting a transfer of a Membership Certificate that, prior to service of a transfer request, the lender shall procure any necessary consent from the appropriate authorities, and shall lodge with the Trustee such sum as the Trustee may require to cover the actual or contingent liability (if any) of the Trustee or the Owning Company in respect of any charge to taxation in relation to the transfer, together with sums sufficient to cover the costs of ascertaining and paying such tax.

19.6 The Trustee is hereby empowered to make such regulations and impose such conditions and prescribe such forms as the Trustee shall in its absolute discretion think fit in connection with the operation of the provisions of this Clause.

## 20 Notices

20.1 A notice may be given to any Member by sending it by post to the Member's address as appearing in the register. Any notice so sent by post shall be deemed to have been given on the second day following that on which the letter containing the same is posted, and in proving such service it shall be sufficient to prove that such letter was properly addressed, stamped and posted.

20.2 Service of a notice or document on any one of several joint Members shall be deemed effective service on the other joint Members.

20.3 Any notice or document sent by post or left at the address of a Member appearing in the register in pursuance of these presents shall, notwithstanding that such Member be then dead or bankrupt and whether or not the Club or the Management Company has notice of his death or bankruptcy, be deemed to have been duly served and such service shall be deemed a sufficient service on all persons in any way interested in or entitled in relation to any Membership Certificate in relation to which the Member was entitled.

20.4 The accidental omission to give notice of a meeting to or the non-receipt of notice of a meeting by any person entitled to receive notice shall not invalidate the proceedings of that meeting and accidental omission shall include an omission which was deliberate but which arose out of or was connected with an honest but mistaken view of law or fact by any officer of the Management Company or the Club.

## 21 Miscellaneous

Any dispute or difference arising out of this Constitution shall be referred to the decision of a single arbitrator to be agreed between the parties or in default of agreement to be appointed upon the application of either party by the Trustee.

## 22 Proper law

This Constitution shall be governed and construed in accordance with the laws of [                    ] and the rights of all persons hereunder and the construction and the effect of each and every one of the provisions hereof shall be subject to and construed in accordance with [                    ] law.

IN WITNESS WHEREOF the Parties hereto have caused their Common Seals to be hereunto affixed this            day of                    [        ]

## Schedule 1 (Form of Appendix)

### Edition:

This is the Appendix referred to in the Constitution of the XYZ Club ('the Constitution') a copy of which is annexed hereto.

This Appendix was revised on [DATE].

We [NAME OF TRUSTEE] HEREBY CERTIFY that the companies listed in paragraph 1 of this Appendix are Owning Companies as defined by the Constitution and are the owners of the Apartments set out opposite their respective names in paragraph 2 of this Appendix and that the weekly period commencement and termination day in respect of each Apartment is that day of the week set opposite its respective name and identity in Paragraph 3 of this Appendix.

| **Paragraph 1** | **Paragraph 2** | **Paragraph 3** |
|---|---|---|
| (Owning Company) | (Apartments) | (Commencement/ Termination Day) |

Executed etc

### Regulations

(see Clause 14.2)

1 Not to use any Apartment forming part of the property of the Club nor permit the same to be used for any purpose whatsoever other than as a private holiday home in the occupation of no more than the maximum number of persons from time to time permitted by the Club nor for any purpose from which a nuisance can arise to other Members or their permitted occupiers or any owner occupier of adjoining land nor for any illegal or immoral purpose whatsoever nor for the purpose of any trade, business, profession or manufacture.

2 No windows belonging to any Apartment shall be stopped-up, darkened or obstructed otherwise than by use of the curtain material or internal blinds provided by the Club and no washing, clothes or other articles shall be hung or exposed anywhere outside any Apartment or in any position visible from outside the building of which any Apartment forms part.

3 Not to throw dirt, rubbish, rags, oil or any deleterious material or other refuse or permit the same to be thrown into the sinks, baths, lavatories and conduits of any Apartment.

4 No music or singing whether by instrument or voices, wireless, gramophone, television or other means shall be allowed in any Apartment so as to cause nuisance or annoyance to any Member or permitted occupier of adjoining land and in particular so as not to be audible outside any Apartment between the hours of 11.30 pm and 9.00 am.

5 No animal or bird shall be brought into or kept in any Apartment.

6 To comply with all arrangements from time to time made by the Club in relation to the disposal of refuse from any Apartment and not to shake, beat, permit to be shaken or beaten any carpets, dusters or other objects from the windows or doors of any Apartment and at no time to throw dirt, rubbish, rags, food or any other material or substance whatsoever out of the windows or doors of any Apartment.

7 To comply at all times with the provisions of the regulations governing the community of owners to which the Apartments belong, copies of which are available from the Management Company on request.

8 Not to store or allow to remain in any Apartment any inflammable or explosive substance.

# XYZ CLUB

## MEMBERSHIP CERTIFICATE

*Certificate No*

XYZ CLUB SALES LIMITED whose registered office is at [ADDRESS] and XYZ CLUB MANAGEMENT LIMITED whose registered office is at [ADDRESS] (together hereinafter referred to as 'the Grantors') as Founder Members of The XYZ Club ('the Club') together with [TRUSTEE COMPANY] who acknowledges membership and in pursuance of the Constitution of the Club HEREBY admit to membership of the Club AND GRANT to the Member whose name and address is stated in paragraph 1 of the Schedule and who has paid to XYZ CLUB SALES LIMITED the appropriate purchase price (receipt whereof is hereby acknowledged) the right to occupy and enjoy the Apartment described in paragraph 2 of the Schedule and all other facilities and amenities of the Club for such Weekly Period or Periods in each calendar year in accordance with and subject to the observance by the Member of the said Constitution and the Trust Deed referred to therein including but without prejudice to the generality of the foregoing the provisions relating to payment of the management charges.

IN WITNESS whereof the Grantors and the Member have executed this Certificate the day and year below written in paragraph 4 of this Schedule

---

1
Member Name _____
       Address _____
              _____
              _____

---

2
Apartment No:                                    Studio/1 bedroomed/
                                                 2 bedroomed/Duplex

---

3
Week(s) No:
Commencement and termination days

---

4
Date of Certificate          SIGNED by the MEMBER(s)
     day of        199

---

THE COMMON SEAL of          THE COMMON SEAL of
XYZ CLUB SALES LIMITED      XYZ CLUB MANAGEMENT LIMITED
was hereunto affixed in the  was hereunto affixed in the
presence of:                 presence of

*Director*                         *Director*

*Secretary*                   *Secretary*

THE COMMON SEAL of
the TRUSTEE
was hereunto affixed in
the presence of:

*Director*

*Secretary*

# XYZ CLUB

## FORM OF SURRENDER AND REQUEST

(Pursuant to Clause 15 of the Constitution of the Club)

I/WE, the within written member(s)

of

being the

of the within written member(s) hereby surrender this Membership Certificate pursuant to Clause 15 of the Constitution of The XYZ Club subject to the issue of the new Membership Certificate in accordance with the Request contained below and hereby agree to use my/our best endeavours at the cost of the person or persons named below to procure that such person or persons is/are admitted to membership of the Club in accordance with the Constitution and pending such admission declare that I/we hold my/our interest as a member(s) of the Club (to the extent that such interest may be so held) upon trust for such person or persons and I/we

(Purchaser's Name)

of

hereby request the issue of a new Membership Certificate to me/us in respect of the weekly periods within mentioned and undertake that with effect from the date mentioned below I/we shall observe and perform all the obligations of membership of the XYZ Club pursuant to the said Constitution.

DATED THE          day of                    199
SIGNED by

}

(Vendor)

SIGNED by

}

(Purchaser)

**Note**

Before paying the Purchase Price, Purchasers are advised to satisfy themselves that the management charge has been paid up to date and that the certificate is still in force. This form should be accompanied by the Transfer Fee and if the person selling is not the registered member, satisfactory evidence of due representation.

THE COMMON SEAL of
XYZ CLUB SALES LIMITED
was hereunto affixed in the
presence of:

THE COMMON SEAL of
XYZ CLUB MANAGEMENT LIMITED
was hereunto affixed in the
presence of

*Director*

*Director*

*Secretary*

*Secretary*

# XYZ CLUB

# DEED OF TRUST

THIS DEED OF TRUST is made the               day of               One thousand nine hundred and [                    ] BETWEEN XYZ CLUB SALES LIMITED a Company incorporated in the Isle of Man (hereinafter called 'the Company') whose registered office is at [ADDRESS] and XYZ CLUB MANAGEMENT LIMITED a Company incorporated in the Isle of Man whose registered office is at [ADDRESS] (hereinafter together called 'the Founder Members') of the first part and the TRUSTEE a Company whose offices are at [ADDRESS] (hereinafter called 'the Trustee') of the second part.

WHEREAS :

A. The Founder Members have together formed a club known as The XYZ Club whose object is to secure for its Members the ownership of exclusive rights of occupation of the Apartments (as hereinafter defined) detailed in the Appendix ('the Appendix') to the Constitution of the Club ('the Constitution') for specific periods in each year during the period mentioned in the Constitution (a copy of which is annexed hereto).

B. It is provided in the Constitution that the ownership and control of those Owning Companies mentioned in the Appendix ('the Owning Companies') shall be vested in an independent Trustee upon trust for the Members of the Club from time to time.

C. The ownership and control of the Owning Companies has been allotted or transferred to the Trustee or as the Trustee may direct (all of such Owning Companies together with all other property which may from time to time be transferred to the Trustee by the Company or otherwise to be held for the benefit of the Club upon the trusts of this Deed shall be hereinafter called 'the Property') and the Trustee has agreed to hold the same upon the trusts and terms hereinafter mentioned.

**NOW THEREFORE THIS DEED WITNESSETH AND IT IS HEREBY AGREED** as follows:

1.1 In this Deed except where the context otherwise requires:

(a) 'Club' means the Club currently known as the XYZ Club referred to in Recital (A).

(b) 'Constitution' means the Constitution of the Club from time to time.

(c) 'Apartments' means the Apartment or Apartments referred to in the Appendix at [                    ], Spain aforesaid and any other residential property in [                    ] which may be vested in an Owning Company and 'Apartment' shall be construed accordingly.

(d) 'the Property' means the Owning Companies together with all other property (real or personal) which may from time to time be transferred to or otherwise vested in the Trustee to be held for the benefit of the Members of the Club from time to time upon the trusts of this Deed.

(e) 'Members' means the Members from time to time of the Club including the Founder Members.

(f) 'holding company' and 'subsidiary company' shall have the meanings respectively attributed to them by s 736 of the Companies Act 1985 (UK).

(g) 'associated company' shall have the meaning attributed to it by s 302(1) of the Income and Corporation Taxes Act 1970 (UK).

(h) 'the Committee' means the body of persons appointed under the provisions of the Constitution to manage the business and affairs of the Club in accordance with the Constitution.

(i) 'the Owning Companies' means the company or companies the names of which are set out in the Appendix each being the owners of one or more Apartments, and any other company the ownership and control of which is issued or transferred to the Trustee or its nominee with the agreement of the Founder Members and the Trustee to be held upon the trusts herein declared, and 'Owning Company' shall be construed accordingly.

1.2 Covenants or warranties given and obligations or liabilities otherwise assumed under the provisions of this Deed by two or more persons shall be deemed to be so given and assumed by such persons jointly and severally.

1.3 (a) Where reference is made herein to directions of the Committee of the Club the Trustee shall be entitled to rely on and accept decisions of the Committee which shall be stated by the Chairman of the committee meeting at which the relevant decision was reached to have been so reached in accordance with the relevant rules of the Constitution and without prejudice to the generality of the foregoing the Trustee shall not be concerned to enquire or satisfy itself in any way as to the election of committee members or of the Chairman of the committee meeting or calling of committee meetings or the procedure adopted or the reaching of decisions thereat; and

(b) where reference is made to the decision of the Club the Trustee shall be entitled to accept and rely on resolutions in writing in respect of which it shall have been certified by the Founder Members that the provisions of Clause 16.7 of the Constitution have been fully observed.

2 The Founder Members hereby appoint the Trustee and the Trustee hereby agrees to act as trustee on behalf of the Club and the Members thereof from time to time on the terms set out in this Deed and the general terms and conditions upon which the Trustee acts as a trustee last published before the date hereof which are more particularly set out in Schedule I hereto. The said general terms and conditions shall apply and be incorporated herein and if there shall be any conflict between the same and the other provisions of this Deed then such terms and conditions set out in Schedule I shall *pro tanto* prevail. The Founder Members will procure that the title deeds evidencing the freehold ownership in each of the Apartments and documents relating to any other Property are delivered to the Trustee as soon as reasonably possible and will remain throughout the period of this Deed in the custody of the Trustee.

3 The Trustee shall hold the ownership and control of each respective Owning Company upon trust to secure the rights of occupation in respect of the Apartment or Apartments owned by such Owning Company under and in accordance with and subject to the Constitution and subject thereto upon trust for all Members from time to time of the Club as provided in the Constitution.

PROVIDED ALWAYS:

(a) that the Trustee shall not be bound to concur in or perform any act or acts which in the opinion of the Trustee shall be illegal or shall be inconsistent with the trusts hereby declared or shall constitute a breach of trust or be prejudicial to the interests of the Members (without the consent of the Members) or shall involve the Trustee in any personal liability or in any action which may be improper or disreputable or which may in the opinion of the Trustee constitute a breach of the conditions or covenants affecting the Property or the Apartments and

(b) that notwithstanding any direction of the Committee or the Founder Members the Trustee shall not be obliged to charge or otherwise encumber the Property or any part thereof nor do anything to prejudice the ownership of the Apartments or the Owning Companies.

4.1 The Trustee shall have no responsibility for the rebuilding repair, maintenance, renewal, upkeep, decoration, administration or management of the Apartments or the contents thereof and shall not be liable for any damage or loss or depreciation which may result in any way therein and the Trustee gives no guarantee or warranty with regard to the validity or otherwise of the title to the Apartments.

4.2 The Trustee shall not be bound to concern itself in any way with the management of the Club nor its assets or finances nor with the rights duties or obligations of Members or any other matter to which Members may be subject nor with the replacement or retrieval or renewal of any of the contents, furniture, fittings or fixtures of the Apartments whether the said contents furniture fittings or fixtures be broken, lost, stolen or damaged or otherwise mislaid or misplaced and the Trustee shall bear no liability to the Members in respect of such matters.

4.3 Pursuant to s 3(2) of the Income Tax (Exempt Companies) Act 1984 (Isle of Man) no person resident in the Isle of Man shall at any time have or be entitled to acquire any beneficial interest (as defined by the said section) under this Trust.

*[4.4 To the extent that any Owning Companies are constituted with a share capital no person or body other than the Trustee or its nominee shall be or become entitled to the shares or to any interest therein and the rights or interests of the Members shall not include any rights to or interest in such shares.]

5 The Trustee shall not be required to take any legal or other action whatever in relation to any matter whatsoever concerning the Property unless fully indemnified by the Club or the Founder Members to the reasonable satisfaction of the Trustee for all costs and liabilities likely to be incurred or suffered by the Trustee.

6 The Trustee shall be entitled at the expense of the Club or the Founder Members to obtain legal advice from its solicitors for the time being and/or the opinion of counsel and/or other legal advisers on any matter relating to the Property or in relation to the trust hereby constituted or the exercise of the Trustee's powers or rights or the observance or performance of the Trustee's liabilities or duties hereunder.

7 The Company shall initially be entitled to occupy the Apartments pursuant to Clause 9 of the Constitution and shall be entitled to grant the rights of occupation of parts thereof in accordance therewith.

8 The Company and the Founder Members on behalf of the Club and as a separate covenant for themselves hereby jointly and severally warrant that save as otherwise ordered by a Court of competent jurisdiction or as provided herein the Trustee shall not by entering into and acting in pursuance of the terms and conditions of this Deed owe any duty or obligation or incur any liability to any person or persons (whether corporate or individual) other than the Members of the Club and that no such person or persons are entitled to require or oblige the Trustee to transfer or deal with the Property or the Apartments.

9 The Company and the Founder Members on behalf of the Club and as a separate covenant for themselves hereby jointly and severally warrant that the Trustee's name shall not appear on any literature or document or on any advertisement issued by or on behalf of the Company, the Founder Members or the Club without the prior approval in writing of the Trustee having first been obtained.

10 (a) The Trustee shall not be responsible for any loss suffered by the Club or any Member thereof arising out of or in respect of any act or omission on the part of the Trustee, its officers, employees or agents in respect of the Property unless the same shall have been caused by or arisen from fraud or negligence on behalf of the Trustee or its said officers, employees or agents.

(b) The Trustee shall not be under any liability on account of anything done or

* insert if Isle of Man is governing jurisdiction.

suffered by the Trustee in good faith in accordance with or in pursuance of any request or advice of the Founder Members (or either of them) the Club or the Committee of the Club.

11 The Founder Members shall pay to the Trustee as remuneration for the performance of its duties hereunder such fees as may from time to time be separately agreed upon between the Founder Members and the Trustee (or failing which between the Committee and the Trustee) and all out-of-pocket expenses incurred by the Trustee in the performance of its duties under this Deed and in default of such payment the Founder Members hereby jointly and severally undertake that the Club will pay to the Trustee all such sums PROVIDED THAT as between the Company and the Founder Members on behalf of the Club the Club shall be primarily liable to pay all such sums.

12 In connection with the Property and/or the Apartments the Founder Members on behalf of the Club and (as a separate covenant) for themselves covenant with the Trustee:
(a) on demand to pay as the Trustee may direct all outgoings whatsoever (including rates, service charges, interest, costs, expenses and damages) covenanted or agreed to be paid (whether contingently or otherwise) in respect of the Property and/or the Apartments;
(b) at all times to observe and perform (and to cause the Owning Companies so to observe and perform) all the covenant's terms and conditions to which the Apartments may from time to time be subject;
(c) to indemnify and keep fully and effectually indemnified the Trustee from and against all actions, claims, demands, losses, damages, costs and expenses made against or suffered or incurred by the Trustee arising from any breach, non-observance or non-performance of any of the agreements and/or covenants contained in this Trust Deed and/or the Constitution and/or the Management Agreement.

13 The Founder Members on behalf of the Club and as a separate covenant for themselves hereby agree jointly and severally to indemnify and hold harmless the Trustee against all claims, actions, proceedings, charges (including without prejudice to the generality of the foregoing charges to tax and breaches of relevant legislation or regulations), fees, costs, liabilities and expenses to which it may be entitled or which may result from or be incurred in connection with the performance by the Trustee of its duties hereunder and the Trustee shall be kept fully indemnified jointly and severally by the Founder Members and the Club against all losses, claims, demands, taxes, actions, damages, costs and expenses made or incurred in connection with the Property or the Owning Companies in connection with the sale of Membership Certificates by the Company or by any Member and/or the Apartments or in any other way in connection with the holding by the Trustee of the office of trustee hereunder (including without prejudice to the generality of the foregoing any taxes assessed on or which are or might ultimately become the liability of the Trustee or the Owning Companies in connection with the sale of Membership Certificates by the Company or any Member). The Trustee shall have the right if at any time it considers it desirable so to do to require that the Founder Members or the Club shall deposit with the Trustee such sum as the Trustee shall reasonably consider to be necessary in support of the indemnities contained in this Deed.

14.1 The Trustee shall be entitled to have recourse to and be indemnified out of the Property and/or the Apartments or the proceeds of the sale thereof for all sums expended by the Trustee in or about or in any way in connection with the trusts of this Deed and for all sums (including remuneration) payable to the Trustee hereunder and to meet and discharge the cost of any indemnity to which it is entitled hereunder and for such purposes shall have all the powers of an absolute owner to sell, let, mortgage or otherwise dispose of the Property or any part thereof unrestricted by Clause 3 hereof or the Constitution.

14.2 If the employment of the Management Company (as defined in the Constitution) or any substitute therefor shall be terminated for any reason then the Trustee shall have the power on each such occasion to appoint another person to administer the subletting in accordance with sub-clause 14.11 of the Constitution the cost and expense of such appointment being borne by the Club.

15.1 This Deed shall continue until:

(a) [DATE]; or

(b) until terminated either by the Club giving not less that six months' notice in writing to the Trustee; or

(c) by the Trustee giving the Company and the Club not less than six months' notice in writing; whichever shall first occur.

Any notice given under this Clause shall expire on the last day of any calendar month and such notice shall not be given in any event before the expiry of one year from the date hereof.

15.2 Upon termination or expiration of this Deed the Founder Members (or failing which the Club) shall pay to the Trustee all remuneration then owing to the Trustee together with any outstanding out-of-pocket expenses and all expenses incurred by the Trustee in conveying or assigning or otherwise disposing of the title to the Property in manner hereinafter provided. The Trustee shall in the event of this Deed being terminated convey or assign the Property or procure the same to be conveyed or transferred (at the expense of the Club or failing which at the expense of the Founder Members) to any succeeding trustee or otherwise as the Committee of the Club in writing may direct.

Upon the termination or expiration of this Deed pursuant to the foregoing provisions or as soon thereafter as is reasonably practicable the Trustee shall as jointly directed by the Committee either:

(a) transfer the Property to the alternative trustee of this or any new trust constituted in accordance with the Constitution, or

(b) retain the Property upon the terms of any new trust constituted in accordance with the Constitution, or

(c) sell the Apartments (or in its sole discretion, the Property) in such manner as it may choose but so that the Trustee shall not be liable to the Founder Members or either to them or to the former Members, or to any other person or persons:

   (i) in the event that the Trustee is unable to find a purchaser for some or all of the Apartments or the Property on acceptable terms, or

   (ii) in respect of the consideration received for any such sale or sales for any loss or damage suffered in respect thereof,

and the Trustee shall be entitled to deduct from the consideration received:

(a) all payments due to the Trustee under this Deed;

(b) all expenses incurred in connection with any sale or sales; and

(c) the Trustee's fees for acting on the termination of the Club and the subsequent distribution of the net proceeds of sale. Such fees to be in addition to any remuneration payable to the Trustee under Clause 11 hereof (but to be determined as therein provided); and

(d) all taxes or fiscal impositions whatsoever relating to the Apartments, the Owning Companies relating thereto and the holding or disposal thereof by the Trustee for which the Trustee and (in the case of the Trustee procuring the sale of an Apartment by an Owning Company) the Owning Company may be liable.

15.3 After deduction of all sums referred to in paragraph 15.2 the Trustee shall distribute the net assets available for distribution to such persons as would be entitled under the Constitution to such proceeds upon dissolution of the Club and pending distribution to invest the net proceeds in any investment authorised by law. PROVIDED THAT the Trustee will have fully discharged its obligations under this sub-clause 15.3 if it distributes the net proceeds of sale to those persons and in such shares as shall be notified to the Trustee by the Management Company as being in accordance with the Constitution (which information the Management Company hereby agrees to supply) and upon distribution in accordance with this information the former members of the Club shall if so required by the Trustee acknowledge in writing that the Trustee has fully discharged its obligations under this Trust Deed.

16.1 The Company and the Founder Members on behalf of the Club and as a separate covenant for themselves jointly and severally undertake:

(a) to give to the Trustee the names and addresses of all officers of the Club

(b) to inform the Trustee within 21 days of any change in the holders of any office with the full name and address of each new officer

(c) to give to the Trustee within 21 days of admission of each Member to Membership the name and address of each such Member and details of any change of address of such Member within 21 days of such change occurring

(d) that within seven days of the relevant meeting there shall be delivered to the Trustee duly certified by the Chairman or Secretary of the Committee of the Club an excerpt from the minutes of any meeting of the Committee or of the Members of the Club minuting the resignation of any officer or other member of the Committee, of the election or appointment of a new officer or Committee member, and any change in the Constitution of the Club approved by the Members thereof

(e) That there shall be delivered to the Trustee:

    (i) a copy of each set of annual audited accounts of the Club as soon as the same is available, and

    (ii) notice of any general meetings of the Club and a copy of the agenda and of any resolution to be proposed at the meeting at least 14 days prior to such meetings, and

    (iii) minutes of any such meeting as soon as the same are available, and

    (iv) a copy of any contract relating to the management of the Club.

16.2 The Trustee shall receive notice of all general meetings of the Club and have the right to attend (at the expense of the Club) at the same but shall have (unless mandated by proxy) no vote in the proceedings.

17 Notwithstanding the provisions of this Deed neither the Trustee nor any holding subsidiary or associated company of the Trustee shall be precluded from acting as insurer, insurance agent or broker or banker, investment manager or adviser to either or both of the Founder Members or the Club nor shall the Trustee nor any holding subsidiary or associated company thereof be precluded from making any advances to either or both of the Founder Members or the Club on such terms as may be agreed or making any contract or entering into any financial or other transaction in the ordinary course of business with either or both of the Founder Members or the Club and shall be entitled to charge interest on overdrawn accounts and make the usual banker's charges and shall not be liable to account to either or both of the Founder Members or the Club for any profit made in connection therewith.

18 Any notice which is required to be given in pursuance to any provision of this Deed shall be given or served by pre-paid first class post, telegram, cable or telex addressed to the Company or to the Founder Members or to the Trustee as the case may be at their respective offices or (in the case of notice to be served on the Club or the Committee) to the Committee of the Club c/o [ADDRESS], and any notice sent by post shall be deemed to have been given or served at the time of despatch.

19 The Trustee and the Founder Members shall be entitled by deed supplemental hereto to modify, alter or add to the provisions of these presents in such manner and to

such extent as they may consider expedient for any purpose; **PROVIDED THAT** unless the Trustee shall certify in writing that in its opinion such modification, alteration or addition does not prejudice the interests of the Members and does not operate to release the Trustee or the Founder Members from any responsibility to the Members no such modification, alteration or addition shall be made without the sanction of a resolution of a special general meeting of Members duly convened and held in accordance with the Constitution of the Club or of a written resolution of the Members in accordance with Rule 16.7 of the Constitution of the Club.

20 This Deed shall be governed and construed in accordance with the present laws of the [                              ], and the Founder Members irrevocably:

(a) submit to the exclusive jurisdiction of the courts of the [                              ]; and

(b) consent to service of process by mail or in any other manner permitted by the laws of the [                              ].

21.1 If a Trustee retires from the trusts hereof or becomes by reason of residence or place of incorporation incapable of acting as a Trustee hereof such Trustee shall be released from all claims, demands, actions, proceedings and accounts of any kind on the part of any beneficiary (whether in existence or not) actually or prospectively interested under this Deed for or in respect of the Property or in the income thereof or the trusts of this Deed or any act or thing done or omitted in execution or purported execution of such trusts other than and except only actions :

(a) arising from any fraud or fraudulent breach of trust to which such trustee or (in the case of a corporate trustee) any of its officers was a party or privy;

(b) to recover from such trustee, trust property or the proceeds of trust property in the possession of such trustee or previously received by such trustee or (in the case of a corporate trustee) any of its officers and converted to his use.

21.2 The perpetuity period applicable to this Deed shall be the period of eighty (80) years from the date hereof.

22 The Trustee declares and it is hereby agreed that it shall have all the additional powers, discretions and rights set out in Schedule 1 hereof.

**IN WITNESS WHEREOF** the parties hereto have hereunto caused their Common Seals to be affixed the day and year first above written.

## Schedule I

General terms and conditions upon which the Trustee accepts appointment.

1 The Trustee may act by a proper officer or officers and may appoint as its proper officer any officers of [                              ] or any associated company or any lawyers for the time being retained by [                              ].

2 The Trustee's remuneration for its services shall be free of all taxes or fiscal impositions whatsoever and the Trustee shall have a first charge upon the estate or trust fund in respect of such remuneration and all legal costs and disbursements, agents' charges, staff travel costs, postages, telephone calls and other expenses properly incurred and paid.

3 Subject to any express provision to the contrary hereinbefore set out, the Trustee may in its absolute discretion determine how remuneration due to the Trustee shall be borne as between different parts of an estate or trust or as between the beneficiaries and every such determination shall be binding upon all persons concerned.

4 The Trustee may without being liable to account for any profit thereby made:

(a) act as insurer or banker and transact any banking or insurance or allied business on normal terms,

(b) retain the customary share of brokerage and other commissions,

(c) perform any service on behalf of the estate or trust and make charges commensurate with the services rendered,

(d) employ at the expense and on behalf of the estate or trust any parent or associated or subsidiary company as banker or to transact any allied business or for any purpose for which a Trustee is entitled to employ any agents,

(e) retain any remuneration received as a result of any appointment of a nominee as a director or officer of any other company whose shares or expenses shall from time to time be held in the estate or trust.

5 The Trustee shall not be required by reason only of the general rule preventing a trustee from deriving a profit from his trusteeship to account to the estate or trust for any profit made in the ordinary course of business by the Trustee or any holding or associated or subsidiary company arising from the exercise of any power or discretion confered by this trust instrument as hereafter amended or by Law.

6 The Trustee may at its discretion vest any property of the estate or trust in any person or corporate body as its nominees.

7 All monies, securities, title deeds and documents belonging to or relating to the Property or this trust shall be under the exclusive custody and control of the Trustee, any other person having all reasonable facilities for verification or inspection and the name of the Trustee or the name of its nominees shall be placed first in the register of all stock, shares, securities or property.

8 Unless otherwise provided in the trust instrument, every appointment whether under the statutory power or under any special power of a new trustee shall be subject to the consent in writing of the Trustee.

|  |  |
|---|---|
| THE COMMON SEAL of [TRUSTEE] was hereunto affixed in the presence of: | THE COMMON SEAL of XYZ CLUB SALES LIMITED was hereunto affixed in the presence of |

*Director*                                    *Director*

*Secretary*                                  *Secretary*

THE COMMON SEAL of
XYZ CLUB MANAGEMENT LIMITED
was hereunto affixed in
the presence of:

*Director*

*Secretary*

# XYZ CLUB

## MANAGEMENT AGREEMENT

**THIS AGREEMENT** is made the          day of          One thousand nine hundred and [          ] BETWEEN XYZ CLUB SALES LIMITED a company incorporated in the Isle of Man having its registered office at [ADDRESS] and XYZ CLUB MANAGEMENT LIMITED a company incorporated in the Isle of Man and having its registered office at [ADDRESS] (hereinafter together called 'the Founder Members') of the one part and the said XYZ CLUB MANAGEMENT LIMITED (hereinafter called 'the Management Company') of the other part WHEREAS :

1 The Founder Members have together formed a club known as the XYZ Club (hereinafter called 'the Club') whose object is to secure for its members the ownership of exclusive rights of occupation of certain Apartments at [ADDRESS], ('the Apartments') for specified periods in each year during the period mentioned in the Club's Constitution ('the Constitution').

2 In pursuance of Clause 11 of the said Constitution the Founder Members have agreed to delegate to the Management Company the general management and administration of the Club.

**NOW THIS AGREEMENT WITNESSETH AND IT IS HEREBY AGREED** as follows:

1 Subject to the rights of the Committee of the Club to intervene where necessary or appropriate the Management Company will undertake on behalf of the Club and the Club hereby delegates to the Management Company the management and administration of the said Apartments and the contents thereof. Without prejudice to the generality of the foregoing the Management Company will be responsible for the provision of all items detailed in Clause 12 of the Constitution of the Club. The Management Company will ensure that the management and administration aforesaid are carried out with all due diligence and in the best interests of the Members of the Club and will comply with all requirements of the Committee of the Club in the performance of its duties hereunder and will effect all maintenance, repairs, renewals and decoration and insurance of the property of the Club when the same shall be necessary and in a good and workmanlike manner with all due speed and diligence but not so as to interfere except in so far as reasonably necessary with the Members' enjoyment of their occupation of the Apartments as aforesaid.

2 The appointment of the Management Company will continue as from [DATE] until determined in accordance with Clause 12 of this Agreement (hereinafter called 'the Management Period').

3 Subject to the right of the Committee to intervene as aforesaid the Management Company shall during the Management Period be entitled to exercise all the powers of the Committee of the Club referred to in the Club's Constitution relating to the management and administration of the Club's property and affairs including the power to collect from each Member any sum or sums due from him pursuant to Clause 12 of the Constitution including any management charge referred to in Clauses 12 and 14 of the Constitution PROVIDED ALWAYS that the exercise of any power or discretion relating to the Club's property which shall require the Trustee of such property to do or concur in any act shall at all times remain vested in the Club and/or (as the Constitution may require) the Committee.

4 (a)  The Committee of the Club may by not less than three (3) months' written notice to the Management Company to that effect require the Management Company

to cease to provide any service for the time being provided by the Management Company hereunder.

(b) Following service of any such notice the Committee of the Club and the Management Company shall use their best endeavours to ascertain the amount by which the Management Charge referred to hereafter shall be reduced. Following the date of expiry of such notice and in default of agreement as to such reduction within two (2) months of the service of such notice the matter shall be referred to an expert in accordance with Clause 15 hereof.

(c) (i) The Committee of the Club may by not less than three (3) months' written notice to the Management Company to that effect request the Management Company to provide such reasonable additional services as may be specified in such notice in addition to all services for the time being provided by the Management Company hereunder

(ii) As soon as reasonably possible after receipt of such notice the Management Company shall submit to the Committee of the Club a written statement setting out its computation of the addition to the Management Charge resulting from the additional services, such computation to be based on the estimated cost to the Management Company of the provision of the additional services.

(iii) Within two (2) months of the receipt of such statement the Committee of the Club shall elect by written notice to the Management Company as to whether or not to accept such computation and if it shall so accept the Management Company shall commence the provision of the relevant services within one (1) month thereafter and the Management Charge shall thenceforth be increased by the amount of such computation.

(iv) In the event of the Committee of the Club electing not to accept such computation and being in a position to enter into an agreement with a third party for the provision of that service at a cost acceptable to the Committee of the Club the Committee of the Club shall not enter into any such agreement unless the Management Company shall have been given at least one (1) month's written notice of such intention and does not offer to provide the service itself on similar terms.

5 The Management Period shall be deemed to commence as from [DATE] and during the first two (2) years of the period each member of the Club shall pay the Management Company by way of a management charge (hereinafter called 'the initial management charge') a fixed sum or sums specified in respect of each Membership Certificate held and category of Apartment (such sum to be determined by the Management Company and notified to the member in writing at the time of issue of his Membership Certificate) and in each subsequent year after the second year he shall pay by way of management charge:

(a) the fixed sum per each Membership Certificate held as aforesaid plus

(b) an increment of such percentage of the management charge as is equal to the percentage increase in the figure at which the retail prices index in [                    ] published by the appropriate Spanish governmental authority stands at each last anniversary of the date of commencement of the Management Period over the index figure of such Index at 1 January [YEAR]. No fall in the figure at which the said index stands shall cause a variation to be made in the management charge or in the amount of any increment previously so determined. In the event of any change in the reference base used to compile the said index the figure taken to be shown in the said index after such change shall be the figure which would have been shown in the said index if the reference base current at [DATE] had been retained PROVIDED THAT in the event of it becoming impossible by reason of any change after the date hereof in the method used to compile the said index or for any other reason whatsoever to calculate the said additional sum payable in any year by reference to the said index or if any dispute or any difference whatsoever shall arise between the Club and the Management Company with respect to the amount of such additional sum or with respect to the construction or effect of this Clause the determination of the additional sum or other matter in difference shall be determined by an expert appointed in pursuance of the terms of this Agreement and he shall have full power to determine on such date as he shall deem appropriate what would have been the increase in the said index had it continued on the same basis and given the information assumed to be available for the operation of this Clause.

6 Not later than three (3) months before the end of the second year of the Management Period either the Committee (acting on the authority of a resolution of the Club in general meeting) may give written notice to the Management Company or the Management Company may give written notice to the Committee that with effect from the commencement of the third year of the Management Period (that is from [DATE] the provision for the ascertainment of the management charge as set out in Clause 5 above ('the First Option') is to be discontinued and replaced by the alternative set out in Clause 7 below (hereinafter referred to as 'the Second Option'). In such event the First Option shall be so discontinued and shall be so replaced. If the said election to discontinue the First Option and replace it by the Second Option shall not be exercised during the period aforesaid the Club and the Management Company shall each have a like right to elect to discontinue the First Option and replace it by the Second Option from any subsequent anniversary of the commencement of the Management Period upon giving at least three (3) months' written notice one party to the other. Thereafter the First Option shall not be reinstated except by the mutual agreement of both the Club and the Management Company.

7 Under the Second Option (as herein defined) each Member of the Club shall (for each Membership Certificate held by him) pay the Management Company by way of annual management charge a proportionate part of the total cost to the Management Company in each year of providing the services it hereby agrees to provide including all the overhead expenses and outlays and outgoings properly incurred by the Management Company in the performance of its duties hereunder and the salaries of all employees of the Management Company to the extent that they are engaged in the provision of these services.

The total cost to the Management Company of providing the aforesaid services shall in the calculation of the sum payable in respect of each Membership Certificate held be firstly apportioned between the respective categories of Studio, one and two bedroomed or Duplex Apartments in accordance with the following ratio:

$$e = \frac{a}{a+b+c+d}; \quad f = \frac{b}{a+b+c+d}; \quad g = \frac{c}{a+b+c+d}; \quad h = \frac{d}{a+b+c+d}$$

Where:

a  = (100)% of the number of Studio Apartments brought into the Club upon the latest anniversary of the commencement of the Management Period

b  = (　　) % of the number of one bedroomed Apartments brought into the Club upon the latest anniversary of the commencement of the Management Period

c  = (　　) % of the number of two bedroomed Duplex Apartments brought into the Club upon the latest anniversary of the commencement of the Management Period

d  = (　　) % of the number of three bedroomed Duplex Apartments brought into the Club upon the latest anniversary of the commencement of the Management Period e = the proportion of the aggregate management costs attributed to Studio Apartments

f = the proportion of the aggregate management costs attributed to one bedroomed Apartments

g = the proportion of the aggregate management costs attributed to two bedroomed Duplex Apartments

h = the proportion of the aggregate management costs attributed to three bedroomed Duplex Apartments

The annual management charge payable in respect of each Membership Certificate in each category of Apartments shall be calculated in accordance with the following formula:

$$A = \frac{B}{51}$$

Where:

A = annual management charge per each Membership Certificate in that category.

B = ll5% of the costs of providing the aforesaid services as attributed to each Apartment in the relevant category of Apartments in accordance with the formula first above appearing.

Under the Second Option the Management Company shall as soon as reasonably practicable after the commencement of each new year of the Management Period give written notice to each Member requiring him to pay an estimated advance payment (hereinafter called 'the advance management charge') of his liability for that year in respect of the annual management charge of each Membership Certificate held by him and each Member shall forthwith pay the Management Company his advance management charge. The amount of the advance management charge shall be such amount as the Management Company shall in their discretion determine to be a fair and reasonable charge but in the event of a dispute as to the amount of the charge the matter shall be resolved as provided in Clause 15 hereof.

Under the Second Option the amount of the total management charge for each year shall be ascertained and certified annually by a certificate signed by the accountants or auditors of the Management Company as soon as reasonably practicable after the end of the year in question and as soon as reasonably practicable after the signature of the certificate every Member shall be furnished with an account of the said total management charge including the 15% addition and secondly the proportionate amount payable by each Member in respect of each Membership Certificate held by him and after giving each Member credit for the advance management charge already paid by him and showing such adjustment if any as may be necessary there shall forthwith be paid by each Member to the Management Company any balance still payable by him in respect of the proportionate amount aforesaid due from him in respect of the annual management charge or (as the case may be) there shall be allowed by the Management Company to the Member against the next following payment of management charge any amount which may have been overpaid by the member by way of an advance management charge.

8 (a) On the issue of each new Membership Certificate to a Member of the Club and if the First Option is in operation such new Member shall forthwith pay in advance the management charge (duly apportioned when necessary by time) due from him in respect of such Membership Certificate for the remainder of the year in which such Membership Certificate shall be issued to him and where the Second Option is in operation the same principle shall apply to the advance management charge subject to any due apportionment by time if necessary.

(b) In the event that the Second Option is in force and thereafter a new Apartment or Apartments is/are added to the Club, the Management Company shall specify in respect of each new Apartment the amount of the initial management charge for each of the 51 weeks in respect thereof for the purpose of calculation of the Management Charge under the Second Option or, as the case may be, pursuant to sub-clause (c) hereof.

(c) Notwithstanding anything to the contrary herein contained or implied the Management Company shall be at liberty at its discretion to alter the apportionment of the total cost as referred to in Clause 7 hereof between different groups or categories of Apartments and/or to alter the basis of the categorisation of the Apartments and then to calculate the management charges for each group or category by reference to the figure apportioned to that group or category and further to provide that in respect of each new Apartment or group or category of Apartments brought into the Club, there shall be payable an initial management charge and the Second Option shall not apply thereto until such time as the First Option is replaced by the Second Option in relation thereto pursuant to Clause 6 hereof.

(d) The Management Company shall have a general discretion to vary the basis of the calculation of the total cost, as hereinbefore referred to, and the basis of its apportionment between Members if in its opinion the then current or applicable basis is unworkable, administratively inconvenient, unduly complex or is unfair or inequitable as between Members or as between the Management Company and the Members. In such event the Management Company shall serve notice of the proposed change upon the Committee who shall within 30 days and by written notice to the Management Company approve or reject the same. If the Committee shall reject the same the dispute shall be referred to arbitration pursuant to Clause 15 hereof.

(e) When the First Option is in operation the Founder Members shall from their own resources pay to the Management Company such amounts as may from time to time be necessary to cover any shortfall between the total cost to the Management Company (plus the 15% addition) of providing the services it hereby agrees to provide and the contributions collected from ordinary Members and shall not pay contributions in respect of Membership Certificates not owned by ordinary Members PROVIDED THAT where the First Option is in operation the Founder Members and the Management Company shall not be obliged or required to provide accounts to the ordinary Members.

9  The Management Company shall arrange for the prompt collection (and payment if necessary) of the management charge payable by each ordinary Member and the Founder Members and shall properly pay and discharge out of all such monies collected by it from ordinary Members and Founder Members all expenses in relation to which such amounts have been collected and shall ensure (subject to the proviso to Clause 8 (e) hereof) that proper records and books of account relating to the management of the Club's property and affairs are maintained at all times on behalf of the members and that such records and books of account are at all reasonable times available for inspection by any Member of the Club or any person on his behalf or the Trustee of the Club's property.

10  During the Management Period the Management Company shall not be entitled to any remuneration in respect of its duties and obligations hereunder save in so far as the aggregate of the management charges collected by it from all ordinary Members and the Founder Members shall in respect of each calendar year be sufficient for that purpose.

11 (a) The Management Company reserves the right to negotiate with the Members for the renting of weekly periods in an Apartment or Apartments such time to

be used for maintenance repairs and redecorations and such rental to be at the market rate for the time being in force and to be recouped by the Management Company as a management charge as hereinbefore defined.

(b) The Management Company reserves the right to delegate all or any of its responsibilities and liabilities hereunder to any person or persons, company or companies as it shall think fit upon such open market terms as it shall think fit, and the total cost thereof shall be and become part of the management charge.

12 The Management Period shall forthwith terminate:

(a) if the Management Company being a corporation shall pass a resolution to wind up or enter into liquidation whether compulsory or voluntary (except for the purpose of amalgamation or reconstruction) or suffer a receiver to be appointed or being an individual or individuals shall commit an act of bankruptcy

or

(b) if the XYZ Club shall be wound up or for any reason shall cease to exist

or

(c) if the Management Company shall have committed a breach of this Agreement and shall neglect or otherwise fail to remedy such breach (whether capable of remedy or not) within one (1) month of being required in writing to do so by the Committee of the Club and the Committee thereafter serves upon the Management Company a notice in writing summarily terminating the Management Period.

13 The Founder Members on behalf of the Members of the Club shall indemnify and keep indemnified the Management Company from and against all claims, demands, proceedings, damages, liabilities and costs and expenses arising out of or incidental to the proper and reasonable performance by the Management Company of its duties under this Agreement.

14.1 A Certificate covering more than one weekly period shall be deemed to be a series of separate Certificates, one for each weekly period it covers, for all the purposes of this Management Agreement and the calculation of management charge.

14.2 The fifteen per cent (15%) addition referred to in Clause 7 of this Agreement represents the agreed remuneration payable to the Management Company in respect of the services agreed to be provided by the Management Company hereunder.

15 Any dispute or difference arising out of this Agreement shall be referred to the decision of a single expert to be agreed between the Committee and the Management Company or in default of agreement to be appointed on the application of either party by the Trustee referred to in the Constitution of the Club or its sucessor or assignees.

16 The Founder Members and the Management Company irrevocably:

(a) submit to the exclusive jurisdiction of the courts of the [                    ] and

(b) consent to service of process by mail or any other manner permitted by [                    ] law.

17 This Agreement shall be governed and construed in accordance with [                    ] law.

IN WITNESS whereof these presents have been executed the day and year first above written.

**SIGNED BY**                              **SIGNED BY**
on behalf of                                on behalf of
XYZ CLUB SALES LIMITED        XYZ CLUB MANAGEMENT LIMITED
in the presence of:                        in the presence of

# XYZ CLUB

## MEMBERSHIP APPLICATION

*Application No*

**THIS** Membership Application is made on the [DATE]:

BETWEEN

on the one hand, **XYZ CLUB SALES LIMITED** of [ADDRESS] ('the Company') of the first part and **XYZ CLUB MANAGEMENT LIMITED** of [ADDRESS] ('the Manager') of the second part. The Company and the Manager are hereinafter together called 'the Founder Members'.

On the other hand, the Applicant ('the Applicant') of the third part as under:

Applicant: _____ Telephone: _____ (Home)
_____ (Office)

Address: _____
_____
_____

The Applicant hereby applies for membership of XYZ Club of which the Company and Manager are Founder Members, in accordance with the following particulars:

| APARTMENT NO(S) | FLOOR PLAN | PERMITTED OCCUPANTS | HOLIDAY PERIOD(S) | OCCUPANCY COMMENCING | MEMBERSHIP FEE |
|---|---|---|---|---|---|
| | | | | | |
| | | | | | |
| | | | | | |

Check in day

| *Membership Terms* | *Payments* | *Method of payment* |
|---|---|---|
| Membership admission fee: | £ _____ | _____ |
| Administrative and contract fee: | £ _____ | _____ |
| International Exchange Organisation affiliation fee: | £ _____ | _____ |
| *Total* | £ _____ | _____ |
| Deposit received: | £ _____ | _____ |
| Balance: | £ _____ | _____ |

Date balance due:_____

All payments must be made in favour of [NAME] ('the Stakeholder') and must be sent to [TRUSTEE] [ADDRESS]. The Stakeholder shall hold the Membership Admission Fee in escrow until the date upon which the conditions mentioned in paragraph 2 of the Membership Application Conditions stated on the reverse of this document have been fulfilled.

THE STAKEHOLDER CANNOT BE RESPONSIBLE FOR ANY PAYMENTS MADE TO ANY OTHER PARTY

The Applicant also hereby agrees to pay the undermentioned initial management charge as described in Clause 12 of the Constitution of the Club as soon as the Membership Certificate is issued:

Initial management charge: £

The Applicant(s) hereby irrevocably agrees by his/her/their signature below to be bound by the MEMBERSHIP APPLICATION CONDITIONS as stated on the reverse of this document, subject to acceptance of this Application by the Founder Members within 28 days of the date of this Application.

SIGNED by Applicant

SIGNED by Applicant                    Witnessed by:

AGREED TO AND ACCEPTED BY
**XYZ CLUB SALES LIMITED**
and
**XYZ CLUB MANAGEMENT LIMITED**
upon the MEMBERSHIP APPLICATION CONDITIONS
stated on the reverse of this document

this              day of                    199

Authorised signatory for and on
behalf of
**XYZ CLUB SALES LIMITED**
and
**XYZ CLUB MANAGEMENT LIMITED**

# XYZ CLUB

## MEMBERSHIP APPLICATION CONDITIONS

1 The Applicant HEREBY AGREES to be bound by the Constitution of the XYZ CLUB and the Trust Deed referred to therein (copies of which have been supplied to the Applicant) and the Applicant shall be bound by the same whether or not the Applicant has actually inspected the same.

2 The Stakeholder is [TRUSTEE]. The Stakeholder shall hold the membership fee received by it from the Applicant in escrow until the date upon which the Apartment referred to overleaf is in all respects completed and ready for occupation (if the same shall not already be completed) and a transfer deed in favour of an Owning Company (as defined in the Constitution) shall have been duly executed and ownership and control of the said Owning Company shall have been vested in the Stakeholder on the trusts of the Deed of Trust ('the Completion Date'). Whereupon the Company shall be entitled to a release of the said membership fee upon production to the Stakeholder of a certificate that the matters specified in this sub-clause have been completed.
Notwithstanding the foregoing, if prior to the Completion Date either:
(a) the Company shall have deposited with the Stakeholder such a guarantee or security or securities for the performance of all the obligations of the Company hereunder as the Stakeholder shall consider reasonable, or
(b) the Company shall have delivered to the Stakeholder a completion guarantee satisfactory to the Stakeholder and a transfer deed in favour of an Owning Company shall have been procured and ownership and control of that Owning Company transferred to the Stakeholder as aforesaid,
then in either such case the Stakeholder may at its discretion release to the Company for stage payments, building and marketing expenses all or part of all membership fees received provided that if the Completion Date shall not have occurred within fifteen (15) months of the date hereof, otherwise than by reason of the default of the Applicant, the Company shall upon the first written demand of the Applicant repay to the Applicant the membership fee received by the Stakeholder, together with interest thereon at 1% (one per cent) below the [                    ] Bank plc offered rate for Sterling deposits. In default thereof the Stakeholder shall enforce any guarantee or guarantees held by it in accordance with the terms thereof.

3 The Company will, within 28 days after the Completion Date, cause to be issued to the Applicant a Membership Certificate in respect of the weekly period or weekly periods (as referred to in Clause 8 of the Constitution of the Club) stated overleaf relating to the Apartment ('the Apartment') specified overleaf and which is shown more particularly on the plan, a copy of which has been made available for inspection by the Applicant and which the Applicant shall be deemed to have inspected.

4 It is hereby agreed between the Founder Members on behalf of the Club and the Applicant that the management charge payable by the Applicant as holder of the said Membership Certificate will in the first year to which the Applicant shall be entitled to occupy the Apartment as Club Member, be at the rate per annum specified overleaf, together with any value added tax or other similar tax which is required by law (whether under the laws of [                    ] or otherwise) to be collected from the Applicant. The said management charge shall become due and payable immediately the Membership Certificate is issued to the Member and thereafter on 1 February in each year.

5 Subject to the payment by the Applicant of the management charge as aforesaid, the Manager, as the Management Company referred to in the Constitution of the Club,

hereby undertakes with the Applicant to observe and perform its obligations imposed upon it by the Management Agreement for the time being in force.

6 In the event of the Applicant failing to make any payment due hereunder within 7 days of being given written notice to that effect by the Company or its legal representatives (of which time shall be of the essence) all monies paid by the Applicant will be forfeited to the Company as liquidated damages and this Agreement shall thereupon be rescinded and neither party shall have any further liability to the other.

7 Where the context so admits and requires the provisions of this Agreement shall remain in full force and effect notwithstanding completion of the issue of the said Membership Certificate to the Applicant.

8 CANCELLATION
In the event that the Applicant wishes to cancel this Agreement, the Applicant must within seven (7) days of the date upon which the Applicant signs this Agreement ('the date of signature') attend in person at the resort and complete a contract annulment form. Alternatively notice of cancellation in writing must be sent to the resort by recorded delivery, such notice to be posted within seven days of the date of signature. In the event of a disruption of postal services preventing the posting of such notice, then such notice shall be communicated by telephone within the same time limit and confirmed in writing by recorded delivery as soon as practicable thereafter.
Following the completion of a contract annulment form or the posting of notice of cancellation as aforesaid this Agreement will be cancelled without further liability on either party save that the Founder Members shall refund any monies received from the Applicant less [                    ] as liquidated damages to cover administration and expenses. The Applicant confirms that he, she or they have read and fully understand this clause.

9 The parties hereto irrevocably:
(a) submit to the exclusive jurisdiction of the courts of the [                    ], and
(b) consent to service of process by mail or in any other manner permitted by the laws in force in the [                    ].

10 This Agreement is constituted under the present laws of the [                    ] and the rights of all persons hereunder and the construction and effect of each and every provision hereof shall be subject to the jurisdiction of and construed in accordance with the laws in force in the [                    ] which shall be the forum for the administration thereof.

# XYZ BEACH CLUB

# (1) [COMPLETION GUARANTEE AND] ESCROW AGREEMENT

THIS [COMPLETION GUARANTEE AND] ESCROW AGREEMENT is made the          day of                    19          BETWEEN XYZ BEACH SALES LIMITED of (hereinafter called 'Sales') of the first part and [                    ] (hereinafter called 'Marketeer') of the second part and the TRUSTEE of [                    ] (hereinafter called 'Trustee') of the third part [and          ] of [                    ] (hereinafter called 'Guarantor') of the fourth part].

WHEREAS :

A [The Guarantor is the owner of land at the Resort (as hereinafter defined) whereon the Apartments are in the course of construction and Guarantor and Sales have agreed that Sales shall acquire the Apartments from Guarantor.] Sales intends to market the Apartments (as hereinafter defined) to members of the public upon a timeshare basis as hereinafter set out. Sales has agreed with Trustee that such marketing shall take the form prescribed by the Timeshare Documentation and that the Trustee shall act as trustee on the terms of the Deed of Trust comprised in the Timeshare Documentation.

B Sales has further agreed with Marketeer for the appointment of Marketeer by Sales to assist in the sales of timeshares to members of the public.

NOW THIS DEED WITNESSETH AS FOLLOWS:

1.1 In this Deed words and phrases shall where the context so admits have the meanings assigned to them by the Timeshare Documentation and subject thereto the following expressions shall bear the following meanings:

'Deed' means this Deed together with its schedules and Appendices.

'Timeshare Documentation' means the Deed of Trust, Club Constitution and Management Agreement entered into by (*inter alia*) Sales and Trustee together with the form of Membership Application annexed thereto and references to 'Deed of Trust', 'Club Constitution' shall bear a corresponding meaning.

'Club' shall mean the XYZ Beach Club, as constituted on the terms of the Club Constitution.

'Applicant' shall mean a purchaser who has contracted to purchase a Timeshare at the Resort who has paid the purchase price therefor (or any part of that price) to the Trustee.

'Timeshare' shall mean all the rights of an Ordinary Member under the Club Constitution and of a beneficiary under the trust constituted by the Deed of Trust.

'Apartments' shall mean all those Apartments at the Resort specified in Schedule 1 hereto (whether complete or in the course of construction or wholly unbuilt).

'Resort' means the land and facilities at [ADDRESS].

'The Apartment Completion Date' shall mean that date being twelve months from the date of this Deed.

'The Required Standard' shall mean the construction, fitting out and finishing of the Apartments to the standards and specifications notified to Applicants by Sales or its agents, not being a lesser standard that that required for affiliation to the Interval International or Resort Condominiums International exchange network.

'Membership Application' shall mean any application made by a member of the public for the purchase of Timeshare in the form annexed to the Timeshare Documentation.

'Procedures Manual' means the manual of procedures agreed between Sales and Trustee annexed hereto as Appendix 1 and any revision of the same from time to time agreed by Sales and Trustee in writing.

'Fee Agreement Letter' means the letter relating to the Trustees' agreed fees annexed hereto as Appendix 2 and any revision of the same from time to time agreed between Sales and Trustee in writing.

'Partially Releasable Funds' means money received from Applicants in connection with the purchase of Timeshares and releasable from escrow under Clause 3.4 but not otherwise releasable.

'Fully Releasable Funds' means money received by Trustee from Applicants in connection with the purchase of Timeshares and releasable from escrow under Clauses 3.2 or 3.5 hereof.

'Releasable Funds' means either Partially Releasable Funds or Fully Releasable Funds as the context shall admit.

'Transferred Apartments' shall mean those Apartments in respect of which a transfer deed in favour of an Owning Company (as defined in the Timeshare Documentation) shall have been duly notarised and ownership and control of such Owning Company shall have been vested in the Trustee on the trusts of the Deed of Trust whether or not such Apartments shall have been constructed at the date hereof or at the date of such transfer.

1.2  This Deed shall apply initially in respect of the Apartments specified in Schedule 1 hereto and shall subsequently be applied to such further Apartments at the Resort as the parties shall from time to time agree in writing.

1.3  Covenants entered into in this Deed by more than one party shall be joint and several covenants.

1.4  In the event of any conflict between the terms of this Deed and the terms of the Procedures Manual this Deed's terms shall prevail. In the event of any conflict between the terms of this Deed and the Timeshare Documentation and/or any Membership Application or Membership Applications the terms of the Timeshare Documentation and/or Membership Application or Membership Applications shall prevail.

2.1  Sales hereby covenants with Trustee to complete or procure the completion of the Apartments by the Apartment Completion Date to the Required Standard.

2.2  Sales and Marketeer hereby covenant with Trustee:

2.2.1  To sell Timeshares to the public on the basis of the Timeshare Documentation and the Procedures Manual annexed hereto and on no other basis and not to make any variation or addition to the Timeshare Documentation or any printed copy or photocopy or summary of the same distributed to the public without the prior written consent of Trustee.

2.2.2  Not to make any misrepresentation to members of the public regarding the Apartments or the Resort or the Timeshare Documentation or the Trustee nor cause the Trustee's name, style or business logo to be used or referred to without the prior written consent of Trustee.

2.2.3  To procure that all funds paid by Applicants in respect of the sales of Timeshares are paid directly by Applicants to Trustee.

2.2.4  To comply in all respects with the provisions of the Timeshare Documentation and of the Procedures Manual.

2.2.5  Not to take any steps to dismiss the Trustee as trustee of the Deed of Trust.

2.2.6  To provide Trustee with all information as from time to time is required by Trustee as to the carrying out of the obligations of Sales and Marketeer hereunder.

2.2.7  To insure and keep insured the Apartments in the name of the relevant Owning Company (as defined in the Timeshare Documentation) against the usual or customary risks in their full value and to deliver up a copy of the insurance policy and a copy of the last premium receipt as and when required by Trustee.

2.2.8  To procure the formation of an Owning Company or Owning Companies if the same shall not already be formed and the assignment of all the ownership and control of the same to Trustee or as Trustee shall direct.

2.2.9  To procure the completion and transfer of the Apartments to Trustee or to the Owning Company as and when required for the purposes of the Timeshare Documentation.

2.2.10  In the event of any overpayment being made by Trustee to any party hereto such party shall forthwith on demand repay the same to Trustee.

3.1  Trustee shall receive all monies from Applicants as Stakeholder on the terms of the Membership Application and in particular upon the 'Membership Application Conditions' specified by the same and subject thereto shall hold such funds in escrow under the provisions of the succeeding Clauses of this Deed.

3.2  Where Sales shall have procured the issue to Trustee of a bank guarantee or guarantee from such other party as shall in Trustee's opinion be of adequate standing (hereinafter referred to as a 'Special Guarantee') then Trustee shall release from escrow all monies received from Applicants up to the maximum aggregate level of indemnity (allowing for interest which may become payable to Applicants) specified by such Special Guarantee. A Special Guarantee shall expressly refer to this Clause of this Deed and the party liable in respect of the same shall undertake to indemnify Trustee in full up to the maximum aggregate level specified in the Special Guarantee in the event of monies becoming refundable to Applicants under the terms of their Membership Applications. Trustee shall have an unfettered discretion as to whether or not to accept a Special Guarantee and as to whether or not to treat funds as releasable from escrow under the provisions of this sub-clause 3.2 and may discontinue at any time without notice the operation of release, from escrow under this sub-clause. Trustee may further unilaterally and without requiring the consent of any party hereto give an undertaking to any third party not to implement the operation of this sub-clause and not to release from escrow funds which will otherwise fall to be released under the provisions of this Clause. Funds releasable from escrow under the provisions of this sub-clause shall be Fully Releasable Funds.

3.3  Subject to sub-clause 3.2 (if applicable) no funds shall be released from escrow unless the Apartment relating to the Membership Application in respect of which such funds are received shall be a Transferred Apartment.

3.4  Where an Apartment shall not have been completed to the Required Standard, notwithstanding that the same shall be a Transferred Apartment, Trustee shall treat same as Partially Releasable Funds and release from escrow such sums as shall not exceed in aggregate eighty per cent (80%) of such amount as a qualified architect shall have certified in writing as being the aggregate value of the Transferred Apartments. Such value shall be assessed upon the basis of a sale at arm's length of the land and Apartments concerned allowing for the extent to which construction shall have been concluded at the date of such valuation and upon the assumption of a sale on a whole ownership as opposed to timeshare basis. If the sums remaining in escrow after release of the Partially Releasable Funds shall total no less than one hundred and ten per cent (110%) (or such greater proportion as Trustee shall consider reasonable) of such aggregate sum as is certified by a qualified architect as being the cost outstanding and unpaid and required to be expended to conclude the construction of uncompleted Transferred Apartments, Trustee may open a designated retention account at          Bank          and credit all such funds remaining in escrow to the same. Thereafter the Trustee may (but shall not be obligated to) treat funds received from Applicants as Fully Releasable Funds.

3.5  Where a Transferred Apartment shall be fully constructed furnished and paid for to no less than the Required Standard thereafter all funds (including any funds standing to the credit of the designated retention account) shall be treated by the Trustee as Fully Releasable Funds.

4  The Trustee shall disperse all Releasable Funds as follows and in the following order of preference:

(a) The agreed contract administration fees of Trustee.
(b) Cancellations or refunds due to Applicants.
(c) The charges and disbursements of Trustees previously agreed.
(d) (If so required by Sales or the Membership Application) such exchange organisation affiliation fee as relates to the Membership Application.
(e) The duly invoiced charges and disbursements of [Trustee's lawyers].
(f) The balance to be divided between Sales and Marketeer or to their credit as hereinafter appears.

5.1 In respect of Partially Releasable Funds there shall be paid to Marketeer [ ] PER CENT ([ ]%) by value of the aggregate of Partially Releasable Funds from time to time to such bank account of Marketeer as shall be notified by Marketeer to Trustee in writing PROVIDED THAT in computing the percentage due to Marketeer sums taken from Partially Releasable Funds under Clauses [4(a), 4(c), 4(d), and 4(f)] above shall be treated as not having been deducted and the balance of Partially Releasable Funds from time to time shall be paid to Sales at such bank account of Sales as Sales shall notify Trustee in writing.

5.2 In respect of Fully Releasable Funds there shall be paid to Marketeer [ ] PER CENT ([ ]%) by value of the aggregate of Fully Releasable Funds from time to time to such bank accounts of Marketeer as shall be notified by Marketeer to Trustee in writing PROVIDED THAT in computing the percentage due to Marketeer sums taken from Fully Releasable Funds under Clauses [4(a), 4(c), 4(d), and 4(f)] above shall be treated as not having been deducted and the balance of Fully Releasable Funds from time to time shall be paid to Sales at such bank account of Sales as Sales shall notify Trustee in writing.

5.3 PROVIDED THAT where in respect of any Transferred Apartments there shall at the date of Releasable Funds becoming released from escrow be any sum outstanding and payable by way of unpaid purchase price in respect of the transfer of an Apartment to an Owning Company or by way of any mortgage charge or lien or any unpaid demand in respect of taxes. Notarial fees, Land Registry fees or any other costs associated with the transfer of the Apartments of whatever nature the Trustee shall apply funds payable to Sales under Clauses 5.1, 5.2 or (if applicable) 3.2 hereof in discharge of all and any such liabilities until Trustee shall have satisfactory evidence of the discharge of the same. Where [                    ] law or notarial or land registry practice requires currency import certificates to be obtained in relation to funds imported on a real property transaction, Sales shall obtain currency import certificates in respect of all such sums and obtain such other evidence of discharge as Trustee shall specify.

6 As between Marketeer and Sales this Deed is terminable upon 21 days' notice in writing from either party to the other and to Trustee SAVE AND EXCEPT that the parties hereto hereby irrevocably agree and authorise Trustee that where either party shall cause a termination of this Deed to be made, Trustee is nevertheless authorised and required to continue to account to the parties hereto in respect of Membership Applications made prior to the date of such termination coming into effect as if this Deed was still in force and effect. [No such termination shall in any event be made until [            ] 19 [ ]]. Save as above it is agreed this Deed is irrevocable and may not be terminated as between Sales and Trustee [or Guarantor and Trustee].

7.1 If [the Guarantor or] Sales shall default in its obligations hereunder Trustee shall at its discretion:
7.1.1 Carry out and complete at the expense in all respects of [Guarantor and/or] Sales the obligations of Sales to Applicants and of [Guarantor and/or] Sales to Trustee (including at the discretion of Trustee payment of any compensation to Applicants or to any of them), or

7.1.2 Realise all assets and possessions under its control relating to the Resort, the Timeshare Documentation, the Timeshares, the Owning Company and/or the Club and after deduction of its costs and expenses account to Applicants in satisfaction or partial satisfaction of the liabilities of Sales to such Applicants.

[7.2] [Guarantor hereby guarantees Trustee that Sales shall duly and faithfully perform all its obligations hereunder and in default thereof Guarantor shall forthwith pay Trustee such sums as shall be required to remedy the said default or (where the same shall be incapable of remedy) such sums as shall in the reasonable opinion of Trustee represent full and adequate compensation in respect of such default. If it be the case that there fall to be payable to Guarantor any sums in respect of Transferred Apartments representing unpaid purchase price owed to Guarantor as vendor of the Transferred Apartments or unpaid construction costs owed in respect of works carried out by Guarantor to the same Guarantor in consideration of Trustee entering into this Deed so as to facilitate the making of Timeshare sales and hence the payment to Guarantor of such sums by virtue of Clause 5.3 hereof HEREBY ACKNOWLEDGES AND DECLARES to Trustee and the Owning Company that it accepts the obligation of Trustee to pay such sums (as and when payable hereunder but not further or otherwise) in substitution for any debt due or expressed to be due from the Owning Company and expressly waives its rights of action against the Owning Company in the event of default.]

8 Trustee shall have the widest and absolute discretion to take any action Trustee shall consider to be desirable in the interests of the Applicants notwithstanding that such acts shall not fall within the provisions of sub-clauses 7.1.1 and 7.1.2 above, or that such actions may be detrimental to the interests of [Guarantor or Sales].

9 Trustee shall be entitled to a full indemnity for all monies or assets under its control in respect of all costs, charges and expenses incurred or to be incurred in the performance of its obligations or discretions hereunder.

10 It is hereby agreed between the parties that the sums paid by the Trustee pursuant to Clauses 3.2 or 5.1 or 5.2 hereof shall be paid to Sales and Marketeer or either of them in partial satisfaction of their liabilities *inter se* and shall be made by Trustee in the proportion specified and Trustee shall not be concerned in computing the said sums due to the respective parties for any claim whether for money due or otherwise which Marketeer may have against Sales or *vice versa* and in particular Trustee shall not be concerned to examine whether either Sales or Marketeer shall have satisfactorily performed any contract with the other.

11 This Deed is constituted under the present laws of the Isle of Man and the rights of persons hereunder and the construction and effect of each and every provision hereof shall be subject to the jurisdiction of and shall be construed in accordance with the laws in force in the Isle of Man which shall be the forum for the administration thereof.

12 The parties hereto IRREVOCABLY submit to the exclusive jurisdiction of the courts of the [                    ] and consent to service of process by mail or in any other manner permitted by the laws in force in the [                    ].

IN WITNESS WHEREOF the parties hereto have hereunto caused their Common Seals to be affixed the day and year first before written.

# Appendix B

# Documentation for an American Club Condominium Timeshare Property Scheme

# Appendix B

# Documentation for an American Club Condominium Timeshare Property Scheme

## Introduction

The attached sample documents were designed for a Florida in-state project. Florida was chosen because of the detail and depth of disclosure Florida law requires. It is important to remember when reviewing the type of provisions included in these sample documents that each state proscribes somewhat different but unique rules. Also, not every document needed for each project is included in these samples, nor is every document annotated because the document is either entirely a product of state law, i.e. the public offering statement, or the document is relatively standard and its use for timeshare does not require substantial modification. For this reason, experienced counsel should be consulted early in order to properly structure the project for that project's unique situation and so that the project complies with federal, state, and local law. For your ease in understanding the following are some of the shorthand terms used in the documents:

'Chapter 718' refers to the Florida Condominium Law as amended.

'Chapter 721' refers to the Florida Real Estate Time-sharing Act as amended.

'Division' is the shorthand method of referring to the administrative body charged with the implementation and enforcement of the Florida Real Estate Time-Sharing Act. The full name of the Division is the Division of Florida Land Sales and Condominiums of the Department of Business Regulation.

'FRETSA' is the shorthand method of referring to the Florida Real Estate Time-Sharing Act.

## TABLE OF CONTENTS

# DECLARATION OF CONDOMINIUM

# FOR

# CLUB "ABC", A CONDOMINIUM

This sample Declaration creates both a condominium and a timeshare property scheme. The condominium regime provides the framework for the imposition of the timeshare program and affords a developer a great deal of flexibility in marketing.

## TABLE OF CONTENTS

# LIST OF EXHIBITS

Please note that the following Exhibits are not included with the timeshare documentation annotated:

Legal Description of Property

Undivided Interests in Common Elements Per Unit/Timeshare Interest; Undivided Interests in Common Furnishings Per Timeshare Interest

Schedule of Vacation Weeks for Initial Fifty (50) years of Timeshare Plan

Survey; Graphic Description; Plot Plan; Certificate of Surveyor

# EXHIBIT 1

## DECLARATION OF CONDOMINIUM

## FOR

## CLUB 'ABC', A CONDOMINIUM

STATE OF FLORIDA

KNOW ALL MEN BY THESE PRESENTS:

COUNTY OF XYZ

THIS DECLARATION OF CONDOMINIUM FOR CLUB 'ABC', a Condominium (hereinafter referred to as 'Declaration'), is executed this ____ day of _____, 19___, by Timeshare Developer, Inc., a Florida corporation (hereinafter called 'Developer'), with its principal place of business and address at 101 Main Street, Anywhere, Florida.

WHEREAS, Developer is the owner in fee simple of certain real property and improvements (hereinafter referred to as the 'Property') situated in XYZ County, Florida, which real property and improvements are more particularly described in Exhibit 'A', which is attached hereto and made a part hereof; and

WHEREAS, Developer desires and intends to submit, and by the recordation thereof in the Public Records of XYZ County, Florida, does submit said Property to the condominium form of ownership, pursuant to Chapter 718, Florida Statutes, for the mutual enjoyment, convenience, benefit, and protection of all Owners; and

*Chapter 718 is the Florida Condominium Act. Timeshare programs which are part of condominiums must still comply with a number of the provisions of the Condominium Act; however, the provisions of the Florida Real Estate Time-Sharing Act ('FRETSA') take precedence in the case of a conflict.*

WHEREAS, Developer desires to establish a uniform plan for the development, sale, and ownership of the Condominium Units and any Timeshare Interests therein, as hereinbelow described, by imposing upon said Property mutual and beneficial restrictions, covenant, conditions, obligations, and easements to apply uniformly to the use, improvement, occupancy, transfer, and encumbrance of all the Property described in Exhibit 'A' hereto, for the mutual enjoyment, convenience, protection, and benefit of all of said Property and the Owners and future Owners thereof.

NOW THEREFORE, Developer hereby declares that all Condominium Units and Timeshare Interests in Club 'ABC', a Condominium, are and shall be held, sold conveyed, mortgaged, hypothecated, encumbered, leased, rented, occupied, improved, and used subject to the covenants, conditions, and restrictions set forth herein, as the same from time to time may lawfully be amended, all of which are established, declared, and agreed to be for the purpose of enhancing and protecting the value and desirability of said Condominium Units, any Timeshare Interests therein, and the Property, which are and shall be binding on and inure to the benefit of Developer, all Owners, and any other persons or entities having or acquiring any right, title, or interest therein and thereto, the Club 'ABC' Condominium Association, Inc., each of their respective heirs, legal representatives, successors, and assigns, and all other persons who are present within or use the Property for any purpose whatsoever.

By the acceptance of a Warranty Deed conveying a Condominium Unit or a Timeshare Interest as herein defined, or of any other instrument of transfer, whether from Developer, its successors or assigns, or from any Owner, each Owner, as herein defined, for himself, his heirs, legal representatives, successors, assigns, or any other person or persons holding or occupying by, through, or under such Owner, and whether or not expressly stated therein, covenants, consents, and agrees to and with Developer and with the other Owners from time to time of each other Condominium Unit and Timeshare Interest, to keep, observe, comply with, and perform the covenants, conditions, and restrictions contained in this Declaration and in the Articles of Incorporation, in the By-Laws, and in the Rules and Regulations of the Club 'ABC' Condominium Association, Inc., as each of the aforesaid documents may lawfully be amended from time to time. Furthermore, the behaviour and conduct of each and every person who comes within Club 'ABC', a condominium, during all such times as such person is present therein, shall be subject to and regulated by the provisions of each of the aforesaid documents.

## ARTICLE 1

### DEFINITIONS

As used in this Declaration and in the Exhibits attached hereto, as well as the By-Laws and the Rules and Regulations of the Club 'ABC' Condominium Association, Inc., and all amendments thereof, unless the context otherwise requires or otherwise expressly provides:

**Section 1** 'Articles of Incorporation' shall mean the Articles of Incorporation of the Club 'ABC' Condominium Association, Inc., attached hereto as Exhibit 'B' and incorporated herein by reference, as they may lawfully be amended from time to time, pursuant to the provisions thereof.

**Section 2** 'Assessment' shall mean any amount which, from time to time, is levied by the Board of Directors upon any Unit Owner(s) or Timeshire Owner(s). The four (4) types of Assessments are:

(a) 'Common Expense Assessment' shall mean an Assessment levied by the Board upon all of the Owners for their proportionate share of the Common Expenses of the Association;

*This assessment is for the expenses of the Condominium as a whole.*

(b) 'Timeshare Maintenance Fee' shall mean an Assessment levied by the Board upon all Timeshare Owners for their proportionate share of the Timeshare Expenses of the Association;

*This type of assessment is for those expenses related to the timeshare operation and would include maid service, reservation services and for timeshare unit furniture and utensil replacement.*

(c) 'Special Assessment' shall mean an Assessment levied by the Board upon all of the Unit Owners and/or Timeshare Owners in the event that the total of all Common Expense Assessments and/or Timeshare Maintenance Fees is inadequate to meet the Common Expenses and/or Timeshare Expenses of the Association; and

*This type of assessment is for an emergency or for an unanticipated expense. It is important to provide a vehicle for levying assessments to meet unexpected and unbudgeted items.*

(d) 'Personal Charge' shall mean an Assessment levied by the Board against a particular Owner for one of the reasons set forth herein.

*This type of assessment requires an owner to pay for his/her own telephone calls and personal expenses which are not generally shared by other owners including payment for any damage caused by the owner to the project facilities.*

**Section 3** 'Association' shall mean the Club 'ABC' Condominium Association, Inc., a Florida not for profit corporation, its successors and assigns. The Association's By-Laws and Rules and Regulations shall govern the operation and administration of the project.

**Section 4** 'Board of Directors' or 'Board' shall mean the Board of Directors of the Association.

**Section 5** 'By-Laws' shall mean the By-Laws of the Club 'ABC' Condominium Association, Inc., attached hereto as

Exhibit 'C' and incorporated herein by reference, as they may lawfully be amended from time to time, pursuant to the provisions thereof.

**Section 6** 'Common Elements' shall mean and include all portions of the Property described in Exhibit 'A' hereto (and any amendments thereof) and all of the improvements thereto and thereon located, except for the Units and the Common Furnishings, and such property as is expressly excluded therefrom, as more fully described herein.

**Section 7** 'Common Expenses' shall mean and include all expenses incurred by the Association or its duly authorized agent(s) for the maintenance, repair, replacement, restoration, improvement, operation, and administration of the Project and the operation and administration of the Association, excluding, however, all Timeshare Expenses, as defined herein.

*Notice that, consistent with the splitting of the type of assessments charged, the expenses are split between timeshare expenses and common or condominium expenses.*

**Section 8** 'Common Furnishings' shall mean all furniture, furnishings, fixtures, and equipment located in a Unit Committed to Timeshared Ownership, except for the telephones and any appurtenant equipment, an undivided interest in which is owned by all of the Timeshare Owners of such Unit in the percentages set forth in Exhibit 'D' hereto.

*The furniture in the timeshare units is owned by the Association in order to provide for its replacement and care and to prevent timeshare owners from attempting to alter the interior scheme of the timeshare units.*

**Section 9** 'Common Surplus' shall mean the excess of all amounts received by the Association, including but not limited to Assessments and rents, profits, and revenues, if any, over the Common Expenses and Timeshare Expenses. Each Owner shall have an undivided interest in the Common Surplus in the same percentage as he owns an undivided interest in the Common Elements, as set forth in Exhibit 'D' hereto.

**Section 10** 'Condominium Parcel' shall mean a Condominium Unit, as defined herein, together with the undivided interest in the Common Elements and Common Surplus which is appurtenant to such Unit.

*Each owner of a condominium parcel owns not only the unit but also the undivided interest in the common elements and common surplus. This 'bundle' of ownership rights may not be severed and separately mortgaged or sold.*

**Section 11** 'Condominium Unit' or 'Unit' shall mean a Unit within Club 'ABC', a Condominium, as described herein.

**Section 12** 'Declaration' shall mean this Declaration of Condominium for Club 'ABC', a Condominium, as it may lawfully be amended from time to time, pursuant to the provisions hereof.

**Section 13** 'Developer' shall mean Timeshare Developer, Inc., its successors and assigns.

**Section 14** 'Exchange User' shall mean any person who occupies a Unit Committed to Timeshared Ownership pursuant to a reciprocal exchange program approved by the Board of Directors.

**Section 15** 'Limited Common Elements' shall mean those Common Elements which are reserved for the use of a certain Condominium Unit or Units, to the exclusion of other Units, as described herein.

*Limited Common Elements usually include balconies and patios because they are open areas with restricted access and use.*

**Section 16** 'Maintenance Week' shall mean the one (1) Vacation Week designated herein as the Maintenance Week for a particular Unit Committed to Timeshared Ownership.

*The purpose of the maintenance week is to allow major cleaning and any necessary repair work to maintain the timeshare unit in usable condition.*

**Section 17** 'Management Agreement' shall mean the then-effective agreement between the Club 'ABC' Condominium Association, Inc., and the Manager which provides for the management of the Project.

**Section 18** 'Manager' shall mean the person or entity, its successors and assigns, engaged by the Association to undertake the duties, responsibilities, and obligations of managing the Project, pursuant to the then-effective Management Agreement.

**Section 19** 'Mortgagee of Record' shall mean any person or entity which has a mortgage on a Condominium Unit or a Timeshire Interest, including but not limited to the holder of a deed trust or a purchase money mortgagee and its successors and assigns, provided that such mortgage is evidenced by a written instrument which has been recorded in the Public Records of XYZ County, Florida, a true and correct copy of which has been provided to the Manager for the Association's records.

*This Declaration provides certain protections for mortgages of record. A lender who has a mortgage on a particular interest needs to be kept apprised of the status of the interest involved in order to monitor the value of its security.*

**Section 20** 'Project' shall mean all of the land and improvements now or hereafter submitted to this Declaration, as it may lawfully be amended from time to time.

**Section 21** 'Project Instruments' shall mean this Declaration and the Articles of Incorporation, the By-Laws, and the Rules and Regulations of the Association, as each may lawfully be amended from time to time.

**Section 22** 'Purchase Contract' shall mean that certain instrument by which Developer agrees to convey one (1) or more Condominium Units or Timeshare Interests in the Project.

**Section 23** 'Rules and Regulations' shall mean the Rules and Regulations of the Club 'ABC' Condominium Association, Inc., as they may lawfully be amended from time to time.

*The Rules and Regulations are the 'nuts and bolts' rules for the enjoyment and use of the Project by owners and generally include reservation procedures, rules for use of the recreational facilities and other use rules such as whether pets are allowed.*

**Section 24** 'Timeshare Expenses' shall mean and include all expenses incurred by the Association or its duly authorized agent(s) which are directly attributable to the commitment of one (1) or more Condominium Units in the Project to timeshared ownership in accordance with the provisions hereof.

*By splitting the timeshare expenses from the common expenses, a developer may sell whole unit condominiums along with the timeshare condominiums and assess each owner accordingly.*

**Section 25** 'Timeshare Interest' shall mean an undivided one fifty-first (1/51) interest in fee simple as tenant in common in and to the specific Condominium Parcel identified in a particular Timeshare Owner's Warranty Deed, together with a corresponding undivided interest in the Common Furnishings which are appurtenant to such Condominium Parcel, as well as the exclusive right each year of said Timeshare Owner to use and occupy his Unit and the Common Furnishings appurtenant thereto, and the non-exclusive right to use and enjoy the Common Elements of the Project, for their intended purposes, during the specific Vacation Week set forth in said Timeshare Owner's Warranty Deed.

*Section 721.05(24) defines a 'timeshare estate' as 'a right to occupy a timeshare unit, coupled with a freehold estate or an estate for years with future interest in a timeshare property or a specified portion thereof.' The above definition fleshes out the statutory definition in a more readily understood fashion.*

**Section 26** 'Timeshare Owner' (sometimes referred to as 'owner') shall mean any person, firm, corporation, partnership, association, trust, or other legal entity in whose name a Warranty Deed to a Timeshare Interest, as defined herein, is recorded in the Public Records of XYZ County, Florida; provided, however, that Developer shall be deemed to be the Timeshare Owner of any Timeshare Interest(s) in a Unit Committed to Timeshared Ownership with respect to which a Warranty Deed has not been recorded in the Public Records of XYZ County, Florida, conveying such Timeshare Interest(s) from Developer to the initial transferee thereof.

*By explicitly reserving the developer's ownership of all units not conveyed by warranty deed, a possible conflict with the Association or other entity is avoided over the ownership of the unsold interests.*

**Section 27** 'Unit Committed to Timeshared Ownership' shall mean a Condominium Unit within the Project with respect to which one (1) or more Warranty Deeds to Timeshare Interest(s) therein have been recorded in the Public Records of XYZ County, Florida.

**Section 28** 'Unit Occupant' shall mean any person occupying a Unit, including but not limited to an Owner, members of his family, his guests, licensees, and invitees, together with any Exchange Users thereof.

**Section 29** 'Unit Owner' (sometimes referred to as 'Owner') shall mean any person, firm, corporation, partnership, association, trust, or other legal entity in whose name a Warranty Deed to a Condominium Unit in the Project is recorded on the Public Records of XYZ County, Florida; provided, however, that Developer shall be deemed to be the Unit Owner of any Condominium Unit(s) with respect to which a Warranty Deed has not been recorded in the Public Records of XYZ County, Florida, conveying such Condominium Unit(s) from Developer to the initial transferee thereof.

**Section 30** 'Vacation Week' shall mean a specific period of seven (7) consecutive days during which time a Timeshare Owner has the exclusive right to use and

occupy the Condominium Unit identified in his Warranty Deed, as well as enjoy such other rights and privileges as are granted to him hereunder.

Vacation Weeks are computed as follows:

Vacation Week number 1 is the seven (7) consecutive days commencing on the first Saturday in each calendar year. Vacation Week number 2 is the seven (7) consecutive days succeeding Vacation Week number 1. The remaining Vacation Weeks, up to and including Vacation Week number 52, may be determined in like manner; provided, however, that every five (5) or six (6) years, a Vacation Week number 53 shall follow the Maintenance Week designated for each Unit Committed to Timeshared Ownership, as indicated on the Schedule of Vacation Weeks which is attached hereto as Exhibit 'E'. Such Vacation Weeks run from 4:00 p.m. on the first Saturday of the Vacation Week to 4:00 p.m. on the immediately succeeding Saturday of the Vacation Week.

*Week 53 may be considered a bonus week and conveyed to the owner of week 52 or kept in a pool of interests to provide scheduling flexibility.*

Notwithstanding the foregoing, each Timeshare Owner shall be required to vacate his Unit at such time prior to the termination of his Vacation Week as shall be set forth from time to time by the Board of Directors in the then-current Rules and Regulations to enable the Association to perform routine cleaning and maintenance, pursuant to the provisions hereof; provided, however, that a Timeshare Owner who owns consecutive Vacation Weeks in the same Unit Committed to Timeshared Ownership shall not be required to vacate his Unit during the period of time between such consecutive Vacation Weeks.

*It is important to make clear that while the ownership interests are divided so that there is no time gap in ownership, there must be a gap period in actuality between timeshare owners to allow cleaning of the timeshare unit.*

**Section 31** 'Warranty Deed' shall mean

that certain instrument by which Developer conveys one or more Condominium Units or Timeshare Interests in the Project, together with any subsequent assignments thereof.

## ARTICLE II

### NAME AND ADDRESS

The name by which this Project shall be known and identified is Club 'ABC', a Condominium, the address of which is 101 Main Street, Anywhere, Florida.

## ARTICLE III

### CONDOMINIUM PROPERTY

**Section 1 Survey, Plot Plan, and Graphic Description** A survey of the land described in Exhibit 'A' hereto, together with a Graphic Description of the improvements in which Condominium Units are located and a Plot Plan thereof, are attached hereto as Exhibit 'F'.

**Section 2 Certificate of Surveyor** Attached hereto as part of Exhibit 'F' is the certificate of a surveyor authorised to practise in the State of Florida which states that construction of the Project is substantially complete such that the Survey, the Plot Plan, and the Graphic Description referred to in Section 1 above, together with the provisions hereof describing the Property, constitute an accurate representation of the location and dimensions of the improvements and that the identification, location, and dimensions of the improvements and the Common Elements can be determined from such materials.

*'Substantially complete' is a key term. The purchase funds held in escrow may not be released under FRETSA until 'completion of construction' of the building which is defined to mean issuance of a certificate of occupancy for the entire building in which a timeshare unit being sold is located or the substantial completion of the building and improvements.*

**Section 3 Description of Condominium Units** The Condominium Units are shown on the Survey which is attached

hereto as Exhibit 'F'. Each such Unit is identified by a number such that no Unit bears the same numerical designation as any other Unit. Each Unit shall be deemed to include all non-load bearing walls and partitions located therein as well as the inner decorated or finished surfaces of all walls, floors, and ceilings. The Units shall not be deemed to include:

(a) The undecorated or unfinished surfaces of the perimeter walls and party walls of each Unit;

(b) All load bearing walls and partitions;

(c) The perimeter walls of the buildings in which the Units are located, including the exterior finishes and surfaces of the perimeter walls;

(d) Any pipes, shafts, wires, conduits, and other utility or service lines located in a Unit;

(e) The undecorated or unfinished floors and ceilings, and all doors, door frames, windows, window frames, and panels located in a Unit; and

(f) All furniture, furnishings, fixtures, and equipment located in a Unit; the same being deemed Common elements or Common Furnishings as provided herein.

**Section 4 Description of Common Elements** The Common Elements of the Project are described as follows:

(a) The land described in Exhibit 'A' hereto;

(b) The undecorated or unfinished surfaces of the perimeter walls and party walls of each Unit;

(c) All load bearing walls and partitions, including the exterior finished or decorated surfaces of such walls and partitions (but not the inner decorated or finished surfaces of such walls in a Unit);

(d) All walls not located in a Unit, including the exterior finished or decorated surfaces of all such walls;

(e) All pipes, wires, shafts, conduits, and other utility or service lines located in a Unit;

(f) The undecorated or unfinished floors and ceilings, and all doors, door frames, windows, window frames, and panels located in a Unit;

(g) The perimeter walls of the buildings in which the Units are located, including the exterior finished surfaces thereof;

(h) Central and appurtenant installations for services such as power, light, gas, water, sewage disposal, and air conditioning, together with the tanks, pumps, motors, fans, compressors, ducts, and, in general, all apparatus, equipment, and installations existing for the common use of all owners, except for the telephones and any appurtenant equipment;

(i) The foundations, floor slabs, beams, columns, supports, girders, walls, partitions, walkways, stairways, stairs, doors, windows, and panels upon the Property existing for the common use of all Owners;

(j) All ducts, electrical equipment, wiring, pipes, and other central and appurtenant transmission facilities and installations over, under, and across the Property which serve more than one Unit for services such as power, light, gas, water, sewage disposal, air conditioning, and radio and television signal distribution; and

(k) Any and all other apparatus and installations of common use which are necessary or convenient for the existence, maintenance, and safety of the Property, or normally in common use, or as are specified in Section 718.108, Florida Statutes.

*Section 718.108 refers to the statutory definition of common elements and is included as part of a catch-all provision of the description.*

Each Owner's undivided interest in the Common elements of the Project is set forth in Exhibit 'D' hereto.

**Section 5 Description of Limited Common Elements** The Limited Common Elements shall consist of such of the above Common Elements, the use of which is reserved exclusively for one (1), or more Units. Such Limited Common elements include, but are not necessarily limited to the following:

(a) Individual patios and balconies appurtenant to a Unit; and

(b) All structures, equipment, and areas designated as Limited Common

Elements on the Survey which is attached as Exhibit 'E' hereto.

## ARTICLE IV

### TIMESHARED OWNERSHIP

**Section 1 Timeshare Estates** Timeshare estates, as that term is defined by Section 721,05(24), Florida Statutes, may be created with respect to some or all of the Units in the project. The maximum number of Units in the Project is _____ _____ (_____) and the maximum number of Timeshare Interests to be conveyed in each such Unit is fifty-one (51). Accordingly, the maximum number of Timeshare Interests which Developer is hereby authorised to create in the Project is _____ _____ (_____).

*A timeshare estate is defined by FRETSA as a 'a right to occupy a timeshare unit, coupled with a freehold estate or an estate for years with future interest in a timeshare property or a specified portion thereof.'*

**Section 2 Committing a Unit to Time-shared Ownership** A Condominium Unit, as shown on Exhibit 'F' hereto, shall become a Unit Committed to Timeshared Ownership upon the recording in the Public Records of XYZ County, Florida, of the first Warranty Deed conveying a Timeshare Interest in such Unit may be committed to a Timeshare Owner. No Condominium Unit may be committed to timeshared ownership by any person or entity other than Developer.

*The last sentence of the above paragraph prevents a whole unit owner from creating his own timeshare scheme separate from the developer's program.*

A Condominium Unit shall no longer be a Unit Committed to Timeshared Ownership if at any time title to all fifty-one (51) Timeshared Interests in such Unit is held by the same legal entity and said legal entity records an instrument in the Public Records of XYZ County, Florida, removing said Unit from timeshared ownership. Notwithstanding the recording of such instrument, such Condominium Unit and the Owner thereof shall remain subject to this Declaration as well as the other Project Instruments. Upon the recording of any such instrument, the Owner of said Unit shall be entitled to use and occupy such Unit during the Maintenance Week which had previously been designated by Developer, pursuant to the provisions of Article IX, Section 7 below.

## ARTICLE V

### DESCRIPTION OF CONDOMINIUM UNITS AND TIMESHARE INTERESTS

Subsequent to the recording of this Declaration in the Public Records of XYZ County, Florida, every lease, mortgage, deed of trust, or other instrument may legally describe a Condominium Unit by its Unit number, as set forth on the Survey which is attached hereto as Exhibit 'F', together with the appropriate recording data for this Declaration and any amendments hereto, and may legally describe a Timeshare Interest in a Unit Committed to Timeshared Ownership by the Unit number and the Vacation Week number, together with the appropriate recording data for this Declaration and any amendments hereto. Each such description shall be good and sufficient for all purposes to sublease, encumber, or otherwise transfer an owner's Condominium Unit or Timeshare Interest.

## ARTICLE VI

### USE RIGHTS AND USE RESTRICTIONS

**Section 1 Residential Use** Each owner shall occupy his Unit as a single family private dwelling for himself, members of his family, his guests, licensees, and invitees, subject to the restrictions contained herein and in the other Project Instruments; provided, however, that Developer may make any lawful use of a Unit or Timeshare Interest of which it is deemed the Owner, pursuant to the provisions hereof.

**Section 2 Occupancy and Constructive Possession of Units Committed to Time-shared Ownership** Each Timeshare Owner shall have the exclusive right to use and occupy his Unit and the Common Furnishings appurtenant thereto, and the non-exclusive right to use and enjoy the Common Elements of the Project, for their intended purposes, during such Vacation Week(s) as are specifically identified in said Timeshare Owner's Warranty Deed. No Timeshare Owner shall occupy his Unit or exercise any of the rights appurtenant to his Timeshare Interest, other than the rights provided to him in this Declaration, during any time period other than his Vacation Week(s), unless expressly authorised to do so by the Timeshare Owner entitled to occupy the Unit during such Vacation Week(s); provided, however, that for purposes of 11 USC Section 365(i), a Timeshare Owner shall be deemed to be in constructive possession of his Unit during all remaining times.

*The above reference is to federal bankruptcy law. The purpose of stating that a timeshare owner remains in constructive possession of his unit is to fall within the special bankruptcy protections of the amended Section 365(i) should consumers have their purchase contracts rejected by a bankruptcy trustee as executory in their developer's bankruptcy.*

**Section 3 Check-In** Upon arrival at the Project, all Timeshare Owners, members of their family, their guests, licensees, and invitees, and any Exchange Users shall check-in at the reception desk available for such purpose. No person shall be admitted into a Unit Committed to Timeshared Ownership until the check-in process has been, completed. Furthermore, proper identification, and in the case of persons other than the Timeshare Owner of a Unit, written authorization to enter and use such Unit, in a form acceptable to the Manager, shall be required.

*The requirement of checking-in allows for greater ease in administration much in the same fashion as a hotel.*

**Section 4 Care of Units** Each Unit Occupant shall exercise reasonable care in the use of his Unit as well as the Common

Elements, Common Furnishings, and any property of the Association.

**Section 5 Responsibility for Damage** Each Owner and Exchange User shall be liable for the uninsured costs and expense of any maintenance, repair, or replacement of the Units, Common Elements, Common Furnishings, or property of the Association, necessitated by his negligent or intentional act or omission. The negligent or intentional act or omission of an Owner's family members, guests, licensees, or invitees (excluding Exchange Users) shall be deemed to be the act of the Owner, and such persons shall be held jointly and severally liable with such Owner.

With respect to Units Committed to Timeshared Ownership, in the event that one (1) or more of such Units are rendered uninhabitable due to the intentional or negligent act or omission of a Timeshare Owner or Exchange User, the Association shall use reasonable efforts to find, and shall initially pay for, alternative accommodations of reasonably comparable quality and location for any person(s) authorized to occupy such uninhabitable Unit(s). The responsible Owner or Exchange User shall be assessed by the Association for the uninsured cost of such alternative accommodations and shall also be liable to the Association for an administrative fee which, unless and until adjusted by the Board of Directors, shall be in the amount of $200.00 per day or any part thereof during the period the Unit(s) remain uninhabitable.

*This type of provision provides the Association with a remedy in the event an Owner or Owner's guest damages a Timeshare Unit and alternative accommodations for the succeeding timeshare owner need to be arranged.*

The Manager shall submit a bill to the responsible Owner or Exchange User for all amounts payable to the Association under this Section, which amounts shall be enforceable as a claim for money damages against such Owner or Exchange User and shall constitute a Personal Charge to such Owner.

Any loss, damage, or destruction caused by an Exchange User to a Unit, a Common Element, a Common Furnishing, or any property of the Association, or any violation of the Project Instruments by the Exchange User, shall be remedied by the Association, and the cost thereof, to the extent not covered by insurance or recovered from the Exchange User, shall be a Timeshare Expense and shall be shared by all Timeshare Owners as a part of their Timeshare Maintenance Fee; provided, however, that if an Exchange User is also a Timeshare Owner, such costs shall constitute a Personal Charge to such Timeshare Owner and shall be borne by such Timeshare Owner exclusively.

*Damage by Exchange Users is not viewed in the same way as damage by an Owner or an Owner's Guest. Since an individual Owner is not directly liable, such damage becomes a common expense of the Association.*

**Section 6 Offensive Use** No Unit Occupant shall cause or permit any unlawful, improper, or offensive use of any Unit, Common Element, Common Furnishing, or property of the Association, nor shall any Unit Occupant permit the Project to be used in any manner contrary to or not in accordance with the provisions of the Project Instruments. Furthermore, no Unit Occupant shall cause or permit anything to be done or kept in a Unit which will increase the rate of any of the Association's insurance coverage, or which will obstruct or interfere with the rights of other Unit Occupants or annoy them by unreasonable noises or otherwise, nor shall any Unit Occupant commit or permit any nuisance, objectionable or disruptive behaviour, or illegal acts in or about the Project.

**Section 7 Hazards to Health and Safety** Any violation which is deemed by the Board of Directors or the Manager to constitute a hazard to health or safety shall be corrected immediately. The responsible Owner or Exchange User shall be liable for any uninsured expense of correcting such violation.

**Section 8 Maximum Occupancy Restriction** No Unit Occupant shall cause or permit his Unit to be occupied overnight by a number of persons in excess of such occupancy limits which are imposed by law and/or set forth in the Rules and Regulations.

**Section 9 Pet Restriction** No pet or animal of any kind shall be permitted within a Unit or elsewhere within the Project.

**Section 10 Vacating Units** Each Unit Occupant of a Unit Committed to Timeshared Ownership shall vacate such Unit on the final day of his Vacation Week (or at the end of his last consecutive Vacation Week in the case of Unit Occupants who are entitled to consecutive Vacation Weeks) at the time specified in the Rules and Regulations. At such time, each Unit Occupant shall take all such steps as are necessary to ensure the removal of all persons occupying his Unit during his Vacation Week(s), along with all of the personal property of such persons. However, Timeshare Owners shall not be responsible for the removal of Exchange Users and/or their personal property. If any Unit Occupant fails to vacate his Unit at the end of his Vacation Week(s), or at such earlier time as may be fixed by the then-current Rules and Regulations, or otherwise uses or occupies a Unit during any period other than his Vacation Week(s) without written authorisation from the Timeshare Owner entitled to occupy such Unit at that time, or prevents another Timeshare Owner from using or occupying the Unit during such Timeshare Owner's Vacation Week(s), then he shall be deemed a 'Holdover Owner' and shall be subject to immediate removal, eviction, or ejection from the Unit wrongfully used or occupied and shall be deemed to have waived any notice required by law with respect to any legal proceedings regarding removal, eviction, or ejection (to the extent that such notices may be waived under Florida law). The Association, acting through the Manager, shall take such prompt and immediate steps as may be necessary to remove such Holdover Owner and his personal property from the Unit wrong-

fully occupied, to the extent permitted by law. The Association shall use its best efforts to secure, at its expense, alternative accommodations for any Timeshare Owner who is unable to occupy his Unit due to the failure to vacate of any Holdover owner. Such accommodations shall be comparable in quality and location to that Owner's Unit, to the extent reasonably possible. Any cost of such alternative accommodations shall initially be borne by the Association. However, such amount, together with all other costs and expenses incurred by the Association due to the Holdover Owner's failure to vacate the Unit in question, as well as an administrative fee which, unless and until adjusted by the Board of Directors, shall be in the amount of $200.00 per day or any part thereof during such holdover period, including the day of surrender, shall be assessed to the Timeshare owner who wrongfully occupied or permitted or otherwise allowed the Holdover Owner to occupy such Unit. The Manager shall submit a bill to the Association pursuant to this Section, which amounts shall be enforceable as a claim for money damages against the Holdover Owner or Exchange User, and shall constitute a Personal Charge to such Timeshare Owner.

*The above provision grants the Manager and Association an enforcement tool to encourage the orderly transition from occupancy to occupancy of Timeshare Owners.*

**Section 11 No Accrual** If for any reason a Timeshare Owner, the members of his family, his guests, licensees, or invitees do not use such Timeshare Owner's entire Vacation Week(s) in a particular calendar year, the unused time cannot be accumulated or otherwise carried forward for future use at the Project, and the Timeshare Owner shall remain responsible for complying with all of the provisions of the Project Instruments, including but not limited to the payment of all Assessments.

**Section 12 Rentals by Developer** Notwithstanding any provision of this Declaration to the contrary, Developer shall have the right to rent any Condominium Unit of which it is deemed the Owner, pursuant to the provisions hereof, or any Unit Committed to Timeshared Ownership during any unused Vacation Week(s) or portion thereof, or during any Vacation Week(s) of which Developer is deemed the Timeshare Owner, pursuant to the provisions hereof, as a hotel accommodation on a transient basis to members of the general public or to make any other use thereof which is permitted by law. Any monies received by Developer from any such rentals or other uses shall inure solely to the benefit of Developer. All guests or tenants of Developer shall be entitled to the same use rights and privileges, and shall be subject to the same use restrictions, as the guests or tenants of other Owners hereunder. The rental of Units on a transient basis to members of the general public shall be governed by Chapter 509, Florida Statutes.

*The above reservation of right to rent Developer-owned Units and Timeshare Interests allows a Developer the use of the unsold timeshare and condominium inventory and clarifies that any income earned from such rentals is the Developer's alone and not for the benefit of the Association.*

**Section 13 Protection of Developer** Notwithstanding any provision of the Project Instruments to the contrary, for so long as Developer holds for sale in the ordinary course of its business one (1) or more Condominium Units and/or Timeshare Interests, none of the following actions may be taken by the Board, the Association, or any Owner other than Developer, without the prior written approval of Developer:

(a) Levying any Assessment against Developer for any capital improvements to the Project; and

(b) Taking any action which would be detrimental to the sale by Developer of Condominium Units and/or Timeshare Interests; provided, however, that an increase in Common Expense Assessments or Timeshare Maintenance Fees without discriminating against Developer shall not be deemed to be detrimental to the sale of Condominium Units or Timeshare Interests.

*This prevents an Association from either drastically modifying the operation of the Project so that Developer sales are jeopardized or levying the cost of major improvements not part of the Developer's agreement with the Owners.*

**Section 14 Easements** The Project shall be subject to the following easements:

(a) Each Unit shall have non-exclusive easements in the Common Elements for support and for the maintenance and repair of such Unit;

(b) If any Common Element now or hereafter encroaches upon any Unit, or if any Unit now or hereafter encroaches upon any other Unit or Common Element, a valid easement for such encroachment and the maintenance thereof, as long as such encroachment continues, does and shall exist. Minor encroachments by any Unit or Common Element upon any other Unit or Common Element due to construction or to the partial or total destruction and subsequent rebuilding of the improvements, shall be permitted, and valid easements for such encroachments and the maintenance thereof shall exist;

(c) Each Owner and Developer, its successors and assigns, shall have an easement in common with all of the Owners to use all pipes, wires, ducts, cables, conduits, public utility lines, and other Common Elements located in any of the other Units or Common Elements which serve his Unit. Each Unit and Common Element shall be subject to an easement in favour of the Owners of all of the other Units and Timeshare Interests and Developer to use the pipes, ducts, cables, wires, conduits, public utilities, and other Common Elements serving such other Units and located in such Units;

(d) Developer shall have and hereby retains for itself, its successors and assigns, an easement to maintain one (1) or more business and sales offices at the Project to enable Developer or its designee(s) to market and sell Condominium Units and Timeshare Interests and to rent available Units on a transient basis to members of the general public in accordance with the provisions of Section 12 above. In connection therewith, Developer or its designee(s) may place signs in or around the Common Elements and may use any of the Common Elements or portions thereof for marketing and rental purposes, in combination with or to the exclusion of all other uses. However, Developer and its designee(s) shall place such signs and conduct such activities in such manner and location as to minimize any inconvenience to the Owners which might be occasioned thereby. Owners, other than Developer, are prohibited from placing signs in or around the Common Elements;

*By explicitly reserving an easement for the right to maintain a sales office at the Project, the Developer's and its successor's ability to sell interests at the Project is protected.*

(e) Developer shall have and hereby retains for itself, its successors and assigns, an easement and right of ingress and egress in and to those portions of the Common Elements which are necessary to Developer for the construction of additions and improvements to the Project or to the Adjacent Condominium Property described in Exhibit 'G' hereto;

(f) Developer shall have and hereby retains for itself, its successors and assigns, an easement over, under, above, and through the Project, as may be required for conduits, ducts, plumbing, wiring, and other facilities necessary for the furnishing of utility services to the Units and the Common Elements;

(g) Developer shall have and hereby retains for itself, its successors and assigns, including all of the Owners, a non-exclusive easement for ingress and egress over, through, and across such streets, walks, paths, stairways, lanes, and other rights-of-way serving the Units and the Common Elements as may be necessary to provide reasonable pedestrian access thereto, as well as an easement for ingress and egress over, through, and across such paved portions of the Common Elements as may be necessary to provide reasonable vehicular access thereto; provided, however, that the latter easement shall not give or create in any

person the right to park upon any portion of the Property not designated as a parking area by the Board of Directors. In the event that any of said easements for ingress or egress shall be encumbered by any mortgage, leasehold, or other lien, other than those on the entire Property, such mortgages, leaseholds, or other liens shall hereby be subordinate to the use rights of any Owner whose Condominium Unit or Timeshare Interest is not also encumbered by said mortgage, leasehold, or other lien;

(h) Developer shall have and hereby retains for itself, its successors and assigns, the right, at its expense and for the benefit of the Project or adjacent property or other property owned or operated by Developer, to utilize and to grant easements over, across, and under the Common Elements for utilities, sanitary and storm sewers, security or other types of monitors, cable television lines, walkways, roadways, and rights-of-way over, across, and under the Common Elements, including without limitation, any existing utilities, sanitary lines, sewer lines, and cable television, and to connect the same over, across, and under the Common Elements, provided that such utilisation, easements, relocations, and connections of lines shall not materially impair or interfere with the use of any Unit. In addition, the Association, through the Board, is authorized to give, convey, transfer, cancel, relocate, and otherwise deal with any and all utility and other easements now or hereafter located on or affecting the Project; and

(i) Developer further reserves for itself, its successors and assigns, the right to establish such additional easements, reservations, exceptions, and exclusions as Developer, in its sole discretion, deems necessary or appropriate and in the best interests of the owners and the Association in order to serve the entire Project.

## ARTICLE VII

## TRANSFER AND ENCUMBRANCE OF CONDOMINIUM UNITS AND TIMESHARE INTERESTS

## Section 1 Transfer of Condominium Units and Timeshare Interests

(a) Any attempt to separate an Owner's interest in his Condominium Unit or Timeshare Interest from its appurtenant undivided interest in the Common Elements, Common furnishings (if applicable), Common Surplus, or membership in the Association shall be null and void.

(b) Except for each Unit Owner's right to lease or rent his Unit and each Timeshare owner's right to lease or rent his Unit during all or a portion of his Vacation Week(s), as provided herein, no Owner may in any way sell, convey, devise, or otherwise transfer any portion of his Condominium Unit or Timeshare Interest without selling, conveying, devising, or otherwise transferring the entire Condominium Unit or Timeshare Interest and all rights related or appurtenant thereto, and any attempt by an Owner to do so shall be null and void. However, an Owner may transfer an undivided interest in his entire Condominium Unit of Timeshare Interest and all rights related or appurtenant thereto to another person or entity.

(c) No transfer of a Condominium Unit or Timeshare Interest shall be permitted unless and until the proposed transferor has paid all Assessments due the Association, and the purported transfer of a Condominium Unit or Timeshare Interest upon which any Assessment is then owing shall be null and void. Upon request, and upon the payment to the Association of a reasonable fee, as determined from time to time by the Board of Directors (except in the case of a Mortgagee of Record, in which instance no fee shall be required), the Association shall issue a written statement setting forth the amounts, if any, which the proposed transferor of a Condominium Unit or Timeshare Interest owes the Association. Such statement shall be conclusive upon the Association in favour of all persons or entities (except the transferor) who rely thereon in good faith as to the amount of such indebtedness as of the date of the statement.

*By conditioning the transfer of a Condominium Unit or Timeshare Interest on the bringing current of any amounts or fees owed to the Association, the Association's collection process is eased.*

(d) Each owner shall be free to transfer his Condominium Unit or Timeshare Interest, subject to the restrictions contained herein. The deed or other instrument of conveyance executed by the transferee shall provide that the Condominium Unit(s) or Timeshare Interest(s) conveyed thereby shall be held by such transferee subject to each of the provisions of the Project Instruments. No transfer of any kind of a Condominium Unit or Timeshare Interest, including a transfer to a Mortgagee of Record which obtains title to the Condominium Unit or Timeshare Interest as a result of the foreclosure of its mortgage thereon or otherwise, shall be valid or effective unless and until an instrument evidencing such transfer is recorded in the Public Records of XYZ County, Florida, and a true and correct copy of each instrument is provided to the Manager for the Association's transferee a reasonable administrative fee for processing the transfer, not to exceed the amount set forth in Section 718.112(2) (j), Florida Statutes.

*This provision allows the Association to collect the amounts owed from either the transferor or transferee. The Section reference is to the Condominium law which places a dollar amount limitation on such administrative fees.*

(e) The transferor of a Condominium Unit or Timeshare Interest shall be jointly and severally liable with the transferee (except a Mortgagee of Record) for all unpaid Assessments levied upon the transferor up to the time of the transfer, without prejudice to the transferee's right to recover from the transferor any amounts paid by the transferee to the Association in satisfaction of such indebtedness. No person or entity (except a Mortgagee of Record) who acquires a Condominium Unit or Timeshare Interest shall be entitled to occupy a Unit or to use and enjoy the Common Elements and Common Furnishings by virtue of the acquisition of such Condominium Unit or Timeshare Interest, until such time as all unpaid Assessments due and owing by the transferor have been paid.

(f) No provision contained herein shall be interpreted so as to prevent a Unit Owner from subleasing or renting his Condominium Unit or to prevent a Timeshare Owner from subleasing, renting, or otherwise making his Unit available for occupancy during his Vacation Week(s) by members of his family, his guests, licensees, invitees, or Exchange Users.

**Section 2 Encumbrance of Condominium Units and Timeshare Interests** Each Owner shall have the right to mortgage or otherwise encumber his Condominium Unit(s) or Timeshare Interest(s); provided, however, that, no Owner may encumber or hypothecate any portion of his Condominium Unit or Timeshare Interest without encumbering or hypothecating the entire Condominium Unit or Timeshare Interest and all rights related or appurtenant thereto, and any attempt by an Owner to do so shall be null and void. No Owner shall have the right to take any action that will encumber the Condominium Unit(s) or Timeshare Interest(s) of any other Owner or any Unit or portion of the Common Elements or Common Furnishings of the Project, and any attempt by an Owner to do so shall be null and void. Any mortgage, deed of trust, or other encumbrance of any Condominium Unit(s) or Timeshare Interest(s) shall be subject to all of the provisions of the Project Instruments.

**Section 3 Waiver of Partition** Each Owner hereby waives any and all right to seek or obtain, through any legal proceeding, judicial partition or sale in lieu of partion of any Unit, Common Element, or other portion of the Project, unless and until the Project is removed from the provisions of Chapter 718, Florida Statutes, as provided in Article XVIII below, or in the case of substantial damage or destruction to the Property as provided in Article XIV below. If, however, any Condominium Unit(s) or Timeshare Interest(s) shall be owned by two (2) or more persons or entities, nothing herein contained shall

prohibit the partition or a judicial sale in lieu of partition of the Condominium Unit(s) or Timeshare Interest(s) as between such co-Owners.

*Section 721.22 of FRETSA states that no action for partition of any timeshare unit will lie unless otherwise provided for in the contract between the seller and the purchaser. The 1984 amendments to FRETSA further added that if a timeshare estate exists as an estate for years with a future interest, the estate for years will not be deemed to have merged with the future interest, and further prevents the conveyance of the estate for years separate from the corresponding future interest.*

**Section 4 Protection of Interest** Except as otherwise provided herein, no Owner shall permit his Condominium Unit(s) or Timeshare Interest(s) to be subject to any lien, claim, or charge, the enforcement of which may result in a sale or threatened sale of any other Condominium Unit(s) or Timeshare Interest(s) or in any interference in the use or enjoyment thereof by any other Owner.

## ARTICLE VIII

### THE CLUB 'ABC' CONDOMINIUM ASSOCIATION, INC.

**Section 1 Membership In Association** Each Owner, including Developer (so long as Developer is deemed the Owner of any Condominium Unit(s) or Timeshare Interest(s), pursuant to the provisions hereof), shall be a member of the Association until he ceases to be an Owner.

**Section 2 Transfer of Membership** The membership of each Owner in the Association is appurtenant to and inseparable from his ownership of a Condominium Unit or Timeshare Interest and shall automatically terminate upon any valid transfer or conveyance of his Condominium Unit or Timeshare Interest to any transferee or grantee, whether voluntary or by operation of law, except to the extent that such transferor retains an interest in any other Condominium Unit or Timeshare Interest in the Project. The transferee of a Condominium Unit or a Timeshare Interest shall, immediately and automatically upon the valid transfer of the Condominium Unit or Timeshare Interest as provided herein, become a member of the Association. If title to a Condominium Unit or Timeshare Interest is vested in more than one (1), person or entity, then all of the persons and/or entities having title to such Condominium Unit or Timeshare Interest shall be members of the Association.

*Membership in the Association cannot be separated from the ownership interest.*

The transfer of any Condominium Unit(s) or Timeshare Interest(s) shall operate to transfer to the new Owner thereof the undivided interest of the prior Owner in all funds held by the Association, even though not expressly mentioned or described in the instrument of transfer and without further instrument of transfer.

### Section 3 Voting

(a) Each Owner (including Developer as to all Condominium Units and Timeshare Interests of which it is deemed the Owner, pursuant to the provisions hereof) shall be entitled to a vote which is equivalent to his undivided interest in the Common Elements, as set forth in Exhibit 'D' hereto. The vote allocated to a Condominium Unit or Timeshare Interest which is owned by more than one (1) person or entity may be cast only by the voting member designated for that Condominium Unit or Timeshare Interest, as provided in the By-Laws.

(b) Voting rights transferred or pledged by any mortgage held by a Mortgagee of Record for any Condominium Unit or Timeshare Interest which has been recorded in the Public Records of XYZ County, Florida, a true and correct copy of which has been filed with the Manager, shall be exercised only by the person designated in such instrument, or such person's proxy, until a written release or other termination thereof has been recorded, and a true and correct copy thereof has been filed with the Manager.

## ARTICLE IX

## MANAGEMENT; MAINTENANCE AND REPAIRS

**Section 1 Administration of the Project** Responsibility for the maintenance, repair, replacement, restoration, improvement, operation, and administration of the Project shall be vested in the Association. The Association shall act as the agent of all of the Owners in collecting Assessments and paying taxes, utility costs, and other Common Expenses and Timeshare Expenses. The Association, through its Board of Directors, Officers, the Manager, and other duly authorized agent(s) may exercise any and all rights and powers granted to it by law by the Project Instruments, as amended from time to time.

**Section 2 Common Elements, Limited Common Elements, and Common Furnishings** Exclusive control and responsibility over the maintenance, repair, modification, and alteration of the Common Elements and the Limited Common Elements is vested in the Association. The Association shall at all times maintain the Common Elements and the Limited in good condition and repair. In the event of any disruption in service, the Association shall immediately make such repairs as may be necessary to restore such service. If Developer believes in good faith that the Association cannot or will not immediately make such repairs, Developer may, but shall not be obligated to, immediately arrange for and make such repairs in order to restore service, and the Association shall be liable to Developer for the cost of such repairs. The Association shall have complete discretion to determine the exterior colour scheme of all Condominium Units as well as the interior colour scheme, the decor, and the furnishings of each Common Element and Limited Common Element, as well as the timing, and nature of all redecorations, repairs, and/or replacements thereof. No Unit Occupant shall make any repairs, modifications, alterations, additions, redecorations, or replacements to a Common Element, Limited Common Element, Common Furnishing, or any property of the Association.

**Section 3 Condominium Units Not Committed to Timeshared Ownership** Each Unit Owner shall maintain his Unit in good condition and repair at all times, and shall be responsible for maintaining, repairing, and replacing, at his sole cost and expense, all portions of such Unit, including but not limited to the interior surfaces of all walls, floors, and ceilings. No Unit Owner may enclose, paint, or otherwise decorate or change the appearance of any patio or balcony appurtenant to his Unit, any portion of the exterior of the building in which his Unit is located, or any other Common Element or Limited Common Element, such responsibilities being vested in the Association as provided in Section 2 above. A Unit Owner may, however, alter or improve his Unit, at his sole and personal cost, provided that all such work is performed without disturbing the rights of other Owners, and further provided that all such work is in compliance with all applicable building codes.

**Section 4 Units committed to Timeshared Ownership** Exclusive control and responsibility over the maintenance, repair, modification, and alteration of all Units Committed to Timeshared Ownership, as well as the Common Furnishings therein, is vested in the Association. No Timeshare Owner shall make any repairs, modifications, alterations, additions, redecorations, or replacements to any Unit Committed to Timeshared Ownership or to any Common Furnishing therein.

*The above restriction allows the Association to administer a uniform scheme among the Timeshare Units and prevents an individual Timeshare Owner from attempting to alter the Association decisions.*

Each Timeshare Owner, during his Vacation Week(s), shall keep the interior of his Unit, including without limitation, the interior walls, windows, glass, ceilings, floors, fixtures, and appurtenances thereto, and all furnishings contained therein, in a clean, sanitary, and attractive condition, and shall be personally liable for any damage or destruction thereto caused by such Timeshare Owner, the members of his family, his guests, invitees, or licensees. The Association shall at all times maintain and keep the Units Committed to Timeshared Ownership, as well as the Common Furnishings therein, in good condition and repair. The Association shall have complete discretion to determine the interior colour scheme, the decor, and the furnishings of each Unit Committed to Timeshared Ownership, as well as the timing, extent, and nature of all redecorations, repairs, and replacements thereof.

**Section 5 Right of Access** Developer and the Association, acting through the Manager or such other person or persons as they shall designate, shall have an irrevocable right of access to each Unit, without liability for trespass, during reasonable hours, as may be necessary to perform and carry out their respective rights, duties, and responsibilities as set forth herein, in the By-Laws, in the Rules and Regulations, and in the Management Agreement, including but not limited to:

(a) Making emergency repairs therein;

(b) Abating any nuisance or any dangerous, unauthorized, prohibited, or unlawful activity in such Unit;

(c) Protecting the property rights and general welfare of the Owners or Unit Occupants; and

(d) Any other purpose reasonably related to the performance by Developer, the Association, and/or the Manager of their respective duties and responsibilities under the Project Instruments.

Such right and authority to enter any Unit shall be exercised in such manner as to avoid any unreasonable or unnecessary interference with the possession, use, and/or enjoyment of any Unit by any occupant thereof, and shall be preceded by reasonable notice to the occupant(s) whenever the circumstances permit. No Owner or Unit Occupant may at any time change a lock on the entrance to any Unit. If an Owner or Unit Occupant changes any such lock, the Association may replace such lock and assess the cost thereof as a Personal Charge to the responsible Owner.

**Section 6 Relocation to Permit Maintenance and Repairs** If it becomes necessary, in the judgment of the Manager, to perform maintenance or repairs within a Unit in order to prevent forseeable personal injury or imminent damage to any of the Units, Common Elements, Common Furnishings, property of the Association, or the personal belongings of any Unit Occupant, and such repairs cannot reasonably be performed while such Unit is occupied, then the occupant(s) of such Unit shall vacate the Unit upon the request of the Manager to do so in order to permit such maintenance or repairs. In such event, the Manager shall use reasonable efforts to relocate the Unit Occupant for the duration of such period of displacement to such reasonably comparable nearby accommodations as possible, at the Association's expense. The decision of the Manager as to whether the Unit is habitable and/or whether relocation to permit maintenance or repairs is necessary shall be conclusive as to all affected persons.

**Section 7 Maintenance Weeks** One (1) specific Vacation Week per year in each Unit Committed to Timeshared Ownership is designated as the Maintenance Week therefor, as shown in the Schedule of Vacation Weeks which is attached as Exhibit 'E' hereto. Subject to the rights of Developer reserved herein, the Association and its agents shall have free access to each Unit Committed to Timeshared Ownership during its designated Maintenance Week for the purpose of effecting any necessary or appropriate maintenance, repairs, modifications, alterations, replacements, and additions to such Unit and/or to the Common Elements and Common Furnishings appurtenant thereto. The Maintenance Week for a particular Unit Committed to Timeshared Ownership may be changed from time to time upon an appropriate amendment of said Exhibit 'E' in the manner hereinafter provided. Whenever the Maintenance Week for a particular Unit Committed to Timeshared Ownership is succeeded by a Vacation Week number 53, as shown in Exhibit 'E' hereto, said Vacation Week number 53 may be utilized by the Association for the same purposes as the Maintenance Week.

*Because of the constant change of occupancy, timeshare units receive more wear and tear and require at least one timeshare period per year for maintenance in order to preserve the quality of the unit.*

## ARTICLE X

### ASSESSMENTS

**Section 1 Common Expense Assessment** Each Owner shall be required to pay a Common Expense Assessment for each Condominium Unit and Timeshare Interest owned. The Common Expense Assessment shall be levied by the Association, through the Board of Directors, to meet the Common Expenses. The Common Expense Assessment shall be shared proportionately by the Owners, based upon each Owner's undivided interest in the Common Elements, as specified and set forth in Exhibit 'D' hereto. The Common Expenses shall include, but shall not be limited to, the costs of the following items:

(a) Personal property taxes, real estate taxes, and any other fees or assessments levied by a governmental authority and not billed directly to the Owners;

(b) The maintenance, repair, modification, alteration, redecoration, and replacement of the Common Elements and Limited Common Elements;

(c) Utility charges;

(d) Basic telephone service;

(e) Insurance coverage, as provided for herein and in the By-Laws;

(f) The purchase, repair, and replacement of any furniture, fixtures, and equipment which may be owned or leased by the Association;

(g) Rental by the Association of any furniture, furnishings, equipment, and/or recreational facilities and other amenities from Developer or other persons or entities;

(h) Administrative costs;

(i) Reserves, as described below;

(j) Management fee; and

(k) Any other costs incurred by the Association in connection with the maintenance, repair, replacement, restoration, redecoration, improvement, operation, and administration of the Project, and in connection with the operation and administration of the Association, but excluding all Timeshare Expenses as provided below.

The initial Common Expense Assessment shall be due and payable by an Owner at the time and in the manner set forth in such Owner's Purchase Contract, to be prorated for the calendar year in question, as appropriate. Subsequent Common Expense Assessments shall be due and payable by an Owner on the fifteenth (15th) day of each month, commencing with the first month immediately succeeding the month in which such Owner's Warranty Deed is recorded in the Public Records of XYZ County, Florida, unless and until the Board of Directors institutes a different payment schedule by providing written notice thereof to each Owner. The Board, in its sole discretion, may elect to establish different payment schedules for Timeshare Owners and Unit Owners such that, for example, all Timeshare owners are required to pay their Common Expense Assessments on a monthly basis, as provided above. Subject to Section 5 below, under no circumstances shall any Owner be required to pay any Common Expense Assessment in a particular calendar year if such Owner is not entitled to use and occupy his Unit during that calendar year for any reason.

**Section 2 Timeshare Maintenance Fee** Each Timeshare Owner shall be required to pay a Timeshare Maintenance Fee for each Timeshare Interest owned. The Timeshare Maintenance Fee shall be levied by the Association, through the Board of Directors, to meet the Timeshare Expenses. The Timeshare maintenance Fee shall be shared proportionately by the Timeshare Owners exclusively, based upon a fraction, the numerator of which shall be the number of Timeshare Interests owned by a particular Timeshare Owner, and the denominator of which shall consist of the total number of Timeshare Interests for which Warranty Deeds have been recorded in the Public Records of XYZ County, Florida, plus the number of Timeshare Interests of which Developer is deemed the Owner, pursuant to the provisions hereof. The Timeshare Expenses shall include, but shall not be limited to, the costs of the following items:

(a) The maintenance, repair, modification, alteration, and redecoration of the Units Committed to Timeshared Ownership;

(b) The maintenance, repair, modification, alteration, redecoration, and replacement of the Common Furnishings;

(c) Insurance coverage on the Units Committed to Timeshared Ownership and the Common Furnishings therein;

(d) Domestic services, including daily cleaning and maid service, furnished to or on behalf of Timeshare Owners; and

(e) Any other costs incurred by the Association in connection with the maintenance, repair, replacement, restoration, redecoration, improvement, operation, and administration of the Project, and in connection with the operation and administration of the Association, which are directly attributable to the commitment of one (1) or more Condominium Units in the Project to timeshared ownership in accordance with the provisions hereof.

The Timeshare Maintenance Fee shall be due and payable by a Timeshare Owner in a single payment along with his Common Expense Assessment, as provided in Section 1 above.

**Section 3 Special Assessments** If the Common Expense Assessments collected from the Owners or the Timeshare Maintenance Fees collected from the Timeshare Owners are at any time inadequate to meet the costs and expenses incurred by or imposed upon the Association for any reason, including but not limited to the non-payment by any Owner of any Assessment, the Board shall immediately determine the approximate amount of such inadequacy, prepare a supplemental budget, and levy a Special Assessment upon each Owner in such amount(s) as the Board determines to be necessary to pay the Association's costs and expenses, which Special Assessment shall be allocated among the Owners based upon each Owner's undivided interest in the Common Elements, as set forth in Exhibit 'D', provided, however, that to the extent any such inadequacy in the funds of the Association is directly attributable to the commitment of one (1) or more Condominium Units in the Project to timeshared ownership in accordance with the provisions hereof, including but not limited to the non-payment by any Timeshare Owner of his Timeshare Maintenance Fee, then a Special Assessment shall be levied only upon the Timeshare Owners in the proportions specified in Section 2 above. Any Special Assessment shall be due and payable within thirty (30) days after the date upon which a written notice of such Special Assessment is mailed to the Owner, unless the Board determines that installment payments shall be permitted and provides each Owner with an approved payment schedule, in which case each Owner's payments must be made no later than is specified in such payment schedule. In the event that the Board authorizes the payment of any Special Assessment in installments, no notice of the due date of each individual installment payment shall be required to be given, other than the aforesaid Special Assessment notice.

**Section 4 Personal Charges** (a) Each Unit Owner shall be responsible for paying to the Association any and all expenses incurred as a result of the act or omission to act of that Unit Owner or any other person(s) occupying such Unit Owner's Unit, including but not limited to the cost to repair any damage to any Unit or Common Element, the cost to satisfy any expenses arising from an intentional or negligent act or omission of the Unit Owner, a member of his family, his guests, invitees, or licensees (to the extent not covered by insurance), or resulting from his or their breach of any of the provisions of the Project Instru-

ments, and any late fees, fines, attorneys' fees, and other amounts which the Project Instruments expressly permit to be assessed upon a particular Unit Owner. Any Common Expenses incurred by the Association in connection with the maintenance, repair, or replacement of a Limited Common Element shall be assessed in equal shares as a Personal Charge against the Owner(s) to whose Unit(s) the Limited Common Element was appurtenant at the time the Common Expense was incurred. All such Personal Charges shall be due and payable within thirty (30) days from the date upon which a notice of such Personal Charges is mailed to the responsible Unit Owner.

(b) Each Timeshare Owner shall be responsible for paying to the Association any and all expenses incurred as a result of the act or omission to act of that Timeshare Owner or any other person(s) occupying such Timeshare Owner's Unit during his Vacation Week(s) (except an Exchange User), including but not limited to the cost of local and long distance telephone charges and other special services or supplies attributable to the occupancy of the Unit during such Timeshare Owner's Vacation Week(s), such as the cost to repair any damage to any Unit or to repair or replace any Common Furnishings located therein, or any Common Element, on account of loss or damage occurring during such Timeshare Owner's Vacation Week(s), the cost to satisfy any expenses arising from an intentional or negligent act or omission of a Timeshare Owner, a member of his family, his guests, invitees, or licensees (to the extent not covered by insurance) or resulting from his or their breach of any of the provisions of the Project Instruments, and any late fees, fines, attorneys' fees, and other amounts which the Project Instruments expressly permit to be assessed upon a particular Timeshare Owner. In connection therewith, the Manager, on behalf of the Association, may require Timeshare Owners or Unit Occupants to surrender upon check-in some form of deposit or credit card imprint to guaranty such Timeshare Owner's or Unit Occupant's payment of any and all Personal Charges incurred by him during the Vacation Week(s) in question. Such Personal Charges shall be paid by each Timeshare Owner as follows:

(i) If the Manager, on behalf of the Association, is able to determine the amount of Personal Charges due from the Timeshare Owner or Unit Occupant at or prior to the time of check-out and to issue a statement therefor, such Personal Charges shall be payable at or before such time.

(ii) Personal Charges due from a Timeshare Owner which are not ascertainable as provided in sub-paragraph (i) above shall be due and payable within thirty (30) days from the date upon which a notice of such Personal Charges is mailed to the responsible Timeshare Owner.

**Section 5 Liability for Assessments** No Owner may exempt himself, his successors or assigns, from his obligation to pay any Assessment(s) by his waiver of the use and enjoyment of his Unit or of any of the Common Elements or the Common Furnishings, or by the abandonment of his Condominium Unit(s) or Timeshare Interest(s).

**Section 6 Surplus Funds** The Association, through its Board of Directors, shall, from time to time, fix and determine the sum or sums which are necessary and adequate to provide for the Common Expenses and Timeshare Expenses of the Project and such other Assessments as are specified herein. The procedure for determining all such Assessments shall be as set forth in the By-Laws, this Declaration, and in the exhibits attached hereto. In the event that the Board determines at any time during the Association's fiscal year that the aggregate amount of Assessments is, or will be, in excess of the amounts needed to meet the Common Expenses and/or Timeshare Expenses of the Project, such excess amount shall appear as a line item on the Association's budget for the immediately succeeding fiscal year, and shall be applied to reduce the amount assessed to meet the Common Expenses and/or Timeshare Expenses, as appropriate, for such fiscal year. Any

such excess shall not relieve any Owner from his obligation to pay any delinquent amounts which he owes the Association, nor shall any Owner be entitled to a refund of all or any portion of any Assessment previously paid on account of such excess.

**Section 7 Reserves** Notwithstanding the foregoing provisions of this Declaration, the Board shall from time to time establish one (1) or more reserves as are necessary for the operation and improvement of the Project by including amounts intended for such purpose in the Association's budget, or by levying Assessments upon all Owners, or upon all Timeshare Owners, to the exclusion of all Unit Owners, if appropriate, to be allocated among Owners in the manner set forth in Sections 1 and 2 of this Article, in such amount(s) as the Board determines to be necessary and appropriate. Said reserves, at the discretion of the Board, may be used to pay any extraordinary expenses for which they were established or intended (such as painting the Units), may be allocated to reserve accounts which were established for different purposes, or may be used to meet any deficiencies in operating funds, as the case may be, from time to time resulting from delinquencies by Owners in the payment of any Assessments, or otherwise; provided, however, that the existence of such reserves shall not operate to exempt any Owner from his obligation to contribute his proportionate share of the Common Expenses and/or Timeshare Expenses or to pay any such Assessments therefor. Any funds used from any of said reserves to meet any deficiencies in operating or maintenance funds resulting from an Owner's delinquencies shall promptly be restored upon the payment of such delinquent Assessment(s) by said Owner. The proportionate interest of each Owner in said reserves and any other funds being held by the Association shall not be withdrawn or assigned separately, but shall be deemed to be transferred with his Condominium Unit(s) or Timeshare Interest(s), even though not mentioned or described expressly in the instrument of transfer. If the Association is ever dissolved, all such funds remaining after full payment of all Common Expenses and Timeshare Expenses shall be distributed to all then-existing Owners in accordance with each Owner's undivided interest in the Common Elements, as set forth in Exhibit 'D' hereto.

**Section 8 Late Charges and Interest** Except as otherwise expressly provided in the Project Instruments, any Assessment levied upon an Owner which is not paid within fifteen (15) days after the date upon which it is due shall bear interest at the highest rate permissible under applicable Florida law, from the date due until paid, compounded monthly, and in the sole discretion of the Board, a late charge in such reasonable and uniform amount as may be set by the Board from time to time may be charged.

**Section 9 Condominium Units and Timeshare Interests Owned by Developer** Notwithstanding any provision to the contrary contained herein, Developer shall not be assessed by the Association for any portion of the Common Expenses or Timeshare Expenses attributable to any Condominium Unit(s) or Timeshare Interest(s) of which it is deemed the Owner, pursuant to the provisions hereof, during such period of time as Developer has guaranteed to each Owner in his Purchase Contract that Common Expense Assessments and Timeshare Maintenance Fees (if appropriate), real estate taxes excluded, will not increase over a specified dollar amount. During any such period of time, Developer shall pay to the Association the amount of any monetary deficiencies (the 'Deficiencies') in the Common Expenses and/or Timeshare Expenses attributable to such Condominium Unit(s) and Timeshare Interest(s) with respect to which a Warranty Deed has been conveyed by Developer and recorded in the Public Records of XYZ County, Florida. The amount of the Deficiencies which Developer shall pay shall be the difference between (a) the Common Expenses and Timeshare Expenses attributable to such Condominium Units and Timeshare Interests

with respect to which a Warranty Deed has been conveyed by Developer and recorded in the Public Records of XYZ County, Florida, real estate taxes excluded; and (b) the Common Expense Assessments and Timeshare Maintenance Fees collected from the Owners of such Condominium Units and Timeshare Interests at the guaranteed levels. Developer shall pay the amount of such Deficiencies when and as the expenses attributable to the maintenance, operation, and administration of the Project become due.

**Section 10 Default in Payment of Assessments; Suspension of Occupancy Privilege; Liens** The Manager shall send a written notice to any Owner who fails to pay any Assessment or any installment thereof when due, which notice shall advise such Owner of its intention to foreclose its lien to collect such unpaid Assessment(s) and of the Owner's right to cure such default by remitting all delinquent amounts, plus late charges and/or interest, within thirty (30) days from the date of such notice. If full payment of all such amounts is not received within the specified period, the unpaid balance of such Owner's remaining installments for such fiscal year, if any, shall then become due. The Association may commence legal action for the recovery of such delinquent amounts and/or exercise its right to foreclose upon such Owner's Condominium Unit or Timeshare Interest as provided hereinafter.

Each Assessment and any late fees, interest, and costs of collection, including reasonable attorney's fees, shall be a personal debt of the Owner against whom they are assessed. A lien as security for the payment of all such amounts shall attach to the Condominium Unit or Timeshare Interest of such Owner, effective as of the date upon which a claim of lien which has been signed and acknowledged by an Officer or agent of the Association is recorded in the Public Records of XYZ County, Florida, as provided in Sections 718.116(4)(a) and 721.16(3), Florida Statutes. Any lien arising hereunder shall continue in full force and effect until fully paid or otherwise discharged. Each Owner shall be deemed to covenant and agree to the attachment of such lien.

As to a Unit Committed to Timeshared Ownership, only the Timeshare Owner(s) thereof who is delinquent in the payment of any Assessment(s) due the Association with respect to such Unit shall be liable for the payment of such Assessment(s). None of the other Timeshare Owners of such Unit shall be jointly or severally liable for the payment of such Assessment(s).

*Section 718.116(b) of the Condominium Law provides that each timeshare owner in a timeshare unit is jointly and severally liable for the payment of all assessments and other charges levied against or with respect to that unit, except to the extent that the declaration or by-laws may provide to the contrary.*

**Section 11 Amount of Unpaid Assessments** Any Owner has the right to require from the Association a certificate showing the amount of any unpaid Assessments due from such Owner with respect to his Condominium Unit or Timeshare Interest. Any Mortgagee of Record has the same rights with respect to any Condominium Unit or Timeshare Interest upon which it has a lien.

## ARTICLE XI

## ENFORCEMENT PROVISIONS

**Section 1 Enforcement of Project Instruments** Default in the payment of any Assessment or the violation of any provision of the Project Instruments by an Owner, members of his family, his guests, licensees, or invitees, or an Exchange User, shall be grounds for an action to recover sums due and/or damages, for injunctive relief, or both, and the reimbursement of all costs and attorneys' fees incurred in connection therewith, as well as late fees and interest on any delinquent amounts, which action shall be maintainable by the Board or the Manager, in the name of the Association, by Developer, or, in a proper case, by an aggrieved Owner. All such amounts, along with any other costs incurred by the Association to obtain the services of an attorney to enforce any provision of the Project Instruments, shall constitute a Personal Charge against the Owner who committed or who is responsible for such violation or who caused the Association to take such action, and shall promptly be reimbursed by such Owner to the Association to take such action, upon demand therefor. Unless otherwise prohibited by law, the violation of any provision of the Project Instruments shall give the Association, the Board, the Manager, and Developer (to the extent of its rights hereunder) the right, in addition to any other rights set forth in the Project Instruments:

(a) To enter the Unit or area in which, or as to which, such violation or breach exists, and to summarily abate and remove, at the expense of the Owner or Exchange User who caused or permitted such violation, any structure, thing, or condition that may exist therein contrary to the intent and meaning of the provisions of the Project Instruments, and neither the Manager, Developer, nor any authorized agent thereof shall thereby be deemed guilty in any number of trespass;

(b) To engage the services of an attorney to initiate such action as is deemed necessary by the Board, the Manager, or Developer, to enforce such provision, including the initiation of a suit for damages and/or to enjoin, abate, or remedy by appropriate legal proceedings, either at law or in equity, the continuance of any such breach;

(c) To foreclose the Association's lien against a Condominium Unit or Timeshare Interest for unpaid Assessments in the same manner as is authorized by the laws of the State of Florida for the foreclosure of mortgages on real property. The Association shall have the right to bid on the Condominium Unit or Timeshare Interest at any foreclosure sale and may acquire, hold, lease, mortgage, and convey the Condominium Unit or Timeshare Interest acquired at such sale;

(d) To impose a reasonable monetary penalty upon such Owner or Exchange User in an amount to be determined by the Board of Directors;

(e) As to Timeshare Owners, to demand and receive from any Unit Occupant during the defaulting Timeshare Owner's Vacation Week(s) the rent due from any Unit Occupant to such Timeshare Owner, up to an amount sufficient to pay all sums due from the Timeshare Owner, including costs, attorneys' fees, and interest. The Unit Occupant shall be discharged from the payment of rent to such Timeshare Owner to the extent of the amount so paid. If the Manager makes a demand upon a Unit Occupant for the payment of rent, the Unit Occupant shall have no right to question the authority of the Manager to make such demand, and shall be obligated to promptly pay the amount demanded by the Manager, with the effect as aforesaid.

**Section 2 Remedies are Cumulative** All of the remedies granted by the Project Instruments are cumulative, and the exercise of one right or remedy shall not impair the right to exercise any other remedy. The Association, the Board, the Manager, and Deveoper shall not be limited to the remedies set forth in this Declaration, and may invoke any other or additional remedies provided for or allowed by law or in equity.

**Section 3 Preservation of Remedies** The failure of the Association, the Board, the Manager, or Developer to enforce any provision of the project Instruments shall not be construed as a waiver of any such provision or right. Rather, such provision shall continue and remain in full force and effect.

## ARTICLE XII

## CONDEMNATION

In the event of a taking in condemnation or by eminent domain of all or any portion of the Project, each Owner shall be entitled to notice thereof and to participate in the proceedings incident thereto, unless otherwise prohibited by law. In addition, all Mortgagees of Record shall be given timely notice of any such proceedings. Unless otherwise required by law at the time of such taking, any award made therefor shall be disbursed to Developer and the Association, as appropriate. Any dispute as to the proper allocation of condemnation proceeds between Developer and the Association shall be determined by distributing such proceeds based upon an appraisal of the fair market value of each party's respective interest in the Project by two (2) reputable and established Florida real estate appraisers, one of which shall have been chosen by the Association, the other of which shall have been chosen by Developer. The aforesaid appraisers shall elect a third appraiser with similar qualifications in the event that they are unable to agree upon a proper allocation of such condemnation proceeds, and the determination of such third appraiser shall be conclusive upon the parties.

In the event of a partial taking in condemnation or by eminent domain, the Board shall arrange for any necessary repairs and restoration of the remaining portion of the Project, in accordance with the design thereof, at the earliest possible date. If such repairs and restoration in accordance with such design are not permissible under the laws then in force, the Board shall nonetheless repair and restore the premises as nearly as is reasonably possible to its condition immediately prior to such taking. The Board is expressly authorized to pay any excess cost of such restoration as a Common Expense, and to levy a Special Assessment, if necessary, in the event that the available Association funds are insufficient for such purpose. In the event that any such sums are received by the Association in excess of the cost of repairing and restoring the Project, such excess proceeds shall be divided proportionately among the Owners, based upon each Owner's undivided interest in the Common Elements, and their Mortgagees of Record, if any, as their respective interests may appear.

In the event of a partial taking in which any portion of the Project is eliminated or not restored, the Board shall disburse that portion of the proceeds allocable to such portion, less the proportionate share of said portion in the cost of debris removal, to the Owners, based upon each Owner's undivided interest in the Common Elements, and their Mortgagees of Record, if any, as their respective interests may appear.

## ARTICLE XIII

### INSURANCE

*Section 721.165 of FRETSA requires the maintenance of insurance on the Project to protect the accommodations and facilities of the timesharing plan in an amount equal to the replacement cost of such accommodations and facilities.*

**Section 1 Property Insurance** The Association shall, at its sole cost and expense, keep all of the Condominium Units, Common Elements, and Common Furnishings, as well as any property of the Association, insured for the benefit of the Association and all Owners and Mortgagees of Record:

(a) For the full replacement value thereof (excluding foundation and excavation costs), against loss or damage by fire and lightning, and, by an extended coverage endorsement, by wind, storm, hail, explosion, riot, riot attending a strike and civil commotion, damage from aircraft and vehicles, smoke damage, vandalism, theft, and malicious mischief;

(b) Against such other risks of a similar or dissimilar nature as are or shall be customarily covered with respect to projects similar in construction, general location, use, and occupancy; and

Full replacement value shall be determined from time to time, at least annually, or more frequently if so determined by the Board, in its sole discretion. Such determination shall be made by one of the insurers, or at the option of the Board, by an appraiser, architect, or contractor who shall be chosen by the Board.

**Section 2 Liability Insurance** The Association shall, at the Association's sole cost and expense, procure and maintain, for the mutual benefit of the Association and all Owners, a general liability insurance policy against claims for personal injury, death, or property damage occurring upon, in, or about the premises, or in or about the adjoining streets and passageways, such insurance to afford protection to such limits as the Board may deem reasonable and appropriate, it being agreed that as of the date hereof, limits of not less than $_____ _____ in respect to injury or death to one (1) or more persons as the result of any one (1) occurrence, and $_____ _____ in respect to property damage are deemed reasonable.

**Section 3 Directors' and Officers' Liability Insurance** The Association shall, at the Association's sole cost and expense, procure and maintain a policy of Directors' and Officers' liability insurance in such amount as the Board may decide, but not less than $_____ _____ per claim and/or aggregate occurrence.

**Section 4 Workers' Compensation** The Association shall, at the Association's sole cost and expense, procure and maintain such worker's compensation and other insurance coverage as is required by law, upon each of the employees of the Association, if any.

**Section 5 Officers, Directors, Employees, and Agents of Association** The Association shall, at the Association's sole cost and expense, procure and maintain insurance on behalf of any person who is a Director, Officer, employee, or agent of the Association against any liability asserted against or received by him in such capacity or arising out of his status as such, whether or not the Association would have the power to indemnify him against such liability under the provision of Article IV, Section 16 of the By-Laws.

**Section 6 Insurance Against Additional Risks** The Association may also procure insurance against such additional risks as the Board deems advisable for the protection of the Owners.

**Section 7 General Insurance Requirements** All insurance provided for in this Article shall be effected under valid and enforceable policies in forms which are reasonably satisfactory to Developer (to the extent it is deemed the Owner of any Condominium Unit(s) or Timeshare Interest(s), pursuant to the provisions hereof), issued by insurers of recognized responsibility which are duly authorized to transact business in Florida, and distributed among such insurers in amounts reasonably satisfactory to Developer. Not less than thirty (30) days prior to the expiration dates of the expiring policies theretofore furnished pursuant to this Article, originals of the policies bearing notations evidencing the payment of premiums or accompanied by other evidence satisfactory to Developer shall be delivered by the Association to Developer (to the extent it is deemed the Owner of any Condominium Unit(s) or Timeshare Interest(s), pursuant to the provisions hereof). All policies of insurance referred to in this Article shall contain appropriate waivers of subrogation for the benefit of Developer, the Association, and all Owners.

**Section 8 Additional Named Insureds** All policies of insurance provided for in this Article shall name Developer (to the extent it is deemed the Owner of any Condominium Unit(s) or Timeshare Interest(s), pursuant to the provisions hereof), and the Association, including each of the Owners, as insureds, as their respective interests may appear, and also, with respect to the policies described in this Article, shall inure to the benefit of the holder of any mortgage, as the interest of any such mortgagee may appear, by standard mortgagee clause, without contribution, if obtainable. The loss, if any, under such policies shall be adjusted with the insurance companies by the Association in the case of any particular casualty resulting in damage or destruction not exceeding $_____ in the aggregate and, except as aforesaid, the loss, if any, under such policies shall be adjusted with the insurance companies by Developer, the Association, and the holder of any mortgage, and the proceeds of any such insurance, as so adjusted, shall be payable to the Association. Any dispute between the Association and Developer, its suc-

cessors or assigns, as to the allocation of such proceeds, shall be submitted to binding arbitration. Each such policy shall, to the extent obtainable, contain a provision that no act or omission of Developer, the Association, the Board, the Manager, or any Owner shall affect or limit the obligation of the insurance company so to pay the amount of any loss sustained. Each such policy issued by the insurer shall, to the extent reasonably obtainable, contain an agreement by the insurer that such policy shall not be cancelled without at least thirty (30) days' prior written notice to Developer and to any mortgagee named therein.

**Section 9 Inspection of Policies** A copy of each policy of insurance in effect shall be made available for inspection at reasonable hours by Owners and their authorized agents at the office of the Manager.

### ARTICLE XIV
### DAMAGE, DESTRUCTION, AND OBSOLESCENCE

**Section 1 Association as Attorney In Fact** Each Owner hereby irrevocably appoints the Association as his Attorney In Fact in his name, place, and stead for the purpose of dealing with the Property upon its damage, destruction, or obsolescence, as hereinafter provided. As Attorney In Fact, the Association, by its authorized Officers, shall have full and complete authorization, right, and power to make, execute, and deliver any contract, deed, or other instrument with respect to the interest of a Unit Owner or Timeshare Owner which is necessary and appropriate in order for the Association to exercise the powers herein granted.

**Section 2 Reconstruction and Repair of Units and Common Elements** Any insurance proceeds which are paid to the Association on account of any damage or loss to all or any portion of the Project shall be used by the Association to restore the project to substantially the same condition in existence prior to the damage, unless all of the Owners and all Mortgagees of Record agree not to rebuild in accordance with the following provisions:

(a) In the event of damage or destruction due to fire or other disaster, the insurance proceeds, if sufficient to reconstruct the improvement(s), shall be applied by the Association, as Attorney In Fact, to such reconstruction, and the improvement(s) shall be promptly repaired and reconstructed. Any excess insurance proceeds shall be distributed by the Association to the Owners, based upon each Owner's undivided interest in the Common Elements, as set forth in Exhibit 'D' hereto. To the extent that any such damage or loss is covered by insurance, neither the Board, the Manager, the Association, nor any Owner shall have a claim or cause of action for damage or loss against any responsible Owner or Unit Occupant, provided that this waiver of claim shall in no way prevent the Board from obtaining similar insurance coverage at similar premium cost in the future. To the extent that any damage or loss to the personal property of any Owner or Unit Occupant is covered by insurance, such Owner or Unit Occupant shall have no claim or cause of action for such damage or loss against the Board, the Manager, the Association, or any other Owner. No damage to, or loss of, all or any portion of the Project shall relieve any Owner of his obligation to pay his proportionate share of the Common Expenses, Timeshare Expenses (if applicable), and all other impositions becoming due, except as otherwise expressly provided herein.

(b) If the insurance proceeds are insufficient to repair and reconstruct the improvement(s), and if such damage is to not more than sixty-six and two-thirds per cent ($66\frac{2}{3}\%$) of all of the Common Elements, not including the land, such damage or destruction shall promptly be repaired and reconstructed by the Association, as Attorney In Fact, using the proceeds of insurance and the proceeds of a Special Assessment to be levied against all of the Owners, based upon each Owner's undivided interest in the Common Elements, as set forth in Exhibit 'D' hereto. The Association shall have the

authority to cause the repair or reconstruction of the improvements using all of the insurance proceeds for such purpose, notwithstanding the failure of an Owner to pay such Special Assessment. The Special Assessment provided for herein shall be the debt of each Owner and a lien on his Condominium Unit or Timeshare Interest, and may be enforced and collected as provided in Article XI hereof.

(c) If more than sixty-six and two-thirds per cent ($66\frac{2}{3}\%$) of all of the Common Elements, not including the land, are destroyed or damaged, and if the Owners representing an aggregate undivided ownership interest of sixty-six and two-thirds per cent ($66\frac{2}{3}\%$) of the Common Elements submitted hereto do not voluntarily, within one hundred (100) days thereafter, make provision for reconstruction, which plan must have the approval or consent of Mortgagees of Record with mortgages on Condominium Units and/or Timeshare Interests representing sixty-six and two-thirds per cent ($66\frac{2}{3}\%$) of the Common Elements submitted hereto, the Association shall forthwith record a notice setting forth such fact or facts, and upon the recording of such notice by the Association's President and Secretary, the entire remaining Property shall be sold by the Association, as Attorney In Fact for all of the Owners, free and clear of the provisions contained in this Declaration. The insurance proceeds shall be collected by the Association, and such proceeds shall be divided by the Association according to each Owner's undivided interest in the Common Elements, as set forth in Exhibit 'D' hereto, and paid into separate accounts, one (1) for each Unit Owner and Timeshare Owner in the Project. Each such account shall be in the name of the Association, and shall be further identified by the applicable Condominium Unit or Timeshare Interest designation and the name of the Owner thereof. From each separate account, the Association, as Attorney In Fact, shall use and disburse the total amount in each of such accounts, without contribution from any one (1) account to another, toward the full payment of the lien of any first mortgage against the Condominium Unit or Timeshare Interest represented by such separate account. There shall be added to each such account the apportioned amount of the proceeds derived from the sale of the entire Property. Such apportionment shall be based upon each Owner's undivided interest in the Common Elements. The total funds in each account shall be used and disbursed, without contribution from one (1) account to another, by the Association, as Attorney In Fact, for the same purposes and in the following order:

(i) For payment of taxes and special assessment liens in favour of any governmental assessing entity;

(ii) For payment of the balance of the lien of any first mortgage;

(iii) For payment of any unpaid Common Expenses or Timeshare Expenses;

(iv) For payment of junior liens and encumbrances in the order and extent of their priority; and

(v) The balance remaining, if any, shall be paid to the Owner.

(d) If the owners representing an aggregate undivided ownership interest of sixty six and two-thirds per cent (66⅔%) of the Common Elements submitted hereto adopt a plan for reconstruction, which plan has the approval of Mortgagees of Record with mortgages on Condominium Units and/or Timeshare Interests representing sixty-six and two-thirds per cent (66⅔%) of the Common Elements submitted hereto, then all of the Owners shall be bound by the terms and provisions of such plan. Any Special Assessment levied in connection with such plan shall be a Common Expense and made *pro rata* according to each Owner's undivided interest in the Common Elements, as set forth in Exhibit 'D' hereto, and shall be due and payable as provided in Article X above. The Association shall have the authority to cause the repair and restoration of the improvements using all of the insurance proceeds for such purpose, notwithstanding the failure of any Owner to pay the Special Assessment. The Special Assessment provided for herein shall be a debt of

each Owner and a lien on his Condominium Unit or Timeshare Interest and may be enforced and collected as provided in Article XI hereof.

### Section 3 Obsolescence

(a) The Owners representing an aggregate undivided ownership interest of at least sixty-six and two-thirds per cent (66⅔%) of the Common Elements submitted hereto may agree that the Common Elements of the Project are obsolete and that the same should be renewed or reconstructed. In such instance, the expenses thereof shall be payable by all of the Owners as Common Expenses.

(b) If the Owners representing an aggregate undivided ownership interest of sixty-six and two-thirds per cent (66⅔%) of the Common Elements submitted hereto adopt a plan for reconstruction, which plan has the approval of Mortgagees of Record with mortgages on Condominium Units and/or Timeshare Interests representing sixty-six and two-thirds per cent (66⅔%) of the Common Elements submitted hereto, then all the Owners shall be bound by the terms and provisions of such plan. In such instance, the Association shall record a notice setting forth such fact or facts, and upon the recording of such notice by the Association's authorized officers, the entire Project shall be sold by the Association, as Attorney In Fact, for all of the Owners, free and clear of the provisions contained in the Declaration. The proceeds from any such sale shall be apportioned between the Owners and their Mortgagees of Record, as their respective interests may appear, based upon each Owner's undivided interest in the Common Elements, as set forth in Exhibit 'D' hereto, and such apportioned proceeds shall be paid into separate accounts, one for each Unit Owner and Timeshare Owner in the Project. Each such account shall be in the name of the Association, as Attorney In Fact, and shall be further identified by the applicable Condominium Unit(s) or Timeshare Interest(s) designation and the name of the Owner thereof. From each separate account, the Association, as Attorney In Fact, shall use and disburse the total amount in each of such accounts, without contribution from one (1) fund to another, for the same purposes and in the same order as provided in sub-Sections 2(c)(i) through (v) above.

**Section 4 Damage or Destruction to Common Furnishings** In the event of any damage or destruction to the Common Furnishings other than by ordinary wear and tear, the Association shall promptly cause such damage to be repaired and shall use any available insurance proceeds for such purpose. If the damage is not covered by insurance, or if the available insurance proceeds are insufficient, the Association shall levy a Special Assessment upon each of the Timeshare Owners, to be allocated in the manner set forth in Article X above. In the event the damage or destruction was caused by the intentional or negligent act or omission of a Timeshare Owner, a member of his family, his guests, invitees, or licensees, then the cost of such repair or the amount of such deficiency shall be a Personal Charge to such Timeshare Owner, to be paid in the manner provided in Article X above.

ARTICLE XV

MORTGAGE PROTECTION

**Section 1 Priority of Lien** The Association's lien upon any Condominium Unit or Timeshare Interest for delinquent Assessments shall be subordinate to the lien of any Mortgagee of Record upon such Condominium Unit or Timeshare Interest made in good faith and for value; provided, however, that a lien may be created after the foreclosure of any such mortgage on the interest of the person or entity acquiring a Condominium Unit or Timeshare Interest at such foreclosure sale to secure all amounts assessed to such person or entity, as an Owner, after the date of such acquisition.

**Section 2 Status of Liens** In the event a Mortgagee of Record forecloses upon a Condominium Unit or Timeshare Interest, the purchaser at such foreclosure sales, the Association shall remain enti-

tled to recover any unpaid Assessments from the Owner whose Condominium Unit or Timeshare Interest was foreclosed upon.

**Section 3 Mortgagee Consent to Amendment** No amendment of this Article shall affect the rights of any Mortgagee of Record which has recorded its mortgage in the Public Records of XYZ County, Florida, and has provided a true and correct copy thereof to the Manager prior to the effective date of such amendment, which does not consent in writing to such amendment.

ARTICLE XVI

THIRD PARTY LIENS

**Section 1 Limitation on Scope of Liens** Any liens against an Owner's interest in the Project shall be limited to the interest of such owner in his Condominium Unit or Timeshare Interest only, and shall not entitle any lienholder to assert any claim against the Condominium Unit or Timeshare Interest of any other Owner, the Common Elements, the Common Furnishings, or any property of the Association.

**Section 2 Notice of Liens** Each Owner shall give written notice to the Association of every lien upon his Condominium Unit or Timeshare Interest, other than liens for the non-payment of Assessments by the Association, within seven (7) days after the Owner receives notice thereof.

*The above two provisions provide additional protection to the Association and other timeshare interest owners in the timeshare unit.*

**Section 3 Protection of Property** All liens against a Condominium Unit or Timeshare Interest, other than for mortgages, taxes, or Assessments, shall be satisfied or otherwise removed within thirty (30) days from the date of the attachment of such lien. In the event of a threatened sale of the Project or the Condominium Unit(s) or Timeshare Interest(s) or any Owner, or any part thereof, or should the use and enjoyment of any portion thereof by any Owner be threatened by reason of any lien, claim, or charge, including a mechanics' lien, against the Condominium Unit(s) or Timeshare Interest(s) of any other Owner, or should proceedings be instituted to effect any such sale or interference, any Owner, acting on his own behalf or through the Association, or the Association, acting on behalf of any one (1) or more Owners, may, but shall not be required to, pay or compromise the lien, claim, or charge without inquiry into the proper amount or validity thereof and, in such event, the Owner whose interest was subjected to the lien, claim, or charge shall forthwith pay the amount so paid or expended to the Owner or the Association, whomsoever shall have paid or compromised the lien, claim, or charge, together with such reasonable attorneys' fees and related costs as he or it may have incurred. No Owner shall permit his interest in any funds from time to time in possession of the Association to be subjected to any attachment, lien, claim, charge, or other legal process, and an Owner shall promptly restore any funds held by the Association with respect to his Condominium Unit(s) or Timeshare Interest(s) to the extent depleted by any such attachment, lien, claim, charge, or other legal process, and shall reimburse the Association for all reasonable attorneys' fees and other costs incurred with respect thereto. All taxes and Assessments upon a Condominium Unit or Timeshare Interest shall be paid before becoming delinquent. The Association may, at its election, pay any such delinquent sums, which shall then constitute a Personal Charge against the responsible Owner.

## ARTICLE XVII

## TERMINATION

**Section 1 Consent of Owners** The Project may be terminated and removed from the provisions of Chapter 718, Florida Statutes, upon the affirmative vote to do so of Owners casting sixty-six and two-thirds per cent (66⅔%) of the total votes eligible to be voted by all of the members of the Association, and upon the consent of Mortgagees of Record having mortgages on Condominium Units and/or Timeshare Interests representing an aggregate undivided ownership interest of sixty-six and two-thirds per cent (66⅔%) of the Common Elements submitted to this Declaration. Such termination shall be effective upon the recording of an instrument, signed and acknowledged by any two (2) Officers of the Association, in the Public Records of XYZ County, Florida, certifying that the afore-described vote has been taken, and that the owners and their respective mortgagees of Record have elected to terminate the Project.

**Section 2 Other Grounds for Termination** The project may be terminated and removed from the provisions of Chapter 718, Florida Statutes, upon its substantial damage or destruction, or upon its obsolescence, upon the vote of Owners and Mortgagees of Record representing an aggregate undivided ownership interest of sixty-six and two-thirds per cent (66⅔%) of the Common Elements submitted hereto, as provided in Article XIV, Sections 2(c) and 3(b) above, or upon the total condemnation of the Project, as provided in Article XII above.

**Section 3 Effect of Termination** Upon any termination of the Project as provided herein, the Owners shall thereupon be deemed to hold title to an undivided interest in the entire Property as tenants in common in an amount equivalent to each Owner's undivided interest in the Common elements, as set forth in Exhibit 'D' hereto.

## ARTICLE XVIII

## AMENDMENT OF DECLARATION

**Section 1 By Owners** This Declaration may be amended at any regular or special Association Meeting, called and convened in accordance with the provisions of the By-Laws, by the affirmative vote of Owners (including Developer as to all Condominium Units and Timeshare Interests of which it is deemed the owner, pursuant to the provisions hereof) casting a majority of the total votes eligible to be voted by all of the members of the Association.

Each such amendment of this Declaration shall be evidenced by an instrument in writing, signed and acknowledged by any two (2) Officers of the Association, setting forth in full the text of such amendment, the appropriate recording data of this Declaration, and certifying that such amendment has been approved by the affirmative vote of Owners casting a majority of the total votes eligible to be voted by all of the members of the Association. Said amendment shall become effective upon the recording of said instrument in the Public Records of XYZ County, Florida.

No amendment which materially affects the rights and privileges of Developer shall become effective unless and until approved, in writing, by Developer. Notwithstanding any provision to the contrary contained herein, the Owners shall not amend this Declaration in such manner as to materially change the configuration or size of any Unit or to materially alter or modify the appurtenances to any Unit, or change the proportion or percentage by which the Owner of a Unit or a Timeshare Interest shares the Common Expenses and Timeshare Expenses (if applicable) and owns the Common Elements and Common Surplus, without the consent of Owners representing an aggregate undivided ownership interest of sixty-six and two-thirds per cent (66⅔%) of the Common Elements submitted to this Declaration. Any vote to amend this Declaration which relates to a change in the percentage ownership of the Common Elements or sharing of the Common Expenses shall be by secret ballot. Furthermore, the Owners shall have no power to enact an amendment to this Declaration which materially affects the rights or security interests of any Mortgagee of Record, without first obtaining the written consent of such affected Mortgagee of Record.

**Section 2 By Developer** Developer reserves the right, prior to the recording of the first Warranty Deed conveying a Condominium Unit or a Timeshare Interest from Developer to an Owner, and thereafter (to the extent permitted by law), to unilaterally amend this Declaration as may be required by any lending institution, title insurance company, or public body, or as may be necessary to conform the same to the requirements of law, to facilitate the operation and management of the Project or the sale of Condominium Units and/or Timeshare Interests therein.

*The above reservation gives the Developer the flexibility to amend the Project Documents to obtain financing or to conform to the requirements of the reviewing state authority. As the Division of Florida Land Sales and Condominiums of the Department of Business Regulation conducts a thorough review of all project documents, the Developer needs the ability to unilaterally amend the recorded Declaration.*

Developer further reserves the right, as long as it is deemed the Owner of Condominium Units and/or Timeshare Interests representing an aggregate undivided ownership interest of ten per cent (10%) of the Common Elements submitted to this Declaration, to change the interior design and/or arrangement of the Units, the Common Elements, and the Common Furnishings, to change the number of Units within the Project, to add Common Elements or enlarge Common Elements already submitted hereto, and to unilaterally effectuate any such amendments to this Declaration and/or the By-Laws as may be necessary or required in connection with the exercise of said reserved right. Any such amendments to this Declaration shall become effective upon the recording in the Public Records of XYZ County, Florida, of an instrument executed solely by Developer, setting forth the text of such amendment in full, together with the appropriate recording data of this Declaration. No amendment of this Declaration not hereby expressly permitted to be unilaterally made by Developer shall be permitted if such amendment would prejudice or impair to any material extent the rights of any Owner or any Mortgagee of Record.

## ARTICLE XIX

## MISCELLANEOUS PROVISIONS

**Section 1 Compliance With Project Instruments** Each Owner and any other person who in any way uses the Project shall comply strictly with the provisions of the project Instruments, as amended from time to time, as well as the decisions and resolutions of the Board and the Association adopted pursuant thereto, and hereby acknowledges that time is of the essence with respect to his compliance with each of the provisions of the Project Instruments.

**Section 2 No Right to Participate in Profit** Neither the Project Instruments nor any of the Warranty Deeds shall be deemed to evidence a joint venture, partnership, or any other similar arrangement, and no party shall have the right to participate in the individual profits, if any, of any other party arising out of the operation of the Project created hereunder.

**Section 3 Latent Conditions** Neither Developer, the Manager, nor the Association shall be liable for injury or damage caused by any latent condition existing at the Project.

**Section 4 Captions** The captions used in the Project Instruments and in any exhibits annexed thereto are inserted solely as a matter of convenience and shall not be relied upon and/or used in construing the effect or meaning of the provisions thereof.

**Section 5 Number and Gender** Whenever the context so requires, the use of any gender in the Project Instruments and in any exhibits annexed thereto shall be deemed to include both genders, and the use of the singular shall be deemed to include the plural, and the plural shall include the singular.

**Section 6 Interpretation** The provisions of the Project Instruments shall be liberally construed to effectuate the purpose of ensuring that the Project shall at all times be operated and maintained in a manner so as to optimize and maximize its enjoyment and utilization by each Owner as a vacation resort.

**Section 7 Severability** The provisions hereof shall be deemed to be independent and severable, and the invalidity or partial invalidity or unenforceability of any other provision hereof.

**Section 8 Waiver** No restriction, condition, obligation, or provision contained in the Project Instruments shall be deemed to have been abrogated or waived by reason of any failure to enforce the same, irrespective of the number of violations or breaches thereof which may occur.

**Section 9 Binding Effect** The provisions of the Project Instruments shall be binding upon all parties having or acquiring any Condominium Unit(s) or Timeshare Interest(s) or any right, title, or interest therein, and shall be for the benefit of each Owner, his heirs, successors, and assigns. Each Owner (including Developer) shall be fully discharged and relieved of liability on the covenants contained therein, in his capacity as Owner, insofar as such covenants relate to each Condominium Unit or Timeshare Interest, upon ceasing to own such Condominium Units(s) or Timeshare Interest(s) and upon paying all sums and performing all obligations thereunder, up to the time his ownership interest terminates, as provided herein.

**Section 10 Choice of Law** This Declaration shall be construed in accordance with the laws of the State of Florida.

IN WITNESS WHEREOF, Developer has executed these presents this _____ day of _____, 199___
Signed, sealed and
delivered in the
presence of:

_____

_____

TIMESHARE DEVELOPER, INC.
'DEVELOPER'
By: _____
    President

STATE OF FLORIDA        )
                        ) SS.
COUNTY OF _____)

On this ____ day of _____, 199__, before me appeared ____, to me personally known, who, being by me duly sworn, did say that he is the President of Timeshare Developer, Inc., a Florida corporation, that the foregoing instrument was signed in the name of and in behalf of said corporation, and acknowledged that he executed the same as his free act and deed and as the free act and deed of said corporation.

_____
Notary Public
My Commission expires: _____

**EXHIBIT 2**

# ARTICLES OF INCORPORATION
## OF
## CLUB 'ABC' CONDOMINIUM ASSOCIATION, INC.

In compliance with Chapter 617, Florida Statutes, the undersigned persons, acting as Subscribers, sign and acknowledge the following Articles of Incorporation for this corporation.

### ARTICLE 1

### NAME

The name of this Corporation is:

Club 'ABC' Condominium Association, Inc., hereinafter referred to as the 'Association.'

### ARTICLE II

### PURPOSES

The purposes for which this Association is formed are:

A To exercise all of the powers and privileges, perform all of the duties, and fulfill all of the obligations of the Association as set forth in the Association's By-Laws and in the Declaration of Condominium for Club 'ABC', A Condominium ('Declaration'), duly recorded or to be recorded in the Public Records of XYZ County, Florida, as it may be amended from time to time, and to provide an entity for the furtherance of the interests of all of the Owners, including Developer, of Condominium Units and Timeshare Interests in Club 'ABC', A Condominium (the 'Project') (or such additional condominiums as may be combined with the Project), with the objective of establishing and maintaining the Project as a condominium of the highest possible quality and value and enhancing and protecting its value, desirability, and attractiveness. Unless expressly indicated to the contrary, the terms used herein shall have the meanings given to them in the Declaration.

B To fix, levy, collect, and enforce payment by all lawful means of all charges and Assessments made pursuant to the terms of the Declaration, to pay all expenses in connection therewith and all administrative and other expenses incurred in exercising the Association's powers and performing its functions; to enforce the terms, covenants, restrictions, reservations, conditions, uses, limitations, and obligations set forth in the Declaration and the Association's By-Laws, and to make and enforce Rules and Regulations as provided therein.

C To purchase, acquire, own, hold, lease, either as lessee or lessor, sell, convey, exchange, encumber, borrow against, improve, construct, maintain, equip, operate, and generally deal in real property and all property of any and every kind or description, whether real or personal, or any interest therein.

D To perform and carry on any lawful activity whatsoever which the Association may deem proper and convenient in connection with any of the foregoing purposes or otherwise, or which may be calculated directly or indirectly to promote the interest of the Association or to enhance or further the accomplishment of any of its powers, purposes, and objectives; to conduct its business either inside or outside the State of Florida; to have and to exercise all of the powers conferred by the laws of the State of Florida upon not for profit corporations formed under the laws pursuant to and under which this Association is formed, as such laws are now in effect and may at any time hereafter be amended.

E To carry out all or any part of the foregoing purposes as principal, agent, or otherwise, either alone or in conjunction with any person, firm, association, or other corporation and in any part of the world; to employ or engage independent contractors and employees, including specifically one or more managing agents to carry out its purposes; and for the purpose of obtaining or furthering any of its purposes, to make and perform contracts of any lawful kind and description with any person, firm, corporation, government, or governmental subdivision, to do such acts and things, to sue and be sued in its own name, and to exercise any and all such powers as a natural person could lawfully make, perform, do, or exercise, provided that the same shall not be inconsistent with the Declaration, the By-Laws, or the laws of the State of Florida.

F  To exercise all other common law or statutory powers of a corporation not for profit which are not in conflict with the Declaration, the Association's By-laws, or any applicable provision of law.

The foregoing statement of purposes shall be construed as a statement of both purposes and powers, and, except where otherwise expressed, the purposes and powers stated in each clause shall be in no way limited or restricted by reference to the terms or provisions of any other clause, but shall be regarded as independent purposes.

## ARTICLE III

### NO DISTRIBUTION

This Association is organised pursuant to Chapter 617, Florida Statutes, and accordingly, no portion of the income or profits of this Association shall be distributed to its members, Directors, or Officers.

## ARTICLE IV

### TERM

The period of duration of this Association shall be perpetual.

## ARTICLE V

### MEMBERS

A  Each Owner including Developer (so long as Developer is deemed the Owner of any Condominium Units(s) or Timeshare Interest(s), pursuant to the provisions of the Declaration), shall be a member of the Association until he ceases to be an Owner.

B  Each member shall have such rights and privileges, and be subject to such duties, obligations, and restrictions, including restrictions governing the transfer of his membership, as are set forth in the Declaration.

## ARTICLE VI

### BOARD OF DIRECTORS

A  The affairs of the Association shall be governed by a Board of Directors composed of at least three (3) but no more than nine (9) persons; provided, however, that the Board shall at all times be composed of an odd number of Directors. Provisions regarding the qualification, election, term, removal, and resignation of Directors shall be set forth in the Association's By-Laws.

B  The initial Board of Directors shall be appointed by Developer and shall serve until such time as Developer appoints replacement Directors or until their successors have been qualified and duly elected by the members of the Association in the manner provided in the By-Laws. The names and addresses of the persons who are to serve as the initial Directors are:

Address:_____
_____

_____
Address:_____
_____

_____
Address:_____
_____

## ARTICLE VII

### OFFICERS

A  The affairs of the Association shall be administered by a President, Vice-President, Secretary, Treasurer, and such additional Officers as the Board of Directors may deem necessary or appropriate from time to time. The Officers of the Association shall be elected annually by the Board of Directors at the organisational meeting of each newly constituted Board, and shall serve at the pleasure of the Board. The names and addresses of the Officers who shall serve until their successors are designated by the Board are as follows:

_____

President and Secretary
Address:_____

_____

Vice-President
Address:_____

_____

_____

Treasurer
Address:_____

_____

## ARTICLE VIII

### BY-LAWS

The initial By-Laws of the Association shall be adopted by the initial Board of Directors and may be altered, amended, or rescinded by the members of the Association or Developer in the manner provided therein.

## ARTICLE IX

### AMENDMENTS

A Amendments to these Articles of Incorporation may be proposed by any Director or member of the Association.

B Any such proposed amendment shall be adopted upon the affirmative vote of members casting a majority of the total votes eligible to be voted by all of the members of the Association, and shall become effective upon the filing of an instrument with the Secretary of State, State of Florida, and the recording of said instrument in the Public Records of XYZ County, Florida, signed and acknowledged by any two (2) Officers of the Association, setting forth the text of such amendment in full.

C Notwithstanding the foregoing provisions of this Article IX to the contrary, no amendment to these Articles of Incorporation which materially affects the rights and privileges of Developer shall become effective unless and until approved, in writing, by Developer. Furthermore, so long as Developer is deemed the Owner of Condominium Units and/or Timeshare Interests representing an aggregate undivided ownership interest of ten per cent (10%) of the Common Elements submitted to the Declaration, Developer may unilaterally amend these Articles of Incorporation to effectuate any of the purposes set forth in Article XIX, Section 2 of the Declaration.

## ARTICLE X

### SUBSCRIBERS

The names and addresses of the Subscribers to these Articles of Incorporation are as follows:

_____

_____

_____

_____

_____

_____

_____

_____

## ARTICLE XI

### REGISTERED OFFICE AND AGENT

The address of the initial registered office of the Association shall be _____ Anywhere, Florida and the name of the initial registered agent at such address shall be Registered Agent.

IN WITNESS WHEREOF, the Subscribers hereto have hereunto set their hands and seals and caused these Articles of Incorporation to be signed this _____ day of _____, 19____.

Signed, Sealed, and

Delivered in the
Presence of:

_____  _____
_____
Subscriber

_____
_____
Subscriber

_____
_____
Subscriber

STATE OF FLORIDA                )
                                )
COUNTY OF _____)

BEFORE ME, the undersigned authority, personally appeared

_____, _____,
and _____, as Subscribers, to me known to be the persons who executed the foregoing Articles of Incorporation of Club 'ABC' Condominium Association, Inc., and being by me duly sworn, acknowledged that they executed the same for the purposes therein expressed.

WITNESS my hand and official seal at the State and County aforesaid, this____ day of _____, 19____.

_____
        Notary Public
My Commission Expires:

# EXHIBIT 3

# BY-LAWS
# OF
# CLUB "ABC" CONDOMINIUM ASSOCIATION, INC.

*The by-laws provide for the operation of the association and set forth the method of electing the Board of Directors, rules on the transfer of interests, and other organizational provisions.*

## TABLE OF CONTENTS

# BY-LAWS
# OF
# CLUB 'ABC' CONDOMINIUM
# ASSOCIATION, INC.

## ARTICLE I

### INTRODUCTION

Club 'ABC' Condominium Association, Inc. (hereinafter referred to as the 'Association') is a Florida not for profit corporation, organized and existing under the laws of the State of Florida for the purpose of administering the condominium project created by the Declaration of Condominium for Club 'ABC', a Condominium (hereinafter referred to as the 'Declaration').

## ARTICLE II

### GENERAL PROVISIONS

**Section 1 Definitions** Unless expressly indicated to the contrary, the terms used herein shall have the meanings given to them in the Declaration.

**Section 2 Conflicts** In the event of any conflict between these By-laws, as amended from time to time, and the Declaration, the Declaration shall control.

**Section 3 Application** All present and future owners, Mortgagees of Record, and occupants of the Units located within the Project, as well as members of their family, their guests, licensees, and invitees, and any other persons who may use the said Project in any manner are subject to the Declaration, these By-Laws and the Rules and Regulations promulgated hereunder, as the provisions of each of said instruments may be amended from time to time. The acceptance of a legal or equitable interest in a Condominium Unit or Timeshare Interest, or the act of occupancy of a Unit, or the entering into a Purchase Contract to acquire a Condominium Unit or Timeshare Interest shall constitute an agreement that the Declaration, these By-Laws, and the Rules and Regulations, as each may lawfully be amended from time to time, are accepted, ratified, and will be strictly observed.

**Section 4 Membership** Each Owner and Developer, so long as it is deemed to be the owner of any Condominium Unit(s) or Timeshare Interest(s), in accordance with the provisions of the Declaration, shall constitute the members of the Association. Transfer of a Condominium Unit or Timeshare Interest, whether such transfer occurs voluntarily or by operation of law, shall immediately and automatically terminate the transferor's membership in the Association, except to the extent that such transferor retains an interest in any other Condominium Unit(s) or Timeshare Interest(s) in the Project. The transfer of a Condominium Unit or Timeshare Interest shall be deemed to have occurred upon the recording in the Public Records of XYZ County, Florida, of the instrument transferring title from the transferor to the transferee, the filing of a true and correct copy of such instrument with the Manager, and the payment of any transfer fees required or authorized by the Project Instruments. The transferee shall, immediately and automatically upon the occurrence of the foregoing events, become a member of the Association. If a Condominium Unit or Timeshare Interest is owned by more than one (1) person, then all of the persons so owning said Condominium Unit or Timeshare Interest shall be members of the Association and shall be eligible to hold office, attend meetings, and exercise all of the other rights of an Owner which are granted by the Project Instruments. However, the vote of a Condominium Unit or Timeshare Interest shall be cast only by the 'voting members', as provided herein.

## ARTICLE III

### ASSOCIATION MEETINGS

**Section 1 Annual Association Meetings** An organizational meeting shall be held within twelve (12) months of the date on which the first Warranty Deed conveying a Condominium Unit or Timeshare Interest from Developer is recorded in the Public Records of XYZ County, Florida. Thereafter, an annual Association Meeting shall be held within the first ninety (90) days of each calendar year, at such date and time as the Board of Directors shall designate, commencing with the year immediately following the year in which the organizational meeting was held. At the organizational Association meeting, and at all subsequent annual meetings, the members shall elect a Board of Directors in accordance with the provisions of these By-Laws, subject to Article IV, Section 2 below, and shall transact such other business as may properly come before them.

*An annual meeting is required by Section 718.112(d) of the Condominium Act.*

**Section 2 Special Association Meetings** Special Association meetings for any purpose or purposes, unless otherwise prescribed by statute, may be called by the President, and shall be called by the President or the Secretary at the request, in writing, of a majority of the Board of Directors, or at the request, in writing, of members representing twenty per cent (20%) of the total votes eligible to be voted by all of the members of the Association. Each such request shall state the purpose or purposes of the proposed meeting. The business transacted at all special Association meetings shall be confined to the subject(s) stated in the notice thereof.

**Section 3 Place of Meetings** All Association meetings shall be held at the Project, or at such other suitable place which is reasonably convenient to the members as shall be designated by the Board and stated in the notice of the meeting. Each Association meeting shall be open to all of the members and such other persons as are not expressly excluded from such meeting by the affirmative vote of members representing a majority of the total votes eligible to be voted by the members present at such meeting, either in person or by proxy.

**Section 4 Notice of Meetings** Unless a member waives in writing his right to receive notice of an Association meeting, the Manager shall mail or deliver written notice of all Association meetings to each member at his address as shown in the records of the Association. Such notice shall be delivered or mailed to each member, by first class or bulk mail, postage prepaid, at least fourteen (14) but not more than sixty (60) days prior to the date of such meeting. Each such notice shall state the time, date, and place of such meeting, and shall also state whether it is an annual or special meeting. In the case of a special Association meeting, the notice thereof shall briefly state the business to be transacted at such meeting. All notices of Association meetings shall also be posted conspicuously at the Project at least fourteen (14) days prior to the meeting time, except in an emergency. Notice of any Association meeting at which the amount of any Assessments to be levied against the Owners is to be considered shall contain a specific statement to such effect along with a reference to the nature of any such Assessments. Upon receipt by the manager of a written request therefor, any Mortgagee of Record shall be mailed a copy of each notice of an Association meeting. Upon notice being given in accordance with the provisions hereof, the failure of any member or Mortgagee of Record to receive actual notice of any Association meeting shall not in any way invalidate the meeting or any business transacted thereat.

*Section 718.12 (d) requires an officer of the Association to provide an affidavit for inclusion in the Association records that notice of the meeting was given in compliance with Section 718.12.*

**Section 5 Quorum** Except as otherwise provided in the Project Instruments, the presence in person or by proxy of members representing twenty per cent (20%) of the total votes eligible to be voted by all of the members of the Association shall constitute a quorum at all meetings of the Association.

### Section 6 Voting

(a) Each Owner (including Developer as to all Condominium Units and Time-share Interests of which it is deemed the Owner, in accordance with the provisions of the Declaration) shall be entitled to a vote which is equivalent to his undivided interest in the Common Elements, as set forth in Exhibit 'D' to the Declaration.

(b) The votes of members, present either in person or by proxy at any duly called Association meeting at which a quorum has been established, casting a majority of the total votes eligible to be voted by such members shall decide any question under consideration, and shall constitute the act of and be binding upon the Association, except as otherwise provided by law, by the Declaration, or by these By-Laws.

*'Voting interest' means the voting rights distributed to the association members pursuant to the Declaration; a 'voting certificate' is the document which designates one of the record title owners, or the corporate, partnership, or entity representative who is authorised to vote on behalf of the unit or interest owned by more than one owner or by any entity. The purpose of having a voting member designated by certificate is to avoid controversy as to who is the proper party to cast the unit or interest vote.*

### Section 7 Designation of Voting Member

If a Condominium Unit or Time-share Interest is owned by more than one person, one (1) person only shall be entitled to cast the vote for such Condominium Unit or Timeshare Interest. Such person shall be designated in a certificate, to be signed by each of the record Owners of such Condominium Unit or Timeshare Interest, and filed with the Manager (or the Secretary of the Association during any period of time in which the Association is temporarily without a Manager). If a Condominium Unit or Timeshare Interest is owned by a corporation, the officer or employee thereof entitled to cast the vote of the Condominium Unit or Time-share Interest for the corporation shall be designated in a certificate which is signed by the President or Vice-President of said corporation and filed with the Manager (or the Secretary of the Association during any period of time in which the Association is temporarily without a Manager). The person so designated in such certificate who is entitled to cast the vote for a Condominium Unit or Time-share Interest shall be known as the 'voting member'. Such certificate shall be valid until revoked or until superseded by a subsequent certificate, or until a transfer of such Condominium Unit or Timeshare Interest, whichever occurs earlier. If such a certificate is not on file for a particular Condominium Unit or Timeshare Interest which is owned by more than one (1) person or entity, or a combination thereof, the following three (3) provisions shall apply:

(a) Such persons or entities may, but shall not be required to, designate a voting member.

(b) If such persons or entities do not designate a voting member, and if more than one (1) of the co-Owners of such Condominium Unit or Timeshare Interest are present at a meeting, then any one (1) of them may cast the vote for their Condominium Unit or Timeshare Interest; provided, however, that no vote for the Condominium Unit or Timeshare Interest may be cast if any of the other co-Owners of such Condominium Unit or Timeshare Interest promptly object to the casting of such vote.

(c) If the co-Owners of a Condominium Unit or Timeshare Interest do not designate a voting member, and only one such co-Owner is present at an Association meeting (either in person or by proxy), then the person present may cast the Condominium Unit's or Time-share Interest's vote, just as though he owned the Condominium Unit or Time-share Interest individually, and without establishing the concurrence of the absent co-Owner(s) of such Condominium Unit or Timeshare Interest.

### Section 8 Proxies

Votes may be cast in person or by proxy. All proxies shall be in writing and signed and dated by the person entitled to vote (as set forth in Section 7 above). A proxy shall be effective only for the specific meeting for which it was originally given and any lawful adjournments thereof. In no event shall any proxy be valid for a period longer than ninety (90) days from the date of the first meeting for which it was given. A proxy shall be revocable at any time in the sole discretion of the Owner who executed it. If a Condominium Unit or Timeshare Interest is owned by more than one (1) person or entity, or a combination thereof, and if such co-Owners have not designated one (1) of them as the voting member, a proxy which designates a third person to cast their vote must be signed by each co-Owner.

**Section 9 Waiver and Consent** Whenever the vote of members at an Association meeting is required or permitted by any provision of these By-Laws to be taken in connection with any action of the Association, the meeting and vote of members may be dispensed with, and the matter(s) in question may be voted upon by mail-in ballot if members representing a majority of the total votes eligible to be voted by all of the members consent in writing to dispense with the meeting and to vote upon the matter(s) in question by mail-in ballot. Mail-in ballots may accompany the requisite consent forms sent to members, and may be completed and returned simultaneously therewith; however, written notice of such action shall be given to all members, unless all members approve of such action.

**Section 10 Order of Business** The order of business at all annual Association meetings shall be as follows:

(a) Proof of notice of meeting;
(b) Summary of business conducted and actions taken at preceding annual meeting;
(c) Report of Officers;
(d) Reports of committees, if any;
(e) Nomination of candidates for election to the Board of Directors;
(f) Appointment of election inspectors;
(g) Election of Directors;

(h) Unfinished business; and
(i) New business.

**Section 11 Adjournment** Any Association meeting, whether or not a quorum is present, may be adjourned from time to time by the affirmative vote of members casting a majority of the total votes represented at said meeting, in person or by proxy. In the absence of a quorum, no other business may be transacted at such Association meeting; provided, however, that any Association meeting which is adjourned due to the failure to establish a quorum shall be re-convened in thirty (30) days, and any business which properly could have been conducted at the original meeting, pursuant to the provisions hereof, may be conducted at the adjournment thereof, without the need to establish a quorum at such adjournment. It shall not be necessary to give any notice of any adjournment of the business to be transacted at any adjourned meeting, other than by an announcement at the meeting at which such adjournment occurs.

**Section 12 Parliamentary Rules** Robert's Rules of Order (latest edition) shall govern the conduct of all Association meetings when not in conflict with the Declaration, these By-Laws, the decisions of the President, or the rulings of the Board of Directors.

**Section 13 The Manager** Each Manager, as long as its Management Agreement with the Association remains in effect, shall be entitled to notice of all Association meetings, shall be entitled to attend the Association's meetings, and may designate such person(s) as it desires to attend such meetings on its behalf.

## ARTICLE IV

## BOARD OF DIRECTORS

*Florida non-profit corporations are required by Section 718.12(a) to have at least three members for the board of administration.*

**Section 1 Number, Term, and Qualification** The affairs of the Association shall be governed by a Board of Directors composed of three (3) persons, each of whom, with the exception of the Directors appointed by Developer, pursuant to Section 2 below, shall be a member of the Association or the spouse of a member; provided, however, that in no event shall a member and his or her spouse both serve on the Board of Directors concurrently; further provided, that at the first annual Association meeting following the date as of which Warranty Deeds to Condominium Unit and/or Timeshare Interest representing an aggregate undivided ownership interest of ninety per cent (90%) of the Common Elements submitted to the Declaration have been recorded in the Public Records of XYZ County, Florida, in the names of Owners other than Developer, the total number of Directors shall be increased from three (3) to five (5). Except for those Directors appointed by Developer, each Director shall serve for a term of three (3) years or until the election of his successor, whichever occurs later, or until his death, incapacity, resignation, or removal; provided, however, that initially one (1) of the first Directors elected by the members shall serve for a one (1) year term, one (1) of the first Directors shall serve for a two (2) year term, and the remaining Director first elected by the members shall serve for a three (3) year term, and thereafter, the term of no more than one (1) of the Directors (for so long as there are only three (3) Directors) shall expire annually.

## Section 2  Election

(a) Notwithstanding any provision of the Project Instruments to the contrary, Developer shall have the right initially to appoint and remove all Directors. Any such Director appointed by Developer shall serve until such time as Developer appoints a replacement Director or until his successor has been qualified and duly elected by the members of the Association, pursuant to the provisions hereof.

(b) At such time as members other than Developer hold title to Condominium Units and/or Timeshare Interests representing an aggregate undivided ownership interest of fifteen per cent (15%) or more of the Common Elements submitted to the Declaration, the members other than Developer shall be entitled to elect no less than one-third ($\frac{1}{3}$) of the Directors.

*The procedures outlined provide for an orderly transition from developer control to member control.*

(c) Members other than Developer shall be entitled to elect not less than a majority of the Directors upon the earliest to occur of the following:

(i) Three (3) years after the date as of which Warranty Deeds to Condominium Units and/or Timeshare Interests representing an aggregate undivided ownership interest of fifty per cent (50%) of the Common Elements submitted to the Declaration have been recorded in the Public Records of XYZ County, Florida in the names of the owners other than Developer; or

(ii) Three (3) months after Warranty Deeds to Condominium Units and/or Timeshare Interests representing ninety per cent (90%) of the aggregate undivided ownership interest of the Common Elements submitted to the Declaration have been recorded in the Public Records at XYZ County, Florida in the names of owners other than Developer; or

(iii) The date as of which all of the Units within the Project have been completed, all or some of such Units have been sold by Developer, and Developer has notified the Association, in writing, that none of the unsold Units or Timeshare Interests therein are being offered for sale by Developer in the ordinary course of its business; or

(iv) The date as of which some of the Units within the Project have been sold by Developer, and Developer has notified the Association, in writing, that none of the remaining Units or Timeshare Interests therein are being constructed or offered for sale by Developer in the ordinary course of its business.

(d) Notwithstanding the foregoing, Developer shall be entitled to elect at least one (1) Director for as long as Developer holds for sale, in the ordinary course of its business, Condominium Units and/or Timeshare Units representing five per cent (5%) of the aggregate undivided ownership interest of the Common Elements submitted to the Declaration.

(e) Within sixty (60) days from the date as of which members other than Developer are entitled to elect one (1) or more Directors, the Association shall call a special Association meeting for the purpose of electing such Director(s) by mailing or delivering written notice thereof to each member, not less than thirty (30) days nor more than forty (40) days from the date of said meeting. The meeting may be called and the notice thereof given by any member in the event the Association fails to do so. Upon the election of the first Director(s) by the members other than Developer, Developer shall promptly forward the name(s) of such person(s) to the Division of Florida Land Sales and Condominiums.

(f) Prior to, or not more than sixty (60) days after the date upon which the members actually elect a majority of the Directors, Developer shall comply fully with the provisions of Section 718.301(4), Florida Statutes.

*The section cited above sets forth in statute the transfer procedures including delivery of books and records, funds, insurance policies, permits, leases and contracts.*

**Section 3 Removal of Directors** At any annual Association meeting, or at any special Association meeting duly called for such purpose by members representing ten per cent (10%) of the total votes eligible to be voted by all of the members of the Association, any one or more of the Directors, other than those Directors appointed by Developer, may be removed, with or without cause, by the affirmative vote of members casting a majority of the total votes eligible to be voted by all of the members of the Association, or by the written agreement of members representing a majority of the total votes eligible to be voted by all of the members of the Association. A successor shall be elected at such meeting for the remainder of the term to fill the vacancy thus created. Should the membership fail to elect such a successor, the Board of

Directors shall fill the vacancy in the manner provided in Section 5 below. Any Director whose removal has been proposed by the members shall be given prompt written notice of his proposed removal and shall be provided with a reasonable opportunity to attend and be heard at the meeting at which his removal is voted upon.

*Section 718.12(f) sets the above recall procedure for use after transfer of control from the developer to the Association.*

**Section 4 Resignation of Directors** Any Director may resign at any time by sending written notice of his resignation to the Manager. Such resignation shall take effect upon receipt thereof by the Manager. Except for those Directors appointed by Developer, any Director who ceases to be an Owner shall automatically be deemed to have resigned. Any Director who is more than thirty (30) days delinquent in the payment of any Assessment or other amount owed to the Association shall be deemed to have resigned from the Board of Directors, effective upon the Board's receipt of notification of such deliquency from the Manager.

**Section 5 Vacancies** If the office of any Director becomes vacant by reason of his death, incapacity, resignation, removal from office, or otherwise, a majority of the remaining Directors, though less than a quorum, shall choose a successor or successors to fill the vacancy. The election for the purpose of filling such vacancy may be held at any annual or special meeting of the Board of Directors.

**Section 6 Organizational Board Meeting** The organizational meeting of each newly constituted Board of Directors shall be held immediately following each annual Association meeting. No notice of the organizational Board meeting shall be required.

**Section 7 Regular Board Meetings** Regular meetings of the Board of Directors may be held at such time, date, and place as shall be determined from time to time by the President; provided, however, that at least one (1) such meeting shall be held during each calendar year. Notice of regular meetings of the Board of Directors shall be given to each Director and to the Manager, personally or by mail, telephone, or telegraph, at least fourteen (14) but not more than sixty (60) days prior to the scheduled meeting date. Adequate notice of all Board meetings shall also be posted conspicuously at the Project at least forty-eight (48) hours prior to the scheduled meeting time, except in an emergency. Such Board meetings shall be open to all members. The members shall be given written notice of the time, date, and place of all Board meetings at which the Association's annual budget will be considered. Not less than thirty (30) days prior to any such meeting, a copy of the proposed annual budget shall be mailed or delivered to each member.

**Section 8 Special Board Meetings** Special meetings of the Board of Directors may be called by the President, and in his absence, by the Vice-President, or by a majority of the Directors by giving at least fourteen (14) but not more than sixty (60) days' notice to each Director and to the Manager, personally or by mail, telephone, or telegraph; provided, however, that notice of special Board meetings by telephone conference, if given personally or by telephone, shall only be required to be given at least forty-eight (48) hours prior to such meeting. Notices of special Board meetings shall state the time, date, place, and purpose of the special Board meeting to which they pertain.

**Section 9 Meetings by Telephone Conference** Both regular and special Board meetings may be conducted by telephone conference. To the extent permitted by law, any Director who is not physically in attendance at any regular or special meeting of the Board of Directors, but who is in telephone contact with the other Directors during such meeting and is thereby able to participate in the discussions, reports, debates, votes, and other matters conducted thereat, shall be deemed to be in attendance at said meeting for all purposes, including but not limited to the

purpose of creating a quorum.

**Section 10 Action by Written Consent** Any action required or permitted to be taken at any meeting of the Board of Directors may be taken without a meeting if all of the Directors consent in writing to the action taken or to be taken at any time prior or subsequent to the intended effective date of such action.

**Section 11 Waiver of Notice** Any Director may at any time waive notice of any meeting of the Board of Directors, in writing, and such waiver shall be deemed to be the equivalent of that Director having actually been given notice of such meeting. Attendance by a Director at any meeting of the Board, either physically or by telephone, shall constitute a waiver by him of notice of the time, date, and place thereof, except when a Director attends a meeting for the express purpose of objecting to the transaction of any business because the meeting is not lawfully called or convened. If all of the Directors are present at any meeting of the Board, no notice thereof shall be required, and any business which could properly come before the Board of Directors may be transacted at such meeting.

**Section 12 Quorum of Board of Directors** At all meetings of the Board of Directors, a majority of the Directors shall constitute a quorum for the transaction of business. The vote of a majority of the Directors present at a Board meeting at which a quorum has been established shall constitute the decision of the Board of Directors. If at any meeting of the Board of Directors a quorum is not established, a majority of those Directors present may adjourn the meeting, one or more times, to a subsequent time, date, and place. At any such adjourned meeting of the Board at which a quorum has been established, any business which might have been transacted at the meeting prior to its adjournment may be transacted without further notice.

**Section 13 Attendance by Manager** Each Manager, as long as its Management Agreement with the Association remains in effect, shall be entitled to notice of all Directors' meetings, shall be entitled to attend the Directors' meetings, and may designate such person(s) as it desires to attend such meetings on its behalf.

**Section 14 Compensation** No Director shall receive any compensation from the Association for acting as such, and no Director shall be reimbursed for any costs incurred for travel, meals, accommodations, or related expenses incurred in order to attend meetings of the Board of Directors, unless such compensation is approved by the affirmative vote of members casting a majority of the total votes eligible to be voted by all of the members of the Association.

**Section 15 Fidelity Bonds** The Board of Directors shall obtain fidelity bonds, in reasonable and prudent amounts, for all Officers, Directors, and employees of the Association who handle or are responsible for Association funds, as provided in Section 718.112(2)(k), Florida Statutes. The premiums for such bonds shall constitute a Common Expense.

*Section 718.112(2)(k), sets a $10,000 minimum bonding requirement for officers or directors who control or disburse funds of the association.*

**Section 16 Liability and Indemnification**

(a) No Director, Officer, employee, or agent of the Association, and no heir, executor, or administrator of any such person, shall be liable to the Association for any loss or damage suffered by it on account of any action or omission by him as a Director, Officer, employee, or agent if he acted in good faith and in a manner reasonably believed to be in or not opposed to the best interests of the Association, unless with respect to an action or suit by or in the right of the Association to procure a judgment in its favour such person shall have been adjudged to be liable for gross negligence or wilful misconduct in the performance of his duty to the Association.

(b) The Association shall indemnify each person who was or is a party or is threatened to be made a party to any threatened, pending, or completed action, suit, or proceeding, whether civil, criminal, administrative, or investigative (other than an action by or in the right of the Association) because he is or was a Director, Officer, employee, or agent of the Association, against expenses (including reasonable attorneys' fees), judgments, fines, and amounts paid in settlement, actually and reasonably incurred by him in connection with such action, suit, or proceeding if he acted in good faith and in a manner reasonably believed to be in or not opposed to the best interests of the Association, and, with respect to any criminal action or proceeding, had no reasonable cause to believe that his conduct was unlawful. The termination of any action, suit, or proceeding by judgment, order, settlement, conviction, or upon a plea of *nolo contendere* or its equivalent, shall not, of itself, create a presumption that the person did not act in good faith and in a manner which he reasonably believed to be in or not opposed to the best interests of the Association, and with respect to any criminal action or proceeding, had reasonable cause to believe that his conduct was unlawful.

The Association shall indemnify each person who was or is a party or is threatened to be made a party to any threatened, pending, or completed action or suit by or in the right of the Association to procure a judgment in its favour because he is or was a Director, Officer, employee, or agent of the Association against expenses (including reasonable attorneys' fees) actually and reasonably incurred by him in connection with the defence or settlement of such action or suit if he acted in good faith and in a manner reasonably believed to be in or not opposed to the best interests of the Association, except that no indemnification shall be made with respect to any claim, issue, or matter as to which such person shall have been adjudged to be liable for gross negligence or wilful misconduct in the performance of his duty to the Association, unless and only to the extent that the court in which such action or suit was brought shall determine, upon application, that despite the adjudication of liability but in view of all the circumstances of the case, such person is fairly and reasonably entitled to indemnification for such expenses which such court shall deem proper.

To the extent that a Director, Officer, employee, or agent of the Assocition has been successful on the merits or otherwise in defence of any action, suit, or proceeding referred to in this Section, or in defence of any claim, issue, or matter therein, he shall be indemnified against expenses (including reasonable attorneys' fees) actually and reasonably incurred by him in connection therewith.

Any indemnification under this Section (unless ordered by a court) shall be made by the Association only as authorized in the specific case upon a determination that indemnification of the Director, Officer, employee, or agent is proper under the circumstances because he has met the applicable standard of conduct set forth in this Section. Such determination may be made (1) by the Board upon a majority vote of a quorum consisting of Directors who were not parties to such action, suit, or proceeding; or (2) if such a quorum is not obtainable, or even if obtainable, a quorum of disinterested Directors so directs, by independent legal counsel in a written opinion to the Association.

Expenses incurred in defending a civil or criminal action, suit, or proceeding may be paid by the Association in advance of the final disposition of such action, suit, or proceeding as authorized by the Board of Directors in a particular case, upon receipt of an undertaking by or on behalf of the Director, Officer, employee, or agent to repay such amount, unless it shall ultimately be determined that he is entitled to be indemnified by the Association as authorized in this Section.

The indemnification provided by this Section shall not be deemed exclusive of any other rights to which those indemnified may be entitled, shall continue as to a person who has ceased to be a Director, Officer, employee, or agent, and shall inure to the benefit of the heirs, executors, administrators, and personal representatives of such person.

*Among the powers listed below for the Board are those necessary for the administration of the timeshare program including maintenance, repair and replacement of the timeshare unit furniture and supplies, the power to enter into agreements for the exchange of timeshare privileges and other more common powers for the operation of the project.*

**Section 17 Powers and Duties** The Board of Directors shall have all of the powers and duties necessary for the maintenance, repair, replacement, restoration, improvement, and operation of the Project, and for the operation and administration of the Association, and may do all such acts and things except as by law, by the Declaration, or by these By-Laws may not be delegated to the Board of Directors by the members. The powers and duties of the Board of Directors shall be subject to approval by the members only when such approval is specifically required by law or by the Project Instruments. Such powers and duties shall include, but shall not be limited to, the following:

(a) To exercise all of the powers specifically set forth in the Declaration and in these By-Laws, and to exercise all powers incidental thereto;

(b) To repair, maintain, repaint, improve, alter, furnish, or refurnish the interior and exterior portions of all Units Committed to Timeshared Ownership, together with the Common Elements and the Common Furnishings; to establish reserves for anticipated costs, including but not limited to the costs of acquisition and replacement of the Common Furnishings, to acquire and pay for equipment, materials, supplies, furniture, Common Furnishings, labour, or services which the Board deems necessary or proper for the maintenance and repair of the Units Committed to Timeshared Ownership, the Common Elements, and the Common Furnishings;

(c) To levy, collect, and enforce Assessments against the Owners in the manner provided in the Declaration in order to pay all the costs of the Project operation, and to do all things necessary to enforce each Owner's obligations under the Project Instruments;

(d) To employ, dismiss, and control the personnel necessary for the maintenance and operation of the Project, including the right and power to employ legal counsel, accountants, contractors, and other professionals, as needed;

(e) To delegate all or a portion of the responsibilities of the Board for the physical and fiscal management of the Project and the Association, respectively, to one (1) or more agents, including without limitation, the Manager;

(f) To adopt, publish, and enforce, from time to time, Rules and Regulations pertaining to the possession, use, and enjoyment of the Units, the Common elements, and the Common Furnishings, which Rules and Regulations shall be consistent with the provisions of the Declaration and these By-Laws;

(g) To open bank accounts on behalf of the Association and its members, and to designate the signatures required therefor;

(h) To procure insurance, pursuant to the provisions of the Declaration and these By-Laws;

(i) To procure whatever legal, accounting, or other professional services as are necessary or proper for the operation of the Project and/or for the enforcement of the Project Instruments;

(j) To pay the amount necessary to discharge any lien or encumbrance against a Condominium Unit, Timeshare Interest, Common Element, or Common Furnishing, if deemed appropriate by the Board, in its sole discretion; provided, that if the Board determines that one (1) or more Owners are responsible for such lien or encumbrance, such Owner(s) shall by jointly and severally liable to the Association for any cost incurred by the Association in discharging it, and for any other cost incurred by the Association by reason of such lien or encumbrance;

(k) To appoint such committee(s) as the Board may deem appropriate, which, to the extent provided in the resolution appointing such committee(s), shall have the powers of the Board of Directors in the affairs and business of the Association. The committee(s) shall keep regular minutes of their proceedings and shall report their findings and recommendations to the Board of Directors, as appropriate;

(l) To enter into and terminate agreements, on behalf of the Association, providing for the rental of furniture, furnishings, equipment and/or recreational facilities and other amenities from Developer or other persons or entities.

(m) To enter into and terminate agreements with organizations allowing Timeshare Owners to exchange the use of their Timeshare Interests with owners, lessees, or certificate holders of time periods at other resorts; and/or to otherwise provide for the trading by Timeshare Owners of Timeshare Interests with other Timeshare Owners within the Project and/or with owners, lessees, or certificate holders of time periods at other resorts; and

(n) To perform all other acts deemed by the Board to be necessary, desirable, or appropriate in order to ensure the proper maintenance, repair, replacement, restoration, improvement, and operation of the Project, and to ensure the proper operation and administration of the Association.

## ARTICLE V

## OFFICERS

**Section 1 Designation** The Officers of the Association shall be the President, Vice President, Secretary, and Treasurer, all of whom shall be elected by the Board of Directors. The Board of Directors may also elect an Assistant Treasurer, an Assistant Secretary, and such other Officers as in its judgment may be necessary or appropriate. One person may hold up to two (2) of the aforementioned positions. The President, the Secretary, and the Treasurer shall all be Directors.

**Section 2 Election of Officers** The Officers of the Association shall be elected annually by the Board of Directors at the organizational meeting of each newly constituted Board of Directors.

**Section 3 Term and Removal of Officers**
Each Officer of the Association shall hold office until his successor is elected, except that each Officer's position shall immediately become vacant when and if he ceases to be an Owner or, in the case of the President, Secretary, and Treasurer, if he ceases to be a Director, whether by resignation, removal, death, incapacity, ineligibility, or otherwise. Any Officer may be removed at any Board meeting, with or without cause, by the Board of Directors; provided, however, that no Officer shall be removed except by the affirmative vote for removal of a majority of the Directors. Any Officer whose removal has been proposed shall be given prompt notice of his proposed removal and shall be provided with a reasonable opportunity to attend and be heard at the Board meeting at which his removal is voted upon. If the office of an Officer becomes vacant, for any reason, the vacancy shall promptly be filled through the election of a successor by the Board of Directors.

**Section 4 President** The President shall be the chief executive officer of the Association. He shall preside at all meetings of the Association and of the Board of Directors. He shall have all of the general powers and duties which are incident to the office of President of a stock corporation organized under the laws of the State of Florida.

**Section 5 Vice-President** The Vice-President shall assume the powers and duties of the President whenever the President is absent from any meeting of the Association or the Board of Directors or is unable to act in his capacity as President. If neither the President nor Vice-President is able to act, a majority of the remaining Directors shall appoint some other Officer to act in the place of the President, on an interim basis. The Vice-President shall also perform such other duties as shall from time to time be delegated to him by the Board of Directors or by the President.

**Section 6 Secretary** The Secretary shall keep the minutes of all meetings of the Association and the Board of Directors and shall make such minutes available for inspection by members, their authorised representatives, and the Directors at reasonable times. The Secretary shall take such steps to assure that the Association retains such minutes for a period of not less than seven (7) years from the date of the meetings to which they pertain. The Secretary shall also perform all of the duties incident to the office of Secretary of a stock corporation organized under the laws of the State of Florida, to the extent that such duties have not been delegated to the Manager. In addition, the Secretary shall, during any period of time in which the Association is temporarily without a Manager, issue notices of all meetings of the Association and the Board of Directors, have charge of the Association's books and records, and receive and incorporate into the records of the Association all notices which are required or permitted to be transmitted to the Manager, including notices from Owners designating voting members and providing changes of address, and also including requests from Mortgagees of Record for copies of notices from the Association to their respective mortgagors.

**Section 7 Treasurer** The Treasurer shall, during any period of time in which the Association is temporarily without a Manager, keep full and accurate financial records and books of account pursuant to Section 718.111(7)(b), Florida Statutes,

*(The reference is to the requirement that books and records be kept in compliance with the standards of the Florida Board of Accountancy for certified public accountants)*

be responsible for the preparation of all required financial data, and be responsible for the deposit of all money and other valuables in such depositories as may from time to time be designated by the Board of Directors. The Treasurer shall perform all of the duties incident to the office of Treasurer of a stock corporation organized under the laws of the State of Florida, to the extent that such duties have not been delegated to the Manager.

**Section 8 Execution of Instruments** All agreements, contracts, deeds, leases, checks, and other instruments of the Association shall be executed by any two (2) Officers, or by such other person or persons, including the Manager, as may be designated by the Board of Directors.

**Section 9 Compensation of Officers** No Officer shall receive any compensation from the Association for acting in his capacity as an Officer unless such compensation is approved by an affirmative vote of members casting a majority of the total votes eligible to be voted by all of the members of the Association.

ARTICLE VI

MANAGER

**Section 1 Management Agreement** The Board, on behalf of the Association, shall at all times employ a responsible managing agent as the Manager, and shall, following the expiration of the initial Management Agreement, enter into subsequent Management Agreements with reasonable terms and renewal periods, and subject to non-renewal by the Board or the Manager.

**Section 2 Discharge of Manager** Members other than Developer casting sixty-six per cent (66%) of the total votes eligible to be voted by the members present, either in person or by proxy, at any duly called Association meeting at which a quorum has been established, so long as such members present represent at least fifty per cent (50%) of the total votes eligible to be voted by all of the members of the Association other than Developer, may discharge the Manager at any time.

*FRETSA provides an easier method for discharge of the manager every three years when the managing contract is up for renewal at Section 721.14(1).*

**Section 3 Compensation** The compensation of the Manager shall be determined by the Board and set forth in each Management Agreement.

*The powers and duties of the Board are statutorily set forth at Section 721.13(3), the following listing expands on the statute.*

**Section 4 Powers and Duties** The Manager shall have such powers and duties as are delegated to or imposed upon it by the Board, from time to time, as set forth in the Management Agreement. Such powers and duties shall at all times include, but shall not necessarily be limited to the following:

(a) To be responsible for the immediate management and operation of the Project and the affairs of the Association, subject to the direction of the Board;

(b) To arrange for the regular cleaning, maintenance, repair, replacement, and restoration of the Common Elements and the Units Committed to Timeshared Ownership and the contents thereof, including all Common Furnishings, and any additions or alterations thereto, as needed and/or as directed to do so by the Board;

(c) To employ, dismiss, and control, on behalf of the Association, such personnel as it deems necessary for the maintenance and operation of the Project and the Association, including attorneys, accountants, contractors, and other professionals, as needed;

(d) To enter into contracts (and subcontracts), in the name and on behalf of the Association, for the furnishing of such services as it deems necessary and appropriate for the proper execution of its duties;

(e) To arrange for the preparation and submission of a proposed budget and schedule of Assessments to the Board for its review and approval, at least thirty (30) days prior to the end of each fiscal year;

(f) To arrange for and submit an annual financial statement and balance sheet of the Association to the Board of Directors within sixty (60) days after the close of each fiscal year;

(g) To assess and collect from the Owners all Assessments, taxes, and any other amounts due and owing the Association or a third party pursuant to the provisions of any applicable law or the Project Instruments;

(h) To arrange for the payment of all of the Association's bills, to the extent of available Association funds;

(i) To procure and maintain in effect

insurance on behalf of the Association, as required by the Declaration and these By-Laws.

(j) To assure that a copy of the then-current Rules and Regulations is kept in each Unit Committed to Timeshared Ownership and/or is furnished to the persons occupying each such Unit at check-in or otherwise, upon request, as directed by the Board, and to assure that the provisions of the Project Instruments are observed and enforced;

(k) To maintain at the Project all books and records of the Association, including but not limited to detailed and accurate records of the Association's receipts and disbursements, an individual account for each Owner designating such Owner's name and address and the amounts of any Assessments paid and/or due by such Owners, minutes of meetings, correspondence, amendments to the Declaration, the By-Laws, and the Rules and Regulations, and a list of the names and current mailing addresses of Association members and Mortgagees of Record;

(l) To make available for inspection by the Division of Florida Land Sales and Condominiums all books and records of the Association, upon the request of said agency;

(m) To establish and maintain federally insured deposits of the Association's funds in a manner so as to indicate the custodial nature thereof;

(n) To procure all necessary supplies, equipment, and services on the Association's behalf;

(o) To arrange for an inspection and inventory of each Unit Committed to Timeshared Ownership to be conducted at the end of each Unit Occupant's stay;

(p) To the extent reasonably possible, to arrange for comparable alternative accommodations for Timeshare Owners unable to occupy their Units because of the occupancy thereof by a Holdover Owner or as a result of needed maintenance or repairs; and

(q) To organize and attend all Association and Board meetings.

**Section 5 Change in Scope of Duties** The Board of Directors may, in its discretion,

from time to time, grant additional powers to and/or impose additional duties upon the Manager, or limit any powers previously granted to the Manager, but only to the extent that such powers and duties are not expressly granted to or imposed upon the Manager by law or by the Project Instruments.

**Section 6 Delinquent Account Statements** Upon receipt of a written request therefor, the Manager shall mail to a Mortgagee of Record, during any month in which its mortgagor is delinquent in any payments owed to the Association, a statement showing the status of the mortgagor's account.

**Section 7 Legal Action** The Manager, subject to the direction of the Board of Directors, may represent the Association in any action, suit, or other proceeding concerning one or more Owners or one or more Condominium Units or Timeshare Interests, provided that any such action shall be brought in the name of the Association.

ARTICLE VII

FINANCES AND ASSESSMENTS

**Section 1 Collection of Assessments** Assessments shall be paid by the members and collected by the Manager, on behalf of the Association, in the manner and according to the terms and provisions set forth in Article X of the Declaration.

**Section 2 Depositories** The funds of the Association shall be deposited in a federally insured institution, in a manner designed to indicate the custodial nature thereof, and shall be withdrawn by the Manager (or the Association during any period of time in which the Association is temporarily without a Manager) for the payment of the Association's expenses in accordance with the provisions of the Project Instruments.

**Section 3 Fiscal Year** The Association shall operate on a fiscal year which begins on the first day of January of each year; provided, however, that the Board of Directors may, in its sole discretion, change to a different fiscal year in the event that the Board of Directors deems it advisable to do so.

**Section 4 Application of Payments and Commingling of Funds** All sums collected by the Association, from Assessments or otherwise, may be commingled in a single fund or divided into more than one (1) fund, as determined by the Board of Directors. All Assessments paid by an Owner shall be applied to interest, delinquencies, costs, attorneys' fees, and other charges, expenses, and advances in such manner and amounts as the Manager determines to be appropriate, unless otherwise directed by the Board and except as otherwise provided in the Project Instruments. All Owners, Mortgagees of Record, and the authorized agents thereof, shall be entitled to inspect the Association's records of the receipts and disbursements at the office of the Manager, during normal business hours, and upon ten (10) days' notice to the Manager or the Board of Directors, any Owner shall be furnished with a statement of his account setting forth the amount of any unpaid Assessments or other charges due and owing from such Owner. The Manager shall be responsible, as the agent of each Owner, for paying the Common Expenses and Timeshare Expenses of the Project, subject to the supervision and direction of the Board. Neither the Board nor the Manager shall be individually liable for the payment of any of the Common Expenses or Timeshare Expenses; rather, they shall merely serve to direct and authorize the payment of the Common Expenses and Timeshare Expenses on behalf of the Owners.

**Section 5 Accounting   Records** Within sixty (60) days following the end of the Association's fiscal year, the Board or the Manager shall mail or deliver to each Owner a complete financial report of the actual receipts and disbursements of the Association for the previous fiscal year, as required by Section 718.111(13), Florida Statutes.

**Section 6 Audit** An audit of the accounts of the Association shall be prepared each year by such independent accounting firm as the Board selects, in its sole discretion, in accordance with generally accepted auditing standards as defined by the rules of the Florida Board of Accountancy or as otherwise permitted by law. A copy of said audit shall be forwarded to the Officers of the Association, and shall be made available to the members of the Association for inspection at reasonable times in the office of the Manager.

**Section 7 Annual Budget** Notwithstanding any provision herein to the contrary, in the event the Board approves an annual budget for a fiscal year which requires an Assessment against members which exceeds one hundred fifteen per cent (115%) of the Assessments against members for the preceding fiscal year, the Board, upon the written application of members eligible to cast at least ten per cent (10%) of the total votes eligible to be voted by all of the members of the Association, shall call a special Association meeting within thirty (30) days, upon not less than ten (10) days' written notice thereof to each member, at which meeting the members may consider and enact a replacement budget. The enactment of any such replacement budget shall require a vote of members casting not less than a majority of the total votes eligible to be voted by all of the members of the Association. If no replacement budget is so enacted, then the budget previously approved and adopted by the Board shall remain in effect until revised or superseded. Notwithstanding the foregoing, the Board may propose its own replacement budget to the members at an Association meeting or in writing. If said budget is approved by members present at said meeting, either in person or by proxy, casting a majority of the total votes eligible to be voted by such members, or in writing by members casting a majority of the total votes eligible to be voted by all of the members of the Association, then said budget shall be adopted; provided, however, that until members other than Developer are entitled to elect a majority of the Board of Directors, the Board shall not impose an Assessment for any fiscal year which is greater than one hundred fifteen per cent (115%) of the prior fiscal year's Assessment without the approval of members eligible to cast a majority of the total votes of all the members of the Association.

In determining whether Assessments exceed one hundred fifteen per cent (115%) of similar Assessments in prior fiscal years, any authorized provisions for reasonable reserves, as discussed in Article X, Section 7 of the Declaration, or for Common Expenses or Timeshare Expenses which are not anticipated to be incurred on a regular or annual basis, or Assessments for betterments to the Project, shall be excluded from the computation.

## ARTICLE VIII

### AMENDMENTS TO THE BY-LAWS

The provisions of these By-Laws may be amended at any duly called Association meeting upon the affirmative vote of members casting a majority of the total votes eligible to be voted by all of the members of the Association; provided, however, that these By-Laws shall not be amended in any manner that will materially impair or prejudice the rights and priorities of any Mortgagee of Record without the written consent of each such Mortgagee of Record so affected. Amendments to these By-Laws shall be effective only upon the recording of an instrument in the Public Records of XYZ County, Florida, signed and acknowledged by any two (2) Officers of the Association, setting forth the text of such amendment, and otherwise complying with Section 718.112(2)(i), Florida Statutes. Notwithstanding any provision to the contrary contained herein, Developer reserves the right to amend these By-Laws by recording an instrument in the Public Records of XYZ County, Florida, setting forth the text of such amendment in full, to accomplish any of the purposes stated in Article XIX, Section 2 of the Declaration, subject to the limitations and restrictions contained therein.

*Any amendments proposed must be fully disclosed to members by either showing the amended provisions with lines through the deleted sections and the additions highlighted, or labelling the amendment as substantially rewording the affected section so that members do not have to find and compare their copy of the existing by-laws to the proposed amendatory language.*

## ARTICLE IX

### RULES AND REGULATIONS

**Section 1 Adoption** The Board of Directors shall have the right to establish and amend, from time to time, such uniform Rules and Regulations as the Board may deem necessary and appropriate for the management, preservation, safety, control, and orderly operation of the Project and for the benefit of all of the Owners and Unit Occupants. Such Rules and Regulations may, to the extent not in conflict with the provisions of the Declaration and these By-Laws, impose reasonable restrictions upon the use and occupancy of any portion of the Project as the Board, in its sole discretion, deems necessary or appropriate.

**Section 2 Compliance with Rules and Regulations** Each Owner shall obey the Rules and Regulations, as the same may be lawfully amended from time to time, and shall ensure that the same are faithfully observed by the members of his family, his guests, invitees, and licensees. Each person who comes within the Project shall be subject to the Rules and Regulations for the duration of his presence therein. A copy of the Rules and Regulations, as amended from time to time, shall be made available to Owners upon request.

**Section 3 Conflict** In the event of any conflict between the Rules and Regulations, as amended from time to time, and the Declaration or these By-Laws, the latter instruments shall control.

## ARTICLE X

### MISCELLANEOUS PROVISIONS

**Section 1 Association's Records** Any member shall have the right to demand and receive from the Manager a complete list of the names and addresses of all the members of the Association, upon reasonable notice and upon the payment of a reasonable fee to the Manager for reproduction costs. The Association's accounting records and the minutes of all Association and Board meetings shall be available for inspection by the members, at reasonable times, in the office of the Manager. Said minutes shall be retained by the Manager, on behalf of the Association, for a minimum of seven (7) years from the date of the meetings to which they pertain.

**Section 2 Notices** Each Owner shall register his mailing address with the Manager upon becoming an Owner, and shall promptly notify the Manager of any subsequent changes of address. Any notices required by the Project Instruments to be given to the Association or the Board of Directors shall be sent by registered or certified mail to the Manager, or in the event that the Association is temporarily without a Manager, to the office of the Association or to such other address as the Board of Directors may hereafter designate from time to time, by notice in writing to all of the Owners. All notices required by the Project Instruments to be given to any Owner shall be sent by first class or bulk mail, postage prepaid, to such Owner's most recent address as shown in the records of the Association. All notices required by the Project Instruments to be given to Mortgagees of Record shall be sent to their respective addresses, as designated by them from time to time, in writing, to the Manager. All notices shall be deemed to have been given when mailed, postage prepaid, except notices of changes of address, which shall be deemed to have been given when received.

**Section 3 Liability Survives Transfer of Condominium Unit or Timeshare Interest** The transfer of a Condominium Unit or Timeshare Interest shall not relieve or release the former Owner from any liabilities or obligations incurred in connection with the Project during the period of his ownership, or impair any rights or reme-

dies which the Association may have against such former Owner arising out of or in any way connected with such ownership and the covenants and obligations incident thereto.

**Section 4 Severability** The provisions hereof shall be deemed to be independent and severable, and the invalidity or partial invalidity or unenforceability of any one (1) provision shall not affect the validity or enforceability of any other provision hereof.

**Section 5 Captions** The captions used in the By-Laws are inserted solely as a matter of convenience and for reference, and in no way define, limit, or describe the scope of these By-Laws or the intent of any of the provisions hereof.

**Section 6 Number and Gender** Whenever the context so requires, the use of any gender in these By-Laws shall be deemed to include both genders, and the use of the singular shall be deemed to include the plural, and the plural shall include the singular.

**Section 7 Waiver** No restriction, condition, obligation, or provision contained in these By-Laws shall be deemed to have been abrogated or waived by reason of any failure to enforce the same, irrespective of the number of violations or breaches thereof which may occur.

**Section 8 Interpretation** The provisions of these By-Laws shall be liberally construed to effectuate the purpose of ensuring that the Project shall at all times be operated and maintained in a manner so as to optimize and maximize its enjoyment and utilization by each Owner as a vacation resort.

IN WITNESS WHEREOF, the undersigned have hereunto set their hands this _____ day of _____, 19____.

BOARD OF DIRECTORS

_____

_____

_____

KNOW ALL MEN BY THESE PRESENTS: That the undersigned Secretary of the Association does hereby certify that the above and foregoing By-Laws were duly adopted by the Board of Directors of the Association as the By-Laws of said Association on the ____ day of _____, 19____, and that they do now constitute the By-Laws of the Association.

ATTEST:

_____

Secretary

# EXHIBIT 4

## INITIAL RULES AND REGULATIONS
### OF
## CLUB 'ABC' CONDOMINIUM ASSOCIATION, INC.

These Rules and Regulations, promulgated the ____ day of _____, 19____, shall govern the use and occupancy of the Units, Common Elements, and Common Furnishings of Club 'ABC', a Condominium (the 'Project') and shall be deemed in effect until amended by the Board of Directors of the Club 'ABC' Condominium Association, Inc. (the 'Association') and shall apply to and be binding upon all Owners. Owners shall at all times obey said Rules and Regulations and shall use their best efforts to ensure that such Rules and Regulations are faithfully observed by members of their families, their guests, invitees, and licensees. All of these Rules and Regulations are subordinate to and designed to supplement the Declaration of Condominium for Club 'ABC', a Condominium (the 'Declaration'), and in the event that there is a conflict between these Rules and Regulations and the Declaration, the Declaration shall control. Said initial Rules and Regulations are as follows:

### I DEFINITIONS
All terms used in these Rules and Regulations shall have the same meanings given to them in the Declaration.

### II USE RESTRICTIONS
A Except in areas which may be designated for such purpose by the Manager, the personal property of all Owners shall be stored within their Units. The Manager shall not be responsible for any belongings left by a Timeshare Owner, members of his family, or his guests, invitees, or licensees at the expiration of his Vacation Week(s).

B No garbage cans, supplies, milk bottles, or other articles shall be placed on the patios, decks, balconies, or entry ways, nor shall any linens, cloths, cloth-ing, curtains, rugs, mops, laundry of any kind, or other articles be shaken or hung from any of the windows, doors, patio, decks, balconies, or entry ways, or exposed in any part of the Common Elements. The Common Elements shall be kept free and clear of refuse, debris, and other unsightly material.

C No Owner or Unit Occupant shall allow anything whatsoever to fall from the windows, patios, decks, balconies, entry ways, or doors of the premises, nor shall he sweep or throw from his Unit any dirt or other substances outside of his Unit or in the Common Elements of the Project.

D Refuse and bagged garbage shall be deposited only in the area provided therefor.

E No Owner shall store or leave boats, trailers, mobile homes, or other recreational vehicles on the Project, except in such areas as are specifically designated for same.

F Employees of the Association or the Manager shall not be sent outside of the Project premises by any Owner at any time for any purpose. No Owner or Unit Occupant shall direct, supervise, or in any manner attempt to assert any control over the employees of the Manager or the Association.

*The above rule allows the Manager to properly operate and control his employees without additional suggestions from the timeshare and condominium owners.*

G No Owner or Unit Occupant shall make or permit any disturbing noises by himself, members of his family, his guests, invitees, or licensees, nor do or permit anything by such persons that will interfere with the rights, comfort, or convenience of the other Owners or Unit Occupants. No Owner or Unit Occupant shall play upon or suffer to be played upon any musical instrument, or operate or suffer to be operated a phonograph, television, radio, or sound amplifier in his Unit in such manner as to disturb or annoy other occupants of the Units in the Project. All Unit Occupants shall lower the volume as to the foregoing from 11:00 p.m. to 8:00 a.m. each night. The Board of Directors shall have the right to abate all nuisances in or about the Project.

H No radio, television installation, or other wiring shall be made without the prior written consent of the Board of Directors.

I An Owner may rent or lend his Unit or Vacation Week, to others, and may invite guests to share occupancy of his Unit, provided that the maximum occupancy limit for such Unit is not exceeded. Owners are responsible for the conduct of their guests, and for all financial obligations incurred by their guests at the Project.

J Owners and Unit Occupants shall be responsible for the conduct of members of their family, their guests, invitees, and licensees. Owners and Unit Occupants shall ensure that such persons' behaviour is neither offensive to any occupant of the Project nor damaging to any Unit or portion of the Common Elements.

K Rules governing the use of the swimming pool are posted thereat. Children twelve (12) years of age or under shall not be permitted in the pool area unless accompanied by an adult. Pool hours and rules are subject to change at the discretion of the Association or the Manager.

L No sign, advertisement, notice, or other lettering shall be exhibited, displayed, inscribed, painted, or affixed in, on, or upon any part of the Units, the Common Elements, the Common Furnishings, or other property in the Project by an Owner or Unit Occupant without the prior written permission of the Board of Directors.

M Complaints regarding the operation and maintenance of the project shall be made in writing to the Manager, as long as any Management Agreement remains in effect, and thereafter, to the Board of Directors.

N No inflammable, combustible, explosive, or otherwise dangerous fluid, chemical, or substance shall be kept in any Unit, except such as are required for normal household use.

O No Unit shall be occupied overnight by a number of persons in excess of such occupancy limits as are imposed by law.

P No animals or pets of any kind may be kept in any Unit or elsewhere within the Project.

Q The parking facilities shall be used in accordance with such regulations pertaining thereto as shall be adopted from time to time by the Association.

R The Manager, as long as any Management Agreement remains in effect, and thereafter, the Board of Directors of the Association, reserves the right to promulgate additional Rules and Regulations as may be required from time to time without the consent of the Association and its members. Such additional Rules and Regulations shall be as binding upon the members as all other Rules and Regulations previously adopted.

S The Association shall be entitled to recover reasonable costs and attorneys' fees in the event it prevails in an action brought against an Owner or Unit Occupant to enforce these Rules and Regulations.

### III UNITS COMMITTED TO TIME-SHARED OWNERSHIP

A *Check-In and Check-Out Time*

Check-in time shall be 4:00 p.m. on the first day of a Timeshare Owner's Vacation Week. All Timeshare Owners and Unit Occupants shall vacate their Units no later than 10:00 a.m. on the last day of their Vacation Week(s). The six (6) hour period between check-in and check-out is reserved exclusively as a service period to permit the routine cleaning, repair, and maintenance of the Units. However, a Timeshare Owner who owns or is otherwise entitled to consecutive Vacation Weeks shall not be required to vacate his Unit during the period of time between such consecutive Vacation Weeks.

*The check-in and check-out times provide the necessary gap period for clearing and cleaning the units.*

**B** *Inventory of Furnishings and Equipment*

Upon check-in, each Timeshare Owner will be given an inventory checklist which lists all of the furniture and furnishings which should be contained within the Owner's Unit. Each owner should inspect his Unit carefully and promptly report to the Manager any discrepancies between the inventory checklist and such items as are actually contained within the Owner's Unit, together with the condition thereof. If a Timeshare Owner fails to report any such discrepancy and a particular item is found to be damaged or missing immediately following the termination of such Timeshare Owner's Vacation Week, such Timeshare Owner shall be charged for the cost of such item.

*The inventory discourages disputes as to when an item was broken or found missing and allows for assessment for the item against the responsible party.*

# EXHIBIT 5

*Section 721.06 of FRETSA is specific as to those provisions which must be included in the timeshare purchase contract. Subsection (1) states that no seller of a timeshare plan shall fail to utilize and furnish each purchaser of such plan a fully completed copy of his contract.*

## PURCHASE CONTRACT
## OF
## CLUB 'ABC', A CONDOMINIUM

THIS PURCHASE CONTRACT is made and entered into this ____ day of _____, 19____, by and Between Timeshare Developer, Inc., a Florida corporation (hereinafter referred to as 'Seller'), the address of which is 101 Main Street, Anywhere, Florida, and

_____
Names(s)

_____
Street Address

_____
City          State          Zip Code

(____) _____
Home Telephone Number

(____) _____
Business Telephone Number
hereinafter referred to as 'Purchaser.'

### WITNESSETH:

That for and in consideration of the mutual convenants contained herein. Seller does hereby agree to sell unto Purchaser and Purchaser does hereby agree to purchase from Seller the following described real property situated at 1110 Main Street, Anywhere, Florida (the 'Property') upon the price, terms, and conditions hereinafter set out:

A Timeshare Interest consisting of an undivided one fifty-first ($\frac{1}{51}$) interest in fee simple as tenant in common in and to the Condominium Parcel identified below, together with a corresponding undivided interest in the Common Furnishings which are appurtenant to such Condominium Parcel, as well as the exclusive right each year, in perpetuity, to use and occupy the Unit within Club 'ABC', a Condominium (the 'Project'), identified below, as well as the Common Furnishings appurtenant thereto, and the non-exclusive right to use and enjoy the Common Elements of the Project, for their intended purposes, during the specific Vacation Week set forth below, subject to the Declaration of Condominium for Club 'ABC', a Condominium, duly recorded in the Public Records of XYZ County, Florida, in Official Record Book ____, at Page _____.

*Section 721.06(1)(e) requires the purchase contract to contain a description of the nature and duration of the timeshare period being sold, whether any interest in real property is being conveyed, and the specific number of years constituting the term of the timeshare plan.*

Parcel (unit) Number: _____
Vacation Week Number: _____

### PURCHASE TERMS

1 Purchase Price of Timeshare Interest:
$_____

2 Initial Deposit          $_____

3 Balance of Downpayment due on or before _____. 19__
$_____

4 Total Downpayment (item 2 plus item 3):          $_____

5   Amount to be Financed or Amount Due at Closing (item 1 minus item 3):                     $_____
6   Estimated Closing Costs:    $_____
7   Initial Exchange Fee:        $_____
8   Estimated Total Cost of Timeshare Interest:          $_____

Purchaser desires to pay for his Timeshare Interest, in US dollars, by using the following method (check one), subject to the Terms and Conditions described in greater detail on the reverse side hereof and incorporated herein by reference: [ ] Cash Payment [ ] Seller Financing [ ] Third Party Lender Financing.

In addition to the financial obligations of Purchaser set forth above, Purchaser will be subject to the payment of the Common Expense Assessment and Timeshare Maintenance Fee described in Paragraph 5 below, together with any ad valorem taxes levied against his Timeshare Interest, to the extent that such taxes are individually billed to Purchaser. If Purchaser obtains mortgage financing, Purchaser will be responsible for the payment of all charges incident to the extension of credit, which charges are specified in the Federal Truth-in-Lending Disclosure Statement to be furnished to Purchaser. Closing costs in connection with the purchase of the above-described Timeshare Interest, including but not limited to all real estate transfer taxes and documentary stamps, notary fees, escrow fees, mortgage recording fees, title insurance fees, attorneys' fees, and unless otherwise agreed upon, all other Closing costs incident to the subject transaction, are to be paid by Purchaser prior to or at the time of Closing.

*Section 721.06(1)(5) requires the purchase contract to disclose the total financial obligation of the purchaser, including the initial purchase price and any additional charges such as financing, reservation, maintenances, management and recreation charges.*

### Form of Ownership
[ ] Sole Owner
[ ] Joint Tenancy with Right of Survivorship
[ ] Tenancy in common
[ ] Tenancy by the Entirety

**YOU MAY CANCEL THIS CONTRACT WITHOUT ANY PENALTY OR OBLIGATION WITHIN 10 DAYS FROM THE DATE YOU SIGN THIS CONTRACT, AND UNTIL 10 DAYS AFTER YOU RECEIVE THE PUBLIC OFFERING STATEMENT, WHICHEVER IS LATER.**

**IF YOU DECIDE TO CANCEL THIS CONTRACT, YOU MUST NOTIFY THE DEVEOPER IN WRITING OF YOUR INTENT TO CANCEL. YOUR NOTICE OF CANCELLATION SHALL BE EFFECTIVE UPON THE DATE SENT AND SHALL BE SENT TO TIMESHARE DEVELOPER AT 101 MAIN STREET, ANYWHERE, FLORIDA. ANY ATTEMPT TO OBTAIN A WAIVER OF YOUR CANCELLATION RIGHTS IS UNLAWFUL. WHILE YOU MAY EXECUTE ALL CLOSING DOCUMENTS IN ADVANCE, THE CLOSING, AS EVIDENCED BY DELIVERY OF THE DEED OR OTHER DOCUMENT, BEFORE EXPIRATION OF YOUR 10-DAY CANCELLATION PERIOD, IS PROHIBITED.**

*The above dislosures are required by Section 721.06(1)(f) and must be in conspicuous type immediately prior to the space reserved in the contract for the purchaser's signature.*

IN WITNESS WHEREOF, Purchaser has executed this Contract on the day and year first written above.
PURCHASER:

_____

_____

SELLER:
TIMESHARE DEVELOPER, INC.
By: _____
      Authorized Representative
Acceptance Date:

_____

*Section 721.06(1)(a) requires the seller to give a purchaser a copy of the contract which shows the date of the seller's signature and execution of the contract.*

[end of first page]

## TERMS AND CONDITIONS
### 1 PURCHASER'S PROMISE TO BUY; SELLER'S RIGHT TO ACCEPT OR REJECT THIS CONTRACT

It is understood that Seller can accept or reject this Purchase Contract. If Seller rejects this Purchase Contract, Purchaser is only entitled to a refund of his deposit and any additional payments made by him, without interest. If Seller accepts this Purchase Contract, then Seller agrees to sell the Timeshare Interest described herein to Purchaser, and Purchaser agrees to make all of the payments required to be made under this Purchase Contract when due. Purchaser understands that the sales-person cannot accept this Purchase Contract for Seller. Only Seller or its authorized representative(s) can accept this Purchase Contract and only by signing it.

*Please note that any delay by the Seller in executing the Purchase Contract acts to delay the running of the cancellation period due to the FRETSA requirement that the cancellation period does not begin to run until the Buyer receives a copy of the Purchase Contract signed by both parties and dated the date of Seller's signature (Sections 721.06 (1)(a) and 721.10(1)).*

### 2 DEPOSITS

Pursuant to Section 721.08, Florida Statutes, Purchaser's initial deposit and any subsequent payments made by Purchaser to Seller prior to Closing shall be held in an escrow account by Attorney-at-Law, 1515 Main Street, Anywhere, Florida (hereinafter referred to as 'Escrow Agent'). Purchaser may obtain a receipt for his deposit from Escrow Agent upon request. Any and all interest which accrues in Purchaser's deposit shall be payable to Seller.

*Until the expiration of the cancellation period, completion of construction of the building containing the unit in which the timeshare interest has been sold, and closing, one hundred per cent (100%) of all funds received from a purchaser of*

*a timeshare must be held in escrow pursuant to Section 721.08.*

*Further, if the contract fails to state to whom the interest on the escrow account is payable, purchasers may have a claim on the interest pursuant to Section 721.08(4).*

### 3 REFUND PRIVILEGE

In the event Purchaser cancels this Agreement during the 10-day cancellation period described on page 1 hereof, Seller will refund to Purchaser the total amount of all payments made by Purchaser under this Contract, reduced by the proportion of any contract benefits Purchaser has actually received under this Contract prior to the effective date of such cancellation. Such refund shall be made by Seller within twenty (20) days after Seller's receipt of the notice of cancellation, or within five (5) days after Seller's receipt of funds from Purchaser's cleared check, whichever is later.

*The above provision is required to be in the purchase contract by Section 721.06(1)(i). The refund periods for cancellations are set forth in Section 721.08(1)(a).*

### 4 CHECK-IN AND CHECK-OUT

Vacation Weeks begin at 4:00 p.m. on the first day of the Vacation Week and end at 4:00 p.m. on the last day of the Vacation Week. However, all Purchasers shall be required to vacate their Units on the last day of their Vacation Week no later than the time set forth in the then-current Rules and Regulations of the Association. The initial Rules and Regulations state that all persons must check-out of their Units by 10:00 a.m. on the last day of their Vacation Week. However, the Board of Directors of the Association ('Board') may, in its sole discretion, change this check-out time by amending the Rules and Regulations. Any Purchaser who fails to vacate his Unit by the required time shall be subject to the penalties and legal actions described in the Declaration.

### 5 CHARGES AND ASSESSMENTS

(a) Purchaser understands and agrees that in accordance with the provisions of the Declaration, Purchaser shall be responsible for his proportionate share of the Common Expenses; and Timeshare Expenses, including but not limited to real estate taxes and other fees and assessments levied by a governmental authority, utility charges, insurance premiums, reserves, domestic services, and all other expenses incurred by the Association in the maintenance, repair, operation, and administration of the Project. Each Purchaser's proportionate share of the normal and ordinary operating expenses of the Association is called his 'Common Expense Assessment,' and his proportionate share of the costs incurred by the Association which are directly attributable to the commitment of one or more Units in the Project to timeshared ownership is called his 'Timeshare Maintenance Fee.' The amount of the Common Expense Assessment and Timeshare Maintenance Fee will be determined by the Board of Directors of the Association, pursuant to the annual budget which will be prepared by the Manager and approved by the Board at the start of each fiscal year. The initial Common Expense Assessment and Timeshare Maintenance Fee shall be combined into a single payment and shall be due at Closing, to be prorated for the calendar year in question, as appropriate. All subsequent Common Expense Assessments and Timeshare Maintenance Fees shall be due and payable on January 15 of each year, or at such other time and in such manner as shall be determined from time to time by the Board. The Common Expense Assessment and Timeshare Maintenance Fee may be revised periodically, based upon the projected expenses of operating the Project for the period in question; provided, however, that Seller guarantees that from the date hereof through _____, 19___, the combined Common Expense Assessment and Timeshare Maintenance Fee payable by Purchaser, exclusive of real estate taxes, shall not exceed $_____ per Timeshare Interest per year. During the guarantee period, the Seller will be excused from paying the Common Expense Assessments and Timeshare

Maintenance Fees allocable to the Units and Timeshare Interests owned by Seller, but Seller agrees to pay all expenses incurred by the Association during such guarantee period, exclusive of real estate taxes, to the extent that such expenses exceed the amounts received by the Association from Owners other than Seller.

*Section 721.15(2) permits the developer to be excused from the payment of his common expenses which would have been assessed against those units during the period the developer has agreed to guarantee that assessments will not exceed a stated amount; provided that the developer makes up any shortfall in assessments collected.*

*Further, since FRETSA requires that the contract specify a purchaser's annual assessment, the contract should provide a mechanism for increases in assessments in the future.*

(b) In addition to the Common Expense Assessment and Timeshare Maintenance Fee, Purchaser understands and agrees that he will be responsible for the timely payment to the Association or its designee of any Special Assessments levied upon him by the Board, or any Personal Charges which he incurs, in accordance with the provisions of the Declaration and the By-Laws.

(c) Any portion of the Common Expense Assessment and Timeshare Maintenance Fee and any Special Assessments or Personal Charges, if not paid by Purchaser within thirty (30) days from the date they are due, shall become a lien on Purchaser's Timeshare Interest and shall bear interest at the rate then allowed by Florida law, compounded monthly. The Board, in its sole discretion, may impose upon Purchaser a late charge for all Assessments and charges not paid within fifteen (15) days from the date they are due, pursuant to the Declaration.

## 6 SOURCE OF PURCHASE FUNDS

Purchaser may pay for the Timeshare Interest described herein in cash or by borrowing a part of the purchase price from Seller (if Seller financing is available at the time Purchaser executes this Contract) or from a third party lender. Purchaser's desired method of payment is indicated on Page 1 of this Contract.

Each Purchaser who desires to finance his purchase shall receive a Federal Truth-in-Lending Disclosure Statement and will read and sign it before Purchaser signs this Contract, That Disclosure Statement will show the terms of the loan that will be made available to Purchaser if Seller or a third party tender designated by Seller agrees to make financing available to Purchaser. Thereafter, Purchaser's promises in this Contract and his obligation to buy will not be dependent upon whether Purchaser later changes his mind about the terms of such financing. If Purchaser requests financing, Seller or a third party lender designated by Seller may agree to finance the Purchaser's purchase, but is not required to do so.

If Purchaser's purchase is made by means of financing provided by Seller or a third party lender designated by Seller, the loan will be evidenced by a Promissory Note and will be secured by the placing of a Purchase Money Mortgage on Purchaser's Timeshare Interest. Purchaser agrees that all personal financial information submitted to Seller or to any third party lender in connection with this Contract will be accurate. Purchaser authorises Seller and Purchaser's proposed third party lender (if applicable) to make credit inquiries regarding Purchaser. Purchaser agrees to provide immediate written notice to Seller or any third party lender of any material adverse change in Purchaser's financial condition which occurs prior to Closing.

## 7 CLOSING

For purposes of this Contract, the term 'Closing' shall mean the date following the expiration of Purchaser's ten (10) day right of rescission without such right having been exercised as of which both parties hereto have properly executed all documents necessary to effect the transfer of title of a Timeshare Interest hereunder, including this Contract, a Warranty Deed, and a Promissory Note and Purchase Money Mortgage, if applicable. Upon Closing, Seller shall cause all necessary documents to be recorded in

the Public Records of XYZ County, Florida, at Purchaser's expense, and copies thereof subsequently to be mailed or delivered to Purchaser. Closing is estimated to occur within thirty (30) days of Seller's acceptance of this Contract. In the event of a default by Purchaser hereunder prior to Closing, Seller may terminate this Contract and shall be entitled to such additional remedies as are set forth in Paragraph 13 hereof.

*The estimated date of closing is required to be disclosed pursuant to Section 721.06(1)(d).*

## 8 TITLE AND TITLE INSURANCE

Seller is not the sole owner of the underlying fee of the Condominium Unit described herein without any liens or encumbrances thereupon; Seller owns fee simple title to said Condominium Unit, subject to a mortgage held by First Federal Bank, Anywhere, Florida. Seller will cause Purchaser's Timeshare Interest to be released from said mortgage at or prior to Closing by the payment of a release fee to the mortgagee or by the full satisfaction of said mortgage.

*Section 721.06(1)(k) requires disclosure of Seller's actual interest in the Project including whether or not it is the sole owner free and clear of all liens and encumbrances of the underlying fee, and if not, then the names and addresses of all persons or entities having an ownership interest.*

Upon Closing, Purchaser will be provided with a policy of title insurance from a title insurance company of Seller's choosing, at Purchaser's expense, insuring Purchaser's title to his Timeshare Interest.

## 9 RIGHT OF OCCUPANCY

Purchaser may not use or occupy a Unit until Closing occurs, as described above. All Units and Common Elements of the Project are presently completed.

## 10 TAXATION

For the purposes of ad valorem assessment, taxation and special assessments, the Association will be considered the taxpayer as your agent, pursuant to Section 192.037, Florida Statutes.

*The above provision is required to be included in the purchase contract by Section 721.06(1)(h).*

## 11 RISK OF LOSS

Seller assumes the risk of loss from fire or otherwise until Closing occurs.

## 12 LATE PAYMENTS

Purchaser shall pay to Seller or its designated assignee a late charge of five per cent (5%) of any monthly payment, not to exceed five dollars ($5.00), which is not received by Seller or its designated assign within ten (10) days after the payment is due.

## 13 DEFAULT

(a) Purchaser shall be in default under this Purchase Contract if he fails to pay on time, keep any promise, or fulfill any agreement or obligation contained herein. Purchaser expressly waives notice of default or breach of any term of this Purchase Contract.

If Purchaser defaults in the performance of his obligations under this Purchase Contract, as described above, Seller, or a successor or assign of Seller, if applicable, may, at its option: 1. Seek a judgment for the amount due and hold Purchaser personally liable; 2. Terminate this Purchase Contract if a Warranty Deed to Purchaser's Timeshare Interest has not been recorded and retain or cause Escrow Agent to deliver to Seller (whichever is applicable) any sums already paid by Purchaser as liquidated damages and not a penalty; 3. Foreclose under the Purchase Money Mortgage upon the property described herein if a Warranty Deed to Purchaser's Timeshare Interest has been recorded, and hold Purchaser personally liable for any monetary deficiency; 4. Pursue any other legal or equitable remedies available to it. Each remedy may be exercised alone or in combination with any other remedies. Failure to exercise any remedy in one default shall not constitute a waiver of the right to exercise such remedy in the event of a later default.

(b) If for any reason Seller is unable to comply with the provisions of this Contract, the sole obligation of Seller shall be to refund or cause Escrow Agent to refund (whichever is applicable) to Purchaser all payments made hereunder, without interest, and upon making such refund, this Contract shall be deemed cancelled, and all rights and obligations hereunder shall terminate.

## 14 DELAY OR IMPOSSIBILITY OF PERFORMANCE

If Seller is delayed or prevented, in whole or in part, from performing any of its duties or obligations hereunder by reason of or as a result of any *force majeure*, Seller shall be excused from performing such duties or obligations. The term *'force majeure'* as used herein shall include: acts of God, strikes, lockouts, wars, epidemics, landslides, earthquakes, fires, storms, floods, governmental restraints, explosions, and other causes beyond the control of Seller. If such *force majeure* delays or prevents Seller's performance hereunder, Seller may, in its sole discretion, provide Purchaser with reasonably comparable accommodations during any period of Seller non-performance or cancel this Purchase Contract and refund or cause Escrow Agent to refund (whichever is applicable) to Purchaser all payments made hereunder, without interest.

## 15 THE CLUB 'ABC' CONDOMINIUM ASSOCIATION, INC.

Upon the recording of Purchaser's Warranty Deed in the Public Records of XYZ County, Florida, Purchaser will automatically become a member of the Club 'ABC' Condominium Association, Inc., and agrees to be subject to and to abide by the By-Laws and Rules and Regulations thereof, as each may lawfully be amended from time to time.

## 16 FURNITURE AND FURNISHINGS

Although the model Unit and descriptive materials are for display purposes only, all Units shall have furniture, appliances, equipment, and accent furnishings which are substantially similar to, or of equal quality to, those shown or used in the model Unit or descriptive materials.

## 17 PURCHASER'S ACKNOWLEDGMENTS

Purchaser acknowledges that prior to signing this Purchase Contract, Purchaser received and had a reasonable opportunity to read the Florida Public Offering Statement prepared pursuant to Chapter 721, Florida Statutes, together with the Exhibits attached thereto, including the Declaration, the By-Laws, and Rules and Regulations of the Association, and Purchaser agrees to be strictly bound and to abide by all of the provisions of those documents, as each may lawfully be amended from time to time. Purchaser further acknowledges and represents that the Timeshare Interest described herein is being purchased for Purchaser's personal use, and not for its investment potential or any possible rent returns, tax advantages, depreciation, or as Purchaser's principal residence. Purchaser also acknowledges that no representations of any nature whatsoever have been made to Purchaser concerning investment potential, rent returns, tax advantages, or depreciation by Seller or any of its agents, employees, or associates. Seller has no resale or rental program for Timeshare Interests, and neither Seller or any of its sales agents, employees, or associates has represented that Purchaser will be assisted in the resale or rental of his Timeshare Interest in the future.

*The above provision is included to attempt to remove the sale of timeshare interests from the definition of a security which would need to be sold in compliance with the federal and state securities laws. In addition, FRETSA includes a statement that Florida-located timesharing plans are not securities under the provisions of Florida securities law.*

Purchaser shall be entitled to the use of his Unit and the Common Furnishings located therein, as well as the Common Elements of the Project, during Purchaser's Vacation Week only. Purchaser's rights under this Purchase Contract shall not entitle him to use any Unit or the Common Elements or Common Furnishings at any other times except during his Vacation Week. The Association shall retain the right to inspect such property, make periodic repairs thereto, and in the sole discretion of the Association, replace such property. While he occupies his Unit, Purchaser shall be responsible for the care and maintenance of the furniture, appliances, equipment, and accent furnishings contained therein, and any damage done to such property caused by the negligent or intentional acts of Purchaser, members of Purchaser's family, his guests, licensees, or invitees, to the extent not covered by insurance, shall be corrected by the Association, and the cost thereof shall be assessed against Purchaser as a Personal Charge. Upon demand by the Association, Purchaser shall pay to the Association the sum expended to repair any such damage. In the event the cost to repair the damage is not promptly paid by the Purchaser, the Association is authorized to place a lien on the Timeshare Interest described herein, and to exercise any of the other remedies granted to it by the Declaration and/or the By-Laws, and by any applicable provision of law.

## 18 EXCHANGE PROGRAM

Seller has executed an agreement with Exchange Company pursuant to which Exchange Company will offer its reciprocal exchange service to Purchaser. The purpose of this service is to allow Purchaser the option of temporarily exchanging the use of his Vacation Week in this Project for occupancy at other timeshare projects participating in the Exchange Company exchange program. Each Purchaser's participation in the exchange program is voluntary and subject to the payment by each Purchaser of such membership and other fees as are required by Exchange Company. Seller makes no representations concerning the current or future services to be provided by Exchange Company, or as to the availability, continuance, success, or failure of the Exchange Company exchange program. Any representations made regarding the exchange program, either orally by Exchange Company employees or within the brochures and literature provided by Exchange Company, are solely the representations of Exchange Company and should not be interpreted as being the representations of Seller.

*Section 721.18 sets forth specific and detailed disclosure requirements for exchange programs. The seller must deliver these disclosures to the purchaser (together with the public offering statement and prior to the offering or execution of any contract between the purchaser and the company offering the exchange program). The purchaser must certify that he or she has received the required disclosures. The disclosures must be approved by the Division of Florida Land Sales and Condominiums. Among the required disclosures is the fact that participation in the exchange program is voluntary.*

## 19 ASSIGNMENT OF PURCHASE CONTRACT

Purchaser may not assign his rights under this Purchase Contract without the prior written consent of Seller, which consent shall not be unreasonably withheld. Purchaser acknowledges Seller's right to assign its rights and interests hereunder.

## 20 NOTICES

All notices which either party desires or is required to give the other party under this Purchase Contract shall be in writing, and shall be delivered personally or by mail, and addressed as follows:

(a) To the Purchaser in care of the address stated in this Purchase Contract or at the last known address provided by the Purchaser to the Seller in writing. If more than one person is listed in this Purchase Contract as the Purchaser, delivery or mailing of notice to any one of such persons shall be deemed to constitute notice to all of them. If Purchaser is a corporation or a partnership, notices may be delivered or mailed to any officer or partner thereof.

(b) To the Seller at its offices at 101 Main Street, Anywhere, Florida, or at such other place as Seller may designate from time to time in writing.

## 21 PAYMENTS

All amounts due hereunder shall be payable at the office of Seller at its address as stated on Page 1 hereof, or at such other place as Seller may designate from time to time in writing.

## 22 TIME IS OF THE ESSENCE

Time is of the essence of this Purchase Contract and of each and all of the conditions contained herein.

## 23 SURVIVAL OF PURCHASE CONTRACT

This Purchase Contract and the agreements and covenants herein set forth shall be binding upon and inure to the benefit of the parties hereto, their respective heirs, successors, assigns, and personal representatives, and said provisions of this Purchase Contract shall survive the Closing of this transaction.

## 24 SEVERABILITY

The terms and provisions hereof shall be deemed independent and severable, and the invalidity of any one provision or portion thereof shall not affect the validity or enforceability of any other provision hereof.

## 25 CHOICE OF STATE LAW

This Purchase Contract shall be governed by and construed in accordance with the laws of the State of Florida.

## 26 MISCELLANEOUS

The captions used in this Purchase Contract are for informational purposes only and do not amplify or limit in any way the provisions hereof. Purchaser is advised to read each and every Paragraph very carefully, and not just the captions alone. Whenever the context so requires, the use of any gender in this Purchase Contract shall be deemed to include both genders, and the use of the singular shall be deemed to include the plural, and the plural shall include the singular. All terms used in this Purchase Contract which are defined in the Declaration shall have the same meanings herein as are given to them in the Declaration.

# EXHIBIT 6

*A receipt for documents is required by Rule 7D–18 (promulgated pursuant to Chapter 718). It is a useful summary of all the Project documents and if a purchaser were to read all of the documents listed, the purchaser would have adequate Project information on which to base a decision to buy.*

## RECEIPT FOR TIMESHARE DOCUMENTS

The undersigned acknowledges that the items listed below have been received and, as to plans and specifications, such plans and specifications have been made available for inspection.

*Name of TimeShare Plan:* CLUB 'ABC', A CONDOMINIUM
*Address of TimeShare Plan:* 1110 Main Street, Anywhere, Florida

| *DOCUMENT* | *DOCUMENT* |
|---|---|
| Offering Statement Text | Plot Plan |
| Declaration of Condominium | Executed Escrow Agreement |
| Articles of Incorporation | Exchange Disclosure Documents |
| By-Laws | TimeShare Period Schedule for |
| Management Agreement | Initial Fifty (50) Years of the |
| Purchase Contract | TimeShare Plan |
| Rules and Regulations | Receipt for TimeShare Documents |
| Lease for Recreational and Other | Plans and Specifications (made |
| Commonly Used Facilities | available) |

REFER TO OFFERING STATEMENT TEXT FOR IMPORTANT
DISCLOSURES OF PURCHASER RIGHTS UNDER FLORIDA LAW.

YOU MAY CANCEL YOUR CONTRACT WITHOUT ANY PENALTY OR OBLIGATION WITHIN 10 DAYS FROM THE DATE YOU SIGN YOUR CONTRACT, AND UNTIL 10 DAYS AFTER YOU RECEIVE THE PUBLIC OFFERING STATEMENT, WHICHEVER IS LATER. IF YOU DECIDE TO CANCEL YOUR CONTRACT, YOU MUST NOTIFY THE DEVELOPER IN WRITING OF YOUR INTENT TO CANCEL. YOUR NOTICE OF CANCEL-LATION SHALL BE EFFECTIVE UPON THE DATE SENT AND SHALL BE SENT TO TIMESHARE DEVELOPER, INC. AT 101 MAIN STREET, ANY-WHERE, FLORIDA. ANY ATTEMPT TO OBTAIN A WAIVER OF YOUR CANCELLATION RIGHTS IS UNLAWFUL. WHILE YOU MAY EXECUTE ALL CLOSING DOCUMENTS IN ADVANCE, THE CLOSING, AS EVI-DENCED BY DELIVERY OF THE DEED OR OTHER DOCUMENT, BEFORE EXPIRATION OF YOUR 10 DAY CANCELLATION PERIOD IS PROHIBITED.

Executed this _____ day of _____, 19____.

_____     _____

Purchaser                                             Purchaser

## EXHIBIT 7

*Section 721.07 of FRETSA requires every developer to file a public offering statement with the Division for approval and each developer must furnish a purchaser with a copy of the approved public offering statement. Until the Division approves the filing, any contract regarding the sale of the timeshare plan will voidable by the purchaser.*

## PUBLIC OFFERING STATEMENT
## FOR
## CLUB 'ABC', A CONDOMINIUM

THIS PUBLIC OFFERING STATE-
MENT CONTAINS IMPORTANT
MATTERS TO BE CONSIDERED IN
ACQUIRING A TIMESHARE PER-
IOD. THE STATEMENTS CON-
TAINED HEREIN ARE ONLY
SUMMARY IN NATURE. A
PROSPECTIVE PURCHASER
SHOULD REFER TO ALL REFER-
ENCES, EXHIBITS HERETO, CON-
TRACT DOCUMENTS, AND SALES
MATERIALS. YOU SHOULD NOT
RELY UPON ORAL REPRESEN-
TATIONS AS BEING CORRECT.
REFER TO THIS DOCUMENT AND
ACCOMPANYING EXHIBITS FOR
CORRECT REPRESENTATIONS.
THE SELLER IS PROHIBITED
FROM MAKING ANY REPRESEN-
TATIONS OTHER THAN THOSE
CONTAINED IN THE CONTRACT
AND THIS PUBLIC OFFERING
STATEMENT.

*Section 721.07(5)(a) requires that the cover page state only the name of the timeshare plan and the above disclosure statement.*

## TABLE OF CONTENTS

*Section 721.07(05)(c) requires each public offering statement to contain a separate index of its contents and exhibits.*

## EXHIBITS

*The listing of exhibits is included for informational purposes to show the detailed nature of a Florida filing. The exhibit listing is set forth as a requirement under FRETSA.*

## SUMMARY

*Section 721.07(5)(b) requires a summary containing all statements required to be in conspicuous type in the offering statement and in all the exhibits. This means that all of the conspicuous type statements in the purchase contract, declaration and other Project documents must be included in the Summary.*

Important matters to be considered in purchasing a Timeshare Interest:

1 **THERE IS A RECREATIONAL FACILITIES LEASE ASSOCIATED WITH THIS TIMESHARE PLAN.**
2 **PURCHASERS ARE REQUIRED TO PAY THEIR SHARE OF THE COSTS AND EXPENSES OF MAINTENANCE, MANAGEMENT, UPKEEP, REPLACEMENT, RENT, AND FEES UNDER THE RECREATIONAL FACILITIES LEASE.**

3 RECREATIONAL FACILITIES MAY BE EXPANDED OR ADDED WITHOUT CONSENT OF THE PURCHASERS OR THE ASSOCIATION.

4 THE DEVELOPER HAS THE RIGHT TO RETAIN CONTROL OF THE ASSOCIATION AFTER A MAJORITY OF THE TIME-SHARE INTERESTS HAVE BEEN SOLD.

5 The following statements appear in conspicuous type in the Purchase Contract, which is attached as Exhibit 5 to this Public Offering Statement:
YOU MAY CANCEL THIS CON-TRACT WITHOUT ANY PENALTY OR OBLIGATION WITHIN 10 DAYS FROM THE DATE YOU SIGN THIS CON-TRACT, AND UNTIL 10 DAYS AFTER YOU RECEIVE THE PUBLIC OFFERING STATE-MENT, WHICHEVER IS LATER. IF YOU DECIDE TO CANCEL THIS CONTRACT, YOU MUST NOTIFY THE DEVELOPER IN WRITING OF YOUR INTENT TO CANCEL. YOUR NOTICE OF CANCELLATION SHALL BE EFFECTIVE UPON THE DATE SENT AND SHALL BE SENT TO TIMESHARE DEVELOPER, INC. AT 101 MAIN STREET, ANY-WHERE, FLORIDA. ANY ATTEMPT TO OBTAIN A WAIVER OF YOUR CANCEL-LATION RIGHTS IS UNLAWFUL. WHILE YOU MAY EXECUTE ALL CLOSING DOCUMENTS IN ADVANCE, THE CLOSING, AS EVIDENCED BY DELIVERY OF THE DEED OR OTHER DOCU-MENT, BEFORE EXPIRATION OF YOUR 10-DAY CANCEL-LATION PERIOD, IS PROHIBITED.
FOR THE PURPOSE OF AD VALOREM ASSESSMENT, TAX-ATION AND SPECIAL ASSESS-MENTS, THE CONDOMINIUM ASSOCIATION WILL BE CON-SIDERED THE TAXPAYER AS YOUR AGENT PURSUANT TO SECTION 192.037, FLORIDA STATUTES.

6 The following statement appears in conspicuous type in the Declaration of Condominium for Club 'ABC', a Condominium (the 'Declaration'), a copy of which is attached hereto as Exhibit 1.
TIME-SHARE ESTATES, AS THAT TERM IS DEFINED BY SECTION 718.103(19), FLORIDA STATUTES, MAY BE CREATED WITH RESPECT TO SOME OR ALL OF THE UNITS IN THE PROJECT.
*Each provision of the Public Offering Statement is required by FRETSA and its regulations. The requirements are lengthy and quite detailed.*

### I DESCRIPTION OF THE CONDOMINIUM

A *Condominium Name*
The name of the Condominium herein-described is Club 'ABC', a Condominium (the 'Project').

B *Condominium Location*
The Project is located at 1110 Main Street, Anywhere, Florida, and is situated upon the real property described in Exhi-bit 'A' to the Declaration.

C *Description of Condominium Property*
The Condominium consists of a total of _____ (__) residential Units located in _____ (__) buildings, each of which Units contains two (2) bedrooms and two (2) bathrooms. The construction and the initial furnishings and equipping of the Condominium Units has been completed.

### II FEE SIMPLE TITLE

Although the Developer reserves the right to sell one (1) or more Units within the Project on a whole Unit basis, the Deve-loper currently plans to divide each Unit into fifty-one (51) Timeshare Interests. Since the maximum number of Units in the Project is _____ (__), the maxi-mum number of Timeshare Interests being offered for sale by the Developer is _____ (__). A purchaser of a Timeshare Interest will acquire an undi-vided one fifty-first ($\frac{1}{51}$) interest in fee simple absolute as tenant in common in and to his Unit and the Common Elements and Common Furnishings appurtenant thereto.

A Purchaser's rights will be evidenced by a Warranty Deed conveyed to him by the Developer and recorded in the Public Records of XYZ County, Florida. A specimen copy of the Warranty Deed is attached hereto as Exhibit 2.

### III VACATION WEEKS

A *Use and Occupancy of Units*
Appurtenant to each Timeshare Interest is a specific Vacation Week, during which time the Owner of said Timeshare Interest, in perpetuity, shall have the exclusive right to use and occupy his Unit and the Common Furnishings located therein, as well as the non-exclusive right to use and enjoy the Common Elements of the Project. Please refer to the Schedule of Vacation Weeks which is attached to the Declaration as Exhibit 'E'.

B *Check-in and Check-out*
Vacation Weeks begin at 4:00 p.m. on the first Saturday of the Vacation Week and end at 4:00 p.m. on the last Saturday of the Vacation Week. However, each purchaser will be required to vacate his Unit on the last day of his Vacation Week no later than the time set forth in the then-current Rules and Regulations of the Association. The initial Rules and Regulations, a copy of which is attached hereto as Exhibit 3, state that all persons must check-out of their Units by 10:00 a.m. on the last day of their Vacation Week. However, the Board of Directors of the Association (the 'Board') may, in its sole discretion, change this check-out time by amending the Rules and Regulations. Any purchaser who fails to vacate his Unit by the required time shall be subject to such penalties and legal actions as are described in Article VI of the Declaration.

C *No Rental of Vacation Weeks by the Developer*
This offering does not involve any rental arrangement or other similar service with emphasis on the economic benefits to the purchaser to be derived from the managerial efforts of the Developer, nor does it involve any form of rental pool arrangement whereby the purchaser must make his Unit available to others for a specific period of time each year, must use an exclusive rental agent, or is otherwise similarly restricted materially in the occupancy or rental of his Unit during his Vacation Week(s).

D *The Developer's Use of Unsold Vacation Weeks*
The Developer has the right, pursuant to Article VI of the Declaration, to use any Unit within the Project during any unsold or otherwise available Vacation Week(s) as a hotel accommodation for rental on a transient basis to members of the general public.

### IV RECREATIONAL AND OTHER COMMONLY USED FACILITIES

A *Common Elements*
Construction by the Developer of a swimming pool located adjacent to the Units, as shown in Exhibit 'F' to the Declaration, has been completed. Such pool can accommodate approximately _____ (__) persons at any given time. The pool is a minimum of _____ (__) feet and a maximum of _____ (__) feet in depth, measures approximately _____ (__) feet by _____ (__) feet, and is heated. A deck extends outward from the pool approximately _____ (__) feet in all directions and can accommodate approximately _____ (__) persons at any given time. A whirlpool will be located adjacent to the pool and will be able to accommodate approximately _____ (__) persons at any given time.

As a portion of the Common Elements, each Purchaser will own an undivided interest in the pool, pool deck, and whirlpool.

B *Leased Facilities*
The following facilities and amenities, all presently completed, will be leased by the Developer to the Club 'ABC' Condominium Association, Inc. (the 'Association') of which all purchasers will be members (see Paragraph VII A below), pursuant to the Lease which is attached hereto as Exhibit 3:
1 Two (2) tennis courts of standard

dimensions and able to accommodate up to eight (8) persons at any given time.

2 Portions of a Clubhouse, including an apartment for the Resident Manager and the Management Office, each of which is fully furnished.

3 The clothes washing machines and dryers which are located on the first (1st) floor of each of the _____ (__) buildings within the Project.

C *Nature of Lease*

**THERE IS A RECREATIONAL FACILITIES LEASE ASSOCIATED WITH THIS TIMESHARE PLAN.**

Each of the facilities described in subparagraph B above will be leased by the Developer to the Association for an initial term of one (1) year at the following annual rental amounts:

1 Tennis Courts            $_____
2 Resident Manager's
  Apartment               $_____
3 Management Office        $_____
4 Washer/Dryers            $_____

**PURCHASERS ARE REQUIRED TO PAY THEIR SHARE OF THE COSTS AND EXPENSES OF MAINTENANCE, MANAGEMENT, UPKEEP, REPLACEMENT, RENT, AND FEES UNDER THE RECREATIONAL FACILITIES LEASE.**

The annual total rent of $_____ will be a Common Expense of the Association, to be shared by all of the Owners in the manner described in Paragraph X below. However, any and all income accruing to the Association as a result of its operation of the above equipment, facilities, and amenities shall inure solely to the benefit of the Association and not the Developer, and may be used by the Association to offset such rental amounts. At present, the Developer has not granted to the Association any option to purchase the above equipment, facilities, and amenities.

D *Developer's Right to Add Recreational Facilities*

**RECREATIONAL FACILITIES MAY BE EXPANDED OR ADDED WITHOUT CONSENT OF THE PURCHASERS OR THE ASSOCIATION.**

The Developer reserves the right, pursuant to Article XVIII of the Declaration, to add additional recreational facilities or to expand the existing facilities of the Project, without the consent of the Owners or the Association. However, the Developer has no plans for any such additions or enlargements at the present time.

E *Maximum Use of Facilities*

It is presently contemplated that the maximum number of Units and Timeshare Interests that will use the accommodations and facilities is _____ (__) and _____ (__), respectively.

F *Use of Facilities By Hotel Guests*

As discussed in Paragraph III above, the Developer plans to rent the Units within the Project during any unsold or otherwise available Vacation Week(s) as hotel accommodations on a transient basis to members of the general public. All such hotel guests shall have the same use rights with respect to the facilities and amenities described in this Paragraph IC as do the Owners. However, once all Timeshare Interests within the Project have been sold by the Developer, the use of such facilities and amenities will be limited to the Owners, members of their families, their guests, invitees, and licensees.

G *Value of Personal Property Within Recreational Facilities*

The Developer has spent or intends to spend at least __ _____ Dollars ($_____) to purchase the various items of personal property to be located in or upon the recreational and other commonly used facilities described above.

## V STATUS OF TITLE

The Developer holds title in fee simple absolute to the Condominium Units and real property upon which the Project is situated, subject to a mortgage held thereon by _____

_____. Each purchaser's Timeshare Interest will be released from said mortgage prior to Closing, as more fully discussed in the Purchase Contract. Purchasers will receive their Timeshare Interests, free and clear of any blanket liens or encumbrances.

# VI TERMS OF PURCHASE

A *Purchase Contract and Escrow Agreement*

Upon a purchaser's execution of a Purchase Contract, a specimen copy of which is attached hereto as Exhibit 5, all deposits and other payments made to the Developer will be held in escrow by Attorney-at-Law (the 'Escrow Agent'), pursuant to an Escrow Agreement entered into between said Escrow Agent and the Developer, a copy of which is attached hereto as Exhibit 6, and may not be disbursed to the Developer until certain conditions which are set forth in the Escrow Agreement have been satisfied. This escrow arrangement is designed to protect each purchaser's deposit and other payments in the event that he elects to cancel his Purchase Contract in the manner discussed in Paragraph XV below, or in the event the Developer fails to perform any of its duties and obligations under said Contract.

B *Method of Payment*

A purchaser may pay for his Timeshare Interest in cash or he may finance the purchase through either the Developer or a third party lender approved by the Developer. If a credit-worthy purchaser chooses to finance the purchase of his Timeshare Interest through the Developer, he will be required to pay such interest or financing charges as are set forth in the Federal Truth-in-Lending Disclosure Statement provided by the Developer. Such purchaser will also be required to execute a Promissory Note and a Purchase Money Mortgage which will secure the payment by the purchaser of the deferred portion of the purchase price of his Timeshare Interest.

At the present time, a minimum down payment of ten per cent (10%) is generally required. The balance of the purchase interest on the unpaid balance to be fixed at the time of purchase at between _____ per cent (____%) and _____ per cent (____%). Any modification to such financing terms shall not be considered to be a material change to this offering.

# VII MANAGEMENT AND OPERATION OF THE PROJECT

A *Club 'ABC' Condominium Association, Inc.*

The Club 'ABC' Condominium Association, Inc. is a Florida not for profit corporation. Each purchaser of a Timeshare Interest automatically becomes a member of the Association upon the recording of his Warranty Deed in the Public Records of XYZ County, Florida, and only such purchasers and the Developer (to the extent that there are any unsold Timeshare Interests or Condominium Units) will be members. If a Timeshare Interest is purchased by more than one (1) person or entity, then each such person or entity shall be a co-member of the Association. The rights and duties of Association members are set forth in the Declaration and in the Association's By-Laws, attached to the Declaration as Exhibit 'C'. The members will elect a Board of Directors to govern the Association.

**THE DEVELOPER HAS THE RIGHT TO RETAIN CONTROL OF THE ASSOCIATION AFTER A MAJORITY OF THE TIMESHARE INTERESTS HAVE BEEN SOLD.**

Pursuant to Article IV of the Association's By-Laws, the initial Board of Directors has been appointed by the Developer. The Developer shall continue to have the right to appoint and remove Directors for a limited period of time, subject to the conditions set forth in said Article IV of the By-Laws.

B *The Manager*

1 Responsibility for the operation, management, and administration of the Project is vested in the Association. The Association, the address for which is 1110 Main Street, Anywhere, Florida, has delegated these responsibilities to ABC Management, Inc. (the 'Manager'), the office of which is located at 101 Main Street, Anywhere, Florida, pursuant to the Management Agreement entered into between said Manager and the Association. A copy of the Management Agreement is attached hereto as Exhibit 7.

2 The initial term of the Management Agreement is three (3) years from the date of its execution. The Management Agreement is automatically renewable every three (3) years unless the Owners vote to discharge the Manager in the manner provided in said Agreement. By virtue of its temporary control of the Association (see sub-Paragraph A, above), the Developer shall be entitled, in its sole discretion, to terminate the initial Management Agreement and to engage a replacement Manager until such period of Developer control ceases, to the extent of the Association's rights under the Management Agreement.

3 The Management Agreement provides that for the first year of the initial term of the Management Agreement, the Manager is entitled to receive a fee from the Association in the amount of $_____ (approximately $_____ per year and $_____ per month per Timeshare Interest). This fee may be renegotiated each year during the term of the Management Agreement on the anniversary date of its execution.

4 The Manager's duties, responsibilities, and obligations are set forth in the Management Agreement and include, but are not necessarily limited to the following:

(a) To be responsible for the immediate management and operation of the Project and the affairs of the Association, subject to the direction of the Board;

(b) To arrange for the regular cleaning, maintenance, repair, replacement, and restoration of the Common Elements and the Units Committed to Timeshared Ownership and the contents thereof, including all Common Furnishings, and any additions or alterations thereto, as needed and/or as directed to do so by the Board;

(c) To employ, dismiss, and control, on behalf of the Association, such personnel as it deems necessary for the maintenance and operation of the Project and the Association, including attorneys, accountants, contractors, and other professionals, as needed;

(d) To enter into contracts (and subcontracts), in the name and on behalf of the Association, for the furnishing of such services as it deems necessary and appropriate for the proper execution of its duties;

(e) To arrange for the preparation and submission of a proposed budget and schedule of Assessments to the Board for its review and approval, at least thirty (30) days prior to the end of each fiscal year;

(f) To arrange for and submit an annual financial statement and balance sheet of the Association to the Board of Directors within sixty (60) days after the close of each fiscal year;

(g) To assess and collect from the Owners all Assessments, taxes, and any other amounts due and owing the Association or a third party pursuant to the provisions of any applicable law, the Declaration, the By-laws, or the Rules and Regulations;

(h) To arrange for the payment of all of the Association's bills, to the extent of available Association funds;

(i) To procure and maintain in effect insurance on behalf of the Association, as required by the Declaration and the By-Laws;

(j) To assure that a copy of the then-current Rules and Regulations is kept in each Unit Committed to Timeshared Ownership and/or is furnished to the persons occupying each such Unit at check-in or otherwise, upon request, as directed by the Board, and to assure that the provisions of the Declaration, the By-Laws, and the Rules and Regulations are observed and enforced;

(k) To maintain at the Project all books and records of the Association, including but not limited to detailed and accurate records of the Association's receipts and disbursements, an individual account for each Owner designating such Owner's name and address and the amounts of any Assessments paid and/or due by such Owner, minutes of meetings, correspondence, amendments to the Declaration, the By-Laws, and the Rules and Regulations, and a list of the names and current mailing addresses of Association members and Mortgagees of Record;

(l) To establish and maintain federally insured deposits of the Association's funds in a manner so as to indicate the custodial nature thereof; and

(m) To organize and attend all Association and Board meetings.

## VIII RESTRICTIONS

A *Sale, Transfer, and Encumbrance*
There are no restrictions on the sale, transfer, or encumbrance of Timeshare Interests other than those set forth in Article VII of the Declaration. A purchaser's Timeshare Interest may be mortgaged or otherwise encumbered in the same manner as any other interest in real property. A purchaser will not be allowed to sell or otherwise transfer legal title to one (1) or more, but less than all seven (7) of the days included in the Vacation Week appurtenant to his Timeshare Interest, nor may such Timeshare Interest be sold or otherwise transferred separate from the undivided interest in the Common Elements and Common Furnishings appurtenant thereto. However, a purchaser may sell, rent, or otherwise transfer his entire Timeshare Interest or an undivided interest therein, so long as the purchaser is current with respect to all amounts assessed by the Association as of the time of the proposed transfer.

A purchaser can sell or otherwise transfer his Timeshare Interest at any price and on any terms he chooses, so long as such terms are consistent with the Declaration, the By-Laws, and the Rules and Regulations of the Association. However, no transfer of a Timeshare Interest will be valid until a legal document evidencing the transfer has been recorded in the Public Records of XYZ County, Florida, and a copy of such document has been provided to the Manager for the Association's records.

B *Use Restrictions*
1 Restrictions governing the use of purchasers' Units and the Common Elements of the Project are contained in Article VI of the Declaration. Among other things, the Declaration includes check-in requirements, prohibits the offensive and hazardous use of Units, and provides that no pet or animal of any kind shall be permitted within a Unit or elsewhere within the Project.

2 The Board of Directors of the Association is authorized to promulgate various Rules and Regulations governing the use and occupancy of the Project. The initial Rules and Regulations, a copy of which is attached hereto as Exhibit 3, require Owners to observe specific rules, including but not limited to the following:

(a) Owners are responsible for the conduct of their family members and guests and for any expense incurred by the Association as a result of any violation of the Rules and Regulations.

(b) Restrictions regarding the use of the swimming pool must be observed, including the requirement that no children under twelve (12) years of age use the pool unless accompanied by an adult.

(c) No Unit shall be occupied overnight by a number of persons in excess of such occupancy limits as are imposed by law.

(d) Except in areas which may be designated for such purpose, the personal property of all Owners shall be stored within their Units. The Manager shall not be responsible for any belongings left by an Owner, members of his family, or his guests, invitees, or licensees at the expiration of his Vacation Week(s).

(e) No Owner shall make or permit any disturbing noises by himself, members of his family, his guests, invitees, or licensees, nor do or permit anything by such persons that will interfere with the rights, comfort, or convenience of the other Owners.

The Board of Directors may amend the Rules and Regulations as it, in its sole discretion, deems necessary or appropriate. At the present time, there are no additional restrictions imposed upon children in connection with their use and occupancy of the Project other than those described above.

## IX UTILITIES AND SERVICES

A *Water*
Water is supplied to the Project by means of a private well which the Developer owns and has leased to the Association.
B *Electricity*
Electrical service is supplied to the Project

by Anywhere Electrical Utilities, City of Anywhere, Florida.

C *Sewage Disposal*

Sewage collection and treatment service is supplied to the Project by a sewage treatment plant owned by Sewage, Inc., 101 Water Street, Anywhere, Florida. Said sewage treatment plant, which is not located within the Project, is the subject of a written agreement between Sewage, Inc. and the Developer.

D *Storm Drainage*

Storm drainage facilities are owned by the Developer and have been leased to the Association.

E *Telephone*

Telephone service is provided to the Project by Telephone Company, Anywhere, Florida.

F *Cable Television*

Cable television service is provided to the Project by Cable TV, Inc., Anywhere, Florida.

## X CHARGES AND ASSESSMENTS

A *Common Expense Assessments; Timeshare Maintenance Fees*

Pursuant to Article X of the Declaration, each owner will be required to pay a proportionate share of the Common Expenses and Timeshare Expenses of the Association, based upon each Owner's undivided interest in the Common Elements of the project, as set forth in Exhibit 'D' to the Declaration. The Common Expenses of the Association include each Owner's share of real estate taxes not billed directly to the Owners, the maintenance, repair, and replacement of the Common Elements, utility charges, insurance coverage, reserves, and administrative costs. Each Owner's proportionate share of the Common Expenses is called his 'Common Expense Assessment'. The Timeshare Expenses of the Association include each Owner's share of the maintenance, repair, and replacement of the Common Furnishings as well as domestic services, including daily cleaning and maid service. Each Owner's proportionate share of the Timeshare Expenses is called his 'Timeshare Maintenance Fee'.

The initial Common Expense Assessment and Timeshare Maintenance Fee shall be due and payable to the Association in the manner set forth in each purchaser's Purchase Contract. All subsequent Common Expense Assessments and Timeshare Maintenance Fees shall be due and payable to the Association on January 15 of each year, unless the Board elects, in its sole discretion, to change the time and manner of payment.

B *Annual Budget*

The amount of the Common Expense Assessment and Timeshare Maintenance Fee will be determined by the Board of Directors, based upon the annual budget which will be prepared by the Manager and approved by the Board at the start of each fiscal year. The current annual budget, a copy of which is attached hereto as Exhibit 8, requires Owners to be responsible for a combined Common Expense Assessment and Timeshare Maintenance Fee of $_____ per Timeshare Interest in 19___.

The Common Expense Assessment and Timeshare Maintenance Fee may be revised periodically, based upon the projected expenses of operating the Project for the period in question. Nevertheless, the Developer has guaranteed that through _____, 19_____. the combined Common Expense Assessment and Timeshare Maintenance Fee payable by purchasers, exclusive of real estate taxes, shall not exceed $_____ per Timeshare Interest per year. During the guarantee period, the Developer will be excused from paying the Common Expense Assessments and Timeshare Maintenance Fees allocable to the Units and Timeshare Interests owned by the Developer, but the Developer has agreed to pay all expenses incurred by the Association during such guarantee period, exclusive of real estate taxes, to the extent that such expenses exceed the amounts received by the Association from its members other than the Developer.

C *Special Assessments*

The Board also has the power to levy a Special Assessment upon its Owners if the Common Expense Assessments and Timeshare Maintenance Fees collected from Owners are for any reason inadequate to pay all of the Common Expenses and Timeshare Expenses of the Association. Each Owner's proportionate share of any Special Assessment will be based on such owner's undivided interest in the Common Elements of the Project, as set forth in Exhibit 'D' to the Declaration.

D *Personal Charges*

Each Owner will be responsible for paying all Personal Charges which he incurs. Personal Charges include, but are not limited to late fees, fines, costs of repair for damage to a Unit, Common Element, or Common Furnishing, to the extent not covered by insurance, and such other costs as are described in Article X of the Declaration.

## XI ESTIMATED CLOSING EXPENSES; TITLE INSURANCE

Purchasers will be responsible for paying any and all Closing Costs in connection with the purchase of one or more Timeshare Interests at the Project. Such costs include, but are not necessarily limited to ad valorem taxes (to the extent such taxes are individually billed to the purchaser), all charges incident to the extension of credit, real estate transfer taxes and documentary stamps, notary fees, escrow fees, mortgage recording fees, and attorneys' fees. In addition, upon Closing, each purchaser will be provided with a title insurance policy, at the purchaser's expense, insuring the purchaser's title to his Timeshare Interest.

## XII IDENTITY OF THE DEVELOPER

The Developer of Club 'ABC', a Condominium, is Timeshare Developer, Inc., a Florida corporation with no prior timesharing development experience. The Managing Director of Timeshare Developer, Inc. is Mr. Managing Director. Mr. Director, who is supervising and coordinating the development and sale of Timeshare Interests at the Project, has been involved in the development of other timesharing projects in Florida since 19____.

## XIII JUDGMENTS OR LAWSUITS

As of the date of this Public Offering Statement, the Developer is unaware of any pending or anticipated lawsuits against the Developer, its mortgagee, the Manager, or any other party which might affect their ability to perform any obligations relating to this offering, or which would in any way affect the Units or the Project.

## XIV TOTAL FINANCIAL OBLIGATION OF PURCHASERS

A purchaser's total financial obligation consists of the purchase price of his Timeshare Interest, all Closing Costs associated with the transaction, as discussed in Paragraph XI above, any applicable financing charges, as discussed in Paragraph VI above, any charges or Assessments becoming due, as discussed in Paragraph X above, and any ad valorem taxes levied upon his Timeshare Interest by XYZ County, Florida.

## XV PURCHASER'S RIGHT OF CANCELLATION

Under Florida law and pursuant to the terms of each Purchase Contract, a purchaser may cancel his Purchase Contract, without penalty or obligation, within ten (10) days from the date such Contract is signed or until ten (10) days from the date the purchaser receives this Public Offering Statement, whichever occurs later. If a purchaser decides to cancel his Purchase Contract, he must notify the Developer in writing of his intent to do so. Such notice of cancellation shall be sent to:

Timeshare Developer, Inc.
101 Main Street
Anywhere, Florida

Any attempt by the Developer to obtain a waiver of a purchaser's cancellation right is unlawful. As discussed in each Purchase Contract, Closing of a particular transaction cannot occur until the purchaser's cancellation right has expired without having been exercised.

## XVI INSURANCE COVERAGE

Article XIII of the Declaration requires

the Association to procure and maintain insurance for the benefit of the Association, its members, and their respective mortgagees. All premiums for such insurance shall constitute either a Common Expense or a Timeshare Expense, as appropriate, and accordingly, each Owner will pay a proportionate share of such premiums through his Common Expense Assessment and/or Timeshare Maintenance Fee.

The insurance coverage required by the Declaration to be obtained by the Association includes, but is not limited to, the following:

A Property insurance on all of the Units, Common Elements, and Common Furnishings against loss or damage by fire, lightning, theft, and other casualties.

B Liability insurance against damage for personal injury, death, or property damage occurring within the Project.

C Directors' and Officers' liability insurance.

D Workers' compensation.

## XVII EXCHANGE OF VACATION WEEKS

A *External Exchange Program*
The Developer has executed an agreement with Exchange Company, P.O. Box _____, Anywhere Else, USA, under which Exchange Company will offer its reciprocal exchange service to each purchaser. The purpose of this service is to allow purchasers the option of temporarily exchanging the use of their Vacation Weeks for occupancy at other resorts participating in the Exchange Company exchange program.

Each purchaser's participation in the program will be voluntary and subject to the payment by each purchaser of such membership and other fees as are required by Exchange Company. Currently, participants must pay an initial subscription fee of $_____, a yearly renewal subscription fee of $_____, and an additional fee of $_____ for each confirmed exchange.

Exchange Company is not controlled by the Developer, and consequently, any representations made regarding the exchange program, either orally by Exchange Company's employees or within the brochures and literature to be provided by Exchange Company, will be solely the representations of Exchange Company and not those of the Developer. The Developer makes no guarantee that a purchaser will be able to exchange his Vacation Week in a particular year, or even that a service such as that offered by Exchange Company will continue to exist.

B *Internal Exchange*
The Board of Directors may, in its sole discretion, elect to implement an internal exchange program within the Project, pursuant to which a purchaser would be entitled to exchange the use of his Vacation Week in a particular calendar year for the use, at the Project, of a different Vacation Week in such year. The procedures for exchanging a purchaser's Vacation Week for another Vacation Week at the Project will be set forth in such Rules and Regulations relating thereto as shall from time to time be promulgated by the Board.

# Appendix C

# French legislation

# Appendix C

**LAW NO 86–18 OF 6 JANUARY 1986 COMPANIES WHICH ALLOCATE BUILDINGS TO BE USED ON A TIMESHARE BASIS**

## Chapter 1: General Provisions

### ARTICLE 1

Companies constituted to attribute, wholly or partly, buildings which are to be used principally for periodic occupation by the shareholders who would not be entitled to the ownership of the building nor to any real rights in consideration of their contribution to the companies' capital, are governed by general prescription applicable to companies subject to prescriptions of this law.

The objects of such companies include constructing the companies' buildings, acquiring buildings or real property rights, converting and upgrading acquired buildings or the buildings of real property rights referred to.

(The objects) also include administration of the property and acquisition of furniture and other equipment consistent with the purpose of the property. They can be extended to provide for services, the operation of equipment which will be collectively used by the occupants of the apartment or of the building and the operation of equipment consistent with, or directly related to, the purpose of the building.

### ARTICLE 2

Companies referred to in art 1 cannot undertake to guarantee obligations of a third party.

### ARTICLE 3

The shareholders are answerable to the company for the supply of funds which are necessary for the construction, acquisition, conversion or upgrading of the company's buildings to the extent of their share in the company's capital, and the shareholders must contribute towards the maintenance charges according to the prescriptions set out in art 9 of this law.

If a shareholder does not comply with the above requirements, the provisions contained in art L212–4 of the Code of Construction and Dwelling (*Code de la Construction et de l'Habitation*) may be enforced against him.

The defaulting shareholder is not entitled to commence occupation or to maintain the occupation of the portion of the property to which he would otherwise have been entitled.

### ARTICLE 4

By dispensation of art 1857 of the Civil Code, the shareholders of companies which are constituted under the form of a civil company (*Société Civile*) are liable for the company's debts to the extent of their contribution to the company's capital.

## ARTICLE 5

The manager(s) of a company constituted for the purposes already set out in art 1 of this law is (are) appointed by a decision of the shareholders representing more than half of the company's share capital, notwithstanding any contrary provision of the company's articles of association.

## ARTICLE 6

The manager(s) of a company constituted for the purposes already set out in art 1 of this law is (are) dismissed by a decision of shareholders representing more than half of the company's share capital, notwithstanding any contrary provision of the company's articles of association.

## ARTICLE 7

Any clause of the articles of association providing for the appointment of a person or a corporate body, other than the representative of the company, to carry out the duties as set out in art 1 of this law is null and void.

## ARTICLE 8

A description of the division defines different parts of the property and distinguishes between the parts for private use and common use.

The shares are allocated amongst the shareholders according to the characteristics of the portion of the building allocated to each of them, and to the duration and period of occupation of the premises to which the shares relate.

The value of the shareholders' rights is assessed at the date of allocation of the shares to the groups to which the shares relate.

A table of allocation of shares according to the portion of the building and period of occupation is annexed to the description of the division.

The regulations define both the purpose of the property as a whole and the purpose of its different parts and set out the means of use of the collective equipment.

If an advertisement, whatever its form may be, refers to a service of exchange of the occupation periods, of the sale of shares or of renting of the premises which would benefit the shareholder, such services must be referred to in the regulations. They may also be referred to in the form of a subscription or of sale of the shares.

The regulations set out particular conditions of such services.

## ARTICLE 9

Unless specified by laws or regulations in force, a decree distinguishes, amongst charges relating to common services, equipment and the use of the property, the common charges and charges related to the occupation.

The shareholders are bound to contribute to the charges of both categories, having regard to both the situation and details of the premises and to the duration and period of occupation.

However, if the premises over which the shareholder exercises his rights of occupation are not occupied, such a shareholder is not bound to contribute to the charges of the second category during the relevant period.

The shareholders are bound to contribute to charges relating to the administration of the company, to the conservation, maintenance and administration of the common parts in proportion to the share capital they hold.

The regulations define in each category of charges the proportion of charges relating to each specified group of action, such proportion being defined according to the situation of the premises, to the duration and period of occupation.

Alternatively, the regulations set out the criteria according to which such apportionment is to be made.

## ARTICLE 10

Any shareholder may apply, in the future, for the review of apportionment of charges, referred to in art 9, to the locally competent court if the contribution relating to his portion of shares is greater than one-quarter, or if the contribution of another shareholder is smaller than one-quarter, in comparison to the contribution fixed according to art 9. If the court considers such an application as justified, the court shall apportion charges.

The application for review referred to in the first paragraph may be filed during the first five years from the establishment of the description of the division, the regulations and relevant clauses in the articles of association.

## ARTICLE 11

Description of the division, the regulations and relevant provisions of the articles of association must be adapted prior to the beginning of building works or, in case of acquisition of the property which is already built, prior to the commencement of occupation of the property by the shareholders.

## ARTICLE 12

Companies referred to in art 1 which are set up for the purpose of construction of a building must comply with the provisions of art L 212–10 of the Code of Construction and of Dwelling requiring either to conclude a development contract or to instruct the company's representative appointed by law or by virtue of the articles of association to carry out property development operations.

Companies referred to in art 1 set up for the purpose of acquiring a property to be upgraded or converted are subject to the same obligations where the total amount of the works exceeds 50 per cent of the acquisition price of the property.

Companies referred to in art 1 set up for the purpose of acquiring a property to be built must conclude a contract or benefit of an assignment of the same according to the provisions of arts L261–10 *ff* of the Code of Construction and Dwelling. If the sale takes the form of a sale in state of future completion, the contract must include the completion guarantee provided for in art 261–11 of the same Code.

## ARTICLE 13

At the beginning of each financial year, the company, constituted in whatever form, may require from each shareholder the payment of the provisional contribution to maintenance charges which do not exceed the contribution to maintenance charges imputed to the same shareholder's previous financial year, or in the case of a new shareholder, imputed to the shareholder who occupied the same premises during the same period in the previous financial year.

The regulations may provide for a down payment of contributions to maintenance charges relating to the first financial year starting after the completion of operations referred to in art 1 of this law.

A general meeting of shareholders is held at least once a year. A general meeting is also to be convened at the request of the shareholders who control together more than one-fifth of the company's capital within three months from the date of such a request.

The shareholders are always entitled to attend and to vote at general meetings. Vote by correspondence is allowed. Notice of general meetings must be addressed to all shareholders. Such a notice must contain all questions to be put on the agenda. Without prejudice to the first paragraph of art 14, a shareholder can always be represented at the general meeting by any person or corporate body, even if such a person or corporate body is not a shareholder. Any stipulation in the articles of association to the contrary is null and void.

Within 15 days preceding the general meeting, any shareholder may request a company to supply a copy of its accounts and consult the register of shareholders.

## ARTICLE 14

The articles shall provide that each group of shareholders exercising their rights of occupation within the same period may appoint one or several shareholders chosen among the members of such a group in order to represent that group at general meetings, such representatives being appointed by a simple majority. Each representative can appoint one or several deputies chosen among the shareholders.

The representatives of the period and their deputies are appointed for not more than three years but such an appointment may be renewed; they cannot appoint a proxy.

The provisions of the first paragraph are not applicable to the decisions referred to in the second and the last paragraph of art 16.

## ARTICLE 15

Each shareholder has a number of votes in proportion to the number of his shares in the company's capital.

However, with respect to the decisions relating to charges referred to in the first paragraph of art 9, each shareholder disposes of a number of votes proportional to his contribution to charges.

Furthermore, where the regulations require from certain shareholders the payment of maintenance costs of a part of the property only, or of maintenance and functioning costs of one piece of equipment, such shareholders or their representatives vote only on the decisions concerning those costs.

In any case, each representative of a period, or his deputy, has a number of votes equal to the total amount of votes of shareholders of the group which he represents, subject to deduction of the votes of the shareholders personally attending or being represented pursuant to paragraph four of art 13.

## ARTICLE 16

All decisions at general meetings are taken by a simple majority of the votes of shareholders in attendance, either personally or through their representative, subject to the paragraphs hereafter and the provisions of arts 5 and 6 of this law.

A majority of two-thirds of the votes of shareholders in attendance either personally or through their representative is required for all decisions relating to the alteration of existing equipment, the addition of new equipment or the alteration or creation of the common parts of the building.

In respect of decisions referred to in the second and third paragraphs, and by dispensation to the first paragraph of art 15, the sellers of shares of a company constituted for the purpose of allocating the property on a timeshare basis cannot have more than 50 per cent of votes.

The allocation of the rights in the company's capital as defined in the second, third and fourth paragraphs of art 8, can only be modified by a majority which is not less than two-thirds of the shareholders' votes. Such a modification must be approved by each shareholder concerned by such a modification.

## ARTICLE 17

The first paragraph of art 23 of Law No 65–557 of 10 July 1965, defining the status of the co-ownership of completed buildings, does not apply to shareholders of companies governed by this law where such companies are members of an owners' association.

Where the companies governed by this law are members of such an association, the companies are represented at general meetings of the association by any person appointed by the general meeting of the company.

## ARTICLE 18

Where the provisions relating to the form of the company chosen by its members do not require the setting up of a board of directors, a supervisory board is to be appointed. The company's directors, their associates and employees cannot be appointed to the supervisory board.

The supervisory board gives its advice respectively to the company's directors or general meetings on any matter on which it has been consulted or on any matter on which it has decided to deliver an opinion.

It may request a copy of any document relating to the company.

Where the articles of association do not require the appointment of a company's auditor, the control of the management shall be carried out each year by a professional accountant who is not a shareholder and who is appointed by a general meeting to which such an accountant has to render an account of his mission.

## ARTICLE 19

The directors, their spouses and their employees and any other person or body acting directly or indirectly on their behalf cannot be appointed as a representative of period or be appointed as a shareholder's proxy.

## ARTICLE 20

Any subscription or sale of shares must be put in writing or take the form of a notarized deed which shall precis the nature and content of the rights related to each share as they result from the situation of the property and premises corresponding to the relevant group of shares and from the definition of the allocated period of occupation.

Where there is a sale of shares the document must mention, *inter alia*, the state of accounts of the seller certified by the company and the price to be paid to the seller. This provision does not apply where the transfer of shares is gratuitous.

The document recording the subscription or transfer must mention the registration with a notary of the contract of sale of the property to be built, or of the contract for development of the property or of a deed replacing the above contracts or of a document recording their assignment.

The document recording the subscription of shares or sale of shares must include the articles of association of the company, a description of the division, the table of allocation of shares, the regulations provided for in art 8, a summary of technical details of the property and the premises and if necessary the balance sheet of the last financial year, the total amount of contribution towards maintenance charges due for the previous financial year or, if there is none, the amount of down payment payable in advance in this respect and an inventory of equipment and furniture. Such a document may only refer to the above schedules if the schedules are deposited with the notary. In such a case, a copy of the schedules is to be handed over to the shareholder and the document recording the subscription or sale of shares must mention such a communication.

The provision of this article does not apply where the subscription of shares takes place when the company is set up subject to general provisions applicable to the relevant type of company.

## ARTICLE 21

The shareholder and the company manager or his duly appointed representative have to establish an inventory of the premises at the end of the occupation period. The next shareholder/occupier has an unfettered right to have the inventory communicated.

## ARTICLE 22

Save between shareholders, no contract of sale of shares can be concluded prior to the completion of the building except where a guarantee referred to in the second paragraph of this article has been granted and where there has been shown evidence of a contract of sale of a building to be completed according to arts L261–10 *ff* of the Code of Construction and Dwelling or evidence of a development contract.

Save between shareholders, any voluntary transfer of shares carried out prior to the completion of the building must include evidence of a guarantee of payment of the funds necessary for payment of the price of the company's assets or of the works of construction, conversion or upgrading of the building. Such a guarantee is to be granted either by a bank authorized to grant financial guarantees or to carry out property finance operations or by an insurance company having relevant licence or by a mutual guarantee society set up persuant to the provisions of the Law of 13 March 1917 for the purpose of organization of finance of small and middle-sized commercial and manufacturing businesses. Where a shareholder selling his shares is one of the above organizations, such shareholder is not required to provide such an undertaking.

The provisions of the first and the second paragraphs of this article apply to subscription of shares taking place prior to the completion of the building except the subscription which takes place at the time of the formation of the company.

The representative of the company who would carry out a subscription of shares, or a shareholder who would have agreed to a transfer of shares in breach of this article, shall be guilty of an offence and punished with imprisonment from two months to two years and with a fine from 6,000 to 100,000 FF or one of the above penalties only.

## ARTICLE 23

The shareholder has a right to rent or lend the premises which he has been allocated for the period during which he is entitled to occupy the premises.

Any stipulation of articles of association or of regulations is null and void.

\* \* \*

## ARTICLE 33

Any document relating to acquisition of shares of the companies governed by this law should state clearly that such an acquisition confers on the purchaser the status of a shareholder and not the status of an owner of the property.

The use of any expression which includes the word 'owner' to define the status of shareholder with respect to the operations of attribution of the properties to be used mainly for dwelling, to be occupied on a timeshare basis by the shareholders, having no ownership entitlement or any other real right over the property granted in consideration of a shareholder's contribution to the company's capital, is null and void.

## ARTICLE 34

Companies set up for the purpose of operations referred to in art 1 prior to the date of this law must amend their articles of association so as to be consistent with the provisions of this law within two years from the date of its publication persuant to the requirements provided for in the third and fourth paragraphs of art 499 of Law No 66/

537 of 24 July 1966 on commercial companies and subject to penalties provided for in the first paragraph of art 500 and in art 501 of the same Law. However, with respect to civil companies, the jurisdiction normally attributed to the president of the Tribunal de Commerce is in the present case attributed to the president of the Tribunal de Grande Instance.

The provisions of art 4 do not apply to companies' liabilities arisen prior to the amendment putting the articles of association in compliance with this law.

## ARTICLE 35

The provision of art 1655 of the General Tax Code does not apply to companies whose articles of association comply with the provisions of this law.

## ARTICLE 36

This law is applicable to the territorial collectivity of Mayotte.

# FIRST DRAFT OF THE LAW OF TRUST INTRODUCED BY MINISTRY OF JUSTICE ON 3 FEBRUARY 1990

## Chapter 1: General Provisions

### ARTICLE 1

Chapter XVI bis called 'On Trust' is inserted in the third volume of the Civil Code and drafted as follows:

\* \* \*

### ARTICLE 2062

The trust is a contract whereby a settlor transfers wholly or partly his property or rights to a trustee who is to act in a specified capacity for the benefit of the beneficiaries or the settlor himself.

The trust is governed by the provisions set out hereafter without prejudice of specific provisions or public order applicable to appropriate situations.

### ARTICLE 2063

The contract specifies the property and rights subject to trust and defines the extent of the powers of administration or of disposition granted to the trustee.

The contract sets out the duration of the trust.

It specifies the names of the beneficiaries or the provisions persuant to the beneficiaries to be designated and the conditions subject to which the property shall either revert to the settlor or be transferred to the beneficiaries at the termination of the trust.

The trust cannot be implied, it must be expressly set out.

### ARTICLE 2064

The trustee must carry out his mission by himself. However, he may delegate the execution of certain acts to a person remaining under the trustee's control and responsibility.

### ARTICLE 2065

A person subject to interdiction to manage or control a business or being declared bankrupt persuant to Chapter 6 of Law No 85/98 of 25 January 1985 governing the bankruptcy proceedings of businesses or by virtue of Chapter 2 of the Law No 67/563 of 13 July 1967 governing the bankruptcy procedure of natural persons or a person subject to a penalty for an offence against honour or good behaviour cannot be appointed as trustee.

The capacity to be appointed as a trustee is defined, *inter alia*, by the provisions specifically applicable to the operations relating to the property to be held on trust.

### ARTICLE 2066

The trust can be declared void only persuant to the provisions of art 2063 or persuant to the general rules under which contracts or settlements can be made void.

### ARTICLE 2067

The property and rights tranferred to the trustee constitute an entity separated from his own estate.

The trustee must take any relevant step in order to avoid any encroachment of such properties and rights and to debts related thereto and of his personal property or other properties held on trust.

Without prejudice to the rights of settlors' creditors entitled to trace a property subject to a charge arisen prior to the conclusion of the contract of the trust and, except for the case of fraud, to the rights of ordinary settlors' creditors, the property transferred to trustee can be attached or removed from the trust only by the persons having claims arising from conservation or the management of the property on trust.

### ARTICLE 2068

In relation to a third party, the trustee is deemed to be granted all powers over the properties on trust except where it is shown that the third party had knowledge of the actual extent of the trustee's powers.

### ARTICLE 2069

Where the trust relates to a rights or properties transfer, which is subject to a formality of registration, the registry must mention the name of the trustee as a trustee.

### ARTICLE 2070

The trustee must carry out his mission trustworthily.

If the trustee fails in his duties or endangers the interests by failing to take due care, the settlor or the beneficiaries may apply to the court for the appointment of a temporary administrator. They can also claim damages and apply for termination of the trust.

### ARTICLE 2070–1

In case of the trustee's death the properties and rights held on trust do not belong to the trustee's estate.

### ARTICLE 2070–2

The trust is ended:
1 At the stipulated date or where the purpose of the trust has been completed prior to the stipulated date.
2 By winding up of trustee where trustee is a corporate body. The parties may agree that the contract of trust may be upheld in case of voluntary winding up until the winding up operations are terminated.
3 By virtue of a judgment ordering the trustee to be put into receivership.
4 By a decision of justice undertaken either where the trust cannot be carried out particularly in cases where the trustee or the beneficiaries have renounced the continuation of the trust or in case provided for in art 2070, second paragraph, in such a case the judgment implies automatically a discharge of a trustee's duties. Except where the deed of trust stipulated otherwise the death of the trustee does not terminate the contract. In such a case the settlor or the beneficiaries are to apply to the court for the transfer of the properties or rights held on trust to another trust.

### ARTICLE 2070–3

Where the trust is terminated and the contract does not provide for allocation of subsisting properties or rights, the properties and rights revert to the settlor, or if the settlor is deceased to the settlor's estate.

# Appendix D

# Greek legislation

# Appendix D

## Law No 1652 ON TIMESHARE LEASE CONTRACTS AND REGULATION OF RELEVANT MATTERS

### ARTICLE I

1  By force of the timeshare lease contract the lessor undertakes the obligation to grant the use of tourist accommodation in his possession to the lessee each year, for the duration specified by the contract, and to offer the lessee relevant services for a time again specified by the contract, while the lessee undertakes the obligation to pay the agreed upon lease premium (rent).

As tourist accommodation for the application of this law is defined as hotel units and tourist developments in general operation under licence by the Greek Tourism Organisation and has been classified under the provisions of this law by decision of the General Secretary of the GTO. The timeshare lease is convened for a period of five to 60 years.

2  The timeshare lease must be in the form of a notarial document and is submitted for transfer formalities.

3  If the lessee resides in a country other than Greece, or his head office is in a country other than Greece, the lease premium is to be paid in foreign currency, which is assigned by the lessee to the Bank of Greece within one month of receipt (collection).

The details of this paragraph can be regulated by force of an Act of the Manager (Administrator) of the Bank of Greece.

### ARTICLE II

1  General and specific successors of both the lessor and the lessee enter upon their rights and obligations from the timeshare lease contract emanating from the lessor and the lessee respectively.

In case of succession of the lessee, art 612 of the Greek Civil Code applies, but lease premiums already paid can not be refunded.

2  The lessee retains the right to sublet or grant the use of the accommodation lease to third parties for one or more timeshare periods (years).

3  General and specific successors of the Lessor have no claim over lease premiums that have been paid to their scheme. The same is true for lease premiums seized by their scheme's creditors.

### ARTICLE III

1  Mortgages, prenotations of mortgages, temporary seizures or attachments for the security of claims by the state, legal entities of public law, municipalities, reputable security organisations, banks or other loan and financial institutions, that concern property leased according to art I of this law are lifted and extinguished if a letter of guarantee covering the (whole) amount of the claim is offered by a Greek or a foreign bank.

2  To extinguish and lift the encumbrances mentioned in item 1 of this article, it is

possible to assign the lease premiums to the creditor or the guarantor bank: in this case the provision of item 3 of art I applies.

3 Every dispute concerning the application of this article shall be resolved by the competent of justice First Instance Court by means of Security proceedings; also for the application of this article, arts 1323 *ff* of the Greek Civil Code shall apply.

## ARTICLE IV

1 The lessor is obliged to notify the GTO in writing about the signing of timeshare lease contracts. The GTO has a right to observe and control the execution of such contracts.
2 By decisions of the Minister of National Economy, published in the *Government Gazette* the following are regulated:

(a) the terms of total or partial classification (subjection) to the provisions of this law of tourist accommodation, by areas of the country,
(b) every issue concerning the function and organisation of the accommodation and services based on the provisions of this law,
(c) terms that must be included in the timeshare lease contract or in the contracts of subletting or of granting of the use of the lessee,
(d) every issue concerning the application of para 1 of this article.

## ARTICLE V

The provisions of the Greek Civil Code concerning the lease of an object also apply for issues not regulated by the provisions of this law, with subject for the second part of art 2 para 1 of this law.

## ARTICLE VI

Violation of the provisions of this law or of the acts issued by authorisation emanating from this law, constitutes reason for revoking the GTO General Secretary's decision concerning the classification (subjection) of the enterprise under the provisions of this law.

## ARTICLE VII

The foreseen law expenses, duties, rights of notarial associations, contributions to the Insurance Fund of Notaries Public, proportional and fixed expenses and rights of Mortgage Registries and any rights of third parties are hereby reduced by half, with the exception of stamp duties.

## ARTICLE VIII

The decision under No 503007/1976 (GGI166) of the GTO General Secretary 'On Regulation of Relation of Hoteliers—Client's' which is hereby ratified and is valid as a law, is as follows:

### Sub-Article 11

'Agreements—contracts between hoteliers and tourist offices or travelling organisations or client groups for the reservation of a number of beds for predetermined periods of time for continual flow of interchanging clientele—ALLOTMENT AGREE-MENTS—in addition to other terms must include:

(a) the agreed upon price for simple lodging for one night or including breakfast or half board or full board.

1 the agreed upon breakfast meals and table d'hôte meals must meet price and composition requirements as determined by the Market Police Ordinances in force from time to time.

2 it is hereby prohibited to Hotels that do not have restaurants and bars within their premises to enter into lodging agreements that include breakfast, half board or full board.

3 similarly, the lease or sublease of the bars and restaurants, operating in the hotel premises, to third parties, not related to the enterprise, is prohibited; it is hereby clarified that responsibility of the enterprise is unique for all the sections of the enterprise.

(b) the type of room (single bed, double bed, plain or with bathroom)

(c) the precise duration of the lease

(d) the agreed upon number of lodgings per month by lower and higher limit.

## Sub-Article 12

1 The Hotelier is entitled to demand a down payment in consideration of up to 25 per cent of the total of the sum resulting from the agreement entered.

2 In case of breach of the agreement by the hotelier, he is obliged to immediately repay the down payment with interest due, in addition to any other rights resulting in favour of the other contracting party and at the same time such behaviour of the Hotelier shall be deemed a most serious fault and shall bring upon him most serious administrative penalties from the EOT.

3 In the case that the tourist office or the travelling organisation does not cover the agreed upon lower ALLOTMENT limit, the Hotelier is entitled to damages, which shall be calculated on the agreed upon price of lodging per night and up to half of the remaining uncovered higher ALLOTMENT limit.

The above-mentioned damages may be offset against the down payment mentioned above.

## Sub-Article 13

1 A tourist office or a travelling organisation is entitled to cancellation of part or whole of the agreed upon number of beds without the obligation to pay damages, if the hotelier is obviously notified twenty-one (21) days prior to the agreed arrival date of the clients (RELEASE PERIOD).

2 Correspondingly the Hotelier is also entitled to a release time limit (RELEASE PERIOD) of twenty-one (21) days prior to each determined date of arrival for those of the agreed beds that have not been confirmed by VOUCHER or ROOMING LIST.

3 In the case that the tourist office or the travelling organisation makes use of the right of cancellation during low season, the hotelier is entitled with a warning of twenty-one (21) days to restrict the ALLOTMENT to the high season correspondingly, but in any case not below the agreed upon lower limit of the month.

## TAX CIRCULAR NO E 10976/5/88

**Subject: implementation of provisions concerning income taxation, tax code elements and VAT on timeshare leases or tourist accommodation**

In relation to the above subject please note the following:

### A INCOME TAXATION

1 According to the provisions of para 1 of art 1 of Law No 1652/1986 (*Government Gazette*, Issue 167/30–10–1986, section A) by force of the timeshare lease contract the lessor undertakes the obligation to grant to the lessee every year for the time specified in the contract the use of tourist accommodation and to offer him related services for a time specified in the contract, while the lessee must pay the agreed upon lease premium.

As tourist accommodation for the purposes of this law is hereby defined as hotel units and tourist developments in general operating under licence by the EOT and has been classified under the provision of this law by decision of the EOT's Secretary General. The timeshare lease is agreed for a period of five to 60 years.

2 Furthermore, by force of the provisions of para 3 of art 2 of Law No 1652/86 it is set out that general and special heirs to the lessee have no claim for lease premiums that were paid in advance to their predecessor. The same is valid for lease premiums seized by their predecessor's creditors.

3 Also, by force of the provisions of para 2 of art 5 of the decision of the Deputy Minister of National Economy under No A 9953/DIONOSE 1789/11–12–1987, issued by authorisation of the provisions of para 2 of art 4 of Law No 1652/86, it is set out that the lease premium of the timeshare lease contracts in drachmae or in foreign currency can be paid in cash or in instalments. In any case, however, full payment of the lease premium must be completed within 18 months from the signing of the contract.

4 The above-mentioned decision also sets the limit for the maximum percentage of the tourist accommodation's capacity which may be devoted to timeshare business; the same decision specifies that the lessor is under the obligation to keep the leased premises in a good standard of repair, to staff the accommodation with the specialised personnel required for full functioning of the unit's total capacity and to bear the cost of the personnel's salaries together with any other expense of the tourist accommodation (art 2).

5 As has been established by our Order No E 13457/POL 176/1985 (following decision No 3301/1981 of the State Council), in the case that an enterprise uses the property together with its machinery and industrial installations for commercial activity, and for certain days of the week or hours of the day, during which the enterprise does not use the property and the machinery for its own purposes, grants the use of such installations to third parties, for the same purposes of commercial activity together with some of the means necessary for production, then the income from commercial activities (section d, para 2, art 31 of Law No 3323/1955), is not deemed income from real estate.

On the contrary, income generated by the lease of the whole or part of the property together with machinery and other installations situated on it or the whole or part of the industrial installations, is deemed as income from real estate, provided that the parties by signing the lease and accepting its terms aimed at the lease of the whole or of part of the property or the industrial installations, alienating the lessor from the use of either the property or the industrial installations.

6 Also, by force of our Order No E 2312/POL 25/11–02–1982 it has been accepted that where an enterprise leases rooms, furnished holiday apartments or villas to clients and at the same time systematically offers related services, the income generated is deemed as income from commercial activities taxable under source of income D.

If, on the other hand, such a business leases rooms without offering client related services (hotel services), the income generated is deemed as income from lease or real estate and as such is taxable under source of income A.

7 As a result of the above points, the lessor, by force of the timeshare lease, undertakes the obligation to offer his clients hotel services and is hence not alienated from the use of his tourist accommodation. Consequently, income generated by the timeshare lease is income from commercial activities and with regard to tax classification it will be spread, under the principle of the independence of each fiscal year, over as many fiscal years as the number of years of the timeshare lease contract, since that is what is paid in advance against services that will be offered to the lessee in the future.

## B TAXATION ELEMENTS CODE

1 According to the provisions of para 3 of art 13 of the Taxation Elements Code (TEC), the operator of a hotel or hostel keeps a record of client registration (door book) in which the full name of the client, the date of arrival and departure and his room number are registered. The above operator issues in any case at the time of the client's departure an endorsed receipt in duplicate for the offer of services, on which his full name and address appear together with the itemised amounts of fees and expenses incurred for the said client. The entrepreneur who lets furnished rooms, apartments and villas to whom an operating licence has been granted by the EOT or by any other authority is under the same obligations.

2 As accepted by this Directorate, taxation elements on services rendered (receipts and invoices for services rendered) are issued at the time the services rendered have been completed. In the case that services are rendered by hotels, client's departure coincides with the completion of the services. Where, after an agreement, the services are rendered for a longer period of time, the taxation elements are issued for precise shorter periods (month, week etc) that cannot be longer than the management period.

3 As a result of the above points the fee amount in timeshare lease contracts, which are always long term, must be divided in proportion to the time of the lease and for every management period an endorsed receipt for services rendered must be issued in duplicate, irrespective of whether the lessee's nationality is Greek or foreign.

That is to say if a travel office enters a lease contract with a hotel for 20 years leasing 50 rooms during the month of August for every year and pays the sum of 20 million, the hotel operator must, according to the provisions of the TEC, on the first day of August every year register in his client registration record the travel office's company name together with the full names of the clients and the room numbers corresponding to each client; also at the latest on the last day of August, a receipt for services rendered must be issued for the sum of 1 million (20 million for 20 years).

## C VALUE ADDED TAX

Finally, concerning the application of VAT provisions and in particular with regard to the time of income taxation, which is of an unusual nature, as this income is generated before the corresponding services are rendered, note the following:

As regulated by the provisions of para 1 of art 13 of Law No 1642/86 'the taxation obligation exists and the tax is due to the State at the time the goods are delivered and the services are rendered'.

According to this provision and in conjunction with the aforementioned regulation of timeshare leases by the TEC and the Income Tax Provisions, the VAT due on the lease premiums will be paid to the State at the time the services are rendered by the operator of the tourist accommodation (hotel, hostel etc) at which point the relevant Tax Element (receipt, invoice) will be issued, as mentioned in part B of this circular concerning TEC issues.

The Minister of Finance
Head of Secretariat   DIM TSOVOLAS

# Appendix E

# Portuguese legislation

*Translator's note*: Throughout the following translation use is made of the expressions 'right to periodic habitation' and 'holder of the title to the periodic habitation'. These are full legal descriptions of the popularly termed rights of TIME-SHARE AND TIME-SHARERS.

# Appendix E

## MINISTRY FOR TRADE AND TOURISM—DECREE NO 130/89 dated 18 April 1989

The right to periodic habitation, created by Decree No 355/81 of 31 December was a pioneer development which came to fill a serious gap felt in the holiday market. It was through the introduction of such right that a system which allowed guaranteed access, through the creation of a property right, for all those who wanted short-term holiday accommodation, appeared for the first time in Portuguese legislation.

However, experience came to show that the system had certain deficiencies as far as tourism was concerned. This was because the right of periodic habitation concerned itself fundamentally with immovable property and real estate aspects, virtually ignoring the tourism aspect.

Nevertheless, it is considered essential that, without losing the benefit of the necessary real estate aspects of such right, the legal provisions governing its discipline should be revised in such a way as to be appropriate to the regulation of tourist developments. Thus, it is now envisaged that the right to periodic habitation can only be constituted in relation to certain categories of tourism developments or enterprises, the functioning of which is compatible with the existence of such rights.

For the same purpose, legal provisions have been introduced aimed at allowing the holders of such rights, in certain cases, to ensure the functioning of tourist enterprises.

At the same time, clarification of certain aspects of the present legal system governing such rights was intended, the practical application of which had been causing some difficulties. It was also considered appropriate to regulate simultaneously the rights of usage of tourist complexes which give to their holders only contractual or obligational type rights. In fact, the absence of minimum regulations governing such rights threatens the good name of the Portuguese tourist industry.

Therefore, without the rigidity of legal provisions required for governing rights on immovable property or real estate, new regulations were created which will allow the holders of rights to periodic habitation to define their interests. Lastly, sanctions were introduced to be applied against any enterprises not complying with the regulations governing these rights. Therefore, in accordance with item 1(a) of art 201 of the Constitution, the Government decrees as follows:

## Chapter I

### The real right to periodic habitation

### ARTICLE 1

### OBJECT

1 Over buildings, or over any fractions thereof, which are part of tourist complexes property rights may be created limited to a certain period of time during each year.
2 For the purposes of the provisions in the previous item tourist enterprises are considered to be those which, under the terms of Decree No 328/86 of 30 September,

were classified as aparthotels or tourist apartments and also those which qualified as tourist complexes in accordance with item 1(b) of art 17 of the same Decree.

3 In order that the right to periodic habitation may be created, the enterprise must cover a total building and must be situated in one or more autonomous fractions of the said building or buildings.

4 The right to periodic habitation can only be established in relation to buildings containing accommodation units and apartments being part of the said developments, which in addition to being independent are differentiated and separated amongst each other and have their own access to common areas of the building of which they are part or to the tourist complex or to the public street.

5 The right to periodic habitation can be constituted only over a proportion of the habitation units and apartments which form the tourist enterprise.

6 The property subject to the right of periodic habitation cannot be treated in the same way as beds available as hotel accommodation.

7 All legal transactions concerning the property rights of periodic habitation are always considered as being carried out in the place where the tourist development or enterprise concerned is built.

## ARTICLE 2

### DURATION

1 The right to periodic habitation is, unless otherwise stipulated, perpetual, but a limited period of duration can be fixed in the pertinent title creating the said rights, which, however, cannot be less than 20 years.

2 The period of time envisaged in item 1 of art 1 may vary between a minimum of seven and a maximum of 30 consecutive days, in accordance with the provisions of the pertinent title creating the right.

3 The last period of time in each year may end in the subsequent calendar year.

## ARTICLE 3

### TITLE

1 The fractions of a building subject to the right to periodic habitation cannot belong to more than one individual person or one corporate body.

2 The right to periodic habitation may belong to individuals or corporate bodies.

3 The constitution of the right to periodic habitation does not prejudice the provisions of arts 44 and 48 of Decree No 328/86 of 30 September, with the exception of the provision contained in item 1 of this article.

## ARTICLE 4

### CONSTITUTION OF THE RIGHT OF PERIODIC HABITATION

1 The right to periodic habitation is created by public deed, in which the proprietor identifies the immovable or immovables or the autonomous fractions thereof where the tourist enterprise is installed, the classification of that enterprise, the number of habitation units and apartments which form the tourist development, as well as the specific description of those subject to this right and also the parts into which the respective use is divided and the periods of time to which they relate.

2 In the description and naming of the habitation units and apartments the regulations in force concerning the ownership of flats (horizontal property) will apply with any necessary adaptations.

3 If the construction of the development has been approved in stages, the public deed mentioned in item 1 will also identify the stage to which it relates.

4 The public deed of constitution of the right to periodic habitation will be

compulsorily attached to the document issued by the General Directorate for Tourism or by the authority competent to approve and classify the tourist enterprise, which by law must contain:
(a) identification of the development stating its location and classification;
(b) the date of approval of the pertinent project and, if the building is to be carried out in stages, identification of the stage to which it relates;
(c) date of opening of the enterprise;
(d) identification of the habitation units and apartments which will be subject to the right to periodic habitation in accordance with the date supplied by the proprietor;
(e) list of sport, leisure and entertainment facilities existing in the development;
(f) statement indicating that the habitation units and or apartments subject to the right to periodic habitation comply with the provisions of item 4 of art 1.

## ARTICLE 5

### DATA WHICH MUST COMPULSORILY FIGURE IN THE TITLE CREATING THE RIGHT

1 Besides all the other specifications imposed or allowed by the present regulations, namely those mentioned in the previous article, the title creating the right to periodic habitation must compulsorily state:
(a) the beginning and end of each period of the habitation rights;
(b) the powers of the respective title holder, namely regarding the parts of the complex subject to communal use;
(c) the duties of the respective title holder, ie those relating to the actual exercise of his right and to the period of time, place and form of payment of the periodic fee described in art 18;
(d) the powers and duties of the owner of the tourist development, regarding equipment and furniture for the habitational units and apartments subject to the right to periodic habitation, their replacement, normal and extraordinary repairs, maintenance and cleaning and further services offered depending on the classification of the development;
(e) the maximum number of people allowed to occupy simultaneously the habitation unit or apartment;
(f) the system applicable in the event of partial or total destruction of the enterprise and of every habitation unit or apartment, for the purposes of apportioning, among the holders of the right to the period of habitation, the risk or insurance value, compensation or the remainder thereof.
2 The fixing of the specifications envisaged in the previous item or of any other such specifications can be carried out by applying by analogy the provisions relating to usufruct or right of ownership of flats (known as 'horizontal property').
3 The title creating the right to periodic habitation cannot create any limitations or obligations for the title holders different from those imposed upon all the other users of the development in accordance with the regulations governing its operation, namely those regarding the use of its infrastructure or facilities for communal use.

## ARTICLE 6

### ALTERATIONS TO THE TITLE

1 Any alteration to the title creating the right to periodic habitation must be embodied in a public deed, compulsorily attached to the document issued by the General Directorate for Tourism or by the entity which approved and classified the tourist development, which, besides the data mentioned in item 4(a) and (c) of art 4, must certify whether the alterations requested correspond to the building project approved and whether further specifications required by the said article are met.

2 If any property registration certificates have already been issued, the alteration can only be carried out if the holders of those certificates also take part in the pertinent public deed of alteration or authorise the owner of the complex by means of a public instrument in which it is stated that the alteration is specifically and expressly authorised thereby.

3 In any event, the alteration is only legally effective after being registered.

4 Annulment on the basis that the alteration was not authorised or that the intervention mentioned in item 2 did not take place can only be invoked by the holders of the certificate mentioned in the same item.

## ARTICLE 7

### REGISTRATION

1 The right to periodic habitation can only be established upon registration of pertinent title at the property registry office.

2 In the event of the tourist complex, which is subject to the system of the right to periodic habitation, consisting of more than one building, only one descriptive entry will be made at the property registry office covering all the buildings, even though the construction in stages of the complex may be envisaged in the relevant building licence.

3 In the cases envisaged in the latter part of the previous item, the registration of the right to periodic habitation relating to each stage will be effected by means of a marginal note in the respective entry.

## ARTICLE 8

### PROPERTY CERTIFICATE

1 A property certificate relating to each right to periodic habitation will be issued by the competent property registry office, which thus becomes the title corresponding right and will permit the creation of charges or encumbrances upon the title or the transfer thereof.

2 The property certificate mentioned in the previous item will show the data pertinent to the right as mentioned in item 1 of art 4, as well as the rights and duties of the respective title owner and of the proprietor shown in the public deed of creation of the right in accordance with the provisions of item 1 of art 5.

3 The form to be used as property certificate will be approved by means of an official order of the Minister of Justice.

## ARTICLE 9

### ISSUE OF PROPERTY CERTIFICATES

1 Property Certificates can only be issued after the final registration of the title creating the property right to periodic habitation has been registered.

2 The issue of the certificates can be made in favour of the owner of the tourist enterprise or of the holder of the property right to periodic habitation.

3 The issue of the certificate in favour of the holder of the right to periodic habitation can also be applied by the owner of the enterprise.

4 The issue of the certificate in favour of the holder of the right to periodic habitation, whoever may have applied for it, will be carried out on the basis of the declaration of sale, which may be signed by the vendor only, showing his or her signature certified by a notary who must be present at the time when the document is signed.

## ARTICLE 10

## CONTENTS AND EXERCISE OF THE RIGHT TO PERIODIC HABITATION

1 The holder of the right to periodic habitation has the following rights:
(a) to occupy the habitation unit or apartment, subject to the said rights;
(b) to use all the rooms, facilities, equipment and services (the use of which is, by law or by virtue of the regulations, considered as being included in the price of the habitation unit or the apartment) of the development in which the habitation unit or the apartment is situated and all the other developments the use of which is permitted in the title creating the said right of habitation.

2 In the exercise of his rights, the holder of the title must act as a good *pater familias* would do, namely by not using the respective habitation unit or apartment or the communal areas of the complex for any purposes other than those for which they were designed, or committing any acts forbidden by the title creating the right or by the rules governing the operation of the enterprise.

3 The rights and duties referred to in the previous items are extended to the persons living with the title holder.

## ARTICLE 11

## TRANSFER OF AND CREATION OF CHARGES UPON THE RIGHT TO PERIODIC HABITATION

1 The holder of the right to periodic habitation may create charges or encumbrances upon or transfer the said right.

2 The transfer or charging by means of a *inter vivos* act or contract is carried out by means of an endorsement or marginal note in the pertinent property registry certificate.

3 The endorsement is only valid if it shows the following data:
(a) identification of the endorser, together with all the details required for the property registration;
(b) price or value of the transfer;
(c) signature of the endorser.

4 The signature of the endorser has to be certified by a notary who must be present when the document is signed and legalised in accordance with the formalities required by the law of the place where the document is signed.

5 The entry recording mortgages or any other encumbrances will be carried out on the basis of a judicial certificate or on the basis of a private document showing the signatures of the person creating the encumbrance and of its beneficiary certified by a notary who must be present when the document is signed and legalised in accordance with the formalities of the law of the place where the encumbrance is created.

6 The right to periodic habitation is transferred at the time of death of the title holder in accordance with the general principles of the law.

7 The transfer, in life by means of an act or contract, or after the death of the holder, of the right to periodic habitation implies automatically the transfer of the position of the respective holder and any contractual clauses to the contrary will be deemed as non-existent.

## ARTICLE 12

## ASSIGNMENT OF USE

1 The holder of the right to periodic habitation may assign its use.

2 The assignment of the use of the habitation unit or apartment subject to the right must be reported, in writing, to the entity responsible for the management of the enterprise before or on the date when the period for exercising such right starts, under the penalty of the said entity opposing the assignment.

## ARTICLE 13

### EXCLUSION OF THE RIGHT OF PRE-EMPTION

1 The holders of the right to periodic habitation do not enjoy the right of pre-emption concerning the sale either of the ownership of the habitation units or apartments subject to such right, or of any of the constituent parts or the whole of the tourist complex where the said units or apartments are situated.

2 The owner of the habitation units or apartments subject to the right to periodic habitation does not enjoy the right of pre-emption in the transfer of the said right.

3 The owner of the enterprise may establish in the title creating the right to periodic habitation that the title holders enjoy the right of pre-emption on the transfer of their rights corresponding to the period immediately before or after the transfer.

4 In the case described in the previous item, the clause concerning the right of pre-emption must be stated in the relevant certificate and registration.

5 The notice of the transfer must be given by means of a registered letter with acknowledgment of receipt and the right of pre-emption must be exercised within 30 days from the receipt of such notice otherwise it will become void.

## ARTICLE 14

### MANAGEMENT

1 The management, conservation and repair of the habitation units and apartments subject to the right of periodic habitation, as well as their equipment and contents are the liability of the respective owner.

2 Whenever the owner of the habitation units and apartments is not the entity responsible for the management of the tourist development where the said units are situated, the latter has the powers and duties, which according to the terms of the present Decree fall upon the owner, without the need of any further formalities, other than those envisaged by the following item.

3 In the case envisaged in the previous item the owner must advise the General Directorate for Tourism and the holders of the right to periodic habitation who the entity responsible for the management of the development is, within a month as from the date of the document which is the title of the transfer of the management, under penalty of not producing any legal effects even in relation to the parties concerned.

## ARTICLE 15

### MAINTENANCE AND CLEANING

1 The habitation units and apartments subject to the right to periodic habitation, as well as their equipment and furniture, must be maintained by the entity responsible for the management of the development in accordance with the maintenance and cleaning standards suitable for the purposes for which the said units were designed and the classification thereof.

2 Without prejudice of his normal exercise of his right, the holder of the right to periodic habitation must by law allow the entity responsible for the management of the development, or his/their representatives, access to the respective habitation unit or apartment to enable them to fulfil his/their obligations as stated in the previous item.

## ARTICLE 16

### REPAIRS

1 The repairs indispensable for the normal exercise of the right to periodic habitation to be carried out in the habitation units or apartments subject to the said right or in the communal parts of the development, as well as their equipment and furniture, which

cannot be carried out without the temporary surrender or sacrifice of the said right, must take place at a time and in such conditions as to annul or minimise that sacrifice, at the discretion of the entity responsible for the management of the development, without prejudice of the right to compensation belonging to those who have suffered any loss of amenity accorded by the terms of the title creating their rights.

2 The repairs envisaged in the previous item which correspond to deterioration for which the holder of the title of the right to periodic habitation is liable and which cannot be deemed to have arisen as a consequence of fair wear and tear of the habitation unit or apartment or their equipment and furniture or the parts of the tourism complex designed for communal use, will also be carried out by the entity responsible for the management, but the title holder responsible will be liable for the cost of such repairs.

## ARTICLE 17

### NEW WORKS

1 The owner of the development can only carry out works which constitute innovations or new works, in the habitation units or apartments, even at his own expense, with the consent of the respective holder or holders of the right to periodic habitation.

2 If the new works relate to the communal parts of the development, consent must be given by the majority of the holders of the right mentioned in the previous item.

## ARTICLE 18

### PERIODIC FEE PAYABLE BY THE HOLDER OF THE RIGHT TO PERIODIC HABITATION

1 The holder of the right to periodic habitation must pay annually, to the entity responsible for the management of the development, a fee which is fixed in the title creating his right.

2 The said fee may vary in time or may be calculated in accordance with the criterion defined in the title creating the right and must take into account the apportioning of expenses such as taxes and rates, municipal taxes, maintenance, repairs, cleaning, administration and other expenses envisaged in the said title which must correspond proportionately to the size of each holding.

3 The fee due as per the previous item can vary depending on the time of year during which the right is to be exercised.

4 In the title creating the right to periodic habitation it can be envisaged that certain expenses such as water, light or repairs to specific habitation units or apartments will be allocated individually to the holders of the relevant rights to periodic habitation.

5 The periodic fee mentioned in item 1 may include a percentage covering the said management fees which must not exceed 20 per cent of the said fee.

6 With the exception of the amount corresponding to the percentage envisaged in the previous item, the periodic payments are to be used to cover the expenses for which they are charged and cannot be used for any other purposes.

## ARTICLE 19

### FAILURE TO PAY THE PERIODIC FEE OR COMPENSATION

1 The creditors enjoy rights to the periodic fee or to compensation from the title holders and any interest due for late payment and also enjoy immovable property credit rights on the said right of periodic habitation, to rank after those mentioned in arts 746 and 748 of the Civil Code.

2 In the event of failure by the title holder to pay the periodic fee up to the date when the exercise of the right to periodic habitation starts, the entity responsible for the

management of the enterprise may deny the use of the habitation unit or apartment, providing that such power is expressly contained in the title creating the right to periodic habitation.

## ARTICLE 20

### RESERVE FUND

1 From the amount mentioned in item 1 of art 18, a percentage of no less than 2.5 per cent will be deducted for the creation of a reserve fund for carrying out repair and renovation work and for the replacement of equipment and furniture.

## ARTICLE 21

### EXPENSES AND CHARGES

The owner of the development is always responsible for payment of taxes, rates, dues and other annual charges which may fall upon the habitation units and apartments subject to the right of periodic habitation, even when these are assessed on the basis of the respective income, as well as for fulfilling any ancillary obligations, even when he is not responsible for the management of the enterprise.

## ARTICLE 22

### GUARANTEE DEPOSIT

1 As guarantee of the fulfilment of the obligations resulting from the creation of the right to periodic habitation, the owner of the development must provide a guarantee in favour of all the holders of such right.
2 The guarantee can consist of an insurance bond, a bank guarantee or deposit.
3 The amount of the guarantee will correspond to at least half the value of the annual total of all the periodic amounts payable by the title holders.
4 The guarantee document must be lodged with the General Directorate for Tourism together with the request for issue of the document mentioned in item 4 of art 4, failing which the guarantee document will not be issued.
5 The deposit mentioned in item 1 can be paid by the entity responsible for the management of the enterprise, providing that the owner so declares in his request for the issue of the document mentioned in item 4 and attaches the document proving the transfer of the management of the enterprise.
6 Whenever there is an alteration in the amount of the periodic payments, the amount of the guarantee deposit must be updated and the pertinent document lodged at the General Directorate for Tourism by the end of the month prior to the date when the new periodic fees are payable.
7 In addition to the updating of the guarantee, the person responsible for providing such guarantee must submit to the General Directorate for Tourism, by the end of each year, evidence showing that such guarantee is in force.

## ARTICLE 23

### SUBMISSION OF ACCOUNT

1 The entity responsible for the management of the development must draw up annual accounts concerning the use of the annual fees paid by the title holders of the right to periodic habitation and any allocations to the reserve fund and submit them to assessment by a professional firm of auditors or an official accountancy expert.
2 The accounts mentioned in the previous item will be sent to each title holder during the first three months of the year following that to which the accounts relate, together with a report on the audit carried out, the title holders or their representatives having

the right to examine the records justifying the account submitted.

3 The firm of auditors or the accountant mentioned in item 1 of this article will be appointed by the title holders of the right to periodic habitation, and in this case the provisions of items 1 and 2 of art 26 will apply.

4 If by the end of the year when rights to periodic habitation have been sold, no firm of auditors or accountant has been appointed, the entity responsible for the management of the enterprise must request the Chamber of Official Accountants (*Camera do Rivisores Oficais de Contas*) during the following month of January to appoint an official accountant for the purposes of complying with the provisions of item 1 hereof.

5 The official accountant appointed in accordance with the previous item will carry out his duties until such time as he is replaced by a firm of auditors or an accountant appointed in accordance with item 3 of this article.

## ARTICLE 24

### ALTERATION IN THE PERIODIC FEE

1 Regardless of the criterion used for fixing the periodic fee stipulated in the title creating the right to periodic habitation, the entity in charge of auditing the respective accounts, whenever they consider that the periodic fee is excessive or insufficient in relation to the expenses for payment of which it is charged, must propose in their report that the periodic fee be revised and indicate the new amount.

2 The periodic fee that becomes due after the date of the proposal envisaged in the previous item will be that proposed by the said report.

3 If the revision of the periodic fee takes place in accordance with the provisions of the previous items, any holder of the right to periodic habitation or the entity responsible for the operation of the enterprise may apply for a judicial assessment and alteration of the amount fixed by the firm of auditors or the accountant within 60 days from the date of becoming aware of the new periodic fee.

4 The request for a judicial assessment suspends the obligation to pay the amount in question.

## ARTICLE 25

### REPLACEMENT OF THE ENTITY RESPONSIBLE FOR THE MANAGEMENT OF THE DEVELOPMENT

1 Whenever the entity responsible for the management of the development is absent without leaving a legal representative, or ceases to guarantee the proper management of the development, the title holders of the rights to periodic habitation can replace such entity in the management, maintenance and repair of the development and appoint a reputable firm to carry out these functions.

2 For the purpose envisaged in the previous item, it is deemed that the entity responsible for the management of the development has ceased to guarantee its normal operation in the following cases:

(a) if it lets the guarantee deposit mentioned in art 22 lapse;

(b) if it fails to organise and submit the annual accounts in accordance with the provisions of art 23;

(c) if it fails to create the reserve fund envisaged by art 20.

3 When the entity responsible for the management of the development is not the owner himself, the power granted by item 1 can only be used if the owner, after receiving written notice from any title holders of the right to periodic habitation, fails to take the appropriate measures within 30 days thereafter.

4 The appointment of a new manager which has taken place pursuant to item 1 must be notified to the owner of the development within 30 days from the appointment of the new management entity.

5 The appointment of a new manager will not cause the termination of the guarantee given by the replacement entity, which will remain in force up to the end of the respective validity period and can be enforced by the new entity so appointed.

6 The entity appointed in accordance with item 1 must notify the title holders of the right to periodic habitation of the appointment of the new entity within 30 days from the date when the new entity takes up its duties.

## ARTICLE 26

### APPOINTMENT OF THE MANAGEMENT COMPANY AND DISCHARGE OF DUTIES

1 The Management company referred to in the previous article will be appointed by the majority votes of the holders of the rights to periodic habitation submitted in writing or in person during a meeting of title holders held for that purpose.

2 For that purpose any title holder may convene a meeting of the holders of the rights to periodic habitation or request their votes in writing regarding the appointment of a specific company.

3 The management company will discharge its duties for the period of time fixed by the holders of the rights to periodic habitation, unless there is a court order to the contrary.

4 The duties of the management company will be remunerated by the development under the usual terms of a management contract, without prejudice of the remuneration envisaged in item 5 of art 18.

5 The management company can only start to discharge its duties after having provided the guarantee envisaged in art 22.

6 The duties of the management company will cease as soon as a manager appointed by a court order takes up his position.

## ARTICLE 27

### RIGHTS AND DUTIES OF THE MANAGEMENT COMPANY

1 The management company appointed in accordance with art 25 has the duty to manage the enterprise, exercising all the rights and discharging all duties of the entity responsible for the operation of the enterprise and in particular:

(a) will receive the periodic fees mentioned by art 18 and pay all the charges envisaged by art 21;

(b) will rest out any periods of time corresponding to rights of periodic habitation not yet sold;

(c) will guarantee the management of the development until the time when a manager has been appointed by court order.

2 The management company is not allowed to:

(a) sell or otherwise charge any periodic habitation rights or any asset or equipment belonging to the development;

(b) sign any operational contracts or assignments, for any reason whatsoever, for periods longer than one calendar year;

(c) authorise the carrying out of (or itself carry out) any work other than mere repair or maintenance, without prejudice to the replacement of the equipment and furniture required to guarantee the normal and correct management of the development.

3 The management company may enforce the guarantee provided by the entity it replaces, if such guarantee is in force and this is necessary.

4 At the end of each year, the management company must submit the accounts concerning the use of the amounts of money received and the allocations made to the reserve fund, in accordance with the provisions of art 23.

5 The managing company must also render accounts to the owner regarding the management both annually and at the end of the management contract.

## ARTICLE 28

### TRANSFER OF THE RIGHTS TO PERIODIC HABITATION SUBJECT TO MANAGEMENT

1 The management company must respect the rights to periodic habitation sold by the owner, even after the said company has started its duties as manager, providing that the holder can produce a title document issued in his name.

2 In the case envisaged in the previous item, the owner must advise the management company of any rights to periodic habitation that the said owner may have sold, within eight days after the sale thereof, under penalty of being liable for any damage caused.

## ARTICLE 29

### JUDICIAL APPOINTMENT OF A MANAGER

1 Without prejudice to the provisions contained in art 26, any holder of the title to the right of periodic habitation may apply to the court in the judicial district where the development is situated for the judicial appointment of a manager for the purpose of assuring the management of the development, on the grounds of any of the situations envisaged in item 1 of art 25.

2 The action for the judicial appointment of a manager mentioned in the previous item must be brought against the owner of the enterprise, and the procedure envisaged for the judicial appointment of a manager of 'horizontal property' [*'horizontal property' is the name given under Portuguese law to the full ownership of an apartment, constituting a separate habitation unit in a block of flats or apartments purpose-built to be sold as separate units*] will apply with the necessary adaptations.

3 The provision of items 2 and 4 of art 25 will apply with the necessary adaptations to the judicial appointment of the manager.

4 In the originating petition for the above-mentioned court case, the applicant must, besides stating the grounds for the petition, state the following:

(a) identify the individual or corporate body, the appointment of which is sought;

(b) declare his professional qualifications;

(c) indicate the criteria to be followed in fixing the remuneration of the judicially appointed manager.

5 The petition mentioned in the previous item must be submitted attached to the following documents:

(a) Authenticated photocopy of the pertinent property registry certificate or certificate issued by the competent property registry office.

(b) Authenticated photocopies of the receipts corresponding to the payment of the periodic fees referring to the year when the petition is submitted, if they have already been sold, and to the previous year if the petitioner was already the holder of the right to periodic habitation at that date.

(c) Document issued by the entity appointed for carrying out the management, declaring that they accept the appointment for such position, together with a certificate from the commercial registry office if they are a company.

6 In the absence of any opposition, the individual or corporate body indicated by the petitioner will be appointed.

7 The functions of the judicially appointed manager will cease as soon as the owner of the development declares that he will carry out the management himself or appoints for that purpose a manager with the required powers.

8 For the purposes of the provisions of the previous item, the owner must apply to the court and in the same judicial case opened for the judicial appointment of the manager, to request termination of the said functions of the manager, after producing evidence that the guarantee envisaged by art 22 has been provided and that the remuneration to

the manager has been paid to date or that the payment of such remuneration is guaranteed by appropriate and reputable means.

9  The provisions of item 6 of art 25, item 4 of art 26 and arts 27 and 28 are applicable to the judicially appointed manager with the required adaptations.

10 The judicially appointed manager's remuneration will be fixed by court order appointing him.

## ARTICLE 30

### PROMISSORY CONTRACTS OF PURCHASE AND SALE OF PERIODIC HABITATION RIGHTS

1  The promissory contracts of purchase and sale rights to periodic habitation must contain all the following essential data:

(a ) identification of the owner of the development;

(b)  identification of the intending buyer;

(c)  identification of the estate agent company, if any;

(d)  identification of the company in charge of the management of the enterprise, if different from the owner;

(e)  identification of the development, including its location and relevant phase in the development, if applicable, as well as the number of the relevant case at the General Directorate of Tourism;

(f)  property registry office description of the tourist development or clear reference that the right to periodic habitation is being created, and that case, property registry office description of the building or buildings of which the development forms part;

(g)  date of start of the development;

(h)  characteristics of the habitation unit or apartment to which the right of habitation pertains, together with an itemised list of the equipment and furniture contained therein;

(i)  duration and dates for the period during which the right of habitation will be exercised;

(j)  list of ancillary, sport, recreation and leisure facilities which the development has available or which it is envisaged will be made available;

(l)  indication of the rights and obligations of the holder of the right and of the owner of the development, in the terms shown in the relevant property registry certificate;

(m)  indication as to the existence or otherwise of any mortgage or charge upon the development or upon the buildings in which the development is situated and, when such mortgage or charge does exist, identification of the respective beneficiary.

2  If the enterprise is under construction, the data mentioned in items 1(d) and (g) are not required, and in such cases the contracts must state clearly that situation and contain also the following data:

(a)  date of approval of the relevant building project;

(b)  date envisaged for the opening of the development or for that stage in the construction;

(c)  statement as to the existence or otherwise of the guarantee or insurance guaranteeing to the buyer the reimbursement of all amounts paid within the scope of the contract, in the event of the contract not being fulfilled within the period of time and in its terms and conditions for reason other than the buyer's default.

3  Any provision making the signing of the final public deed of creation of the right to periodic habitation depend on the sale of the remainder of the habitation units or apartments forming the relevant development will be null and void.

4  The intending buyer may revoke the contract, by means of recorded delivery letter with acknowledgment of receipt, within seven days of signing the contract, without incurring any charges or obligations, and with the right to be reimbursed for any amount which he may have already paid at the time of signing the contract, after

deducting any amount paid by the intending vendor as taxes.

5 The right to revoke the contract in the conditions envisaged in the previous item exists whatever the contractual terms state, and any agreement excluding, limiting or prejudicing such right is null and void.

6 The data mentioned in item 1(h) (f) and (l) may be shown in the document to be attached to the contract, providing that the existence of such document is clearly and expressly referred to in the text of the contract.

### ARTICLE 31

### PROHIBITION AS TO THE USE OF CERTAIN TERMS

In each and every contract and document concerning the rights to periodic habitation the word owner or any other expressions capable of creating in the minds of the buyers of such rights the false idea that they will be the owners of the development cannot be used.

### ARTICLE 32

### POSSIBILITY OF ANNULMENT

1 Without prejudice to the application of the legal provisions regarding the nullity and annulment of the legal transactions, the promissory contracts of purchase and sale of right to periodic habitation can also be annulled on any of the following grounds:

(a) the absence of approval, in accordance with the law, of the building project for the development on the date of signature of the contract;

(b) the absence of data as specified in items 1 and 2 of art 30;

(c) the use of words or expressions contrary to the provisions of item.

2 The annulment of contracts on the basis of any of the reasons mentioned in the previous item can only be invoked by the intending buyer up to the date when the property registry certificate is delivered to him or the date of declaration of sale mentioned in item 4 of art 9.

3 If the contract is annulled on any of the grounds mentioned in item 1, the intending buyer has the right to receive double the amount of the moneys that he may have paid in respect of the cancelled contract, together with interest as from the date when the payment was originally made until repayment.

### ARTICLE 33

### PUBLICITY

1 All publicity or promotion material regarding the sale or marketing of property rights to periodic habitation must contain at least the data mentioned in item 1(a), (c), (f), (g), (h), (i), (j), and (l) or item 2 of art 30, as the case may be.

2 No publicity or promotion material regarding those rights can be circulated before the enterprise is finally approved by the competent authorities.

3 The provisions of art 31 apply to publicity and promotion of the said rights.

## Chapter II

### The Contractual Rights of Tourist Habitation

### ARTICLE 34

### CONTRACTUAL RIGHTS OF TOURIST HABITATION

1 The rights of habitation of accommodation units or apartments with a duration equal to or greater than two years, which have a mere contractual character, whatever

name may be given to them, can only be sold or promoted after the pertinent contracts have been approved by the General Directorate of Tourism, after provision of the guarantee described in art 35.

2  For this purpose, only contracts concerning habitation units or apartments which form part of any tourist enterprise as referred to in item 2 of art 1 already in operation and fulfilling all requirements prescribed in this Decree can be approved.

3  The period of duration of the said rights cannot in any case be longer than the period of the contract which gives to the entity promoting them the operation of the tourist enterprise to which they relate, if the operator is not the owner.

4  The petition for the approval of the contract must be submitted to the General Directorate of Tourism together with at least the following data:

(a)  written document in which the promoting entity proves the existence of the said rights (such document must show at least the data specified in items 1 and 3 of art 4 and item 1 of art 5);

(b)  contract of assignment of the operation of the enterprise, if applicable;

(c)  photocopy of the licence for the opening of the enterprise;

(d)  document issued by the entity who is going to supply the deposit described in art 35, stating his willingness to do so;

(e)  specimen of the title document to be delivered to the buyer, representing the right bought;

(f)  indication as to the number of contracts to be signed and the value thereof.

5  The title document of the right will show compulsorily at least the data mentioned in item 2 of art 8, in accordance with the stipulations of the document mentioned in item 4(a) and also an express and unequivocal statement that the document does not give to its holder the right of ownership of immovable property or any property right, either in relation to the habitation unit or apartment the use of which is allowed by the said document, or in relation to the development where the habitation unit or apartment is situated.

6  The provisions of items 4, 5 and 6 of art 1, items 2 and 3 of art 2, items 2 and 3 of art 3, item 2 of art 4, item 3 of art 5, item 2 of art 6 and arts 11 to 17 and 21 are applicable to such rights with the required adaptations.

## ARTICLE 35

### GUARANTEE DEPOSIT

1  Besides compliance with the requirements set out in the previous article, the vendor company of those rights must also provide a guarantee for the purpose of securing the fulfilment of their obligations arising from the contracts approved.

2  The amount of the guarantee will be equal to a third of the value of the rights to be sold and its initial value cannot be less than 10,000,000 Esc (10,000 contos—1 conto equals 1,000 Esc).

3  The provisions contained in art 22 will apply to this guarantee with the necessary adaptations.

## ARTICLE 36

### JUDICIAL APPOINTMENT OF A MANAGER

1  When the entity responsible for the operation of the development is absent, without leaving a legal representative, or fails to guarantee the normal operation of the development, the holders of the contractual right to periodic habitation may apply, on those grounds, to the district court of the area where the development is situated for the judicial appointment of a manager, for the purpose of guaranteeing the operation and maintenance of the enterprise.

2  For the purposes described in the previous item, it is considered that the entity

responsible for the operation of the enterprise has ceased to guarantee its normal operation if it lets the guarantee deposit mentioned in item 1 of the previous article lapse.

3 The provisions of item 1 of this article are applicable to the judicially appointed manager and his appointment is governed by the provisions of art 29 with the necessary adaptations.

## ARTICLE 37

### OBLIGATORY DECLARATIONS

1 Each and every contract and document concerning the rights mentioned in art 34 must contain an obligatory declaration of the fact that such right does not give to the holder the right of ownership of the habitation unit or apartment to the use of which such contract or document relates, or of the development where the habitation unit or the apartment is situated.

2 An identical statement must be contained compulsorily in any publicity or promotion material relating to the said rights.

## ARTICLE 38

### ANNULMENT

1 Without prejudice of the application of the legal provisions regarding nullity and annulment of legal transactions, contracts relating to the sale of contractual rights of tourist accommodation may be annulled on the basis of any of the following grounds:
(a) the said contracts have not been approved by the General Directorate of Tourism;
(b) the title documents do not contain the data and statement as required by item 5 of art 34.

2 In this case the provisions of items 2 and 3 of art 32 will apply with the necessary adaptations.

3 The annulment of contracts on the grounds of item 1 of this article can only be invoked by the buyers and providing that they have not been legalised or the holder has not exercised his right.


# Chapter III

**Infringements and Penalties**


## ARTICLE 39

### CONTRAVENTIONS

1 The following are contraventions:
(a) the establishment of any limitations or obligations for the holders of the right to periodic habitation infringing the provisions in item 3 of art 5;
(b) the lack of maintenance and cleaning of the habitation units and apartments subject to the right to periodic habitation in breach of the provisions of item 1 of art 15;
(c) failure to present the document showing the updating of the amount of the guarantee deposit in breach of the provisions of item 6 of art 22;
(d) failure to submit the document proving that the guarantee is in force, therefore breaching the provisions of item 7 of art 22;
(e) failure to organise accounts in breach of the provisions of item 1 of art 22;
(f) failure to send the accounts in breach of item 2 of art 22;

(g) signing promissory contracts of purchase and sale of property rights óf periodic habitation in breach of the provisions of art 30;
(h) infringement of the provisions of art 31 and item 1 of art 37;
(i) carrying out publicity or promotion in breach of the provisions of art 33 and item 2 of art 37;
(j) the sale or promotion of contractual rights of tourist habitation in breach of item 1 of art 34.

2 The contraventions envisaged in the previous items carry the following penalties:
(a) from 20,000 Esc to 100,000 Esc in the cases described in item 1(a), (b) and (f);
(b) from 50,000 Esc to 150,000 Esc in the cases described in item 1(h) and (i);
(c) from 100,000 Esc to 200,000 Esc in the cases described in item 1(c), (d), (e), (g) and (j).

## ARTICLE 40

### POSSIBILITY OF APPLICATION OF PENALTIES IN CASES OF NEGLIGENCE AND INTENT

In the cases described in item 1 of art 39, negligence and intent to commit the said breaches are always punishable.

## ARTICLE 41

### ANCILLARY PENALTIES

The contravention described in item 1 of art 39 may, under the general terms of the law, be punishable with the following ancillary penalties:
(a) seizure of all the material used in the cases described in item 1(h), (i) and (j);
(b) a ban on the carrying on of the business for a period of up to two years, in the cases described in item 1(a), (c), (e), (g) and (f) of the same number.

## ARTICLE 42

### COMPETENCE

1 The General Directorate for Tourism is the competent entity for the imposition of penalties and respective ancillary sanctions.
2 The General Directorate for Tourism is also competent to organise and prosecute the cases concerning infringements of the provisions of this Decree.

## Chapter IV

**Temporary and Final Provisions**

## ARTICLE 43

### TERMINOLOGY

In all legal provisions relating to the property right of periodic habitation, namely those concerned with property registration:
(a) the words 'habitation parts' are replaced by 'habitation units' or 'apartments', regarding the type to which the right to periodic habitation relates;
(b) the words 'building' or 'building complex' are replaced by the words 'tourist enterprise'.

## ARTICLE 44

### TIME OF APPLICATION OF LEGISLATION REGARDING RIGHTS TO PERIODIC HABITATION

1 The present Decree is applicable to the rights of periodic habitation created under the provisions of Decree No 355/81, of 31 December with the wording given by Decree No 368/83, of 4 October, with the exception of any effects thereof already produced.
2 The property certificates issued in accordance with the above-mentioned legal regulations remain valid for all purposes.

## ARTICLE 45

### TIME OF APPLICATION OF LEGISLATION REGARDING CONTRACTUAL RIGHTS

1 The provisions of the Decree apply to the promotion and sale of the rights mentioned in art 34 even when the marketing commenced prior to the date when this Decree becomes law, without prejudice to the effects already produced by the matters that this legislation aims at controlling.
2 Companies interested in the promotion and sale of those rights must regularise their respective situations, to coincide with the provisions hereof, within a maximum period of twelve months from the date when this Decree becomes valid.

## ARTICLE 46

### APPLICATION IN THE AUTONOMOUS REGIONS OF PORTUGAL

The competence given by present Decree to the General Directorate for Tourism will be taken up in the Autonomous Regions of the Azores and Madeira by the respective organs of self-government.

## ARTICLE 47

Decree No 355/81 of 31 December with the exception of art 15 of the same is hereby revoked.

## ARTICLE 48

### DATE WHEN THIS DECREE BECOMES VALID

This Decree becomes valid and enforceable 30 days after its publication.
  Seen and approved in Council of Ministers on the 16 February 1989—Anibal Antonio Cavaco Silva, Joaquim Fernando Nogueira, Joaquim Martins Ferreira do Amaral.
  Promulgated on the 4 April 1989.
  To be published.

The President of the Republic, Mario Soares.
signed as Prime Minister on 7 April 1989.

The Prime Minister, Anibal Antonio Cavaco Silva.

## PERIODIC OCCUPANCY REGISTRATION (predial certificate)

TRANSLATION OF:

DESPACHO from the Direccao Geral dos Registos e do Notariado (General Directorate for Registrations and Notaries)

DIRECTIVE: In accordance with the provisions of art 3 of Decree 130/89 of 18–4, the attached designs of the certificate relating to Periodic Occupancy Registration (predial certificate), printed in black on a white ground, have been approved.

Owners of tourist developments may with the authorisation of the Direccao Geral dos Registos e do Notariado, use their company colours in the panel and in the space reserved for the identity of the proprietor, giving prominence to his emblem or insignia, but in such cases the forms must be supplied by the interested parties.

### 'CERTIFICATE A'

## REPÚBLICA PORTUGUESA

## TÍTULO
## DE REGISTO DO DIREITO
## DE HABITAÇAO PERIÓDICA

### (CERTIFICADO PREDIAL)

CONSERVATÓRIA DO REGISTO PREDIAL DE

PRÉDIO Nº

EMPREENDIMENTO TURÍSTICO

LOCALIZAÇAO

CLASSIFICAÇAO DO EMPREENDIMENTO TURÍSTICO

FRACÇAO AUTÓNOMA

UNIDADES DE ALOJAMENTO OU APARTAMENTO

PROPRIETÁRIO DO EMPREENDIMENTO TURÍSTICO

TITULAR DO DIREITO DE HABITAÇAO PERIÓDICA

PERÍODO DE TEMPO DO DIREITO DE HABITAÇAO

INÍCIO

TERMO

LIMITE DE DURAÇAO DO DIREITO DE HABITAÇAO PERIÓDICA

O CONSERVADOR DO REGISTO PREDIAL

**TRANSLATION OF CERTIFICATE 'A'**

PORTUGUESE REPUBLIC

CERTIFICATE
OF REGISTRATION OF RIGHT
TO PERIODIC OCCUPANCY
(Predial Certificate)

Predial Registration Office at . . . . . . . . . .
Predial No: . . . . . . . . . .
Tourist Development . . . . . . . . . .
Location: . . . . . . . . .
Classification of the Tourist Development: . . . . . . . . . .
Autonomous Fraction: . . . . . . . . . .
Accommodation Unit or Apartment: . . . . . . . . . .
Proprietor of the Tourist Development: . . . . . . . . . .
Holder of the Right to Periodic Occupancy: . . . . . . . . . .
Beginning: . . . . . . . . . .
Ending: . . . . . . . . . .
Date of Termination of the Right to Periodic Occupancy . . . . . . . . . .

O Conservador do Registo Predial
(The Registrar)

**'CERTIFICATE B'**

CERTIFICO QUE O PRÉDIO Nº.          SE ENCONTRA SUJEITO AO
REGIME DE HABITAÇAO PERIÓDICA, CONFORME TÍTULO CONSTITU-
TIVO INSCRITO NESTA CONSERVATÓRIA SOB O Nº          E QUE SOBRE
O MESMO PRE DIO, FRACÇAO AUTÓNOMA OU PARCELA HABITACIO-
NAL INCIDEM OS SEGUINTES ÓNUS OU ENCARGOS:

**TRANSLATION OF CERTIFICATE 'B'**

I CERTIFY THAT BUILDING NO:          IS SUBJECT TO THE SYSTEM
OF PERIODIC OCCUPATION IN ACCORDANCE WITH THE DEED OF
CONSTITUTION RECORDED IN THIS REGISTRATION OFFICE UNDER
THE NUMBER . . . . . AND THAT SUCH AUTONOMOUS FRACTION OR
HABITATIONAL UNIT OR BUILDING INCURS THE FOLLOWING TAXES
AND CHARGES:-

'CERTIFICATE C'

# PRINCIPAIS DIREITOS E OBRIGAÇOES DO TITULAR DO DIREITO DE HABITAÇAO PERIÓDICA

## TRANSLATION OF CERTIFICATE 'C'

### PRINCIPAL RIGHTS AND OBLIGATIONS OF THE HOLDER OF THE RIGHT TO PERIODIC OCCUPANCY

'CERTIFICATE D'

# PRINCIPAIS DIREITOS E OBRIGAÇOES DO PROPRIETÁRIO DO EMBRE ENDIMENTO TURÍSTICO

## TRANSLATION OF CERTIFICATE 'D'

### PRINCIPAL RIGHTS AND OBLIGATIONS OF THE PROPRIETOR OF THE TOURIST DEVELOPMENT

'CERTIFICATE E'

## ENDOSSOS E
## AVERBAMENTOS

**TRANSLATION OF CERTIFICATE 'E'**

ENDORSEMENTS AND ANNOTATIONS

# Appendix F

# Draft Spanish Timeshare Law

# Appendix F

# Draft Spanish Timeshare Law
# Borrador de Anteproyecto de Ley de Tiempo Compartido

El concepto de tiempo compartido, multipropiedad o 'time-sharing' como se le conoce generalmente es una nueva manifestación de la capacidad del sector turístico y del mercado inmobiliario para buscar productos que respondan a las necesidades cambiantes del mercado y a las legítimas aspiraciones de los consumidores y usuarios.

La idea de ofrecer al público el derecho a disfrutar unas vacaciones en una vivienda turística que cuente con todos los servicios, mobiliario e instalaciones durante un periodo de tiempo determinado de cada año ha venido así a contribuir a la innovación del mercado de productos turísticos cubriendo una verdadera necesidad, que no siempre se ve atendida por la compra de un inmueble que sólo se ocupa durante un mes o menos al año, y que sin embargo requiere una cuantiosa inversión inicial e importantes gastos anuales de mantenimiento.

Como ha ocurrido en otros casos, la capacidad de la sociedad para plasmar en esquemas jurídicos este nuevo concepto se ha adelantado al legislador, de forma que en la actualidad nuestro país, líder en materia turística, es ya el principal mercado europeo del 'time-sharing' sin que hasta el momento exista una normativa directamente reguladora del mismo, produciéndose un importante vacío legal.

The concept of shared time, multi-ownership, or 'timesharing', as it is more generally known, is a new proof of the ability of both the tourism and the real estate business communities, in looking for products corresponding to the ever changing demand within the market and to consumers' aspirations.

The idea of offering the public the right to enjoy their holidays in a resort which is fully furnished and equipped and provides all facilities, during one or more specific periods of time each year has contributed towards the modernisation of the market of tourist products thus responding to a genuine necessity, which is not normally satisfied by the purchase of a property which will only be occupied for one month or less per year, and which yet requires a substantial sum of initial investment and further large expenses for upkeep and maintenance.

As has been the case on other occasions, the ability of society to shape into legal moulds this new concept has taken place before the Legislature has regulated it, in such a way that at present our country, leader in the field of tourism, has already also become the leader in the European timesharing market, without there having existed any rules or regulations over this sector of the market up to now and resulting in a major legal vacuum.

La aparición de este fenómeno en nuestro país tiene además una clara dimensión internacional, al ser el tiempo compartido un producto de especial atractivo para los compradores extranjeros e intervenir mayoritariamente en él promotores extranjeros, lo cual obliga a incluir en esta ley normas específicas que tengan en cuenta este factor.

La reciente evolución del mercado ha hecno que un número creciente de promotores españoles tenga gran interés en adoptar esta fórmula, sintiendo la necesidad de una regulación legal que dé confianza y garantías a los consumidores, a los promotores y al mercado en general.

Otro de los rasgos distintivos del 'timesharing' es su variedad de formas y conceptos, entre los que únicamente es común la idea dc disfrutar unas vacaciones durante una o más semanas al año en un complejo inmobiliario turístico a lo largo de varios años y con pago por adelantado de una cantidad, seguido por pagos anuales para cubrir gastos generales de administración y mantenimiento.

La inexistencia de una orientación legislativa mayoritaria entre los paises de nuestro entorno en esta materia es prueba adicional de que se trata de un fenómeno que puede calificarse de muy distintas maneras.

Así, en Portugal se califica tanto como derecho real de habitación periódica como derecho personal, en Grecia se basa en la idea del arrendamiento periódico, en Francia en esquemas societarios, entre otros, y en otros paises, como Reino Unido, que son pioneros en este campo, no hay legislación específica ni se ha considerado necesaria hasta ahora debido a la existencia de mecanismos jurídicos de aplicación generalizada y que gozan de la total confianza de los consumidores, aunque recientemente se ha empezado a solicitar la promulgación de una legislación específica.

The appearance of this phenomenon in our country has a clear international dimension, timesharing being a product that proves especially attractive to foreign buyers, and being marketed mainly to them. This factor must be borne in mind when laws governing this sector of tourism are passed, and specific provisions need to be taken in consequence.

Recent development of the market has meant that a growing number of Spanish developers are showing increasing interest in this sector, and are beginning to recognise the need for legal regulations establishing guidelines and guarantees for the consumer, the developer and for the market in general.

Another of the features that mark the concept of timesharing is the variety of forms and concepts that it adopts; among which the single common element is the idea of enjoying a holiday for one or more weeks a year in a resort over a period of several years, for a fixed price paid in advance and followed by further annual payments in order to cover general administrative expenses and maintenance charges.

The lack of major legislative guidelines between countries participating in this same sector is proof that this is a concept that can be qualified in many different ways.

Thus, in Portugal, it is qualified as a real right of periodic habitation as well as a personal right; in Greece, it is based on the idea of periodic rental; in France as a corporate scheme or in some other form; and in other countries, such as the United Kingdom, pioneer in this field, where no specific legislation has been considered necessary up to now, due to the fact that the consumer has found confidence and satisfaction and the application of general legislation has proved adequate, the situation has changed and there is a growing demand for legislation.

En consecuencia, no parece conveniente imponer una única modalidad jurídica, siendo preferible implantar un esquema básico de garantías y contenidos mínimos que aseguren la adecuada protección de los consumidores, sea cual fuere la fórmula elegida por cada promotor, junto con una serie de requisitos obligatorios para las diferentes modalidades jurídicas aplicadas en la práctica.

Así, as normas sobre publicidad, defensa de los consumidores, competencia desleal y condiciones generales de contratación son especialmente aplicables al concepto de tiempo compartido, siendo además necesarias otras normas específicas que en esta ley tienen su acogida.

Por otro lado, la competencia de las Comunidades Autónomas en materia turística hace que estas disposiciones que constituyen el marco jurídico mínimo que habrá de aplicarse en todo el territorio nacional, puedan complementarse con las normas turísticas que cada Comunidad considere oportunas, limitándose la ley a señalar que los conjuntos inmobiliarios en régimen de tiempo compartido estarán siempre sometidos a la normativa turística en todos los aspectos que le sean aplicables por su naturaleza y destino.

En cuanto a la terminología adoptada, si bien es cierto que el término 'time-sharing' se ha impuesto con facilidad en todas las zonas turísticas en las que se ha desarrollado hasta el momento este nuevo concepto en España, su conocimiento por el público español dista de ser general, por lo que no puede hablarse de un nuevo término aceptado en la práctica con carácter general.

El término 'tiempo compartido', traducción literal de aquel y habitualmente empleado en los países iberoamericanos parece así plenamente adecuado para designar este nuevo concepto, reservándose el de 'propiedad por periodos' o 'multipropiedad' a aquella modalidad del mismo en que el derecho del adquirente se configura como derecho real.

In consequence, it does not seem sufficient to impose one single legal overall scheme, but rather to form a basic scheme of minimum guarantees and contents which would ensure sufficient consumer protection, and would be the formula chosen by every developer, together with a series of mandatory requirements for the various legal schemes applied in practice.

Rules especially applicable to timesharing would cover advertising, consumer protection, competition and general contractual conditions, in addition to other specific regulations that the present law contemplates.

On the other hand, the competence of the Autonomous Communities in the field of tourism means that the provisions that form the basic legal framework will have to be applied to all national territory, and can be complemented with the tourist legislation which each Community deems suitable, the law limiting itself to stating that the timeshare resorts always conform to tourist legislation in all aspects applicable by their nature or aim.

As far as the terminology adopted is concerned, whether or not it is true that the term 'timesharing' has been readily adopted in all tourist areas where this new concept has been developed in Spain, the term is certainly not yet a familiar one to the Spanish public in general and cannot be accepted as a new legal term.

The term 'tiempo compartido', a literal translation of 'timesharing' commonly used in Latin American countries seems to be perfectly adequate and the terms 'property for periods' and 'multi-ownership' are reserved for the legal regulations with reference to the buyer, and which is conceived as a real right.

La promulgación de la presente ley contribuirá a consolidar lo que ya es una realidad de importancia creciente en España, permitiendo el acceso a esta fórmula a la mayoría de la población en lo que se podría ciertamente considerar como un fenómeno de socialización de las vacaciones en promociones y conjuntos inmobilia rios de calidad superior a la media y a precios económicos, contribuyéndose así a la creación de nuevos servicios y a una mejor y más racional utilización del patrimonio inmobiliario.

Finalmente, no puede olvidarse el importante componente extranjero que el tiempo compartido atrae en España, por lo que resulta también indispensable incluir en la ley una serie de disposiciones que tiendan a proteger específicamente los intereses de los consumidores extranjeros proporcionándoles una adecuada información del producto que se les ofrece, al menos en un idioma que puedan entender Asimismo, respecto de las numerosas promociones ya existentes en España, organizadas conforme a esquemas de derechos personales nacidos en virtud de contratos celebrados en el extranjero, no es posible ignorar su existencia y validez en la generalidad de los casos, pero no puede asimismo olvidarse que su localización en España comporta la imperativa aplicación de las normas españolas relativas a la propiedad, la posesión, y demás derechos sobre los inmuebles sitos en nuestro país, así como de la normativa sobre protección de los consumidores respecto de las ventas y actividades comerciales realizadas en él. De aquí que se imponga la adaptación de todos esos esquemas y promociones de forma que respondan a las garantías contempladas por la ley.

The enactment of this law serves to consolidate what is already an important and growing reality in Spain, facilitating the access to it to the majority of the population, in what could to a certain extent be considered to be a phenomenon of socialisation of holidays in resorts of an above average quality and at economic prices, thus contributing to the creation of new services and a better and more adequate use of property.

Finally, the significant number of foreigners that are attracted to Spain by timesharing must not be forgotten, and thus it is vital to include within the timeshare law a series of provisions that specifically protect the interests of the foreign consumer and provide them with sufficient information about the product which is being offered to them in a language they can understand. In addition, with respect to the large number of resorts that already exist in Spain, which are organised according to schemes of personal rights, by virtue of contracts signed abroad, it is impossible to forget the fact that Spain is where the resorts are located and that this means that Spanish legislation will apply to the property, possession and other laws affecting real estate property in this country, as well as legislation affecting consumer protection regarding sales and commercial activities carried out here. Due to this fact, all marketing and promotional activities carried out in this country must be governed by the guarantees established by the law.

## Titulo preliminar – Preliminary title

### Disposiciones generales – General regulations

| | |
|---|---|
| **Artículo 1.   Definición** | **Article 1.   Definition** |

1. Por el contrato de tiempo compartido una de las partes se obliga a facilitar a la otra la ocupación y disfrute exclusivos, durante una o más semanas al año de un alojamiento determinado de carácter turístico, amueblado y equipado, que se integra en un conjunto inmobiliario, así como la utilización de todas las instalaciones y servicios comunes con que este cuente o vaya a contar durante un número de años superior a tres, a cambio de un precio cierto, pagadero por adelantado en uno o más plazos, así como a organizar la administración y el mantenimiento del conjunto inmobiliario. Cada adquirente habrá de contribuir al pago de los gastos originados por la administración y el mantenimiento del conjunto inmobiliario en régimen de tiempo compartido mediante una cuota anual, que deberá satisfacer en fecha fija y cuya determinación se hará por procedimientos objetivos en los que el titular ha de poder participar con su voto.

1. By virtue of the timeshare contract, one of the parties is to provide the other party the exclusive occupation and use of a fully furnished and equipped touristic accommodation which forms part of a resort, as well as the use of all its facilities and community services already in existence or to be included in the future, during one or more weeks each year, over a period of more than three years, as well as to organise the administration and upkeep of the timeshare resort, in exchange for a fixed price, paid in full in advance or in several installments. Each timeshare member will have to contribute to the administration and maintenance, by means of an annual sum, which must be paid by a certain date and determined by objective procedures in which the timeshare member has to be able to participate with his/her vote.

2. A los efectos de esta ley se entiende por conjunto inmobiliario tres o más inmuebles destinados a vivienda, ya estén integrados en un único edificio, dividido o no en régimen de propiedad horizontal, o en varios edificios contiguos o situados en una misma manzana o urbanización, que tengan salida propia a la vía pública o a un elemento o zona común del inmueble o de la manzana o urbanización y cuenten con zonas e instalaciones comunes adecuadas a la finalidad turística propia del mismo.

2. For the purposes of this law, the term 'resort' is understood to mean three or more properties intended as dwellings, and which are situated in the same building, whether or not horizontally divided, or in several buildings which are adjacent or belong to the same community and which have communal areas and services adequate to the purpose of tourism.

| | |
|---|---|
| **Artículo 2.   Normativa aplicable** | **Article 2.   Applicable rules** |

1. El contrato de tiempo compartido se regirá por las disposiciones de la presente ley, por las normas reguladoras de la protección de los consumidores y por los pactos y condiciones establecidos por las partes en todo aquello que no esté en contradicción con las citadas disposiciones.

1. The timesharing contract will be governed by the regulations of the present law, and by the regulations for consumer protection rights and the agreements and conditions established by the parties regarding all factors that are not in contradiction to the above provisions.

En el caso de que como consecuencia del contrato se cree o transmita a favor del adquirente un derecho real su constitución, contenido y extinción se regularán por las disposiciones de esta ley en primer lugar y supletoriamente por las del Código Civil relativas a la comunidad de bienes y al usufructo, según los casos.

2. Las disposiciones de la presente ley no serán aplicables a los proyectos de tiempo compartido que se refieran a menos de tres viviendas.

**Artículo 3.    Aplicación de las normas españolas**

1. Las relaciones contractuales creadas válidamente al amparo de ordenamientos jurídicos extranjeros podrán referirse a viviendas y conjuntos inmobiliarios situados en el territorio español sin perjuicio de que la creación, regulación o extinción de derechos reales sobre los mismos haya de regirse imperativamente por las normas españolas conforme a lo dispuesto en el artículo 10 de Código Civil. En todo caso, los conjuntos inmobiliarios situados en territorio español y respecto de los cuales se haya celebrado un contrato de tiempo compartido al amparo de un ordenamiento jurídico extranjero estarán igualmente sometidos con carácter imperativo a las normas españolas en materia turística, urbanística ye de protección de los consumidores.

2. La actividad de promoción y celebración de contratos de tiempo compartido creados y regulados al amparo de ordenamientos jurídicos extranjeros que tenga lugar en territorio español, estará sometida a las normas españolas sobre protección de los consumidores, tributación, régimen laboral y de extranjería y legislación vigente sobre control de cambios. En especial serán aplicables a esta actividad las diposiciones de los artículos 5 y 6, y 9 a 19, ambos inclusive, con independencia del contenido de las relaciones contractuales y de su validez conforme al ordenamiento jurídico a que se hayan sometido.

In the event where as a consequence of the contract a real right is created or transmitted in favour of the acquiring party, its constitution, content and extinction will be governed by the provisions of this law in the first instance and supplemented by the Civil Code regarding communal ownership and usufruct, as the case might be.

2. The provisions of this law are not applicable to timesharing projects where fewer than three properties are involved.

**Article 3.    Application of Spanish regulations**

1. The clauses of contracts validly executed under foreign legislation can relate to property situated within Spanish territory. However the creation, regulation, transmission or extinction of real rights on such property must compulsorily be governed by Spanish legislation as required by article 10 of the Civil Code. In all cases, property situated on Spanish territory for which timeshare contracts have been signed according to foreign laws will equally be submitted compulsorily to the Spanish laws regarding tourism, urban rights and consumer protection rights.

2. The promotional and marketing activities and the execution of timeshare contracts created and governed by foreign laws and which take place on Spanish territory will be subject to the Spanish legislation regarding consumer protection, taxation, labour rules and rules regarding alien status and also to the applicable legislation regarding exchange control. In particular, the provisions of articles 5 and 6, and 9 to 19 will be applicable to such activities, independently of terms of the respective contracts and their validity in accordance with the foreign regulations governing them.

3. En todo caso, con carácter previo al inicio de la actividad de comercialización y celebración en España de los contratos mencionados en el apartado anterior, tanto si el conjunto inmobiliario radica en España o en el extranjero, será necesario protocolizar previamente ante notario español el documento a que se refiere el artículo 5, junto con la traducción oficial al castellano de la documentación que sirva para configurar las relaciones jurídicas surgidas de ellos, esté o no mencionada en el citado artículo, y en particular el texto del contrato tipo y la identidad de las entidades en torno a las que se centralizan las relaciones jurídicas de los titulares. Cuando se trate de personas jurídicas deberá asimismo indicarse la identidad de sus administradores, así como sus datos de inscripción registral.

### Artículo 4.   Modalidades del tiempo compartido

1. Por la identificación del periodo anual de disfrute y de la vivienda sobre la que el mismo recae, el tiempo compartido puede ser fijo, flotante, sobre espacio flotante o mixto.

En el tiempo compartido de carácter fijo el disfrute recae cada año sobre la misma vivienda y en la misma semana o semanas del año.

En el de carácter flotante, el periodo anual de disfrute es variable dentro de ciertas temporadas o estaciones del año y su determinación se hace de forma periódica conforme a procedimientos objetivos que respeten el principio de igualdad de oportunidades.

En el tiempo compartido sobre espacio flotante, el derecho del usuario recae sobre una vivienda indeterminada del conjunto inmobiliario, dentro de una categoría o tipo determinado y su determinación se hace cada vez según la disponibilidad y mediante procedimientos objetivos que respeten la igualdad de oportunidades de todos los titulares.

3. In all cases, on order to start such business activities and to execute in Spain the abovementioned contracts, both for property located in Spain and abroad, it will be necessary to legalise the document referred to in article 5 before a Spanish Notary, together with its official translation into Spanish as well as all the documents detailing the legal relations between the parties, whether they are included or not in the list of the abovementioned article, and in particular the specimen of timeshare contract and the identity of the parties around which the legal relations of the timeshare owners will be centred. Where legal persons are concerned, the identity of their administrators must be given, in addition to their registration details.

### Article 4.   Timeshareing modalities

1. Depending on whether the annual period of time during which the property can be used be fixed or variable, timeshare can be fixed, floating, on floating space or a combination of these.

In the case of fixed timeshare, the use is to be provided on the same property for the same week or weeks of the year on an annual basis.

Floating timeshare entitles to the use of the property within certain seasons or at certain times of the year, the specific weekly periods being determined annually by objective proceedings which ensure equal opportunities for all timeshare members.

Timeshare over floating space entitles to the use and occupation of one of the timeshare dwellings of the resort within a certain category or of a certain type and its allocation will depend on availability and will be done by means of objective procedures which shall ensure equal opportunities for all timeshare members.

En el tiempo compartido de tipo mixto se combinan las dos modalidades anteriores, de manera que el derecho del titular será ejercitable en un periodo indeterminado dentro de una cierta temporada y en una cualquiera de las viviendas de un tipo determinado dentro del mismo conjunto inmobiliario.

2. Por la naturaleza del derecho que adquiera el titular el proyecto de tiempo compartido será de carácter real o de carácter obligacional. En el primer caso los titulares adquieren un derecho real sobre el inmueble y en el segundo caso su derecho a la utilización y disfrute del mismo está basado en relaciones jurídicas obligacionales.

3. Las modalidades, de tiempo compartido cuando el contrato dé lugar a la creación de derechos reales en favor del adquirente, son la multipropiedad o propiedad por periodos, y el usufructo por periodos, cuyo concepto y régimen específico se establecen en el Título.

Mixed timeshares combining the two above types means that the timeshare member is entitled to an undetermined timeshare period within a certain season of the year to be spent in one of the timeshare properties of a given type within the resort.

2. In accordance with the nature of the rights acquired by the owner, the timeshare scheme shall be of a real or obligational character. In the first case, the owners acquire real rights on the property and in the second case, the right of use, is based on personal rights acquired by contractual relations.

3. When the timeshare contract provides for the creation of real rights in favour of the purchaser the timeshare right is called multi-ownership or ownership for periods, and is specifically regulated by the provision contained in Title 1.

## Capítulo 1 Formalización del proyecto de tiempo compartido
## Chapter 1 Legalisation of the timeshare scheme

**Artículo 5.  Protocolización previa**

1 Antes de la celebración del primer contrato de tiempo compartido, el pro motor deberá otorgar un documento, que se elevará a escritura pública, en el que constará, como mínimo:

a) la descripción e identificación registral del conjunto inmobiliario ye de cada una de las viviendas que van a ser objeto del proyecto de tiempo compartido, así como de sus instalaciones comunes, con referencia expresa a la existencia de cargas o gravámenes y con indicación del número máximo de personas que en cada periodo de tiempo compartido podrán ocupar simultáneamente cada una de las dichas viviendas.

**Article 5.  Prior Notarisation**

1. Prior to the signature of the first timeshare contract, the developer must execute a notarised deed in which at least the following information must be included:

a) Description and identification in the Land Registry of the resort and of each of the individual units which will be included in the timesharing project, as well as the communal facilities, with express reference to any charges or encumbrances that might exist, and with an indication of the maximum number of persons who could occupy each of the units at the same time.

Asimismo se acompañará copia de la documentación acreditativa de la situación urbanística del conjunto inmobiliario.

b) En el caso de que el conjunto inmobiliario no haya empezado a construirse o se encuentre en construcción, la descripción e identificación registral del solar, y todos los documentos exigidos por la legislación vigente en materia urbanística para la ejecución de la obra y en especial el modelo de contrato de seguro o aval bancario que se otorgará en favor de los adquirentes de conformidad con lo dispuesto en el artículo 15.

c) la identificación de los periodos de disfrute exclusivo de cada vivienda conforme a letras, nombres, números o cualquier combinación de lo anterior, con indicación precisa de las fechas de inicio y de terminación de cada periodo. El periodo unitario en que se dividirá el uso y disfrute de cada vivienda será de una semana. No podrán comercializarse nunca más de cincuenta y un periodos por vivienda.

En el caso de la modalidad flotante de tiempo compartido, la identificación de los periodos se hará igualmente de forma que se asegure que no se venderán más de cincuenta y un periodos por vivienda. Deberá indicarse en todo caso a qué temporada corresponde el periodo o entre qué fecha inicial y que fecha final puede quedar establecido dicho periodo cada año.

d) la enumeración de los servicios mínimos cuyo coste estará cubierto por la cuota anual, que deberán incluir la administración y el mantenimiento del inmueble y sus instalaciones, y en particular la limpieza semanal de los elementos e instalaciones comunes, de todas las viviendas.

e) la indicación expresa, en su caso, de que, a parte de las destinadas al tiempo compartido, el promotor tiene el propósito de vender una o más viviendas en pleno dominio en el mismo conjunto inmobiliario.

A copy of the documents authorising the construction and granting planning permission to the resort is also to be enclosed with the above.

b) In the case that the resort has not yet been constructed, or is still under construction, the description and identification in the Land Registry of the plot, and all documents required by current legislation regarding urban matters for the execution of the construction and in particular, the insurance policy or bank guarantee to be granted in favour of the purchasers in accordance with the provisions of article 15.

c) Identification of the periods of exclusive right of use of each unit, by means of letters, names, numbers, or any combination of these, with a precise indication of dates of commencement and end of each time period. The unitary period of time will be one week, the use of each resort being divided into this time factor. No single timeshare property may be marketed for a total number of periods exceeding fifty one per resort.

In the case of floating timeshares the identification of the timeshare periods will be carried out in a similar way so that the number of timeshare periods sold never exceeds fifty one per single property. In all cases, the season to which the timeshare period corresponds or the dates of commencement and termination of the timeshare period each year must be indicated.

d) The enumeration of minimum services the cost of which is to be covered by an annual charge and which must include administration, upkeep of the property and its facilities, and in particular, weekly cleaning of the units and communal services and facilities.

e) Express mention of the fact if applicable that, apart from those properties that have been designated as timeshare properties, the developer also intends to sell one or more units on an outright basis within the same resort.

f) el procedimiento para el cálculo anual de los gastos de administración, conservación, y mantenimiento de cada vivienda y de los elementos comunes del conjunto inmobiliario con indicación del tiempo, lugar y forma del pago de las mismas.

g) los votos asignados al titular de cada periodo de tiempo compartido, en la Junta u órgano que haga sus veces, en el caso de que por cualquier razón alguno de los titulares tenga derecho a más de un voto por semana de tiempo compartido.

h) la identificación de los periodos del año en los que está prevista la realización de trabajos de mantenimiento o reparación del conjunto inmobiliario y durante los cuales la totalidad o parte de las viviendas no podrán ser ocupadas. La duración mínima de estos periodos, cada año, deberá ser de una semana.

i) copia del contrato de administración del conjunto inmobiliario celebrado con una sociedad de las reguladas en el capítulo 1 del Título II y copia del aval bancario o de la póliza de caución presentados por dicha sociedad en cumplimiento de lo dispuesto en el artículo 40 cuando sean exigibles.

j) si se prevé la adición de nuevas viviendas a un mismo proyecto de tiempo compartido, el procedimiento establecido para ello y la fórmula para la determinación o corrección de las cuotas anuales de los titulares que resulten después de la incorporación de aquellas. Asimismo, si se prevé la posibilidad de separar del conjunto inmobiliario las viviendas respecto de las cuales no se haya llegado a celebrar ningún contrato de tiempo compartido, deberá expresarse la forma o procedimiento en que ello se hará y las medidas adoptadas para que en tal supuesto no se vean perjudicados los derechos de los titulares.

f) The procedure for the annual calculation of administration and services charges, and costs for the upkeep of each property and communal charges for the resort with an indication of the type of unit to which they correspond, as well as the place and form of payment of the same.

g) The votes corresponding to the owner of each timeshare period, at the General Meetings, in the event that for some reason more than one vote corresponds to one timeshare period.

h) The identification of the periods of the year when maintenance or repair works are to be carried out in the resort, during which periods all or part of the units will not be occupable. The minimum duration of such periods will be of one week per year.

i) Copy of the management contract of the resort, signed with one of the companies regulated in Chapter 1 of Title II, and copy of the bank guarantee or insurance policy presented by the aforesaid company in accordance with the provisions of article 40 when applicable.

j) If the addition of new units is foreseen to the same timeshare project, the procedures established for this and the formula for the determination or change of the annual charges which may result from the incorporation of these new units. Similarly, if it were contemplated that the units in respect of which no timeshare contract has been executed can be taken away from the timeshare scheme, it shall be necessary to describe the procedure to follow in that case and the specific guarantees for the rights acquired by the timeshare owners.

k) Descripción de las instalaciones deportivas, de ocio y de recreo con que cuenta el conjunto inmobiliario, así como de las que el promotor se compromete a proporcionar al mismo, con especificación de los derechos que los titulares tienen sobre ellas.

l) indicación de la fecha de apertura del conjunto inmobiliario;

m) en el caso de proyectos de tiempo compartido de duración limitada, la identificación de los derechos que corresponderán a los titulares al expirar el contrato o el procedimiento para el cálculo de las cantidades a percibir por cada uno, o la indicación expresa de que a la extinción del contrato los titulares no tendrán derecho a ninguna compensación. Si el derecho adquirido por el titular va a ser de usufructo, deberá ofrecerse asimismo una breve descripción de la naturaleza de este derecho y del alcance de su derecho de transmisión en caso de fallecimiento.

n) los estatutos por los que se han de regir las relaciones del conjunto de titulares de tiempo compartido, en los que podrán figurar los extremos anteriores y en todo caso deberán contener la regulación de los que se enumeran en el artículo 43.

Además habrá de establecerse en ellos el procedimiento y requisitos para su modificación, así como las reglas aplicables en los supuestos de destrucción parcial o total del conjunto inmobiliario o de alguna de las viviendas que lo integran.

2. Al elevar a público el documento a que se refiere el apartado anterior, el promotor expresará que son ciertas y veraces todas las manifestaciones que consten en el mismo.

3. El promotor estará obligado a protocolizar notarialmente el documento descriptivo de cualquier modificación posterior en el Proyecto de tiempo compartido que se refiera a los puntos mencionados en el párrafo primero.

k) Description of sports, leisure and recreational facilities that each resort includes, in addition to those that the developer undertakes to provide, with specification of the rights that the owners have over such facilities.

l) Indication of the date of opening of the resort.

m) In the case of timeshare projects of limited duration, the identification of the rights which will correspond to the owners upon expiry of the contract or the procedure for calculation of the quantities to be received by each one, or express indication of the fact that upon expiry of the contract, the owners will not have any right to a compensation. If the right to be acquired by the purchaser is to be a usufruct a brief explanation of the nature of his right and the extent of the right to transfer it in case of death.

n) The statutes governing the relations among the timeshare owners in which there shall appear the abovementioned points including in all cases the regulations set out in article 43.

In addition to the above document the rules applying in the event of partial or total destruction of the resort or of any of the units belonging to it.

2. At the time of the issuance of the Public Deed referred to in the paragraph above, the developer must confirm that all statements made in the same are true and may be verified.

3. The developer will be under obligation to notarise as well the document describing any further changes made to the resort or the timeshare project referred to in the first paragraph.

4. Copia simple de la escritura pública a que se refiere el apartado anterior deberá estar a disposición para su examen por toda persona interesada en la celebración de un contrato de tiempo compartido sobre el conjunto inmobiliario correspondiente. El adquirente que así lo desee podrá solicitar, a su costa, copia de dicha escritura.

**Artículo 6.    Comunicación de los proyectos de tiempo compartido a la Autoridad Turística**

Para la válida comercialización del tiempo compartido en cualquiera de sus modalidades será necesario que con carácter previo el Notario autorizante remita una copia de la escritura pública a que se refiere el artículo anterior o de la escritura a que se refiere el artículo 3.3, en su caso, a la autoridad competente en materia turística de la Comunidad Autónoma en que radique el conjunto inmobiliario, si se encuentra en territorio español y en todo caso a la Secretaría General de Turismo.

**Artículo 7.**

En los conjuntos inmobiliarios en régimen de comunidad de bienes o de propiedad horizontal que se construyan o dividan horizontalmente con posterioridad a la entrada en vigor de esta ley, no podrá constituirse un régimen de tiempo compartido si los estatutos de la comunidad lo prohiben expresamente, pudiendo establecerse tal prohibición por acuerdo de más del 50% de los propietarios.

**Artículo 8.    Derechos y obligaciones de los titulares**

1. Los derechos y obligaciones de los titulares deberán constar con claridad en los Estatutos.

2. Son derechos de los titulares:

a) El derecho a la ocupación y disfrute exclusivo de una vivienda dentro del conjunto inmobiliario durante uno o más periodos de una semana en el año;

4. A simple copy of the Public Deed referred to in the above paragraph must be available for examination by all persons interested in signing a timeshare contract regarding any of the units belonging to the resort. The purchaser may, upon request and at his own cost, receive a copy of the aforementioned Deed.

**Article 6.    Notification of the timeshare projects to the Tourist Authorities**

In order to carry out any marketing activities regarding a timeshare project, it will be necessary that the authorising Notary gives a copy of the Public Deed referred to in the previous article or of the Deed referred to in Article 3.3, to the authorities competent in matters of tourism of the particular Autonomous Community in which the resort is situated, if on Spanish territory, and, in all cases, to the Secretariat General of Tourism.

**Article 7.**

In resorts under the horizontal ownership regulations constructed as such or divided horizontally after this present law has come into force, timeshare schemes may not be established if the statutes of the community expressly forbid it, such prohibition requiring the vote of more than 50% of the owners.

**Article 8.    Rights and obligations of the timeshare owners**

1. The rights and obligations of the owners must be clearly defined in the Statutes.

2. The owners' rights are as follows:

a) The right of exclusive occupation and enjoyment of a unit within a resort for one or more weekly periods a year.

b) El derecho a la utilización de todos los servicios e instalaciones comunes del conjunto inmobiliario;

b) The right of use of all communal services and facilities of the resort.

c) Los derechos de asistencia y voto en la Junta de titulares;

c) Voting and attendance rights at the Meeting of Owners.

d) El derecho a ser elegido para los cargos de Presidente y de Secretario siempre que se reunan los requisitos establecidos para ello en los Estatutos;

d) The right to be elected as President or Secretary, provided that the statutory requirements are met.

e) El derecho de solicitar información al Promotor o, en su defecto, a la sociedad de administración en cualquier momento sobre cualquier extremo referido al régimen de tiempo compartido o al conjunto inmobiliario respectivo.

e) The right to request information from the developer or in his absence from the management company at any time regarding the timeshare scheme or the resort, in accordance to the statutes.

f) El derecho a examinar las cuentas y el presupuesto anual, con quince días de antelación, como mínimo, a la fecha de celebración de la Junta en que habrán de ser censuradas y, en su caso, aprobadas;

f) The right to examine accounts and the annual budget, at least fifteen days in advance of the date on which the General Meeting is to take place, when these have to be examined and, as the case may be, approved.

g) El derecho a los servicios mínimos especificados en el contrato de tiempo compartido, que no podrán ser reducidos más que por acuerdo válidamente adoptado con el número de votos previsto en el artículo 49.4.

g) The right to receive minimum services as specified in the timeshare contract, which cannot be further reduced except than by resolution adopted with the number of votes provided for in article 49.4.

h) El derecho a la transmisión por actos inter vivos o mortis causa, a título oneroso o gratuito, de los derechos y obligaciones adquiridos como consecuencia del contrato de tiempo compartido, sea cual fuere su forma y naturaleza jurídicas, con arreglo a lo dispuesto en los estatutos de la Asociación de Titulares.

h) The right to transfer by acts *inter vivos* or *mortis causa*, by onerous means or gratuitously, the rights and obligations acquired as a consequence of the timeshare contract, whatever their form or legal nature, in accordance with the Statutues of the Association of Timeshare Owners.

3. Para el ejercicio de sus derechos el titular deberá estar al corriente en el pago de las cuotas que le correspondan de conformidad con lo establecido en la presente Ley. La sociedad de administración podrá requerir al titular para acreditar su condición de tal.

3. In order to exercise his rights, the owner must be up-to-date in all payments corresponding to him according to the present law. The management company may require the owner to make payment to such effect.

4. Los derechos que la presente ley otorga a los titulares de tiempo compartido, cualquiera que sea la modalidad conforme a la que éste se organice, son irrenunciables.

4. The rights granted by the present law to timeshare owners, whatever the modality of the timeshare scheme, cannot be waived.

5. Son obligaciones de los titulares:

a) Cumplir las normas de régimen interior y demás acuerdos válidamente adoptados por los órganos de gobierno de la Asociación;

b) Pagar las cuotas anuales.

c) Satisfacer los gastos que puedan ser imputados con carácter individual y correspondan a la vivienda sobre la que el titular ejercita sus derechos de uso y disfrute durante el periodo respectivo.

d) Usar la vivienda, sus instalaciones y mobiliario y las instalaciones y zonas comunes del conjunto inmobiliario conforme a su destino respectivo y con la diligencia propia de un buen padre de familia.

e) Responder frente a la Asociación de titulares por los daños causados en la vivienda, en su mobiliario o en las instalaciones comunes del conjunto inmobiliario por él; por cualquiera de sus acompañantes o por las personas que haya autorizado. En ningún supuesto el titular será responsable de forma exclusiva por los desperfectos y averías causados por el mero transcurso del tiempo o por la normal utilización de la vivienda, del mobiliario o de las instalaciones comunes;

f) Comunicar a la sociedad de administración las averías y desperfectos que sufra la vivienda a que corresponda su derecho de tiempo compartido durante el periodo de utilización que le corresponda;

g) Autorizar la realización de obras o reparaciones que tengan el caracter de urgentes o inaplazables, con derecho a ser compensado, a su elección, en estos casos, económicamente o mediante el disfrute de su periodo de tiempo compartido en otra de las viviendas de similares características del mismo conjunto inmobiliario.

h) Designar un domicilio a efecto de notificaciones;

5. The owners' obligations are as follows:

a) To comply with the domestic regulations and further agreements adopted by the governmental bodies and by the Association of Timeshare Owners.

b) To pay the annual charges for general expenses.

c) To pay all charges and expenses that may correspond to him individually or to the property over which he exercises his rights of use and which he occupies for the respective period of time.

d) To use the property, its facilities and furniture and the communal areas of the resort in accordance with its intended use and with due diligence.

e) To take responsibility before the Association of Owners for any damages caused to the property, furniture or communal facilities of the resort, either by himself or his guests or by anybody authorised by him. In no case will the owner be held exclusively responsible for the imperfections or damage caused by mere wear or normal use of the property or of the communal facilities.

f) To inform the management of all deficiencies or damages caused to the property during the period of time corresponding to him.

g) To authorise all works and repairs that may be urgent or may not be delayed, with the right to compensation, if he so chooses, in such cases, either in cash or by being allowed to spend his timeshare period in another of the timeshare units of a similar type in the same resort.

h) To designate an address, giving due notice of any changes thereof.

i) Comunicar a la Sociedad de Administración la identidad de las personas que ocuparán la vivienda que corresponda al titular durante el periodo respectivo, con una antelación mínima de 48 horas, siempre que el titular no vaya a estar presente;

i) To communicate to the Management Company the identity of persons who will be occupying the unit during the allocated weekly period, with a minimum notice of 48 hours, if the owner will not himself be present.

j) Notificar al Secretario y a la sociedad de administtración la transmisión por cualquier título de su derecho, con indicación de la indentidad y domicilio del nuevo titular.

j) To notify the Secretary and the management company of any transfer of the timeshare rights indicating the identity and address of the new timeshare owner.

6. En el caso de que en el contrato de tiempo compartido se haya convenido el pago aplazado del precio, el adquirente gozará de los mismos derechos y obligaciones que la presente ley reconoce a todos los titulares de tiempo compartido, desde el momento de la celebración, de aquel, y le serán aplicables las normas de la presente ley.

6. If the timeshare contract provides for the payment in installments of the price, the buyer will acquire the rights and obligations that the present law imposes upon all timeshare owners from the moment the contract is signed, and the general rules of the law will apply from that moment.

## Capítulo II Garantías en favor de los adquirentes
## Chapter II Guarantees in favour of the Owners

**Artículo 9.**

**Article 9.**

Sólo podrán celebrarse contratos de tiempo compartido referidos a viviendas que se hallaren libres de cargas y gravámenes al tiempo de la celebración del contrato, salvo las servidumbres legales o las derivadas del régimen de propiedad horizontal en que en su caso se haya constituido el conjunto inmobiliario, a menos que el promotor garantice mediante aval bancario, contrato de seguro, o cuenta bloqueada, la devolución a los adquirentes de todas las cantidades pagadas más el interés legal del dinero en el caso de no levantarse dichas cargas o gravámenes dentro del plazo máximo de dos años a contar desde la fecha de primera ocupación por el titular indicada en la escritura pública a que alude el artículo 5 o en el contrato de tiempo compartido.

Timeshare contracts will only be permissible in respect of units free of any charges and encumbrances at the time of signature, with the exception of legal easements or those deriving from regulations for horizontal ownership, when the resort is organized under this system, unless the developer guarantees by means of a bank guarantee, insurance contract, or escrow deposits the reimbursement to the purchasers of all payments plus accrued interests at the legal rate in the event that such charges or encumbrances are not paid off within a maximum period of two years from the day of first occupation of the unit by the timeshare owner as specified in the Notarial Deed referred to in Article 5 or in the sales contract.

**Artículo 10.   Contenido mínimo del contrato**

El contrato de tiempo compartido en cualquiera de sus modalidades sólo podrá celebrarse por escrito en el que constarán, al menos, los siguientes extremos:

a) La fecha de celebración del contrato así como la de elevación a Escritura Pública del documento a que se refiere el artículo 5, con identificación del Notario autorizante y del número de su protocolo;

b) Los nombres y direcciones de las partes contratantes y en especial la identidad del promotor y de sus ad-ministradores;

c) El importe total que debe satisfacer el adquirente, como consecuenia de su obligación de pago, que incluirá el precio inicial y cualquiera otra cantidad adicional que por cualquier concepto haya de pagar;

d) La identificación del conjunto inmobiliario, con indicación del lugar donde radica y de sus fases de desarrollo, así como la fecha estimada de terminación de su construcción si no estuviese terminada al tiemo de la celebración del mismo, y la fecha estimada de otorgamiento de la escritura pública en el caso de crearse o transmitirse al propio tiempo un derecho real sobre la vivienda respectiva o sobre el conjunto inmobiliario en su totalidad;

e) La descripción de la vivienda a que se refiere el contrato de tiempo compartido;

f) La descripción de la modalidad y duración del proyecto de tiempo compartido a que se refiere el contrato, con mención particular acerca de si la misma comporta la adquisición o no de algún derecho real.

g) La indicación, con tipo de imprenta bien visible y en el espacio inmediatamente anterior a la firma del adquirente de la siguiente frase:

**Article 10.   Minimum contents of the contract**

The timeshare contract, whatever its form, may only be executed in writing and shall include at least the following:

a) The date of signature of the contract, as well as the date of notarisation of the document referred to in article 5, with the indication of the name of the authorising Notary and the number of the document in his protocol.

b) The names and addresses of the contracting parties and in particular details of the identity of the developer and his directors.

c) The total amount which must be paid by the buyer, which includes the initial price and any other additional sum that has to be paid for any reason whatsoever.

d) The exact details of the resort, indicating its exact location and the phases of development contemplated, as well as the dates by which construction is planned to be completed should this not already have been completed at the time of signature, and the granting of the Public Deed in the case of a real right being created or transferred on the unit or on the timeshare resort as a whole.

e) Description of the timeshare unit to which the timeshare contract refers.

f) Description of the form and duration of the timeshare project to which the contract refers, with particular reference as to whether this includes the acquisition or not of a real right.

g) The following clause, printed in bold type which can be clearly read, and placed directly before the signature of the buyer at the end of the contract:

EL ADQUIRENTE DE UNO O MAS PERIODOS DE TIEMPO COMPARTIDO EN VIRTUD DEL PRESENTE CONTRATO TIENE DERECHO A RESOLVERLO SIN SUFRIR NINGUNA PENALIDAD DENTRO DEL PLAZO DE SIETE DIAS A CONTAR DESDE LA FIRMA DEL MISMO.

EN CASO DE OPTAR POR LA RESOLUCION DEL CONTRATO, EL ADQUIRENTE DEBERA NOTIFICARLO AL PROMOTOR POR CUALQUIER MEDIO QUE DEJE CONSTANCIA DEL CONTENIDO DE LA COMUNICACION Y DE SU RECEPCION, ASI COMO DE LA FECHA DE SU ENVIO. LA RESOLUCION TENDRA EFECTO INMEDIATO EN LA FECHA DE ENVIO DEL ESCRITO AL PROMOTOR.

h) La indicación de que, en caso de resolverse el contrato por el adquirente dentro del plazo de siete días a que se refiere el apartado anterior, el promotor devolverá a aquel todas aquellas cantidades que hubiera recibido del mismo en virtud del contrato hasta la fecha de la resolución, con deducción únicamente de las cantidades correspondientes al valor razonable de los servicios que haya percibido el adquirente hasta el momento de la resolución en virtud del contrato.

i) En el caso de que el contrato dé lugar a la adquisición de algún derecho real, la expresión de la fecha prevista para el otorgamiento de la escritura pública, así como de la indicación de la necesaria inscripción de la misma en el Registro de la Propiedad por parte del adquirente para obtener la plena protección de su derecho. Si el derecho adquirido por el titular ha de ser un usufructo deberá ofrecerse asimismo una breve descripción de la naturaleza de este derecho y del alcance de su derecho de transmisión en caso de fallecimiento.

THE PURCHASER OF ONE OR MORE TIMESHARE PERIODS BY VIRTUE OF THE PRESENT CONTRACT HAS THE RIGHT TO ANNUL IT WITHOUT SUFFERING ANY PENALTY WITHIN A PERIOD OF SEVEN DAYS AS FROM THE DATE OF SIGNATURE OF THE SAME.

IN THE CASE OF ANNULMENT OF THE CONTRACT, THE PURCHASER MUST NOTIFY THE DEVELOPER BY WHATSOEVER MEANS THAT PROVIDES WRITTEN EVIDENCE OF THE CONTENTS OF SUCH NOTIFICATION AND ITS RECEPTION, IN ADDITION TO THE DATE ON WHICH IT WAS SENT. ANNULMENT WILL TAKE IMMEDIATE EFFECT AS FROM THE DATE ON WHICH THE WRITTEN NOTIFICATION WAS SENT TO THE DEVELOPER.

h) Indication that, in the case of the contract being annulled by the purchaser within the period of seven days referred to above, the developer will return to the purchaser in total all sums that he may have received from the same by virtue of the contract up to the date of its annullment, with the only admissible deduction of the sums corresponding to the total fair value of the services which the purchaser may have received up to the moment of annullment of the contract.

i) In the case where the contract leads to the acquisition of a real right, the date must be given on which it is expected that the Public Deed will be granted, and the necessity must be expressed of registration of the same in the Land Registry by the purchaser, in order to have full protection of his rights. In case the right to be granted is a usufruct a brief explanation of the nature of his right and the extent of the right to transfer it in case of death.

j) En el caso de que el promotor o la sociedad de administración ofrezca la prestación de los servicios de administración y mantenimiento a un tanto alzado, deberá indicarse expresamente la duración de dicha obligación así como el compromiso del promotor o de la sociedad de administración de asumir a su cargo el pago de cualesquiera cantidades que excedan del presupuesto estimado. Este compromiso será obligatorio para el promotor en el caso de que de conformidad con lo prevenido en la artículo 61.4, quede excusado del pago de cuotas anuales respecto de los periodos sobre los que no se hayan celebrado contratos de tiempo compartido en cada vivienda;

k) La cifra a pagar inicialmente en concepto de cuota anual de gastos, con copia del presupuesto que ha servido para su determinación, que deberá contener las menciones a que se refiere el artículo 13.

2. La omisión de cualquiera de estos extremos en el contrato de tiempo compartido dará derecho al adquirente a resolver el mismo dentre del plazo de treinta días contados desde la fecha de firma del contrato de tiempo compartido.

**Artículo 11.   Inventario**

La persona a quien se proponga la celebración de un contrato de tiempo compartido tendrá derecho a examinar antes de la firma del mismo y a recibir una copia en el momento en que ésta tenga lugar, de un inventario completo de todos los muebles, instalaciones y ajuar con que cuenta la vivienda a que el contrato se refiere.

Dicho inventario deberá ser actualizado cada vez que se añada una nueva instalación, equipo o elemento del ajuar a la vivienda o a las instalaciones comunes del conjunto inmobiliario, y se entregará a todos los titulares copia del mismo.

j) In the case where the developer or the management company offer their services for administration and maintenance at a fixed price, express reference must be made of the exact duration of such obligation and the developer or the management company shall undertake to assume themselves any sum in excess of the fixed amount. Such commitment shall be compulsory for the developer in the case that, in accordance with the provisions of article 61.4, the developer has been excused from the payment of charges with respect to unsold timeshare periods.

k) The sum to be paid initially in the concept of annual charges with a copy of the budget on which such sum is based, which must contain the information given in article 13.

2. The omission of any of the above informations in the timeshare contract will give the purchaser the right to annul the same within a period of thirty days as from the date on which the purchaser signs the timeshare contract.

**Article 11.   Inventory**

The person to whom the signature of a timeshare contract is proposed will have the right to examine the same before signing, and to receive a copy at the moment of signing, of a complete inventory of all items of furniture, equipment and furnishings contained in the timeshare property to which the contract refers.

Such inventory must be updated each time that a new item of furniture, piece of equipment or furnishing is added to the property or to the timeshare resort, where copies of the same inventory are to be distributed to all owners.

**Artículo 12.  Información adicional**

En la documentación a que se refieren los artículos anteriores deberá hacerse referencia a los contratos de suministro de agua, luz, gas, teléfono, y cualquier otro suministro con que cuente el conjunto inmobiliario y la vivienda objeto del contrato de tiempo compartido.

El titular tendrá asimismo derecho a examinar la documentación requerida por la legislación vigente respecto de toda venta de viviendas, en especial la mencionada en el Real Decreto 515/89, de 21 de abril, así como a recibir una copia de dicha documentación a su solicitud.

**Artículo 13.  Presupuesto de gastos**

El presupuesto figurará como anexo al contrato de tiempo compartido y expresará los gastos comunes del conjunto inmobiliario, que incluirán, en todo caso, los correspondientes a administración, gastos generales, manteni miento, alquileres de instalaciones deportivas o de recreo, impuestos y demás tributos que graven los inmuebles, vigilancia y seguridad, seguros y reservas para sustitución de mobiliario e instalaciones averiadas o deterioradas y para reparación o conservación del inmueble.

El presupuesto incluirá asimismo información acerca de los demás gastos que puedan afectar al titular y que no están incluidos en la cuota anual a pagar a la sociedad de administración, tales como los correspondientes a servicios pagaderos en función del consumo directo efectuado por cada titular o que se prestan a su solicitud.

La Junta de titulares aprobará anualmente, después del primer año de existencia del proyecto de tiempo compartido, el presupuesto de gastos conforme a la propuesta que le someta la sociedad de administración, en la que podrá introducir, no obstante, las modificaciones que tenga por conveniente.

**Article 12.  Additional information**

In addition to the documentation referred to in the above articles there shall be given reference to the contracts for the supply of water, electricity, gas, telephone, and any other facilities which the resort or timeshare property to which the contract refers may be supplied with.

The owner will have the right to examine all documents required by the law with respect to Real Decree 515/89, of 21 April, and also to receive a copy of such documentation on request.

**Article 13.  Estimate for expenses**

The estimate of expenses will figure as an annexe to the timeshare contract, and will express communal charges for the resort, which will include, in all cases, administrative charges, general expenses, maintenance, use of sports facilities, taxes and further payments attaching to the property, vigilance and security, insurance and a sinking fund for substitution of furniture and broken or deteriorated equipment, and for major repairs and upkeep of the property.

In the estimate shall appear as well information regarding all other expenses that might affect each timeshare owner and which are not included in the annual charges to be paid to the management company, such as those corresponding to services that can be paid on the basis of actual expenditures made by each timeshare owner, and which are rendered at his request.

The General Meeting of Timeshare Owners will approve on an annual basis – after the first year of existence of the resort – the estimate of charges and expenses in accordance with the proposal that the Management makes to them, to which, however, amendments that are deemed appropriate may be made.

## Artículo 14.   Seguro

Con anterioridad a la comercialización de un proyecto de tiempo compartido el promotor deberá contratar un seguro de responsabilidad civil de cualquiera de sus dependientes, y de los ocupantes de las viviendas, y un seguro de daños del conjunto inmobiliario y de sus instlaciones y equipos, cuyos costes anuales deberán incorporarse al presupuesto de gastos del proyecto de tiempo compartido. Copia de dichos contratos deberá estar a disposición de todos los adquirentes.

## Artículo 15.   Garantías en el supuesto de inmuebles en construcción

1. Los promotores que vayan a celebrar contratos de tiempo compartido que se refieran a inmuebles por construir o en curso de construcción están obligados a garantizar a los adquirentes la devolución de todas las cantidades entregadas más el interés legal que corresponda mediante contrato de seguro otorgado con entidad aseguradora, aval solidario o fianza bastante prestados por entidad bancaria o constitución de cuentas bloqueadas en garantía para el caso de que la construcción no se inicie o no llegue a buen fin por cualquier causa en el plazo convenido.

2. El promotor está obligado en el momento de la celebración del contrato a entregar al adquirente documento en el que se acredite la garantía referida en el párrafo anterior.

3. El derecho del adquirente a obtener la garantía mencionada en el apartado primero es irrenun-ciable. El adquirente podrá resolver el contrato en cualquier momento si aquella no se hubiera prestado.

## Article 14.   Insurance

Prior to the commercialisation of a timeshare project, the developer must contract an insurance covering civil liability for each of its dependants, and for the occupants of the units, and an insurance covering damages to the timeshare resort and to its installations and equipment, for which the annual costs must be included in the estimate of expenses of the timesharing project. Copies of such contracts must be accessible to all purchasers.

## Article 15.   Guarantees in the event of units under construction

1. The developers that are going to sign timeshare contracts with reference to buildings for construction or under construction must compulsorily guarantee the purchaser the reimbursement of all sums paid, together with the corresponding legal interest by means of an insurance contract undertaken with an insurance company, by a full bankers' guarantee, or by an escrow deposit in the event that construction is not started or is not completed, for whatsoever reason, within the agreed time period.

2. The developer is obliged to deliver to the purchaser at the time of the signature of the contract a copy of the document in which the guarantee referred to in the above paragraph is verified.

3. The purchaser's right to obtain the above mentioned guarantee (paragraph 1) cannot be waived. The purchaser may annul the contract at any moment if this is not presented to him.

**Artículo 16. Publicidad**

1. Todos los materiales publicitarios, anuncios, ofertas, folletos y mensajes publicados por cualquier medio de difusión por el promotor deberán cumplir con los requisitos establecidos por la Ley General de Publicidad y la Ley de Competencia Desleal y sus disposiciones reglamentarias.

2. En particular ninguno de dichos materiales y mensajes publicitarios podrá ofrecer información engañosa o dar lugar a error en el público respecto de la modalidad del contrato, la naturaleza jurídica de los derechos surgidos del mismo y sus condiciones o sobre las características del conjunto inmobiliario, la vivienda y los derechos y obligaciones de los titulares, ni hacer predicciones específicas acerca de los incrementos de valor que los periodos de tiempo compartido ofrecidos a la venta vayan a experimentar. Tampoco podrá aludirse al tiempo compartido como una forma de inversión financiera o inmobiliaria.

3. En toda promoción escrita o verbal, publicidad u oferta de contratos de tiempo compartido el promotor deberá expresar siempre si el conjunto inmobiliario se encuentra en construcción o si la edificación ha concluido. Deberá asimismo indicar cuando resulte oportuno si el conjunto inmobiliario cuenta con accesos y facilidades para minusválidos.

**Article 16. Advertising**

1. All advertising materials. advertisements, brochures, offers, leaflets and messages, printed and distributed by whatsoever means by the developer must conform to the requirements established by the General Law of Publicity, the legislation regarding unfair competition and the regulations enacted in their execution.

2. In particular, none of the above material or messages may advertise false or untrue information which could be misconstrued by the general public with respect to the form of the contract, the legal nature of the rights and conditions stipulated therein, or to the features of the timeshare resort, property or rights and obligations of the owners, nor may they make specific predictions as to the increase in value which the timeshare periods at present on sale may gain. Nor may any reference be made to timesharing as a source of financial or real estate investment.

3. With all types of promotion, whether verbal or written, advertising or offers of timeshare contracts, the developer must always state whether the timeshare resort is still under construction or whether it has been completed. At the same time, he must state if relevant whether or not the timeshare resort has facilities available for the handicapped.

**Artículo 17. Organizaciones de consumidores**

Las organizaciones de consumidores y usuarios legalmente constituidas tendrán derecho a recibir copia de toda la documentación relativa al proyecto de tiempo compartido elaborada por el promotor con objeto de verificar el cumplimiento de todos los requisitos legales, y a tal efecto podrán visitar sus representantes debidamente acreditados las oficinas del promotor y de la entidad comercializadora en su caso y recabar del personal responsable de las mismas la información y documentación respectiva.

**Artículo 18. Garantías en favor de los adquirentes extranjeros**

1. El promotor o la sociedad vendedora, en su caso, deberán tener a disposición de los adquirentes extranjeros una traducción a un adioma que ellos entiendan, del contrato de compra y de los documentos que, con arreglo al artículo 5, deban entregarse o manifestarse a los adquirentes, así como del acta notarial mencionada en dicho artículo.

En caso de discrepancia entre la versión castellana y la extranjera prevalecerá siempre la primera.

2. Los extranjeros no residentes que celebren en España contratos de tiempo compartido sobre una vivienda situada en territorio español al amparo de un ordenamiento jurídico extranjero, podrán invocar el auxilio de las autoridades y tribunales españoles respecto de la aplicación de las normas españolas en materia de turismo y de protección de los consumidores.

**Article 17. Consumers' organisations**

The legally constituted organisations of consumers and users will have the right to receive copies of all documentation related to the timeshare project formulated by the developer with the object of verifying the fulfillment of all legal requirements, and to such effect their representatives may, with due authorisation, visit the offices of the developer and of the marketing company, as the case may be, and request from the persons responsible for the same information and documentation in this respect.

**Article 18. Guarantees in favour of foreign purchasers**

1. The developer or the marketing company must, if necessary, make available to foreign purchasers a translation into a language they understand of the purchase contract and of the documents which, according to Article 5, must be produced or handed over to the purchasers, as well as of the Notarial Act therein referred to.

In the case of any discrepancy between the Spanish and translated versions, the former will always prevail.

2. Foreign non residents signing timeshare contracts in Spain for properties located on Spanish territory governed by a foreign legislation may benefit from the protection of the Spanish authorities and Spanish Courts in order to apply Spanish regulations within the field of tourism and for consumer protection.

### Capitulo III   Aplicación de la normativa turística
### Chapter III   Application of tourism regulations

**Artículo 19.**

1. Todos los conjuntos inmobiliarios en régimen de tiempo compartido deberán cumplir las disposiciones en materia turística vigentes en la Comunidad Autónoma en que rediquen en lo referente a clasificación, inspección, publicidad, requisitos de apertura, y medidas de seguridad.

2. La sociedad de administración quedará sujeta en el desarrollo de sus actividades a la clasificación, disciplina, inspección y sanciones establecidas para las actividades turísticas en la legislación aplicable en la Comunidad Autónoma respectiva.

**Article 19.**

1. All the timeshare resorts must comply with the existing regulations for tourism of the corresponding Autonomous Communities, regarding classification, inspection, advertising, requirements for opening and security precautions.

2. The management company will be subject in all its activities to the regulations regarding classification, discipline, inspection and penalties established for tourist activities by the legislation of the Autonomous Community concerned.

## TITULO I—TITLE 1

### Garantía de la ocupación exclusiva, uso y disfrute de la vivienda
### Guarantee of exclusive occupation, use and enjoyment of the timeshare property

**Artículo 20.**

El promotor deberá garantizar el cumplimiento de su obligación de facilitar la ocupación exclusiva, uso y disfrute de las viviendas del conjunto inmobiliario en favor de todos los titulares de tiempo compartido mediante cualquiera de los medios siguientes o cualquier combinación de los mismos:

a) transmitiendo a cada adquirente, como parte del contenido del contrato, un derecho de propiedad por periodos o de usufructo por periodos sobre la vivienda objeto del contrato con arreglo a lo que se establece en el Capítulo I;

b) transmitiendo a cada adquirente, como parte del contenido del contrato, una acción de la sociedad propietaria del conjunto inmobiliario, con arreglo a lo que se dispone en el Capítulo II;

**Article 20.**

The developer must guarantee compliance with his obligation to provide exclusive occupation, use and enjoyment of the timeshare units to all the timeshare owners by any of the following methods or any combination of the following methods:

a) by, as part of the arrangements, transferring to each purchaser the right of ownership by periods or the usufruct by periods over the unit which is the object of the timeshare contract pursuant to Chapter 1.

b) by, as part of the arrangements, transferring to each purchaser of a timeshare period one share of the company owning the resort pursuant to Chapter II.

c) cediendo en prenda todas las acciones de la sociedad propietaria del conjunto inmobiliario en favor de la Asociación de titulares de tiempo compartido, como parte del contenido del contrato y de conformidad con lo dispuesto en el Capítulo III;

c) by, as part of the arrangements, pledging all the shares of the said owning company in favour of the Association of Timeshare Owners in accordance with Chapter III.

d) constituyendo, como parte del contenido del contrato, una hipoteca en favor de la Asociación de titulares, con arreglo a lo dispuesto en el Capítulo IV;

d) by, as part of the arrangements, granting a mortgage over the property in accordance with Chapter IV in favour of the Association of timeshare owners.

e) asegurando, como parte del contenido del contrato, mediante aval bancario o póliza de seguro, la devolución del precio total de compra más el interés legal del dinero en caso de incumplimiento por parte del Promotor, con arreglo a lo dispuesto en el Capítulo V.

e) by, as part of the arrangements, providing a bank guarantee or insurance policy insuring the full repayment of the full price plus interest at the legal rate in the event of default by the developer pursuant to Chapter V.

## Capítulo I    Propiedad y usufructo por periodos
## Chapter I    Ownership and usufruct by periods

### Artículo 21.    Disposiciones generales

### Article 21.    General regulations

1. En el régimen de propiedad o de usufructo por periodos la propiedad de la vivienda se distribuye en cincuenta y dos cuotas indivisas iguales, transmitiendo el promotor la propiedad o el usufructo de una de ellas por cada periodo de tiempo compartido contratado, junto con una cuota indivisa igual a una cincuenta y un ava parte de la cuota correspondiente a la semana destinada a arreglos anuales de la vivienda, que de esta forma pertenecerá por igual a todos los titulares. Las relaciones entre los propietarios o los usufructuarios se regirán por los estatutos previstos en el artículo 43, que tendrán el carácter de estatutos de la comunidad de propietarios y deberán inscribirse en el Registro de la Propiedad.

1. In the case of ownership or usufruct by periods ownership of the unit is divided in fifty two equal undivided parts, the developer transferring full ownership or usufruct of one of them for each weekly period of timeshare contracted for, together with an undivided portion equal to one fifty second part corresponding to the week destined for annual maintenance which in this way will belong equally to all timeshare owners. Relations between the owners or usufructuaries shall be governed by the statutes provided for in article 43, which shall have the nature of statutes of the community of owners, having to be registered in the Land Registry.

2. Cuando el contrato de tiempo compartido de lugar a la creación o transmisión de la propiedad o el usufructo por periodos deberá formalizarse exclusivamente por medio de escritura pública, en la que se hará constar expresamente al adquirente que la plena protección de su derecho se obtiene únicamente por medio de la inscripción de la misma en el Registro de la Propiedad.

3. El régimen de propiedad o de usufructo por periodos es compatible con el de propiedad horizontal.

4. La identificación de cada una de las cincuenta y una cuotas indivisas que pueden venderse individualmente se hará mediante cualquiera de los procedimientos establecidos en el artículo 5 que impidan que puedan venderse individualmente en ningún caso más de cincuenta y una por cada vivienda. El uso y disfrute exclusivo podrá no recaer sobre la vivienda objeto del derecho real, si así está previsto en los estatutos, pudiendo asimismo variar cada año el periodo de disfrute y ocupación exclusiva.

5. La celbración de la Junta de titulares de tiempo compartido podrá coincidir en el tiempo y en el espacio con las de las juntas de propietarios de las viviendas del conjunto inmobiliario.

6. Los copropietarios y los co-usufructuarios podrán acordar que la presidencia de las Comunidades corresponda a cualquiera de los copropietarios o co-usufructuarios de viviendas del conjunto inmobiliario y que todas las reuniones de las juntas de copropietarios coincidan y se celebren en el mismo acto. Podrán recaer sobre una misma persona los cargos de Presidente de la Asociación de titulares y de Presidente de todas o alguna de las comunidades de propietarios de las viviendas del conjunto inmobiliario.

2. Whenever the timeshare contract entails the creation or transmission of a right of ownership or usufruct by periods, it shall have to be executed by means of a public deed in which it shall be stated that the purchaser will only benefit from the full protection of the law by means of its registration in the Land Registry.

3. Ownership or usufruct by periods shall be compatible with 'horizontal ownership' schemes.

4. The identification of each of the fifty one undivided interests that can be sold separately shall be made in any of the forms provided for in article 5 which will prevent that more than fifty one such interests are separately sold in each unit. The exclusive use and enjoyment may not take place in the unit on which the real right has been established, if this possibility is contemplated in the statutes, it being equally possible that the period of exclusive occupation and use varies from year to year.

5. The celebration of a General Meeting of Timeshare Owners can coincide in time and space with the General Meeting of the Community of Owners of the resort.

6. The co-owners or the co-usufructuaries may resolve to allow that the Presidency of the Communities of owners falls on any of the co-owners or co-usufructuaries of units belonging to the same resort, and that all the General Meetings take place at the same time and in the same place. The same person may be appointed as President of the Association of Timeshare Owners and President of some or all the Communities of owners of units in the resort.

7. El los casos de mora en el pago de los gastos de comunidad, la sociedad de administración estará facultada para impedir la entrada en la vivienda al titular y a arrendarla durante el periodo respectivo en la forma prevista en el artículo 69. Asimismo, en los casos de falta de pago de dos anualidades consecutivas podrá procederse a la ejecución judicial con cargo al derecho de propiedad o de usufructo por periodos, y durante la tramitación de dicha ejecución podrá la sociedad de administración negar la entrada a la vivienda al titular.

7. In the event of delay in the payment of community charges, the management company shall have the authority to prevent the access to the unit and its occupation during the corresponding weekly period as provided for in article 69. It shall equally be possible, in the event of non payment of the annual charges during two consecutive years, to terminate judicially the right of ownership or usufruct and during the time it takes to complete the judicial procedure the management company shall have the authority to refuse access to the unit to the timeshare owner.

### Artículo 22.  Propiedad por periodos

### Article 22.  Ownership by periods

1. La propiedad por periodos de una vivienda integrada e un conjunto inmobiliario en régimen de tiempo compartido comporta el dominio sobre una cuota indivisa de la misma y el derecho exclusivo a la ocupación y disfrute durante un periodo de tiempo de cada año de la misma.

1. Ownership by periods of a unit belonging to a timeshare resort entails full ownership of an undivided portion of it together with the exclusive right to use and enjoy it during a certain period of time every year.

2. En la propiedad por periodos no tendrá lugar la acción divisoria ni el retracto de comuneros, dada la especial finalidad de la misma y la naturaleza del objeto sobre que recae.

2. In the case of ownership by periods there shall be no division rights nor preemption rights for the co-owners, given the special purpose of the scheme and the nature of the property on which it is set up.

3. El derecho de propiedad por periodos será hipotecable.

3. The right of ownership by periods can be mortgaged.

4. E. los casos de pago aplazado del precio de compra y en cualesquiera otros en los que el otorgamiento de la escritura de compra quede demorado por cualquier causa, las cantidades pagadas a cuenta por el comprador deberán quedar bloqueades en una cuenta bancaria establecida al efecto, a menos que el promotor haya contratado una póliza de seguro de caución que asegu-re el buen fin de todas las cantidades recibidas hasta el momento del otorgamiento de la escritura.

4. In the event of payment in installments as well as in all others in which the granting of the public deed is delayed for any reason, all amounts paid towards the total price shall be blocked in a special bank account to be opened for this purpose, unless the developer has obtained an insurance that guarantees the proper use of these funds until the moment of issuance of the public deed.

5. La extinción del proyecto de tiempo compartido configurado como propiedad por periodos sin limitación temporal sólo podrá acordarse por unanimidad de los titulares o por decisión judicial firme adoptada en interés de la comunidad a solicitud de la mayoría de los titulares que posean asimismo la mayoría de las cuotas de propiedad del conjunto inmobiliario.

5. The extinction of a timeshare scheme devised as multi-ownership for an unlimited period of time shall only take place by unanimous agreement of all the owners or by a firm Court injunction adopted for the common benefit of the respective community at the request of the majority of the co-owners representing as well the majority of the undivided rights of ownership of it.

**Artículo 23.   El usufructo por periodos**

**Article 23.   Usufruct for periods of time**

1. En el usufructo por periodos el usufructuario tendrá derecho a usar y disfrutar del inmueble objeto del mismo durante un periodo fijo del año a lo largo de un número determinado de años, que no podrá exceder de cincuenta, correspondiendo la nuda propiedad al promotor.

1. Where the usufruct for periods of time is concerned, the user will have the right to use and enjoy the property which is the object of the same over a fixed period of time during the year and over a determined number of years, which may not exceed fifty, the bare legal ownership corresponding to the developer.

2. En el usufructo por periodos no se aplicará la limitación del artículo 515 del Código civil.

2. The limitations expressed in article 515 of the Civil Code will not apply to the usufruct for periods of time.

3. El nudo propietario responderá ante los usufructuarios del cumplimiento de las responsabilidades de la sociedad de administración para con ellos con esta última.

3. The bare owner will be jointly liable with the management company for the provision of the services of the same.

4. El usufructo por periodos podrá constituirse èn favor de una o màs personas, quienes lo disfrutarán simultánea o sucesivamente. En el caso de Ilamamientos sucesivos al usufructo por periodos no habrá limitación en el número de Ilamamientos.

4. The usufruct can be created in favour of one or more persons, who may enjoy it either simultaneously or successively. In the case of successive calls to the usufruct, there will be no limitation to the number of such calls.

5. Las relaciones entre los usufructuarios por periodos estarán reguladas por unos estatutos que podrán formar parte integrante de los estatutos de la Asociación de titulares, regulados en el artículo 43.

5. The relations between the usufructuaries will be regulated by their statutes which may be included in the statutes of the Association of timeshare owners, referred to in article 43.

6. En la Junta de titulares el promotor, nudo propietario, tendrá derecho de asistencia y podrá participar en todas las deliberaciones, pero sólo le corresponderá el derecho de voto en los casos en que se trate de la enajenación o reforma estructural del inmueble. A los efectos de dicha votación exclusivamente, tendrá asignado el Promotor un número de votos inversamente proporcional al tiempo que quede hasta la extinción del usufructo, de forma que, teniendo en cuenta el número de votos correspondientes a los usufructuarios, los que correspondan al promotor representen un 30% al inicio del régimen de tiempo compartido y un 70% a final del mismo.

7. El derecho de usufructo por periodos se extinguirá por cualquiera de las causas de extinción del usufructo contempladas en el Código civil. Al extinguirse el derecho de usufructo por periodos la propiedad plena de la vivienda revertirá en favor del Promotor.

6. The developer, who holds the bare ownership of the resort, will have the right to attend General Meetings of Timeshare Owners, and to participate in all deliberations, although he will have the right to vote in cases concerning the sale or structural reform of the building. To the effects of such voting only, the developer will have assigned to him a number of votes inversally proportional to the time that remains until the expiry of the usufruct, in such a way that, taking into account the number of votes corresponding to all the users, those that will correspond to the developer will represent 30% at commencement of the usufruct and 70% at the end of it.

7. The right of usufruct over periods of time will be extinguished for any of the causes regarding usufruct expressed in the Civil Code. On expiry or termination of the right of usufruct, the property concerned will again come under full ownership of the developer.

## Capítulo II: Transmisión de acciones de la sociedad propietaria
## Chapter II: Transfer of shares of the owning company

### Artículo 24.

### Article 24.

El promoter podrá cumplir su obligación de asegurar a cada adquirente de tiempo compartido el uso y disfrute exclusivo de la vivienda a que se refiere el contrato de tiempo compartido mediante la transmisión a cada uno de ellos de una transmisión de la sociedad propietaria del conjunto inmobiliario por cada periodo de tiempo adquirido. Para ello será necesario que dicha sociedad reuna los siguientes requisitos:

The developer may comply with his obligation to guarantee to every timeshare purchaser the exclusive use and enjoyment of the timeshare property by means of the transfer to each one of them of a share of the company owning the resort for each timeshare period purchased. To this effect, it will be necessary that the aforementioned company fulfills the following requirements:

a) tratarse de una sociedad anónima.

a) to be a 'sociedad anónima'.

b) tener su capital íntegramente desembolsado y dividido en un número de acciones igual al de periodos de tiempo compartido en que pueda repartirse la totalidad de las viviendas del conjunto inmobiliario;

b) to have its stock capital divided into a number of shares equal to the number of timeshare periods into which the total number of timeshare units of the resort can be divided.

c) disponer en sus estatutos que la enajenación y gravámen de sus bienes inmuebles, así como la modificación de los estatutos, únicamente puede tener lugar previo acuerdo de la Junta General adoptado con el voto favorable de accionistas que representen al menos el 75% del capital;

d) disponer en sus estatutos que en caso de prenda de acciones, el ejercicio de los derechos políticos corresponderá en todo caso al acreedor pignoraticio.

e) disponer en sus estatutos que el órgano de administración no puede asumir deudas ni avalar deudas u obligaciones en nombre de la sociedad sin el consentimiento previo de la Junta General adoptado con las mismas ma yorías contempladas en el apartado c) del presente artículo.

f) ser propietaria del conjunto inmobiliario en pleno dominio y libre de cargas y gravámenes.

g) no tener deuda alguna pendiente ni haber prestado garantía de ninguna clase en favor de teceros ni de sus socios hasta el momento de la celebración del primer contrato de tiempo compartido.

**Artículo 25.**

1. Cuando el Promotor tenga el propósito de transmitir a los adquirentes de tiempo compartido las acciones de la sociedad propietaria del conjunto inmobiliario, a los documentos que deben protocolizarse notarialmente de conformidad con lo dispuesto en el artículo 5 deberán añadirse los siguientes:

a) el documento justificativo de haberse cumplido con todos los requisitos establecidos por la Ley del Mercado de Valores para poder llevar a cabo la oferta pública de venta de las acciones de la sociedad propietaria del conjunto inmobiliario;

c) to include in its bye-laws the condition that the sale and encumbrance of its immovable properties, as well as the amendment of the statutes, may only take place with the previous consent of the General Meeting of Shareholders, given with the favourable vote of at least 75% of the stock capital.

d) to determine in its bye-laws that in the case of a pledge of shares, the exercise of political rights will correspond in all cases to the pledge creditor.

e) to determine in its bye-laws that the Board of Directors or the managers of the company may not assume debts or obligations in the name of the company without previous consent of the General Shareholders' Meeting, the same rules applying to the vote in favour as in point c) of the present article.

f) to have full ownership of the resort, free of charges and encumbrances.

g) not to have any outstanding debt, nor have given any kind of securities to a third party or to its shareholders up to the time of signature of the first timeshare contract.

**Article 25.**

1. Where the developer intends to transfer the shares of the owning company to the purchasers of timeshares, the following documents have to be added to the list of those to be notarised in accordance with the conditions expressed in article 5:

a) Proof of compliance with all the requirements established by the stock-market legislation for permission to carry out a public sale of shares of the owning company.

b) el documento en el que se formalice la prenda de todas las acciones de dicha sociedad en favor de la Asociación de titulares, en garantía del cumplimieno de la obligación de facilitar la ocupación exclusiva, uso y disfrute de cada una de las viviendas del conjunto inmobiliario. En dicho documento deberá figurar expresamente la aceptación del depósito y de todas sus obligaciones formulada por la entidad bancaria o de seguros a que se refiere el artículo siguiente;

c) copia de los estatutos de la sociedad propietaria del inmueble en los que figurarán expresamente los extremos mencionados en los apartados a, b, c, d y e del artículo anterior;

d) balance de la sociedad proietaria del conjunto inmobiliario, del que resulte la inexistencia de deudas y la presencia del mismo como único activo, debidamente auditado;

e) declaración escrita del promotor de que la sociedad no ha prestado garantía alguna ni tiene ningún pasivo oculto.

f) copia del contrato de arrendamiento del conjunto inmobiliario a la Asociación de titulares, a que se refiere el artículo 28 y del aval prestado por el Promotor.

**Artículo 26.**

El promotor deberá asimismo dar en prenda las acciones de la sociedad poipietaria del conjunto inmobiliario para garantizar a la asociación de titulares el cumplimiento de sus obligaciones.

La prenda sobre las acciones de la sociedad propietaria del conjunto inmobiliario deberá comportar su depósito en una entidad bancaria o de seguros, quien asumirá el ejercicio de los derechos políticos de las mismas en la sociedad hasta su extinción, asumiendo la obligación de no permitir la enajenación ni el gravámen del conjunto inmobiliario.

b) A document in which is recorded the pledge of shares of the said company in favour of the Association of Timeshare Owners as guarantee of compliance of the obligation to provide the exclusive right of occupation of each of the timeshare properties of the resort. Such document must also contain the express acceptance of the deposit and of all obligations expressed by the bank or insurance company referred to in the following article.

c) Copies of the bye-laws of the owning company, in which are expressly stated the details given in points a), b), c), d) and e) of the above article.

d) Balance sheet and accounts of the owning company, demonstrating the absence of debts and that the resort is its only asset, duly audited.

e) Written declaration by the developer that the company has not given any securities nor has any liabilities.

f) Copy of the lease contract for the resort in favour of the Association of Timeshare Owners, as referred to in article 28, and the guarantee given by the developer.

**Article 26.**

The developer shall equally pledge all the shares of the Company owning the resort as guarantee to the association of timeshare owners for the proper compliance with all his obligations.

The pledge of shares of the owning company must entail their deposit in a bank or insurance company, who will assume the exercise of political rights of the same in the company until its expiry, with the obligation not permit the sale or encumbrance of the resort.

**Artículo 27.**

La prenda a que se refiere el artículo anterior quedará liberada respecto de cada una de las acciones, en el momento de su adquisición por uno de los titulares de tiempo compartido, quien se integrará en el mismo acto a la Asociación de titulares.

**Artículo 28.**

La sociedad propietaria deberá arrendar el conjunto inmobiliario a la Asociación de titulares por tiempo igual al de la duración del proyecto inmobiliario. El Promotor deberá avalar la obligación del pago de la renta asumida por la Asociación, hasta que concluya la venta de las acciones de la compañia propietaria.

**Artículo 29.**

En el caso de quiebra o insolvencia del promotor no podrá acordarse la disolución de la sociedad propietaria del inmueble a menos que se reembolse previamente a los titulares de acciones de la misma el mismo importe pagado por ellos para su adquisición disminuido únicamente en el importe estimado de la ocupación y disfrute de la vivienda respectiva desde la adquisición de la acción.

**Article 27.**

The pledge of shares referred to in the respect to each of the shares, at the above article will be released with moment of their purchase by one of the timeshare owners, who will thereby become a member of the Association of Timeshare Owners.

**Article 28.**

The owning company must rent the resort to the Association of Timeshare Owners for a length of time which is equal to that of the duration of the timeshare scheme. The developer must guarantee the obligation to pay the rent assumed by the Association until the sale of shares of the company is concluded.

**Article 29.**

In the case of bankruptcy or insolvency of the developer, it will not be permissible to dissolve the owning company unless previous payment is made to the shareholders of the same of a sum equal to that paid by them for their purchase, only deducting from such sum the estimated amount for occupation and enjoyment of the respective property from the time of purchase of the share.

## Capítulo III: prenda de las acciones de la sociedad propietaria
## Chapter III: Pledge of the shares of the owning company

**Artículo 30.**

El promotor podrá cumplir su obligación de asegurar a cada adquirente de tiempo compartido el uso y disfrute exclusivo de la vivienda a que se refiere el contrato de tiempo compartido constituyendo sobre la totalidad de las acciones de la sociedad propietaria del conjunto inmobiliario una prenda en favor de la Asociación de titulares.

**Article 30.**

The developer may comply with his obligation to guarantee to each purchaser of timeshares the exclusive use and enjoyment of the property referred to in the timeshare contract by constituting a pledge in favour of the Association of Timeshare Owners for all the shares in the owning company.

En tal caso la sociedad propietaria del conjunto inmobiliario deberá reunir los mismos requisitos establecidos en el artículo 24 y el Promotor deberá cumplir asimismo lo dispuesto en los artículos 25 y 26.

In such a case, the owning company must fulfil the same requirements established in article 24, and the developer must fulfil those established in articles 25 and 26.

**Artículo 31.**

**Article 31.**

La entidad bancaria o de seguros que acepte el depósito de las acciones asumirá asimismo el control del órgano de administración de la sociedad propietaria del conjunto inmobiliario.

The bank or insurance company accepting the deposit of shares assumes thereby the control of the Board of Directors of the owning company.

**Artículo 32.**

**Article 32.**

La prenda de las acciones deberá mantenerse en existencia hasta el momento de extinción del régimen de tiempo compartio o hasta su ejecución en caso de incumplimiento por el Promotor de su obligación de facilitar la ocupación exclusiva, uso y disfrute de cada vivienda objeto de contratos de tiempo compartido.

The pledge of shares must be kept up to the moment of expiry of the timeshare scheme or until its execution in the case of default by the developer of his obligation to provide exclusive use and enjoyment of each timeshare unit which is the object of the timeshare contracts.

## Capítulo IV    Hipoteca del conjunto inmobiliario
## Chapter IV    Mortgage of the resort

**Artículo 33.**

**Article 33.**

1. El Promotor podrá cumplir su obligación de asegurar a cada adquirente de tiempo compartido el uso y disfrute exclusivo de la vivienda a que se refiere el contrato de tiempo compartido constituyendo una hipoteca en favor de la Asociación de titulares sobre el inmueble objeto del proyecto de tiempo compartido, por importe equivalente al valor total de venta estimado de los derechos de tiempo compartido que vayan a ser vendidos por aquel, que permanecerá en vigor durante todo el tiempo de existencia de la obligación citada.

1. The developer may fulfil his obligation to guarantee to each timeshare purchaser the exclusive use and enjoyment of the timeshare property referred to in the Timeshare Contract by constituting in favour of the Association of timeshare owners a guarantee secured by mortgage over the property which is the object of the obligation for the total estimated sales value of all timeshare interests to be sold by the developer in respect of the property and for the total period during which the right originating from the said obligation is to have legal effect.

2. La Asociación de titulares estará facultada para revisar el importe de la hipoteca y el Promotor estará obligado, si así lo solicita la Asociación, a ampliar la hipoteca hasta dicho importe.

2. The Association of timeshare owners will be empowered to review the amount of the mortgage and the developer will be obliged, if the Association so requires, to increase the amount of the mortgage.

3. El importe de la hipoteca no podrá ser inferior al valor del conjunto inmobiliario al tiempo de otorgarse la escritura pública a que se refiere el artículo 5.

3. The value of the mortgage may not be less than the value of the property at the date of the Notarial Deed envisaged by Article 5.

4. El Promotor estará facultado para repercutis sobre los titulares la parte proporcional de los impuestos y gastos originados por el otorgamiento de la hipoteca y por las sucesivas ampliaciones de la misma. En el supuesto de sucesivas ampliaciones podrá exigir el Promotor como condición previa para atender al requerimiento de la Asociación que ésta presente aval bancario que garantice el pago de los citados impuestos y gastos.

4. The developer will be entitled to charge the timeshare owners with a proportionate part of the taxes and expenses originated by the guarantee and any subsequent increases in the value of the mortgage, and in the case of subsequent increases may as a pre-condition of complying with the requirement demand that the Association of Timeshare Owners provide a bank guarantee for payment of the said taxes and expenses.

## Capítulo V   aval bancario o póliza de seguro
## Chapter V   Bank guarantee or insurance policy

### Artículo 34.

### Article 34.

1. El Promotor podrá cumplir su obligación de asegurar a cada adquirente de tiempo compartido el uso y disfrute exclusivo de la vivienda a que se refiere el contrato de tiempo compartido mediante aval bancario o póliza de seguro que garantice la devolución a cada titular de tiempo compartido de la totalidad del precio pagado incrementada con el interés legal, sin más deducción que la correspondiente a los periodos de uso y disfrute transcurridos hasta el momento del incumplimiento por parte del Promotor. A los efectos del presente artículo se entiende por incumplimiento la falta grave y material por parte del Promotor de sus obligaciones en el contrato de tiempo compartido.

1. The developer may fulfil his obligation to guarantee to each timeshare purchaser the exclusive use and enjoyment of the timeshare property referred to in the timeshare contract by means of a bank guarantee or an insurance policy, which guarantees the reimbursement to each timeshare owner of the total sum paid plus legal interest, without any deduction other than that corresponding to the periods of use and enjoyment that may have elapsed up to the moment of default by the developer. For the purpose of this clause default shall mean substantial and material default by the developer in performing his written obligations as set out in the Timeshare sales contract.

2. En tal caso, el Promotor deberá añadir copia de dicho aval o póliza a la documentación que debe protocolizar notarialmente con arreglo a lo dispuesto en el artículo 5.

2. In this case, the developer must include a copy of such guarantee or insurance policy to the list of documents accompanying the declaration to be notarised as provided for in article 5.

3. El aval o la póliza podrán ser sustituidos en cualquier momento por cualquiera de las demás garantías del cumplimiento de las obligaciones del Promotor previstas en el artículo 20.

3. The guarantee or insurance may be terminated in the event of any of the other methods of guaranteeing the developer's obligation envisaged by Article 20 being substituted.

## TITULO II – TITLE II

### Capítulo I  Garantías del cumplimiento de la obligación de administrar y mantener el conjunto inmobiliario
### Chapter I  Guarantees of the fulfillment of the obligation to administrate and maintain the resort

**Artículo 35.**

**Article 35.**

1. El Promotor será responsable del mantenimiento y administración del conjunto inmobiliario desde el momento de la protocolización notarial del documento a que se refiere el artículo 5.

1. The developer will be responsible for the upkeep and administration of the resort from the moment of the notarisation of the document referred to in article 5.

2. Esta obligación irá pasando paulatinamente a los titulares de tiempo compartido a medida que se vayan celebrando contratos de tiempo compartido sobre todos los periodos en que puede dividirse el conjunto inmobiliario.

2. This obligation will be gradually passed on to the timeshare owners as the timeshare contracts are be signed for all time periods into which the resort may be divided.

3. Para asegurar el cumplimiento de esta obligación, el Promotor deberá contratar los servicios de mantenimiento y administración del conjunto inmobiliario a una sociedad que habrá de reunir los requisitos establecidos por la presente Ley, tal como se dispone en el artículo siguiente.

3. In order to ensure the fulfillment of this obligation, the developer must contract the services of a management that meets the requirements established by the present law which will take care of the maintenance and administration of the resort, as is provided for in the next article.

4. Asimismo deberá el Promotor constituir con los primeros titulares de tiempo compartido una Asociación encargada del gobierno del régimen de tiempo compartido desde su constitución hasta su extinción y en la que estarán integrados todos los titulares.

4. In addition, the developer must constitute with the first timeshare owners an Association responsible for the control of the timesharing scheme from its commencement until its termination and to which all the timeshare owners will belong.

**Artículo 36.**

1. El promotor, antes de comenzar la comercialización del conjunto inmobiliario en régimen de tiempo compartido, y como requisito indispensable para ello, deberá contratar con una de las sociedades reguladas en el presente capítulo la administración del conjunto inmobiliario. El adquirente podrá resolver el contrato de tiempo compartido dentro de los treinta días siguientes a la fecha prevista en el mismo para el comienzo de uso y disfrute de la vivienda respectiva, si llegada esta fecha la sociedad de administración no hubiere iniciado la prestación de sus servicios.

El promotor será responsable de la administración mantenimiento y reparación de las instalaciones comunes del conjunto, de las viviendas que lo integran y del mobiliario de los mismos hasta el momento en que la sociedad de administración comience la prestación de los mismos.

2. La sociedad de administración deberá revestir la forma de sociedad anónima y su capital social, que no podrá ser inferior a cincuenta millones de pesetas, deberá estar íntegramente desembolsado.

3. La sociedad de administración deberá prestar sus servicios durante el periodo convenido en el respectivo contrato, que no podrá ser inferior a cinco años. Al término del plazo convenido, si no hubiese sido renovado el contrato ni se hubiese contratado la prestación de los servicios de administración y mantenimiento del conjunto inmobiliario con otra sociedad de administración, la que los estuviera prestando deberá seguir haciéndolo durante un máximo de tres meses. En tal caso y durante dicho plazo la sociedad de administración que vencido su contrato continúe por virtud de lo preceptuado por este artículo en la prestación de los servicios percibirá la remuneración del ejercicio inmediato anterior actualizada conforme a la variación que haya experimentatdo el índice de precios al consumo, subgrupo de servicios de hostelería.

**Article 36.**

1. The developer, before the start of the marketing of the resort, and as prerequisite for it, must contract with one of the companies governed by the provisions of this chapter the administration of the resort. The purchaser shall able to cancel the timeshare contract within thirty days from the date given in the same for the commencement of use and enjoyment of the timeshare unit, should the management company not have begun to render its services by that date.

The developer will be responsible for the administration, maintenance and repairs of the general installations of the resort, the units included in it and the furniture of the same up to the time when the management company begins to render its services.

2. The management company must adopt the form of a 'sociedad anónima' and its stock capital, which may not be of less than fifty million Pesetas, must be completely paid up.

3. The management company must render it services over the agreed period of time stated in the respective contract which may not be less than five years. On termination of the agreed period of time, if the contract has not been renewed nor a services contract signed with another management company, then the company that has been rendering these services must continue to do so over a maximum period of three months. In such case, and for the aforementioned period of time, the company that has continued to render services after the expiry of its contract by virtue of what is expressed in this article will receive payment to this effect, taking into account any changes in the consumer index relating to hotel services.

El mismo procedimiento se aplicará en el supuesto de que la sociedad de administración decidiera poner término al contrato antes del término contemplado en el mismo, en caso de incumplimiento grave por parte de la Asociación de Titulares.

The same procedure will be followed in the event of the resignation of the management company before the end of the period contemplated in the contract in the event of substantial and material default by the Association of Timeshare Owners.

**Artículo 37.**

**Article 37.**

1. La sociedad de administración será responsable del empleo correcto de los fondos recibidos para tal fin y en general para el cuidado, mantenimiento, conservación y administración del conjunto inmobiliario y la gestión de los intereses comunes de los titulares en relación con el mismo, ateniéndosea los acuerdos e instrucciones de la Junta y del Presidente, dentro de los términos de su contrato, que deberá atribuirle como mínimo la responsabilidad de la organización necesaria para la prestación de las siguientes funciones:

1. The management company is responsible for utilising the money received by it for that purpose in or towards the care, upkeep, maintenance and administration of the resort, and for the management of common interests of the owners in respect of the same, according to the resolutions and the instructions of the General Meeting and the President, within the terms of its contract, which must assign to the said company at least the responsibility for making proper arrangements for the provision of the following duties:

a) la aprobación y modificación de reglamentos de régimen interior;

a) Approval and amendments of the internal regulations of the resort.

b) la preparación del presupuesto anual de ingresos y gastos del conjunto inmobiliario en régimen de tiempo compartido.

b) Preparation of an annual budget covering income and expenditures of the resort.

c) el cobro de las cuotas anuales a los titulares, así como de cualquier otra cantidad que éstos o terceras personas hayan de pagar en aplicación de los Estatutos y la expedición de los correspondientes recibos y certificaciones;

c) Collection of annual payments from the owners, and also any other quantity that they or any third party might have to pay in accordance to the statutes and to issue the corresponding receipts or certificates.

d) el pago, por cuenta de los titulares, con los fondos destinados a la administración que estén en su poder o bajo su control, del importe de los suministros, impuestos, contribuciones y cualesquiera otros gastos que con carácter periódico deban ser satisfechos por aquellos o recaigan sobre la propiedad.

d) Payment, on behalf of the timeshare owners from any management funds in its possession or under its control, of the total cost of services, taxes, contributions and any other expenses that must be paid periodically by the timeshare owners or which are charged to the resort.

e) la contratación en nombre de la Asociación de Titulares o del promotor o de la persona o entidad designada a tal efecto, del personal necesario para la prestación de los servicios que le corresponden;

e) The contracting in the name of the Association of Timeshare Owners or the developer or any third party appointed for that purpose, of the necessary personnel for the rendering of the services for which it is responsible.

f) la celebración en nombre de la Asociación de Titulares o del promotor o de la persona o entidad designada a tal efecto, de los contratos de suministro necesarios para el normal funcionamiento del conjunto inmobiliario. El otorgamiento del contrato de administración llevará consigo el apoderamiento en favor de la sociedad de administración para celebrar en nombre de la asociación de titulares estos contratos que habrán de quedar especificados en el mismo apoderamiento;

g) el mantenimiento, reparación, y sustitución de las instalaciones y mobiliario del conjunto, y la ejecución de las mejoras acordadas por la Junta, que deberán realizarse durante los periodos anuales previstos para cada vivienda en el documento a que se refiere el artículo 5, salvo en caso de urgencia o necesidad, en que se aplicará lo dispuesto en la letra siguiente;

h) la adopción de medidas urgentes y ejecución de obras de conservación y reposición extraordinarias, dando cuenta al Presidente y ateniéndose a las determinaciones que éste o la Junta, en su caso, adopten al respecto;

i) el ejercicio de la facultad sancionadora respecto de los usuarios del conjunto inmobiliario de acuerdo con lo establecido en los Estatutos;

j) el ejercicio de cualesquiera otras facultades atribuidas por los Estatutos o encomendadas por la Junta;

k) la contratación en nombre de la asociación de titulares de seguros de daños y de responsabilidad civil exigidas por el artículo 15.

l) la determinación, para los titulares de tiempo compartido en las modalidades de espacio o tiempo flotante, de las viviendas específicas o de los periodos concretos de ocupación exclusiva que les corresponderán cada año.

f) The execution in the name of the Association of Timeshare Owners or the developer or any third party appointed for that purpose, of contracts for the provision of all the services required for the normal functioning of the resort. The granting of the management contract will also include a power in favour of the management company to sign in the name of the Association of Timeshare Owners contracts that are to be specified within the same abovementioned power.

g) The upkeep, repairs and replacement of the equipment and furniture of the resort, and the carrying out of improvements agreed by the General Meeting, these having to be carried out during the annual periods as foreseen for each timeshare unit in the document referred to in article 5, except in the case of urgency or extreme need, in which case the provisions of the following letter (h) applies:

h) The adoption of urgent measures and the carrying out of extra works for conservation and replacement, informing the President and abiding by his decisions or those of the General Meeting, as the case may be, in this respect.

i) The exercise of the faculty to impose penalties to the users of the resort in accordance with the provisions of the Statutes.

j) The exercise of any other powers attributed by the Statutes or granted by the General Meeting.

k) To contract in the name of the Association of Timeshare Owners the insurance against damage and civil liability as required by article 15.

l) In the case of floating space or time, to allocate to each timeshare owner the specific unit and/or weekly periods of exclusive occupation corresponding to them each year.

2. Para el desempeño de sus funciones la sociedad de administración tendrá acceso al libro de actas y al libro-registro o a cualquier otra base de información de los titulares Ilevados por el Secretario.

2. For the fulfillment of its tasks, the management company will have access to the book of Acts and to the registry book or other records of the identity of timeshare owners, which are held by the Secretary.

3. La sociedad de administración no será responsable respecto de las cuotas anuales no pagadas por los titulares de tiempo compartido.

3. The management company shall not be responsible for any deficiencies deriving from annual fees not paid by the timeshare owners.

**Artículo 38.**

**Article 38.**

La Sociedad de administración someterá anualmente a auditoría las cuentas de la Asociación de titulares. El resultado de dicha auditoría estará a disposición del Presidente y de los titulares para su examen con quince días como mínimo de antelación a la celebración de ¹a Junta Ordinaria, y en todo caso se someterá a la misma.

The management company will submit for audit on an annual basis the accounts of the Association of Timeshare Owners. The results of such audit shall be available to the President and the timeshare owners for their examination, at least fifteen days before the General Meeting of Shareholders, and in any case they will be presented at the meeting.

**Artículo 39.**

**Article 39.**

1. El promotor deberá contratar los servicios de la sociedad de administración por un periodo mínimo de cinco años. El contrato se renovará automáticamente por periodos de cinco años, a menos que la Junta de titulares acuerde su extinción con un preaviso de seis meses de antelación a término del periodo que corresponda, o que la sociedad de administración decida terminar el contrato antes del término previsto, dando para ello un preaviso de tres meses.

1. The developer may contract the services of the management company for a minimum period of five years. The contract will be renewed automatically for periods of five years, unless the General Meeting of Timeshare Owners agree to its termination giving six months notice before the end of the corresponding period or the management company decides to terminate the contract before the agreed term giving three months notice.

2. No obstante lo dispuesto en el apartado anterior, en caso de incumplimiento grave del mismo, el contrato de administración podrá ser resuelto en cualquier momento por acuerdo de la Junta de titulares, cesando la sociedad de administración en sus funciones, sin perjuicio de la determinación y exigencia de responsabilidades que podrá llevarse a efecto después de dichos cese y resolución del contrato. A los efectos de este artículo se entiende por incumplimiento grave la no prestación o la prestación gravemente deficiente de los servicios mínimos contratados.

La Junta, al acordar la resolución del contrato y el cese de la sociedad de administración, deberá encomendar al Presidente o a un comité designado al efecto la selección de una nueva entidad.

Hasta que tenga lugar dicha designación el Presidente o el comité deberán asumir transitoriamente las obligaciones propias de la misma y en especial contratar la prestación de los servicios mínimos a una o varias empresas o personas capaces de asumir sus funciones sin solución de continuidad respecto de las de la sociedad cesada.

**Artículo 40.**

Antes de entrar a prestar los servicios a que se refiere el artículo 21 la Sociedad de administración, si su capital social desembolsado es inferior a la cifra de cincuenta millones de pesetas deberá presentar un aval bancario o una póliza de caución por importe equivalente al de las cuotas anuales de gastos que puede recaudar en el año siguiente año, en beneficio e interés de la asociación de titulares, para responder de cualesquiera responsabilidades derivadas de su gestión. En caso de renovación o prórroga del contrato dicho aval o póliza deberán ser actualizados.

2. Notwithstanding what is provided for in the above paragraph, in the case of a serious breach of contract the management contract may be cancelled at any moment by resolution of the General Meeting of Timeshare Owners and the management company will cease in the provision of its services, without prejudice to the assessment of liabilities incurred and the right to ask for their compensation after the end of the provision of services and cancellation of the contract. For the purpose of this article, it will be considered as serious breach the failure to render or a serious deficiency in the rendering of the minimum services contracted.

The General Meeting must request, when resolving to cancel management contract and to cease the functions of the management company, that the President or a committee appointed for this purpose select a new management company.

Until the said selection and appointment takes place, the President or the committee will temporarily take over the obligations of the same, in particular the contracting of minimal services by one or more persons or companies fit to carry out such tasks so that the said services are rendered without interruption from those of the removed company.

**Article 40.**

Before commencement of services to which article 21 refers, the management company, if it does not have a paid up capital of at least fifty million pesetas, must present a bank guarantee or an insurance policy for an amount equivalent to that of the expected annual charges to be collected over the next year, for the benefit and interest of the Association of Timeshare Owners, in order to discharge its liabilities during the time of provision of its services. In the event of the said contract being renewed or extended, the aforementioned guarantee or insurance policy must be equally renewed or extended.

**Artículo 41.**

Podrá acordarse con la sociedad de administración que, como retribución por sus servicios, explote, mientras presta los mismos, determinados locales, elementos, instalaciones o servicios comunes del conjunto.

**Article 41.**

It will be possible to authorise the management company, in compensation for its services, to use for its own benefit and for the duration of its services to the resort certain shops, elements, installations and communal services of the resort.

## Capítulo II. Gobierno del conjunto inmobiliario
## Chapter II. Control of the resort

### Sección primera. Disposiciones generales
### First section. General regulations

**Artículo 42.  La asociación de titulares. Constitución, órganos, carácter democrático y servicios mínimos**

**Article 42.  The Association of Timeshare Owners. Constitution, Democratic Character and Minimum Services**

1. E. gobierno del conjunto inmobiliario corresponde a la Asociación de titulares. Serán órganos de la misma, la Junta de titulares, el Presidente y el Secretario. En los Estatutos de la asociación pueden preverse, además, Junta Directiva, Tesorero u otros órganos de gobierno, sin menoscabo de los poderes y facultades de los órganos que la Ley establece.

1. The task of controlling the timeshare scheme will be the responsibility of the Association of Timeshare Owners which will be governed by a President and a Secretary. The Statutes of the Association may also provide for an Executive Committee, a Treasurer and other governing bodies, without detriment to the powers and faculties of the bodies established by the law.

2. La asociación de titulares, a la que pertenecerán todos los titulares de tiempo compartido, se constituirá entre el promotor, y dos al menos de los titulares de tiempo compartido, y se adherirán a la misma los sucesivos adquirentes al tiempo de celebrar el contrato de tiempo compartido. El funcionamiento de la asociación responderá en todo caso a principios democráticos y de respeto a las minorías. Dentro de los primeros dieciocho meses de existencia la Asociacion deberá renovar los cargos de Presidente y Secretario así como dos tercios de los puestos del Comite, caso de existir éste.

2. The Association of Timeshare Owners, to which all the timeshare owners shall belong, will be formed by the developer and at least two of the timeshare owners, who will ensure that all successive purchasers of timeshares will be included in the above once they have signed the timeshare contract. The functioning of the Association will respect in all cases democratic principles and minority rights. Within the first eighteen months of existence the Association shall have to renew its President and Secretary, as well as to thirds of the members of the Committee if it exists.

3. En interés de todos los titulares, el contenido de los servicios mínimos establecidos al constituirse el proyecto de tiempo compartido no podrá ser reducido más que por acuerdo adoptado por la Junta de titulares con las mayorías y requisitos exigidos para acordar la extinción del régimen de tiempo compartido.

**Artículo 43. Estatutos que rigen la asociación titulares**

1. La composición y el funcionamiento de los órganos de gobierno de la asociación de titulares, a adquisición, transmisión y pérdida de la condición de miembro de la misma, sus derechos y obligaciones, y su régimen disciplinario, se regularán, cualquiera que sea la modalidad del contrato de tiempo compartido, et unos estatutos, que podrán formar parte, en su caso, de los estatutos de la sociedad propietaria del inmueble o de los de la comunidad de propietarios del mismo, y en los que como mínimo deberán constar:

a) las normas sobre la adquisición, transmisión y extinción de la condición de titular de uno o más periodos de tiempo compartido;

b) la modalidad del contrato de tiempo compartido con indicación expresa de si comporta la adquisición de algún derecho real;

c) los derechos y obligaciones de los titulares, con especial referencia al pago de cuotas anuales y a la responsabilidad por daños;

d) los órganos de administración y control del conjunto de la asociación de titulares, su composición, los criterios para la elección de sus miembros, funciones, el régimen de impugnación de acuerdos de la asociación, los criterios por la atribución de votos, las reglas de representación, las reglas de la convocatoria y para la cobertura de vacantes;

e) las sanciones por incumplimiento de las obligaciones estatutarias; la competencia para su imposición; y las garantías y el procedimiento;

3. In the interest of all timeshare owners, the contents of the minimum ∘ervices established on incorporation of the timeshare scheme may not be reduced other than by resolution of the General Meeting of timeshare owners, adopted with the same formalities required for the termination of the timeshare scheme.

**Article 43. Statutes governing the Association of Timeshare Owners**

1. The composition and functioning of the governing bodies of the Association of Timeshare Owners, as well as the acquisition, transfer and loss of the quality of member of the same, the members' rights and obligations, and their disciplinary regime, will be governed, whatever form the timeshare contract may take, by its statutes, which can be included in those of the owning company of the resort or of the community of owners of the same, as the case might be. The statutes have to include at least the following:

a) The regulations regarding acquisition, transfer and expiry of the ownership of one or more timeshare periods.

b) The form of timeshare contract, expressly indicating whether the purchase entails the acquisition of a real right.

c) The rights and obligations of the owners, with special reference to the payment of annual charges and liability for damages.

d) The bodies of administration and control of the association of owners, its composition, the criteria for the election of its members, tasks, the regime for the exception to the agreements of the association, the criteria for the distribution of votes, rules of representation, rules for notice of meetings and for cover of vacancies.

e) Penalties for failure to fulfil statutory obigations, capacity for imposing these, and guarantees and procedures.

f) en el caso de que se prevea la posibilidad de ampliar el conjunto inmobiliario en régimen de tiempo compartido, o sus instalaciones recreativas o deportivas de uso común, la indicación de la fórmula o criterios con arreglo a los que se calcularán el importe máximo en que podrá incrementarse la cuota anual de gastos como consecuencia de ello, o la indicación expresa de que tal ampliación no determinará incremento alguno de la misma.

g) La descripción de las demás zonas o instalaciones de uso común no sólo para los titulares del proyecto de tiempo compartido, sino para otras personas, cuyo uso requiera el pago de alguna cantidad por los titulares o por la comunidad, sociedad o asociación en que estén organizados.

h) En el caso de que el uso de alguna de las instalaciones o zonas comunes por los titulares del proyecto de tiempo compartido esté condicionado al pago de un alquiler o comporte la afiliación a una asociación por parte de cada uno, se hará mención de ello en caracteres de imprenta claramente legibles y con indicación en su caso de si la afiliación a tales asociaciones resulta obligatoria o automático para cada titular. En tal caso, si resulta asimismo obligatorio el pago de alguna cuota de socio deberá hacerse constar en los mismos caracteres de imprenta claramente legibles. Deberá también indicarse el lugar y forma de acceso a toda la información disponible acerca de la organización de la asociación y sus correspondientes estatuos.

2. El promotor estará obligado a facilitar una copia de los estatutos por los que se rigen las relaciones entre los titulares a cada adquirente en el momento de la formalización del contrato de tiempo compartido.

f) When the possibility of expanding the resort, or its recreational or sports facilities for common use is contemplated, the indication of the form or criteria to be used to calculate the maximum increase in the annual expenses that such expansion can produce, or the express indication that it will not entail an increase in expenses.

g) Description of any further areas or facilities that may be of common use not only for the timeshare owners, but also for other persons, which use will entail payment of a certain price by the timeshare owners, the community of owners, or the company or association under which they are organised.

h) In the event that the use of any of the facilities or communal areas by one of the timeshare owners being conditioned to the payment of a rent or membership of a club, this fact shall be referred to in clear print indicating, where necessary, whether the membership of such club is obligatory or automatic for each timeshare owner. If that were the case, if the membership would imply the obligation to pay an annual fee this fact should be equally indicated in the same print. It shall be equally indicated the place and form of access to all the information available regarding the statutes of the Association and its organisation.

2. The developer will be under obligation to make available to each purchaser, at the time of execution of the timeshare contract a copy of the statutes governing the relations between the members of such club or association.

## Sección segunda. La Junta de titulares
## Second Section.   The General Meeting of Timeshare Owners

### Artículo 44.   Composición y competencia

La Junta es el órgano supremo de deliberación y decisión de la asociación de titulares. Está integrada por todos los titulares de periodos de tiempo compartido en el conjunto inmobiliario, así como por el promotor del proyecto en relación con los periodos de tiempo compartido que no hayan sido aún objeto de contrato. Le corresponde la adopción de las principales decisiones relacionadas con el conjunto imobiliario y con el régimen de derecho compartido no atribuidas expresamente a otros órganos.

No podrán existir derechos de voto en relación con las viviendas del conjunto inmobiliario que no estén terminadas.

### Artículo 45.   Convocatoria

1. El. Presidente de la Junta convocará la misma en las ocasiones que impongan la Ley o los Estatutos o cuando lo estime oportuno. Los titulares que representen al menos un 10% de los periodos de tiempo compartido del conjunto inmobiliario podrán pedir al Presidente la convocatoria si hubiere causa razonable para ello, y si no fueran atendidos, podrán acudir al Juez quien, oído el Presidente, decidirá.

En los casos de vacante o de imposibilidad del Presidente o de quien haga sus veces, podrá convocar la Junta el Secretario a solicitud de los titulares que representen al menos un 10% de los periodos de tiempo compartido.

2. En la convocatoria se expresarán los asuntos a tratar y el día, hora y lugar de la reunión, que habrá de efectuarse dentro del municipio en que se encuentra el conjunto inmobiliario, a menos que se haya establecido otra cosa en los Estatutos o se haya acordado así por la Junta.

### Article 44.   Composition and Competence

The General Meeting is the supreme body for deliberation and decision of the Association of Timeshare Owners. It is composed of all the timeshare owners in the same resort, as well as the developer in relation to the timeshare periods which have not yet been sold. The General Meeting of Timeshare Owners has authority to take decisions in relation with the resort and with the timeshare scheme not expressly attributed to other bodies.

There will be no voting rights for uncompleted units of the resort.

### Article 45.   Calling of meetings

1. The President of the Association of owners will call a General Meeting whenever he considers necessary for the normal functioning of the timeshare scheme. Timeshare owners representing at least 10% of the timeshare periods of the same resort are entitled to request that the President call a meeting of timeshare owners whenever there may be reasonable cause for this. If such requests are not met, they may appeal to a Judge who, having heard the President, will decide.

In case of vacancy of the Presidency or impossibility on the part of the President or the person acting on his behalf in his absence, the Secretary will be able to call a General Meeting at the request of owners representing a minimum of 10% of the timeshare periods in the same resort.

2. The notice calling for a General Meeting shall state the matters to be discussed, the day, time and place of the meeting this having to be within the municipality in which the resort is located, unless the Statutes indicate otherwise or it had been so agreed by the Board.

3. La convocatoria se enviará con un mes, como mínimo, de antelación – a menos que en los Estatutos se establezca un plazo mayor – al domicilio que cada uno de los titulares tenga señalado a estos efectos en el libro registro de socios. Para aquellos titulares cuyo domicilio no constara en tiempo oportuno en el libro de domicilios, bastará el anuncio expuesto durante ese plazo en la recepción del conjunto inmobiliario o en el lugar habilitado al efecto.

El Secretario hará constar en el libro de Actas el cumplimiento de las anteriores diligencias.

4. La Junta podrá reunirse, aun sin convocatoria, cuando, presentes todas las personas con derecho a voto, lo acuerden así por unanimidad.

### Artículo 46.   Derecho de asistencia y voto en los casos de titularidad múltiple o compartida

El derecho de asistencia y voto correspondiente a cada periodo de tiempo compartido será ejercitado por una sola persona, sea cual fuere el número de titulares del mismo.

### Artículo 47.   Ejercicio del dere-cho de asistencia y voto

1. A efectos del ejercicio del derecho de asistencia y voto de una persona física podrá ser representante suyo cualquiera de los demás titulares, así como las personas que tengan poder notarial a tal efecto. La representación deberá conferirse por escrito y con carácter especial para cada Junta.

3. Notice of a meeting shall be given at least one month in advance – unless the Statutes establish a longer length of time – and sent to the domicile of each of the owners as recorded to this effect in the register of timeshare owners. For those timeshare owners whose addresses were not recorded in due time in the above mentioned book, the notice placed during this period of time in the reception of the resort, or similar place used for such purpose, will be sufficient.

The Secretary must record that the above actions have been undertaken in the minutes book.

4. The General Meeting shall convene without prior notice in the event that all its voting members were present and unanimously would agree to celebrate the meeting.

### Article 46.   Rights for attendance and voting in the case of multiple or shared ownership

The right of attendance and voting corresponding to each timeshare period will be exercised by one single person, whatever the number of owners of the same may be.

### Article 47.   Exercise of attendance and voting rights

1. Any other timeshare owner of the resort may represent another in the exercise of attendance and voting rights, such representation being conferred in writing and applying exclusively for one meeting. This right may also be granted to any other person having notarial power to this effect.

2. El. titular podrá votar por carta, fechada y firmada, con expresión del nombre y apellidos, indicación de los periodos de tiempo compartido de que es titular el remitente y la indicación bien del sentido de su voto o de la delegación hecha en otra persona designada en la carta, para el ejercicio del voto. Dicha carta deberá ser dirigida al Secretario, al Presidente o a cualquier otro funcionario de la Asociación habilitado al efecto y estar en poder del destinatario con una antelación de al menos 24 horas respecto de la fecha de celebración de la Junta. La delegación de voto hecha de esta forma se entenderá igualmente aplicable a todas las eventuales reanudaciones de la reunión de la Junta que tengan lugar después de una suspensión de la misma.

3. La persona con derecho a asistir podrá ir acompañada de otra persona e intervenir a través de ésta en la deliberación. También puede ir acompañada de Notario a fin de levantar acta de las incidencias y acuerdos.

### Artículo 48. Presidencia de la Junta

Corresponderá la presidencia de la Junta el Presidente de la Asociación o quien haga sus veces. En su defecto, será designado por la Junta de entre los titulares asistentes, en el momento de su constitución.

### Artículo 49. Quora de decisión

1. Salvo que otra cosa disponga a Ley o se establezca en los Estatutos, los acuerdos podrán adoptarse por la mayoría de votos presentes o representados en la reunión de la Junta. Es suficiente esta mayoría para cambiar el domicilio de la Asociación de titulares.

2. The timeshare owner may cast his vote by a letter, dated and signed and giving his name, address and the identification of the timeshare periods he owns and either indicating how he wishes to vote, or delegating the authority to vote to any other party named in the letter, provided the letter is delivered to the Secretary, the President or any other authorised officer of the Association of Timeshare Owners not later than 24 hours before the date appointed for the meetings. It will be implied in such authority that the authority is given to vote in any adjournments of such meeting.

3. The person with a right of attendance may do so accompanied by another person, and may participate in the deliberations through this person. He may also attend accompanied by a Notary who will formalise the records he takes of the matters discussed and agreements taken.

### Article 48. Presidency of the General Meeting

Presidency of the General Meeting will be undertaken by the President of the Association or the person representing him in his absence. If this were not possible, the General Meeting shall appoint a President from among the timeshare owners present at the moment of its constitution.

### Article 49. Decision Quora

1. Unless the law or Statutes decree otherwise, agreements may be adopted by a vote cast by the majority of those timeshare owners present or represented at the General Meeting. This majority will be sufficient in order to change the domicile of the Association of owners.

2. A estos efectos la titularidad de un periodo de tiempo compartido llevará siempre aparejado un voto como mínimo. El promotor será el titular de los periodos sobre los que no se haya aún celebrado contrato de tiempo compartido pero no tendrá derecho de voto en relación con los periodos correspondientes a viviendas no terminadas. Los estatutos podrán atribuir más de un voto a los titulares de aquellos periodos que recaigan sobre viviendas de tamaño superior, debiendo en todo caso respetar el principio de proporcionalidad en la atribución del número de votos.

3. Deberá reunirse como mínimo la mayoría de los votos presentes o representados, para la adopción de los siguientes acuerdos:

a) la contratacion de la prestación de todos los servicios del proyecto de tiempo compartido de interés común por un precio alzado, respecto de cualquier años posterior a los tres primeros ejercicios completos posteriores al otorgamiento de la escritura a que se refiere el artículo 5;

b) el establecimiento de instalaciones o servicios comunes o la mejora de los existentes, siempre que comporten el incremento de la cuota anual ordinaria, salvo lo dispuesto en la escritura a que se refiere el artículo 5;

c) la remoción del Presidente o del Secretario.

4. Deberá reunirse como mínimo la mayoría del 75% de los votos presentes o representados, siempre que ésta, a su vez, represente más de la mitad de los titulares y de los votos de la Asociación de titulares, para la adopción de los siguientes acuerdos:

a) la modificación de los Estatutos;

b) la extinición del régimen de tiempo compartido.

2. To the effects of the above paragraph, ownership of a timeshare period will always entail the right of at least one vote. The developer will own all timeshare periods for which timeshare contracts have not yet been signed but should not have a vote in respect of uncompleted units. The statues may assign more than one vote to timeshare owners with larger properties, but in all cases the principle of proportion must be respected for the number of votes assigned.

3. A majority of votes cast by those present and represented shall be required, for the adoption of the following resolutions:

a) contracting at a fixed price, the provision of services that are of communal interest in respect of any year following the first three complete years after the date of the Notarial Deed envisaged by article 5.

b) establishment of facilities or communal services or the improvement of those already existing, whenever this means an increase in the annual ordinary charges, except as envisaged in the Notarial Deed envisaged in Article 5;

c) the removal of the President or Secretary.

4. A majority of 75% of the votes of those present or represented, provided that they add up to over half the owners and votes of the Association, will be necessary in order to adopt the following resolutions:

a) amendment of the Statutes;

b) extinction of the timeshare scheme.

5. Hasta el momento en que el promotor haya vendido la mitad de los derechos de tiempo compartido de que conste el proyecto, no podrá participar en votaciones relativas a la modificación de los Estatutos ni alteración de las cuotas de gastos anuales. Estos acuerdos sólo podrán adoptarse por decisión judicial si el promotor se opusiera al acuerdo de los demás titulares.

5. Up to the time when the developer has sold half of the timeshare rights of which the project consists, he will not be able to participate in voting regarding amendments to the Statutes or alteration of the annual expenses. These resolutions shall only be adopted, if the developer opposes them, by a court resolution.

**Artículo 50. Actas de las sesiones**

**Article 50. Minutes of the Meetings**

1. De cada sesión y sus incidencias se levantará en el correspondiente libro, acta de la Junta, en la que se incará el porcentaje de titulares presentes o representados. Se expresará, respecto de cada acuerdo, el número de votos que concurran en su favor y el porcentaje que representen respecto de los presentes y representados, así como respecto del total del proyecto de tiempo compartido, cuando así lo exija la Ley o los Estatutos.

1. The Secretary shall draft the Minutes of the Meeting in which the percentage of owners present or represented is to be stated, and, with respect to each vote, the number of votes in favour and the percentage represented with respect to the number of persons present and represented, and with respect to the total timeshare project, whenever the law of the Statutes so require.

Podrán nombrarse dos interventores del acta por cada acuerdo, uno en representación de los titulares que votaron a favor y otro en representación de los demás.

Two persons may be appointed to supervise the contents of the minutes, one representing the majority and the other, the minority.

2. El acta deberá terminarse y cerrarse dentro de los cinco días siguientes, con la firma del Secretario y con la del Presidente de la Junta. Los interventores podrán hacer constar a continuación sus propias observaciones siempre dentro de los diez días siguientes al de la reunión. Dentro de los noventa días siguientes a su aprobación, la sociedad de administración deberá enviar copia del acta a cada uno de los titulares.

2. The minutes must be concluded and closed within the five days following the meeting, with the signatures of the Secretary and President of the same. The above supervisors may record thereafter their own comments, within ten days following the meeting. Thereafter within ninety days following the approval of the minutes a copy shall be circulated to each timeshare owner by the management company.

3. El Secretario guardará unidas la convocatoria, las cartas, las copias o referencias suficientes de las delegaciones o poderes y los demás dogaciones o poderes y los demás documentos relativos a cada sesión.

3. The Secretary will keep together the notice of the General Meeting, and all the letters, copies and sufficient references of the delegations or powers and further documents relating to each session.

## Artículo 51.    Decisión por el Juez

1. Cuando la Junta convocada no se reúna o no adopte acuerdo sobre uno de los asuntos del orden del día, cualquier titular que, en su caso, hubiere asistido a la Junta o emitido su voto en la forma prevista en el artículo 49.3 podrá solicitar del Juez que adopte, de acuerdo con lo dispuesto en el artículo 1.428 de la Ley de Enjuiciamiento Civil, las medidas necesarias a fin de evitar graves perjuicios para los intereses comunes de los titulares o para los legítimos intereses propios.

2. La solicitud habrá de presentarse al Juez dentro de los treinta días siguientes al de celebración de la Junta indicado en la convocatoria. Los demás titulares serán citados por anuncio expuesto en la recepción del conjunto inmobiliario o en el lugar designado al efecto durante diez días, lo que podrá acreditarse por certificación del Secretario. El Juez dará audiencia al Presidente y a los titulares que se presentaren y después de examinar las pruebas presentadas por los interesados y las acordadas de oficio, decidirá lo que proceda.

## Artículo 52.    Ineficacia de los acuerdos

1. Son nulos los acuerdos de la Junta que recaigan sobre materias que excedan de su competencia, los adoptados sin las mayorías específicamente exigidas o los que, por su causa o contenido, sean contrarios a las leyes o al orden público.

## Article 51.    Court decision

1. In the event that the General Meeting for which notice has been given does not take place or if no agreement is reached about one of the points of the agenda, any owner who had intended to attend or to vote at the Meeting, in the manner decreed by article 49.3 may request from the Judge, in accordance with what is established by article 1.428 of the Civil Procedures Law, the adoption of necessary measures in order to avoid serious infringement against the common interests of the owners or his own legitimate interests.

2. The above request will have to be made to the Judge within thirty days following the date set for the General Meeting in the notice calling it. The other owners will be notified by an announcement placed in the reception of the resort or place used to that effect for a period of ten days, the Secretary being able to certify this. The Judge will give a hearing to the President and owners who attend, and following examination of the evidence presented by those interested persons and that produced at his own request, will decide accordingly.

## Article 52.    Inefficacity of the resolutions

1. Agreements of the General Meeting regarding matters exceeding the limits of its authority, or those adopted without the majorities expressly decreed, or those resolutions which, because of their contents, breach the law or are contrary to public order, will be null and void.

2. Son anulables los demás acuerdos que produzcan graves perjuicios para la comunidad de titulares o para los legítimos intereses de un titular y los demás acuerdos que vulneren los2. Son estatutos o hayan sido adoptados sin las formalidades precisas. La acción de impugnación deberá ejercitarse dentro de los tres meses siguientes al anulables los demás acuerdos que produzcan graves perjuicios para la comunidad de titulares o para los legítimos intereses de un titular y los demás acuerdos que vulneren losdía de celebración de la Junta en que se adoptaron los acuerdos respectivos. Presentada la demanda, el Juez podrá, de conformidad con lo dispuesto en el artículo 1.428 de la Ley de Enjuiciamiento Civil, ordenar la suspensión del acuerdo impugnado y adoptar las medidas necesarias a fin de evitar daños de difícil reparación.

2. It will be possible to annul resolutions which incur serious prejudice to the community of timeshare owners or to the legitimate interests of any individual timeshare owner, or agreements which violate the statutes or which have been adopted without the necessary formalities. Action to challenge these resolutions may be lodged within three months following the day of the Meeting at which the resolutions concerned were made. Once a claim has been made, the Judge may, in accordance with what is decreed in article 1.428 of the Civil Procedures Law, order the suspension of the challenged resolution and adopt the necessary measures in order to avoid damages that may be difficult to remedy.

3. Cualquier titular podrá intervenir en el proceso para defender la validez del acuerdo.

3. Any of the owners may intervene in this case in order to defend the validity of the resolution challenged.

4. Las costas procesales que correspondan a la Asociación de titulares se repartirán entre ellos como los demás gastos comunes.

4. Whenever the judicial expenses of the case were imposed on the Association of Timeshare Owners they shall be divided among them all as all other communal expenses.

**Artículo 53.  Junta Ordinaria**

**Article 53.  Ordinary General Meeting**

1. La Junta ordinaria habrá de celebrarse como mínimo una vez al año, debiendo celebrarse la primera junta ordinaria dentro de los dieciocho meses siguientes al otorgamiento de la escritura a que se refiere el Artículo 5.

1. The Ordinary General Meeting must take place at least once a year, provided that the first ordinary general meeting may take place at any time within 18 months of the date of the Notarial Deed envisaged by Article 5.

2. Con la convocatoria se acompañará el estado de las cuentas que rinde la sociedad de administración y el proyecto de presupuesto para el ejercicio anual en curso.

2. Notice of the Meeting will be given together with a statement of accounts submitted by the management company and the budget for the present year.

3. En la Junta se censurarán las cuentas y la actuación de la sociedad de administración y demás personas nombradas para los distintos cargos y se decidirán las partidas del presupuesto.

3. At the Meeting, the accounts and actions undertaken by the management company and by other persons appointed for certain tasks will be examined and all the items appearing on the budget will be approved or refused.

4. En la misma Junta se decidirá cualquier otro asunto que figure en el orden del día.

### Artículo 54. Juntas especiales

1. En los Estatutos pueden preverse Juntas especiales para decidir cuestiones que afecten sólo a los elementos, instalaciones y servicios cuyos gastos hayan de repartirse conforme a módulos distintos de los ordinarios.

2. Sólo serán convocados aquellos titulares que, en su caso, hayan de soportar los gastos. Para la adopción de acuerdos se computarán los porcentajes en relación con los votos de los titulares afectados por dichos gastos. En ningún caso los acuerdos podrán menoscabar los intereses de los demás miembros de la Asociación.

3. Asumirá su presidencia el Presidente de la Asociación o uno de los titulares en quien el mismo delegue.

4. En todo lo no previsto en este artículo serán de aplicación las normas relativas a la Junta Ordinaria.

4. At the same Meeting, a decision will be taken regarding any other matter which may appear in the agenda.

### Article 54. Special General Meetings

1. The Statutes may authorise Special General Meetings in order to take decisions regarding matters that affect exclusively the elements, equipment and services for which the expenses are to be divided according to methods different from the general ones.

2. Only those timeshare owners will be summoned who, where applicable, are to bear the corresponding expenses. For the adoption of these resolutions, percentages will be calculated in relation to the votes of the timeshare owners affected by the above expenses. In no case may the agreements damage the interests of the other members of the Association.

3. The President of the Association or one of the timeshare owners designated by him will preside over the Extraordinary General Meeting.

4. In all instances not foreseen in this article, the regulations will apply as for the Ordinary General Meeting.

## Sección tercera. Organos de gestión
## Third Section. Governing authorities

### Artículo 55. Enmeración y nombramiento

1. La Junta proveerá los cargos de Presidente y de Secretario, con arreglo a lo dispuesto en los artículos 57 y 58;

2. Corresponderá a la Junta decidir si, además, han de ser nombrados suplentes para los cargos de Presidente y Secretario;

3. Los nombramientos se harán por un año y podrán ser prorrogados indefinidamente por iguales periodos;

### Article 55. Enunciation and Appointment

1. The General Meeting Shall designate a President and a Secretary of the association, according to what is established in articles 57 and 58.

2. It is the responsibility of the General Meeting to decide whether or not deputies are to be appointed for the President and Secretary.

3. Nominations will be made for one year and may be extended indefinitely for equal periods of time.

4. El Presidente y el Secretario podrán ser removidos por la Junta en cualquier momento. Pero si la cuestión no figura en el orden del día, se exigirá para el acuerdo lel voto del 75% de los titulares presentes o representados.

4. The President and Secretary may be removed by the General Meeting at any time. However, if this matter is not included in the agenda, the resolution will require at least 75% of the votes of the timeshare owners present or represented.

**Artículo 56. Responsabilidad de los nombrados**

**Article 56. Responsibility of Appointed Persons**

Todo titular podrá exigir ya en interés propio, ya en beneficio común, el cumplimiento de las obligaciones y la indemnización por daños y perjuicios causados por cualquiera de los órganos de gobierno de la Asociación en el ejercicio de sus funciones.

All the timeshare owners may request, in their own interest or for communal benefit, compliance of obligations and penalties for damages and prejudice caused by any of the governing authorities of the Association in the carrying out of their tasks.

**Artículo 57. El Presidente**

**Article 57. The President**

1. El. Presidente representará en juicio y fuera de él a la Asociación de titulares. Le corresponde también exigir a la sociedad de administración, al Secretario y a los titulares, el cumplimiento de sus respectivos deberes.

1. The President will represent in or out of Court the Association of Timeshare Owners. It will also be his responsibility to ensure that the management company, the Secretary and all other Timeshare Owners comply with their respective obligations.

2. El Presidente será elegido por la Junta de titulares de entre aquellos que tengan su residencia habitual dentro de la misma Comunidad Autónoma en que radique el conjunto inmobiliario. El requisito de residencia podrá ser suprimido por acuerdo de la Junta siempre que ello no menoscabe la correcta ejecución de las funciones del Presidente.

2. The President shall be elected by the General Meeting of Timeshare Owners among those having their permanent residence within the Autonomous Community where the resort is located. The requirement to reside there can be waived by resolution of the General Meeting provided this causes no detriment to the proper execution of the duties of the President.

3. El Presidente sólo podrá celbrar los contratos a cuyo cumplimiento la Asociación pueda hacer frente con las partidas específicamente previstas en el presupuesto anual y aquellos otros para los que esté autorizado por acuerdo especial de la Junta. Para concertar relaciones laborales se requiere además que los puestos de trabajo respectivos estén previstos estatutariamente o que se autorice la contratación por la Junta.

3. The President shall only be authorised to execute those contracts the Association can carry out and pay for with the normal provisions of the budget and those others for which he is expressly authorised by special resolution of the General Meeting. In order to celebrate labour contracts it shall be necessary that the corresponding jobs are provided for in the statutes or else that the contract be expressly authorised by the General Meeting.

4. El Presidente no requiere acuerdo especial de la Junta para ejercitar las acciones y excepciones que correspondan a la Asociación de titulares sin perjuicio de la obligación de dar cuenta a la Junta de las incidencias del pleito y de atenerse a las instrucciones recibidas de ella. No podrá, sin embargo, renunciar a la acción, allanarse, transigir o comprometer en árbitro sin previo acuerdo de la Junta adoptado con las mayorías que correspondan por razón de la trascendencia del acto.

5. El cargo de Presidente es obligatorio. Si nadie quiere voluntariamente el cargo, el nombramiento se decidirá, en reunión de la Junta, por la suerte entre quienes no lo hubieran desempeñado y reunan el requisito necesario de domicilio antes citado cuando éste fuera exigible, o bien, alternativamente, la Junta podrá decidir en tal caso nombrar Presidente a cualquier persona, incluso no titular de tiempo compartido, y en el caso de que se trate de persona cuyos servicios hayan de ser remunerados, el importe de tal remuneración deberá incluirse entre los gastos de administración.

**Artículo 58. El Secretario**

1. El Secretario será elegido por la Junta pudiendo recaer el cargo en persona que no sea titular de tiempo compartido, con tal de que sea residente en la provincia en que radique el conjunto inmobiliario.

2. Corresponde al Secretario llevar los libros de la Asociación, mencionados en el apartado siguiente, y custodiar la documentación de los órganos de gobierno, levantar actas de las Juntas, notificar a los titulares cuando proceda y expedir certificaciones de la documentación a su cargo.

4. The President does not require a special resolution by the General Meeting in order to execute all legal actions or objections corresponding to the Association, although he shall have to inform about it the said General Meeting and abide to its resolutions. He will not be authorised, however, to waive an action, transact or appoint arbitrators without previous resolution by the General Meeting adopted with the formalities corresponding to the importance of the matter.

5. The position of President is mandatory. If no timeshare owner wishes to serve this position, the appointment shall be decided at a General Meeting by chance, among those timeshare owners not having served it and complying with the residency requirement whenever exigible or alternatively the general meeting may elect any person to be president, whether or not he is a timeshare owner, and if on terms that such president is to be a paid official, that his fees will form part of the management charge.

**Article 58. The Secretary**

1. The Secretary shall be designated by the General Meeting the appointed person not requiring to be a timeshare owner, provided he resides in the same province where the resort is located.

2. The Secretary will have the responsibility of the books of Association, mentioned in the following paragraph, the custody of the documents of the governing authorities, drafting of minutes of all meetings, notification to the timeshare owners when these are to take place and issuance of certifications from the documents in his charge.

3. En el Libro de Actas se reflejarán, por orden cronológico, los acuerdos adoptados por la Junta. En el Libro Registro de Titulares se consignarán, agrupados por cada vivienda, los nombres y direcciones, de todos los titulares. El domicilio designado a efectos de notificaciones podrá ser alterado por simple voluntad del titular, siempre que se haga constar el nuevo domicilio.

4. En ambos libros, los folios estarán numerados con caracteres indelebles, debiendo en todo caso practicarse una diligencia de apertura autorizada por Notario, quien asimismo dará fe de la fecha de incorporación de adiciones a los mismos y de la numeración respectiva de los nuevos folios. El Libro Registro de Titulares podrá llevarse por procedimientos informáticos, siendo en estos casos necesarios legalizar ante notario el listado de titulares anualmente y con anterioridad a la convocatoria de la Junta de Titulares.

5. Los Libros y la documentación en poder del Secretario deberán manifestarse a las personas autorizadas por la Asociación de Titulares, mediante exhibición en el propio conjunto inmobiliario o expedición de fotocopia autorizada por el Secretario, siendo los gastos que ello ocasione a cargo del solicitante. Cualquier persona con interés legítimo y directo podrá asimismo solicitar certificaciones, abonando los gastos que su expedición y remisión originen.

6. Para acreditar los nombramientos y, en general, los acuerdos de las Juntas, bastará el certificado expedido a tal efecto por el Secretario con el visto bueno del Presidente o, en su defecto, el testimonio notarial por exhibición de la correspondiente acta del Libro si éste está debidamente legalizado.

3. The Minutes Book will record, in chronological order, the resolutions adopted by the General Meeting. The names and addresses of all the timeshare owners, will be recorded for each unit in the Register Book of Timeshare Owners. The address given for the purpose of notification may be changed if the owner so wishes, as long as the new address is recorded.

4. In both of the above mentioned books, the pages will be numbered with indelible characters, and in all cases the opening must be authorised by a Notary, who at the same time will attest the date of incorporation of new additions to the same, and the corresponding numeration of the pages. The Register Book of Timeshare Owners may be maintained by computer, provided that a written record is produced and notarized at the time when notices convening a General Meeting are sent out.

5. The books and documents entrusted to the Secretary must be shown to any person authorised by the Association, either by exhibition in the same resort or by means of a photocopy obtained by the Secretary, and any expenses incurred will be charged to the person making the request. Any person with a legitimate interest can obtain certificates, at his request, having to sustain the cost of their issuance and delivery.

6. In order to prove the various appointments and in general all resolutions of the General Meetings the certificate issued by the Secretary duly approved by the President, or failing this a notarial testimony issued after examination of the minutes book if it were properly legalised, will be sufficient.

## Sección cuarta. Las cuentas anuales y el presupuesto
## Fourth Section. Annual Expenses and Budget

**Artículo 59.**

**Article 59.**

La sociedad de administración deberá someter a la Junta de titulares, dentro de los seis primeros meses de cada año, las cuentas anuales de su gestión, con indicación individualizada por capítulos de las cantidades y conceptos a que corresponden todos los gastos, así como el presupuesto a que se refiere el artículo siguiente. Dichas cuentas anuales deberán acompañarse del informe de auditoría emitido por la entidad independiente contratada para dicha función.

The management company must produce before the General Meeting of Timeshare Owners, within the first six months of each year, the annual accounts and the report of its activities, with an indication of each of the individual amounts and concepts which correspond to the total expenses, in addition to the budget referred to in the following article. These annual sums must be accompanied by an auditing report issued by the independent auditing firm contracted for such task.

**Artículo 60.   Fondo de reserva**

**Article 60.   Sinking Fund**

1. En el presupuesto deberán figurar junto a la totalidad de los gastos previstos por todos los conceptos, una cantidad destinada a la constitución de un fondo de reserva del que sólo podrá disponerse para gastos de reposición de elementos esenciales del conjunto o las viviendas, realización de reparaciones extraordinarias o gastos imprevistos de carácter urgente, sometiendo dichos gastos a la posterior aprobación de la Junta. La cifra destinada al fondo de reserva será equivalente a la décima parte de los gastos comunes, a menos que en los Estatutos se establezca cantidad superior.

1. In the budget, there must appear together with the total amount of expenses foreseen for all concepts, an amount which is destined for the constitution of a sinking fund which may only be used for replacement of capital items, extraordinary repairs and unforeseen expenses of an urgent nature, where such expenses are submitted to the General Meeting for its subsequent approval. The amount destined for reserve funds will be equivalent to a tenth of the communal expenses, unless a greater quantity is required by the Statutes.

2. El sobrante de los fondos anuales, tal como resulte del balance de las cuentas anuales, incrementará el fondo de reserva establecido en el número anterior o, si la Asociación así.lo decidiera, podrá ser deducido del presupuesto de gastos del año siguiente.

2. The surplus annual funds, resulting at the end of the year will be used to increase the sinking fund established in the previous paragraph or, if the Association so wishes, can be deducted from the budget for the following year.

**Artículo 61.   Ingresos y gastos**

**Article 61.   Income and Expenditure**

1. La sociedad de administración deberá someter a la Junta un proyecto de presupuesto anual de ingresos y gastos para el siguiente ejercicio.

1. The management company must submit to the General Meeting an annual budget for income and expenditure for the next year.

2. Los ingresos estarán constituidos por las cuotas anuales de los titulares y las cantidades que hayan de pagar los mismos por servicios que no tengan carácter común o por sanciones o indemnización de daños y perjuicios. Dentro de los gastos comunes sufragados mediante dichas cuotas se incluirá expresamente el importe cobrado por la sociedad de administración por sus servicios.

3. El pago de las cuotas anuales deberá hacerse dentro de los dos primeros meses de cada ejercicio. La Junta deberá aprobar no sólo el presupuesto de gastos sino también las cuotas individuales correspondientes a cada periodo de tiempo compartido, que habrán de cobrarse en el siguiente ejercicio.

4. Ninguno de los titulares podrá quedar excusado del pago de su cuota anual, a excepción del promotor, que podrá serlo durante los tres primeros ejercicios de existencia del proyecto respecto de todos los periodos de tiempo compartido no vendidos, siempre que asuma la obligación de que las cuotas anuales de los titulares sean fijas durante el mismo plazo, siendo de cargo de aquel exclusivamente las cantidades en que excedan los gastos anuales de la recaudación global por cuotas de los titulares, con tal de que garantice mediante aval bancario o póliza de seguro el cumplimiento de esta obligación.

La no utilización de un servicio común no eximirá al titular del periodo de tiempo compartido de la contribución por los gastos que correspondan al mismo.

5. Las cuotas anuales se considerarán vencidas al final del periodo señalado por la Junta para su pago. Las cuotas vencidas podrán devengar intereses en favor del conjunto de los titulares, si así se estableciere en los Estatutos, a un tipo que no podrá exceder en más de cinco puntos al tipo de interés legal del dinero, desde la fecha de vencimiento a la de su pago por el titular moroso.

2. All income consists of the annual sums to be paid by the timeshare owners, and the sums to be paid by the same for services that are not of a communal nature and for penalties or compensation for damages. The communal charges covered by the aforementioned sums will also expressly include the amount collected by the management company for its services.

3. The payment of annual charges must be made within the first two months of each year. The General Meeting must approve not only the budget of expenses but also the individual charges that correspond to each timeshare period, which have to be collected in the next year.

4. None of the timeshare owners may be excused from payment of his annual charges, with the exception of the developer, who may be excused during the first three years of existence of the timeshare scheme with respect to all the timeshare periods that have not been sold, provided that he undertakes the obligation to maintain the annual charges to be paid by the owners at a fixed sum over the same period of time, accepting exclusive responsibility for the expenses exceeding the annual collection of charges from the timeshare owners and provides the Association of Timeshare Owners with a bank or insurance guarantee, for this liability.

No timeshare owner will be exempted from paying the charges corresponding to his timeshare period on the grounds that he does not make use of communal facilities.

5. The annual charges will be considered due at the end of the period designated by the General Meeting for their payment. Past due charges may carry interest in favour of the General Meeting of Timeshare Owners, if the Statutes so decree, at a rate that may not exceed by more than five points the rate of legal interest on the money, from the date of maturity up to the date of payment by the defaulting timeshare owners.

6. A menos que se establezca otra cosa en los Estatutos, los gastos realizados en beneficio de sólo parte de los titulares deberán repartirse únicamente entre los beneficiarios respectivos.

6. Unless the Statutes establish otherwise, expenses incurred into for the benefit of only some of the timeshare owners may only be charged to the respective timeshare owners.

**Artículo 62.   La deuda por gastos**

**Article 62.   Outstanding debts for charges**

1. Resultará personalmente obligado a satisfacer la cuota anual de gastos, quien en el día del vencimiento de la obligación de pago figure como titular del respectivo periodo de tiempo compartido.

1. Responsibility for payment of the annual charges shall fall on the person who, on the date of maturity of the obligation to pay, appears as owner of the respective timeshare period.

2. En todo contrato por el que se transmita un derecho de tiempo compartido a título oneroso deberá el transmitente acreditar por medio de certificación expedida por la sociedad de administración, con el visto bueno del Secretario, que se halla al corriente en el pago y que no hay responsabilidades pendientes a su cargo.

2. In all contracts where a timeshare right is transferred, the seller must verify by means of a certificate obtained by the management company with the consent of the Secretary, that all payments have been made and that there are no pending charges of his responsibility.

3. Para reclamar a cada titular el pago de su cuota y de cualquier otra cantidad debida por el mismo, tendrá aparejada ejecución, a los efectos del artículo 1.429 de la Ley de Enjuiciamiento Civil la certificación expedida por la sociedad de administración acreditativa del importe de la deuda vencida del titular de que se trate. Dicha certificación deberá ser intervenida por un fedatario público que acredite que aquel importe coincide con el que figura en la cuenta abierta al titular en los libros de la sociedad de administración. La certificación deberá venir acompañada por otra expedida por el Secretario con el visto bueno del Presidente, acreditativa de la conformidad del importe reclamado con los Estatutos y acuerdos de la Junta.

3. In order to claim from each owner the payment of the amount that he owes and any other outstanding debt, it shall have executory nature for the purposes of what is stated by article 1.429 of the Civil Procedures Law, the certificate issued by the management company stating the amount of the matured debt owed by the timeshare owner in question. This certificate shall be supervised by a Public Notary who will verify that this amount is the same as the amount given in the account opened to the timeshare owner in the books of the management company. This certificate must be accompanied by another issued by the Secretary with the President's approval, stating that the amount claimed corresponds with the Statutes and agreements of the Board.

**Artículo 63.   Nuevos servicios**

**Article 63.   New services**

La inclusión de un nuevo servicio en la lista de los servicios comunes cubiertos por la cuota anual de los titulares sólo podrá tener lugar por acuerdo de la Junta adoptado de conformidad con lo establecido en el artículo 53.3.

A new service may only be incorporated in the list of communal services covered by the annual charges paid by the timeshare owners on agreement by the General Meeting in accordance with that established in article 53.3.

## Sección quinta. Garantías en favor de la Asociación
## Fifth Section. Guarantees in favour of the Association

**Artículo 64.**

En caso de que el titular permanezca en la vivienda al término del periodo que le corresponde, la sociedad de administración podrá imponer, si así lo autorizan los Estatutos, una sanción pecuniaria al titular por cada día de ocupación indebida que no podrá exceder de una cantidad equivalente a cinco veces la que corresponde, por día de ocupación, a la cuota anual por gastos. Si la permanencia indebida del titular impidiese a otro ocupar la vivienda en el periodo que le corresponde, con independencia de la sanción pecuniaria el titular infractor deberá abonar los gastos originados por el alojamiento del perjudicado. En ambos casos la Junta podrá asimismo acordar su expulsión, para lo que podrá delegar esta potestad en la sociedad de administración.

**Artículo 65.**

La sociedad de administración estará facultada en cualquier caso para arrendar a terceros dicha vivienda durante el periodo que correspondiese al deudor con objeto de reintegrar a la Asociación la deuda pendiente.

El remanente que quedare, en su caso, deberá incrementar el fondo de reserva, salvo en el caso de que los servicios comunes se presten por una cantidad alzada, en cuyo caso podrá hacer suyo dicho remanente la sociedad de administración.

**Artículo 66.**

El titular que deje de satisfacer sus cuotas anuales durante dos anualidades consecutivas podrá ser expulsado del conjunto inmobiliario mediante un procedimiento adecuado a la naturaleza de su derecho, previamente establecido en los Estatutos.

**Article 64.**

In the event that the timeshare owner continues to occupy the unit after the timeshare period corresponding to him is over, the management company may impose, where the Statutes so authorise, a penalty against the timeshare owner for every day of unlawful occupation, which may not exceed an amount equal to five times that which is applicable for each day of occupation calculated on the annual expenses. If unlawful occupancy by the timeshare owner prevents another owner from occupying the unit for the period which corresponds to him, then independently of the penalty imposed, the responsible owner shall pay all costs of the accommodation of the injured party. In either case the General Meeting may order his expulsion and can delegate this power to the management company.

**Article 65.**

The management company will in any case have the faculty to rent out to third parties the said unit for the period corresponding to the debtor with the object of recuperating the pending debt for the Association.

The remaining amount, when applicable, will be paid into the sinking fund, except for the case in which the communal services are rendered for a fixed flat amount, in which case the said balance can be kept by the management company.

**Article 66.**

Any timeshare owner who fails to pay his annual charges during two consecutive years will be expelled from the Association by means of procedures that correspond to the nature of his rights, previously established in the Statutes.

El titular podrá evitar la expulsión mediante el pago de todas las cantidades debidas incrementadas con el intereses legal que corresponda.

En caso de expulsión los derechos del titular expulsado serán extinguidos en beneficio de la Asociación de titulares, que podrá revender tales derechos y que, en tal supuesto, deberá rendir cuentas al titular expulsado devolviéndole el remanente que quedare una vez deduciods los pagos debidos por gastos anuales atrasados y otros coneptos, así como las comisiones, honorarios y gastos de venta relacionados con tal venta. La Asociación podrá delegar el ejercicio de esta facultad en la sociedad de administración.

The timeshare owner may avoid expulsion by means of a payment of all quantities owed increased by the legal interests that correspond.

In the case of expulsion, the rights of the expelled owner shall be forfeited to the Association of Timeshare Owners, who may resell the right and who shall, in the event of such resale account to the expelled owner for any surplus (after payment of the timeshare owner's arrears of annual charges and other monies due from him, and the commissions fees and expenses relating to the sale). The Association may delegate this power to the management company.

### Artículo 67.

1. La sociedad de administración podrá exigir al titular una declaración escrita y firmada por él en la que manifieste haber encontrado a su llegada la vivienda en estado correcto para su utilización y con su inventario completo. Igual obligación recaerá sobre la persona autorizada por el titular para ocupar la vivienda en su ausencia.

2. La sociedad de administración podrá asimismo verificar, antes del final del periodo de ocupación exclusivo, la integridad de los elementos del inventario y el estado de conservación de la vivienda.

3. En el caso de apreciar daños imputables a los ocupantes, la sociedad de administración podrá requerir el pago inmediato de los gastos que origine su reparación. En el caso de que estos gastos no pudieran ser satisfechos en el momento por el ocupante, la sociedad de administración podrá exigirle una declaración en la que reconozca la existencia de los daños causados, o, en caso de disconformidad solicitar al Presidente o al Secretario su presencia para la comprobación de estos extremos.

### Article 67.

1. The management company may request from the timeshare owner a declaration, written and signed by him, in which he states to have found the unit upon his arrival in a correct state adequate for its use and with the inventory complete. A similar obligation will apply to the person authorised by the timeshare owner to occupy the property in his absence.

2. The management company may at the same time verify, immediately before termination of the period of occupancy, the integrity of the items of the inventory and the state of conservation of the unit.

3. In the case of estimation of damages attributable to the occupants, the management company may demand immediate payment of expenses for repairs. In the case where such expenses cannot be paid by the occupant at the time, the management company may request from him a statement in which he declares his acknowledgement of the damage, or, in the case of disagreement, may request that the President or Secretary confirm the extent of the damage.

## Sección sexta. Garantías en favor de los titulares
## Sixth Section. Guarantees in favour of the timeshare owners

### Artículo 68. Garantías en caso de expulsión

1. La expulsión de un titular sólo podrá ser acordada por la Junta, y procederá únicamente en los casos previstos en la presente Ley, si bien podrá ser delegada esta facultad por la Junta en la sociedad de administración.

2. El titular expulsado podrá recurrir el acuerdo en vía judicial dentro del plazo de tres meses desde la fecha de la misma.

### Artículo 69. Garantías en caso de realización de obras

La realización de obras o mejoras que comporten la imposibilidad de ocupar el inmueble o cualquiera de las viviendas del mismo por un periodo igual o inferior a tres meses dará derecho a los titulares afectados a ocupar, con cargo al presupuesto anual de la Asociación de titulares, una vivienda análoga en el mismo conjunto inmobiliario o en su defecto en la misma localidad durante el periodo respectivo.

### Artículo 70. Extinción del régimen de tiempo compartido

El proyecto de tiempo compartido puede terminar por el transcurso del tiempo establecido en el documento a que se refiere el artículo 5, o por la destrucción de más del 50% de las viviendas del conjunto inmobiliario, o por acuerdo de la Junta de Titulares adoptado con los votos señalados en el artículo 49.4.

### Article 68. Guarantees in the case of expulsion

1. The expulsion of a timeshare owner may only be agreed by the General Meeting, and may only be carried out in the cases contemplated in this law but the General Meeting may delegate the power of expulsion to the management company.

2. The expelled timeshare owner may challenge the said agreement by legal means within the space of three months from the date of the same.

### Article 69. Guarantees in the event of repair works

The execution of works or improvement or repairs which mean that the building of any one of the units thereof cannot be occupied for a period equal to or less than three months, will give the timeshare owners the right to occupy, at the expense of the Association, a similar unit in the same resort or if this is not possible, in the same location, for the respective timeshare period.

### Article 70. Extinction of the timeshare scheme

The timeshare shemes may terminate by the lapse of the period of time established in the document referred to in article 5, or by the destruction of more than 50% of the units of the resort, or by resolution of the General Meeting adopted with the votes indicated in article 49.4.

En el momento de la terminación del proyecto de tiempo compartido la Junta de Titulares deberá designar un comité ejecutivo encargado de la tarea de enajenar el conjunto inmobiliario y distribuir el producto de la enajenación entre los titulares en proporción a sus respectivos derechos, a menos que en el documento de constitución del proyecto hubiese quedado expresamente señalado que al término del proyecto de tiempo compartido se produciría la total extinción de los derechos de los titulares, como es el caso de la extinción del usufructo por periodos.

At the time of termination of a timeshare scheme, the General Meeting shall appoint an executive committee charged with the task of disposing of the resort and distributing the proceeds among the timeshare owners in proportion to their respective rights unless in the constitution of the scheme it was specifically stated that termination would entail the complete disappearance of the rights of the timeshare owners, as is necessarily the case in the event of the usufruct by periods.

**Disposición transitoria**

**Transitory provision**

1. Las sociedades de administración que estuviesen prestando sus servicios en virtud de contratos celebrados con anterioridad a la entrada en vigor de la presente ley deberán adaptarse a los requisitos establecidos en la misma dentro del plazo de dos años desde la fecha de publicación de la ley en el B.O.E.

1. The management companies rendering their services by virtue of contracts signed before the present law comes into force must adapt to the requirements established by the same within a period of two years as from the date of publication of the law by the Official State Bulletin (B.O.E.).

2. Los proyectos de tiempo compartido que estuviesen en funcionamiento a la fecha de la entrada en vigor de la presente Ley deberán adoptar las medidas necesarias para el cumplimiento de lo dispuesto en la misma dentro del plazo de dos años desde la fecha de publicación de la ley en el B.O.E.

2. Any timeshare projects that may have been started before the present law comes into force must take the necessary measures to ensure compliance with what is decreed by this law within a period of two years from the date of publication of the law in the Official State Bulletin.

3. La actividad de comercialización de contratos de tiempo compartido en cualquiera de sus modalidades deberá ajustarse a las disposiciones del Título Preliminar dentro del plazo de un año a contar desde la fecha de publicación de la ley en el B.O.E.

3. The activities of marketing of timeshare contracts in any form must comply with the provisions of the Preliminary Title within one year as from the date of publication of the law by the Official State Bulletin.

4. Los conjuntos inmobiliarios en régimen de tiempo compartido ya existentes y cuya comercialización hubiera comenzado con anterioridad a la entrada en vigor de la presente ley, el Promotor estará en vigor de la presente ley, el Promotor estará obligado a constituir la hipoteca a que se refiere el artículo 20.d, con tal de que sea requerido para ello por la Asociación de Titulares. En tal caso, el Promotor estará facultado para repercutir a la Asociación la parte proporcional de los impuestos y gastos originados por la constitución de dicha hipoteca y su inscripción, así como para hacerlo en los casos de ampliación de hipoteca que en lo sucesivo le sean requeridos por la Asociación.

En el supuesto de que la Asociación de Titulares requiriese la constitución o la ampliación de la citada hipoteca el Promotor estará facultado para solicitar como requisito para atender al requerimiento la presentación de garantía bancaria por parte de aquella para responder de su obligación de pago de impuestos y gastos.

5. Con objeto de adoptar la decisión a que se refiere la disposición anterior, la Junta de Titulares deberá ser convocada dentro del plaze de un año a partir de la publicación de la presente Ley. El acuerdo de requerir al Promoton la coustitución de hipoteca requerirá el voto afirmativo de al menos el 75% de los titulares, presentes o representados.

4. In respect of timeshare resorts established and where sales have been initiated before the coming into force of the present law, the developer will be obliged to execute the mortgage and guarantee referred to in Article 20.d, provided that this is requested by the Association of Timeshare Owners. In this case the Developer will be entitled to charge the Association of Timeshare Owners with the proportional part of the taxes and expenses originated in the execution and registration of the mortgage guarantee and will also be entitled to apply the said charge to the Association of Timeshare Owners in the case of up-dating the guaranteed value as described in the said Article.

In the event of the Association of Timeshare Owners requesting a mortgage guarantee or any increase of the same, the Developer may as a precondition of complying with the request, require the Association to provide a bank guarantee for payment of the said taxes and expenses.

5. In order to decide on the above point, the General Meeting shall be convened within a period of one month from the date of publication of the present law. The resolution to request the mortgage guarantee shall require the vote of 75% of the timeshare owners present or represented.

# Appendix G

# United States Legislation

# Appendix G

## FLORIDA REAL ESTATE TIMESHARING ACT

### CHAPTER 721: REAL ESTATE TIMESHARE PLANS

## TABLE OF CONTENTS

## Chapter 721

### Real Estate timeshare Plans

**Section 721.01 Short title** This chapter shall be known and may be cited as the 'Florida Real Estate Time-Sharing Act.'

**Section 721.02 Purposes** The purposes of this chapter are to:

(1) Give statutory recognition to real property time sharing in the state.

(2) Establish procedures for the creation, sale, exchange, promotion, and operation of timeshare plans.

(3) Provide full and fair disclosure to the purchasers and prospective purchasers of timeshare plans.

(4) Require every timeshare plan offered for sale or created and existing in this state to be subjected to the provisions of this chapter.

**Section 721.03 Scope of chapter**

(1) This chapter applies to all timeshare plans consisting of more than seven timeshare periods over a period of at least 3 years in which the facilities or accommodations are located within this state.

(2) All timeshare accommodations or facilities which are located outside the state but offered for sale in this state are subject only to the provisions of ss. 721.01–721.05, 721.06–721.12, 721.18, 721.20, 721.21, 721.26, and 721.28.

(3) When a timeshare plan is subject to both the provisions of this chapter and the provisions of chapter 718 or chapter 719, the plan shall meet the requirements of both chapters unless exempted as provided in this section. In the event of a conflict between the provisions of this chapter and the provisions of chapter 718 or chapter 719, the provisions of this chapter shall prevail.

(4) A timeshare plan which is subject to the provisions of chapter 718 or chapter 719, if fully in compliance with the provisions of this chapter, is exempt from the following:

(a) Sections 718.202 and 719.202, relating to sales or reservation deposits prior to closing.

(b) Sections 718.502 and 719.502, relating to filing prior to sale or lease.

(c) Sections 718.503 and 719.503, relating to disclosure prior to sale.

(d) Sections 718.504 and 719.504, relating to prospectus or offering circular.

(5) The treatment of timeshare estates for ad valorem tax purposes and special assessments shall be as prescribed in chapters 192 through 200.

**Section 721.04 Saving clause** All timeshare plans filed pursuant to chapter 2–23, Florida Administrative Code, prior to July 1, 1981, shall be deemed to be in compliance with the filing requirements of chapter 81–172, Laws of Florida.

**Section 721.05 Definitions** As used in this chapter, the term:

(1) 'Accommodations' means any apartment, condominium or cooperative unit, cabin, lodge, hotel or motel room, campground, or other private or commercial structure which is situated on real property and designed for occupancy or use by one or more individuals.

(2) 'Agreement for deed' means any written contract utilized in the sale of timeshare estates which provides that legal title will not be conveyed to the purchaser until the contract price has been paid in full and the terms of payment of which extend for a period in excess of 180 days after either the date of execution of the contract or completion of construction, whichever occurs later.

(3) 'Assessment' means the share of funds required for the payment of common expenses which is assessed from time to time against each purchaser by the managing entity.

(4) 'Closing' means:

(a) For any plan selling timeshare estates, conveyance of the legal title to a timeshare period as evidenced by the delivery of a deed to the purchaser or to the clerk of the court for recording or conveyance of the equitable title to a timeshare period as evidenced by the irretrievable delivery of an agreement for deed to the clerk of the court for recording.

(b) For any plan selling timeshare licenses, the final execution and delivery by all parties of the last document necessary for vesting in the purchaser the full rights available under the plan.

(5) 'Common expenses' means those expenses properly incurred for the maintenance, operation, and repair of the accommodations or facilities, or both, constituting the timeshare plan.

(6) 'Completion of construction' means:

(a)1 That a certificate of occupancy has been issued for the entire building in which the timeshare unit being sold is located, or for the improvement, or that the equivalent authorization has been issued, by the governmental body having jurisdiction; or

2 In a jurisdiction in which no certificate of occupancy or equivalent authorization is issued, that the construction, finishing, and equipping of the building or improvements according to the plans and specifications have been substantially completed; and

(b) That all accommodations of the timeshare unit and facilities of the timeshare plan are available for use in a manner identical in all material respects to the manner portrayed by the promotional material, advertising, and public offering statements filed with the division.

(7) 'Conspicuous type' means type in boldfaced capital letters no smaller than the largest type exclusive of heading, on the page on which it appears and, in all cases, at least 10-point type. Where conspicuous type is required, it must be separated on all sides from other type and print. Conspicuous type may be utilized in contracts for purchase or public offering statements only where required by law.

(8) 'Contract' means any agreement conferring the rights and obligations of a timeshare plan on the purchaser.

(9) 'Developer' includes;

(a) A 'creating developer,' which means any person who creates the timeshare plan;

(b) A 'successor developer,' which means any person who succeeds to the interest of the persons in this subsection by sale, lease, assignment, mortgage, or other transfer, but the term includes only

those persons who offer timeshare periods for sale or lease in the ordinary course of business and does not include an owner of a timeshare period who has acquired his unit for his own occupancy; or

(c) A 'concurrent developer,' which means any person acting concurrently with the persons in this subsection with the purpose of creating, selling, or leasing timeshare periods in the ordinary course of business, but the term does not include a person who has acquired a unit for his own occupancy.

(10) 'Division' means the Division of Florida Land Sales, Condominiums, and Mobile Homes of the Department of Business Regulation.

(11) 'Enrolled' means paid membership in an exchange program or membership in an exchange-program evidenced by written acceptance or confirmation of membership.

(12) 'Escrow account' means an account established solely for the purposes set forth in this chapter with a financial institution located within this state.

(13) 'Escrow agent' includes only:

(a) A savings and loan association, bank, trust company, or other financial lending institution located in this state having a net worth in excess of $5 million;

(b) An attorney who is a member of The Florida Bar and who has posted a fidelity bond issued by a company authorized and licensed to do business in this state as surety in the amount of $50,000: or

(c) A real estate broker who is licensed pursuant to chapter 475 and who has posted a fidelity bond issued by a company authorized and licensed to do business in this state as surety in the amount of $50,000.

(14) 'Exchange company' means any person owning or operating, or owning and operating, an exchange program.

(15) 'Exchange program' means any opportunity or procedure for the assignment or exchange of timeshare periods among purchasers in the same timeshare plan or other timeshare plans.

(16) 'Facilities' means amenities

including any structure, service, improvement, or real property, improved or unimproved, other than the timeshare unit, which is made available to the purchasers of a timeshare plan.

(17) 'Managing entity' means the person responsible for operating and maintaining the timeshare plan.

(18) 'Memorandum of agreement' means a written document, in recordable form, which includes the names of the purchaser and seller, a legal description of the timeshare property and timeshare period, and a description of the type of timeshare license sold by the seller.

(19) 'Offer to sell,' 'offer for sale,' 'offered for sale,' or 'offer' means the solicitation, advertisement, or inducement, or any other method or attempt, to encourage any person to acquire the opportunity to participate in a timeshare plan.

(20) 'Owner of the underlying fee' means any person having an interest in the real property underlying the accommodations or facilities of the timeshare plan at or subsequent to the time of creation of the timeshare plan or any person who purchases 15 or more timeshare periods for resale in the ordinary course of business.

(21) 'Owners' association' means the association made up of all purchasers of a timeshare plan who have purchased timeshare estates.

(22) 'Purchaser' means any person, other than a developer, who by means of a voluntary transfer acquires a legal or equitable interest in a timeshare plan other than as security for an obligation.

(23) 'Seller' means any developer or any other person, or agent or employee thereof, who is offering timeshare periods for sale to the public in the ordinary course of business, except a person who has acquired a timeshare period for his own occupancy and later offers it for resale.

(24) 'Timeshare estate' means a right to occupy a timeshare unit, coupled with a freehold estate or an estate for years with a future interest in a timeshare property or a specified portion thereof.

(25) 'Timeshare instrument' means one or more documents, by whatever name denominated, creating or governing the operation of a timeshare plan.

(26) 'Timeshare license' means a right to occupy a timeshare unit, which right is neither coupled with a freehold interest, nor coupled with an estate for years with a future interest, in a timeshare property.

(27) 'Timeshare period' means that period of time when a purchaser of a timeshare plan is entitled to the possession and use of the accommodations or facilities, or both, of a timeshare plan.

(28) 'Timeshare plan' means any arrangement, plan, scheme, or similar device, other than an exchange program, whether by membership, agreement, tenancy in common, sale, lease, deed, rental agreement, license, or right-to-use agreement or by any other means, whereby a purchaser, in exchange for a consideration, receives ownership rights in or a right to use accommodations or facilities, or both, for a period of time less than a full year during any given year, but not necessarily for consecutive years, and which extends for a period of more than 3 years.

(29) 'Timeshare property' means one or more timeshare units subject to the same timeshare instrument, together with any other property or rights to property appurtenant to those units.

(30) 'Timeshare unit' means an accommodation of a timeshare plan which is divided into timeshare periods.

**Section 721.056 Supervisory duties of developer** Notwithstanding obligations placed upon any other persons by this chapter, it is the duty of the developer to supervise, manage, and control all aspects of the offering of a timeshare plan, including, but not limited to, promotion, advertising, contracting, and closing. Any violation of this section which occurs during such offering activities shall be deemed to be a violation by the developer as well as by the person actually committing such violation.

**Section 721.06 Contracts for purchase of timeshare periods**

(1) No seller of a timeshare plan shall fail to utilize, and furnish each purchaser

of such plan a fully completed copy of, a contract pertaining to the sale, which contract shall include the following information:

(a) The actual date the contract is executed by each party.

(b) The names and addresses of the developer, any owner of the underlying fee, and the timeshare plan.

(c) The total financial obligation of the purchaser, including the initial purchase price and any additional charges to which the purchaser may be subject, such as financing, reservation, maintenance, management, and recreation charges.

(d) The estimated date of completion of construction of each accommodation or facility which is not completed at the time the contract is executed by the seller and purchaser and the estimated date of closing.

(e) A description of the nature and duration of the timeshare period being sold, including whether any interest in real property is being conveyed and the specific number of years constituting the term of the timeshare plan.

(f) Immediately prior to the space reserved in the contract for the signature of the purchaser, in conspicuous type, substantially the following statements:

YOU MAY CANCEL THIS CON-TRACT WITHOUT ANY PENALTY OR OBLIGATION WITHIN 10 DAYS FROM THE DATE YOU SIGN THIS CONTRACT, AND UNTIL 10 DAYS AFTER YOU RECEIVE THE PUBLIC OFFERING STATEMENT, WHICH-EVER IS LATER.

IF YOU DECIDE TO CANCEL THIS CONTRACT, YOU MUST NOTIFY THE DEVELOPER IN WRITING OF YOUR INTENT TO CANCEL. YOUR NOTICE OF CAN-CELLATION SHALL BE EFFECTIVE UPON THE DATE SENT AND SHALL BE SENT TO (Name of Devel-oper) AT (Address of Developer). ANY ATTEMPT TO OBTAIN A WAIVER OF YOUR CANCELLATION RIGHT IS UNLAWFUL. WHILE YOU MAY EXECUTE ALL CLOSING DOCU-MENTS IN ADVANCE, THE CLOS-ING, AS EVIDENCED BY DELI-VERY OF THE DEED OR OTHER DOCUMENT, BEFORE EXPI-RATION OF YOUR 10-DAY CAN-CELLATION PERIOD, IS PRO-HIBITED.

(g) If a timeshare license is being con-veyed, the following statement in conspi-cuous type:

YOU MAY ALSO CANCEL THIS CONTRACT AT ANY TIME AFTER THE ACCOMMODATIONS OR FACILITIES ARE NO LONGER AVAILABLE AS PROVIDED IN THIS CONTRACT AND THE PUBLIC OFFERING STATEMENT.

(h) If a timeshare estate is being con-veyed, the following statement in conspi-cuous type:

FOR THE PURPOSE OF AD VALOREM ASSESSMENT, TAXA-TION AND SPECIAL ASSESS-MENTS. THE MANAGING ENTITY WILL BE CONSIDERED THE TAX-PAYER AS YOUR AGENT PUR-SUANT TO SECTION 192.037, FLOR-IDA STATUTES.

(i) A statement that, in the event the purchaser cancels the contract during a 10-day cancellation period, the developer will refund to the purchaser the total amount of all payments made by the purchaser under the contract, reduced by the proportion of any contract benefits the purchaser has actually received under the contract prior to the effective date of the cancellation. The statement shall further provide that the refund will be made within 20 days after receipt of notice of cancellation or within 5 days after receipt of funds from the purchaser's cleared check, whichever is later.

(j) If the timeshare period is being sold pursuant to an agreement for deed, a statement that the signing of the agree-ment for deed does not entitle the pur-chaser to receive a deed until all payments under the agreement have been made.

(k) Unless the developer is at the time of offering the plan the owner in fee simple absolute of the accommodations and facilities of the timeshare plan, free and clear of all liens and encumbrances, a statement that the developer is not the sole owner of the underlying fee of the accommodations or facilities without liens or encumbrances, which statement shall include:

1 The names and addresses of all persons or entities having an ownership interest or other interest in the accommodations or facilities: and

2 The actual interest of the developer in the accommodations or facilities.

(l) If the contract is for the sale or transfer of a timeshare period in which the accommodations or facilities are subject to a lease, the following statement within the text in conspicuous type: THIS TIMESHARE PERIOD IS SUBJECT TO A LEASE (OR SUBLEASE). A copy of the executed lease shall be attached as an exhibit.

(2) An agreement for deed shall be recorded by the developer, who shall pay all recording costs associated therewith.

(3) The escrow agent shall provide every seller with a receipt for all funds paid to the seller.

**Section 721.07 Public offering statement** Prior to offering any timeshare plan, the developer must file a public offering statement with the division for approval. The developer shall furnish every purchaser with a copy of the approved public offering statement. Until the division approves such filing, any contract regarding the sale of the timeshare plan which is the subject of the public offering statement is voidable by the purchaser.

(1) The division shall, upon receiving a public offering statement from a developer, mail to the developer an acknowledgment of receipt. The failure of the division to send such acknowledgment will not, however, relieve the developer from the duty of complying with this section.

(2) Within 45 days of receipt of a public offering statement, the division shall determine whether the proposed public offering statement is adequate to meet the requirements of this section and

shall notify the developer by mail that the division has either approved the statement or found specified deficiencies in the statement. If the division fails to approve the statement or specify deficiencies in the statement within 45 days, the filing will be deemed approved. The developer may correct the deficiencies; and, within 20 days after receipt of the developer's corrections, the division shall notify the developer by mail that the division has either approved the filing or found additional specified deficiencies in it, if the division fails to approve or specify additional deficiencies within 20 days after receipt of the developer's corrections, the filing will be deemed approved.

(3)(a) Any change to an approved filing shall be filed with the division for approval as an amendment prior to becoming effective. The division has 20 days to approve or cite deficiencies in the proposed amendment. If the division fails to act within 20 days, the amendment will be deemed approved. If the developer fails to file corrections to any deficiency citation within 30 days, the division may reject the amendment. Each approved amendment shall be delivered to a purchaser prior to closing, but in no event later than 10 days after the amendment is approved.

(b) At the time amendments, as provided in paragraph (a), are delivered to purchasers, the developer shall provide to those purchasers who have not closed a written statement that if any of such amendments materially alter or modify the offering in a manner which is adverse to the purchaser, the purchaser or lessee will have a 10-day voidability period.

(4) Upon the filing of a public offering statement, the developer shall pay a filing fee of $1 for each timeshare period which is to be part of the proposed timeshare plan.

(5) Every public offering statement shall contain the following:

(a) A cover page stating only:

1 The name of the timeshare plan; and

2 The following statement, in conspicuous type:

THIS PUBLIC OFFERING STATE-

MENT CONTAINS IMPORTANT MATTERS TO BE CONSIDERED IN ACQUIRING A TIME-SHARE PERIOD. THE STATEMENTS CONTAINED HEREIN ARE ONLY SUMMARY IN NATURE. A PROSPECTIVE PURCHASER SHOULD REFER TO ALL REFERENCES, EXHIBITS HERETO, CONTRACT DOCUMENTS, AND SALES MATERIALS. YOU SHOULD NOT RELY UPON ORAL REPRESENTATIONS AS BEING CORRECT. REFER TO THIS DOCUMENT AND ACCOMPANYING EXHIBITS FOR CORRECT REPRESENTATIONS. THE SELLER IS PROHIBITED FROM MAKING ANY REPRESENTATIONS OTHER THAN THOSE CONTAINED IN THE CONTRACT AND THIS PUBLIC OFFERING STATEMENT.

(b) A summary containing all statements required to be in conspicuous type in the offering statements and in all exhibits thereto.

(c) A separate index of the contents and exhibits of the public offering statement.

(d) A text, which shall include, where applicable, the disclosures set forth in paragraphs (e)–(hh) and cross-references to the location in the public offering statement of each exhibit.

(e) A description of the timeshare plan, including, but not limited to:

1 Its name and location.

2 An explanation of the form of timeshare ownership that is being offered, including a statement as to whether any interest in the underlying real property will be conveyed to the purchaser. If the plan is being created or being sold on a leasehold, the location of the lease in the exhibits to the public offering statement shall be stated.

3 An explanation of the manner in which the apportionment of common expenses and ownership of the common elements has been determined.

(f) A description of the accommodations and facilities, including, but not limited to:

1 The number of buildings, the number of units in each building, the number of timeshare periods in each unit, the total number of timeshare periods being offered, the number of bathrooms and bedrooms in each unit, and the total number of units and unit weeks.

2 The latest date estimated for completion of constructing, finishing, and equipping.

3 The maximum number of units and timeshare periods that will use the accommodations and facilities. If the maximum number of units or timeshare periods will vary, a description of the basis for variation and the minimum amount of dollars per timeshare period to be spent for additional recreational facilities or for enlargement of such facilities. If the addition or enlargement of facilities will result in a material increase of a purchaser's maintenance expense or rental expense, the maximum increase and limitations thereon shall be stated.

4 A statement of whether the developer intends to offer whole units in addition to timeshare units.

5 The duration, in years, of the timeshare plan.

(g) A description of the recreational and other commonly used facilities that will be used only by purchasers of the plan, including, but not limited to:

1 Each room and its intended purposes, location, approximate floor area, and capacity in numbers of people.

2 Each swimming pool and its general location, approximate size, depths, and capacity; its approximate deck size and capacity; and whether the pool is heated.

3 Each additional facility; the number of each such facility; and its approximate location, approximate size, and approximate capacity.

4 A general description of the items of personal property and the approximate numbers of each item of personal property that the developer is committing to furnish for each room or other facility or, in the alternative, a representation as to the minimum amount of expenditure that will be made to purchase the personal property for the facility.

5 The estimated date when each room

or other facility will be available for use by the purchaser.

6 An identification of each room, accommodation, or other facility to be used by purchasers that will not be owned by the purchasers or the association.

7 A reference to the location in the disclosure materials of the lease or other agreements providing for the use of those facilities.

8 A description of the terms of the lease or other agreement, including the length of its term; the rent payable, directly or indirectly, by each purchaser; and the total rent payable to the lessor, stated in weekly, monthly, and annual amounts for the entire term of the lease; and a description of any option to purchase the property under any such lease, including the time the option may be exercised, the purchase price or how it is to be determined, the manner of payment, and whether the option may be exercised for a purchaser's share or only as to the entire leased property.

9 A statement as to whether the developer may provide additional facilities not described above; the general locations and types of such facilities; improvements or changes that may be made: the approximate dollar amounts to be expended; and the estimated maximum additional common expense or cost to the individual purchaser that may be charged during the first annual period of operation of the modified or added facilities.

(h) A description of the recreational and other commonly used facilities which will not be used exclusively by purchasers of the timeshare plan and which require the payment of any portion of the maintenance and expenses of such facilities, either directly or indirectly, by the purchasers. The description shall include, but not be limited to, the following:

1 Each building or facility committed to be built.

2 Facilities not committed to be built except under certain conditions, and a statement of those conditions or contingencies.

3 As to each facility committed to be built, or which will be committed to be built upon the happening of one of the

conditions in subparagraph 2, a statement as to whether it will be owned by the purchasers having the use thereof or by an association or other entity which will be controlled by the purchasers, or others, and the location in the exhibits of the lease or other document providing for use of those facilities.

4 The year in which each facility will be available for use by the purchasers or, in the alternative, the maximum number of purchasers in the project at the time each of the facilities is committed to be completed.

5 A general description of the items of personal property and the approximate numbers of each item of personal property that the developer is committing to furnish for each room or other facility or, in the alternative, a representation as to the minimum amount of expenditure that will be made to purchase the personal property for the facility.

6 If there are leases, decriptions thereof, including the length of their terms, the rents payable, and descriptions of any options to purchase.

(i)1 If any recreational facilities or other facilities offered by the developer for use by purchasers are to be leased or have club membership associated with them, one of the following statements in conspicuous type: THERE IS A RECREATIONAL FACILITIES LEASE ASSOCIATED WITH THIS TIMESHARE PLAN; or, THERE IS A CLUB MEMBERSHIP ASSOCIATED WITH THIS TIME-SHARE PLAN. There shall be a reference to the location in the disclosure materials where the recreation lease or club membership is described in detail.

2 If it is mandatory that unit owners pay fees, rent, dues, or other charges under a recreational facilities lease or club membership for the use of the facilities, the applicable statement in conspicuous type:

a MEMBERSHIP IN THE RECREATIONAL FACILITIES CLUB IS MANDATORY FOR PURCHASERS;

b PURCHASERS ARE REQUIRED, AS A CONDITION OF OWNERSHIP, TO BE LESSEES UNDER THE

RECREATIONAL    FACILITIES
LEASE;

c PURCHASERS ARE REQUIRED
TO PAY THEIR SHARE OF THE
COSTS AND EXPENSES OF MAIN-
TENANCE, MANAGEMENT, UP-
KEEP, REPLACEMENT, RENT,
AND FEES UNDER THE RECREA-
TIONAL FACILITIES LEASE (OR
THE OTHER INSTRUMENTS PRO-
VIDING THE FACILITIES); or

d A similar statement of the nature of
the organization or the manner in which
the use rights are created, and that purchasers are required to pay.

Immediately following the applicable
statement, the location in the disclosure
materials where the development is described in detail shall be stated.

3 If the developer, or any other person
other than the purchasers and other
persons having use rights in the facilities,
reserves, or is entitled to receive, any rent,
fee, or other payment for the use of the
facilities, the following statement in conspicuous type: THE PURCHASERS OR
THE ASSOCIATION(S) MUST PAY
RENT OR LAND USE FEES FOR
RECREATIONAL OR OTHER COM-
MONLY USED FACILITIES. Immediately following this statement, the
location in the disclosure materials where
the rent or land use fees are described in
detail shall be stated.

4 If, in any recreation format, whether
leasehold, club, or other, any person
other than the association has the right to
a lien on the timeshare periods to secure
the payment of assessments, rent, or other
exactions, a statement in conspicuous
type in substantially the following form:

a THERE IS A LIEN OR LIEN
RIGHT AGAINST EACH TIME-
SHARE PERIOD TO SECURE THE
PAYMENT OF RENT AND OTHER
EXACTIONS UNDER THE REC-
REATION LEASE. A PURCHASER'S
FAILURE TO MAKE THESE PAY-
MENTS MAY RESULT IN FORE-
CLOSURE OF THE LIEN; or

b THERE IS A LIEN OR LIEN
RIGHT AGAINST EACH TIME-
SHARE PERIOD TO SECURE THE

PAYMENT OF ASSESSMENTS OR
OTHER EXACTIONS COMING DUE
FOR THE USE, MAINTENANCE,
UPKEEP, OR REPAIR OF THE
RECREATIONAL OR COMMONLY
USED    FACILITIES.    A    PUR-
CHASER'S FAILURE TO MAKE
THESE PAYMENTS MAY RESULT
IN FORECLOSURE OF THE LIEN.

Immediately following the applicable
statement, the location in the disclosure
materials where the lien or lien right is
described in detail shall be stated.

(j) If the developer or any other person
has the right to increase or add to the
recreational facilities at any time after the
establishment of the timeshare plan, without the consent of the purchasers or
association being required, a statement in
conspicuous type in substantially the
following    form:    RECREATIONAL
FACILITIES MAY BE EXPANDED
OR ADDED WITHOUT CONSENT
OF THE PURCHASERS OR THE
ASSOCIATION(S). Immediately following this statement, the location in the
disclosure materials where such reserved
rights are described shall be stated.

(k) An explanation of the status of the
title to the real property underlying the
timeshare plan, including a statement of
the existence of any lien, defect, judgment, mortgage, or other encumbrance
affecting the title to the property, and how
such lien, defect, judgment, mortgage, or
other encumbrance will be removed or
satisfied prior to closing.

(l) A description of any judgment
against the developer, the managing
entity; or owner of the underlying fee,
which judgment is material to the timeshare plan; the status of any pending suit
to which the developer, the managing
entity, or owner of the underlying fee is a
party, which suit is material to the timeshare plan; and any other suit which is
material to the timeshare plan of which
the developer, managing entity, or owner
of the underlying fee has actual knowledge. If no judgments or pending suits
exist, there shall be a statement of such
fact.

(m) A description of all unusual and

material circumstances, features, and characteristics of the real property.

(n) A description of any financing to be offered to purchasers by the developer or any person or entity in which the developer has a financial interest, together with a disclosure that the description of such financing may be changed by the developer and that any change in the financing offered to prospective purchasers will not be deemed to be a material change.

(o) A detailed explanation of any financial arrangements which have been provided for completion of all promised improvements.

(p) A statement as to whether the plan of the developer includes a program of leasing units or timeshare periods rather than selling them, or leasing and selling them subject to such leases. If so, there shall be a description of the plan, including the number and identification of the units and the provisions and term of the proposed leases, and a statement in conspicuous type that: THE UNITS (OR TIMESHARE PERIODS) MAY BE TRANSFERRED SUBJECT TO A LEASE.

(q) The name and address of the managing entity; a statement whether the seller may change the managing entity or its control and, if so, the manner by which the seller may change the managing entity; a statement of the arrangements for management, maintenance, and operation of the accommodations and facilities and of other property that will serve the purchasers; and a description of the management arrangement and any contracts for these purposes having a term in excess of 1 year, including the names of the contracting parties, the term of the contract, the nature of the services included, and the compensation, stated for a month and for a year, and provisions for increases in the compensation. Copies of all described contracts shall be attached as exhibits.

(r) If the developer, or any person other than the purchaser, has the right to retain control of the board of administration of the association for a period of time which may exceed 1 year after the closing of the sale of a majority of the units in that timeshare plan to persons other than successors or concurrent developers and the plan is one in which all purchasers automatically become members of the association, a statement in conspicuous type in substantially the following form: THE DEVELOPER (OR OTHER PERSON) HAS THE RIGHT TO RETAIN CONTROL OF THE ASSOCIATION AFTER A MAJORITY OF THE UNITS HAVE BEEN SOLD. Immediately following this statement, the location in the disclosure materials where this right to control is described in detail shall be stated.

(s) If there are any restrictions upon the sale, transfer, conveyance, or leasing of a timeshare period, a statement in conspicuous type in substantially the following form: THE SALE, LEASE, OR TRANSFER OF TIMESHARE PERIODS IS RESTRICTED OR CONTROLLED. Immediately following this statement, the location in the disclosure materials where the restriction, limitation, or control on the sale, lease, or transfer of timeshare periods is described in detail shall be stated.

(t) If the timeshare plan is part of a phase project, a statement to that effect and a complete description of the phasing.

(u) A summary of the restrictions, if any, to be imposed on timeshare periods concerning the use of any of the accommodations or facilities, including statements as to whether there are restrictions upon children and pets, and references to the volumes and pages of the timeshare plan documents where such restrictions are found, or, if such restrictions are contained elsewhere, then a copy of the documents containing the restrictions shall be attached as an exhibit. If there are no restrictions, there shall be a statement of such fact.

(v) If there is any land that is offered by the developer for use by the purchasers and which is neither owned by them nor leased to them, the association, or any entity controlled by the purchasers, a statement describing the land, how it will serve the timeshare plan, and the nature and term of service. Immediately following this statement, the location in the disclosure materials where the declaration or other instrument creating such servitude is found shall be stated.

(w) A description of the manner in which utility and other services, including, but not limited to, sewage and waste disposal, water supply, and storm drainage, will be provided and the names of the persons or entities furnishing them.

(x) An estimated operating budget for the timeshare plan and the association or managing entity and a schedule of the purchaser's expense shall be attached as an exhibit and shall contain the following information:

1 The estimated annual expenses of the timeshare plan collectible from purchasers by assessments. The estimated payments by the purchaser for assessments shall also be stated in the estimated amounts for the times when they will be due. Expenses shall also be shown for the shortest timeshare period offered for sale by the developer. If the timeshare plan provides for the offer and sale of units to be used on a non-timeshare basis, the estimated monthly and annual expenses shall be set forth in a separate schedule.

2 The estimated weekly, monthly, and annual expenses of the purchaser of each timeshare period, other than assessments payable to the managing entity. Expenses which are personal to purchasers that are not uniformly incurred by all purchasers or that are not provided for or contemplated by the timeshare plan documents may be excluded from this estimate.

3 The estimated items of expenses of the timeshare plan and the managing entity, except as excluded under subparagraph 2 including, but not limited to, the following items, which shall be stated either as management expenses collectible by assessments or as expenses of the purchaser payable to persons other than the managing entity:

a    Expenses for the managing entity.
(I)    Administration of the managing entity.
(II)    Management fees.
(III)    Maintenance.

(IV)    Rent for recreational and other commonly used facilities.
(V)    Taxes upon timeshare property.
(VI)    Taxes upon leased areas.
(VII)    Insurance.
(VIII)  Security provisions.
(IX)    Other expenses.
(X)    Operating capital.
(XI) Reserves for deferred maintenance and reserves for capital expenditures. All reserves shall be calculated by a formula which is based upon estimated life and replacement cost of each reserve item. Reserves for deferred maintenance shall include accounts for roof replacement, building painting, pavement resurfacing, replacement of unit furnishings and equipment, and any other component the useful life of which is less than the useful life of the overall structure.
(XII) Fees payable to the division.
b    Expenses for a purchaser.
(I)    Rent for the unit, if subject to a lease.
(II)    Rent payable by the purchaser directly to the lessor or agent under any recreational lease or lease for the use of commonly used facilities, which use and payment is a mandatory condition of ownership and is not included in the common expense or assessments for common maintenance paid by the purchasers to the association.

4 The estimated amounts shall be stated for a period of at least 12 months and may distinguish between the period prior to the time that purchasers elect a majority of the board of administration and the period after that date.

5 If the developer intends to guarantee the level of assessments, a description of such arrangement, including, but not limited to:

a The specific time period during which the guarantee will be in effect.

b A statement that the developer will pay all expenses incurred in excess of the amounts collected from purchasers or unit owners other than the developer if the developer has excused himself from the payment of assessments during the guarantee period.

c The level, expressed in total dollars, at which the developer guarantees the budget.

6 If the developer intends to provide a trust fund to defer or reduce the payment of annual assessments, a copy of the trust instrument shall be attached as an exhibit and shall include a description of such arrangement, including, but not limited to:

a The specific amount of such trust funds and the source of the funds.

b The name and address of the trustee.

c The investment methods permitted by the trust agreement.

d A statement in conspicuous type that the funds from the trust account may not cover all assessments and that there is no guarantee that purchasers will not have to pay assessments in the future.

(y) A schedule of estimated closing expenses to be paid by a purchaser or lessee of a timeshare period and a statement as to whether a title opinion or title insurance policy is available to the purchaser and, if so, at whose expense.

(z) The identity of the developer and the chief operating officer or principal directing the creation and sale of the timeshare plan and a statement of the experience of each in this field or, if no experience, a statement of that fact.

(aa) A statement of any service, maintenance, or recreation contracts or leases that may be cancelled by the purchasers.

(bb) A statement of the total financial obligation of the purchaser, including the initial purchase price and any additional charges to which the purchaser may be subject.

(cc) The name of any person who will or may have the right to alter, amend, or add to the charges to which the purchaser may be subject and the terms and conditions under which such alterations, amendments, or additions may be imposed.

(dd) An explanation of the purchaser's right of cancellation.

(ee) A description of the insurance coverage provided for the benefit of the purchasers.

(ff) A statement as to whether the timeshare plan is participating in an exchange program and, if so, the name and address of the exchange company offering the exchange program.

(gg) Any other information that the seller, with the approval of the division, desires to include in the public offering statement.

(hh) Copies of the following documents and plans, to the extent they are applicable, shall be included as exhibits:

1 The declaration of condominium, or the proposed declaration if the declaration has not been recorded.

2 The cooperative documents, or the proposed cooperative documents if the documents have not been recorded.

3 The declaration of covenants and restrictions, or proposed declaration if the declaration has not been recorded.

4 The articles of incorporation creating the association.

5 The bylaws of the association.

6 The ground lease or other underlying lease of the real property on which the timeshare plan is situated.

7 The management agreement and all maintenance and other contracts regarding the management and operation of the timeshare property which have terms in excess of 1 year.

8 The estimated operating budget for the timeshare plan and the requirement schedule of purchasers' expenses.

9 The floor plan of each type of accommodation and the plot plan showing the location of all accommodations and facilities of the timeshare plan.

10 The lease of recreational facilities and other facilities which will be used only by purchasers of the timeshare plan.

11 The lease of facilities used by purchasers and others.

12 The form of timeshare period lease, if the offer is of a leasehold.

13 A declaration of servitude of properties serving the accommodations or facilities but not owned by purchasers or leased to them or the association.

14 The statement of condition of the existing building or buildings, if the offering is of timeshare periods in an operation being converted to condominium or cooperative ownership.

15 The statement of inspection for termite damage and treatment of the existing improvements, if the timeshare property is a conversion.

16 The form of agreement for sale or lease of timeshare periods.

17 The executed agreement for escrow of payments made to the developer prior to closing.

18 The documents containing any restrictions on use of the property required by paragraph (u).

19 The documents creating the timeshare plan.

20 Any contract or lease to be signed by the purchasers.

(ii) Such other information as is necessary to fully and fairly disclose all aspects of the timeshare plan. However, if a developer has, in good faith, attempted to comply with the requirements of this section, and if, in fact, he has substantially complied with the disclosure requirements of this chapter, nonmaterial errors or omissions shall not be actionable.

For purposes of this section, descriptions shall include locations, areas, capacities, numbers, volumes, or sizes and may be stated as approximations or minimums.

### Section 721.08 Escrow accounts; nondisturbance instruments, alternate security arrangements

(1) Prior to the filing of the public offering statement with the division, the developer shall establish an escrow account with an escrow agent for the purpose of protecting the deposits of purchasers. All escrow agents shall be independent of the developer and seller: and no developer or seller, nor any officer, director, affiliate, subsidiary, or employee thereof, may serve as escrow agent. An escrow agent shall maintain the accounts called for in this section only in such a manner as to be under the direct supervision and control of the escrow agent. The escrow agent shall have a fiduciary duty to each purchaser to maintain the escrow accounts in accordance with good accounting principles and to release the purchaser's funds or other property from escrow only in accordance with this chapter. The escrow agent shall retain all affidavits received pursuant to this section for a period of 5 years. Should

the escrow agent receive conflicting demands for the escrowed funds or property, the escrow agent shall immediately either, with the consent of all parties, submit the matter to arbitration or, by interpleader or otherwise, seek an adjudication of the matter by court.

(2) One hundred percent of all funds or other property which is received from or on behalf of purchasers of the timeshare plan or timeshare period prior to the occurrence of events required in this subsection shall be deposited pursuant to an escrow agreement approved by the division. The escrow agreement shall provide that the funds or property may be released from escrow only as follows:

(a) *Cancellation*—In the event a purchaser gives a valid notice of cancellation pursuant to s. 721.10 or is otherwise entitled to cancel the sale, the funds or property received from or on behalf of the purchaser, or the proceeds thereof, shall be returned to the purchaser. Such refund shall be made within 20 days of demand therefor by the purchaser or within 5 days after receipt of funds from the purchaser's cleared check, whichever is later. If the purchaser has received benefits under the contract prior to the effective date of the cancellation, the funds or property to be returned to the purchaser may be reduced by the proportion of contract benefits actually received.

(b) *Purchaser's default*—Following expiration of the 10-day cancellation period, if the purchaser defaults in the performance of his obligations under the terms of the contract to purchase or such other agreement by which the seller sells the timeshare period, the developer shall provide an affidavit to the escrow agent requesting release of the escrowed funds or property and shall provide a copy of such affidavit to the purchaser who has defaulted. The developer's affidavit, as required herein, shall include:

1 A statement that the purchaser has defaulted and that the developer has not defaulted;

2 A brief explanation of the nature of the default and the date of its occurrence;

3 A statement that pursuant to the terms of the contract the developer is

entitled to the funds held by the escrow agent; and

4 A statement that the developer has not received from the purchaser any written notice of a dispute between the purchaser and developer or a claim by the purchaser to the escrow.

(c) *Compliance with conditions—*

1 If the timeshare plan is one in which timeshare licenses are to be sold and no cancellation or default has occurred, the escrow agent may release the escrowed funds or property upon presentation of:

a An affidavit by the developer that all of the following conditions have been met:

(I) Expiration of the cancellation period.

(II) Completion of construction.

(III) Closing.

(IV) Execution and recordation of the nondisturbance and notice to creditors instrument, as described in this section.

b A certified copy of the recorded nondisturbance and notice to creditors instrument.

c A copy of a memorandum of agreement, as defined in s. 721.05(18), which has been irretrievably delivered for recording.

2 If the timeshare plan is one in which timeshare estates are to be sold and no cancellation or default has occurred, the escrow agent may release the escrowed funds or property upon presentation of:

a An affidavit by the developer that all of the following conditions have been met:

(I) Expiration of the cancellation period.

(II) Completion of construction.

(III) Closing.

b If the timeshare estate is sold by agreement for deed, a certified copy of the recorded nondisturbance and notice to creditors instrument, as described in this section.

If the deveoper has previously provided a certified copy of any document required by this section, he may for all subsequent disbursements substitute a true and correct copy of the certified copy, provided no changes to the document have been made or are required to be made.

(3) The nondisturbance and notice to creditors instrument, when required, shall be executed by every person having an interest in the accommodations or facilities or having a lien, mortgage, or other encumbrance to which the facilities or accommodations are subject. The instrument shall state that:

(a) If the party seeking enforcement is not in default of its obligations, the instrument may be enforced by both the seller and any purchaser of the timeshare plan;

(b) The instrument shall be effective as between the timeshare purchaser and interestholder despite any rejection or cancellation of the contract between the timeshare purchaser and developer during bankruptcy proceedings of the developer;

(c) So long as the interestholder has any interest in the accommodations, facilities, or plan, the interestholder will fully honor all the rights of the timeshare purchasers in and to the timeshare plan, will honor the purchasers' right to cancel their contracts and receive appropriate refunds, and will comply with all other requirements of this chapter and rules promulgated hereunder.

The instrument shall contain language sufficient to provide subsequent creditors of the developer and interestholders with notice of the existence of the timeshare plan and of the rights of purchasers and shall serve to protect the interest of the timeshare purchasers from any claims of subsequent creditors. A copy of the recorded nondisturbance and notice to creditors instrument, when required, shall be provided to each timeshare purchaser at the time the purchase contract is executed.

(4) In lieu of any escrow provisions required by this act, the director of the division shall have the discretion to permit deposit of the funds or other property in an escrow account as required by the jurisdiction in which the sale took place.

(5) In lieu of any escrows required by this section, the director of the division shall have the discretion to accept other assurances, including, but not limited to a

surety bond issued by a company authorized and licensed to do business in this state as surety or an irrevocable letter of credit in an amount equal to the escrow requirements of this section.

(6) An escrow agent holding funds escrowed pursuant to this section may invest such escrowed funds in securities of the United States Government, or any agency thereof, or in savings or time deposits in institutions insured by an agency of the United States Government. The right to receive the interest generated by any such investments shall be paid to the party to whom the escrowed funds or property are paid unless otherwise specified by contract.

(7) Each escrow agent shall maintain separate books and records for each timeshare plan and shall maintain such books and records in accordance with good accounting practices.

(8) Any developer, seller, or escrow agent who intentionally fails to comply with the provisions of this section concerning the establishment of an escrow account, deposits of funds into escrow, and withdrawal therefrom is guilty of a felony of the third degree, punishable as provided in s. 775.082, s. 775.083, or s. 775.084, or the successor thereof. The failure to establish an escrow account or to place funds therein as required in this section is prima facie evidence of an intentional and purposeful violation of this section.

### Section 721.09 Reservation agreements; escrows

(1)(a) Prior to filing the public offering statement with the division, a seller shall not offer a timeshare plan for sale but may accept reservation deposits upon approval by the division of a fully executed escrow agreement and reservation agreement properly filed with the division.

(b) Reservations shall not be taken on a timeshare plan unless the seller has an ownership interest or leasehold interest, of a duration at least equal to the duration of the proposed timeshare plan, in the land upon which the timeshare plan is to be developed.

(2) Each executed reservation agreement shall be signed by the developer and shall contain the following:

(a) A statement that the escrow agent will grant a prospective purchaser an immediate, unqualified refund of the reservation deposit upon the written request of either the purchaser or the seller directed to the escrow agent.

(b) A statement that the escrow agent may not otherwise release moneys unless a contract is signed by the purchaser, authorizing the transfer of the escrowed reservation deposit as a deposit on the purchase price. Such deposit shall then be subject to the requirements of s. 721.08.

(c) A statement of the obligation of the developer to file a public offering statement with the division prior to entering into binding contracts.

(d) A statement of the right of the purchaser to receive the public offering statement required by this chapter.

(e) The name and address of the escrow agent and a statement that the escrow agent will provide a receipt.

(f) A statement that the seller assures that the purchase price represented in or pursuant to the reservation agreement will be the price in the contract for the purchase or that the price represented may be exceeded within a stated amount or percentage or a statement that no assurance is given as to the price in the contract for purchase.

(3)(a) The total amount paid for a reservation shall be deposited into a reservation escrow account.

(b) An escrow agent shall maintain the accounts called for in this section only in such a manner as to be under the direct supervision and control of the escrow agent.

(c) The escrow agent may invest the escrowed funds in securities of the United States Government, or any agency thereof, or in savings or time deposits in institutions insured by an agency of the United States Government. The interest generated by any such investments shall be payable to the party entitled to receive the escrowed funds or property.

(d) The escrowed funds shall at all reasonable times be available for withdrawal in full by the escrow agent.

(e) Each escrow agent shall maintain separate books and records for each timeshare plan and shall maintain such books and records in accordance with good accounting practices.

(f) Any seller or escrow agent who intentionally fails to comply with the provisions of this section regarding deposit of funds in escrow and withdrawal therefrom is guilty of a felony of the third degree, punishable as provided in s. 775.082, s. 775.083, or s. 775.084, or the successor of any of such sections. The failure to establish an escrow account or to place funds therein as required in this section is prima facie evidence of an intentional and purposeful violation of this section.

### Section 721.10  Cancellation

(1) A purchaser has the right to cancel the contract until midnight of the 10th calendar day following whichever of the following days occurs later:

(a) The execution date; or

(b) The day on which the purchaser received the last of all documents required to be provided to him.

This right of cancellation may not be waived by any purchaser or by any other person on behalf of the purchaser. Furthermore, no closing may occur until the cancellation period of the timeshare purchaser has expired. Any attempt to obtain a waiver of the cancellation right of the timeshare purchaser, or to hold a closing prior to the expiration of the cancellation period, is unlawful and such closing is voidable at the option of the purchaser for a period of 1 year after the expiration of the cancellation period. However, nothing in this section precludes the execution of documents in advance of closing for delivery after expiration of the cancellation period.

(2) Any notice of cancellation shall be considered given on the date postmarked if mailed, or when transmitted from the place of origin if telegraphed, so long as the notice is actually received by the developer or escrow agent. If given by means of a writing transmitted other than by mail or telegraph, the notice of cancellation shall be considered given at the time of delivery at the place of business of the developer.

(3) In the event of a timely preclosing cancellation, or in the event the plan is one in which timeshare licenses are sold and at any time the accommodations or facilities are no longer available, the developer shall honor the right of any purchaser to cancel the contract which granted the timeshare purchaser rights in and to the plan. Upon such cancellation, the developer shall refund to the purchaser all payments made by the purchaser which exceed the proportionate amount of benefits made available under the plan, using the number of years of the proposed plan as the base. Such refund shall be made within 20 days of demand therefor by the purchaser or within 5 days after receipt of funds from the purchaser's cleared check, whichever is later.

### Section 721.11  Advertising    materials; oral statements

(1)(a) Any advertising material relating to a timeshare plan, including prize and gift promotional offers, shall be filed with the division by the developer 10 days prior to use. All such advertising materials must be substantially in compliance with this chapter and in full compliance with the mandatory provisions of this chapter. In the event that any such material is not in compliance with this chapter, the division may require the developer to correct the deficiency by notifying the developer of the deficiency; and, if the developer fails to correct the deficiency, the division may file administrative charges against the developer and exact such penalties or remedies as provided in s. 721.26.

(b) The director of the division shall have the discretion to accept other assurances from the developer to assure the developer will comply with the provisions of this chapter regarding all advertising materials, including prize and gift promotional offers, used by the developer. Such assurances shall include, but not be limited to, a surety bond issued by a company authorized and licensed to do business in this state as surety or an irrevocable letter of credit in the amount of $10,000. Upon the acceptance by the director of such assurances from the developer, the developer shall be entitled to file and use advertising materials, including prize and gift promotional offers, in accordance with paragraph (c). In the event the developer intends to file and use any lodging or vacation certificates as advertising material pursuant to paragraph (c), the director shall have the discretion to increase the assurances to an amount deemed sufficient by the director to fully secure the performance of the certificate promoter, or to provide refunds to certificateholders in the event of nonperformance by the certificate promoter. The purpose of such other assurances, if accepted by the director, shall be to provide the division with a source of funds to secure the developer's promise in any prize and gift promotional offer to deliver the prize or gift represented in such offer to any prospective purchaser not receiving the represented prize or gift.

(c) A developer from whom other assurances have been accepted by the director of the division pursuant to paragraph (b) shall file all advertising material, including prize and gift promotional offers with the division at the time of use. All such advertising materials must be substantially in compliance with this chapter and in full compliance with the mandatory provisions of this chapter. In the event that any such material is not in compliance with this chapter, the division may require the developer to correct the deficiency by notifying the developer of the deficiency: and, if the developer fails to correct the deficiency after receiving such notice, the division may file administrative charges against the developer and exact such penalities or remedies as provided in s. 721.26. So long as the developer prepares and disseminates the advertising material in good faith, the division shall not penalize the developer for any deficiencies which the division determines to exist in any advertising material which the developer uses prior to receipt of a notice of deficiency from the division regarding the advertising material. For purposes of this section, 'good faith' shall mean that the developer has

reasonably attempted to comply with the provisions of this chapter relating to advertising material, and that any deficiency determined to exist by the division is not material and adverse to a prospective purchaser.

(2) The term 'advertising material' includes;

(a) Any promotional brochure, pamphlet, advertisement, or other material to be disseminated to the public in connection with the sale of a timeshare plan.

(b) A transcript of any radio or television advertisement.

(c) Any lodging or vacation certificate.

(d) A transcript of any standard oral sales presentation.

(e) Any billboard or other sign posted on or off the premises, except that such billboard or sign shall not be required to contain the disclosure set forth in paragraph (5)(a) or (5)(b), unless it relates to a prize and gift promotional offer. For purposes of this section, a 'sign' shall mean advertising which is affixed to real or personal property and which is not disseminated by other than visual means to prospective purchasers.

(f) Any photograph, drawing, or artist's representation of accommodations or facilities of a timeshare plan which exists or which will or may exist.

(g) Any paid publication relating to a timeshare plan which exists or which will or may exist.

(h) Any other promotional device or statement related to a timeshare plan, including any prize and gift promotional offer as described in s. 721.111.

(3) The term 'advertising material' does not include:

(a) Any stockholder communication such as an annual report or interim financial report, proxy material, registration statement, securities prospectus, registration, property report, or other material required to be delivered to a prospective purchaser by an agency of any other state or the Federal Government.

(b) Any communication addressed to and relating to the account of any person who has previously executed a contract for the sale and purchase of a timeshare period in the timeshare plan to which the communication relates, except when directed to the sale of additional timeshare periods.

(c) Any audio, written, or visual publication or material relating to an exchange company or exchange program.

(d) Any audio, written, or visual publication or material relating to the promotion of the availability of any accommodations or facilities, or both, for transient rental, so long as a mandatory tour of a timeshare plan or attendance at a mandatory sales presentation is not a term or condition of the availability of such accommodations or facilities, or both, and so long as the failure of any transient renter to take a tour of a timeshare plan or attend a sales presentation does not result in any reduction in the level of services which would otherwise be available to such transient renter.

(4) No advertising or oral statement made by any seller shall:

(a) Misrepresent a fact or create a false or misleading impression regarding the timeshare plan or promotion thereof.

(b) Make a prediction of specific or immediate increases in the price or value of timeshare periods.

(c) Contain a statement concerning future price increases by the seller which are nonspecific or not bona fide.

(d) Contain any asterisk or other reference symbol as a means of contradicting or substantially changing any previously made statement or as a means of obscuring a material fact.

(e) Describe any improvement to the timeshare plan that is not required to be built or that is uncompleted unless the improvement is conspicuously labelled as 'NEED NOT BE BUILT,' 'PROPOSED,' or 'UNDER CONSTRUCTION' with the date of promised completion clearly indicated.

(f) Misrepresent the size, nature, extent, qualities, or characteristics of the offered accommodations or facilities.

(g) Misrepresent the amount or period of time during which the accommodations or facilities will be available to any purchaser.

(h) Misrepresent the nature or extent of any services incident to the timeshare plan.

(i) Make any misleading or deceptive representation with respect to the contents of the public offering statement and the contract or the rights, privileges, benefits, or obligations of the purchaser under the contract or this chapter.

(j) Misrepresent the conditions under which a purchaser may exchange the right to use accommodations or facilities in one location for the right to use accommodations or facilities in another location.

(k) Misrepresent the availability of a resale or rental program offered by or on behalf of the developer.

(l) Contain an offer or inducement to purchase which purports to be limited as to quantity or restricted as to time limit unless the numerical quantity or time limit applicable to the offer or inducement is clearly stated.

(m) Imply that a facility is available for the exclusive use of purchasers if the facility will actually be shared by others or by the general public.

(n) Purport to have resulted from a referral unless the name of the person making the referral can be produced upon demand of the division.

(o) Misrepresent the source of the advertising or statement by leading a prospective purchaser to believe that the advertising material is mailed by a governmental or official agency, credit bureau, bank, or attorney, if that is not the case.

(p) Misrepresent the value of any prize, gift, or other item to be awarded in connection with any prize and gift promotional offer, as described in s. 721.111.

(5)(a) No written advertising material, including any lodging certificate, gift award, premium, discount, or display booth, may be utilized without a disclosure in conspicuous type that: THIS ADVERTISING MATERIAL IS BEING USED FOR THE PURPOSE OF SOLICITING SALES OF TIMESHARE PERIODS.

(b) This subsection does not apply to any advertising material which involves a project or development which includes sales of real estate or other commodities or services in addition to timeshare periods, including, but not limited to, lot sales, condominium or home sales, or the rental of resort accommodations. However, if the sale of timeshare periods, as compared with such other sales or rentals, is the primary purpose of the advertising material, a disclosure shall be made in conspicuous type that: THIS ADVERTISING MATERIAL IS BEING USED FOR THE PURPOSE OF SOLICITING THE SALE OF (Disclosure shall include timeshare periods and may include other types of sales). Factors which the division may consider in determining whether the primary purpose of the advertising material is the sale of timeshare periods include:

1 The retail value of the timeshare periods compared to the retail value of the other real estate, commodities, or services being offered in the advertising material.

2 The amount of space devoted to the timeshare portion of the project in the advertising material compared to the amount of space devoted to other portions of the project, including, but not limited to, printed material, photographs, or drawings.

### Section 721.111 Prize and gift promotional offers

(1) As used herein, the term 'prize and gift promotional offer' means any advertising material wherein a prospective purchaser may receive goods or services other than the timeshare plan itself, either free or at a discount, including, but not limited to, the use of any prize, gift, award, premium, or lodging or vacation certificate.

(2) No game promotion, such as a contest of chance, gift enterprise, or sweepstakes, in which the elements of chance and prize are present may be used after January 1, 1985, in connection with the offering or sale of timeshare periods. All gift promotions used until that time shall meet all requirements of this chapter and of ss. 849.092 and 849.094(1), (2), and (7).

(3) Any prize, gift, or other item offered pursuant to a prize and gift promotional offer must be delivered to the prospective purchaser on the day he appears to claim it, whether or not he purchases a timeshare period.

(4) A separate filing for each prize and gift promotional offer to be used in the sale of timeshare periods shall be made with the division pursuant to s. 721.11(1). One item of each prize or gift, except cash, must be made available for inspection by the division.

(5) Each filing of a prize and gift promotional offer with the division shall include, when applicable:

(a) A copy of all advertising material to be used in connection with the prize and gift promotional offer.

(b) The name, address, and telephone number (including area code) of the supplier or manufacturer from whom each type or variety of prize, gift, or other item is obtained.

(c) The manufacturer's model number or other description of such item.

(d) The information on which the developer relies in determining the verifiable retail value.

(e) The name, address, and telephone number (including area code) of the promotional entity responsible for overseeing and operating the prize and gift promotional offer.

(f) The name and address of the registered agent in this state of the promotional entity for service of process purposes.

(g) The number of anticipated recipients of each item of advertising material related to the prize and gift promotional offer.

(h) Full disclosure of all pertinent information concerning the use of lodging or vacation certificates, including the terms and conditions of the campaign and the fact and extent of participation in such campaign by the developer. The division may require reasonable assurances that the obligation incurred by a seller or his agent in a lodging certificate program can be met.

(6) Each developer shall pay to the division a fee of $100 for the filing of each prize and gift promotional offer, at the time of filing. Those developers utilizing

game promotions in which the elements of chance and prize are present shall pay an additional $400 fee at the time of filing of the prize and gift promotional offer. No additional fee may be charged for the submission of corrected advertising material related to a prize and gift promotional offer or for the submission of additional material related to a prize and gift promotional offer for which a prior filing has been made.

(7) All advertising material to be distributed in connection with a prize and gift promotional offer shall contain, in addition to the information required pursuant to the provisions of s. 721.11, the following disclosures;

(a) A description of the prize, gift, or other item that the prospective purchaser will actually receive, including the manufacturer's suggested retail price or, if none is available, the verifiable retail value.

(b) All rules, terms, requirements, and preconditions which must be fulfilled or met before a prospective purchaser may claim any prize, gift, or other item involved in the prize and gift promotional plan, including whether the prospective purchaser is required to attend a sales presentation in order to receive the prize, gift, or other item.

(c) The date upon which the offer expires.

(d) If the number of prizes, gifts, or other items to be awarded is limited, a statement of the number of items that will be awarded.

(e) The method by which prizes, gifts, or other items are to be awarded.

(8) All developers shall file with the division by March 1 of each year the following information regarding each prize and gift promotional offer used during the prior calendar year.

(a) The total number of each prize, gift, or other item actually awarded or given away.

(b) The name and address of each person who actually received a prize, gift, or other item which had a verifiable retail value or manufacturer's suggested retail price in excess of $200. This regulation does not apply to recipients of lodging or vacation certificates.

(9) All prizes, gifts, or other items represented by the developer to be awarded in connection with any prize and gift promotional offer shall be awarded by the date referenced in the advertising material used in connection with such offer.

**Section 721.12 Recordkeeping by seller**
Each seller of a timeshare plan shall maintain among its business records the following:

(1) A copy of each contract for the sale of a timeshare period, which contract has not been cancelled. If a timeshare estate is being sold, the seller is required to retain a copy of the contract only until a deed of conveyance, agreement for deed, or lease is recorded in the office of the clerk of the circuit court in the county wherein the plan is located.

(2) A list of all salespersons of the seller and their last known addresses. The names and addresses of such salespersons whose employments terminate shall be retained for 3 years after termination of employment. If the seller has a contract with any entity not owned or controlled by the seller for the sale of the timeshare plan, that entity shall be responsible for maintaining a record of current employees involved in the sale of the timeshare plan and a record of any former employees involved in the sale of such plan within the previous 3 years.

**Section 721.13 Management**
(1) Before the first sale of a timeshare period, the developer shall create or provide for a managing entity which may be the developer, a separate management firm, or an owners' association, or some combination thereof.

(2) The managing entity shall act in the capacity of a fiduciary to the purchasers of the timeshare plan.

(3) The duties of the managing entity include, but are not limited to:

(a) Management and maintenance of all accommodations and facilities constituting the timeshare plan.

(b) Collection of all assessments for common expenses.

(c) Providing each year to all purchasers an itemized annual budget which shall include all receipts and expenditures.

(d) Maintenance of all books and records concerning the timeshare plan on the premises of the accommodations or facilities of such plan and making all such books and records reasonably available for inspection by any purchaser or the authorized agent of such purchaser.

(e) Arranging for an annual independent audit of all the books and financial records of the timeshare plan by a certified public accountant in accordance with generally accepted auditing standards as defined by the rules of the Board of Accountancy of the Department of Professional Regulation. A copy of the audit shall be forwarded to the officers of the owners' association, or, if no association exists, the owner of each timeshare period shall be notified that such audit is available upon request.

(f) Making available for inspection by the division any books and records of the timeshare plan upon the request of the division.

(g) Scheduling occupancy of the timeshare units, when purchasers are not entitled to use specific timeshare periods, so that all purchasers will be provided the use and possession of the accommodations and facilities of the timeshare plan which they have purchased.

(h) Performing any other functions and duties which are necessary and proper to maintain the accommodations or facilities as provided in the contract and as advertised.

(4) The managing entity shall maintain among its records and provide to the division upon request a complete list of the names and addresses of all purchasers and owners of timeshare units in the timeshare plan. The managing entity shall update this list no less frequently than quarterly.

(5) Any managing entity, or employee or agent thereof, who willfully misappropriates the property or funds of a timeshare plan is guilty of a felony of the third degree, punishable as provided in s. 775.082, s. 775.083, or s. 775.084, or the successor thereof.

(6)(a) The managing entity of any timeshare plan located in this state, including, but not limited to, those plans created with respect to a condominium pursuant to chapter 718 or a cooperative pursuant to chapter 719, may deny the use of the accommodations and facilities of the timeshare plan to any purchaser who is delinquent in the payment of any assessments made by the managing entity against such purchaser for common expenses or for ad valorem real estate taxes pursuant to this chapter or pursuant to s. 192.037. Such denial of use shall also extend to those parties claiming under the delinquent purchaser described in paragraphs (b) and (c). For purposes of this subsection, a purchaser shall be considered delinquent in the payment of a given assessment only upon the expiration of 60 days after the date the assessment is billed to the purchaser or upon the expiration of 60 days after the date the assessment is due, whichever is later. For purposes of this subsection, an affiliated exchange program shall be any exchange program which has a contractual relationship with the creating developer or the managing entity of the timeshare plan, or any exchange program that notifies the managing entity in writing that it has members that are purchasers of the timeshare plan, and the exchange companies operating such affiliated exchange programs shall be affiliated exchange companies. Any denial of use shall be implemented only pursuant to this subsection.

(b) A managing entity desiring to deny the use of the accommodations and facilities of the timeshare plan to a delinquent purchaser and to those claiming under the purchaser, including his guests, lessees, and third parties receiving use rights in the timeshare period in question through a nonaffiliated exchange program, shall, no less than 30 days prior to the first day of the purchaser's use period, notify the purchaser in writing of the total amount of any delinquency which then exists or which will exist as of the first day of such use period, including any accrued interest and late charges permitted to be imposed under the terms of the public offering statement for the timeshare plan or by law and including a per diem amount, if any, to account for further accrual of interest and late charges between the stated effective date of the notice and the first date of use. The notice shall also clearly state that the purchaser will not be permitted to use his timeshare period until the total amount of such delinquency is satisfied in full or until the purchaser produces satisfactory evidence that the delinquency does not exist. The notice shall be mailed to the purchaser at his last known address as recorded in the books and records of the timeshare plan, and the notice shall be effective to bar the use of the purchaser and those claiming use rights under the purchaser, including his guests, lessees, and third parties receiving use rights in the timeshare period in question through a nonaffiliated exchange program, until such time as the purchaser is no longer delinquent. The notice shall not be effective to bar the use of third parties receiving use rights in the timeshare period in question through an affiliated exchange program without the additional notice to the affiliated exchange program required by paragraph (c).

(c) In addition to giving notice to the delinquent purchaser as required by paragraph (b), a managing entity desiring to deny the use of the accommodations and facilities of the timeshare plan to third parties receiving use rights in the delinquent purchaser's timeshare period through any affiliated exchange program shall notify the affiliated exchange company in writing of the denial of use. The receipt of such written notice by the affiliated exchange company shall be effective to bar the use of all third parties claiming through the affiliated exchange program, and such notice shall be binding upon the affiliated exchange company and all third parties claiming through the affiliated exchange program until such time as the affiliated exchange company receives notice from the managing entity that the purchaser is no longer delinquent. However, any third party claiming through the affiliated exchange program who has received a confirmed assignment of the delinquent purchaser's use rights from the affiliated exchange company

prior to the expiration of 48 hours after the receipt by the affiliated exchange company of such written notice from the managing entity shall be permitted by the managing entity to use the accommodations and facilities of the timeshare plan to the same extent that he would be allowed to use such accommodations and facilities if the delinquent purchaser were not delinquent.

(d) Any costs reasonably incurred by the managing entity in connection with its compliance with the requirements of paragraphs (b) and (c), together with any costs reasonably incurred by an affiliated exchange company in connection with its compliance with the requirements of paragraph (c), may be assessed by the managing entity against the delinquent purchaser and collected in the same manner as if such costs were common expenses of the timeshare plan allocable solely to the delinquent purchaser. The costs incurred by the affiliated exchange company shall be collected by the managing entity as the agent for the affiliated exchange company. In no event shall the total costs to be assessed against the delinquent purchaser pursuant to this paragraph at any one time exceed 5 percent of the total amount of delinquency contained in the notice given to the delinquent purchaser pursuant to paragraph (b) per timeshare period or $15 per timeshare period, whichever is less.

(e) An exchange company may elect to deny exchange privileges to any member whose use of the accommodations and facilities of the member's timeshare plan is denied pursuant to paragraph (b), and no exchange program or exchange company shall be liable to any of its members or third parties on account of any such denial of exchange privileges.

(f) A managing entity shall have breached its fiduciary duty described in subsection (2) in the event it enforces the denial of use pursuant to paragraph (b) against any one purchaser or group of purchasers without similarly enforcing it against all purchasers, including all developers and owners of the underlying fee. A managing entity shall also have breached its fiduciary duty in the event an error in the books and records of the timeshare plan results in a denial of use pursuant to this subsection of any purchaser who is not, in fact, delinquent. In addition to any remedies otherwise available to purchasers of the timeshare plan arising from such breaches of fiduciary duty, such breach shall also constitute a violation of this chapter and shall subject the managing entity to the penalties set forth in s. 721.26 and to the purchaser remedies set forth in s. 721.21. In addition, any purchaser receiving a notice of delinquency pursuant to paragraph (b), or any third party claiming under such purchaser pursuant to paragraph (b), may immediately bring an action for injunctive or declaratory relief against the managing entity seeking to have the notice invalidated on the grounds that the purchaser is not, in fact, delinquent, that the managing entity failed to follow the procedures prescribed by this section, or on any other available grounds. The prevailing party in any such action shall be entitled to recover his reasonable attorney's fees from the losing party.

**Section 721.14 Discharge of managing entity**
(1) If timeshare estates are being sold to purchasers of a timeshare plan, the contract retaining a managing entity shall be automatically renewable every 3 years, beginning with the third year after the managing entity is first created or provided for the timeshare plan, unless the purchasers vote to discharge the managing entity. Such a vote shall be conducted by the board of the owners' association. The managing entity shall be discharged if at least 66 percent of the purchasers voting, which shall be at least 50 percent of all votes allocated to purchasers, vote to discharge the managing entity.
(2) In the event the managing entity is discharged, the board of the owners' association is responsible for obtaining another managing entity. If the board fails to do so, any timeshare owner may apply to the circuit court within the jurisdiction of which the accommodations and facilities lie for the appointment of a receiver to manage the affairs of the association. At least 30 days before applying to the circuit court, the timeshare owner shall mail to the association and post in a conspicuous place on the timeshare property a notice describing the intended action, giving the association the opportunity to fill any vacancies on the board. If during such time the association fails to fill the vacancies, the timeshare owner may proceed with the petition. If a receiver is appointed, the association is responsible for payment of the salary of the receiver, court costs, and attorney's fees. The receiver shall have all powers and duties of a duly constituted board of administration and shall serve until the association fills vacancies on the board sufficient to constitute a quorum.
(3) The managing entity of a timeshare plan subject to the provisions of chapter 718 or chapter 719 may be discharged pursuant to chapter 718 or chapter 719, respectively, or its successor or pursuant to this section.

**Section 721.15 Assessments for common expenses**
(1) Until a managing entity is created or provided, the developer shall pay all common expenses.
(2) After the creation or provision of a managing entity, the managing entity shall make an annual assessment against each purchaser for the payment of common expenses, based on the projected annual budget, in the amount specified by the contract between the seller and the purchaser. No owner of a timeshare period may be excused from the payment of his share of the common expenses unless all unit owners are likewise excused from payment, except that the developer may be excused from the payment of his share of the common expenses which would have been assessed against those units during a stated period of time during which he has guaranteed to each purchaser in the timeshare documents, or by agreement between the developer and a majority of the owners of timeshare periods other than the developer, that the assessment for common expenses imposed upon the owners would not

increase over a stated dollar amount. In the event of such a guarantee, the developer is obligated to pay any amount of common expenses incurred during the guarantee period which was not produced by the assessments at the guarantee level from other unit owners.

(3) Past-due assessments may bear interest at the legal rate or at some lesser rate established by the managing entity.

(4) Unless otherwise specified in the contract between the seller and the purchaser, any common expenses benefiting fewer than all purchasers shall be assessed only against those purchasers benefited.

(5) Any assessments for common expenses which have not been spent for common expenses during the year for which such assessments were made shall be shown as an item on the annual budget.

(6) Notwithstanding any contrary requirements of s. 718.112(2)(h) or s. 719.106(1)(g), for timeshare plans subject to this chapter, assessments against purchasers need not be made more frequently than annually.

(7) A purchaser, regardless of how his timeshare estate or timeshare license has been acquired, including a purchaser at a judicial sale, is personally liable for all assessments for common expenses which come due while he is the owner of such interest. A successor in interest is jointly and severally liable with his predecessor in interest for all unpaid assessments against such predecessor up to the time of transfer of the timeshare interest to such successor without prejudice to any right a successor in interest may have to recover from his predecessor in interest any amounts assessed against such predecessor and paid by such successor. The predecessor in interest shall provide the managing entity with a copy of the recorded deed of conveyance if the interest is a timeshare estate or a copy of the instrument of transfer if the interest is a timeshare license, containing the name and mailing address of the successor in interest within 15 days after the date of transfer. The managing entity shall not be liable to any person for any inaccuracy in the books and records of the timeshare

plan arising from the failure of the predecessor in interest to timely and correctly notify the managing entity of the name and mailing address of the successor in interest. Nothing in this subsection shall be construed to impair the operation of s. 718.116(6) for timeshare condominiums.

**Section 721.16 Liens for overdue assessments; mechanics' liens**

(1) The managing entity has a lien on a timeshare period for any assessment levied against that timeshare period from the date such assessment becomes due.

(2) The managing entity may bring an action in its name to foreclose a lien for assessments in the manner a mortgage of real property is foreclosed and may also bring an action to recover a money judgment for the unpaid assessments without waiving any claim of lien. However, in the case of a timeshare plan in which no interest in real property is conveyed, the managing entity may bring an action under the Uniform Commercial Code.

(3) The lien is effective from the date of recording a claim of lien in the public records of the county or counties in which the accommodations or facilities constituting the timeshare plan are located. The claim of lien shall state the name of the timeshare plan and identify the timeshare period for which the lien is effective, state the name of the purchaser, state the assessment amount due, and state the due dates. Notwithstanding any provision of s. 718.116(4)(a) to the contrary, the lien is effective until satisfied or until 5 years have expired after the date the claim of lien is recorded unless, within that time, an action to enforce the lien is commenced pursuant to subsection (2). The claim of lien may include only assessments which are due when the claim is recorded. A claim of lien shall be signed and acknowledged by an officer or agent of the managing entity. Upon full payment, the person making the payment is entitled to receive a satisfaction of the lien.

(4) A judgment in any action or suit brought under this section shall include

costs and reasonable attorney's fees for the prevailing party.

(5) Labor performed on a unit, or materials furnished to a unit, shall not be the basis for the filing of a lien pursuant to the mechanics' lien law against the timeshare unit of any timeshare-period owner not expressly consenting to or requesting the labor or materials.

### Section 721.165 Insurance

(1) The seller, initially, and thereafter the managing entity, shall be responsible for obtaining insurance to protect the accommodations and facilities of the timeshare plan in an amount equal to the replacement cost of such accommodations and facilities.

(2) A copy of each policy of insurance in effect shall be made available for reasonable inspection by purchasers and their authorized agents.

### Section 721.17 Transfer of interest

Except in the case of a timeshare plan subject to the provisions of chapter 718 or chapter 719, no developer or owner of the underlying fee shall sell, lease, assign, mortgage, or otherwise transfer his interest in the accommodations or facilities of the timeshare plan except by an instrument evidencing the transfer recorded in the public records of the county in which the accommodations or facilities are located. The instrument shall be executed by both the transferor and transferee and shall state:

(1) That its provisions are intended to protect the rights of all purchasers of the plan.

(2) That its terms may be enforced by any prior or subsequent timeshare purchaser so long as that purchaser is not in default of his obligations.

(3) That the transferee will fully honor the rights of the purchasers to occupy and use the accommodations and facilities as provided in their original contracts and the timeshare instruments.

(4) That the transferee will fully honor all rights of timeshare purchasers to cancel their contracts and receive appropriate refunds.

(5) That the obligations of the transferee under such instrument will continue to exist despite any cancellation or rejection of the contracts between the developer and purchaser arising out of bankruptcy proceedings.

Should any transfer of the interest of the developer or owner of the underlying fee occur in a manner which is not in compliance with this section, the terms set forth in this section shall be presumed to be a part of the transfer and shall be deemed to be included in the instrument of transfer. Notice shall be mailed to each purchaser of record within 30 days of the transfer. Persons who hold mortgages on the property constituting a timeshare plan before the public offering statement of such plan is approved by the division shall not be considered transferees for the purposes of this section.

### Section 721.18 Exchange programs; filing of information and other materials; filing fees; unlawful acts in connection with an exchange program

(1) If a purchaser is offered the opportunity to subscribe to an exchange program, the seller shall deliver to the purchaser, together with the public offering statement, and prior to the offering or execution of any contract between purchaser and the company offering the exchange program, written information regarding such exchange program; or, if the exchange company is dealing directly with the purchaser, the exchange company shall deliver to the purchaser, prior to the initial offering or execution of any contract between the purchaser and the company offering the exchange program, written information regarding such exchange program. In either case, the purchaser shall certify in writing to the receipt of such information. Such information shall include, but is not limited to, the following information, the form and substance of which shall first be approved by the division in accordance with subsection (2):

(a) The name and address of the exchange company.

(b) The names of all officers, directors, and shareholders of the exchange company.

(c) Whether the exchange company or

any of its officers or directors has any legal or beneficial interest in any developer, seller, or managing entity for any timeshare plan participating in the exchange program and, if so, the name and location of the timeshare plan and the nature of the interest.

(d) Unless otherwise stated, a statement that the purchaser's contract with the exchange company is a contract separate and distinct from the purchaser's contract with the seller of the timeshare plan.

(e) Whether the purchaser's participation in the exchange program is dependent upon the continued affiliation of the timeshare plan with the exchange program.

(f) A statement that the purchaser's participation in the exchange program is voluntary.

(g) A complete and accurate description of the terms and conditions of the purchaser's contractual relationship with the exchange program and the procedure by which changes thereto may be made.

(h) A complete and accurate description of the procedure to qualify for and effectuate exchanges.

(i) A complete and accurate description of all limitations, restrictions, or priorities employed in the operation of the exchange program, including, but not limited to, limitations on exchanges based on seasonality, unit size, or levels of occupancy, expressed in boldfaced type, and, in the event that such limitations, restrictions, or priorities are not uniformly applied by the exchange program, a clear description of the manner in which they are applied.

(j) Whether exchanges are arranged on a space-available basis and whether any guarantees of fulfillment of specific requests for exchanges are made by the exchange program.

(k) Whether and under what circumstances a purchaser, in dealing with the exchange program, may lose the use and occupancy of his timeshare period in any property applied for exchange without his being provided with substitute accommodations by the exchange program.

(l) The fees or range of fees for partici-pation by purchasers in the exchange program, a statement whether any such fees may be altered by the exchange company, and the circumstances under which alterations may be made.

(m) The name and address of the site of each accommodation or facility included in the timeshare plans participating in the exchange program.

(n) The number of the timeshare units in each timeshare plan which are available for occupancy and which qualify for participation in the exchange program, expressed within the following numerical groupings: 1–5; 6–10; 11–20; 21–50; and 51 and over.

(o) The number of currently enrolled purchasers for each timeshare plan participating in the exchange program, expressed within the following numerical groupings: 1–100; 101–249; 250–499; 500–999; and 1,000 and over, and a statement of the criteria used to determine those purchasers who are currently enrolled with the exchange program.

(p) The disposition made by the exchange company of timeshare periods deposited with the exchange program and not used by the exchange company in effecting exchanges.

(q) The following information, which shall be independently audited by a certified public accountant or accounting firm in accordance with the standards of the Accounting Standards Board of the American Institute of Certified Public Accountants and reported annually beginning no later than July 1, 1982:

1 The number of purchasers currently enrolled in the exchange program.

2 The number of accommodations and facilities that have current affiliation agreements with the exchange program.

3 The percentage of confirmed exchanges, which is the number of exchanges confirmed by the exchange program divided by the number of exchanges properly applied for, together with a complete and accurate statement of the criteria used to detrmine whether an exchange request was properly applied for.

4 The number of timeshare periods for which the exchange program has an

outstanding obligation to provide an exchange to a purchaser who relinquished a timeshare period during the year in exchange for a timeshare period in any future year.

5 The number of exchanges confirmed by the exchange program during the year.

(r) A statement in boldfaced type to the effect that the percentage described in subparagraph (q)3 is a summary of the exchange requests entered with the exchange program in the period reported and that the percentage does not indicate the probabilities of a purchaser's being confirmed to any specific choice or range of choices.

(2) Each exchange company offering an exchange program to purchasers in this state shall file the information specified in subsection (1) at least 20 days prior to July 1 of each year. However, an exchange company shall make its initial filing at least 20 days prior to offering an exchange program to any purchaser in this state. Each filing shall be accompanied by an annual filing fee of $500. Within 20 days of receipt of such filing, the division shall determine whether the filing is adequate to meet the requirements of this section and shall notify the exchange company in writing that the division has either approved the filing or found specified deficiencies in the filing. If the division fails to respond within 20 days, the filing shall be deemed approved. The exchange company may correct the deficiencies; and, within 10 days after receipt of corrections from the exchange company, the division shall notify the exchange company in writing that the division has either approved the filing or found additional specified deficiencies in the filing. If at any time the division determines that any of such information supplied by an exchange company fails to meet the requirements of this section, the division may undertake enforcement action against the exchange company in accordance with the provision of s. 721.26.

(3) No developer shall have any liability with respect to any violation of this chapter arising out of the publication by the developer of information provided to it by an exchange company pursuant to this section. No exchange company shall have any liability with respect to any violation of this chapter arising out of the use by a developer of information relating to an exchange program other than that provided to the developer by the exchange company.

(4) Audio, written, or visual publications or materials relating to an exchange company or an exchange program shall be filed with the division within 3 days of their use.

(5) The failure of an exchange company to observe the requirements of this section, or the use of any unfair or deceptive act or practice in connection with the operation of an exchange program, is a violation of this chapter.

**Section 721.19 Provisions requiring purchase or lease of timeshare property by owners' association or unit owners; validity** In any timeshare plan in which timeshare estates are sold, no grant or reservation made by a declaration, lease, or other document, nor any contract made by the developer, managing entity, or owners' association, which requires the owners' association or unit owners to purchase or lease any portion of the timeshare property shall be valid unless approved by a majority of the purchasers other than the developer, after more than 50 percent of the timeshare periods have been sold.

**Section 721.20 Licensing requirements; suspension or revocation of license**

(1) Any seller of a timeshare plan must be a licensed real estate salesman, broker, or broker-salesman as defined in s. 475.01, except as provided in s. 475.011. Solicitors licensed under the provisions of paragraph (2)(a) who engage only in the solicitation of prospective purchasers, and purchasers engaging in solicitation activities as described in paragraph (2)(e), are exempt from the provisions of chapter 475.

(2)(a) Pursuant to rules adopted by the division, each off-premises solicitor or other person who engages in the solicitation of prospective purchasers of units in a timeshare plan must purchase annually a timeshare occupational license for a fee of $25. The license shall expire on July 1 of each year. The division may deny a license to any individual whom the division finds not to be of good moral character, in addition to, or in lieu of, a suspension or revocation provided for in this section for violation of the rules of the division.

(b) It is unlawful for any person to solicit prospective purchasers of a timeshare plan without first having secured a timeshare occupational license and paid the occupational license fee.

(c) Prior to issuing an occupational license, the division shall receive an application, on forms designed by the division, containing such pertinent background information as is necessary to properly identify the applicant; however, the fingerprinting of applicants is not required. The division may deny a license to any individual whom the division finds not to be of good moral character.

(d) The division may deny, suspend, or revoke any occupational license when the holder thereof has violated the provisions of this chapter or the rules and regulations of the division governing timesharing. If any occupational license expires by division rule while administrative charges are pending against the license, the proceedings against the license shall continue to conclusion as if the license were still in effect. The division may impose a civil fine of up to $500 in addition to, or in lieu of, a suspension or revocation provided for in this section for violation of the rules of the division.

(e) Any purchaser who refers no more than 20 people to a developer per year or who otherwise provides testimonials on behalf of a developer shall not be subject to licensure under the provisions of paragraph (a).

(3) This section does not apply to those individuals who offer for sale only timeshare periods in timeshare property located outside this state and who do not engage in any sales activity within this state or to timeshare plans which are registered with the Securities and Exchange Commission. For the purposes of this section, both timeshare licenses and timeshare estates are considered to be interests in real property.

**Section 721.21 Purchasers' remedies** An action for damages or for injunctive or declaratory relief for a violation of this chapter may be brought by any purchaser or association of purchasers against the developer, a seller, an escrow agent, or the managing entity. The prevailing party in any such action, or in any action in which the purchaser claims a right of voidability based upon either a closing before the expiration of the cancellation period or an amendment which materially alters or modifies the offering in a manner adverse to the purchaser, may be entitled to reasonable attorney's fees. Relief under this section does not exclude other remedies provided by law.

**Section 721.22 Partition**

(1) No action for partition of any timeshare unit shall lie, unless otherwise provided for in the contract between the seller and the purchaser.

(2) If a timeshare estate exists as an estate for years with a future interest, the estate for years shall not be deemed to have merged with the future interest, but neither the estate for years nor the corresponding future interest shall be conveyed or encumbered separately from the other.

**Section 721.23 Securities** Timeshare plans are not securities under the provisions of chapter 517 or its successor.

**Section 721.25 Zoning and building** All laws, ordinances, and regulations concerning buildings or zoning shall be construed and applied with reference to the nature and use of the real estate timeshare plan property, without regard to the form of ownership.

**Section 721.26 Regulation by division** In addition to other powers and duties prescribed by chapters 498, 718, and 719, the division has the power to enforce and ensure compliance with the provisions of this chapter. In performing its duties, the division shall have the following powers and duties:

(1) To aid in the enforcement of this chapter, the division may make necessary public or private investigations within or

outside this state to determine whether any person has violated or is about to violate this chapter.

(2) The division may require or permit any person to file a written statement under oath or otherwise, as the division determines, as to the facts and circumstances concerning a matter under investigation.

(3) For the purpose of any investigation under this chapter, the director of the division or any officer or employee designated by the director may administer oaths or affirmations, subpoena witnesses and compel their attendance, take evidence, and require the production of any matter which is relevant to the investigation, including the identity, existence, description, nature, custody, condition, and location of any books, documents, or other tangible things and the identity and location of persons having knowledge of relevant facts or any other matter reasonably calculated to lead to the discovery of material evidence. Upon failure to obey a subpoena or to answer questions propounded by the investigating officer and upon reasonable notice to all persons affected thereby, the division may apply to the circuit court for an order compelling compliance.

(4) The division may prepare and disseminate a prospectus and other information to assist prospective purchasers, sellers, and managing entities of time-share plans in assessing the rights, privileges, and duties pertaining thereto.

(5) Notwithstanding any remedies available to purchasers, if the division has reasonable cause to believe that a violation of this chapter has occurred, the division may institute enforcement proceedings in its own name against any developer, exchange program, seller, managing entity, association, or other person as follows:

(a) The division may permit any person whose conduct or actions may be under investigation to waive formal proceedings and enter into a consent proceeding whereby an order, rule, or letter of censure or warning, whether formal or informal, may be entered against that person.

(b) The division may issue an order requiring a developer, exchange program, seller, managing entity, association, or other person, or other assignees or agents, to cease and desist from an unlawful practice under this chapter and take such affirmative action as in the judgment of the division will carry out the purposes of this chapter.

(c) The division may bring an action in circuit court for declaratory or injunctive relief or for other appropriate relief, including the appointment of a receiver or restitution.

(d)1 The division may impose a civil penalty against any developer, exchange program, seller, association, managing entity, escrow agent, or other person for a violation of this chapter. A penalty may be imposed on the basis of each day of continuing violation, but in no event may the penalty for any offence exceed $10,000. All accounts collected shall be deposited with the Treasurer to the credit of the Division of Florida Land Sales, Condominiums, and Mobile Homes Trust Fund.

2a If a developer, exchange program, seller, escrow agent, or other person fails to pay a civil penalty, the division shall thereupon issue an order directing that such developer, exchange program, seller, escrow agent, or other person cease and desist from further operation until such time as the civil penalty is paid; or the division may pursue enforcement of the penalty in a court of competent jurisdiction.

b If an association or managing entity fails to pay a civil penalty, the division shall thereupon pursue enforcement in a court of competent jurisdiction.

(e) In order to permit the developer, exchange program, seller, managing entity, association, or other person an opportunity either to appeal such decision administratively or to seek relief in a court of competent jurisdiction, the order imposing the civil penalty or the cease and desist order shall not become effective until 20 days after the date of such order.

(f) Any action commenced by the division shall be brought in the county in which the division has its executive offices or in the county where the violation occurred.

(6) The division is authorized to promulgate rules pursuant to chapter 120 as necessary to implement, enforce, and interpret this chapter.

**Section 721.27 Annual fee for each timeshare period in plan** On or before January 1 of each year, each managing entity shall collect as a common expense and pay to the division an annual fee of $1 for each timeshare period within the timeshare plan.

**Section 721.28 Division of Florida Land Sales, Condominiums, and Mobile Homes Trust Fund** All funds collected by the division and any amounts paid as fees or penalties under this chapter shall be deposited in the State Treasury to the credit of the Division of Florida Land Sales, Condominiums, and Mobile Homes Trust Fund created by s. 498.019.

**Section 721.30 Application of ch. 83–264, Laws of Florida**

(1) It is the intent of the Legislature that chapter 83–264, Laws of Florida, apply to timeshare plans existing on or after July 1, 1983, but that chapter 83–264 not be construed to effect the impairment of any existing contract.

(2) Timeshare plans which were filed and approved by the Division of Florida Land Sales and Condominiums of the Department of Business Regulation before July 1, 1983, shall submit all amendments necessary to bring such timeshare plans into compliance with the provisions of chapter 83–264 and shall obtain approval of such amendments no later than October 1, 1983.

(3) With respect to contracts entered into before July 1, 1983, amendments made only for the purpose of bringing a timeshare plan into compliance with chapter 83–264 shall, for purposes of voidability, be determined not to be material or adverse.

(4) If a timeshare plan was filed and approved by the division prior to the effective date of this act, the developer may rely upon the provisions of s. 718.202, relating to the use of sales or reservation deposits for construction purposes prior to closing. However, with regard to phase condominiums, the developer may only rely upon the provisions of s. 718.202 if the filing fees and documents for the proposed phase were submitted to the division on or before July 1, 1983.

# Appendix H

# Further United States Legislation

# Appendix H

# Further United States Legislation

## MODEL TIMESHARE ACT

Drafted By

National TimeSharing Council of the
American Land Development Association

and

National Association of Real Estate
Licence Law Officials

February, 1983
Washington, DC

Endorsed by
National Association of Realtors

---

**NOTE**

This Model Act is subject to change. You are encouraged to contact the Model Act's sponsor to determine whether or not revisions have been made. American Land Development Association's National TimeSharing Council ☆, 1220 L Street, N.W., Suite 510, Washington D.C. 20005.

---

## Preface

This Model Law is designed primarily to regulate the *sale* of timeshared real estate. Inherent in all timeshare ownership are aspects of real property ownership. This law will therefore include specific provisions which are designed to protect those real property interests.

The jurisdiction of this Model Law includes: (1) timeshare projects located within the situs state; (2) out-of-state projects sold within the state; and (3) projects located in-state although not sold within the state.

This Model Law does not distinguish between fee and right-to-use timeshare ownership, as such.

# MODEL TIMESHARE ACT: TABLE OF CONTENTS

# NTC/NARELLO MODEL TIMESHARE ACT

## Part 1: Timeshare Dispositions

### ARTICLE 1

### GENERAL PROVISIONS

**Section 1–101 Short Title** This Act shall be known and may be cited as the [          ] Timeshare Act.

**Section 1–102 Certain Definitions**   As used in this Act, the following terms shall have the following meanings:

1 'Affiliate' means any person who controls, is controlled by, or is under common control with a developer. A person 'controls' a developer if the person (a) is a general partner, officer, director, or employer of the developer. (b) directly or indirectly or acting in concert with one or more other persons, or through one or more subsidiaries, owns, controls, holds with power to vote, or holds proxies representing more than 20 per cent of the voting interest in the developer, (c) controls in any manner the election of a majority of the directors of the developer, or (d) has contributed more than 20 per cent of the capital of the developer. A person 'is controlled by' a developer if the developer (a) is a general partner, officer, director, or employer of the person, (b) directly or indirectly or acting in concert with one or more other persons, or through one or more subsidiaries, owns, controls, holds with power to vote, or holds proxies representing more than 20 per cent of the voting interest in the person, (c) controls in any manner the election of a majority of the directors of the person or (d) has contributed more than 20 per cent of the capital of the person. A person is also controlled by a developer if such person is a project broker or sales agent for any timeshare property of the developer. Control does not exist if the powers described in this paragraph are held solely as security for an obligation and are not exercised.

2 'Agency' means (insert appropriate administrative agency).

3 'Association' means the association of owners provided for and described in Section 11–101.

4 'Blanket Encumbrance' means any mortgage, deed of trust, option to purchase, mechanic's lien, vendor's lien or interest under a contract or agreement of sale, judgment lien, federal or state tax lien or any other lien or encumbrance which (i) affects timeshares owned by more than one owner, either directly or by reason of affecting the timeshare property, or any portion, in which the timeshare is sold, and (ii) secures or evidences the obligation to pay money or to sell or convey the timeshare property, or any portion, and which authorizes, permits or requires the foreclosure or other disposition of the property affected. The following shall not be considered blanket encumbrances:

(a) A lien for taxes and assessments levied by any public authority which are not yet due and payable.

(b) A lien for common expenses in favour of a homeowners' or community association which is not a judgment lien.

(c) Any lien for trustee's fees charged by a trustee holding title to the timeshare property pursuant to a trust created under Sections 3–104 or 3–105.

(d) A lease.

5 'Board' means the board of directors of the association provided for and described in Section 11–103.

6 'Common Areas' means all portions of a project other than units.

7 'Common Property' means all furniture, furnishings, appliances, fixtures, equipment and all other personal property from time to time owned, leased or held for use by the association or by the owners or some of them.

8 'Declaration' means the document required by Section 10–101, including all exhibits thereto.

9 'Developer' means any person in the business, primarily or otherwise, of creating or disposing of that person's timeshares in such timeshare property, but

does not include a person acting solely as a project broker or a sales agent.

10 '*Dispose or disposition*' means a voluntary transfer of any legal or equitable interest in a timeshare, but does not include the transfer or release of a security interest.

11 '*Exchange Company*' means any person owning and/or operating an Exchange Program.

12 '*Exchange Program*' means any arrangement allowing owners to exchange occupancy rights with persons owning other timeshares; provided, however, that an exchange program shall not exist if all of the occupancy rights which may be exchanged are in the same timeshare property.

13 '*Managing Agent*' means any Person engaged by the association to manage the timeshare plan and the timeshare property.

14 '*Multi-Location Plan*' means a timeshare plan respecting more than one timeshare property pursuant to which owners may, by reservation or other similar procedure, occupy timeshare units in more than one timeshare property.

15 '*Multi-Location Developer*' means a developer creating or selling its own timeshares in a multi-location plan.

16 '*Nondisturbance Agreement*' means an instrument by which the holder of a blanket encumbrance agrees that (i) its rights in the timeshare property shall be subordinate to the rights of owners from and after the recordation of the instrument; (ii) the holder and all successors and assigns, and any person who acquires the property through foreclosure or by deed in lieu of foreclosure of such blanket encumbrance, shall take the timeshare property subject to the rights of owners, and (iii) the holder and any successor acquiring the timeshare property through the blanket encumbrance shall not use or cause the timeshare property to be used in a manner which would prevent the owners from using and occupying the timeshare property in a manner contemplated by the timeshare plan.

17 '*Offer*' means any advertisement, inducement, solicitation, or attempt to encourage any person to acquire a timeshare, other than as security for an obligation. An advertisement in a newspaper or other periodical of general circulation, or in any broadcast medium to the general public, is not an offer if the advertisement states that is it not an offer in any state where applicable state registration requirements have not been completed.

18 '*Owner*' means any person who owns or co-owns a timeshare other than as security for an obligation; provided that to the extent, and for such purposes as are provided in any agreement of sale or contract for deed, the purchaser under such agreement or contract shall be considered the owner of the timeshare. The developer shall be treated as the owner of all timeshares with respect to a timeshare plan which is not owned by another.

19 '*Person*' means, one or more natural persons, corporations, partnerships, joint ventures, associations, estates, trusts, governments, governmental subdivisions or agencies, other legal or commercial entities, or any combination thereof.

20 '*Personal Charges*' means timeshare expenses resulting from an act or failure to act by an owner, his visitors or any person using a timeshare unit as a result of the exercise by such owner of his exchange rights pursuant to an exchange program.

21 '*Project*' means real property containing more than one unit. Project includes but is not limited to condominiums and cooperative housing corporations. A project may include units that are not timeshare units.

22 '*Project Broker*' means, at any applicable time, with respect to any timeshare property, the person in this State who has been designated as the project broker for this State by the developer of such timeshare property, or, if no such designation has been made, the person to whom sales agents acting within this State are responsible.

23 '*Project Instruments*' means all of the documents, by whatever names denominated, and any amendments thereto, which create and govern the rights and

relationships of owners of units in a project and govern the use and operation of the project, exclusive of the timeshare documents.

24 '*Purchaser*' means any person other than the developer who has contracted to purchase a timeshare.

25 '*Purchase Money Lien*' means a lien on a timeshare that is:

(1) Taken or retained by the developer to secure payment by the purchaser of all or part of its price; or

(2) Given by a purchaser to a person who provides financing to the purchaser to enable him to buy the timeshare.

26 '*Remainderman*' means a person, including but not limited to a developer, in whom title to the timeshare property is vested or who is the beneficiary of a trust created to satisfy the requirements of Section 3–106, but excluding the lessor under a ground lease.

27 '*Reaffirmation Instrument*' means the instrument provided for and described in section 2–103.

28 '*Sales Agent*' means any person who, for compensation or in expectation of compensation, on behalf of another person, including, but not limited to developer or an affiliate, disposes or offers to dispose, buys or offers to buy, leases or offers to lease, solicits prospective purchasers of, solicits or obtains listings of, negotiates the disposition of a timeshare by direct contact (personal or telephone) with a prospective purchaser, or provides information concerning a timeshare property with the intent of inducing such prospective purchaser to purchase a timeshare. Sales agent shall not include a person whose activity does not extend beyond attempts to induce a person to attend a sales presentation concerning a timeshare property.

29 '*Sales Contract*' means the written contract which provides for the sale by developer and the purchase by purchaser of one or more timeshares in a timeshare property.

30 '*Service Period*' means the time period or periods allocated for maintenance of a timeshare unit.

31 '*Sheltered Property*' means a timeshare property in which timeshares are created which, under the laws of this State, create an interest in real property which is not subject to levy or sale by creditors of the developer or by the holders of liens against the timeshare property recorded after the date of conveyance of such timeshares.

32 '*Subordination Agreement*' means a written agreement executed by the holder of the blanket encumbrance by which the priority of the declaration is made senior to the blanket encumbrance even though the blanket encumbrance was recorded prior to the declaration.

33 '*Timeshare*' means the right, however evidenced or documented, to use and occupy one or more timeshare units on a periodic basis according to an arrangement allocating such use and occupancy rights between other similar users.

34 '*Timeshare Documents*' means all of the documents, by whatever names denominated, and any amendments thereto, which establish the timeshare plan, create and govern the rights and relationships of owners, and govern the use and operation of the timeshare property, excluding project instruments. Such documents include, but are not limited to, the declaration, the articles of incorporation, and by-laws of the association, and the rules and regulations for the timeshare plan.

35 '*Timeshare Expenses*' means expenditures, fees, charges, or liabilities (i) incurred with respect to the timeshare plan, including allocations to reserves and (ii) imposed on the timeshare units, timeshares or owners by the association, or, if there is no association, by the developer, a managing agent or any other person.

36 '*Timeshare Plan*' means the rights, obligations and program created by the timeshare documents for a timeshare property or, in the case of a multi-location plan, for timeshare properties.

37 '*Timeshare Property*' means one or more timeshare units subject to the same declaration, together with any common areas or any other real estate, or rights therein, appurtenant to those units.

38 '*Timeshare Unit*' means a unit which is the subject of a timeshare plan.

39 '*Unit*' means real property, or a portion thereof, designated for separate occupancy.

40 '*Unit Ownership Plan*' means a timeshare plan with respect to which each owner has a distinct ownership interest in or the right to use a particular timeshare unit.

41 '*Use Period*' means the increments of time into which a timeshare unit or the timeshare property is divided for the purpose of allocating rights of use, occupancy or possession among the owners.

**Section 1–103 Severability** If any provision of this Act or its application to any person or circumstance is held invalid, the invalidity does not affect other provisions or applications of this Act which can be given effect without the invalid provision or application. To that end, the provisions of this Act are severable.

**Section 1–104 Local Ordinance Regulation of Timeshare Sales**

1 This Act shall preempt any local ordinance or regulation which requires (pursuant to the jurisdiction of the local agency adopting such ordinance or regulation) disclosure statements or registration over and above the requirements of this Act within the jurisdiction of the local agency adopting such ordinance or regulation.

2 This Act shall preempt any local business license ordinance or regulation which requires acts, bonds, fees, deposits, procedures or items not called for in business licenses for hotels, motels or other similar activities within the jurisdiction of the local agency adopting such ordinance or regulation.

**Section 1–105 Exclusivity** This Act shall be the sole law of the State governing the creation and disposition of timeshares. No timeshare property shall be subject to the following acts, except as provided in this Section:

1 (State Securities Act), provided, however, that the (State Securities Act) shall be applicable to any investment contract sold or offered for sale with, or as a part of, any timeshare. An investment contract shall not be considered to exist

by reason of the fact that a timeshare is free from restrictions on sale or exchange.

2 (State Lands Sale Act).

3 Any other State act which, but for the existence of this Act, requires registration with this agency or another state agency as a condition to the offer for sale or sale of timeshares.

**Section 1–106 Security Exemption** An owner shall not be considered to hold an investment contract, nor shall his purchase be considered risk capital, because income derived from the real and personal property dedicated to the timeshare project reduces the assessment for timeshare expenses, provided that the income inures directly to the benefit of the association and not to the direct benefit of any individual owners.

## ARTICLE II

## TIMESHARE PERMIT AND LICENSING REQUIREMENTS FOR TIMESHARE SALES

**Section 2–101 Timeshare Permit** Except as provided in Sections 2–102 and 2–103, it shall be unlawful for any person to offer or to dispose of any timeshare to purchasers in this State or to offer or to dispose of any timeshare in any timeshare property located in this State to purchasers located in any other jurisdiction without a timeshare permit.

**Section 2–102 Exceptions** Part 1 of this Act shall not apply to and no timeshare permit shall be required with respect to any of the following:

1 The disposition of timeshares in a timeshare property comprising 13 or fewer timeshares unless the developer offers or intends to offer timeshares in additional units in the same real estate subdivision aggregating more than 26 timeshares within any 12 month period. This right of exemption may only be exercised provided the developer notifies the Agency indicating an intention to exercise this right and setting forth all facts upon which the exemption is based.

2 Any offer or disposition not entered into for the purposes of evading the provisions of this Act which constitutes:

(a) an offer or disposition evidencing indebtedness secured by a mortgage or deed of trust;

(b) an offer or disposition in any timeshare or timeshare project by reason of any forfeiture, foreclosure action taken or by deed in lieu thereof;

(c) a gratuitous disposition;

(d) a disposition by devise, descent, or distribution or a disposition to an inter vivos trust;

(e) a transaction normal and customary in the hotel and motel business including but not limited to acceptance of advance reservations, provided that the person engaging in such transaction operates or owns a motel or hotel substantially engaged in the business of accepting short-term, single reservation contracts with customers who obtain no associated long-term use rights;

(f) a disposition or offer of a timeshare by an owner other than the developer, except dispositions or offers made by such owner in the ordinary course of a business conducted by such owner.

3 Any other offer or disposition which the Agency exempts from the provisions of this Act or from the provisions of this Act requiring a timeshare permit.

## Section 2–103 Preliminary Timeshare Permit

A The Agency shall issue a preliminary timeshare permit in advance of the satisfaction of all requirements for the issuance of a timeshare permit if the developer has applied for a preliminary timeshare permit and has paid the appropriate filing fee. The preliminary timeshare permit shall be in the form prescribed by the Agency and shall contain the information and disclosures required by the Agency, if any.

B If the Agency issues a preliminary timeshare permit, the developer may solicit and accept reservations to purchase timeshares along with good faith deposits if:

1 The purchaser making the reservation receives a copy of the preliminary timeshare permit and executes a receipt for a copy of the preliminary timeshare permit before any money or anything of value is accepted by or on behalf of the developer in connection with the reservation.

2 The good faith deposit is in the form of a check or other instrument made payable to an escrow agent meeting the requirements of Section 3–103 and is delivered to such escrow agent to hold pursuant to an escrow agreement, approved with the provisions of the reservation instrument.

3 The instrument by which the reservation is taken is in a form previously approved by the Agency and:

(a) Provides the purchaser and, if the developer elects, the developer, with the right to cancel unilaterally the reservation at any time prior to the execution, after the date of issuance of the timeshare permit, of a sales contract.

(b) Provides for payment to the purchaser of the total deposit (and, if the reservation instrument so states, any interest earned on the deposit) within 15 days of cancellation of the reservation.

C If a preliminary timeshare permit has been issued by the Agency, the developer may enter into sales contracts with prospective purchasers, provided that the following conditions are satisfied:

1 The form of the sales contract has been approved by the Agency.

2 All instruments received from or on behalf of the prospective purchaser are made payable to an escrow agent satisfying the requirements of Section 3–103 and are deposited with that escrow agent pursuant to an escrow agreement approved by the Agency. No cash may be accepted by the developer.

3 The sales contract and escrow agreement shall expressly prohibit the release of funds from escrow prior to the close or termination of the escrow.

4 The sales contract and the escrow agreement shall provide that the prospective purchaser is not bound and the escrow may not close unless and until all of the following, in addition to all other requirements, for the close of escrow provided for in Article III, have occurred:

(a) A timeshare permit has been issued.

(b) The prospective purchaser has been notified in writing that the timeshare permit has been issued.

(c) All deliveries required to be made pursuant to Section 3–102 have been made to the prospective purchaser.

(d) The purchaser has executed and delivered to the escrow agent an instrument (the 'Reaffirmation Instrument'), in a form approved by the Agency, reaffirming the sales contract and expressly agreeing to be bound by its terms, subject to the purchaser's right to cancel the sales contract as provided in Section 3–101.

5 The sales contract and escrow agreement shall provide that the failure of the prospective purchaser to execute and deliver the reaffirmation agreement within the period prescribed in the sales contract shall establish the prospective purchaser's conclusive election to lawfully rescind the sales contract, and, to be eligible for the return of all funds and instruments deposited in escrow.

D It shall be unlawful to enter into any agreement or arrangement with a purchaser with respect to the purchase of a timeshare under the authority of a preliminary timeshare permit except as provided in this Section.

## Section 2–104 Application for Timeshare Permit

A Any person may file an application for a timeshare permit with the Agency. It shall be in the form prescribed by the Agency and accompanied by the appropriate filing fee. The application shall include all other documents and information as the Agency may, by regulation, prescribe, but shall include in all instances:

1 A current preliminary title report or commitment to issue a title policy for the timeshare property (or, if it is common practice in the state for lawyers to issue opinions as to title in lieu of title policies, the customary lawyer's opinion as to title) and copies of the documents reported and exceptions in the preliminary title report or commitment.

2 Copies of all project instruments and timeshare documents.

3 Copies of the forms of escrow instructions (if different from the sales contract), deed, sales contract and all other written materials to be used in the normal course of the sale of the timeshares.

4 If a trust is to be used in connection with the sale of the timeshares pursuant to the provisions of Sections 3–105 and 3–106 of this Act, a copy of the proposed trust agreement establishing the trust.

5 A statement as to how the local taxing authority is currently assessing the timeshare property for property tax purposes.

6 Evidence that timeshare use complies with the zoning laws of the local government in which the timeshare property is located or, a copy of a letter from the developer to the local government notifying it of the proposed use of the property as a timeshare property.

7 If the timeshare units are subject to any project instrument, evidence that the project instruments do not prohibit the use of units for timeshare purposes and, if the project instruments do not expressly authorize timeshare use, a copy of a letter to the president of the governing entity of the project stating the developer's intent to use units for timeshare purposes, together with evidence of its receipt by the addressee.

8 The budget for the association.

9 Copies of the materials, if any, required to be delivered to purchasers in Article VIII, relating to exchange programs or multi-location plans.

10 The name and address of the project broker(s).

11 If an exchange program is to be part of the timeshare plan, evidence of acceptance by an exchange program.

12 Any other information and documents the Agency shall, by its rules and regulations, require to be furnished, or that the developer may desire to present.

B Items 9, 10 and 11 need not be furnished at the time the application is filed, but must be furnished prior to issuance of a timeshare permit. After the application for a timeshare permit is received, the Agency may require the developer to submit any additional information the Agency finds necessary for compliance with this Act. It shall be unlawful for any person to submit any information to the Agency in connection with an application for a timeshare permit which that person knows to be untrue or misleading or to fail to submit information which that person knows to be material. Any information submitted to the Agency, shall be deemed disseminated to and relied upon by each purchaser.

### Section 2–105 Issuance or Denial of Timeshare Permit

A  Upon receipt of an application for a timeshare permit, the Agency shall review such application to determine if it substantially complies with all of the requirements of 2–104 and the regulations of the Agency concerning materials to be submitted with an application for a timeshare permit. An application which meets such criteria is herein called a 'substantially complete application.' The grant or denial of a timeshare permit shall be in the form of order.

B  The Agency shall determine and notify the developer within 20 days of receipt of the application (i) whether or not it is a substantially complete application, (ii) if it is not, the requirements which must be met in order that it become a substantially complete application, and (iii) if it is a substantially complete application, any additional information or items which the Agency requires. The Agency shall similarly respond within 20 days following any additional submittals to the Agency.

C  Within 45 days of mailing notice to the developer that the application is substantially complete, the Agency shall:

1  Issue a timeshare permit;

2  Issue to developer an itemization of all deficiencies which it has determined exist, and which, if corrected, will entitle the developer to a timeshare permit;

3  Deny the application or advise the developer of its intent to deny the application. In either case, the Agency shall notify the developer of the purported grounds for denial.

D  Nothing in this section shall require the Agency to issue a timeshare permit if grounds for denial exist. The grounds for denial of a timeshare permit are the following:

1  The failure of the timeshare plan to comply with any of the provisions of this Act of the regulations of the Agency pursuant thereto.

2  The failure of any evidence submitted pursuant to Section 2–104 to establish the proposition for which it is submitted.

3  The determination that the developer, or any affiliate has, within five years preceding the date of filing the application for a timeshare permit or, at any time thereafter:

(a)  Been convicted of a felony involving fraud or misrepresentation;

(b)  Been permanently enjoined by order, judgment or decree of a court of competent jurisdiction from engaging in the sale of timeshares, real estate or securities or entered into a consent decree or other stipulation to such effect.

(c)  Had a license to act as a real estate broker or salesman, securities broker or dealer, project broker or sales agent revoked;

(d)  Been subject to a cease and desist order under Section 7–103 that remains in force;

(e)  Had a timeshare permit for a timeshare property revoked under Section 7–104.

E  Although grounds for denial exist, the Agency may, notwithstanding, issue a timeshare permit if it finds that the developer has complied with alternative requirements, approved by the Agency in accordance with Section 7–108 that serve to protect the interests of purchasers as substantially as exact compliance with the provisions of the Act.

F  The Agency may, by regulation, establish an expedited procedure for the application for and issuance of a timeshare permit for a timeshare property subject to a currently effective timeshare permit issued under the law of another state, substantially similar to this Act.

### Section 2–106 Contents of Timeshare Permit

The timeshare permit shall be prepared by the Agency. It shall contain the notice required by Section 3–101 and may otherwise be in the form and contain such other information and disclosures that the Agency may, in its discretion, determine to include. The Agency may require that the developer prepare and submit to the Agency a proposed form of timeshare permit.

### Section 2–107 Filing Fees

The fee for filing an application for a preliminary timeshare permit shall not exceed $_____. The fee for filing an application for a timeshare permit shall not exceed the sum of $_____ plus $_____ for each timeshare, the sale of which is sought to be authorized by the issuance of a timeshare permit. The Agency shall, periodically by its regulations, review and re-set the fee schedule to offset reasonable costs and expenses incurred in the administration of this Act. The Agency shall maintain filing fees lower than the maximum permitted if the Agency determines that the costs and expenses incurred will be sufficiently covered.

The Agency may conduct an inspection of the timeshare property or properties and if it does so, the Agency may require the person making the application for a timeshare permit to pay to the Agency the estimated amount of travel costs and expenses to be incurred by the Agency in making the inspection, in advance. The Agency may engage an independent consultant to review the budget for the association and if it does so, the Agency may require the person making the application for a timeshare permit to pay the fees of such independent consultant in advance.

### Section 2–108 Use of Timeshare Permit

A copy of the timeshare permit shall be given to each purchaser prior to the execution of a sales contract. A receipt for the timeshare permit in the form the Agency prescribes, shall be obtained from the purchaser. A copy of the timeshare permit, and a statement advising that a copy of the timeshare permit may be obtained from the developer at any time, shall be posted in a conspicuous place in any office where dispositions or offers are regularly made. The developer shall retain each receipt for a timeshare permit for a period of 24 months from the date of receipt. A developer may make copies of a timeshare permit issued and retained on file by the Agency.

### Section 2–109 Material Changes

A A material change in the timeshare plan includes, but is not limited to, the following:

1 Any material change in the timeshare documents or the project instruments.

2 Any material change, other than typographical corrections and the like, in the escrow instructions, sales contract or other documents made available to or executed by any purchaser.

3 If a trust is established pursuant to Sections 3–105 and 3–106 of this Act, any resignation or proposed resignation of the trustee or any material change in the trust agreement creating such trust.

4 Any material adverse change in the financial condition of the developer or the association, but only if such change is likely to harm any owner's interest in the timeshare property.

5 Any governmental action or proposed governmental action which would have a material effect on the timeshare plan or on the developer, but only if such effect on the developer is likely to adversely affect owners.

6 Any action by the owners' association or other management entity of the project in which the timeshare property is located which would have a material adverse affect on the timeshare plan.

7 Any change which would cause the information in the timeshare permit to be materially incorrect or misleading, including the suspension or expiration of a timeshare permit issued by another State.

8 Any change of a project broker.

9 Any suspension by an exchange program.

B It shall be unlawful for a developer to intentionally cause a material change in the timeshare plan without at least 10 days advance notice to the Agency. As long as a developer is engaged in the offer or disposition of timeshares respecting a timeshare plan, it shall be unlawful for such developer to fail to notify the Agency of any material change within 10 days from the date on which the developer first knew of it.

C Upon the occurrence of a material change, the Agency may:

1 Request that sales be voluntarily suspended by the developer pending a determination of the effect of the material change on the timeshare permit or pending an amendment to the timeshare plan and/or the timeshare permit.

2 Require that the timeshare permit be amended, and that sales be suspended until the amendment is complete or for a period not to exceed 15 days, whichever comes first.

3 Invoke the remedies and procedures provided in Sections 7–103 and 7–104.

**Section 2–110 Existing Timeshare Property** As used in this Act, the term 'existing timeshare property' means a timeshare property with respect to which, by _____, 19___ (recommended date is a date by which timeshare developers could be expected to know of the introduction of the Bill resulting in the enactment of the Act) at least _____ persons who are not affiliates and who are residents of this State have either purchased a timeshare in the timeshare property or have entered into a sales contract for a timeshare within the timeshare property.

Provided the provisions of Article III are satisfied, if the developer of an existing timeshare property files with the Agency an application for a timeshare permit containing the documents and information specified in items 1 through 11 of Section 2–104 and, if by _____ _____, 19___ (recommended date is 30 days prior to the next mentioned date), the Agency has issued regulations requiring additional information be provided under Section 2–104, such additional information and items, shall be filed by _____, 19___ (recommended date is approximately 90 days from the date of enactment of this Act), timeshares in the existing timeshare property may be offered for sale and sold without a time-

share permit until the Agency denies the application for a timeshare permit, if at all. The agency shall not deny an application for a timeshare permit for an existing timeshare property without first providing the developer with written notice of intent to deny the application and a statement of specific reasons for the Agency's intended denial. The notice shall advise the developer that unless written objection to the notice of intention to deny is received from the developer within 15 days following the date of actual delivery of the notice to the developer, the denial shall become effective upon the time, place and date (not earlier than 30 days following the date of actual delivery to the developer of the notice) on which a show cause hearing shall take place, if the developer files an objection to the notice. The developer has the right to present evidence to cross examine, and to be represented by counsel. Upon the expiration of the 15 day period, the developer must immediately cease and desist from entering into any additional sales contracts unless the developer delivers written objection to the Agency together with a copy of the written disclosure which the developer shall provide to each purchaser, thereafter, until a decision is rendered following the hearing. The disclosure document must inform the purchaser in writing, that the Agency has issued a notice of intention to deny developer's application for a timeshare permit; that developer has requested a hearing on the denial; and that if, following a hearing, the order of denial is issued, any monies deposited by the purchaser shall be promptly returned to the purchaser without deduction and the sales contract shall be of no further force or effect.

The Agency may accept a timeshare plan for an existing timeshare property which does not comply with all of the provisions of this Act if it complies with Article III and if the Agency determines that it would be impossible or impractical to modify the timeshare plan in order to comply with other provisions of this Act and that the basic interests of the purchasers of timeshares in the existing timeshare property and of the owners in the existing timeshare project will be adequately protected by the timeshare plan (subject to modification of the timeshare plan in the manner required by the Agency) for the existing timeshare property.

**Section 2–111 Right to Hearing** Any developer whose application for a timeshare permit has been denied may, within 30 days after receipt of the order of denial, file a written request with the Agency for a hearing on such denial. If a request is filed, a hearing shall be held in accordance with the laws of this state applicable to administrative adjudications.

**Section 2–112 Sales Agents and Project Brokers**

A It is unlawful for any person to sell or offer to sell a timeshare in this State unless the developer of the timeshare property in which the timeshare is located has designated a person as a project broker and that person is then serving as the project broker for the timeshare property. The timeshare property shall be considered a separate real estate office for purposes of the real estate licensing laws of this State.

B It is unlawful for any person to engage in the business, act in the capacity of or advertise or assume to act as a project broker within this State unless such person is a licensed real estate broker under the laws of this State.

C It is unlawful for any person to engage in the business, act in the capacity of or advertise or assume to act as a sales agent within this State unless such person is a real estate licensee under the laws of this State.

## ARTICLE III

### SALES DOCUMENTS, ESCROW PROVISIONS; PROTECTION AGAINST BLANKET ENCUMBRANCES; PRESALE REQUIREMENTS

**Section 3–101 Cancellation Rights of Purchasers** A purchaser shall have the right to cancel the purchase transaction until midnight of the 5th calendar day

following the date ('execution date') on which the purchaser executed (i) the sales contract, (ii) the receipt for a timeshare permit, or (ii) the reaffirmation instrument. The right of cancellation shall be set forth conspicuously in boldface type (i) on the first page of any timeshare permit, (ii) immediately above the signature of the purchaser on any sales contract and (iii) immediately above the signature of the purchaser on a reaffirmation instrument and, in each case shall include an explanation of the conditions and manner of exercise of such right. The right of cancellation shall not be waivable by any purchaser. The developer shall furnish to each purchaser a form, as prescribed by the agency, for the exercise of the right.

Any notice of cancellation given by mail or telegraphic communication shall be effective on the date postmarked or when transmitted from the place of origin, respectively, if actually received by developer or escrow agent within 15 days of the execution date. A notice given by mail or telegraphic communication which is not actually received within said fifteen (15) day period shall not be effective. A mailed notice of cancellation shall be certified, with return receipt requested, if possible. Any written notice of cancellation delivered other than by mail or telegraph shall be effective at the time of delivery at the place of business of the developer or escrow agent designated in the form of notice of cancellation.

**Section 3–102 Required Deliveries** It shall be unlawful for any developer, affiliate or agent of either to execute a contract for the disposition of a timeshare without first delivering true copies to the purchaser of:

1 The timeshare documents;

2 The project instruments, if any;

3 The sales contract;

4 The escrow instructions, if not incorporated in the sales contract; and

5 The current budget of the Association.

**Section 3–103 Escrow or Trust Account Required**

A It shall be unlawful for any person who is not an escrow agent meeting the requirements of Subsection B to accept, pursuant to any sales contract, any of the following:

1 Cash;

2 Any instrument, including, but not limited to, a credit card authorization, made payable to any person other than the escrow agent.

B Except as provided in Subsection C all funds and any instruments received from or on behalf of a purchaser or reservation of a timeshare shall be deposited pursuant to an escrow agreement approved by the Agency (the 'escrow agreement') with either (i) a person, acceptable to the Agency, qualified to conduct escrow business in this State or the state in which the sales contract was executed by the purchaser and who is not an affiliate or (ii) a person, acceptable to the Agency, who is the trustee under a trust meeting the requirements of Subsection B, Section 3–105. Either such person is herein referred to as the 'escrow agent.'

C The developer or project broker may hold, until the 10th day following the execution date (or any longer cancellation period provided the purchaser in the sales contract), an instrument made by a purchaser which is payable to the escrow agent or to the order of the escrow agents.

After the expiration of said period, if no notice of cancellation is received, such negotiable instrument shall be deposited as provided in Subsection B.

D The requirements of this Section shall not apply to payments and instruments made by a purchaser after the close of escrow.

**Section 3–104 Release of Purchaser's Funds and Instruments from Escrow–In General** Payments and instruments made by a purchaser may be released from escrow only as follows and the escrow agreement shall so provide:

1 If a purchaser gives a valid notice of cancellation of the sales contract pursuant to Section 3–101, all payments and any instruments made by the purchaser (or proceeds) shall be returned to the purchaser no later than 15 days after receipt by developer or escrow agent of the notice of cancellation.

2 If a purchaser otherwise terminates a sales contract pursuant to its terms, all payments and any instruments made by the purchaser (or proceeds) shall be delivered in accordance with the provisions of the sales contract.

3 If the purchaser or the developer defaults in the performance of his obligations under the sales contract, the payments and any instruments (or proceeds) made by the purchaser under the sales contract shall be delivered in accordance with the provisions of the sales contract.

4 Upon the close of escrow, payments and instruments (or proceeds) made by purchaser shall be delivered to either (i) the developer or as directed by the developer or (ii) to the trustee of a trust meeting the requirements of Subsection B of Section 3–106 to the extent required to satisfy the requirements of that Subsection. No payments or instruments made by purchaser shall be delivered to developer or trustee unless either:

(a) Escrow agent has received written confirmation from the purchaser, given after the expiration of the 5-day cancellation period under Section 3–101, evidencing that the purchaser did not exercise such right of cancellation; or

(b) At least 16 days from the execution date have expired, and the escrow agent has not received any cancellation notice given within the 5-day cancellation period and has received a sworn statement from the developer that developer has not received any cancellation notice given within the 5-day cancellation period.

**Section 3–105 Requirements for Close of Escrow for a Property Which is Not Sheltered Property**

A An escrow for a sale of a timeshare in a property which is not a sheltered property may close only if title to the timeshare property has been conveyed to a trustee of a trust which meets the rquirements of Subsection B and the sales contract is between the trustee and the purchaser.

B A trust agreement for a property which is not a sheltered property must provide that:

1 The trustee shall be a company qualified to conduct trust business in this State, shall be acceptable to the Agency and shall not be an affiliate.

2 The trust shall be irrevocable so long as any owner has a right to occupancy of any portion of the timeshare property, unless the Agency consents to the earlier revocation or termination of the trust.

3 The trustee shall not convey or transfer any portion of the timeshare property for which any owner has a right of occupancy.

4 The trustee shall not encumber the timeshare property, or any portion thereof, without the Agency's consent. Consent shall be given only if the trust, after such encumbrance, will meet all the requirements of Subsection B of Section 3–106 or if one of the other requirements of Section 3–106, Subsection A, Paragraph 2 is satisfied.

5 The association shall expressly be a third party beneficiary.

6 The trustee shall not resign upon less than 30 days prior written notice to the association and the Agency. No resignation shall become effective until a substitute trustee, approved by the Agency, is appointed by the association, and accepts the appointment.

### Section 3–106 Blanket Encumbrances– Requirements for Close of Escrow

A An escrow for the sale of a timeshare in a timeshare property which is subject to a blanket encumbrance may close only:

1 If the lien of the blanket encumbrance does not affect such timeshare because it has been released as to such timeshare, or for any other reason; or

2 If one of the following requirements is satisfied:

(a) Each and every person holding an interest in a blanket encumbrance has executed and delivered a recorded non-disturbance agreement approved by the Agency.

(b) There has been posted with the Agency a surety bond or letter-of-credit satisfying the following requirements. Any surety bond or letter-of-credit furnished to the Agency pursuant to this Section shall be to the Agency for the

benefit of purchasers and must be in an amount which is not less than 105 per cent of the remaining principal balance of every indebtedness secured by a blanket encumbrance affecting the timeshare project. The surety must be authorized to do business in this State and have sufficient net worth to satisfy the indebtedness. Any letter-of-credit must be irrevocable and must be drawn upon a bank, savings and loan association or other financial institution acceptable to the Agency. The bond or letter-of-credit shall provide for payment of all amounts secured by the blanket encumbrance, including costs, expenses and legal fees of the lien-holder, if for any reason the blanket encumbrance is enforced. The bond or letter-of-credit may be reduced periodically in proportion to the reduction of the amounts secured by the blanket encumbrance.

(c) Title to the timeshare property has been conveyed to the trustee of a trust meeting the requirements of Subsection B.

(d) Any alternative arrangement accepted by the Agency pursuant to Section 7–108 has been made.

B A trust created to satisfy the requirements of subparagraph (c), Paragraph 2 of Subsection A must comply with each of the requirements of Subsection B of Section 3–105 and, in addition, with the following:

1 Prior to the close of escrow for the sale of the first timeshare in the timeshare property, the trustee shall hold:

(a) Blanket encumbrance security meeting the requirements of Paragraph 6, below;

(b) Cash or cash equivalent (the 'cash deposit') in an amount equal to:

(i) If the blanket encumbrance(s) are fully amortized by equal periodic installments, (A) if the installments are payable monthly–three monthly installments, or (B) if the installments are payable less frequently than monthly, the amount of all installments which will be due within the six months next succeeding the date of close of escrow, or, (C) when no installments are due within the six month period, an amount equal to the next installment due.

(ii) If the blanket encumbrance(s) are not fully amortized in equal periodic installments, an amount established by the Agency.

2 The trustee may use all or a portion of the cash deposit to make any payments with respect to the blanket encumbrances which are more than ten days past due. The developer shall promptly restore the cash deposit to its required amount should the trustee deplete the cash deposit. Should the developer fail to restore the amount of the cash deposit, any distributions due from the trustee to the developer shall be first applied to restore the cash deposit.

3 The trustee may sell, transfer, hypothecate, encumber or otherwise dispose of the blanket encumbrance security, or any portion of it, necessary in the judgment of the trustee, to make any payment needed to prevent foreclosure of the blanket encumbrance.

4 The priority of distributions by the trustee from the trust shall be as follows:

(a) First, to pay current debt service due under blanket encumbrances.

(b) Second, if one or more of the blanket encumbrances is not fully amortized by equal periodic payments, to pay the sinking fund established under Paragraph 5.

(c) Third, to pay the trustee's reasonable fees and costs; and

(d) Fourth, to pay any obligation to the developer.

5 If any blanket encumbrance affecting the timeshare property is not amortized by equal periodic payments, the trust instrument shall establish a sinking fund requiring a monthly installment sufficient to pay, when due, all balloon payments under the encumbrance.

6(a) The blanket encumbrance security shall be comprised of either nondelinquent project receivables or nondelinquent other qualifying assets or a combination thereof. 'Project receivables' means installment sales contracts and/or promissory notes given by purchasers as all or a portion of the consideration for the purchase of a timeshare in the timeshare project. 'Other qualifying assets' means assets other than project receivables but similar in nature (such as receivables from another project) approved by the Agency for the blanket encumbrance security. A project receivable or other qualifying asset shall be considered delinquent if any required payment is more than 59 days past due.

(b) The blanket encumbrance security shall, at the time of the close of escrow for the sale of the first timeshare sold in the timeshare project, meet the following test (the 'security test'):

The payments provided to be made with respect to the blanket encumbrance security if all paid when due shall (i) equal or exceed 125 per cent of the difference between (x) principal and interest and other amounts required to be paid under the blanket encumbrances and (y) the cash deposit and any other cash or cash equivalents which the developer has deposited in trust and authorized the trustee to hold for the payment of amounts due under blanket encumbrances, and (ii) provide, at any point in time 115 per cent of the monies needed to enable the trustee to make any payment with respect to the blanket encumbrance(s) when the same is due.

7 The trust instrument shall prohibit the distribution from the trust to the developer or the application as directed by the developer of any project receivable, other qualifying asset, or other cash deposited by developer to be used for the payment of the blanket encumbrance if, as result of such distribution or application, the security test would not then be met.

**Section 3–107 Requirements Where the Developer's Interest in the Timeshare Property is a Leasehold Interest**

A If the interest which the developer holds in the timeshare property is a leasehold interest, the lease (or an amendment or supplement thereto) must contain a purchaser protection clause satisfactory to the Agency unless the Agency shall determine that the interests of the owners in the timeshare property will be adequately protected in its absence. The purchaser protection clause shall provide that the lessor cannot terminate the lease by reason of the lessee's default without first giving reasonable notice of the default to the association and providing the association with a reasonable opportunity to cure the default. The purchaser protection clause shall also obligate the lessor to enter into a new lease with the association on the same terms and conditions as the old lease so that bankruptcy of the lessee will not disrupt the timeshare owners' continued rights of occupancy.

B In determining whether a purchaser protection clause shall be required, the Agency shall consider, among other factors deemed relevant by the Agency, whether the budget of the association will include the rental payments, whether the association will make the rental payments directly to the lessor as opposed to paying an equivalent sum to the developer-lessee, and the relative size of the rental payments.

The Agency may also require a surety bond or letter-of-credit from the developer, subject to Section 3–107 except as to amount, to secure rental payments.

### Section 3–108 Projects to be Completed

A Payments made by purchasers into escrow may not be released prior to the close of escrow, to pay for contruction costs, or otherwise. Such payments shall be released only as provided in Section 3–104. For purposes of this Section, the timeshare property or the phase thereof for which the timeshare property is sought shall not be considered completed unless and until all physical improvements comprising the timeshare property (or phase) are installed, any refurbishment or remodelling of existing improvements contemplated for the timeshare property (or phase) installed and completed and the common property for the timeshare property (or such phase) are available. If a timeshare property is not completed prior to the issuance of the timeshare permit, the timeshare permit shall disclose the estimated date or dates of completion and one of the following shall be satisfied before the timeshare permit issues:

1 Developer shall furnish to the Agency a lien and completion bond or bonds in an amount and subject to such terms, conditions and coverage as the Agency may approve to assure completion of the timeshare property free of liens. The bond or bonds shall be to the Agency for the benefit of purchasers and must provide, as a condition for the obligation, that the developer, as principal, complete the timeshare property free of liens and claims on or before the estimated date or dates for completion set forth in the timeshare permit (or any extension thereof granted by the Agency), or the obligation is forfeited. Otherwise, it shall remain in full force and effect until the timeshare property is completed free of liens and claims.

2 An amount sufficient to cover the estimated cost to complete the timeshare property is deposited in a neutral escrow depository acceptable to the Agency under an approved written agreement providing for disbursements from escrow as the work is completed.

3 The sales contract prohibits the close of escrow until the timeshare property is completed.

4 The requirements of any alternative arrangement accepted by the Agency shall be satisfied.

### Alternative 3–108

1 Payments made by purchasers into escrow may not be released prior to the close of escrow, to pay for construction costs or otherwise, except as provided in Paragraph 2 of this Section 3–108, and in Section 3–104. (The rest of Paragraph 1 is the same as Section 3–108 – first alternative.)

2 Payments made by purchasers into escrow may, at the discretion of Agency, be released from escrow prior to its close only if all of the following conditions are met:

(a) Payments must be used for construction costs of improvements upon the timeshare property (or the phase for which the timeshare permit is sought). As used herein the term 'construction costs' means any amounts payable under the 'construction contract,' as that term is defined in subparagraph 2(b) and no other costs. Construction costs shall not include architectural fees, engineering fees, finance costs, land acquisition costs, or legal fees, unless provided by the contractor under the construction contract.

(b) For purposes of this section, 'construction contract' means a guaranteed maximum cost contract or a fixed price contract between the developer and a person who is not an affiliate, providing for the construction of all improvements. The construction contract shall prohibit any contractor from engaging developer or any affiliate to perform any service or function in connection with such construction for compensation. Developer shall deposit with Agency a duplicate original of the construction contract together with certification from the contractor that the construction contract delivered to the Agency is true and correct and that it has not been amended or modified.

(c) Developer shall provide evidence to Agency that the following bonds have been issued and remain in full force and effect:

(i) A payment and performance bond to developer, as obligee, in an amount equal to 100 per cent of the fixed price or guaranteed maximum cost, specified in the construction contract, and

(ii) A labor and material bond naming developer as obligee in an amount equal to not less than 50 per cent of the amount of said payment and performance bond.

(d) A construction loan for the construction of such improvements with an institutional lender, which is not an affiliate, shall have been recorded providing for a construction loan of not less than 100 per cent of the fixed price or guaranteed maximum cost specified in the construction loan, may be disbursed for purposes other than payments under the construction contract.

(e) An agreement shall have been entered into among the Agency, developer and the construction lender whereby the construction lender agrees to receive such payments from escrow and to disburse the same to the payment of construction costs in the manner provided for in the construction loan agreement between the construction lender and developer. Such agreement shall specifically provide that no such funds shall be disbursed to developer or an affiliate.

(f) Developer shall furnish to Agency evidence of the existence of such course of construction insurance and insurance against loss or damage covered by an insurance policy written on an all-risk basis, as shall be satisfactory to the Agency.

(g) The developer shall meet any other conditions as the Agency may impose by regulation.

## ARTICLE IV

## ADVERTISING

**Section 4–101 False advertising** It shall be unlawful for any person with intent, directly or indirectly, to offer for disposition timeshares in this State, to authorize, use, direct or aid in the dissemination, publication, distribution or circulation of any statement, advertisement, radio broadcast or telecast concerning the timeshare property in which the timeshares are offered, which contains any statement, or sketch which is false or misleading or contains any representation or pictorial representation of proposed improvements or nonexistent scenes without clearly indicating that the improvements are proposed and the scenes do not exist.

Nothing in this Section shall be construed to hold the publisher or employee of any newspaper, or any job printer, or any broadcaster or telecaster, or any magazine publisher, or any of the employees thereof, liable for any publication herein referred to unless the publisher, employee or printer has actual knowledge of the falsity thereof.

**Section 4–102 Submission of Advertising Materials for an Advisory Opinion** Advertising materials proposed for use by any person in connection with the offer or sale of timeshares in this State may, prior to their use, be submitted to the Agency for an advisory opinion concerning compliance with this Act. The Agency may, but shall be under no obligation to, issue such an advisory opinion unless it has adopted regulations obligating it to issue advisory opinions. Materials shall be submitted in the context and format prescribed by regulations, if any, adopted by the Agency. The Agency may, by regulation, require a fee for an advisory opinion. An advisory opinion issued by the Agency shall bind the Agency, but shall have no effect on any other person.

**Section 4–103 Mandatory Submission of Advertising Materials** The Agency may adopt regulations requiring all or any part of advertising materials, proposed for use by any person in connection with the offer or sale of timeshares in this State to be filed with the Agency at least ten (10) days after their first use. No regulation under this Section shall require a different submission of materials than required under Section 4–102.

Advertising materials include, but are not limited to, the following:

1 Promotional brochures, pamphlets, advertisements, or other materials to be disseminated to the public in connection with the sale of timeshares.

2 Transcripts of all radio and television advertisements.

3 Offers of travel, accommodations, meals or entertainment at no cost or reduced cost, in whatever form.

4 Direct mail solicitations.

5 Advertising copy including testimonials or endorsements.

6 Scripts or standardized narrative for use in making telephone solicitations.

**Section 4–104 Prohibited Advertising** No advertising for the offer or disposition of timeshares shall:

1 Contain any representation as to the availability of a resale program or rental program offered by or on behalf of the developer or its affiliate unless the resale program and/or rental program has been made a part of the offering and submitted to the Agency.

2 Contain an offer or inducement to purchase which purports to be limited as to quantity or restricted as to time unless the numerical quantity and/or time applicable to the offer or inducement is clearly and conspicuously disclosed.

3 Contain statements concerning the availability of timeshares at a particular minimum price if the number of timeshares available at that price comprises less than 10 per cent of the unsold inventory of the developer, unless the number of timeshares then for sale at the minimum price is set forth in the advertisement.

4 Contain any statement that the timeshare being offered for sale can be further divided unless a full disclosure of the legal requirements for further division of the timeshare is included.

5 Contain any asterisk or other reference symbol as a means of contradicting or changing the ordinary meaning of any previously made statement in the advertisement.

6 Misrepresent the size, nature, extent, qualities, or characteristics of the accommodations or facilities which comprise the timeshare property.

7 Misrepresent the nature or extent of any services incident to the timeshare property.

8 Misrepresent or imply that a facility or service is available for the exclusive use of purchasers or owners if a public right of access or of use of the facility or service exists.

9 Make any misleading or deceptive representation with respect to the contents of the timeshare permit, the sales contract, the purchaser's rights, privileges, benefits or obligations under the sales contract or this Act.

10 Misrepresent the conditions under which a purchaser or owner may participate in an exchange program.

11 Purport to have resulted through a referral unless the name of the person making the referral can be produced upon demand of the Agency.

12 Describe any proposed or uncompleted private facilities over which the developer has no control unless the estimated date of completion is set forth and evidence has been presented to the Agency that the completion and operation of the facilities are reasonably assured within the time represented in the advertisement.

13 Describe or portray any improve-

ment which is not required to be built unless the description or portrayal of the improvement is conspicuously labelled or identified as 'NEED NOT BE BUILT.'

**Section 4–105 Disclosure of Intent to Make Sales Presentation**

A It is unlawful for any person to use any promotional device, including, but not limited to sweepstakes, gift awards, lodging certificates or discounts, with the intent to solicit the disposition of time-shares without disclosing in a clear and unequivocal manner, the purpose of soliciting the disposition of timeshares.

B The following unfair acts, practices undertaken by, or omissions of, any person intentionally promoting the disposition of timeshares are prohibited:

1 Failing clearly and conspicuously to disclose all rules, regulations, terms and conditions of the promotional program; the exact nature and approximate retail value of any gifts or similar items when offered or if the item is not available at retail, the cost to the developer or project broker of the item; the date or dates on or before which the offer will terminate or expire; the odds of receiving any gift or similar item.

2 Failing to obtain the express written consent of individuals before their names are used for a promotional purpose in connection with a mailing to a third person.

3 Failing to award items promised in a promotion by the date and year specified in the promotion.

4 Misrepresenting in any manner the odds of receiving any item or gift, the rules, terms or conditions of anticipation in the promotional program.

ARTICLE V

WARRANTIES

**Section 5–101 Express Warranties of Quality**

A Express warranties made by any developer to a purchaser if relied upon by purchaser, are created as follows:

1 Any affirmation of fact or promise which relates to the timeshare, the time-share unit, rights appurtenant to either,

area improvements that would directly benefit the timeshare, or the right to use or have the benefit of facilities not located on the timeshare unit, creates an express warranty that the timeshare, the time-share unit and related rights and uses will conform to the affirmation or promise;

2 Any model or description of the physical characteristics of the timeshare property, including plans and specifications of or for improvements, creates an express warranty that the property will conform to the model or description;

3 Any description of the quantity or extent of the real estate constituting the timeshare property, including plans or surveys, creates an express warranty that the property will conform to the description, subject to customary tolerances; and

4 A provision that a purchaser may put a timeshare unit only to a specified use is an express warranty that the specified use is lawful.

B Neither formal words, such as 'warranty' or 'guarantee,' nor a specific intention to make a warranty, is necessary to create an express warranty of quality, but a statement purporting to be merely an opinion or commendation of the time-share, the timeshare unit, or the value of either does not create a warranty.

C Any transfer of a timeshare transfers to the purchaser all express warranties of quality made by previous sellers.

**Section 5–102 Implied Warranties of Quality**

A A developer warrants that a time-share unit will be in at least as good condition at the earlier of the time of the transfer or of the delivery of possession as it was at the time of contracting, reasonable wear and tear excepted.

B A developer impliedly warrants that a timeshare unit and any other real property owners have a right to use in conjunction therewith are suitable for the ordinary uses of real estate of its type and that any improvements made or contracted for by him, or made by any person before transfer, will be:

1 Free from defective materials; and

2 Constructed in accordance with

applicable law, according to sound engineering and construction standards, and in a workmanlike manner.

C A developer warrants to a purchaser that an existing use of the timeshare unit, continuation of which is contemplated by the parties, does not violate applicable law at the earlier of the time of transfer or of the delivery of possession.

D A developer warrants to a purchaser that for the period in which the developer controls the association the timeshare plan is being operated in accordance with the provisions of this Act and other applicable law and, without limiting the foregoing in any manner, that:

1 The association's current budget is adequate for the normal and necessary functioning of the association;

2 The association has been duly created and is being operated in accordance with applicable law.

E For purposes of this Section, improvements made or contracted for by an affiliate are made or contracted for by the developer.

F Any transfer of a timeshare transfers to the purchaser all of any developer's implied warranties of quality.

## ARTICLE VI

## REMEDIES

**Section 6–101 Unconscionable Agreement or Term of Contract** The court, upon finding as a matter of law that a contract or contract clause was unconscionable at the time the contract was made, may refuse to enforce the contract, enforce the remainder of the contract without the unconscionable clause, or limit the application of any unconscionable clause in order to avoid an unconscionable result.

**Section 6–102 Obligation of Good Faith** Every contract or duty governed by this Act imposes an obligation of good faith which shall mean honesty in fact and the observance of reasonable standards of fair dealing in its performance or enforcement.

**Section 6–103 Remedies to be Liberally Administered**

A The remedies provided by this Act shall be liberally administered to the end that the aggrieved party is put in as good a position as if the other party had fully performed. However, consequential, special, or punitive damages may not be awarded except as specifically provided in this Act or by other rule of law.

B Any right or obligation declared by this Act is enforceable by judicial proceeding.

**Section 6–104 Supplemental General Principles of Law Applicable** The principles of law and equity, including the law of corporations, the law of real property and the law relative to capacity to contract, principal and agent, eminent domain, estoppel, fraud, misrepresentation, duress, coercion, mistake, receivership, substantial performance, or other validating or invalidating cause supplement the provisions of this Act, except to the extent inconsistent with this Act.

**Section 6–105 Effect of Violations on Rights of Action; Attorney's Fees** If a developer or any other person subject to this Act fails to comply with any provision of this Act or of the timeshare documents, any person or class of persons adversely affected by the failure to comply has a claim for appropriate relief. Punitive damages may be awarded for a willful failure to comply with this Act. The court may also award reasonable attorney's fees.

**Section 6–106 Disposition Voidable**

A Any deed or instrument of conveyance, disposition or sales contract is voidable, at the sole option of the grantee or purchaser, his heirs, personal representative or trustee, in insolvency or bankruptcy within two years of the last to occur of (i) the date of execution of the sales contract, (ii) the date of delivery of the deed or other instrument of conveyance, or (iii) the date on which the disposition occurred if such disposition were not effected by deed or other instrument of conveyance, if on any such date, there was no valid effective timeshare permit.

B A deed or instrument of conveyance, disposition or sales contract which is voidable under subsection A is binding upon any successor-in-interest of the grantee or purchaser, other than those enumerated in subsection A and upon the developer or his assignee, heir, devisee or successor-in-interest.

## ARTICLE VII

## POWERS OF THE AGENCY

### Section 7–101 Regulations and Forms

A The Agency may from time to time make, amend and rescind the regulations, forms and orders necessary to carry out the provisions of this Act, including regulations and forms governing applications and reports, and defining any terms, whether or not used in this Act, insofar as such definitions are not inconsistent with the provisions of this Act.

B If it appears that any person has engaged, is engaging, or is about to engage in any act or practice in violation of this Act or any of the Agency's regulations or orders, the Agency without prior administrative proceedings may bring suit in the appropriate court to enjoin that act or practice or for other appropriate relief. The Agency is not required to post a bond or prove that no adequate remedy at law exists.

C The Agency may intervene in any action or suit involving the powers or responsibilities of a developer in connection with any timeshare for which an application for registration is on file.

### Section 7–102 Investigative Powers The
Agency may initiate public or private investigations and conduct hearings within this State to determine whether any representation in any document or information filed with the Agency is false or misleading or whether any person has engaged, is engaging, or is about to engage in any unlawful act or practice. For the purpose of any investigation or proceeding under this Act, the director of the Agency or any officer designated by the director, may administer oaths and firmations, subpoena witnesses, compel their attendance, take evidence, and require the production of any books, papers, correspondence, memoranda, agreements, or other documents or records which the Agency deems relevant or material to the inquiry. If any person in proceedings before the Agency disobeys or resists any lawful order or refuses to respond to a subpoena or refuses to take the oath or affirmation as a witness or thereafter refuses to be examined, or is guilty of misconduct during the hearing or so near the place thereof as to obstruct the proceeding, the Agency shall certify the facts to the appropriate court in and for the county where the proceedings are held. The court shall thereupon issue an order directing the person to appear before the court and show cause why he/she should not be punished for contempt. The order and a copy of the certified statement shall be served on the person. Thereafter the court shall have jurisdiction of the matter. The same proceeding shall be had, the same penalties may be imposed and the person charged may purge himself/herself of the contempt in the same way, as in the case of the person who has committed a contempt in the trial of a civil action before a court in this State.

### Section 7–103 Cease and Desist Order

A If in the opinion of the director of the Agency, the offer or disposition of any timeshare within this State requires a timeshare permit under this Act and the timeshare is being, or has been offered or disposed without a timeshare permit, the Agency may order the developer, project broker or any sales agent to cease and desist from the further offer or disposition of the timeshare unless or until a timeshare permit has been duly issued under this Act. Any person for whom such order is directed may within 30 days after its service, file with the Agency a written request for a hearing to contest the order. If such a request is filed, a hearing shall be held in accordance with the laws of this State applicable to administrative adjudication, and the Agency shall have all the powers granted thereunder.

B Whenever the Agency determines from evidence available to it that a developer is directly, or through its project broker, sales agents, or representatives, violating or failing to comply with any of the provisions of this Act or the regulations of the Agency pertaining thereto, or that representations and assurances given by the developer upon which the Agency relied in issuing a timeshare permit have not been carried out in the timeshare property, or that conditions existing with respect to the timeshare plan would have caused the denial of a timeshare permit, the Agency may order the developer to desist and refrain from such violations, and/or it may order the cessation of a sale of timeshares in the timeshare project. Upon receipt of such an order, the person or persons to whom the order is directed shall immediately discontinue activities in accordance with the terms of the order. Any person to whom an order is directed may, within 30 days after service of the order upon the person, file with the Agency a written request for hearing to contest the order. If such a request is filed, a hearing shall be held in accordance with the provisions of the laws of this State applicable to administrative adjudications, and the Agency shall have all of the powers granted thereunder.

C Whenever the Agency determines from evidence available to it that a person is violating or failing to comply with any of the provisions of this Act or the regulations of this Act or the regulations of the Agency pertaining thereto, or that representations and assurances given by the person upon which the Agency has relied were untrue or have not been carried out or that conditions existing would have caused the denial of the entitlement granted by the Agency, the Agency may order the person to cease and desist from such violations. Upon receipt of such an order, the person or persons to whom the order is directed shall immediately discontinue activities in accordance with the terms of the order. Any person to whom such order is directed may, within 30 days after service of the order upon the person, file with the Agency a written

request for hearing to contest the order. If such a request is filed, a hearing shall be held in accordance with the provisions of the laws of this State applicable to administrative adjudications, and the Agency shall have all of the powers granted thereunder.

D When the Agency has authority to issue a cease and desist order or other proceeding pursuant to the provisions of this Article, it may accept, in lieu thereof or as part thereof, an assurance of discontinuance of any violative practice. An assurance may include a stipulation for the voluntary payment by the alleged violator of the costs of investigation and any action or proceeding by the Agency, and any amount necessary to restore to any person, money or property acquired by means of the violation. Any assurance of discontinuance accepted by the Agency and any stipulation filed with a court as a part of any action or proceeding shall be confidential to the parties to the action or proceeding and to the court and its employees, but if an accepted assurance of discontinuance is violated, or a person engages in the same violative practice which he previously agreed to discontinue as permitted under this subsection, the assurance of discontinuance or stipulation shall become a public record and open to inspection by any person.

**Section 7–104 Revocation of Timeshare Permit** The Agency, after issuance of a cease and desist order pursuant to Section 7–104, subsection A or B, and if no hearing has been requested to contest the order within the time permitted, or if the developer has unsuccessfully exhausted all administrative remedies available to contest the order, may, by order, revoke a timeshare permit.

**Section 7–105 Suspension of Project Broker or Sales Agent** The Agency may, upon its own motion, and shall upon the verified complaint in writing of any person, investigate the actions of any person engaged in the business or acting in the capacity of a project broker or sales agent within this State. The Agency may issue an order to temporarily suspend or permanently revoke the real estate license of a project broker or sales agent, if such person, in performing or attempting to perform any of the acts within the scope of this Act has been guilty of any of the following:

1 Making any material misrepresentation or any false promises of a character likely to influence, persuade or induce.

2 In the case of a project broker, permitting, allowing or suffering to occur, material misrepresentation or the making of false promises by sales agents or any other person.

3 In the case of a project broker, permitting, allowing or suffering to occur, on more than one occasion, unlicensed persons to perform functions for which a licensed sales agent is required.

4 Engaging in any other conduct, whether of the same or a different character than specified in this section, which constitutes fraud or dishonest dealing.

**Section 7–106 Judicial Review of the Agency** Every final order, decision, or other official act of the Agency is subject to judicial review in accordance with the laws of this State.

**Section 7–107 Punishment of Violations Under Other Statutes** Nothing in this Act limits the power of the State to punish any person for any conduct which constitutes a violation under any other statute. Nothing contained in this Article VII limits the other powers of the Agency expressly granted in other Articles of this Act.

**Section 7–108 Waiver of Requirement – Agency Powers**

A The Agency may waive specific requirements or may allow alternative arrangements to the requirements of this Act, or any regulation promulgated pursuant to it, if:

1 Compliance with specific provisions is impracticable or impossible;

2 Any person will suffer severe hardship if strict compliance is required; and

3 Adequate protection for purchasers of timeshares will be maintained.

B Any alternative arrangements must be in keeping with the policies of this Act, including the orderly development of

timeshare projects and purchaser protection, and shall take into account the following factors:

1 The number of owners and/or living units comprising the timeshare property;

2 The laws of the state or county in which the timeshare property is located;

3 The number of owners who are residents of this State in relation to the total number of owners;

4 The number of timeshares sold before the effective date of this Act;

5 The net worth, liquidity and other financial ability of the developer; and

6 Any other factor the Agency finds relevant to permitting an alternative arrangement.

## Part 2: Exchange Programs and Multi/Location Plans

### ARTICLE VIII

### EXCHANGE PROGRAMS

**Section 8–101 Point of Sale Disclosure**

A If a purchaser is offered the opportunity to subscribe to any exchange program, the developer shall, except as provided in subsection B, deliver to the purchaser, prior to the execution of (i) any contract between the purchaser and the exchange company, and (ii) the sales contract, at least the following information regarding such exchange program and the purchaser shall certify in writing to the receipt of such written information:

1 The name and address of the exchange company.

2 The names of all officers, directors, and shareholders owning five per cent (5%) or more of the outstanding stock of the exchange company.

3 Whether the exchange company or any of its officers or directors has any legal or beneficial interest in any developer or managing agent for any timeshare plan participating in the exchange program and, if so, the name and location of the timeshare plan and the nature of the interest.

4 Unless the exchange company is also the developer or an affiliate, a statement that the purchaser's contract with the

exchange company is a contract separate and distinct from the sale's contract.

5 Whether the purchaser's participation in the exchange program is dependent upon the continued affiliation of the timeshare plan with the exchange program.

6 Whether the purchaser's membership or participation, or both, in the exchange program is voluntary or mandatory.

7 A complete and accurate description of the terms and conditions of the purchaser's contractual relationship with the exchange company and the procedure by which changes thereto may be made.

8 A complete and accurate description of the procedure to qualify for and effectuate exchanges.

9 A complete and accurate description of all limitations, restrictions, or priorities employed in the operation of the exchange program, including, but not limited to, limitations on exchanges based on seasonality, unit size, or levels of occupancy, expressed in boldfaced type, and, in the event that such limitations, restrictions, or priorities are not uniformly applied by the exchange program, a clear description of the manner in which they are applied.

10 Whether exchanges are arranged on a space available basis and whether any guarantees of fulfillment of specific requests for exchanges are made by the exchange program.

11 Whether and under what circumstances an owner, in dealing with the exchange company, may lose the use and occupancy of his timeshare in any properly applied for exchange without his being provided with substitute accommodations by the exchange company.

12 The fees or range of fees for participation by owners in the exchange program, a statement whether any such fees may be altered by the exchange company, and the circumstances under which alterations may be made.

13 The name and address of the site of each timeshare property, accommodation or facility which is participating in the exchange program.

14 The number of units in each property participating in the exchange program which are available for occupancy and which qualify for participation in the exchange program, expressed within the following numerical groupings: 1–5; 6–10; 11–20; 21–50; and 51 and over.

15 The number of owners with respect to each timeshare plan or other property which are eligible to participate in the exchange program expressed within the following numerical groupings: 1–100; 101–249; 250–499; 500–999; and 1,000 and over; and a statement of the criteria used to determine those owners who are currently eligible to participate in the exchange program.

16 The disposition made by the exchange company of timeshares deposited with the exchange program by owners eligible to participate in the exchange program and not used by the exchange company in effecting exchanges.

17 The following information, which, except as provided in Subsection B, below, shall be independently audited by a certified public accountant or accounting firm in accordance with the standards of the Accounting Standards Board of the American Institute of Certified Public Accountants and reported for each year no later than July 1, of the succeeding year, beginning no later than _____, 198__:

(a) The number of owners eligible to participate in the exchange program. Such numbers shall disclose the relationship between the exchange company and owners as being either fee paying or gratuitous in nature.

(b) The number of timeshare properties, accommodations or facilities eligible to participate in the exchange program categorized by those having a contractual relationship between the developer or the association and the exchange company and those having solely a contractual relationship between the exchange company and owners directly.

(c) The percentage of confirmed exchanges, which shall be the number of exchanges confirmed by the exchange company divided by the number of exchanges properly applied for, together with a complete and accurate statement of the criteria used to determine whether an exchange request was properly applied for.

(d) The number of timeshares for which the exchange company has an outstanding obligation to provide an exchange to an owner who relinquished a timeshare during the year in exchange for a timeshare in any future year.

(e) The number of exchanges confirmed by the exchange company during the year.

18 A statement in boldfaced type to the effect that the percentage described in subparagraph (17)(c) of Subsection A is a summary of the exchange requests entered with the exchange company in the period reported and that the percentage does not indicate a purchaser's/owner's probabilities of being confirmed to any specific choice or range of choices, since availability at individual locations may vary.

B The information required by Subsection A shall be accurate as of a date which is no more than 30 days prior to the date on which the information is delivered to the purchaser, except that the information required by Subsection A, Paragraphs 2, 3, 13, 14, 15 and 17 shall be provided as at December 31 of the year preceding the year in which the information is delivered, except for information delivered within the first 180 days of any calendar year which shall be provided as at December 31 of the year preceding the year in which the information is delivered. All references in this Section to the word 'year' shall mean calendar year.

C In the event an exchange company offers an exchange program directly to the purchaser or owner, the exchange company shall deliver to each purchaser or owner, prior to the execution of any contract between the purchaser or owner and the company offering the exchange program, the information set forth in Subsection A, above. The requirements of this paragraph shall not apply to any renewal of a contract between an owner and an exchange company.

D Each exchange company offering an exchange program to purchasers in this state must include the statement set forth in Paragraph 18 of Subsection A on all promotional brochures, pamphlets, advertisements, or other materials disseminated by the exchange company which also contain the percentage of confirmed exchanges described in subparagraph (17)(c) of Subsection A.

**Section 8–102 Annual Filings by Exchange Companies** An exchange company whose exchange program is offered to purchasers in connection with the offer or disposition of timeshares in this State shall, on or before July 1, of each year, file with the Agency and secretary of the association for the timeshare plan in which the timeshares are offered or disposed, the information required by Section 8–101 with respect to the preceding year. If the Agency determines that any of the information supplied fails to meet the requirements of this Section, the Agency may undertake enforcement action against the exchange company in accordance with the provisions of Article VII. No developer shall have any liability arising out of the use, delivery or publication by the developer of information provided to it by the exchange company pursuant to this Section. Except as provided in the next sentence, no exchange company shall have any liability with respect to (i) any representation made by the developer relating to the exchange program or exchange company, or (ii) the use, delivery or publication by the developer of any information relating to the exchange program or exchange company. An exchange company shall only be liable for written information provided to the developer by the exchange company. The failure of the exchange company to observe the requirements of this Section, or the use by it of any unfair or deceptive act or practice in connection with the operation of the exchange program, shall be violation of this Article.

**Section 8–103 No Security** The offering of an exchange program in this State in conjunction with the offer or sale of timeshares in this State shall not constitute a security under the laws of this State.

## ARTICLE IX

### MULTI/LOCATION PLANS

**Section 9–101 Point of Sale Disclosures**

A Except as provided in Subsection B, a multi-location developer shall deliver to the purchaser, prior to the execution of the sales contract at least the following information and the purchaser shall certify in writing to the receipt of such written information.

1 A complete and accurate description of the procedure to qualify for and effectuate use rights in timeshare units in the multi-location plan.

2 A complete and accurate description of all limitations, restrictions, or priorities employed in the operation of the multi-location plan, including, but not limited to, limitations on reservations, use or entitlement rights based on seasonality, unit size, levels of occupancy or class of owner, expressed in boldfaced type, and, in the event that such limitations, restrictions, or priorities are not uniformly applied by the multi-location plan, a clear description of the manner in which they are applied.

3 Whether use is arranged on a space-available basis and whether any guarantees of fulfillment of specific requests for use are made by the multi-location developer.

4 The name and address of the site of each timeshare property included in the multi-location plan.

5 The number of timeshare units in each timeshare property which are available for occupancy; with respect to each such timeshare unit, the interest which the multi-location developer has therein (e.g. fee ownership, leasehold, option to purchase), and if less than fee ownership a statement of all relevant terms of the multi-location developer's interest therein; and with respect to each timeshare unit, whether it may be withdrawn from the multi-location plan.

6 The following information, which, except as provided in Subsection B, below, shall be independently audited by a certified public accountant or accounting firm in accordance with the standards of the Accounting Standards Board of the American Institute of Certified Public Accountants and reported for each year on or before July 1 of the succeeding year beginning no later than _____, 198__:

(a) The number of owners in the multi-location plan.

(b) For each timeshare property in the multi-location plan, the number of properly made requests for use of timeshare units in such timeshare property.

(c) For each timeshare property, the percentage of owners who properly requested use of a timeshare unit in such timeshare property who received the right to use a timeshare unit in such timeshare property.

7 A statement in boldfaced type to the effect that the percentages described in Paragraph 6 of Subsection A do not indicate a purchaser's/owner's probabilities of being able to use any timeshare unit since availability at individual locations may vary.

B The information required by Subsection A shall be provided as at a date which is no more than 30 days prior to the date on which the information is delivered to the purchaser, except that the information required by Subsection A, Paragraphs 4, 5 and 6 shall be provided as at December 31 of the year preceding the year in which the information is delivered, except for information delivered within the first 180 days of any calendar year which shall be provided as at December 31 of the year preceding the year in which the information is delivered. All references in this Section to the word 'year' shall mean calendar year.

**Section 9–102 Annual Filings by Multi-Location Developer** A multi-location developer which offers or disposes of timeshares in this State shall, on or before July 1, of each year, file with the Agency the information required by Section 9–101 with respect to the preceding year. If at any time the Agency determines that any of the information supplied fails to meet the requirements of this Section, the

Agency may undertake enforcement action against the multi-location developer in accordance with the provisions of Article VII. The failure of a multi-location developer to observe the requirements of this Section, or the use by it of any unfair or deceptive act or practice in connection with the operation of the exchange program, shall be violation of this Article.

## Part 3: Requirements Respecting the Timeshare Plan and the Contents of Timeshare Documents/Incidents of Timeshares

### ARTICLE X

### CREATION OF AND INCIDENTS OF TIMESHARES; CONTENTS OF DECLARATION

**Section 10–101 Execution and Recordation of Declaration** Prior to the issuance of a timeshare permit pursuant to Section 2–105 above:

A The developer and the holders of the legal and equitable title to the fee or leasehold estate of the timeshare property shall execute a declaration;

B The executed declaration shall be recorded in every county in which any timeshare property is located, and shall be indexed in the name of the timeshare plan and the association, and in the name of each person executing the declaration; and

C The holders of any blanket encumbrance affecting the timeshare property shall execute and cause to be recorded an instrument subordinating the lien and charge thereof to the declaration.

**Section 10–102 Contents of Declaration**

A In every case, the declaration shall:

1 State the name of the timeshare plan and of the association.

2 Contain a legally sufficient description of the timeshare property.

3 State the name or other identification of the project(s), if any, within which the timeshare property is situated.

4 Contain or incorporate by reference a recorded project map. This requirement may be met by any recorded plat or plan which satisfies the requirements for a project map. A project map shall:

(a) State the name of the project, unless it has no name.

(b) Contain each timeshare unit's identifying number or other insignia and floor plans and elevations of the building or buildings, showing the layout, location and dimensions of the timeshare units and any appurtenant portion of the common area designated by the project instruments or timeshare documents for the exclusive use of the owners of one or more, but fewer than all, of the units ('limited common areas').

5 If the declaration is recorded after substantial completion of the timeshare units, contain a verified statement of a registered architect or professional engineer certifying that the project map fully depicts with substantial accuracy the layout, location, unit numbers or identifying insignia and dimensions of the timeshare units and appurtenant limited common areas as built.

6 If the declaration is recorded before substantial completion of the timeshare units, or any of them, contain a preliminary project map and a verified statement of a registered architect or professional engineer certifying that such preliminary map recorded with it is an accurate copy of portions of the plans of the timeshare units as filed with and as approved by the government official having the authority to issue building permits in the jurisdiction in which the timeshare units are located; within forty-five (45) days after the date the timeshare units legally can be occupied, the declaration shall be amended to include the certification required under Paragraph 5 of Subsection A.

7 Provide for the plan for the use, occupancy, or possession of the timeshare units by owners. So long as the basic plan for use, occupancy or possession of the timeshare units is included in the declaration, the details of such plan may be included in any other timeshare document provided that the timeshare document which sets forth the method, if any,

by which owners reserve the use of timeshare units is recorded in the same manner as the declaration.

8 Contain a schedule of use periods identifying the use periods and the use seasons, if any, for each timeshare unit by letter, name, number or other device, or any combination thereof.

9 Provide for an annual service period for each timeshare unit. The service period may be different for different timeshare units and need not be for a specifically designated time period or for consecutive days.

10 Provide for the organization of the association required by Section 11–101.

11 Provide that the association shall be responsible for and have control over the administration and operation of the timeshare property and the timeshare plan.

12 Require that the association enter into and maintain, at all times, a management agreement which satisfies the requirements of Section 11–110.

13 Require that the association obtain the insurance policies required by Section 11–112.

14 Describe and authorize the method by which timeshare expenses shall be allocated to each timeshare and by which timeshare expenses and personal charges shall be assessed to and collected from owners.

15 If not provided for in the by-laws, describe and provide for, in a manner consistent with the provisions of Section 11–104, allocation of the voting rights attributable to each timeshare.

16 Describe and authorize the methods, if any (in addition to those otherwise provided by law) by which the timeshare documents may be enforced, including but not limited to the association's right to enforce the collection of timeshare expenses and personal charges.

17 Specify the term of the timeshare plan.

18 Specify the events, including but not limited to condemnation and damage or destruction, upon and the procedures by which the timeshare plan may or shall be terminated before the expiration of its full term and the consequences of such termination, including but not limited to

the manner in which the timeshare property and/or the proceeds from the disposition thereof shall be held or distributed among owners.

19 Provide for subordination to the declaration by the owners of their rights of partition and all other rights or attributes as tenants-in-common so long as the timeshare plan is in effect and, if desired, during any period of time specified in the declaration for the disposition of the timeshare property after termination of the timeshare plan.

20 Provide for amendment of declaration consistent with the provisions of this Act.

21 If the timeshare units are located in a project with respect to which there is an association of owners of units which is different from the association, provide for the manner in which owners may exercise voting rights in such other association.

22 Contain any other provision necessary to cause the timeshare plan to comply with the requirements of this Act.

B Units may not be added to the timeshare plan and, except as provided in Sections 10–109 and 10–110, timeshare units may not be withdrawn from the timeshare plan unless such addition and/or withdrawal is expressly authorized in the declaration, in which event the declaration, in addition to satisfying the requirements of Subsection A, shall also:

1 Specify that (i) units may be added as timeshare units to or (ii) timeshare units may be withdrawn from the timeshare plan only by execution and recordation of a supplemental declaration to such effect and that such supplemental declaration shall be filed with the secretary of the association prior to recordation; and

2 Specify the method or formula for the allocation of the timeshare expenses to owners of timeshares within units added to the timeshare plan or the reallocation of the timeshare expenses among owners of timeshares within the timeshare units remaining after the withdrawal of timeshare units.

### Section 10–103 Amendment

A Except as provided in Subsections C and D, no amendment or modification to the declaration or any other timeshare document which would materially and adversely change the rights of an owner made after the first sales contract is entered into shall be effective unless the board shall consent thereto. Such consent shall be in writing and signed by the appropriate officers of the association.

B In addition to the requirements of Subsection A, and except as provided in Subsections C and D, for so long as the developer and/or its affiliates own or control timeshares to which a majority of the voting power of the association has been allocated, amendments to or modifications of the declaration shall not be effective unless:

1 Approved by owners through referendum in accordance with the provisions of Section 11–107 or adopted by initiative pursuant to the provisions of Section 11–106; and

2 Filed with the Agency.

C The developer may, if the declaration contains an explicit authorization to do so, amend or modify the declaration or any other timeshare document, with the consent or joinder of only such persons, if any, as shall be required by the terms of the declaration, to comply with the laws of any jurisdiction or the requirements of any governmental agency in connection with the registration of the timeshare plan to permit the sale of timeshares in that jurisdiction, provided that any such amendment or modification shall be consistent with the provisions of this Act.

D If the declaration and the timeshare permit contain an authorization to do so, which explicitly describes the events and conditions upon which the same may occur, the developer may amend or modify the declaration or any other timeshare document with the consent or joinder of only such persons, if any, as shall be required by the terms of the declaration; provided, however, that no such amendment shall change the use period or timeshare unit to be used, the vote allocated to or the proportionate timeshare expense liability of a timeshare without being adopted by the class of owners affected thereby in the manner set forth in Section 11–107.

E No amendment or modification to the declaration or any other timeshare document which would materially and adversely change the rights of the developer or an affiliate may be made without the consent of the developer unless such amendment or modification would affect all other owners in the same way.

F No action to challenge the validity of an amendment adopted pursuant to this section may be brought more than one year after the amendment is effected.

G Every amendment to the declaration must be (i) filed with the secretary of the association to be effective, (ii) recorded in every county in which timeshare units in the plan are located, and (iii) indexed in the name of the timeshare plan, the association and the parties executing such amendment.

**Section 10–104 Partition** No action for partition of a timeshare unit may be maintained except as provided by the timeshare documents. If a timeshare is owned by two or more persons, the provisions of this Section shall not prohibit an action for a judicial sale of the timeshares in lieu of partition as between such co-owners. Notwithstanding any law or authority to the contrary, a provision in a declaration effecting a waiver or subordination of the rights of partition and/or other attributes of tenancy-in-common shall be valid, binding and enforceable.

**Section 10–105 Non-Merger** The acquisition or conveyance of a timeshare consisting of use rights as an estate for years together with a reversion or remainder interest upon termination of the estate for years or upon termination of the timeshare plan shall not merge the estate for years and the remainder interest unless all of the timeshares in the particular timeshare unit are acquired by a single person and such person records a document (i) withdrawing such timeshare unit from the timeshare plan or (ii) expressly effecting such a merger.

**Section 10–106 Character of Real Property Used for Timeshare Purposes** The division of any present or future legally recognized real property interest into timeshares shall not change the real property character of the real property interest so divided.

**Section 10–107 Void Conveyance** Any purported conveyance, encumbrance, judicial sale, or other voluntary or involuntary transfer of a timeshare made without the use period which is part of that timeshare is void.

**Section 10–108 Rights of Secured Lenders** The declaration may require that all or a specified number or percentage of the mortgagees or beneficiaries of deeds of trust encumbering units or timeshares approve specified actions of the owners, developer or association as a condition to the effectiveness of those actions, but no requirement for approval may operate to (i) deny or delegate control over the general administrative affairs of the association by the owners or their elected representatives, or (ii) prevent the association from commencing, intervening in, or settling any litigation or proceeding, or receiving and distributing any insurance or condemnation proceeds pursuant to Section 10–110.

**Section 10–109 Damage and Destruction Condemnation**

A  As used in this Section:

1 'Material Damage' means significant damage or destruction to all or a portion of the timeshare property from any cause, including such damage resulting from or certain to result from a 'Taking.'

2 'Taking' means and shall occur when the timeshare property, or any portion thereof, is possessed by or conveyed to a body politic or corporation having the right to exercise the power of eminent domain as a result of the exercise of such power, or in lieu of or in settlement of eminent domain proceedings, actual or threatened, and in spite of the absence of such proceedings.

3 'Total Taking' means a taking of all of the timeshare property or so much of the timeshare property and/or the buildings and improvements thereon that the use of the remainder for the purposes

provided for in the timeshare plan is impractical or economically unfeasible.

4 'Partial Taking' means a taking which is not a total taking.

B  The consequences of and the procedures to be followed as a result of material damage or a taking shall be as provided for in the timeshare documents, or, to the extent not provided for in the timeshare documents, as provided for in this Section.

C  A total taking shall terminate the timeshare plan. A partial taking shall result in withdrawal from the timeshare plan of the timeshare units taken, the retirement of timeshares and the distribution of condemnation proceeds as provided below.

D  Within a reasonable time after the occurrence of material damage, the board shall adopt a plan for dealing with the material damage which plan shall include (i) a determination whether or not to rebuild all or some of the timeshare property which has suffered material damage, (ii) if the determination is to rebuild all or a portion of the timeshare property, include a determination of the amount, if any, by which the cost of rebuilding will exceed insurance proceeds or condemnation proceeds, and the amount each owner would be assessed in order to provide for the deficiency, (iii) if the board determines not to rebuild the timeshare property or any portion thereof, the estimated amount of distributions which would be received by each class of owner whose timeshare would be retired from the timeshare plan in accordance with the provisions of Subsection F, below. The board shall, within a reasonable time after adoption of the plan, submit the plan to the owners for adoption or rejection, either at a meeting of owners or pursuant to Section 11–107. If the plan is not approved by owners, the board shall revise the plan and submit the revised plan to the owners for adoption or rejection. Such procedure shall be repeated until such time as the plan of the board is adopted by owners, or until the owners shall obtain approval for an alternative course of action pursuant to Section 11–106.

E Timeshare property which is not rebuilt or is taken shall be deemed withdrawn from the timeshare plan. The board shall authorize and direct two officers of the association to record a certificate designating that portion of the timeshare property so withdrawn from the timeshare plan and identifying the timeshares correspondingly retired pursuant to the provisions of Subsection F.

F Whenever timeshare units are withdrawn from the timeshare plan, timeshares shall correspondingly be retired. When a timeshare is retired, its owners shall have no further right to use the timeshare property and shall be entitled to receive a distribution of proceeds as provided below. If the timeshare plan is a unit ownership plan, the timeshares retired shall be those in the timeshare units withdrawn. If the timeshare plan is not a unit ownership plan, the board shall conduct a lottery to determine which timeshares shall be retired. In the case of a unit ownership plan, an owner whose timeshare is retired shall be entitled to receive that portion of the proceeds attributable to his interest in the timeshare unit withdrawn from the timeshare plan. In the case of a timeshare plan which is not a unit ownership plan, an owner whose timeshare is retired is entitled to receive that portion of the total proceeds distributable to all owners whose timeshares are retired equal to the percentage which his timeshare expense liability bears to the total timeshare expense liability of all such owners.

G The association and the board shall have the same authority and power to sell and convey timeshare property which is not rebuilt as is conferred pursuant to Section 10–110 following termination of the timeshare plan.

### Section 10–110 Termination

A The timeshare plan shall terminate at the end of the term of the timeshare plan, or prior to the end of the term:

1 As provided in the timeshare documents.

2 To the extent not provided for in the timeshare documents the timeshare plan shall terminate as follows:

(a) As provided in Section 10–109;

(b) Upon entry of a final judgment by a court of competent jurisdiction in an action brought by the association declaring that the useful life of the improvements has ended.

B Termination of the timeshare plan shall not terminate the existence of the association, which shall continue for so long as is necessary to implement the provisions of the timeshare documents or this Section.

C Unless the timeshare documents expressly provide to the contrary, subject to the provisions of Subsection E, upon termination of the timeshare plan, the association may sell, convey, transfer or otherwise dispose of the owners' interests in the timeshare property, upon such terms and conditions as the board, in its sole discretion, shall determine. The timeshare property may be conveyed by deed or other appropriate instrument of conveyance executed and acknowledged by two officers of the association, which instrument recites that it is made pursuant to the authority provided by this Section and, if the timeshare documents provide any procedure therefor, that the procedure set forth in the timeshare documents for the disposition of the timeshare property was followed. After such conveyance it shall be conclusively presumed that a deed or other instrument of conveyance so executed and acknowledged, and containing such recitals shall vest good and marketable title in the grantee named therein. No action may be instituted by or on behalf of any owner to set aside or invalidate any conveyance so made.

D Any proceeds received by the association in connection with the sale or other disposition of the timeshare property shall be distributed to owners as follows:

1 If the timeshare plan is a unit ownership plan, such proceeds shall be distributed to each owner in accordance with such owner's percentage ownership in his timeshare unit.

2 If the timeshare plan is not a unit ownership plan, such proceeds shall be distributed to owners in the same ratio as

they share timeshare expense liability.

E If the timeshare plan is terminated prior to the end of the term provided in the timeshare documents, and there is a remainderman, the board shall give written notice to the remainderman of the terms and conditions upon which the board proposes to dispose of the timeshare property. If the remainderman agrees to convey the timeshare property on such terms and conditions, the remainderman shall convey the timeshare property on such terms and conditions and the association and the remainderman shall divide the proceeds in a manner acceptable to both the board and the remainderman, or in the event they fail to agree on the division of proceeds, by arbitration as provided below. If the remainderman does not agree to convey the timeshare property on such terms, the remainderman shall purchase the owners' interest in the timeshare property on the same terms and conditions, except the purchase price shall be that percentage of the purchase price equal to that percentage which the owners' interest in the timeshare property bears to its total value. If the board and the remainderman cannot agree on such percentage, it shall be determined by arbitration in accordance with the commercial arbitration rules of the American Arbitration Association.

## ARTICLE XI

## OPERATION AND MANAGEMENT

### Section 11–101 Association

A All timeshare plans having more than 12 timeshares shall have an association of owners. Each owner shall be a member of the association for the timeshare plan and only owners may be members. If the number of timeshare interests in the timeshare plan is 12 or fewer, the owners may form an association meeting the requirements of this section.

B The association shall be organized as a non-profit corporation. The state or foreign jurisdiction of incorporation of the association shall be one of the following:

1 This state;

2 Provided the requirements of Subsection C are satisfied, the state or foreign jurisdiction in which the timeshare property is located, or, in the case of a multi-location, the timeshare property is located; or

3 Provided the requirements of Subsection C are satisfied, any state or foreign jurisdiction in which the developer has obtained authorization to dispose of timeshares in the timeshare plan in such state or foreign jurisdiction provided that such authorization was given pursuant to a law which specifically regulates timeshares.

C The state or foreign jurisdiction in which the association is incorporated shall be a state of foreign jurisdiction, the laws of which (i) empower the association to perform substantially all the powers enumerated in Section 11–102, (ii) allow compliance with the provisions of Sections 11–103 and 11–104, and (iii) insulate the members of the association from personal liability for contractual obligations of the association.

### Section 11–102 Powers of Association

Any other law of this state to the contrary notwithstanding, an association incorporated under the laws of this state may:

1 Institute, defend, or intervene in litigation or administrative or other legal proceedings in its own name on behalf of itself or two or more owners on matters affecting the timeshare property; the timeshare plan; or the timeshares.

2 Indemnify its directors and officers and maintain directors and officers' liability insurance.

3 Exercise any other powers conferred on it by the timeshare documents.

4 Exercise any other powers authorized by this Article or necessary and proper (as determined by the board or pursuant to the provisions of Section 11–106) for the administration and operation of the association.

### Section 11–103 Board of Directors Subject to the limitations of this Article, all powers of the Association shall be exercised by or under the authority of, and the business and affairs of the association

shall be conducted by a board of directors.

### Section 11–104 Allocation of Association Voting Rights

A The declaration or by-laws shall allocate voting rights to each timeshare, including unsold timeshares held by the developer. No distinction in voting rights shall be made between timeshares held by owners other than the developer and those held by the developer. Voting rights may not be allocated to any property except timeshares or to any person who is not an owner. The vote (or, if the laws of the state of incorporation of the association require that one vote be allocated to each timeshare owner, the weight of the vote) allocated to each timeshare shall be determined according to any of the following methods:

1 One vote per timeshare;

2 A single percentage or fractional vote for each timeshare proportionate to the size of its corresponding timeshare unit or type of unit as compared to other timeshare units or types of units in the timeshare plan.

3 A single percentage or fractional vote for each timeshare proportionate to the cost and expenses of operating its corresponding timeshare unit or type of unit as compared to the cost and expenses of operating other timeshare units or types of units in the timeshare plan.

4 Any other method approved by the Agency.

B As to some matters, the vote allocated to each timeshare may be determined according to one method provided in Subsection A. Cumulative voting may be utilized only for the purpose of electing the board. Class voting may be authorized if approved by the Agency.

C If a timeshare is owned by more than one person, the vote for such timeshare shall be exercised as provided in the declaration or by-laws, but in no event shall more than the vote allocated to such timeshare be cast or counted. The declaration of by-laws may require that the vote of a timeshare owned by more than one person be cast as a whole or be split among the co-owners of the time-share in the manner specified in the declaration or by-laws. An owner casting a vote allocated to a certain timeshare will be conclusively presumed for all purposes to be acting with the authority and consent of all other owners of the same timeshare unless a written protest is received from such other owner or such other owner casts a conflicting vote, in which case the vote of that timeshare shall be cast as provided in the declaration or by-laws.

### Section 11–105 Initiative, Referendum and Recall: General Provisions

A The board shall cause the managing agent to maintain and the managing agent shall maintain and make reasonably available for inspection and copying by any owner a roster containing the names and the last known addresses of all owners. Any owner who requests access to the roster shall, if the managing agent so requests, agree in writing not to make any commercial use of the roster, which agreement may contain a liquidated damage clause.

B Each ballot prepared pursuant to Sections 11–106, 11–107 and 11–108 shall contain no material which is not required or authorized by this Article and must contain:

1 A statement that the ballot will not be counted unless signed by an owner.

2 The specification of a date not less than 20 or more than 60 days after the date the ballot is mailed, by which the ballot must be received by the person to whom it is to be returned and a statement that the ballot will not be counted unless received by that date.

3 The name and address of the person to whom the ballot is to be returned.

C Each ballot mailed pursuant to Sections 11–106, 11–107 and 11–108 shall be mailed to the address of the owner to whom it is addressed as shown in the roster maintained by the managing agent, or, if known to the person responsible for mailing it to be different, to such different address. The board shall procure and keep reasonably available for inspection for at least one year after the vote is calculated a certificate of mailing for each ballot and the original or a photocopy of each ballot returned by the date specified pursuant to Paragraph 2 of Subsection B.

D If the managing agent, the developer or anyone on behalf of any of them communicates with any owner, other than as expressly authorized by Sections 11–106, 11–107 and 11–108, on the subject matter of any petition or ballot prepared pursuant to any of those sections, the expense of that communication shall be borne by such person and may not be assessed directly or indirectly in whole or in part to any other owner.

E Any ballot that is not signed by an owner or is not received by the date specified pursuant to Paragraph 2 of Subsection B is void.

F The board shall take action reasonably calculated to notify all owners of the determination of any matter pursuant to Sections 11–106, 11–107 and 11–108.

G The board shall cause an amendment to the declaration or any other recorded timeshare document adopted pursuant to Section 11–106 or approved pursuant to Section 11–107 to be set forth in an instrument which shall also contain a statement of the vote and shall cause the same to be recorded in the same manner as the instrument amended.

H No right or power of an owner under this Section or Sections 11–106, 11–107 or 11–108 may be waived, limited or delegated by contract, power of attorney, proxy or otherwise in favor of the developer, an affiliate of a developer, a managing agent or any person designated by any of them.

### Section 11–106 Direct Initiative by Owners

A Subject to the limitations and requirements set forth elsewhere in this Act, owners may amend the declaration or other timeshare documents or take any action which the board could lawfully take in the manner provided by this Section. The initiative rights of owners provided for in this Section are in addition to the rights of owners, if any, otherwise to effect such action.

B Any owner may deliver to the board a petition containing a proposal to be determined by initiative and signed by owners holding at least five per cent of the voting power of the association. There may be attached to the petition a writing of not more than 750 words in support of the proposal. Within 20 days after receiving the petition, the board shall mail to each owner a ballot setting forth the language of the proposal, and affording an opportunity to indicate a preference between approval and disapproval of the proposal, together with a copy of a writing properly delivered with the petition. The ballot may also be accompanied by a writing of not more than 750 words from the board recommending approval or disapproval of the proposal.

C Within 10 days after the date specified for the return of ballots, the board shall examine the ballots that have been returned and determine the vote. A proposal submitted for determination by initiative shall be adopted only if following requirements are met:

1 If the proposal is an amendment to the declaration or other timeshare document;

(a) The consent of the developer is not required under Subsection E of Section 10–103, or has been given.

(b) In the case of an amendment to the declaration, the requirements of Section 10–102 have been met.

2 The proposal does not violate any other provision of this Act or any other law.

3 Ballots were cast in the initiative representing at least 20 per cent of the voting power of the association and the proposal was favored by at least 15 per cent of the voting power of the association and by at least 50 per cent of the voting power of all owners casting ballots in the initiative favored the proposal.

D A proposal adopted pursuant to this Section may not be repealed or modified within 3 years except by another initiative pursuant to this Section. Thereafter, the board may not repeal or modify the result without the approval of the owners.

### Section 11–107 Referendum of Owners

A Whenever the approval of owners or

a class of owners of board action is required by the timeshare documents or this Act, or the board desires to obtain such approval, such approval may be given by referendum in accordance with this Section 11–107.

B The referendum shall be conducted in accordance with the procedures set forth in Section 11–105. The ballot to be mailed to each owner shall:

1 Describe the board action for which approval is sought.

2 State the vote of the board on the action, and, if less than a unanimous vote, list the board members in favor and those opposed.

3 State whether the approval is required by the timeshare documents.

4 If the vote required for approval is other than a majority of the voting power of all owners casting ballots in the referendum, state the requirement for approval.

5 Provide the opportunity to indicate a preference between approval or disapproval of the action.

C The ballot may be accompanied by a writing of not more than 750 words recommending approval of the action from the members of the board favoring such approval. If the members of the board who do not favor approval of the action so request, the ballot shall be accompanied by a writing of not more than 750 words from such board members recommending disapproval of the action.

D Within 10 days after the date specified for the return of ballots, the board shall examine the ballots that have been returned and determine the vote. A board action submitted for approval by referendum shall be approved only if the following requirements are met:

1 Unless the ballot stated a larger percentage, ballots were cast in the referendum representing at least 10 per cent of the voting power of the association, or, if the approval of a class of owners was sought, 10 per cent of the voting power of such class.

2 Unless the ballot stated a larger majority for approval, ballots representing at least 50 per cent of the voting power

of all owners casting ballots (or, if approval of a class of owners was sought, of all owners of such class casting ballots) in the referendum favored approval.

3 If the ballot stated requirements for approval other than those described in Paragraphs 1 and 2, such requirements were met.

## Section 11–108 Recall of Managing Agent by Owners

A In addition to any manner permitted by other law or by the timeshare documents, the owners may discharge the managing agent with or without cause in the manner provided by this Section.

B Any owner may deliver to the board a petition containing the language of a proposed ballot affording the opportunity to indicate a preference between retaining and discharging the present managing agent. Such petition must be signed by owners holding at least five per cent of the voting power of the association. There may be attached to the petition a writing of not more than 750 words supporting discharge of the managing agent. A copy of the petition and any such writing must be delivered by such owner to the managing agent in the same manner as the petition was delivered to the board. The board shall cause a copy of the petition to be delivered to the managing agent within 5 days of its receipt by the board. Not earlier than 20 days nor later than 30 days after receipt of the petition, the board shall mail to each owner (i) a ballot affording an opportunity to indicate a preference between retaining and discharging of the managing agent, (ii) a copy of any writing properly delivered with the petition, (iii) if submitted by the managing agent, a writing of not more than 750 words, (iv) if it elects to do so, a writing of not more than 750 words from the board recommending retention or discharge of the managing agent.

C Within 10 days after the date specified for the return of ballots, the board shall examine the ballots that have been returned and determine the vote. The vote shall be determined to be in favor of discharge of the managing agent only if the following requirements are met:

1 Ballots are cast representing at least 50 per cent of the voting power of the association.

2 Ballots representing at least 66⅔ per cent of the voting power of all owners casting ballots favored discharge of the managing agent.

D If the vote is determined to be in favor of discharging the managing agent, the managing agent shall be discharged effective 90 days after the date specified for the return of the ballots.

E A managing agent discharged pursuant to this Section is not entitled by reason of such discharge to any penalty or other charge payable directly or indirectly in whole or in part by any owner, except to the extent the developer is obligated under any agreement with the managing agent to pay any such charge or penalty.

**Section 11–109 Duties of Association/ Function of Managing Agent** The association shall be responsible for and have control over the administration of the timeshare plan and the operation and maintenance of the timeshare property except to the extent the project instruments vest control of the operation and maintenance of the common areas in another entity. The actual management of the timeshare plan and the operation and maintenance of the timeshare property shall be performed by a managing agent (or, in the case of a multi-location project, one or more managing agents) selected by the board and engaged by the association pursuant to a written management agreement which satisfies the requirements of Section 11–110. The developer or an affiliate may be a managing agent.

**Section 11–110 Management Agreements**

A The management agreement shall obligate the managing agent to cause to be provided, under the direction and control of the board, all services required to administer the timeshare plan and the affairs of the association and to operate and maintain the timeshare property except to the extent the project instruments vest responsibility for the operation and maintenance of the common areas in an entity other than the association. If, in the case of a multi-location plan, there is more than one managing agent, one of the managing agents shall be primarily responsible for the administration of the timeshare plan.

B Except as provided in Subsection C, the term of the management agreement shall comply with the following provisions:

1 Except for the first management agreement for a timeshare plan, the initial term of a management agreement may not exceed three years. The initial term of the first management agreement for a timeshare plan may have a term of the shorter of (i) five years, or (ii) three years from the date on which the developer shall have sold 25 per cent of the timeshares included in the timeshare plan as it existed at the commencement of the term of the management agreement.

2 Subsequent terms of a management agreement shall not exceed one year. A management agreement may provide for automatic annual renewals upon the expiration of each successive term unless at least 90 days before the end of any term the board or the managing agent gives written notice that it will not renew the management agreement.

3 The term of the management agreement may be terminated, prior to its expiration:

(a) By the board or managing agent for cause by at least 30 days written notice.

(b) By recall as provided in Section 11–108.

(c) By the managing agent, without cause, by at least 90 days written notice.

C For the purpose of this Section, the term 'hotel plan' means a timeshare plan which satisfies the following requirements: (i) the timeshare units are within a hotel which has at least 100 living units for use as transient accommodations ('living units'), (ii) the living units are owned by the developer or the developer has a leasehold interest in the living units with a remaining term of at least 10 years at the time a management agreement for the timeshare plan is made or renewed, and (iii) owners do not have the right to occupy at any one point in time, living units having an aggregate gross floor area in excess of 70 per cent of the aggregate gross floor area of all of the living units (x) by reason of provisions in the declaration or other timeshare documents to such effect, and/or (y) as a function of the number of owners or timeshares. The term of a management agreement for a hotel plan shall either comply with the provisions of Subsection B or comply with the following provisions:

1 Except for the first management agreement for a hotel plan, the initial term of a management agreement may not exceed five years. The initial term of the first management agreement shall not exceed 10 years.

2 Subsequent terms of a management agreement for a hotel plan shall not exceed five years. A management agreement for a hotel plan may provide for automatic five year renewals upon the expiration of each successive term unless at least 180 days before the end of any term the board or the managing agent gives written notice that it will not renew the management agreement.

3 The term of the management agreement may be terminated, prior to its expiration:

(a) By the board or managing agent for cause by at least 30 days written notice.

(b) By recall as provided in Section 11–108.

(c) Subject to the provisions of Paragraph 4, by the managing agent, without cause, by at least 180 days written notice.

4 The resignation of the managing agent shall not be effective and the term of any management agreement which would have otherwise ended shall be extended until the board shall have secured the agreement of a real estate or hotel management firm to act as the successor managing agent and the owners, pursuant to Section 11–107, have approved the action of the board in engaging the successor managing agent.

D Every managing agent shall keep proper books and records with respect to the administration and operation of the timeshare plan and the timeshare property. Such books and records shall be the property of the association.

E A remainderman may be a party to any management agreement entered into by the association. If the remainderman elects to become a party to a management agreement, the management agreement for such timeshare plan shall be an agreement between the association, the managing agent and the remainderman. The declaration for a timeshare plan with respect to which there is a remainderman may contain provisions (i) authorizing assessments in order to pay any obligation to the remainderman under the management agreement, (ii) if the remainderman is not made an express party to any management agreement to which the remainderman has requested it be made a party, making the remainderman a third-party beneficiary of such management agreement with all of the rights specified herein, and (iii) entitling the remainderman to possession of the timeshare property to the extent necessary to effect the remainderman's rights under the management agreement. A management agreement to which the remainderman is a party shall, at the request of the remainderman, contain:

1 A covenant of the association in favor of the remainderman that the association shall cause the timeshare units to be maintained in good condition and repair.

2 The agreement of the association that, if, after the expiration of a reasonable time following written notice from the remainderman to the board and the managing agent of an alleged breach of the association's covenant to maintain the timeshare units in good condition and repair, such breach has not been cured, the remainderman shall have the right to take or cause to be taken those measures required to cure such default if the remainderman shall have given the board and the managing agent 10 days written notice of the remainderman's intent to effect such cure; provided, however, that no such 10 day notice need be given if repairs of an emergency nature are required.

3 The promise of the association to pay to the remainderman, upon demand, the amount of any sums expended by the remainderman to effect a cure of any breach of the covenant to keep the timeshare units in good condition and repair, together with interest at the maximum rate permitted by law from the date the funds are expended until the obligation is repaid.

4 A provision requiring for the submission of any dispute between the remainderman and the association and/ or the managing agent to arbitration in accordance with the Commercial Arbitration Rules of the American Arbitration Association and providing that any award in such arbitration shall be binding upon the parties.

5 The agreement of the association that the board shall cause an assessment to be levied against owners to the extent necessary to obtain any funds which the association may be required to pay to the remainderman by reason of the breach of the association's covenant to maintain the timeshare units in good condition and repair.

### Section 11–111 Tort and Contract Liability

A An owner is personally liable for his own acts and omissions and those of his visitors, employees and agents other than the association and the board.

B An owner shall not be liable for any damage or injury to persons or property occurring on the timeshare property or for any obligation of the association merely because he is an owner.

C A judgment for money against an association [if recorded] [if (insert other procedure required under state law to perfect a lien on real property as a result of a judgment)] is a lien against all of the timeshares, but no other property of an owner is subject to the claims of creditors of the association.

D A judgment against an association must be indexed in the name of the association.

### Section 11–112 Insurance

A Subject to the provisions of Subsection C, before the close of escrow for the sale of any timeshare in a timeshare property in which the number of timeshares is more than 12, the association shall obtain and thereafter maintain:

1 Insurance against loss or damage to the timeshare property, the common property and any other contents of the timeshare units, including without limitation machinery used in the service of the timeshare project, by fire and other risks and hazards customarily covered by an insurance policy written on an all-risk basis, including earthquakes, and, if the timeshare property is located in an area which has been identified by the Secretary of Housing and Urban Development as a flood hazard area and in which flood insurance has been made available under the National Flood Insurance Act of 1968, floods. The stipulated amount of such insurance shall be based on the full replacement cost of such property, and either such stipulated full replacement cost amount shall be updated annually to reflect the then current estimated full replacement cost thereof, or the policy shall include an endorsement which provides for full reimbursement for the actual cost of repair or replacement thereof, without deduction for depreciation.

2 Insurance covering the common property, any other contents of the timeshare units and personal property on the timeshare property owned by any owner or other person who rightfully occupies a timeshare unit, or in the possession of the association, its agents or employees against hazards such as burglary and theft.

3 Insurance against loss of earnings, continuing charges and expenses, and such other risks and hazards customarily covered by business interruption insurance shall be combined with insurance against loss due to extra expenses arising out of operating the timeshare property and the cost of temporary quarters for owners and other persons entitled to use the facilities due to damage to the facilities, the common property and such other risks and hazards customarily covered by such extra expense insurance policies.

4 Insurance against loss for liability due to injury to or destrution of personal

property belonging to owners or other persons who rightfully occupy a time-share unit while located within the time-share property, including without limitation, loss due to claims for bodily injury, death and property damage with a combined single limit liability with regard thereto of not less than $1,000,000.00 per occurrence. There shall also be procured and maintained one or more umbrella liability insurance policies against loss or damage due to claims for personal injury, death and property damage with a limit with regard thereto of not less than $5,000,000.00 per occurrence.

B Each insurance policy carried pursuant to Subsection A must provide that:

1 The association, the managing agent(s), each owner are each an insured person under the policy whether designated as an insured by name individually or as part of a named group or otherwise, as his interest may appear.

2 The insurer waives its right to subrogation under the policy against the association and any owner or member of his household.

3 No act or omission by any owner, unless acting within the scope of his authority on behalf of an association, will void the policy or be a condition to recovery by any other person under the policy.

4 If, at the time of a loss under the policy, there is other insurance in the name of a timeshare owner covering the same risk covered by the policy, the policy maintained pursuant to Subsection A is primary insurance not contributing with the other insurance, and other insurance in the name of an owner applies only to loss in excess of the primary coverage.

5 The insurer shall issue certificates or memoranda of insurance to the association and, upon written request, to any owner, mortgagee, or beneficiary under a deed of trust.

6 The insurance may not be cancelled until 30 days after notice of the proposed cancellation has been mailed to the association and the managing agent and each person to whom a certificate or memoranum of insurance has been issued, at their respective last known addresses.

C The association shall not be required to obtain or maintain any of the insurance described in Subsection A, if:

1 The board determines it is not available at a reasonable cost and gives written notice to each owner of such determination, which notice shall also set forth the annual premium for such insurance and the approximate annual cost to each owner.

2 The owners determine not to maintain such insurance.

3 The insurance is carried by another person in connection with the project in which the timeshare property is located pursuant to a policy which satisfies the requirements of Subsection B.

D The board shall obtain fidelity bonds covering the association, each managing agent, and all directors, officers, employees, agents, independent contractors and volunteers responsible for handling funds belonging to or held in connection with the timeshare plan or the owners. The fidelity bond must name the association as the obligee and provide coverage in an amount not less than three months estimated operating expenses plus the savings and reserves of the association. The coverage shall be adjusted annually. The bonds must also:

1 Provide that they may not be cancelled or substantially modified without at least 30 days prior written notice to the board and the managing agent.

2 Provide coverage for persons who serve without pay and contain a waiver of any defense based upon the exclusion of such persons from the definition of the term 'employee' or similar terms.

E The board shall obtain a policy of errors and omissions insurance covering the association and each managing agent, and all of their respective directors, officers, employees, agents and independent contractors. The policy must name the association as trustee for each owner as insureds. The policy must contain no provision relieving the insurer of liability because of any act or omission by an owner.

### Section 11–113 Unavailable and Unusable Units

A  If for any reason, other than the act or omission to act of the owner affected, a timeshare unit is unavailable or unusable during an owner's use period, the managing agent shall (i) use its best efforts to secure alternate accommodations of comparable or better quality for use by such owner during his use period; (ii) provide transportation for the owner, his family and guests, if any, from the location of the timeshare unit to the alternative accommodations; (iii) allow the owner one telephone call without charge, for the purpose of permitting the owner to contact such person as the owner selects to advise of his change in accommodations; and (iv) advise any telephone answering service or front desk of the change in accommodations to be sure that communications intended for the owner are forwarded.

B  The association shall pay the costs and expenses of satisfying the foregoing requirements. If the managing agent caused the timeshare unit to be rendered unusable or unavailable, the managing agent shall reimburse the association for the amounts expended by the association pursuant to this section.

C  Except to the extent otherwise provided in the declaration, an action may not be maintained by an owner for the loss of the use of the timeshare unit during his use period if the association satisfies the requirements of Subsection A.

### Section 11–114 Dissemination of Information to Owners and the Agency

A  The following shall be disseminated by the board to all owners within the times provided below:

1  The budget for each fiscal year, which shall be disseminated not less than 45 days before the beginning of the fiscal year to which the budget applies.

2  An annual report consisting of the following within 120 days after the cost of the fiscal year:

(a) A balance sheet as of the end of the fiscal year.

(b) An income statement for the fiscal year.

(c) A statement of the net changes in the financial position of the association for such fiscal year.

(d) A list of the names and mailing addresses of the members of the board.

3  Minutes of the first organizational meeting of the association and each annual meeting of the association thereafter within 30 days after the date of such meeting.

B  The annual reports described in Paragraph 2 of Subsection A shall be prepared by an independent certified public accountant and shall be certified, unless the board determines not to certify the reports, the decision of the board shall be submitted to the owners for approval pursuant to Section 11–107. A notice shall accompany the ballot explaining in plain language the difference in cost and the difference in nature between a certified and an uncertified audit.

C  Until the date of expiration of the timeshare permit, the developer shall cause to be provided to the agency, within the same time frames specified above, all items which are required by this Section to be furnished to owners.

### Section 11–115 Budget of Timeshare Expenses

The board shall prepare, or cause to be prepared, and adopt for each fiscal year of the association an estimate of all expenses to be incurred in connection with the operation and administration and maintenance of the timeshare plan and the operation and maintenance of the timeshare property for such fiscal year ('timeshare expenses'). Without limiting the generality of the foregoing, the budget shall include:

1  Funds for a contingency account in such amount as the board determines to be adequate to provide financial stability in the administration of the timeshare plan; provided, however, that the amount budgeted for the contingency account shall not be less than the difference between (i) four per cent of the total amount budgeted for other timeshare expenses, excluding amounts budgeted for the capital improvements reserve account, and (ii) the balance of the contingency account at the end of the preceding fiscal year. The funds in the

contingency account shall be deemed to be savings of the individual owners held by the board for their benefit to pay timeshare expenses not payable or paid from regular assessments.

2 Funds for a capital improvements reserve account in such annual amounts as the board determines to be adequate to provide for specific capital improvements, whether it be the repair, remodeling, restoration, upgrading or replacement of the timeshare units or the common property, or such other improvements as the board determines to be necessary, appropriate or desirable. The funds in the capital improvements reserve account shall be deemed to be savings of the timeshare owners held by the board for their benefit for expenses of a capital nature.

### Section 11–116 Assessments for Timeshare Expenses

A The association shall levy annual assessments against owners to pay for the timeshare expenses. The aggregate amount of annual assessments to be levied, with respect to any fiscal year, shall not be less than the amount of timeshare expenses reflected in the budget for such fiscal year, except to the extent the association had a surplus from a preceding fiscal year or years which is to be applied to the payment of such expenses. The board shall determine whether the annual assessment levied against each owner shall be paid in installments or in a lump sum.

B The declaration shall allocate a portion of the timeshare expense liability to each timeshare. The share of liability for timeshare expenses allocated to each timeshare shall be determined according to any of the methods permitted for the allocation of votes pursuant to Section 11–104, but the allocation of timeshare expense liability to a timeshare may be based on a method different from that allocating voting rights to such timeshare. Except for assessments under Subsection C and G, all timeshare expenses must be assessed against all timeshares in accordance with the allocations of timeshare expense liability set forth in the declaration.

C To the extent provided by the declaration, any timeshare expense benefiting fewer than all of the owners may be assessed exclusively to the timeshares of the owners benefited.

D Commencing with the date any owner is first required to pay assessments, the developer shall be obligated either to (i) pay assessments on all unsold timeshares, or (ii) make payments pursuant to and enter into a subsidy agreement with the association. The subsidy agreement shall obligate the developer to pay to the association the difference between the actual timeshare expenses incurred by the association for which assessments are levied and the amounts payable to the association by owners other than the developer as assessments for timeshare expenses. The actual expenses incurred by the association shall include an amount for reserves which shall be at least equal to that portion of the reserves provided for in the budget attributable to those portions of the timeshare property actually used by owners (including the developer) in connection with the timeshare plan. The actual expenses incurred by the association shall not include that portion of the reserves provided for in the budget attributable to portions of the timeshare property which have not then been used by owners and for which no actual reserves are appropriate. Unless the Agency shall determine that by reason of the net worth, liquidity of assets and financial ability of the developer, security therefor shall not be required, the developer's obligation to pay assessments or, in lieu thereof, to subsidize the operation of the timeshare plan pursuant to a subsidy agreement shall be secured by an irrevocable letter-of-credit, assets of the developer acceptable to the Agency, a surety bond or by some other arrangement satisfactory to the Agency. If a letter-of-credit or bond is furnished as security, the principal amount thereof shall be in an amount equal to 50 per cent of the initial budget. If other security is furnished, the fair market value thereof, after deducting the estimated cost of realizing upon the security and converting the security to cash, shall be at least equal to 50 per cent of the initial budget and in determining the exact amount, the Agency shall consider the estimated time it would take to realize upon the security and convert the same to cash. Any security given pursuant to this Section shall remain in force until 80 per cent of the timeshares shall be owned by owners other than the developer. Any surety bond, letter-of-credit or other security provided pursuant to this Section and furnished to the Agency shall be held by the Agency for the benefit of owners. Any such bond must be issued by a surety authorized to do business in this State and having sufficient net worth to be acceptable to the Agency. Any such letter-of-credit must be drawn upon or issued by a bank, savings and loan association or other financial institution authorized to do business in this State and having a sufficient net worth to be acceptable to the Agency.

E All amounts collected for reserves shall be held in trust and may be used only for the specified purposes for which such amounts have been collected unless the owners, at a meeting of owners or pursuant to either Section 11–106 or 11–107, determine to spend such funds for other purposes. Any ballot for any proposal to spend reserve funds for purposes other than that for which they were collected shall be accompanied by an explanation in plain language of the reasons for and consequences, if any, of doing so.

F Unless otherwise provided in the declaration or by-laws or otherwise determined by the owners at a meeting of owners or pursuant to either Section 11–106 or 11–107, any surplus funds derived from owners or property belonging to them or the association and held by the board remaining after payment of or provision for timeshare expenses must be paid to the owners in proportion to their timeshare expense liability or credited to them in said proportion to reduce their future timeshare expense assessments.

G If any timeshare expense is caused by the act or omission to act by an owner or his guest, the amount of such expense shall be assessed to the timeshare of such owner and the amount so assessed shall be a personal charge. Late charges, fines and interest on past due amounts shall also be personal charges. Personal charges may be assessed to an owner at check-out time or by later billing.

### Section 11–117 Lien for Assessments

A All sums assessed for timeshare expenses or personal charges constitute a lien on the timeshare from the time the assessment becomes due. The lien may be foreclosed (i) in like manner as a mortgage on real estate (or pursuant to a power of sale under [insert appropriate state statute]), or (ii) as provided in Section 11–118. If an assessment is payable in installments, the full amount of the assessment is a lien from the time the first installment becomes due.

B A lien under this Section is prior to all other liens and encumbrances on a timeshare except (i) liens and encumbrances recorded before the recordation of the declaration and, in a cooperative, liens and encumbrances which the association creates, assumes, or takes subject to, (ii) a first mortgage or deed of trust encumbering a timeshare and recorded before the date on which the assessment sought to be enforced became delinquent, (iii) a purchase money mortgage or deed of trust encumbering a timeshare and recorded before the date on which the assessment sought to be enforced became delinquent, (iv) liens for real estate taxes and other governmental assessments or charges against the timeshare, the timeshare unit, or the timeshare property and (v) liens securing assessments or charges made by a person managing a project of which the timeshare property is a part. This Section does not affect the priority of mechanics' or materialmen's liens. (The lien under this Section is not subject to the provision of [insert appropriate reference to state homestead, dower and curtesy or other exemption].)

C Recording of the declaration constitutes record notice and perfection of the lien. No further recordation of any claim of lien for assessment under this Section is required.

D A lien for unpaid assessments is extinguished unless proceedings to enforce the lien are instituted within three years after the full amount of the assessment becomes due.

E This Section does not prohibit actions or suits to recover sums for which Subsection A creates a lien or preclude resort to any contractual or other remedy permitted by law, or prohibit the lienholder from taking a deed or assignment in lieu of foreclosure.

F A judgment or decree in any action or suit brought under this Section must grant costs and reasonable attorney's fees for the prevailing party.

G Upon written request, the board shall provide an owner with a statement, in recordable form, setting forth the amount of unpaid assessments currently levied against his timeshare. The statement must be provided within 15 business days after receipt of the request and is binding in favor of persons reasonably relying thereon.

### Section 11–118 Foreclosure on Timeshares

A The trustee under a deed of trust or the holder of a lien on a timeshare, upon the failure of the owner thereof to pay the sums secured by such lien, may sell the timeshare by complying with this Section. The sale may be by public sale or by private negotiation, and at any time and place, but every aspect of the sale, including the method, advertising, time, place and terms must be reasonable. The lienholder shall give to the owner written notice of the time and place of any public sale or, if a private sale is intended, of the intention of entering into a contract to sell and of the time after which a private disposition may be made. The same notice shall also be sent to any other person who has a recorded interest in the timeshare which would be cut off by the sale, but only if the recorded interest was on record seven weeks before the date specified in the notice as the date of any public sale or seven weeks before the date specified in the notice as the date after which a private sale may be made. The notices required by the Subsection may be sent to any address reasonable under the circumstances. The sale may not be held until five weeks after the sending of the notice. The creditor may buy at any public sale, and, if the sale is conducted by fiduciary or other person not related to the creditor, at a private sale.

B The proceeds of sale shall be applied in the following order:

1 The reasonable expenses of sale.

2 The reasonable expenses of holding, maintaining, and preparing the timeshare for sale, including payment of taxes and other governmental charges, and to the extent provided for by agreement between the creditor and the owner, reasonable attorney's fees and other legal expenses incurred by the lienholder or the creditor.

3 Satisfaction in the order of priority of any liens and subordinate claims or record; and

4 Any excess shall be paid to the owner.

C Unless otherwise agreed, the debtor is liable for any deficiency.

D A good faith purchaser for value acquires the timeshare free of the debt which gave rise to the lien under which the sale occurred and any subordinate lien or interest, even though the lienholder or other person conducting the sale failed to comply with the requirements of this Section. The person conducting the sale shall execute a conveyance to the purchaser sufficient to convey the owner's interest, which conveyance states that it is executed by him after a foreclosure pursuant to this Section. The signature and title or authority of the person signing the conveyance as grantor and a recital of the facts of non-payment of the debt secured by the lien and of the giving of the notices required by this Section are sufficient proof of the facts recited and of his authority to sign. Further proof of authority is not required even though the lienholder or creditor is named as grantee in the conveyance.

E At any time before the lienholder has disposed of a timeshare or entered into a contract for its disposition pursuant to this Section. the owner or the holder of any subordinate lien may cure the owner's default and prevent sale or other disposition by tendering the performance due including any amounts due because of exercise of a right to accelerate, plus the reasonable expenses of proceeding to foreclosure incurred to the time of tender, including reasonable attorney's fees of the lienholder or creditor.

*NOTE: A copy of this Model Act may be obtained from the address on page 599.*

FINAL: As adopted by ARRDA Board of Directors, April 8, 1989.

## ARRDA MODEL TIMESHARE RESALE BROKER REGULATION LEGISLATION

*[Note: These proposals are based upon legislation currently under consideration in Florida. While specific references to Florida statutes have been eliminated, some definitional adjustment may be necessary in other states so that the legislation conforms with existing state law. Insertions marked in* **bold face** *type relate to cross-references to other state laws; insertions not marked in* **bold face** *type are a part of the proposed legislation.]*

### Section 1 Definition of Timeshare Resale Broker

(a) 'Timeshare resale broker' means any real estate salesman, broker or broker-salesman licensed pursuant to **[insert cross-reference to state real estate licensure law]** or any other person or entity who undertakes to list, advertise for sale, promote or sell by any means whatsoever more than 10 timeshare periods per year in one or more timeshare plans on behalf of any number of purchasers. For purposes of this section, 'timeshare periods' shall include membership campground contract interests, and 'timeshare plans' shall include membership campground plans. The term 'timeshare resale broker' shall not include:

(1) any person who has acquired any number of timeshare periods in any number of timeshare plans for his own use and occupancy and who later offers one or more of such periods for resale without the assistance of a timeshare resale broker;

(2) with regard to any resales whatsoever in connection with a given timeshare plan, the developer or the managing entity of the timeshare plan, or any entity licensed as a real estate broker pursuant to **[insert cross-reference to state real estate licensure law]** which is under common ownership or control with the developer of the timeshare plan; or

(3) a publisher of a newspaper or periodical in general circulation, or a broadcaster or telecaster; however, this exemption shall not apply to any publisher, broadcaster or telecaster under common ownership or control with a timeshare resale broker, or to any publisher, broadcaster or telecaster who serves directly or indirectly as the advertising agent or agency for a timeshare resale broker.

### Section 2 Regulation of Resale Broker Advertising

(a) Any advertising material relating to the solicitation of an agreement engaging the services of a timeshare resale broker in connection with the resale of a timeshare period pursuant to Section 4(b) shall be subject to the provisions of **[insert cross-reference to all regulations and restrictions imposed by state law upon developer advertising, if any]**.

(b) The term 'advertising material' includes any oral or written sales pitch, promotional brochure, pamphlet, catalogue, advertisement, sign, billboard or other material to be disseminated to the public by any means relating to the solicitation of an agreement engaging the services of a timeshare resale broker in connection with the resale of a timeshare period pursuant to Section 4(b), including a transcript of any standard oral sales presentation or any radio or television advertisement.

(c) No written advertising material relating to the solicitation of an agreement engaging the services of a timeshare resale broker in connection with the resale of a timeshare period pursuant to Section 4(b) may be utilized by a timeshare resale broker unless the advertising material includes in conspicuous type the disclosure described in Section 4(b)(1).

### Section 3 Resale Broker Licensure

(a) Any timeshare resale broker must be a licensed real estate salesman, broker, or broker-salesman as defined in [insert cross-reference to state real estate licensure law].

### Section 4 Resale Broker Listing Agreements and Resale Contract Disclosures *(for states having existing regulation of real estate broker listing fees)*

(a) It shall be a violation of [insert cross-reference to state timeshare law] for any timeshare resale broker to enter into any agreement with any person engaging the services of the timeshare resale broker in connection with the resale of a timeshare period unless the agreement complies in all respects with the provisions of subsections (b) and (c). It shall be a violation of [insert cross-reference to state timeshare law] for any timeshare resale broker to utilize any form of contract or purchase and sale agreement in connection with the resale of a timeshare period unless the contract or purchase and sale agreement complies in all respects with the provisions of subsection (d). It shall be a violation of [insert cross reference to state timeshare law] for any timeshare resale broker to provide any such services to anyone or to accept any monies or any other thing of value from anyone in connection with such services prior to fully complying with the registration and filing requirements set forth in subsection (e).

(b) In addition to all requirements of and obligations under [insert cross-reference to state real estate licensure law], all agreements engaging the services of a timeshare resale broker in connection with the resale of a timeshare period shall contain all of the following:

(1) The following statement in conspicuous type located immediately prior to the space in the agreement reserved for the signature of the owner: THERE IS NO GUARANTEE THAT YOUR TIMESHARE PERIOD CAN BE SOLD AT ANY PARTICULAR PRICE OR WITHIN ANY PARTICULAR PERIOD OF TIME.

(2) A complete and clear disclosure of any fees, commissions, and other costs or compensation payable to or received by the timeshare resale broker under the agreement, whether directly or indirectly.

(3) The term of the agreement; a statement regarding the ability of any party to extend the term of the agreement; and a description of the conditions under which the agreement may be extended and all related costs.

(4) If a fee or other compensation to be paid in advance of closing of the resale of the timeshare period is charged by the timeshare resale broker, a statement describing the promotional efforts that the timeshare resale broker will undertake, including all methods typically or customarily used by the timeshare resale broker to generate prospective resale purchasers, and including a description of the average circulation and geographical distribution area of any printed or media advertising, including catalogues, used by the timeshare resale broker.

(5) A description of the services to be provided by the timeshare resale broker under the agreement, and a description of the obligations of each party regarding a resale purchase, including any costs to be borne and any obligations regarding notification of the managing entity and any exchange company.

(6) A statement disclosing whether the agreement grants exclusive rights to the timeshare resale broker to locate a purchaser during the term of the agreement; a statement disclosing to whom and when any proceeds from a sale of the timeshare period will be disbursed; a statement whether any party may terminate the agreement and under what conditions; and a statement disclosing the amount of any commission or other compensation due to the timeshare resale broker from any party upon a termination of the agreement prior to the closing of the resale.

(7) A statement disclosing whether the agreement permits the timeshare resale

broker or any other person to make any use whatsoever of the timeshare period in question and a detailed description of any such permitted use rights, including a disclosure of to whom any rents or profits generated from such use of the timeshare period will be paid.

(8) A statement disclosing the existence of any judgments or pending litigation against the timeshare resale broker resulting from or alleging a violation by the timeshare resale broker of **[insert cross-references to state laws governing real estate licensure, land sales, condominiums and timesharing]** or resulting from or alleging consumer fraud on the part of the timeshare resale broker.

(c) All agreements described in subsection (b) must be reduced to writing, and the person engaging the services of the timeshare resale broker must receive a fully executed copy of the written agreement on the day he signs it. If the agreement is initially entered into by telephone or by any other oral means, the timeshare resale broker must make all of the disclosures required by subsection (b) to the person engaging his services prior to accepting anything of value from such person. In any event, a written agreement executed by the timeshare resale broker must be presented for signature to the person engaging his services within 10 days after the date the agreement was initially orally entered into.

(d) All forms of contract or purchase and sale agreement utilized by a timeshare resale broker in connection with the sale of a timeshare period shall contain all of the following:

(1) An explanation of the form of timeshare ownership being purchased and a legally sufficient description of the timeshare period being purchased.

(2) The name and address of the managing entity of the timeshare plan.

(3) The following statement in conspicuous type located immediately prior to the space in the contract reserved for the signature of the purchaser: THE CURRENT YEAR'S ASSESSMENT FOR COMMON EXPENSES ALLOCABLE TO THE TIMESHARE PERIOD YOU ARE PURCHASING IS $_____.

THIS ASSESSMENT, WHICH MAY BE INCREASED FROM TIME TO TIME BY [insert name of entity having authority to increase assessment], IS PAYABLE IN FULL ON OR BEFORE [state payment due date(s)]. THIS ASSESSMENT [INCLUDES/DOES NOT INCLUDE] YEARLY AD VALOREM REAL ESTATE TAXES. [If ad valorem real property taxes are not included in the current year's assessment for common expenses, the following statement must be included: THE MOST RECENT ANNUAL ASSESSMENT FOR AD VALOREM REAL ESTATE TAXES FOR THE TIMESHARE PERIOD YOU ARE PURCHASING IS $_____.] FAILURE TO TIMELY PAY THESE ASSESSMENTS MAY RESULT IN RESTRICTION OR LOSS OF YOUR USE AND/OR OWNERSHIP RIGHTS. In making the disclosures required by this paragraph, the timeshare resale broker may rely upon information provided in writing by the managing entity of the timeshare plan.

(4) A complete and accurate disclosure of the terms and conditions of the purchase and closing, including the obligations of the seller and/or the purchaser for closing costs and title insurance.

(5) A statement disclosing the existence of any mandatory exchange program membership included in the timeshare plan.

(e) All timeshare resale brokers shall register with **[insert the state agency having jurisdiction over registrations by timeshare developers]** prior to offering, advertising or executing any agreement described in subsections (b) or (d) above in this state. Each initial registration shall be accompanied by a $_____ registration fee and shall include the information described in paragraphs (1) through (5) below. The registration shall thereafter be renewed annually on or before the first day of _____ by payment of a $_____ renewal fee and submission of the information described in paragraphs (1) through (5) below, current to at least 30 days prior to the renewal date. Each registration shall include the following:

(1) The names and addresses of the timeshare resale broker and of all officers, directors and holders of in excess of 10 per cent of the shares of the timeshare resale broker; the names and addresses of all employees or agents of the timeshare resale broker who hold current licenses as real estate salesmen, brokers, or broker-salesmen; and the addresses and telephone numbers of each office maintained by the timeshare resale broker in this state, or of the principal office of the timeshare resale broker if no office is maintained in this state.

(2) A sample copy of all forms of resale listing contracts or agreements to be used by the timeshare resale broker.

(3) A sample copy of all forms of contract or purchase and sale agreement to be used by the timeshare resale broker.

(4) A schedule of any fees and commissions charged to customers of the timeshare resale broker.

(5) A summary of any services to be offered to the public by the timeshare resale broker.

**Alternate Section 4  Resale Broker Listing Agreements and Resale Contract Disclosures** *(for states having no existing regulation of real estate broker listing fees)*

(a) It shall be a violation of **[insert cross-reference to state timeshare law]** for any timeshare resale broker to enter into any agreement with any person engaging the services of the timeshare resale broker in connection with the resale of a timeshare period unless a written agreement complying in all respects with the provisions of subsection (b) is first executed by the timeshare resale broker and the person engaging the services of the timeshare resale broker. It shall be a violation of **[insert cross-reference to state timeshare law]** for any timeshare resale broker to accept any monies or any other thing of value from any person engaging the services of the timeshare resale broker in connection with the resale of a timeshare period in advance of the closing of the resale of such timeshare period. It shall be a violation of **[insert cross-reference to state timeshare law]** for any timeshare resale broker to utilize any form of contract or purchase and sale agreement in connection with the resale of a timeshare period unless the contract or purchase and sale agreement complies in all respects with the provisions of subsection (d). It shall be a violation of **[insert cross-reference to state timeshare law]** for any timeshare resale broker to provide any such services to anyone or to accept any monies or any other thing of value from anyone in connection with such services prior to fully complying with the registration and filing requirements set forth in subsection (e).

(b) In addition to all requirements of and obligations under **[insert cross-reference to state real estate licensure law]**, all agreements engaging the services of a timeshare resale broker in connection with the resale of a timeshare period shall contain all of the following:

(1) The following statement in conspicuous type located immediately prior to the space in the agreement reserved for the signature of the owner: THERE IS NO GUARANTEE THAT YOUR TIMESHARE PERIOD CAN BE SOLD AT ANY PARTICULAR PRICE OR WITHIN ANY PARTICULAR PERIOD OF TIME.

(2) A complete and clear disclosure of any fees, commissions, and other costs or compensation payable to or received by the timeshare resale broker under the agreement, whether directly or indirectly.

(3) The term of the agreement; a statement regarding the ability of any party to extend the term of the agreement; and a description of the conditions under which the agreement may be extended and all related costs.

(4) A description of the services to be provided by the timeshare resale broker under the agreement, and a description of the obligations of each party regarding a resale purchase, including any costs to be borne and any obligations regarding notification of the managing entity and any exchange company.

(5) A statement disclosing whether the agreement grants exclusive rights to the timeshare resale broker to locate a purchaser during the term of the agreement; a statement disclosing to whom and when

any proceeds from a sale of the timeshare period will be disbursed; and a statement whether any party may terminate the agreement and under what conditions.

(6) A statement disclosing whether the agreement permits the timeshare resale broker or any other person to make any use whatsoever of the timeshare period in question and a detailed description of any such permitted use rights, including a disclosure of to whom any rents or profits generated from such use of the timeshare period will be paid.

(7) A statement disclosing the existence of any judgments or pending litigation against the timeshare resale broker resulting from or alleging a violation by the timeshare resale broker of **[insert cross-references to state laws governing real estate licensure, land sales, condominiums and timesharing]** or resulting from or alleging consumer fraud on the part of the timeshare resale broker.

(c) The person engaging the services of the timeshare resale broker must receive a fully executed copy of the agreement described in subsection (b) on the day he signs it.

(d) All forms of contract or purchase and sale agreement utilized by a timeshare resale broker in connection with the sale of a timeshare period shall contain all of the following:

(1) An explanation of the form of timeshare ownership being purchased and a legally sufficient description of the timeshare period being purchased.

(2) The name and address of the managing entity of the timeshare plan.

(3) The following statement in conspicuous type located immediately prior to the space in the contract reserved for the signature of the purchaser: THE CURRENT YEAR'S ASSESSMENT FOR COMMON EXPENSES ALLOCABLE TO THE TIMESHARE PERIOD YOU ARE PURCHASING IS $_____. THIS ASSESSMENT, WHICH MAY BE INCREASED FROM TIME TO TIME BY [insert name of entity having authority to increase assessment], IS PAYABLE IN FULL ON OR BEFORE [state payment due date(s)]. THIS ASSESSMENT [INCLUDES/DOES

NOT INCLUDE] YEARLY AD VALOREM REAL ESTATE TAXES. [If ad valorem real property taxes are not included in the current year's assessment for common expenses, the following statement must be included: THE MOST RECENT ANNUAL ASSESSMENT FOR AD VALOREM REAL ESTATE TAXES FOR THE TIMESHARE PERIOD YOU ARE PURCHASING IS $_____.] FAILURE TO TIMELY PAY THESE ASSESSMENTS MAY RESULT IN RESTRICTION OR LOSS OF YOUR USE AND/OR OWNERSHIP RIGHTS. In making the disclosures required by this paragraph, the timeshare resale broker may rely upon information provided in writing by the managing entity of the timeshare plan.

(4) A complete and accurate disclosure of the terms and conditions of the purchase and closing, including the obligations of the seller and/or the purchaser for closing costs and title insurance.

(5) A statement disclosing the existence of any mandatory exchange program membership included in the timeshare plan.

(e) All timeshare resale brokers shall register with **[insert the state agency having jurisdiction over registrations by timeshare developers]** prior to offering, advertising or executing any agreement described in subsections (b) or (d) above in this state. Each initial registration shall be accompanied by a $_____ registration fee and shall include the information described in paragraphs (1) through (5) below. The registration shall thereafter be renewed annually on or before the first day of _____ by payment of a $_____ renewal fee and submission of the information described in paragraphs (1) through (5) below, current to at least 30 days prior to the renewal date. Each registration shall include the following:

(1) The names and addresses of the timeshare resale broker and of all officers, directors and holders of in excess of 10 per cent of the shares of the timeshare resale broker; the names and addresses of all employees or agents of the timeshare resale broker who hold current licenses as

real estate salesmen, brokers, or broker-salesmen; and the addresses and telephone numbers of each office maintained by the timeshare resale broker in this state, or of the principal office of the timeshare resale broker if no office is maintained in this state.

(2) A sample copy of all forms of resale listing contracts or agreements to be used by the timeshare resale broker.

(3) A sample copy of all forms of contract or purchase and sale agreement to be used by the timeshare resale broker.

(4) A schedule of any fees and commissions charged to customers of the timeshare resale broker.

(5) A summary of any services to be offered to the public by the timeshare resale broker.

**Section 5 Regulatory Agency Jurisdiction Over Resale Brokers**

(a) **[Insert necessary provisions to extend all existing state regulatory agency jurisdiction over timeshare developers to timeshare resale brokers.]**

# Index

# Bibliography

## United Kingdom

Cheshire and Burn, *Modern Law of Real Property*, 14th edn (Butterworths)
Cheshire, Fifoot and Furmaston, *The Law of Contract*, 12th edn (Butterworths 1991)
Cheshire and North, *Private International Law*, 11th edn (Butterworths)
*Conveyancer and Property Lawyer—Precedents for the Conveyancer* (Sweet & Maxwell, looseleaf service)
Dawson and Pearce, *Licences Relating to the Occupation or Use of Land* (Butterworths)
Dicey and Morris, *Conflict of Laws*, 12th edn (Sweet & Maxwell 1991)
English Tourist Board Development Guides, *Obtaining Planning Permission, Holiday Home Development, Developing Timeshare*
Goode, *Consumer Credit Legislation* (Butterworths)
Josling, J.F. and Alexander, L., *The Law of Clubs*, 6th edn (Longman 1987)
Karpinski and Fielding, *Truth in Lending* (Waterlow Publishers Ltd)
Megarry and Wade, *The Law of Real Property*, 7th edn (Sweet & Maxwell 1991)
Morris and Leek, *Rules against Perpetuities* (Sweet & Maxwell)
Palmer, *Company Law*, 23rd edn (Sweet & Maxwell)
Underhill and Hayton, *Law of Trusts and Trustees*, 14th edn (Sweet & Maxwell)

## France

Bouyeure, *La Jouissance des Biens Immobiliers à temps Partagé* (Revue Administrer 1.12.82)
Capoulade, P, *Les Professions Immobilières* (Éditions de l'actualité juridique)
*Code Permanent Construction et Urbanisme* (Éditions Législatives et administratives) (2 vols)
Dagot and Spiteri, *A la Recherche de la multipropriété* (JCP 1972)
Dalloz, *Nouveau Répertoire* (Vol IV Sociétés)
Dutrec, *La Commercialisation et la Gestion des Immeubles en Multipropriété* (Revue Administrer 1.04.81)
Houpin and Bosvieux, *Traite General Théorique et Pratique des Sociétés Civiles et Commerciales*
Juris Classeur Civil Vo Contrats de Promotion Immobiliere, Art 1981–1 A 1831–5 FASC 1
Juris Classeur Civil Vo Ventes D'Immeubles à Construrie, Art 1601–1 A 1601–4 FASC B
Juris Classeur Civil Vo Sociétés Civiles, Art 1832 A 1873
Liet Vaux, *Le Droit de la Construction* (Libraires Techniques 1982)
Malinvaud and Ghestaz, *Droit de la Promotion Immobiliére* (Precis Dalloz)
Martin, *Multipropriété ou Multijouissance* (Ann Loyers 1.08.81)
Morand, *La Copropriété Saisonnière ou Multipropriété depuis 10 ans*, (Gaz Palais 8.05.79)

Pelletier, *Le Rérime Juridique et Fiscal des Immeubles à Temps Partagé* (Revue Droit Immob 1.04.82)
Saint Alary, *Droit de la Construction* (PUF Themis)
Stemmer, *Du Probleme des Periodes et leur Évaluation en Matière de Multipropriété* (JCP 1980 (1))

## Spain
Código de las Leyes Civiles, Ed Civitas    Arco (M A Del)
Comentarios al Dódigo Civil y Compilaciones Forales, 32 vols    Albaladejo Garcia (M)
Comunidad de propietarios. Gúia práctica 1982    Alonso Del Alamo
Curso de Derecho Civil Español, Comum y Foral 5 vols    Albaladejo Garcia (M)
Derecho Civil Español, Común y Foral 6 vols    Castan Tobenas (J)
Fiscalidad de las operaciones inmobiliarias    Buireu Guarro (J)
Fundamentos de Derecho Civil 5 vols    Puig Brutau (J)
La Propiedad de Casas por Pisos 1980 Ed Marfil    Batlle Vasquez (M)
Manual de Derecho Mercantil, Ed Tecnos    Broseta Pont (M)
Repertorio de Legislación Tributaria, Ed Estudios Financieros  Diez Aroca (J)
Sistema de Derecho Civil 4 vols    Diez-Picazo (L), Gulon (A)
Sistema fiscal español 3 vols    Albi Ibanez y Ariznavarreta
Temas sobre Inversiones Extranjeras y Control de Cambios, 2 volus Ed de Derecho Reunidas    Lucas Fernandez (F)
Tratado de Derecho Mercantil 3 vols    Garrigues (J)

## USA
Annotated OILSR regulation/Interstate Land Sales Act (1980), Land Development Institute
Annotated Interstate Land Sales Act (1979), Land Development Institute
Burlingame, Carl H, ed, *Directory of Resort and Recreational Development*
*Buyer's Guide to Resort Timesharing* (The CHB Company Inc.)
Davis, Thomas J and Rodriguez, Mario F, *Marketing a Time Sharing Project* and *Structuring the Interval Project—From Conception to Marketing*
*Guide for Sales Personnel* (3rd edn) (Land Development Institute)
*Guide for Timeshare Sales Personnel* (Land Development Institute)
Henze, Mark E., *The Law of Business and Timeshare Resorts* (Clark Boardman Company Limited)
Ingersoll, *The Legal Aspects of Real Estate Timesharing* (Practising Law Institute)
Ingersoll, Bloch and Madsen, eds., *Digest of State Land Sales Regulations* (Land Development Institute)
Ragatz, Richard L, and Burlingame, Carl, *Timeshare Purchasers: Who they are, why they buy* (The CHB Company Inc.)
*Resort Timesharing—A Consumer's Guide* (American Land Development Association)
*Resort Timesharing (1979) Surveys on Timeshare Industry* (American Land Development Association)
*Resort Time Sharing Survey Results: Industry Factbook* (The David Time Share Group)
*Resort Timesharing Today* (The CHB Co, Inc)
*The Timesharing Encyclopedia* (Interval International)
*Timesharing Guide* (Keith Romney Associates)
Tomlin, Donald R and Granieri, William F, *Making Time Sharing Work—A Complete Marketing Guide* (Columbia Management Corp.)
Trowbridge, Keith W., *Resort Timesharing* (Simon & Schuster)